DEFERRED PROSECUTION AGREEMENTS AND DIRECTORS' LIABILITY

LLOYD'S INSURANCE LAW LIBRARY
Series Editors: Robert Merkin
and Malcolm A. Clarke

LLOYD'S INSURANCE LAW LIBRARY
Series Editors: Robert Merkin and Malcolm A. Clarke

Directors' and Officers' Liability Insurance
Adolfo Paolini and Deepak Nambisan

Insurance Law and the Financial Services Ombudsman Service
Judith P. Summer

Reinsuring Clauses
Ozlem Gurses

Insurance Disputes
Third Edition
The Right Honourable Lord Mance, Iain Goldrein QC
and Robert Merkin

The Law of Liability Insurance
Malcolm A. Clarke

Lloyd's
Law and Practice
Julian Burling

Systemic Risk and the Future of Insurance Regulation
Edited by Andromachi Georgosouli
and Miriam Goldby

Chinese Insurance Contracts
Law and Practice
Zhen Jing

The Law of Liability Insurance
Second Edition
Malcolm A. Clarke

Good Faith and Insurance Contracts
Fourth Edition
Peter MacDonald Eggers QC,
Simon Picken
and Patrick Foss

The Law of Compulsory Motor Vehicle Insurance
Özlem Gürses

The Global Insurance Market and Change
Emerging Technologies, Risks and Legal
Edited by Anthony A Tarr, Professor
Julie-Anne Tarr,
Maurice Thompson and Dino Wilkinson

Insurance, Climate Change and the Law
Franziska Arnold-Dwyer

Deferred Prosecution Agreements and Directors' Liability
Natalie Turney

For more information about this series, please visit: www.routledge.com/Lloyds-Insurance-Law-Library/book-series/LILL

DEFERRED PROSECUTION AGREEMENTS AND DIRECTORS' LIABILITY

NATALIE TURNEY

informa law
from Routledge

First published 2024
by Informa Law from Routledge
4 Park Square, Milton Park, Abingdon, Oxon OX14 4RN

and by Informa Law from Routledge
605 Third Avenue, New York, NY 10158

Informa Law from Routledge is an imprint of the Taylor & Francis Group, an informa business

British Library Cataloguing-in-Publication Data
A catalogue record for this book is available from the British Library

Library of Congress Cataloging-in-Publication Data
Names: Turney, Natalie, author.
Title: Deferred prosecution agreements and directors' liability / Natalie Turney.
Description: Abingdon, Oxon [UK]; New York, NY: Routledge, 2024. |
Series: Lloyd's insurance law library | Includes bibliographical
references and index.
Identifiers: LCCN 2023055829 (print) | LCCN 2023055830 (ebook) |
ISBN 9781032599502 (hardback) | ISBN 9781032599540 (paperback) |
ISBN 9781003456964 (ebook)
Subjects: LCSH: Prosecution–Great Britain–Decision making. |
Prosecution–United States–Decision making. | Directors of
corporations–Legal status, laws, etc.–Great Britain | Tort liability
of corporations–Great Britain | Corporation law–Great
Britain–Criminal provisions. | Debtor and creditor–Great Britain. |
Commercial crimes–Law and legislation–Great Britain.
Classification: LCC KD8348 .T87 2024 (print) | LCC KD8348 (ebook) |
DDC 345.41/05042–dc23/eng/20231214
LC record available at https://lccn.loc.gov/2023055829
LC ebook record available at https://lccn.loc.gov/2023055830

ISBN: 978-1-032-59950-2 (hbk)
ISBN: 978-1-032-59954-0 (pbk)
ISBN: 978-1-003-45696-4 (ebk)

DOI: 10.4324/9781003456964

Typeset in Times New Roman
by Deanta Global Publishing Services, Chennai, India

For my family.

CONTENTS

Part V Recommendations and conclusions

FOREWORD

By Professor Adolfo Paolini

Deferred prosecution agreements (DPAs), originally developed in the United States and later in the United Kingdom, have opened the door to correcting market anomalies without severely punishing corporate bodies. The DPA itself is a promise to delay and/or avoid prosecution, should corporate bodies first agree to the alleged breach, second waive their right to challenge the agreement, and most importantly adopt measures to correct the damaging effects of the wrongful act itself.

One should not be confused by the previous statement; in fact, breaching securities regulation must and should lead to rigorous consequences. Otherwise the pillars of integrity, fairness, and transparency, which underpin the financial market, will be seriously undermined. Reality shows, nevertheless, that DPAs have put to the test the directors' and officers' (D&O) liability insurance market in a way that may not have been foreseen by underwriters.

Company directors are exposed to liability as a result of the agreement between the investigated company and the prosecutors because DPAs require companies to accept liability, even though this is done at the expense of directors.

Whether directors could defend such allegations without breaching the DPA and most importantly find refuge in their D&O policy are precisely the answers that this book aims at providing all of us with.

This work is part of Dr Turney's PhD at the University of Buckingham, and for me personally, it is very inspiring to see young professionals being able to produce work of this quality.

PREFACE

In 2014, England and Wales saw the passage of the Crime and Courts Act 2013 and, with it, the introduction of deferred prosecution agreements (DPAs). As the financial crisis of 2008 brought corporate crime and accountability under a renewed spotlight, DPAs were advanced in the battle against difficulties in corporate criminal liability laws and standards. Heavily influenced by the United States DPA model, where DPAs find their origin, the transplantation was not quite "cut and paste". In the United States, DPAs have always been available to individuals, with the original objective being the rehabilitation of young and low-level offenders. In England and Wales, the prospect of DPAs for individuals was outrightly rejected during statutory development, and the provision is thus available to corporates alone.

In their novelty, DPAs raise a number of questions, not least in relation to the position of individuals implicated in the underlying corporate wrongdoing. Answers are few and far between, in statute, case law, prosecutorial guidance, and beyond. This book aims to provide answers on the position of implicated company directors where DPAs arise. In doing so, there is a focus on directors' liability and directors' and officers' (D&O) liability insurance.

Dealing with two different areas in many respects, the book sets out first to provide the reader with the necessary background and law on DPAs, and thereafter on D&O insurance. In assessing the position of company directors, the book aims to establish the extent to which DPAs can be said to be available to individuals or to offer any protection from prosecution. On this basis, there is a detailed discussion on directors' professional duties to the company, in facing the DPA process and acting in the corporate's best interests. Facing the dichotomy of balancing such duties with personal rights and interests, the issue of a director's defence is discussed, with particular focus on the controversial practice of naming directors in DPA documentation.

The book aims to explain the impact of DPAs on D&O insurance, in establishing a wider understanding of directors' liability in these new and evolving circumstances. To this effect, the complexities of "ABC" D&O policies, which provide coverage not only to company directors but also corporate entities, are acknowledged, and a comprehensive analysis of coverage of each insured is set forth. The book aims to establish the complications and necessary cautions where directors and the entity are insured under the same D&O policy. The securing of a D&O policy is discussed, in identifying pre-contractual obligations which may impact the obtaining of the policy and subsequent cover. Thereafter, the process of seeking indemnification and – crucially – advancement of defence costs is analysed in depth.

There is focus on discussing the position of various stakeholders throughout. From an insurance perspective, the focus largely centres on the responsibilities and conduct of the insurer and insured. In respect of the DPA process, the practice of directors, corporates, lawyers, prosecutors, and the judiciary is of central importance. More generally, the book presents best practice in dealing with implicated individuals.

This book emanates from and builds upon my PhD thesis. It is my hope that the book provides some guidance and answers to questions where a lack of clarity currently prevails. Of course, where there are issues not addressed within, it would be invaluable to hear from readers on matters that could be considered in further editions.

I owe thanks to many. First, my thanks to those at the Taylor & Francis Group who have assisted in making this process so enjoyable. On my PhD journey, I wish to thank my supervisor Professor Adolfo Paolini for his constant support and kindness, and Professor Robert Merkin KC and Professor Özlem Gürses for their wisdom during *viva* examination. I cannot end without thanking my family, to whom I owe everything and the deepest thanks: my mum Siobhán and dad Jim, and my siblings Niamh, Joe, and Ciarán, and my grandparents. Finally, my lovely friends.

Dr Natalie Turney
October 2023

TABLE OF CASES

Australia

Canada

European Union

France

Hong Kong

Ireland

New Zealand

Singapore

United Kingdom

United States

TABLE OF LEGISLATION

Singapore

Spain

United Kingdom

United States

TABLE OF STATUTORY INSTRUMENTS AND RULES OF COURT

United Kingdom statutory instruments

United Kingdom rules of court

TABLE OF DEFERRED PROSECUTION AGREEMENTS

Court orders

Deferred prosecution agreements

Judgments

Notice of discontinuance

Related company undertakings

Statements of facts

United States deferred prosecution agreements

LIST OF ACRONYMS AND ABBREVIATIONS

ABC	Sides A, B, and C of a Directors' and Officers' Liability Insurance Policy
(The) Administration	The Regional Administration of Castilla-Léon
AFWEL	Amec Foster Wheeler Energy (UK) Ltd
ASL	Airline Services Ltd
CA 2006	Companies Act 2006
CACA 2013	Crime and Courts Act 2013
CEO	Chief Executive Officer
CIDRA 2012	Consumer Insurance (Disclosure and Representations) Act 2012
CJA 1967	Criminal Justice Act 1967
CJA 1987	Criminal Justice Act 1987
CJIP	*Convention judiciaire d'intérêt public* (France)
CMA	Competition and Markets Authority
CPIA 1996	Criminal Procedure and Investigations Act 1996
CPR	Civil Procedure Rules
CPS	Crown Prosecution Service
CrimPR	Criminal Procedure Rules
CSIL	Cyril Sweett International Ltd
D&O	directors' and officers' (liability insurance)
DARCstar	Directors' All Risk Cover
DIC	(Side A) Difference-in-Conditions
DoJ	Department of Justice (United States)
DPA	deferred prosecution agreement
DPA Code	Deferred Prosecution Agreement Code of Practice, published by the Serious Fraud Office and Crown Prosecution Service (2014)
E&O	Errors and Omissions (Insurance)
ECHR	European Convention on Human Rights
ECtHR	European Court of Human Rights
EGMA	Enterprise Growth Market Advisors Limited
EU	European Union
FCA	Financial Conduct Authority
FRE	Federal Rules of Evidence (United States)
FSA	Financial Services Authority
FWEL	Foster Wheeler Energy Limited
FWL	Foster Wheeler Limited

HRA 1998	Human Rights Act 1998
IA 2015	Insurance Act 2015
IPSO	Independent Press Standards Organisation
JIT	Joint Investigation Team (the Serious Fraud Office and French *Parquet National Financier*)
JLL CIL	Jones Lang LaSalle Capital Investments Limited
JLL EU	Jones Lang LaSalle Europe Limited
JLL Group	Jones Lang LaSalle Group
KC	King's Counsel
LIA	Libyan Investment Authority
LIBOR	London Interbank Offered Rate
LLP	limited liability partnership
LPP	legal professional privilege
Ltd	limited company
MIA 1906	Marine Insurance Act 1906
OECD	Organisation for Economic Co-operation and Development
PDP	Pretrial Diversion Program(me)
PLC	public limited company
PNF	*Parquet National Financier* (France)
PNM	identifier given to party in *Khuja v Times Newspapers Limited* [2017] UKSC 49
QC	Queen's Counsel
SA 2020	Sentencing Act 2020
SAME	Side-A Match Edge
SE	European Public Limited Liability Company
SEC	Securities and Exchange Commission (United States)
(The) Select Committee	The Select Committee on the Bribery Act 2010
SFO	Serious Fraud Office
SFO (Operational) Handbook	handbook published by the Serious Fraud Office providing guidance on approach to matters set out within (2020)
SIL	Skansen Interiors Ltd
SIR	Self-Insured Retention
SME	small and medium enterprise
SOCPA 2005	Serious Organised Crime and Police Act 2005
SOF	statement of facts
UK	United Kingdom
US	United States

PART I

INTRODUCTION

Where deferred prosecution agreements ("DPA(s)") sit within an area of corporate criminal liability, and directors' and officers' ("D&O") liability insurance sits within insurance law and practice, some definition on the two distinct areas is required. Part I of the book provides the necessary introductory material to the two different areas of law and practice. Part I starts with the first chapter, which defines DPAs and offers an insight into the introductory process, the legal framework, and a timeline of the process from negotiation to DPA completion. The first chapter discusses in detail each DPA case to be approved in the UK courts thus far, with reference to the underlying offending, relevant documentation, and – crucially – the position of implicated individuals. The second chapter within Part I introduces insurance more generally, providing a background of the practice and the development into an operational legal framework. D&O insurance is thereafter introduced, covering a brief history of the product and its general and typical nature. Part I concludes with an insight into the convergence of DPAs and D&O and looks to warnings heralded by the D&O market in response to the introduction of the corporate criminal tool.

DOI: 10.4324/9781003456964-1

CHAPTER 1

An introduction to DPAs

1.1 Deferred prosecution agreements in the UK

Deferred prosecution agreements ("DPA(s)") were imported into the laws of England and Wales (hereafter "UK" for ease) from a United States ("US") model.[1] Originally created as a rehabilitative method of sanctioning individuals, the tool thereafter developed in the US into a corporate penalty tool, as an alternative method of criminally penalising companies (**Section 4.1**). In the UK – crucially – DPAs are *only* available to a body corporate, a partnership, or an unincorporated association, and are not available to individuals.[2] A DPA can be agreed with multiple companies, though in such circumstances each company will sign a separate DPA with the prosecutor. A DPA is an agreement between a company suspected[3] to have committed a criminal act and a prosecuting agency (in the UK: the Serious Fraud Office ("SFO") or Crown Prosecution Service ("CPS")). Proceedings are instituted by preferring a bill of indictment for the underlying criminal offence(s), but deferred on the basis that the terms within the agreement are observed.

1.1.1 From Bill to Act

Published in May 2012, the Ministry of Justice's ("MoJ") consultation paper on DPAs as a 'new enforcement tool to deal with economic crime committed by commercial organisations'[4] outlined the existing shortcomings with corporate criminal prosecution: predominantly the difficulties with the identification principle[5] and lack of incentivisation to

1 'I welcome the proposals for deferred prosecution agreements in the proposed new schedule. They provide a comprehensive and workable code for a useful new procedure. The proposals are no worse for being an American import.' *See* HL Deb 30 October 2012, vol 740, col 573 (Lord Marks of Henley-on-Thames).

2 Crime and Courts Act 2013, sch 17 para 4(1).

3 The limitation on judicial involvement and the agreed nature of the statement of facts are key in setting out that the company cannot be said to have definitively committed criminal acts, or rather be culpable to a *criminal* standard. In the context of complex financial activity, for example, there is at times a question as to whether practice which is wrong can be said to be criminal.

4 Ministry of Justice, *Consultation on a New Enforcement Tool to Deal With Economic Crime Committed by Commercial Organisations: Deferred Prosecution Agreements* (Cm 8348, 2012) para 88.

5 Corporate criminal liability standards formed the basis of a Law Commission project, following the request of the government, in November 2020. Interestingly, in 2022, the Law Commission recommended retaining the identification principle (the most debated corporate criminal liability principle). *See* Law Commission, *Corporate Criminal Liability: An Options Paper* (2022) para 1.39. However, in 2023, the government – reportedly following collaboration with prosecutors, the Law Commission, and the private sector – brought forward a proposal to extend the identification doctrine to include "senior managers" within the scope of the "directing mind and will" of the company. Section 196(1) of the Economic Crime and Corporate

DOI: 10.4324/9781003456964-2

self-report.[6] Though the tool was proposed as a result of its success in the US, criticisms of the US model were considered in its implementation within the UK legal framework: 'our proposals are based on the system that operates in the US, but are adapted to make it suitable and appropriate for the specific context of the UK.'[7] The predominant criticisms considered were the purported lack of transparency in the prosecutorial approach and remote judicial oversight,[8] which were said to be in misalignment with UK constitutional arrangements.[9] Despite this, the proposed UK approach remained largely influenced by the US model.[10]

The MoJ's response to consultation followed in October 2012, setting out the government's plan for progression. The paper denoted an overwhelming agreement with DPAs, at 86 percent of those consulted.[11] The objective of incentivising self-reporting remained a persistent theme throughout the response; an admission of guilt would not be necessary, though a statement of facts would need to be agreed.[12] Despite concerns raised by respondents, the government's position on the admissibility of evidence in future proceedings was unchanged (**Section 7.3**).[13] Following the consultation process, DPAs were introduced in the UK (except Northern Ireland and Scotland)[14] on 24 February 2014 under section 45 and Schedule 17 of the Crime and Courts Act 2013 ("CACA 2013").

Transparency Act 2023 sets out that '[i]f a senior manager of a body corporate or partnership ("the organisation") acting within the actual or apparent scope of their authority commits a relevant offence after this section comes into force, the organisation is also guilty of the offence', defining "senior manager" as an individual who plays a 'significant role in – the making of decisions about how the whole or a substantial part of the activities of the body corporate or (as the case may be) partnership are to be managed or organised, or the actual managing or organising of the whole or a substantial part of those activities'. *See* Economic Crime and Corporate Transparency Act 2023, s 196(4).

6 Ministry of Justice, *Consultation on a New Enforcement Tool to Deal With Economic Crime Committed by Commercial Organisations: Deferred Prosecution Agreements* (n 4) para 3.

7 ibid para 71.

8 Lord Edward Garnier KC has commented on the difference between the UK and US in this respect: 'One of the distinctions between the US system and our system … is the active role the judge plays in supervising DPAs. Nobody wants to go to court to be told that this DPA is unjust … People work very hard to make sure that this is going to get past the judge … It's more of a thing in our minds than in the US where it just goes in the inbox of the judge, that the clerk probably/might not even show the judge, and out it comes the other way.' Lord Garnier's comments were made in an event hosted by the Law Commission online due to COVID-19 restrictions: Law Commission, 'Corporate Criminal Liability Project: Launch Event' (online, Law Commission 9 June 2021). Interestingly, though, in a more recent DPA approving judgment, Mrs Justice May states that: 'in deciding whether or not to approve the DPA, the court exercises no fact-finding function … *The court's role is one of oversight only*, making an independent assessment of the public interest in arriving at the DPA and of the reasonableness, fairness and proportionality of the particular terms which the parties have agreed.' *See Director of the Serious Fraud Office v Bluu Solutions Limited and Tetris-Projects Limited* [2023] EWHC 1976 (KB) [15] (Mrs Justice May) (emphasis added).

9 Ministry of Justice, *Consultation on a New Enforcement Tool to Deal With Economic Crime Committed by Commercial Organisations: Deferred Prosecution Agreements* (n 4) paras 63, 65, 67.

10 ibid para 70.

11 Ministry of Justice, *Deferred Prosecution Agreements: Government Response to the Consultation on a New Enforcement Tool to Deal With Economic Crime Committed by Commercial Organisations* (Cm 8463, 2012) para 18.

12 ibid para 96.

13 ibid para 161.

14 Crime and Courts Act 2013, s 61(13)(g). 'As for what the committee says about civil settlements in Scotland—the alternative to the deferred prosecution system in England and Wales—I do not wish to take anything away at all from what my noble and learned friend Lord Saville said about this matter in his introduction. However, the differences between those two systems are perhaps less troublesome than the committee seems to have thought in commenting on the Scottish position… Scotland does not have sentence bargaining, but agreements about pleas and settlements are within the discretion of the prosecutor. I doubt whether anyone

1.1.2 Operating framework

Schedule 17 of the CACA 2013, the statutory framework for DPAs, is supported by the CPS and SFO's Deferred Prosecution Agreements Code of Practice (the "DPA Code") and the SFO's Operational Handbook. The former was published in 2014 upon DPA introduction, with no updates since, and the latter was published in 2020. Schedule 17 of the CACA 2013 sets out the judicial process to be followed upon completion of DPA negotiations and guidance as to the contents of a DPA. The DPA Code is provided by the CPS and SFO pursuant to a requirement set out in paragraph 6 of Schedule 17 of the CACA 2013. According to paragraph 6(1), the DPA Code is required to provide guidance for prosecutors on general principles to be applied in determining whether a DPA is likely to be appropriate, and the disclosure of information by a prosecutor to the company (in the course of negotiations for a DPA and after a DPA has been agreed). The DPA Code provides guidance to prosecutors on the pre-negotiation and negotiation stages of the process, and each stage of the process post-negotiation. The SFO's Operational Handbook is similar, covering largely the same areas as the DPA Code, but is more up to date and provides guidance for SFO staff alone.

1.1.3 Process

1.1.3.1 Pre-negotiation and negotiation period

At the point in which DPA negotiations are considered, there will be a suspicion by the prosecutor of potential criminal conduct committed by the company, and an investigation will be underway. It may be the case that such a suspicion arises following a self-report made by the company, and the prospect of being offered a DPA may be signalled to the company during the investigation process. As DPAs are only available in relation to specific offences, this will be borne in mind by prosecutors from the outset.[15]

The DPA Code sets out the requirements for the pre-negotiation period. During this period, the prosecutor offers to enter DPA negotiations, and the company has the choice as to whether to accept or reject the offer. Should the company accept, undertakings regarding the terms of negotiations are made. The company's "pre-negotiation confidentiality undertaking" with the prosecutor forms the basis of the DPA negotiations which follow thereafter. Within it, there is a mutual understanding that the *fact* of DPA negotiations and information and material exchanged remain confidential, with one exception being disclosure required by law.[16] The fact of DPA negotiations has been shared, for example, where entered into by a listed company.[17] In such instances, in order to uphold the interest

---

in Scotland would want that system to brought under the supervision of the judges.' *See* HL Deb 3 February 2021, vol 809, col 350GC (Lord Hope of Craighead).

15 Crime and Courts Act 2013, sch 17 pt 2.

16 Crown Prosecution Service and Serious Fraud Office, 'Deferred Prosecution Agreements Code of Practice' (*Crown Prosecution Service*, 11 February 2014) <https://www.cps.gov.uk/sites/default/files/documents/publications/dpa_cop.pdf> accessed 9 June 2020, para 3.9.1; Serious Fraud Office, 'Deferred Prosecution Agreements' (*Serious Fraud Office*, 23 October 2020) <https://www.sfo.gov.uk/publications/guidance-policy-and-protocols/sfo-operational-handbook/deferred-prosecution-agreements/> accessed 23 October 2020.

17 *See* Entain, 'Update on HMRC Investigation' (*Entain*, 31 May 2023) <https://www.entaingroup.com/news-insights/latest-news/2023/update-on-hmrc-investigation/> accessed 4 July 2023.

of market integrity, a company might make such a disclosure where it is considered to constitute "insider information".[18]

Though the letter of invitation signals the start of the pre-negotiation period,[19] the formal negotiation period cannot begin until the company provides its acceptance of the invitation. Following acceptance, a second letter will be sent by the prosecutor to the company in respect of undertakings as to the terms of the negotiations. An indication of the potential terms of negotiations is likely to have been given in the first letter, which outlines 'the basis on which any negotiations will proceed'.[20] Notably, an invitation to enter negotiations does *not* guarantee that a DPA will ultimately be offered.

During the negotiation period, the prosecutor and company will negotiate the proposed terms of the agreement and also the statement of facts upon which the DPA is based. The negotiation period is private, and there is no opportunity for third-party individuals (such as former directors) to participate in the drafting of the statement of facts. However, the opportunity for the involvement of related companies (principally the parent company) may arise in order to better effect successful negotiations.

1.1.3.2 Preliminary hearing

Following the period of investigation, negotiation, and drafting of the DPA and statement of facts, the prosecutor applies to the court for a declaration that entering into the DPA in the circumstances *is likely* to be in the interests of justice and that the *proposed* terms are fair, reasonable, and proportionate. This application is made in private, under paragraph 7 of Schedule 17 to the CACA 2013. The judge will provide reasons for approval, which should remain private (though notably have been publicised in three cases), and it has been said that 'a practice has developed of reserving such reasons to the final hearing, and for the open judgment to set out the whole reasoning'.[21] If approval is given (subsequent to

18 The Financial Conduct Authority ("FCA") Handbook's Disclosure Guidance and Transparency Rules ("DTR") apply to Entain, as a company with a premium listing on the London Stock Exchange. DTR 2.2.1 and 2.2.1A require a listed company to disclose "inside information", which is defined as: 'Information which, if it were made public, would be likely to have a significant effect on the prices of financial instruments, derivative financial instruments, related spot commodity contracts, or auctioned products based on emission allowances shall mean information a reasonable investor would be likely to use as part of the basis of his or her investment decisions.' *See* FCA, 'FCA Handbook' (*Financial Conduct Authority*, 3 July 2016) <https://www.handbook.fca.org.uk/handbook/DTR/2/2.html#> accessed 4 July 2023, DTR 2.2.1, citing Regulation (EU) 596/2014 of the European Parliament and of the Council of 16 April 2014 on market abuse (market abuse regulation) and repealing Directive 2003/6/EC of the European Parliament and of the Council and Commission Directives 2003/124/EC, 2003/125/EC and 2004/72/EC [2014] OJ L173/1, art 7(4). Entain, in a press release setting out a £585 million provision taken out in preparation for an approved DPA, cited the Regulation for the purpose of publicising insider information: Entain, 'Update on HMRC Investigation' (*Entain*, 10 August 2023) <https://www.entaingroup.com/media/sbwn1thb/entain-hmrc-update-10-aug-23.pdf> accessed 9 October 2023.

19 The official starting point of the DPA negotiation process is somewhat confused; the Code sets out that the prosecutor will first send the company a 'formal letter of invitation outlining the basis on which any negotiations will proceed', which constitutes the 'beginning of the DPA negotiation period'. However, the Code then sets out that the letter must include a 'request for confirmation of whether [the company] wishes to enter into negotiations' and a timeframe in which the company must notify the prosecutor of whether or not it accepts the invitation 'to enter into negotiations'. *See* Crown Prosecution Service and Serious Fraud Office, 'Deferred Prosecution Agreements Code of Practice' (n 16) paras 3.1–3.2, 3.5.

20 ibid para 3.1.

21 *Bluu Solutions Limited and Tetris-Projects Limited* (n 8) [12] (Mrs Justice May). In the first two DPA cases, the preliminary approved judgments were published, and in the tenth DPA, reasons were given in an annex to the agreement titled 'The private reasons at the paragraph 7 stage': *Director of the Serious Fraud Office v Amec Foster Wheeler Energy Limited (Preliminary)* [2021] Lexis Citation 109.

any further hearings necessary to make amendments to the agreement at the direction of the judge), formal agreement between the prosecutor and company may be reached, and the process can move to the next step of final approval. If approval is not given on the first application, the prosecutor may apply again thereafter.

1.1.3.3 Final hearing

Under paragraph 8 of the CACA 2013, the prosecutor must again apply to the Crown Court for a declaration, this time that the DPA *is* in the interests of justice, and the *final* terms of the DPA are fair, reasonable, and proportionate. The final approved judgment is to be made public, either immediately upon pronouncement of approval or upon the expiry of any court orders to the contrary. A court order to the contrary, made under section 4(2) of the Contempt of Court Act 1981 pursuant to paragraph 12 of Schedule 17 to the CACA 2013, may be made where individuals implicated in the wrongdoing are prosecuted and their cases are ongoing. Where a report is made of an approved DPA in such circumstances, it will typically be limited to a statement setting out that the company – or an unidentified company (where necessary to protect individual identification, for example, where the company is small) – has agreed a DPA. Such a report relates only to the potential criminal liability of the company, and does not address whether liability of any sort attaches to any associated individual.

1.1.3.4 DPA period: breach, challenge, and variation

During the DPA term, the company will be required to comply with the terms set out within the agreement. Upon completion of the DPA term and adherence to the terms set out within, proceedings will be discontinued. If, however, the company fails to comply with the terms of the agreement, breach proceedings may be instituted under paragraph 9 of Schedule 17 of the CACA 2013.[22] Breach proceedings are instigated by the prosecutor on application to the Crown Court, and therefore the company must ensure terms are complied with to the satisfaction of the prosecutor during the DPA term. The power to decide on whether a breach has occurred rests with the court, decided on the balance of probabilities, and the court provides reasons for its decisions. Upon a finding of breach, the court has two options: to invite the prosecutor and the company to agree proposals to remedy the company's failure to comply with the DPA terms; or to terminate the DPA.

Within the statutory framework of Schedule 17 of the CACA 2013, there does not currently exist an alternative route to terminate a DPA, prior to its expiry upon completion of the DPA term. A DPA is not challengeable by appeal, and thus decisions made within the process would be challenged only by judicial review. This is notable due to a number of instances in late 2023 whereby parties have sought to appeal DPAs agreed in the UK and US. In respect of a DPA agreed between the SFO and Airbus SE in the UK (**Section 1.1.5.7**), Indonesia's Minister for Law and Human Rights Yasonna Laoly provided the following statement to the *Financial Times* in September 2023: "'We will file our claim to the English court with the purpose to annul the DPA [deferred prosecution agreement] …

22 Usage of the word "may" is deliberate. There has been criticism of the SFO that the prosecutor elected not to pursue breach proceedings when a company failed to abide by the term of cooperation within its DPA, in disclosing material. When a claim for judicial review was made to the High Court, it was set out that this was the incorrect forum, though the court was critical of the SFO's approach. *See R (on the application of AL) v Serious Fraud Office* [2018] EWHC 856 (Admin) [8]–[11].

and renegotiate and conclude [a] DPA that includes the rights of the victim state."'[23] This follows a dispute in the US whereby families of victims of the Boeing disasters that led to the Boeing DPA with the US Department of Justice ("DoJ") (on the basis of conspiracy to defraud the Federal Aviation Administration) unsuccessfully appealed to have the DPA set aside in late 2022.[24] In the latter instance, a petition for review in the Fifth Circuit was filed in February 2023 (and is ongoing). Whilst the appeal of the US Boeing DPA appears to be motivated more by the families' insistence on ensuring their right to confer, thus looking to revert back to the negotiation stage, the threatened appeal of the UK Airbus DPA appears to be motivated by a claim for 'a share of the fine'.[25] Nevertheless, the statement provided by Laoly, which demonstrates an intention to renegotiate, would also have the effect of reverting back to the negotiation stage if successful. Whilst the first DPA in the UK set a precedent for the provision of compensation to a foreign government, the Airbus SE DPA bore no such provision. Crucially, the Airbus SE DPA expired in 2023, and thus any claim made in respect of compensation would be better made outside the guise of an appeal, particularly if seeking renegotiation. As the DPA expired upon successful completion of its terms, the company cannot be prosecuted again in the UK on the basis of the same underlying offences.

Paragraph 10 of Schedule 17 of the CACA 2013 sets out that, during the DPA term, it is possible for the prosecutor and company to agree variation of the DPA terms, either on account of a finding by the court of breach, or where necessary to avoid a failure by the company to comply in circumstances that were not, and could not have been, foreseen by either the prosecutor or company at the time that the DPA was agreed. However, where such a variation occurs, the prosecutor must apply to the Crown Court for a declaration that the variation is in the interests of justice and that the varied terms of the DPA are fair, reasonable, and proportionate. Details of the variation, or refusal of the court to approve the variation, are ultimately made public (immediately or upon expiry of a court order to the contrary), though the hearing itself can be held in private.

---

23 Penny Hollinger and Sylvia Pfeifer, 'Indonesia Vows to Sue UK Over Airbus Corruption Probe Settlement' (*Financial Times*, 26 September 2023) <https://www.ft.com/content/dc0720ec-b381-4f5b-8bba-44fb09408522> accessed 26 September 2023.

24 The District Court found that the families have status as 'lawful representatives of "crime victims" under the [Crime Victims' Rights Act] and that they therefore have standing to assert rights under the Act', which include the 'right to confer with the Government attorney in the case' and the 'right to be informed in a timely manner of any … deferred prosecution agreement'. The court found violations of the families' rights had arisen in such circumstances. *See United States of America v The Boeing Company* No 4:21-cr-00005-O (ND Tex 2022) 7-8, 18, citing Crime Victims' Rights Act 18 USC § 3771. However, the decision did not comment on the court's supervisory role in respect of DPAs, and in early 2023 the victims' families were denied a remedy. The District Court latterly stated that 'neither the Speedy Trial Act nor this Court's inherent supervisory powers provide a means to remedy the incalculable harm that the victims' representatives have suffered'. The court went on to state: 'The Speedy Trial Act gives the Executive exclusive discretion to negotiate deferred prosecution agreements without judicial oversight, even in response to the most heinous crimes. Despite increasing and perhaps legitimate criticism of these agreements, Congress—not the courts—is the appropriate venue to redress the inadequacies of this statutory enactment. In our system of justice, a judge's role is constitutionally confined to interpreting and applying the law, not revising it. For this Court to step outside those constitutional bounds in an attempt to remedy wrongs it has no legitimate authority to correct would compound injustice, not see justice through.' *See United States of America v The Boeing Company* No 4:21-cr-00005-O (ND Tex 2023) 29-30. A petition for review in the Fifth Circuit was filed in February 2023. At the time of writing (January 2024), it remains to be seen the outcome for the families. However, a January 2024 incident involving Alaska Airlines flight 1282 exposed issues relating to the safety of the Boeing 737 MAX 9 planes, just days before the DPA was due to expire, which may impact the DPA in any event.

25 Hollinger and Pfeifer (n 23).

1.1.3.5 Notice of discontinuance

Upon completion of the DPA term, the prosecutor gives notice in writing to the court and the company discontinuing the prosecution in accordance with paragraph 11(1) of Schedule 17 to the CACA 2013 and rule 11.8 of the Criminal Procedure Rules. The notice may include a brief comment setting out any details of compliance on each of the terms of the DPA. Where such a notice is given, the company cannot be prosecuted for the underlying offence, except (under paragraph 11(3)) where the prosecutor finds that, during the course of the negotiations for the DPA, the company provided inaccurate, misleading, or incomplete information to the prosecutor, and knew or ought to have known that the information was inaccurate, misleading, or incomplete.

1.1.4 Documentation

The DPA documentation can be separated into three key pieces: the DPA (and any attachments); the statement of facts; and the approved judgment(s) (and any court orders prescribed within).

The DPA is the document containing the agreement between the company and the prosecutor. It will contain the indictment and acceptance of responsibility, the term (time period), the scope, attachments, terms of the agreement, and an overview of the key considerations of the prosecutor in offering the DPA.

The indictment may be attached as an appendix and will set out the statement of the offence (detailed as counts where there are multiple offences) and brief particulars of the offence. The acceptance of responsibility comprises two parts. Firstly, the company agrees that the statement of facts is true and accurate to the best of its knowledge and belief. Secondly, the company agrees that – should the deferral be lifted and prosecution proceed – the company will not, in those proceedings, contest the admissibility of, nor contradict, the content within the statement of facts (even where the company enters a guilty plea, and at sentencing hearings).

The statement of facts is a document agreed between the company and the prosecutor, outlining the agreed factual account in relation to the predicate offence(s) forming part of the indictment, and is typically attached to the DPA by appendix. Notably, the statement of facts is an agreed account which is not subject to judge or jury adjudication, and will not feature the input of third parties (such as individuals no longer part of the company). In respect of proceedings reinstated upon cessation of the deferral, the statement of facts is treated as an admission by the company to the content within, under section 10 of the Criminal Justice Act 1967 ("CJA 1967") (provided for under paragraph 13(2) of Schedule 17 of the CACA 2013). For the purpose of obtaining the DPA, however, the company is required only to accept responsibility for the stated wrongdoing, and is not required to make a formal admission to having committed criminal offences.

The term of the DPA will be agreed by the parties and could be a matter of months or years. Considerations in fixing the term may include (but are not limited to) the time period of the investigation leading to the DPA, the extent to which changes have already been effected within the company during that time, the ability to make payments required within the agreement, and the period required to see deliverance of a successful compliance programme.

In respect of attachments, it may be the case that a DPA requires an undertaking – typically provided by the wrongdoer company's parent company (or related company within the corporate group) – in order to guarantee completion of all or a number of DPA terms. The most common use of an undertaking has been to guarantee payment of a financial penalty, though use has also been productive in ensuring abidance by compliance programmes (which may be effected across a corporate group) and cooperation in ongoing investigations (for example). Though such undertakings were not envisaged in the introductory process, and are not reflected in the statutory framework, their use has been seen in a number of cases.[26]

Terms that may be included in the DPA are (non-exhaustively) set out under paragraph 5(3) of Schedule 17 of the CACA 2013. Typical terms seen within DPAs include payment of a financial penalty, payment of costs, payment of compensation, disgorgement of profits, implementation of and adherence to a compliance programme, cooperation with prosecuting agencies in ongoing investigations, and the promise that the company remains in existence to the end of the DPA period (if this is considered a necessary explicit addition). Where the latter term is deemed a requirement, it may be the case that an undertaking provided by a related company – forming an attachment to the DPA – is also required as a guarantee. Such terms agreed by the company may feature within the overview of the prosecutor's key considerations in offering the DPA (within the DPA document). However, considerations may also include conduct already displayed by the company, such as the self-report (or "self-disclosure") of necessary information, past prompt and voluntary cooperation with the investigation, lack of prior record of wrongdoing, financial penalties already paid to other authorities, and remediation already effected (such as changes to senior management).

The DPA is accompanied by the approved judgment(s) delivered by a Crown Court judge in approving the DPA. An approved judgment is not published pursuant to the private preliminary hearing but is published upon final approval (immediately, or upon expiry of any court orders to the contrary under section 4(2) of the Contempt of Court Act 1981). The approved judgment typically refers to the legal framework, the facts presented to the court in relation to the underlying offending (as agreed between the company and prosecutor), factors in favour or against the offering of a DPA (including any involvement by related companies), and any publication orders, and will always set out whether the DPA is in the interests of justice and whether the terms of the DPA are fair, reasonable, and proportionate.

1.1.5 Cases

1.1.5.1 Serious Fraud Office v Standard Bank Plc ("*Standard Bank*")

The first DPA in the UK was agreed between the SFO and Standard Bank Plc ("Standard Bank") in 2015 and predominantly involved three organisations: Standard Bank, Stanbic Bank Tanzania Ltd ("Stanbic") (a subsidiary of Standard Bank), and the Tanzanian company Enterprise Growth Market Advisors Limited ("EGMA"). During the period

26 *Serious Fraud Office v Serco Geografix Ltd* [2019] Lloyd's Rep FC 518 (Crown); *Serious Fraud Office v G4S Care and Justice Services (UK) Ltd* [2021] Crim LR 138 (Crown); *Director of the Serious Fraud Office v Amec Foster Wheeler Limited* [2021] Lloyd's Rep FC 353 (Crown); *Bluu Solutions Limited and Tetris-Projects Limited* (n 8).

of wrongdoing, two directors (and shareholders) of EGMA also served as the (then) Commissioner of the Tanzania Revenue Authority and former Chief Executive Officer of the Tanzanian Capital Markets and Securities Authority, with strong ties to the Tanzanian government.[27]

The underlying wrongdoing related to an agreement reached between Stanbic and EGMA to further the objective of the Tanzanian government in '[raising] funds by way of a sovereign note placement',[28] where Stanbic would act as lead managers.[29] Stanbic was not licensed to 'deal with non-local foreign investors in the debt capital market'[30] but collaborated with sufficiently licensed subsidiary Standard Bank to ensure performance under the agreement. Standard Bank neglected to consider the high risk of corruption and relied entirely on Stanbic's due diligence performance in relation to activities with EGMA, '[making] no [further] enquiry'.[31] The SFO was alerted when $6 million (US) paid by Stanbic into the bank account shared between them and EGMA as the agreed fee was promptly withdrawn in cash.

The SFO found that Standard Bank had failed to prevent bribery contrary to section 7 of the Bribery Act 2010 for the purposes of obtaining or retaining business or an advantage in the conduct of business, based on evidence obtained during negotiations: the first prosecution (though deferred) for a section 7 offence by any UK prosecutor.

The offence related to the actions of Stanbic's 'then Chief Executive Officer (Bashir Awale) and/or Head of Corporate and Investment Banking (Shose Sinare)'.[32] It was alleged within the statement of facts that Awale and Sinare personally sanctioned the payment of $6 million (US) to EGMA, to be used to induce Tanzanian government representatives to show favour to Stanbic and Standard Bank in awarding Stanbic the position as lead managers.[33] Allegations made within the statement of facts have, however, subsequently been vehemently denied by the two individuals.[34] The Right Honourable Sir Brian Leveson importantly noted that the alleged offence under the DPA was in relation to inadequate systems of prevention and lack of appropriate provision and was not directed specifically at the company or its employees.[35]

The DPA expired on 30 November 2018, when the SFO announced the end of the agreement upon Standard Bank's full compliance with its terms.[36]

---

27 *Serious Fraud Office v Standard Bank Plc (now ICBC Standard Bank Plc) (Final)* [2016] Lloyd's Rep FC 102 (Crown) [7].

28 ibid [6].

29 Sarah Garvey, 'First UK Deferred Prosecution Agreement Between the SFO and a Bank' (*Allen & Overy*, 14 April 2016) <http://www.allenovery.com/publications/en-gb/Pages/First-UK-deferred-prosecution-agreement-between-the-SFO-and-a-bank.aspx> accessed 12 May 2018.

30 *Standard Bank Plc (now ICBC Standard Bank Plc) (Final)* (n 27) [6].

31 ibid [7].

32 Serious Fraud Office, 'Deferred Prosecution Agreement – Statement of Facts – SFO v ICBC SB PLC' (*Serious Fraud Office*, 1 June 2016) <https://www.sfo.gov.uk/cases/standard-bank-plc/> accessed 1 March 2018.

33 *Standard Bank Plc (now ICBC Standard Bank Plc) (Final)* (n 27) [128].

34 Prior to her plea agreement in Tanzania, Sinare was reportedly suing Stanbic and Standard Bank in Tanzania in respect of misrepresentations and falsehoods within the DPA process. *See* Daily News, 'Shose Sinare Seeks 30m US Dollars Damages From Stanbic' (*Daily News*, 2 March 2016) <https://allafrica.com/stories/201603021200.html> accessed 1 February 2021. There had been calls in 2016 for the SFO to reopen the *Standard Bank* case, in light of Sinare's claims; however this did not materialise.

35 *Standard Bank Plc (now ICBC Standard Bank Plc) (Final)* (n 27) [11].

36 Serious Fraud Office, 'Standard Bank Plc' (*Serious Fraud Office*, 3 September 2019) <https://www.sfo.gov.uk/cases/standard-bank-plc/> accessed 30 November 2019.

1.1.5.2 Serious Fraud Office v Sarclad Limited ("*Sarclad Ltd*")

Formerly known as *Serious Fraud Office v XYZ Ltd*, the SFO's second DPA was agreed in 2016 with small to medium-sized enterprise Sarclad Ltd ("Sarclad"). Sarclad was acquired in February 2000 by US-owned company Heico Companies LLC ("Heico"), trading primarily in exportation to Asian markets.[37] Upon implementation of a compliance plan in Sarclad in 2011, Heico subsequently became aware of malpractice in the securing of contracts and launched an internal investigation which led to a self-report to the SFO.[38] During the period of June 2004 to June 2012, Sarclad had, through intermediary agents, engaged in the payment of bribes to those '[exerting] influence and control over the awarding'[39] of 28 implicated contracts forming the subject of the DPA.[40] The offences committed preceded and succeeded the introduction of the Bribery Act 2010 and were therefore charged under the 2010 Act, the Criminal Law Act 1977, and the Prevention of Corruption Act 1906.[41]

The Right Honourable Sir Leveson stated that the activities were committed by the company's 'controlling minds'[42] on a 'prolific scale',[43] and several former employees were, at the time of the agreement, subject to individual criminal proceedings.[44] Since the agreement, three implicated individuals, Michael Sorby, Adrian Leek, and David Justice, have been personally acquitted of conspiracy to corrupt and conspiracy to bribe, leading to a removal of reporting restrictions.[45]

Following an agreed period of full compliance, the DPA reached its conclusion on 16 July 2019.[46]

1.1.5.3 Serious Fraud Office v Rolls-Royce Plc ("*Rolls-Royce*")

The SFO's third DPA – agreed in 2017 – was, unlike its predecessors, not triggered by a self-report. Instead, the SFO became aware of concerning posts on the internet and approached Rolls-Royce for further information.[47] The offences subject to the DPA include six counts of conspiracy to corrupt, contrary to section 1 of the Criminal Law Act 1977, five counts of failure to prevent bribery, contrary to section 7 of the Bribery Act 2010, and one count of false accounting, contrary to section 17(1)(a) of the Theft Act 1968.[48] The large scale of corruption within the civil, defence, and energy businesses of Rolls-Royce

37 *Serious Fraud Office v Sarclad Limited (Serious Fraud Office v XYZ Ltd) (Final)* [2016] Lexis Citation 686 (Crown) [5]. *See also Serious Fraud Office v XYZ Limited* [2016] Lloyd's Rep FC 509 (Crown) [5].

38 ibid [11].

39 ibid [8].

40 ibid [7]–[8].

41 ibid [12].

42 ibid [1].

43 ibid [4]; Serious Fraud Office, 'Sarclad Ltd and SFO Deferred Prosecution Agreement' (*Serious Fraud Office*, 23 December 2019) <https://www.sfo.gov.uk/download/sarclad-ltd-and-sfo-deferred-prosecution-agreement/> accessed 9 February 2021, para 1.

44 Jonathan Brogden and Graham Ludlam, 'Second Deferred Prosecution Agreement Approved by the English Court Demonstrates the Value of Self Reporting' (*DAC beachcroft*, 19 July 2016) <https://www.dacbeachcroft.com/en/gb/articles/2016/july/second-deferred-prosecution-agreement-approved-by-the-english-court-demonstrates-the-value-of-self-reporting/> accessed 25 April 2018.

45 Serious Fraud Office, 'Sarclad Ltd' (*Serious Fraud Office*, 3 September 2019) <https://www.sfo.gov.uk/cases/sarclad-ltd/> accessed 30 November 2019; Serious Fraud Office, 'Three Individuals Acquitted as SFO Confirms DPA With Sarclad' (*Serious Fraud Office*, 16 July 2019) <https://www.sfo.gov.uk/2019/07/16/three-individuals-acquitted-as-sfo-confirms-dpa-with-sarclad/> accessed 30 November 2019.

46 Serious Fraud Office, 'Sarclad Ltd' (n 45).

47 *Serious Fraud Office v Rolls-Royce Plc* [2017] Lloyd's Rep FC 249 (Crown) [16].

48 ibid [137].

bore continuous themes of payments of bribes and commissions in order to ensure that Rolls-Royce was shown favour, secured contracts and tenders, and was protected from investigation.[49] The 12 offences subject to the DPA were committed in seven countries over 24 years,[50] demonstrating the monumental scale and 'culture of corruption'[51] within the company. Nonetheless, a DPA was offered to Rolls-Royce due to its commendable conduct and cooperation when approached by the SFO,[52] including waiver of privilege,[53] and the 'severe adverse impact [of a prosecution] on innocent parties'.[54]

The relevant activities were undoubtedly conducted and approved by many individuals and 'controllers';[55] the 12 offences demonstrative of significant involvement of senior individuals, particularly those relating to conspiracy to corrupt and the payment of bribes. One individual in the 'spotlight'[56] at the time was chief executive for 14 of the 23 years of corruption and within this capacity reportedly sanctioned several payments under Rolls-Royce's Code of Business.[57] However, in 2019, the SFO announced that it would not be prosecuting any associated individuals, following an investigation into the available evidence and considered public interest.[58]

The DPA has been criticised following the Right Honourable Sir Leveson's comment within the judgment that 'if Rolls-Royce were not to be prosecuted in the context of such egregious criminality … then it was difficult to see when any company would be prosecuted'.[59] Many opine that Rolls-Royce was a company beyond prosecutorial reach and control, raising questions as to the SFO's power to prosecute high-scale corruption and 'whether Rolls Royce was simply too large and too powerful'.[60] This supports the often-asserted argument that DPAs were introduced to rectify the inherent problem within English law that prosecution of (larger) corporate bodies is 'too difficult',[61] providing an alternative "penalty" for wrongdoers.

The DPA successfully expired on 17 January 2022.[62]

---

49 Serious Fraud Office, 'Deferred Prosecution Agreement – Statement of Facts – SFO v Rolls Royce PLC' (*Serious Fraud Office*, 17 January 2017) <https://www.sfo.gov.uk/cases/rolls-royce-plc/> accessed 15 May 2020, 5.

50 *Rolls-Royce Plc* (n 47) [30].

51 Keith Reid, 'Rolls-Royce: the reality of bribery' [2017] Comp & Risk 10, 11.

52 *Rolls-Royce Plc* (n 47) [141]–[143].

53 Rita Cheung, 'Deferred Prosecution Agreements: Cooperation and Confession' (2018) 77 CLJ 12, 14.

54 Mark Sutton and Karen Boto, 'Rolls Royce: Take Off for the Jumbo DPA' (*Clyde & Co*, 24 January 2017) <https://s3.amazonaws.com/documents.lexology.com/142e5ee3-47c3-4ecb-a250-83ca10d244cb.pdf?AWSAccessKeyId=AKIAVYILUYJ754JTDY6T&Expires=1696874832&Signature=T87%2FoqZO8kZfxl9b13zFiBzScz4%3D> accessed 10 May 2018.

55 Peggy Hollinger and Catherine Belton, 'UK Investigation Into Rolls-Royce Turns its Focus to Individuals' (*Financial Times*, 21 January 2017) <https://www.ft.com/content/f1344464-df23-11e6-9d7c-be108f1c1dce> accessed 1 March 2018.

56 Ibid.

57 'From 2003 the chief executive had to personally authorise all commissions above more than 5 percent of the value of any contract under company rules. He also had to authorise any fixed payments above £150,000 from 2007.' *See* ibid.

58 Serious Fraud Office, 'SFO Closes GlaxoSmithKline Investigation and Investigation Into Rolls-Royce Individuals' (*Serious Fraud Office*, 22 February 2019) <https://www.sfo.gov.uk/2019/02/22/sfo-closes-glaxosmithkline-investigation-and-investigation-into-rolls-royce-individuals/> accessed 30 November 2019.

59 *Rolls-Royce Plc* (n 47) [61].

60 Sutton and Boto (n 54).

61 David Green, 'Pinsent Masons and Legal Week Regulatory Reform and Enforcement Conference' (*Serious Fraud Office*, 24 October 2013) <https://www.sfo.gov.uk/2013/10/24/pinsent-masons-legal-week-regulatory-reform-enforcement-conference-2/> accessed 9 May 2018.

62 Serious Fraud Office, 'Serious Fraud Office and Rolls-Royce Plc, Rolls-Royce Energy Systems Ltd – Discontinuance of Proceedings on Expiry of Deferred Prosecution Agreement' (*Serious Fraud Office*, 2022)

1.1.5.4 Serious Fraud Office v Tesco Stores Ltd ("*Tesco Stores Ltd*")

The fourth UK DPA was agreed in 2017 between Tesco Stores Ltd (a wholly owned subsidiary of Tesco Plc) and the SFO for false accounting from February to September 2014. For this half-year period, Tesco Stores Ltd identified an overstatement of its expected profits on the basis of income pulled forward (earlier than it should have been) in an attempt to fill the gap of an inability to meet targets, with the knowledge of senior management figures.[63] Systemic pressure within the company to meet financial targets led to the wrongful recognition of income, effected by an amalgamation of such pulling forward and legacy misstatements, and thus a 'dishonest'[64] false account of the company's financial position.[65] The inaccurate update on expected corporate group profits (published by Tesco Plc on the basis of figures provided by Tesco Stores Ltd), including Tesco Stores Ltd, was not rectified for almost a month,[66] and reporting of the overstatement led to a drop in share prices and loss in share value by over £2 billion.[67]

The implicated individuals were former finance director Carl Rogberg, former commercial director for food John Scouler, and former managing director of Tesco UK Christopher Bush, each charged with one count of fraud by abuse of position and one count of false accounting.[68] The actions of the three former directors were alleged to have amounted to a deliberate manipulation of figures to mislead the stock market and conceal the true financial position of the organisation. However, the individuals denied the charges,[69] and were acquitted following weaknesses in the case presented by the SFO in the trials of Scouler and Bush, and the failure of the SFO to present any evidence in the trial of Rogberg.[70] The contempt of court order which once restricted reporting on the DPA, to allow for a fair trial of the individual directors, was lifted in 2020. Parallel to the agreement with the SFO, the Financial Conduct Authority (FCA) announced that, as 'Tesco PLC and Tesco Stores Ltd had committed market abuse',[71] a fine was also being imposed by the regulator.

The DPA expired on 10 April 2020.[72]

<https://www.sfo.gov.uk/download/serious-fraud-office-and-rolls-royce-plc-rolls-royce-energy-systems-ltd-discontinuance-of-proceedings-on-expiry-of-deferred-prosecution-agreement/> accessed 12 April 2023.

63 *Serious Fraud Office v Tesco Stores Ltd* [2019] Lloyd's Rep FC 283 (Crown) [32].

64 Serious Fraud Office, 'Deferred Prosecution Agreement – Statement of Facts – SFO v Tesco Stores Ltd' (*Serious Fraud Office*, 23 January 2019) <https://www.sfo.gov.uk/download/deferred-prosecution-agreement-statement-of-facts-sfo-v-tesco-stores-ltd/> accessed 26 June 2020, para 6.

65 *Tesco Stores Ltd* (n 63) [30]–[31].

66 Serious Fraud Office, 'Deferred Prosecution Agreement – Statement of Facts – SFO v Tesco Stores Ltd' (n 64) para 5.

67 ibid para 73.

68 Sarah Butler, 'Tesco Fraud Trial Abandoned After Defendant Taken Ill' (*The Guardian*, 6 February 2018) <https://www.theguardian.com/uk-news/2018/feb/06/tesco-trial-abandoned-after-defendant-taken-ill> accessed 1 March 2018.

69 Sarah Butler, 'Former Tesco Executives Pressured Others to Falsify Figures, Court Told' (*The Guardian*, 29 September 2017) <https://www.theguardian.com/business/2017/sep/29/tesco-executives-court-christopher-bush-carl-rogberg> accessed 12 May 2018.

70 Jane Croft and Jonathan Eley, 'Tesco Fraud Trial Collapse Puts Deferred Prosecution Deals in the Dock' (*Financial Times*, 23 January 2019) <https://www.ft.com/content/b6c2b688-1f29-11e9-b126-46fc3ad87c65> accessed 30 November 2019.

71 Nick Benwell and Charles Mayo, 'Tesco Enters Into DPA With SFO' (*Simmons & Simmons elexica*, 11 April 2017) <http://www.elexica.com/en/legal-topics/corporate-governance-and-compliance/100417-tesco-enters-into-dpa-with-sfo> accessed 8 February 2018.

72 Serious Fraud Office, 'Notice of DPA Discontinuance' (*Serious Fraud Office*, 7 April 2020) <https://www.sfo.gov.uk/download/notice-of-dpa-discontinuance/?wpdmdl=26045&refresh=5ebd721e359611589473822> accessed 14 May 2020.

1.1.5.5 Serious Fraud Office v Serco Geografix Ltd ("*Serco Geografix Ltd*")

The first DPA concerning fraud relating to a public contract (but the fifth DPA in the UK) was agreed in 2019 between the SFO and Serco Geografix Ltd ("Serco Geografix").[73] Serco Geografix, a wholly owned subsidiary of Serco Ltd, was via a holding company wholly owned by Serco Group PLC.[74] Serco Geografix predominantly operated to service two contracts held by Serco Ltd for the supply of electronic monitoring equipment to the UK Government.[75] During an investigation into suspected invoices issued for the monitoring of non-existent individuals, which revealed no evidence of foul play, emails revealing 'manipulation of accounting between [Serco Geografix] and [Serco Ltd] designed artificially to reduce the profit margins reported to the [MoJ]' were found.[76] The DPA which followed was based on three counts of fraud and two counts of false accounting. It was the first DPA in the UK to bear an attached undertaking, provided by parent company Serco Group PLC, assuming responsibility for payment of the financial penalty and costs upon potential default by the wrongdoer subsidiary.

Cases brought against former executives Nicholas Woods and Simon Marshall in relation to the corporate wrongdoing collapsed on the basis of disclosure failings by the SFO. Following the failings, the SFO accepted liability for (defence) costs, which totalled £2.7 million.[77] This prompted the prosecuting agency to commission Sir Brian Altman KC to conduct a review into the matter.[78] Since the case, Marshall – speaking to *The Times* newspaper – accused the SFO of trying to retrofit the case to him, critical of the functioning of the agency and the use of DPAs.[79]

The DPA with Serco Geografix expired on 4 July 2022.[80]

1.1.5.6 Serious Fraud Office v Güralp Systems Ltd ("*Güralp Systems Ltd*")

Agreed in 2019, the SFO's sixth DPA was based on two counts: conspiracy to corrupt, contrary to section 1 of the Prevention of Corruption Act 1906, and failure to prevent bribery, contrary to the Bribery Act 2010. Güralp Systems Ltd, via the statement of facts, accepted that two directors (Dr Cansun Güralp and Andrew Bell) and a senior employee (Natalie

73 Jonathan Ames, 'Serco's "Deliberate Fraud" on Taxpayer' (*The Times*, 5 July 2019) <https://www.thetimes.co.uk/article/serco-s-deliberate-fraud-on-taxpayer-fckbsl6k7> accessed 30 November 2019.

74 *Serco Geografix Ltd* (n 26) [1], [3].

75 ibid [2].

76 ibid [4].

77 *See* Email from A Abed to author (30 September 2021). This email was a response to a Freedom of Information request made under the Freedom of Information Act 2000 by the author to the Serious Fraud Office on 2 September 2021 (Case FOI2021-111). A Abed is the Information Officer from the Public Relations and Information Team who responded.

78 Notably, the review focussed on disclosure failures only. *See* Brian Altman and Rebecca Chalkley, 'Report to the Serious Fraud Office: The Collapse of *R V. Woods & Marshall* on 26 April 2021' (*Serious Fraud Office*, July 2022) <https://www.sfo.gov.uk/download/review-of-r-v-woods-marshall-by-brian-altman-qc/> accessed 8 February 2023, Serious Fraud Office, 'Implementation Update – May 2023: Altman Review' (*Serious Fraud Office*, 24 May 2023) <https://www.sfo.gov.uk/download/implementation-update-may-2023-altman-review/> accessed 3 June 2023.

79 Oliver Gill, 'Abolish Serious Fraud Office Says Acquitted Ex-Serco Boss' (*The Telegraph*, 8 May 2021) <https://www.telegraph.co.uk/business/2021/05/08/abolish-serious-fraud-office-says-acquitted-ex-serco-boss/> accessed 13 May 2021.

80 Serious Fraud Office, 'Deferred Prosecution Agreement – Serco Geografix Ltd & SFO' (*Serious Fraud Office*, 2022) <https://www.sfo.gov.uk/download/deferred-prosecution-agreement-serco-geografix-ltd-sfo/> accessed 12 April 2023.

Pearce) of the company engaged in misconduct over two decades in regard to payments made to and dealings with Dr Heon-Cheol Chi. Chi was an individual who held multiple positions within a government-funded research institute in the Republic of Korea. The involvement of Chi, designed to induce or reward Chi to exploit his senior position in the Korea Institute of Geoscience and Mineral Resources in order to influence the award of contracts to Güralp Systems Ltd,[81] allowed the company to make profits in excess of £2 million which would not otherwise have been made.[82] The alleged involvement of the aforementioned individuals is divulged in detail within the statement of facts and the judgment of Mr Justice William Davis. Such detail includes, though is not limited to, the organisation of the relationship between the company (headed by Cansun Güralp) and Chi; and the scheduling and making of payments to Chi, with considered concealment of such payments and invoices from other employees of Güralp Systems Ltd and colleagues of Chi.

It was announced in December 2019 that the individuals implicated by the statement of facts and DPA – Cansun Güralp, Andrew Bell, and Natalie Pearce – had all been acquitted of conspiracy to make corrupt payments, contrary to section 1(1) of the Criminal Justice Act 1977, for their personal involvement in the misconduct forming part of the company's agreement. On announcement of the acquittal of the three implicated individuals, concerns resurfaced regarding the effectiveness of the SFO's corporate penalty tool and particularly the accountability of related individuals.[83]

The DPA is due to expire on 22 October 2024.

1.1.5.7 Director of the Serious Fraud Office v Airbus SE ("*Airbus SE*")

With a financial sanction nearing one billion euro, the landmark DPA between the SFO and Airbus SE (a Dutch and French domiciled company) was agreed in 2020, based on five counts of failure to prevent bribery contrary to section 7 of the Bribery Act 2010. The seventh DPA in the UK, but the first before approving judge Dame Victoria Sharp, was agreed with Airbus SE as the ultimate parent company of an entity that had evolved throughout the period of wrongdoing (2011 to 2015), due to its growth and conversion into a European public-limited company.

The investigation by the SFO was triggered by a report made by Airbus SE and UK Export Financing in April 2016, following communication between the two latter parties on export credit financing which uncovered red flags for corruption. In January 2017, the SFO joined forces with the French Parquet National Financier (PNF) forming the joint investigation team (JIT) to facilitate investigations. This was an important step in the SFO's investigation due to the French Blocking Statute and the French Code of Criminal Procedure, which impacts the disclosure of information and sharing of documentation in

81 Serious Fraud Office, 'Deferred Prosecution Agreement, Statement of Facts, Approved Judgment – SFO v Güralp Systems Ltd: Statement of Facts' (*Serious Fraud Office*, 20 December 2019) <https://www.sfo.gov.uk/download/deferred-prosecution-agreement-statement-of-facts-approved-judgment-sfo-v-guralp-systems-ltd/> accessed 9 February 2021, para 3.

82 *Serious Fraud Office v Güralp Systems Ltd* [2020] Lloyd's Rep FC 90 (Crown) [25].

83 Michael Cross, 'Fraud Office Under Fire for Deferred Prosecution After "Not Guilty" Verdicts' (*The Law Society Gazette*, 23 December 2019) <https://www.lawgazette.co.uk/law/fraud-office-under-fire-for-deferred-prosecution-despite-not-guilty-verdicts/5102586.article> accessed 10 March 2020; Neil O'May, 'Deferred Prosecution Agreements After Tesco: Whither are we Bound?' (2019) 30(2) PLC Mag 16–17.

foreign proceedings.[84] Airbus SE was also the subject of investigations in the US by the US DoJ and US Department of State. The resolution of the investigations of each body was finalised by way of respective settlement agreements, of which financial sanctions totalled over 3.5 billion euro.

The five counts within the UK DPA relate to failure to prevent bribery concerned with the purchase of aircraft in Malaysia, Sri Lanka, Taiwan, and Indonesia, and the purchase of military transport aircraft in Ghana (though investigations by other bodies encompass further jurisdictions).[85] In the outline of each count, bribery of the directors of purchasing companies in the respective jurisdictions is outlined.[86] However, individual identity is protected to ensure fair trials and due to human rights concerns, as the death penalty exists for corruption in some relevant jurisdictions.[87] The involvement of 'very senior, senior and other employees'[88] is covered in paragraph 65 of the judgment, with identifying information omitted (such as specific roles). Sixty-three top and senior management employees of Airbus have departed since 2015, 31 of whom were dismissed.[89]

Investigation into individuals connected, or previously connected, with Airbus SE was ongoing at the time of DPA approval.[90] However, according to the SFO website: 'Following a detailed review of the available evidence, the SFO will not be prosecuting any individuals in connection with its investigation of Airbus and others.'[91] Such a decision is surprising, as the case comprised over 30.5 million documents surrendered to the JIT. As part of the DPA, the SFO agreed to bring to a close their investigation into Airbus SE (and its controlled subsidiaries).[92]

The DPA with the SFO expired on 31 January 2023.[93]

1.1.5.8 Serious Fraud Office v G4S Care and Justice Services (UK) Ltd (*"G4S C&J"*)

G4S Care & Justice Services UK ("G4S C&J") (previously named "Securicor Justice Services Ltd") was at the time of DPA approval a wholly owned UK registered subsidiary of G4S plc, a public limited company incorporated in the UK. G4S C&J provided electronic monitoring services for use within the UK criminal justice system to the MoJ between 2005 and 2013. Interestingly, in 2003, when the Home Office initially submitted an Invitation to Propose, G4S C&J were successful in their bid for three of the five respective areas, and the remaining two were awarded to Serco Geografix Ltd (contracts which led to a DPA between the SFO and the latter company in 2019).[94]

---

84 *Director of the Serious Fraud Office v Airbus SE* [2021] Lloyd's Rep FC 159 (Crown) [34].

85 ibid [34].

86 ibid [39]–[56].

87 ibid [13].

88 ibid [65].

89 ibid [78].

90 ibid [13].

91 Serious Fraud Office, 'Airbus Group' (*Serious Fraud Office*, 2 March 2023) <https://www.sfo.gov.uk/cases/airbus-group/> accessed 26 September 2023.

92 Serious Fraud Office, 'Deferred Prosecution Agreement Airbus 31.01.20' (*Serious Fraud Office*, 31 January 2020) <https://www.sfo.gov.uk/download/airbus-se-deferred-prosecution-agreement-statement-of-facts/> accessed 28 February 2020, para 8.

93 Serious Fraud Office, 'R v Airbus SE – Deferred Prosecution Agreement' (*Serious Fraud Office*, 2023) <https://www.sfo.gov.uk/download/airbus-se-deferred-prosecution-agreement-statement-of-facts/> accessed 12 April 2023.

94 *G4S Care and Justice Services (UK) Ltd* (n 26) [11].

Following an investigation into a matter referred to the SFO by the MoJ in 2013, the SFO held that there was not sufficient evidence to corroborate allegations that G4S C&J had been dishonestly issuing invoices for the monitoring of individuals where no such monitoring had taken place. Later in 2013, the MoJ referred a separate concern to the SFO regarding G4S C&J's compliance with its financial reporting and notification obligations. A month later, G4S plc reported to the SFO that it had found material suggesting its subsidiary's failure to provide accurate financial reports to the MoJ.[95] The investigation led to a finding of three counts of fraud contrary to section 2 of the Fraud Act 2006, and G4S C&J was offered a DPA.

Within the DPA negotiation period, G4S C&J agreed to work with the Home Office (the body that agreed to the initial contract) to reduce costs and, in doing so, agreed 'that the Home Office would be entitled to recover 50% of the value of "any unanticipated cost efficiencies" which the company achieved'.[96] G4S C&J also agreed to submit a financial model report to the Home Office every six months in an effort to keep pricing transparent and minimal. The three counts of fraud by false representation relate to the financial models provided in 2011 and 2012, which set out historic inaccurate costs from a period of approximately six years.[97] Dishonest reporting within the financial models was carried out in an effort to 'conceal the unanticipated cost efficiencies'[98] and therefore retain money due to be shared between the contracting parties. With great focus on the importance of 'governance changes',[99] a DPA was agreed for such wrongdoing. Notably, the discount applied to the financial penalty for cooperation in the investigation was calculated at 40 percent (in contrast with the more frequently applied 50 percent discount in other DPA prior cases) as the level of cooperation was deemed to be substantial, rather than exemplary.[100] The DPA was approved with an attached parent company undertaking, to ensure that compliance measures ordered would be maintained and enforced.[101]

The publication of the statement of facts was originally postponed until the conclusion of the investigation and 'prospect of proceedings'[102] against individuals allegedly involved in the criminal behaviour. Former directors Richard Morris, Mark Preston, and James Jardine were each charged with seven offences of fraud in connection with the DPA underlying wrongdoing. All three directors were acquitted in March 2023, after the SFO's barrister Crispin Aylett informed the court that it was 'no longer in the public interest' to proceed with the prosecutions.[103] The SFO's conduct in relation to disclosure was again called into question, with Jardine's representative Joanna Dimmock referring to 'ten years of delay, mismanagement and misunderstanding of the evidence', as well as 'a litany of disclosure disasters and breaches by the SFO of over 60 court orders'.[104]

---

95 ibid [4].
96 ibid [14].
97 ibid [25].
98 ibid [20].
99 ibid [32].
100 ibid [40].
101 ibid [43].
102 ibid [18].
103 Kate Beioley, 'Serious Fraud Office Abandons Case Against Former G4S Executives' (*Financial Times*, 10 March 2023) <https://www.ft.com/content/93323263-6617-48c4-8567-ad8c32ba0f1f> accessed 16 March 2023.
104 ibid.

The DPA expired on 17 July 2023.[105]

1.1.5.9 Director of the Serious Fraud Office v Airline Services Ltd ("*Airline Services Ltd*")

Airline Services Limited ("ASL") and the SFO entered into the SFO's ninth DPA in late 2020 on the basis of three counts of failure to prevent bribery under section 7 of the Bribery Act 2010. Following an internal investigation into another agent and airline, it became clear that the conduct of "Agent 1" required further investigation and external solicitors were instructed to do so. As a result of the findings, a self-report was made to the SFO in July 2015 which led to a criminal investigation being opened in December 2015. It was determined that Agent 1 – working as an agent for ASL and as a consultant project manager for Lufthansa (with duties including work on invitation to tender documents, evaluation of bid documents, and making recommendations to the Decision Committee on bids) – had received commission payments from ASL for its part in securing three of four supplemental agreements with Lufthansa, which fed into General Terms of Agreement agreed between ASL and Lufthansa in 2011.[106] Within the three agreements, Agent 1 passed on confidential information obtained by virtue of their employment with Lufthansa to ASL, which consequently led to the awarding of relevant contracts to ASL by Lufthansa.

Prior to the enactment of the Bribery Act 2010, ASL instructed external legal advisers to assess its compliance with the impending legislation. A number of recommendations were made, an "Anti-corruption Policy and Guidelines" document was created for internal use, and the use of agents was identified to be a significant risk. The guidance document was never circulated to staff, and agents continued to be used. As such, the compliance procedures in place during the period of offending were deemed by Mrs Justice May to be 'woefully inadequate'.[107]

ASL, a dormant non-trading entity, was said to plan to be wound up following its conclusion,[108] though according to Companies House it remains active.[109] The DPA expired on 30 October 2021.[110]

1.1.5.10 Director of the Serious Fraud Office v Amec Foster Wheeler Limited ("*AFWEL*")

As part of a global settlement which involved the SFO, US DoJ and SEC, and Brazilian authorities, Amec Foster Wheeler Energy Limited ("AFWEL") entered into a DPA with the SFO in mid-2021. The tenth UK DPA agreed by the SFO was approved on the basis of ten counts of offending: nine relating to conspiracy to corrupt and one relating to failure to prevent bribery. The offending took place in Nigeria, Saudi Arabia, Malaysia, India, and

105 Serious Fraud Office, 'Notice of Discontinuance: G4S Care & Justice Services (UK) Limited' (*Serious Fraud Office*, 25 July 2023) <https://www.sfo.gov.uk/download/details-of-compliance-g4s/> accessed 25 July 2023.

106 *Director of the Serious Fraud Office v Airline Services Ltd* [2021] Lloyd's Rep FC 42 (Crown) [21].

107 ibid [40].

108 ibid [16].

109 Companies House, 'Airline Services Limited' (*Companies House*, 2023) <https://find-and-update.company-information.service.gov.uk/company/01685094> accessed 26 April 2023.

110 Serious Fraud Office, 'Airline Service Ltd – Details of Compliance' (*Serious Fraud Office*, 2021) <https://www.sfo.gov.uk/download/airline-service-ltd-details-of-compliance/> accessed 12 April 2023.

Brazil over an 18-year period, when the company was known as Foster Wheeler Energy Limited ("FWEL") (and was owned by Foster Wheeler Limited ("FWL")), prior to acquisition by AFWEL, and consequently by John Wood Group PLC ("Wood").

FWEL was the UK operating entity of the wider group, and its business was largely in the design and engineering of on- and offshore oil, gas, and petrochemical facilities, a service which operated internationally and generated contracts worth hundreds of millions of pounds. Those contracts would often be agreed with state-owned energy companies, and the statement of facts refers to evidence demonstrating FWEL's use of agents to assist in obtaining or retaining such business, or an advantage in the conduct of business. In order to do so, the SFO's position was that agents were used by FWEL, with the conspiracy of FWEL's employees and directors, to make corrupt payments to relevant public officials. Further, with a lack of adequate procedures in place to address and combat such conduct, FWEL had failed to prevent bribery. Despite the uncovering of evidence between 2007 and 2010 that supported the theory that individuals in FWEL may have engaged in unlawful conduct in relation to such activities, this was not self-reported in the UK or internationally.[111]

The DPA was approved with an attached undertaking provided by parent company Wood, more extensive in its obligations than previously seen in cases with DPA undertakings.[112] Lord Justice Edis was keen to consider the provision of such an undertaking, with Wood being '"twice removed" from the management of FWEL which was responsible for the misconduct'.[113] Nevertheless, within the undertaking, Wood guaranteed to ensure the performance of AFWEL of all obligations within the DPA, in particular in relation to financial liabilities. Wood further guaranteed to ensure that AFWEL would remain in existence (and within Wood's ownership and control) during the DPA term; to enhance and modify Wood's group-wide ethics and compliance policies and procedures (the "E&C Programme"); to report to the SFO annually in relation to the E&C Programme; to cooperate with the SFO and other enforcement and regulatory authorities (at the request of the SFO) in ongoing related investigations; to report any new concerns of serious or complex fraud should they become known; not to make or authorise the making of any public statement contradicting the content of the statement of facts; and to consult with the SFO prior to any related press releases or public statements.

At the time of DPA approval, it was said that a charging decision in respect of individuals (anonymised in the judgment and statement of facts) would be made within three months. The SFO thereafter confirmed that it would not be pursuing any prosecutions of individuals.[114] This is despite the fact that Lord Justice Edis was clear in outlining the wrongdoing

111 Serious Fraud Office, 'Statement of Facts – Amec Foster Wheeler Energy Limited' (*Serious Fraud Office*, 7 February 2022) <https://www.sfo.gov.uk/download/statement-of-facts/> accessed 30 March 2023, paras 12–13.

112 Serious Fraud Office, 'Amec Foster Wheeler Energy Limited – Deferred Prosecution Agreement – Undertaking' (*Serious Fraud Office*, 28 June 2021) <https://www.sfo.gov.uk/download/amec-foster-wheeler-energy-limited-deferred-prosecution-agreement-undertaking/> accessed 2 July 2021.

113 *Amec Foster Wheeler Limited* (n 26) [13] (Edis LJ).

114 Serious Fraud Office, 'Amec Foster Wheeler PLC' (*Serious Fraud Office*, 28 October 2021) <https://www.sfo.gov.uk/cases/amec-foster-wheeler-plc/> accessed 1 December 2021.

of individuals in approving the DPA, setting out that '[a] number of [the] offences did not involve "wilful disregard" but actual *complicity* of senior officers' (emphasis added).[115]

The DPA is due to expire on 2 July 2024.

1.1.5.11 Director of the Serious Fraud Office v Bluu Solutions Limited and Tetris-Projects Limited ("Bluu Solutions Limited" and "Tetris-Projects Limited")

Formerly known as *Director of the Serious Fraud Office v AB Ltd and another*, the DPAs agreed in 2021 between the SFO and Bluu Solutions Limited ("Bluu") and Tetris Projects Limited ("Tetris")[116] represent the first of their kind in the UK. Though the DPAs were agreed separately (and have separate undertakings attached), they share a joint statement of facts and were approved in one approved judgment. The Bluu DPA was approved on the basis of five counts: four counts of bribing another person and one count of failure to prevent bribery. The Tetris DPA was approved on one count of failure to prevent bribery. Bluu and Tetris had been competitors until 2015. Tetris was owned by Jones Lang LaSalle Europe Limited ("JLL EU") within the Jones Lang LaSalle Group ("JLL Group"), and in 2015 Bluu was acquired by Jones Lang LaSalle Capital Investments Limited ("JLL CIL") within the same JLL Group. Bluu originally remained separate in respect of overseeing the completion of existing contracts, though in the beginning of 2016 its staff moved to Tetris, the businesses merged, and two directors of Bluu (originally unidentified, though later named) became directors of Tetris.[117]

According to DPA documentation, the wrongdoing of Bluu was unknown to the JLL Group at the point of Bluu's acquisition, but became known after a post-acquisition audit, which triggered a self-report by the companies to the SFO.[118] The underlying wrongdoing of Bluu, culminating in the five counts, centred on bribes paid between 2014 and 2016 to third parties in order to secure business in relation to five separate contracts.[119] The wrongdoing of Tetris, resulting in one count, related to behaviours in respect of two of the five counts against Bluu. When the two directors had moved from Bluu to Tetris, there was said to have been a period of time whereby those individuals 'continued engaging in the activities vis à vis Roger Dewhirst and [another agent] which they had begun at Bluu Solutions Ltd prior to its acquisition by the JLL Group'.[120]

When first announced, details were very brief pursuant to reporting restrictions which had been imposed pending the outcome of cases against implicated individuals. The statement of facts identifies implicated agent Roger Dewhirst by name, following conviction

115 *Amec Foster Wheeler Limited* (n 26) [13] (Edis LJ). Notably, at paragraph 29 of the judgment, it is set out that those individuals no longer form part of the company (and if they had, a DPA would not have been appropriate).

116 In the approved judgment, Bluu Solutions Limited is referred to as "AB Ltd" and Tetris Projects Limited is referred to as "CD Ltd". This was confirmed in the de-anonymised version of the judgment, subsequently issued: *Bluu Solutions Limited and Tetris-Projects Limited* (n 8).

117 ibid [3].

118 ibid [4].

119 ibid [26]–[56]; Serious Fraud Office, 'Statement of Facts' (*Serious Fraud Office*, 2 March 2023) <https://www.sfo.gov.uk/download/r-v-bluu-solutions-limited-and-tetris-projects-limited/> accessed 28 March 2023, para 8.

120 *Bluu Solutions Limited and Tetris-Projects Limited* (n 8) [63]. In the original anonymised judgment, the agents were anonymised as "Agent 1" and "Agent 2". *See Director of the Serious Fraud Office v AB Ltd and another* [2021] Lexis Citation 1385 (Crown) [65].

on entering a guilty plea in respect of receiving bribes.[121] Dewhirst was not an employee or senior officer of either offending company; instead, he was a third-party recipient of the bribe payments underpinning the corporate criminal wrongdoing. Three further connected individuals were acquitted at trial, yet subsequently named when the expiry of the two DPAs led to the issuing of a de-anonymised version of the approving judgment.[122] Just over two months later, the SFO website containing the link to the de-anonymised judgment and details identifying the individuals by name was re-anonymised, though no further judgment or clarification has been issued on this matter.[123] As such, those individuals are anonymised herein on the basis that this is subject to challenge.[124] An anonymisation order had previously had the effect of concealing names within the statement of facts and judgment, and the statement of facts alone remains anonymised (except Dewhirst).[125]

Two undertakings by the parent companies of each wrongdoing entity attach to the DPAs.[126] JLL CIL guaranteed the performance by Bluu of its DPA obligations, and further guaranteed the financial liabilities of both Bluu and Tetris (in relation to the disgorgement of profits and financial penalties). JLL CIL agreed to retain Bluu within the scope of its control for the DPA term; not to make or authorise the making of any public statement contradicting the content of the statement of facts; and to consult with the SFO prior to any related press releases or public statements.[127] JLL EU similarly agreed to ensure Tetris would remain within its control, and terms in relation to public statements and press releases. Further, JLL EU guaranteed to ensure the cooperation of Tetris with the SFO and other enforcement and regulatory authorities (at the request of the SFO) in ongoing related investigations to ensure the performance by Tetris of its DPA obligations.[128]

The DPAs expired on 20 July 2023.[129]

121 Ruby Hamid and others, 'The DPA Challenge – The SFO's First DPA-Related Conviction of an Individual Bucks the Trend' (*Ashurst*, 10 March 2023) <https://www.ashurst.com/en/news-and-insights/legal-updates/the-dpa-challenge---the-sfos-first-dpa-related-conviction/> accessed 28 March 2023.

122 Upon the issuing of the notice of discontinuance pursuant to both DPAs, the de-anonymised judgment was published, though the statement of facts remains as it was upon original publication. The de-anonymised judgment names individuals acquitted in their own proceedings, though it does not make note of those acquittals. *See Bluu Solutions Limited and Tetris-Projects Limited* (n 8).

123 As of 2 October 2023. *See* Serious Fraud Office, 'R v Bluu Solutions Limited and Tetris Projects Limited' (*Serious Fraud Office*, 2 October 2023) <https://www.sfo.gov.uk/cases/r-v-bluu-solutions-limited-and-tetris-projects-limited/> accessed 2 October 2023.

124 Ana de Liz, 'Acquitted Bluu Solutions Executive Asks to be Left Out of DPA Judgment' (*Global Investigations Review*, 27 November 2023) <https://globalinvestigationsreview.com/article/acquitted-bluu-solutions-executive-asks-be-left-out-of-dpa-judgment> accessed 28 November 2023.

125 Prior to the expiry of the DPAs, the SFO stated: 'The DPA Statement of Facts and Judgment contain anonymised names of individuals subsequently acquitted at trial. These individuals are subject to an anonymisation order and cannot be named.' *See* Serious Fraud Office, 'R v Bluu Solutions Limited and Tetris Projects Limited' (*Serious Fraud Office*, 9 March 2023) <https://www.sfo.gov.uk/cases/r-v-bluu-solutions-limited-and-tetris-projects-limited/> accessed 28 March 2023.

126 *Bluu Solutions Limited and Tetris-Projects Limited* (n 8) [125].

127 Serious Fraud Office, 'Undertaking – Jones Lang LaSalle Capital Investments Limited' (*Serious Fraud Office*, 9 July 2021) <https://www.sfo.gov.uk/download/r-v-bluu-solutions-limited-and-tetris-projects-limited/> 28 March 2023.

128 Serious Fraud Office, 'Undertaking – Jones Lang LaSalle Europe Limited' (*Serious Fraud Office*, 9 July 2021) <https://www.sfo.gov.uk/download/r-v-bluu-solutions-limited-and-tetris-projects-limited/> 28 March 2023.

129 Serious Fraud Office, 'Serious Fraud Office and Bluu Solutions Ltd ["BSL"] and Tétris Projects Ltd ["TPL"]: Discontinuance of Proceedings on Expiry of Deferred Prosecution Agreements' (*Serious Fraud Office*, 28 July 2023) <https://www.sfo.gov.uk/download/bluu-solutions-and-tetris-projects-de-anonymised-judgment-and-details-of-compliance/> accessed 28 July 2023.

1.1.5.12 The CPS and DPAs

Until the end of 2023, the CPS had not agreed a DPA.[130] In July 2021, Director of Public Prosecutions Max Hill KC set out that the CPS continues to look for appropriate cases in which to offer DPAs, but outlined that the SFO had the necessary expertise, and that issues with corporate criminal liability (predominantly the identification principle) often render it too difficult to even consider DPAs – noting the importance of corporate cooperation in the preparatory stages.[131]

Skansen Interiors Ltd ("SIL") was the first company to be convicted following a contested charge under section 7 of the Bribery Act 2010.[132] Skansen Group had in 2014 appointed a new CEO, Ian Pigden-Bennett, who was notified by SIL managing director Stephen Banks about payments made to a third party (Graham Deakin) via a third company,[133] a 'sham, or shell, company'.[134] Following an internal investigation initiated by Pigden-Bennett, Banks and SIL's commercial director were dismissed. Following a self-report by Skansen Group, SIL put forward the defence that it had adequate procedures in place to prevent bribery but was convicted. With no assets available, the company was given an absolute discharge.[135]

Banks and Deakin were charged under sections 1 and 2 of the Bribery Act 2010, and both entered guilty pleas.[136] During Iskander Fernandez's (a member of SIL's defence team) witness evidence to the Select Committee, it was made clear that SIL was extensively cooperative in assisting the City of London Police's investigation into individuals. According to Polly Sprenger, SIL 'thought they were negotiating a DPA'.[137] Pigden-Bennett,

---

130 By contrast, the SFO in its Annual Report and Accounts of 2022–23 reported that – at the time of publication whereupon 12 DPAs had been agreed by the prosecutor – it had '[s]ecured over £1.7bn since 2015–16 to the end of this reporting period through the continued use of Deferred Prosecution Agreements'. *See* Serious Fraud Office, *Annual Report and Accounts 2022–23* (2023, HC 1473) 19. Nevertheless, Lord Edward Garnier KC, in January 2024, noted his disappointment at the small number of DPAs agreed: Catherine Baksi, 'Deal or No Deal' (*The Law Society Gazette*, 15 January 2024) <https://www.lawgazette.co.uk/features/deal-or-no-deal/5118420.article> accessed 20 January 2024.

131 Hill's comments were made in an event hosted by the Law Commission online due to COVID-19 restrictions: Law Commission, 'Corporate Criminal Liability: Options for Reform' (online, Law Commission 20 July 2021).

132 *R v Skansen Interiors Limited* (Southwark Crown Court, 21 February 2018).

133 In 2013, SIL had won two tenders for a refurbishment contract with DTZ Debenham Tie Leung ("DTZ"). A £10,000 payment (two bribes) had been made to DTZ project manager Graham Deakin via a third company, and Pigden-Bennett was notified that a further £29,000 would be due upon contract completion. The third company was Goodier Property Services Limited ("Goodier"), which invoiced and received the bribes, and its sole director and shareholder was Deakin's son. *See* Omar Qureshi and others, 'Failure to Prevent Bribery: First Contested Prosecution' (*Thomson Reuters Practical Law*, 29 March 2018) <https://uk.practicallaw.thomsonreuters.com/w-013-8901?transitionType=Default&contextData=(sc.Default)&firstPage=true> accessed 25 February 2021, 1; City of London Police, 'Two Employees Sentenced for Roles in £6.4 Million Bribery' (*City of London Police*, 24 April 2018) <https://web.archive.org/web/20221128010711/http://news.cityoflondon.police.uk/r/1020/two_employees_sentenced_for_roles_in__6_4_million> accessed 25 February 2021.

134 Select Committee on the Bribery Act 2010, *The Bribery Act 2010: Post Legislative Scrutiny: Evidence Session No 23* (HL 2017–19, 303) question 203 (Iskander Fernandez).

135 Select Committee on the Bribery Act 2010, *The Bribery Act 2010: Post-Legislative Scrutiny* (HL 2017–19, 303) para 220.

136 Both were imprisoned and disqualified as directors: Banks was imprisoned for 12 months and disqualified for six years. The reason on the Companies House register for Banks' disqualification is noted as disqualification on conviction of an indictable offence, under section 2 of the Company Directors Disqualification Act 1986. SIL's commercial director was not charged with any offence. *See* Companies House, 'Stephen Banks' (*Companies House*, 2021) <https://find-and-update.company-information.service.gov.uk/disqualified-officers/natural/5pK_-KyquuxxpbxiuNi-ScISd9A> accessed 25 February 2021; Qureshi and others (n 133) 1.

137 Sprenger's comments were made in an event hosted by the Institute of Advanced Legal Studies (School of Advanced Study University of London) online due to COVID-19 restrictions: The Centre for Financial Law,

on behalf of SIL, provided 'documentary evidence about the individuals concerned', and the company provided both privileged and non-privileged materials.[138] Fernandez stated that SIL, not knowing it was a suspect at the time, had been 'essentially putting forward the individuals and the evidence that backed up the assertions that these individuals were the two to blame for the offending'[139] – demonstrating the focus on individual wrongdoers during corporate criminal investigations.

1.1.5.12.1 R v Entain Plc ("Entain")

In May 2023, global sports betting, gaming, and interactive entertainment group Entain plc announced that it had entered into DPA negotiations with the CPS, whilst simultaneously under investigation by His Majesty's Revenue & Customs.[140] The company announced that the offences in question included failure to prevent bribery (contrary to section 7 of the Bribery Act 2010), but the investigations were not limited to this type of offence. The announcement raised questions as to the permissibility of such disclosure, contrary to the typical pre-negotiation confidentiality undertaking (**Section 1.1.3.1**).[141] However, with premium listing on the London Stock Exchange, Entain is required to disclose inside information in following FCA rules. In line with such requirements, the company posted a further update in August 2023, outlining that it had taken a £585 million provision in respect of its ongoing DPA negotiations (an amount calculated with 'full credit for its extensive co-operation').[142] Interestingly, at the time of the update, an indication of the advancement of negotiations is presented as Entain states that the prospective DPA would provide a four-year payment period. The update provides an estimate of judicial approval being sought in Q4 of 2023, and the company 'believes that it is likely to be able to agree a resolution'.[143] In December 2023, the final approved DPA was published, on the basis of four counts of failure to prevent bribery, contrary to section 7 of the Bribery Act 2010. Publication of the statement of facts is postponed until the conclusion of criminal proceedings of relevant individuals, pursuant to an order of the court under section 4(2) of the Contempt of Court Act 1981.[144] The DPA is amongst the largest (financially) agreed thus far, and includes the novel term of payment of a charitable donation of £20 million.

Regulation and Compliance, 'Deferred Prosecution Agreements' (online, Institute of Advanced Legal Studies 10 December 2020).

138 Select Committee on the Bribery Act 2010, *The Bribery Act 2010: Post Legislative Scrutiny: Evidence Session No 23* (n 134) question 203.

139 ibid.

140 Entain, 'Update on HMRC Investigation' (n 17).

141 Iskander Fernandez and Matthew Poli, 'Entain's DPA Announcement – A Ripple or a Wave?' (*Kennedys*, 29 June 2023) <https://kennedyslaw.com/en/thought-leadership/article/2023/entain-s-dpa-announcement-a-ripple-or-a-wave/> accessed 4 July 2023.

142 Entain, 'Update on HMRC Investigation' (n 18).

143 ibid. Though it is worth noting that Skansen Interiors Ltd is also reported as having believed this to be the case, before it was prosecuted to conviction. *See* Sprenger (n 136).

144 Crown Prosecution Service, 'Deferred Prosecution Agreements' (*Crown Prosecution Service*, 5 December 2023) <https://www.cps.gov.uk/deferred-prosecution-agreements> accessed 13 December 2023.

CHAPTER 2

The problem of corporate DPAs and individuals

Amidst the contemplation of self-reporting and DPA negotiations, individuals undoubtedly take centre stage. A company by nature has 'no mind or morals',[1] and is therefore vulnerable to the acts of human persons incurring liability on its behalf, but also dependent on the acts of human persons to see that any liability is dealt with appropriately in the given circumstances. Individuals naturally become implicated in both instances as a result, and principally the onus falls on directors and senior officers of "wrongdoing" companies to consider the best interests of the company in dealing with such matters. This is a duty inherent within the directorship role, and is one of a number of mandatory duties set out in the Companies Act 2006. The issue becomes complicated where the individuals implicated in the corporate wrongdoing are those bound by such statutory duties, to serve and protect the company over and above themselves.

Upon introduction in the UK, there was a clear lack of consideration of the impact of corporate DPAs on the individuals behind the corporate shell,[2] and disregard of support for broadening the scope of DPAs to individuals in line with the original model's primary objectives.[3] Though adopted as a largely transposed model from the US with minimal distinguishing characteristics, DPAs remain available to individuals in the US, but the

1 Michael Bisgrove and Mark Weekes, 'Deferred Prosecution Agreements: A Practical Consideration' (2014) 6 Crim LR 416, 419.

2 The government consultation focussed more on the enhancement of the opportunity to successfully prosecute individuals, as a by-product of corporate cooperation pursuant to DPA negotiations and terms. *See* Ministry of Justice, *Consultation on a New Enforcement Tool to Deal With Economic Crime Committed by Commercial Organisations: Deferred Prosecution Agreements* (Cm 8348, 2012) para 88.

3 In response to the government's consultation, reportedly from 63 responses to a question regarding the scope of DPAs, '[a]lmost half of respondents (48%) supported a wider application of DPAs … including … [i]ndividuals accused of economic crime and/or working within a commercial organisation that is party to a DPA' (at para 41), though the proportion of responses supporting individual DPAs within that 48 percent was not expressed. The government response set out that DPAs would be introduced to target issues faced with successfully prosecuting corporate (economic) crime, and 'individuals [would] be excluded' (at para 47). *See* Ministry of Justice, *Deferred Prosecution Agreements: Government Response to the Consultation on a New Enforcement Tool to Deal With Economic Crime Committed by Commercial Organisations* (Cm 8463, 2012) paras 39–47. Regarding the origins of DPAs in the US in dealing with low-level offences or juveniles and first-time offenders by taking a rehabilitative approach, *see* Benjamin Greenblum, 'What Happens to a Prosecution Deferred? Judicial Oversight of Corporate Deferred Prosecution Agreements' (Oct 2005) 105(6) Colum L Rev 1863, 1866.

DOI: 10.4324/9781003456964-3

notion was clearly rejected in the UK.[4] Such disregard during the formative stage has led to a significant lack of clarity in the law and has had an adverse impact since.[5]

Such lack of clarity has raised unanswered questions about the position of directors during the DPA process; the impact on directors' ability to effectively discharge their statutory duties; the maintenance of directors' rights in their own defence; the rights of directors to ultimately clear their names; and whether directors can indeed be protected by a corporate DPA. This uncertainty consequently poses substantial risks to directors' and officers' ("D&O") liability insurance coverage, which in its standard form is not typically drafted any (materially) differently to account for corporate DPAs and the potential impacts. Pitfalls in the interpretation of integral D&O provisions – namely defence costs cover – pose further risks to directors where insurance is likely to be the central source of support in determining solutions and answers to the challenges posed by the unanswered questions.

2.1 Consideration of individuals

In the US, following the savings and loan crisis of the 1980s, over 1,000 individuals were prosecuted and 800 convicted.[6] However, when a series of corporate scandals arose in the early 2000s and a hard-line US prosecutorial response ensued, this proved to be problematic. Having agreed a DPA with the US DoJ in 1996 (which did not require an admission of guilt), Arthur Andersen LLP was thereafter offered another DPA in the early 2000s for allegedly shredding accounting documents of Enron Corporation when the latter was collapsing.[7] The '"big five" accounting firm'[8] refused the DPA on the basis that it would have required an admission, and this was perceived to be 'just as devastating to its fortunes as an indictment or guilty plea'.[9] Though convicted in 2002, the verdict was overturned in 2005. Nonetheless, the impact of the original conviction was detrimental, as 28,000 employees lost their jobs when the corporation collapsed. As the leverage held by the DoJ was said to be in the threat of prosecution, the decision to proceed with prosecution was inevitable.[10] The fall of Arthur Andersen LLP led to the increased use of DPAs within the

4 Notably, the role of the judiciary also differs between US and UK DPAs. In the latter instance, the judiciary plays a more prominent role in approving a DPA against a set test. The role of the judiciary in US DPAs – as to whether judicial approval is limited to ensuring the Speedy Trial Act is adhered to, or whether it is extended to an inherent supervisory power to ensure the administration of justice – is a subject of debate.

5 For example, the purportedly irrevocable naming of acquitted individuals as guilty parties within the DPA. *See Serious Fraud Office v Tesco Stores Ltd* [2019] EW Misc 1 (Crown).

6 Vijaya Kumar Rajah, 'Prosecution of Financial Crimes and its Relationship to a Culture of Compliance' (2016) 37(4) Comp Law 122, 125.

7 Linda Greenhouse, 'Justices Unanimously Overturn Conviction of Arthur Andersen' (*The New York Times*, 31 May 2005) <https://www.nytimes.com/2005/05/31/business/justices-unanimously-overturn-conviction-of-arthur-andersen.html> accessed 9 June 2020.

8 Rajah (n 6) 123.

9 Kurt Eichenwald, 'Andersen Refused a Probation Deal' (*The New York Times*, 2 April 2002) <https://www.nytimes.com/2002/04/02/business/andersen-refused-a-probation-deal.html> accessed 9 June 2020.

10 It has been argued that this decision was based upon the preservation of power. *See* James Anderson and Ivan Waggoner, *The Changing Role of Criminal Law in Controlling Corporate Behavior* (RAND Corporation 2014) 54–56.

US,[11] but also fuelled the ongoing debate about whether larger corporations are "too big to jail".[12]

Following the financial crisis of 2008 to 2009, there was greater political appetite to address (corporate) economic crime. In the UK, it was an opportune time to consider enhancing prosecutors' arsenal of measures to hold wrongdoers accountable. The deep public dissatisfaction arising as a result of a perceived failure to hold individuals accountable for their roles in the financial crisis[13] has thus become an undertone of reforms, and proposed reforms,[14] to corporate criminal liability. During the consultative stages of DPA implementation, the rationale for their introduction was to tackle economic crime and to address difficulties associated with corporate prosecutions:[15] difficulties which were not said to exist in prosecuting individuals.[16] The continued requirement to seek prosecutions of individuals was made clear throughout the DPA developmental process, as the government was unwavering on the point that it was not seeking to protect individuals from such accountability.

Before DPAs were introduced, when they faced debate in the House of Lords, there was considerable support for the inclusion of individual DPAs within the proposed framework (**Section 4.2**). It was argued that individual DPAs available to corporate officers may be an attractive and beneficial addition in the corporate sector,[17] but that there must be some measure of appropriateness.[18] However, Lord McNally fundamentally exclaimed that '[i]ndividual directors of companies will not be immune from prosecution if their company is part of a plea bargain',[19] and the framework was left unamended in this regard. Thus, the CACA 2013 expressly excludes DPAs for individuals.[20] This exclusion sits in line with the general support for individual prosecution within academic literature,[21] and by prosecutors.[22]

11 'The outcome sent a chill through the Department of Justice, prompting them to turn to deferred prosecution agreements or non-prosecution agreements as a less severe alternative to combating major corporate crimes.' *See* Rajah (n 6) 123. *See also* James Gilsinan and others, 'Whose Fault Is It? Shifting Spheres of Responsibility' (2018) 39(4) Comp Law 122, 127.

12 Thus also fuelling criticism of DPAs. *See* Rachel Delaney, 'Congressional Legislation: The Next Step for Corporate Deferred Prosecution Agreements' (2009) 93(2) Marq L Rev 875, 882; Polly Sprenger, *Deferred Prosecution Agreements: The Law and Practice of Negotiated Corporate Criminal Penalties* (Sweet & Maxwell 2015) 74, 84.

13 For example, in respect of Barclays. *See* Iris Chiu, 'Regulatory Duties for Directors in the Financial Services Sector and Directors' Duties in Company Law: Bifurcation and Interfaces' (2016) 6 JBL 465, 468–469.

14 Proposed reforms which are continuing beyond the passage of the Bribery Act 2010 and Schedule 17 to the Crime and Courts Act 2013. The Law Commission recently investigated Corporate Criminal Liability in a project which started in 2021. *See* Law Commission, *Corporate Criminal Liability: An Options Paper* (2022).

15 Ministry of Justice, *Deferred Prosecution Agreements: Government Response to the Consultation on a New Enforcement Tool to Deal With Economic Crime Committed by Commercial Organisations* (n 3) paras 15, 47.

16 HL Deb 30 October 2012, vol 740, col 583 (Lord McNally).

17 ibid col 579 (Lord Woolf).

18 ibid col 577 (Lord Goldsmith).

19 ibid col 584 (Lord McNally). Lord Phillips of Sudbury also outlined that shielding wrongdoer directors and executives would be a failure of the regime. *See* ibid col 581.

20 Crime and Courts Act 2013, sch 17 para 4(1).

21 Vicky Comino, 'The GFC and Beyond – How do we Deal With Corporate Misconduct?' (2018) 1 JBL 15, 39; Jennifer Arlen, 'The Potential Promise and Perils of Introducing Deferred Prosecution Agreements Outside the U.S.' in Tina Søreide and Abiola Makinwa (eds), *Negotiated Settlements in Bribery Cases: A Principled Approach* (Edward Elgar Publishing Ltd 2020) 176.

22 Crown Prosecution Service and Serious Fraud Office, 'Deferred Prosecution Agreements Code of Practice' (*Crown Prosecution Service*, 11 February 2014) <https://www.cps.gov.uk/sites/default/files/documents/publications/dpa_cop.pdf> accessed 9 June 2020, para 2.9.1.

However, there have been concerns raised that individuals are insufficiently protected and are disregarded by the prosecution-focussed approach to individual criminality. Dr Radha Ivory and Professor Tina Søreide have observed that the OECD Working Group on Bribery has 'acknowledge[d] concerns that individuals may be unfairly impacted by negotiations between prosecutors and companies, but failed to endorse those concerns or to incorporate them into its country-specific recommendations'; this is criticised as being an 'inadequate response' in respect of the rights of 'individual lower-level employees'.[23] Notably, this does not appear to include company directors; nevertheless, the OECD Working Group's report does not respond to concerns regarding directors, nor does it offer recommendations.[24] Similar lack of consideration of directors (despite concerns regarding lower-level employees) is posed by Dr Vicky Comino, who questions whether 'individuals might be scapegoated by companies, sacrificing "lower-down" employees but protecting "higher ups"'.[25]

Scapegoatism is a concern supported by Federico Mazzacuva, who places some responsibility on prosecutors to consider individuals' actual position when faced with corporate disclosures: 'prosecutors should be very careful to ascertain if the individual indicated by the target company as the wrongdoer is really responsible or a mere scapegoat.'[26] Mazzacuva supports cooperation in ensuring successful individual prosecutions,[27] but nevertheless highlights the impact on those with little to no involvement in the wrongdoing. The use of corporate cooperation in assisting individual prosecutions is provided for within the SFO's Operational Handbook,[28] and has also been incorporated as a term in all of the 13 UK DPAs.

The extent of the encouragement and incentivisation of companies in the implication of individuals has further raised concerns regarding the use of DPA materials against those individuals.[29] Ivory and Søreide have criticised the OECD Working Group's missed opportunity to consider the impact of corporate settlements (including DPAs) on individuals' right to defence.[30] Though only one individual prosecution relating to UK DPAs has thus far been successful (that of a third-party individual receiving bribes from the

23 Radha Ivory and Tina Søreide, 'The International Endorsement of Corporate Settlements in Foreign Bribery Cases' (2020) 69(4) ICLQ 945, 975.

24 OECD Working Group on Bribery, *Implementing the OECD Anti-Bribery Convention: Phase 4 Report: United Kingdom* (OECD 2017).

25 Comino (n 21) 32.

26 Federico Mazzacuva, 'Justifications and Purposes of Negotiated Justice for Corporate Offenders: Deferred and Non-Prosecution Agreements in the UK and US Systems of Criminal Justice' (2014) 78(3) J Crim L 249, 261. Mazzacuva is a research fellow of Università degli Studi di Milano-Bicocca.

27 ibid 251.

28 Serious Fraud Office, 'Deferred Prosecution Agreements' (*Serious Fraud Office*, 23 October 2020) <https://www.sfo.gov.uk/publications/guidance-policy-and-protocols/sfo-operational-handbook/deferred-prosecution-agreements/> accessed 23 October 2020.

29 Ren-En Lim, 'Parting the Fog of the UK Bribery Act 2010: A Critical Discussion of What We Do Know about the Act and Why It Is in the Company's Interests to Comply With Its Provisions' (2014) 25(1) ICCLR 1, 12–13.

30 '[T]he examiners acknowledge the interaction between settlements and the fundamental rights of the defence. However, this concern is configured, not as a matter of criminal procedure or human rights, but as a constraint on the capacity of States to enforce foreign bribery laws or disclose information about particular deals. Consequently, the Working Group misses the opportunity to engage with well-known problems of defendants who waive their privileges to benefit from the speed, certainty and savings of settlement options.' *See* Ivory and Søreide (n 23) 975.

DPA-agreeing companies),[31] Hickman & Rose partner Ross Dixon has expressed concern about the impact of these prosecutions on the individuals involved.[32] Conversely, some argue that individuals remain sufficiently protected: one might contest that the lack of successful prosecutions *prima facie* demonstrates a minimal exposure to criminal liability. Indeed, Comino and Corruption Watch present the position that individuals 'are let off the hook by DPAs',[33] and 'have become a substitute for individual accountability'.[34]

Some commentators – following the implementation of DPAs into the statute books – go further than expressing concern and suggest that individual DPAs should be included within the framework. Whilst some US proponents of individual DPAs tend to rationalise their support by limiting it to lower-level and/or non-violent offenders in ensuring parity in the law,[35] this argument often refers back to the US DPA's original objective of individual rehabilitation (**Section 4.1.1**).[36] Moreover, arguably, since the UK model is effectively an import (albeit with some notable differences), it carries with it the historical formative development.[37] A number of UK commentators have also demonstrated support of individual DPAs. Lord Edward Garnier KC, Solicitor General between 2010 and 2012 (when DPAs were debated), has stated that '"[i]f we are going to convict companies and convict individuals, but also enter into DPAs with companies, there is a logic in thinking about arranging DPAs with individuals"'.[38] Lawyers Eoin O'Shea and Emma Shafton also support the extension of DPAs to individuals 'in marginal cases', suggesting that there would be 'significant benefits, including clear accountability of an individual'.[39] Furthermore, support for individual DPAs does not necessarily amount to a wholly protectionist approach, but an amelioration of the current individual accountability standards.

In the middle ground, between support for individual DPAs and the strong advocacy for increased individual prosecutions backed by corporate support, some academics argue for the increased use of leniency measures for individuals involved in corporate crime. Such support for leniency does not necessarily amount to non-conviction, but also mitigation

31 Serious Fraud Office, 'R v Bluu Solutions Limited and Tetris Projects Limited' (*Serious Fraud Office*, 2 October 2023) <https://www.sfo.gov.uk/cases/r-v-bluu-solutions-limited-and-tetris-projects-limited/> accessed 2 October 2023.

32 The conviction followed Dixon's publication. *See* Ross Dixon, 'Great Expectations?' (2021) 171(7939) NLJ 15, 16.

33 Comino (n 21) 31; Corruption Watch, 'Out of Court, Out of Mind: Do Deferred Prosecution Agreements and Corporate Settlements Fail to Deter Overseas Corruption' (*Corruption Watch UK*, March 2016) <https://drive.google.com/file/d/1sLCoenXwiDocwcRwOQ8Jfj_twtK_ZUdd/view?usp=sharing> accessed 8 October 2021, 23.

34 Comino (n 21) 32; Corruption Watch (n 33) 10.

35 Andrea Amulic, 'Humanizing the Corporation While Dehumanizing the Individual: The Misuse of Deferred-Prosecution Agreements in the United States' (2017) 116(1) Mich L Rev 123, 127.

36 '[P]rosecutors should offer more deferred-prosecution and nonprosecution agreements to these individuals.' *See* ibid 152–153. *See also* Peter Reilly, 'Sweetheart Deals, Deferred Prosecution, and Making a Mockery of the Criminal Justice System: U.S. Corporate DPAs Rejected on Many Fronts' (2018) 50 Ariz St LJ 1113, 1136–1138, citing *United States v Aegerion Pharmaceuticals Inc* 280 F Supp 3d 217, 224–225 (D Mass 2017): 'Judge William G. Young writes of the "shocking disparity between the treatment of corporations and individuals in our criminal justice system."'

37 The argument for parity has also been signalled within the UK since the Crime and Courts Bill debating stage. *See* HL Deb 30 October 2012 (n 16) col 581 (Lord Phillips of Sudbury).

38 James Booth, 'Is the SFO Giving Executives an Easy Ride in Bribery Cases?' (*CityAM*, 25 February 2020) <https://www.cityam.com/are-executives-getting-off-easily-in-bribery-cases/> accessed 8 October 2021.

39 Eoin O'Shea and Emma Shafton, 'DPAs: Time to Extend the Regime?' (2019) 169(7851) NLJ 7, 7–8.

on account of a guilty plea.[40] O'Shea and Shafton note the existing repertoire of leniency measures available to prosecutors under the Serious Organised Crime and Police Act 2005 and Sentencing Act 2020, giving the example of immunity notices.[41]

Irrespective of the omission of individuals from the statutory framework, directors are exposed to liability and/or adversity as a result of the operation of DPAs in practice, and are not protected by the existing framework. Whilst the implementation of individual DPAs might somewhat mitigate *some* of the exposures to directors – for example in permitting a joint DPA with the company as opposed to prosecution inflamed by a company-versus-individual backdrop – this book does not explore potential implementation and is limited in scope to determining the impact of the *existing* framework.

2.2 Targeting individuals

Sir Brian Leveson, responsible for approving the first four UK DPAs, has stated that

> [c]ritical to my approach to DPAs over the four that I have done has been that those who are responsible for the criminality face prosecution … It is absolutely *critical* that the individuals in these circumstances are prosecuted, however senior or junior in the company they are (emphasis added).[42]

This is echoed in his preliminary judgment of the *Standard Bank* DPA, whereby he held that 'it is obviously in the public interest that individuals involved in the conduct at issue are investigated and prosecuted and this term [relating to corporate cooperation] will obviously be critical to this (and any) DPA'.[43]

However, of the four DPAs approved by Sir Leveson, only two led to or involved individual UK prosecutions (albeit that one could not have led to prosecutions due to territorial issues). The third DPA with Rolls-Royce was approved whilst the investigation into individuals was ongoing, but the investigation subsequently ceased without prosecution; this is despite the fact that the underlying criminality spanned several decades and was described as being 'egregious'.[44] Furthermore, it has been observed that in the US 'approximately two-thirds of settlement agreements [including DPAs and non-prosecution agreements] are

40 ibid 7 (regarding reduction in sentence following an agreement under section 73 of the Serious Organised Crime and Police Act 2005, and guilty plea). *See also* Arlen in Søreide and Makinwa (eds) (n 21) 177 (in respect of the US and overseas). This position was also advanced by the US government in *United States v Transport Logistics International Inc*: '"we're hopeful that through both, you know, the [DPA] with the company but also through the charges against the individuals and the pleas with the individuals, that that will be a sufficient deterrent to other companies and other individuals when viewing conduct like this."' *See* Reilly (n 36) 1133, citing *United States v Transport Logistics International Inc* No 8:18-cr-00011-TDC (D Md Mar 12 2018) (Transcript of Proceedings at 16–17).

41 O'Shea and Shafton (n 39) 7. *See also* Serious Organised Crime and Police Act 2005, s 71.

42 This comment was made in an evidence session on the Bribery Act 2010, where Sir Brian Leveson discussed his interaction with the Act through DPAs. *See* Select Committee on the Bribery Act 2010, *The Bribery Act 2010: Post Legislative Scrutiny: Evidence Session No 16* (HL 2017–19, 303) question 153. *See also* Select Committee on the Bribery Act 2010, *The Bribery Act 2010: Post-Legislative Scrutiny* (HL 2017–19, 303) para 313.

43 *Serious Fraud Office v Standard Bank Plc (now ICBC Standard Bank Plc) (Preliminary)* [2016] Lloyd's Rep FC 91 (Crown) [59] (Sir Brian Leveson).

44 *Serious Fraud Office v Rolls-Royce Plc* [2017] Lloyd's Rep FC 249 (Crown) [61]. *See also* Serious Fraud Office, 'SFO Closes GlaxoSmithKline Investigation and Investigation Into Rolls-Royce Individuals' (*Serious Fraud Office*, 22 February 2019) <https://www.sfo.gov.uk/2019/02/22/sfo-closes-glaxosmithkline-investigation-and-investigation-into-rolls-royce-individuals/> accessed 30 November 2019.

not accompanied by the prosecution of the individuals that run those companies',[45] a figure which also reflects the number of individual prosecutions which have failed to materialise from UK DPAs.[46] There must therefore be some consideration as to the nature of such purported criticality: where DPAs are agreed and expire without individual prosecution, it cannot be said that individual prosecution is critical to the success of a DPA.

However, the argument has arisen that the failure to successfully prosecute individuals accused of the predicate wrongdoing of an approved DPA not only undermines the provision, but actually renders the relevant corporate DPA unenforceable.[47] This position advanced by Karl Laird is based upon the fact that a breach of an identification principle offence-based DPA and subsequent prosecution of the company would likely be unsuccessful where the respective directors representing the 'directing mind and will'[48] are acquitted in the interim.[49] Whilst the statement of facts attached to the DPA is admissible against the company in such circumstances as a formal admission under section 10 of the CJA 1967,[50] this admission may be challenged on the basis that the relevant directing mind and will would likely not have contributed to it. In such circumstances, it is the extrinsic evidence which supports the establishing of the identification principle that will be vital in ensuring a corporate conviction. Furthermore, Laird's position demonstrates that the criticality of supporting individual prosecution(s) may not arise on successful completion of a DPA, but instead in the ensuring of successful corporate prosecution upon DPA breach. The criticality cannot centre on ensuring that the DPA is "enforceable", as the DPA is not an enforceable agreement in the same way one might consider enforceability within the lens of the law of contract: a DPA breach is either rectified by agreed variation,[51] or is dealt with by DPA termination[52] and (likely) prosecution, and thus there is no cause of action to conventionally *enforce* the DPA terms *per se*.

Rather than critical, Dr Susan Hawley (Policy Director of Corruption Watch) denotes individual prosecutions to be a 'crucial' factor in ensuring public confidence post-DPA.[53] The Select Committee on the Bribery Act 2010 ("Select Committee") in its post-legislative scrutiny report stated: 'We share the strongly held views of our witnesses that the DPA process, far from being an alternative to the prosecution of individuals, makes it all

45 Deidre Healy and Joe McGrath, '"Comparing Apples with Oranges Disguised as Apples" (But Still Producing Fruit): The Methodological Difficulties in Conducting Comparative White-Collar Crime Research and a Way Forward' (2020) 63 Irish Jurist 61, 79, citing Brandon Garrett, *Too Big to Jail: How Prosecutors Compromise with Corporations* (Harvard University Press 2014).

46 Seven DPAs (of 13) (counting Bluu Solutions Limited and Tetris Projects Limited separately) have led to known individual prosecutions, those with: Sarclad Ltd (unsuccessful); Tesco Stores Ltd (unsuccessful); Serco Geografix Ltd (unsuccessful); Güralp Systems Ltd (unsuccessful); and G4S Care & Justice Services Ltd (unsuccessful); Bluu Solutions Limited and Tetris Projects Limited (successful, but of a third-party individual to the offending company).

47 Karl Laird, 'Deferred Prosecution Agreements: The Latest Developments' (2021) 4 Crim LR 283, 297–298.

48 *Tesco Supermarkets Ltd v Nattrass* [1972] AC 153 (HL) 180.

49 Laird (n 47) 297–298.

50 Crime and Courts Act 2013, sch 17 para 13(2).

51 ibid sch 17 paras 9(3)(a), 10.

52 ibid sch 17 para 9(3)(b).

53 This comment was made in an evidence session on the Bribery Act 2010, where Dr Susan Hawley discussed DPAs. *See* Select Committee on the Bribery Act 2010, *The Bribery Act 2010: Post-Legislative Scrutiny* (n 42) para 311, citing Select Committee on the Bribery Act 2010, *The Bribery Act 2010: Post Legislative Scrutiny: Evidence Session No 3* (HL 2017–19, 303) question 46.

the more important that culpable individuals *should* be prosecuted'[54] (emphasis added). The discretionary language adopted by the Select Committee thus emulates a realism approach, somewhat in line with that of Hawley.

The statutory framework does not provide that individual prosecutions are critical. Schedule 17 to the CACA 2013 is silent on individuals, except in noting that DPAs are not available to them.[55] This echoes the sentiment of Lord McNally – who introduced the relevant amendment of the Crime and Courts Bill to the House of Lords – that individuals would remain 'best dealt with through criminal prosecution'.[56] The DPA Code, published jointly by the CPS and the SFO when DPAs were introduced, sets out that '[i]t will ordinarily be appropriate that those individuals [incriminated by the company] be investigated and where appropriate prosecuted'.[57] The SFO's 2020 Operational Handbook does not set out that individuals must, or should, be prosecuted, but does outline that cooperation in the investigations into and prosecutions of individuals will be a considered term of inclusion within the DPA.[58]

As part of the consultation process, the MoJ commissioned the fulfilment of impact investigations to assess the risk of DPAs to involved parties. The Equality Impact Assessment makes no mention of the potential detriment of DPAs to individuals generally, as it is solely focussed on those with protected characteristics.[59] The more general Impact Assessment is useful in determining the continuing objectives of the government in introducing DPAs. The intention to pursue action against individuals is clear within the Impact Assessment, with one noted objective of DPAs being to ensure that 'offenders are appropriately dealt with'.[60] The intention to use evidence amassed against individuals within an offending company is mentioned within the Impact Assessment, with the objective result being accountability.[61]

Furthermore, though individual prosecutions would complement DPAs (particularly those based upon identification principle offences), and would provide further support to the basis of the deferred prosecution and any subsequent proceedings upon breach, it cannot be said that such prosecutions are *critical* to the successful operation of the existing

54 ibid para 315.

55 Crime and Courts Act 2013, sch 17 para 4(1).

56 HL Deb 30 October 2012 (n 16) col 568.

57 This statement is made within a discussion about the incrimination of individuals within the corporate self-report. *See* Crown Prosecution Service and Serious Fraud Office, 'Deferred Prosecution Agreements Code of Practice' (n 22) para 2.9.1.

58 This has been a common term in all of the 12 published SFO DPAs, which demonstrates the prosecutor's objectives but does not evidence criticality. *See* Serious Fraud Office, 'Deferred Prosecution Agreements' (n 28). The CPS DPA with Entain plc does not specify cooperation in cases against individuals, but instead 'in any and all matters relating to the conduct that is the subject of the Indictment or otherwise described in the Statement of Facts'. *See* Crown Prosecution Service, 'Deferred Prosecution Agreements: R v Entain DPA' (*Crown Prosecution Service*, 5 December 2023) <https://www.cps.gov.uk/deferred-prosecution-agreements> accessed 13 December 2023, para 11.

59 Sophie Langdale, 'Equality Impact Assessment Initial Screening – Relevance to Equality Duties' (*Ministry of Justice*, 23 October 2012) <https://consult.justice.gov.uk/digital-communications/deferred-prosecution-agreements/results/dpa-eia.pdf> accessed 6 February 2020.

60 Ministry of Justice, 'Impact Assessment: A New Enforcement Tool to Deal With Economic Crime by Commercial Organisations: Deferred Prosecution Agreements' (*Ministry of Justice*, 23 October 2012) <https://consult.justice.gov.uk/digital-communications/deferred-prosecution-agreements/results/dpa-ia.pdf> accessed 21 February 2020, 1.

61 ibid 21.

framework.[62] However, the general consensus – despite different interpretations of the "criticality" – appears to be that individual prosecutions *should* (as a minimum) follow DPAs.

2.3 Action against individuals

Though there is a clear trend in efforts to prosecute individuals connected with the corporate criminality underpinning UK DPAs, this has evidently been unsuccessful thus far in the UK, with no resulting convictions of implicated individuals within the offending companies. Individual prosecution post-DPA has not been as unsuccessful for foreign jurisdictions, particularly considering those party to global settlements which include UK DPAs. However, from Table 2.1, it can be observed that there is some reliance upon plea agreements within foreign jurisdictions in ensuring individual accountability.

A key issue arising from DPAs is the naming of third-party individuals, who have no input in the drafting process.[63] It can be observed from recent UK DPAs – with the exception of the case(s) of *Bluu Solutions Limited* and *Tetris Projects Limited* – that greater efforts have been made to anonymise individuals, though this is not on the basis of any authoritative statutory requirement or case precedent. Therefore, it remains to be seen whether future DPAs will name individuals prior to their own trials. In some DPAs – those that have formed part of global settlements – efforts have been made to anonymise individuals so as to avoid human rights concerns in foreign jurisdictions.[64] However, such consideration has not been made in respect of individuals across all DPAs. The naming of individuals within earlier DPAs caused, and continues to cause,[65] great concern. Though reporting restrictions have often been deployed in order to protect individuals' own proceedings, the stain the records leave upon publication has been adjudicated to be irreversible.[66]

In more recent DPAs, greater effort has been made to outline that the DPA does not set out the liability of individuals. This is prudent as, previously, language used has appeared somewhat determinative of wrongdoing. For example, non-convicted directors in *Tesco Stores Ltd* were said to have acted dishonestly;[67] and in *Standard Bank* it was outlined that

62 The DPAs of Standard Bank Ltd, Sarclad Ltd, Rolls-Royce, Tesco Stores Ltd, Serco Geografix Ltd, Airbus SE, and Airline Services have all expired successfully without successful individual prosecution.

63 For example, in respect of the statement of facts drafted pursuant to the *Bluu Solutions Limited* and *Tetris Project Limited* DPAs, Mrs Justice May stated: 'the facts … have not been agreed by any of the individuals to which I refer in this judgment, nor have they been asked for their comments.' *See Director of the Serious Fraud Office v Bluu Solutions Limited and Tetris-Projects Limited* [2023] EWHC 1976 (KB) [16].

64 Consideration of the potential human rights concerns of those residing in jurisdictions which sanction corruption with the death penalty (which would be regarded in the UK as a contravention of Article 3 of the European Convention on Human Rights) was made in ensuring anonymity. *See Rolls-Royce Plc* (n 44) [32]; *Director of the Serious Fraud Office v Airbus SE* [2021] Lloyd's Rep FC 159 (Crown) [13].

65 As the cessation of such naming has not been authoritatively confirmed.

66 In January 2019, Sir Brian Leveson held that despite the acquittals of the directors, their names would continue to feature within the statement of facts upon the expiration of reporting restrictions. The judge set out that the court had no jurisdiction to alter or modify the terms of the DPA or the statement of facts and could only enforce its terms upon approval. *See Serious Fraud Office v Tesco Stores Ltd* (n 5) [4].

67 In the statement of facts, three former directors are referred to by name under paragraph 9 where it states that they 'were aware of and dishonestly perpetuated the misstatement'. *See* Serious Fraud Office, 'Deferred Prosecution Agreement – Statement of Facts – SFO v Tesco Stores Ltd' (*Serious Fraud Office*, 23 January 2019) <https://www.sfo.gov.uk/download/deferred-prosecution-agreement-statement-of-facts-sfo-v-tesco-stores-ltd/> accessed 26 June 2020, para 9.

Table 2.1 UK DPAs and the resulting action taken against individual(s) implicated.

Defendant company name	*Date of DPA*	*Individual named in DPA*	*UK prosecution of individual*	*UK conviction of individual*	*Overseas prosecution of individual*	*Overseas conviction of individual*
Standard Bank Plc	30 Nov 2015–30 Nov 2018	Yes	No	No	Yes (Tanzania)	Yes (plea agreement)
Sarclad Ltd	11 Jul 2016–16 Jul 2019	Yes	Yes	No	No	N/A
Rolls-Royce	17 Jan 2017–17 Jan 2022	No	No	No	Yes (US and Brazil)	Yes (plea agreement, one guilty plea without agreement)
Tesco Stores Ltd	10 Apr 2017–10 Apr 2020	Yes	Yes	No	No	N/A
Serco Geografix Ltd	4 Jul 2019–4 Jul 2022	No	Yes	No	No	N/A
Güralp Systems Ltd	22 Oct 2019–ongoing	Yes	Yes	No	No	N/A
Airbus SE	31 Jan 2020–31 Jan 2023	No	No	No	Ongoing	N/A
G4S Care & Justice Systems Ltd	10 Jul 2020–ongoing	No	Yes	No	No	N/A
Airline Services Ltd	30 Oct 2020–30 Oct 2021	No	Investigation seemingly ongoing	N/A	No	N/A
Amec Foster Wheeler Energy Ltd	1 Jul 2021–ongoing	No	No	No	Ongoing	N/A

(Continued)

Defendant company name	*Date of DPA*	*Individual named in DPA*	*UK prosecution of individual*	*UK conviction of individual*	*Overseas prosecution of individual*	*Overseas conviction of individual*
Bluu Solutions Limited Tetris Projects Limited	20 Jul 2021–28 Jul 2023	Yes	Yes	Yes (however, the individual is a third party to the companies that agreed the DPAs. Intra-corporate individuals were acquitted)	No	N/A
Entain Plc	5 Dec 2023–ongoing	No	Unknown (reporting restrictions in place pending conclusion of criminal proceedings against individuals)	No	Unknown	No

named individuals *would* be guilty.[68] Somewhat concerningly, despite efforts to outline the non-inclusion of individuals in the process, Lord Justice Edis in the *AFWEL* DPA considered that the anonymised statement of facts may later be substituted by a statement of facts identifying individuals; it is not stated when such substitution would be appropriate (though a hearing would precede such a decision),[69] and the only appropriate circumstances would be upon individual conviction (**Section 9.1.4**). Prompting further concern, the expiry of the DPAs of *Bluu Solutions Limited* and *Tetris Projects Limited* led to the issuing of a subsequent "de-anonymised" judgment, despite the fact that all but one of the individuals identified had been acquitted in their own proceedings.[70]

DPAs have, unsurprisingly, attracted deep criticism from the individuals who have been prosecuted and acquitted following the corporate agreements. In two DPAs in particular, the impact of the proceedings upon individuals' health has been publicly reported.[71] Following the *Serco Geografix Ltd* DPA, one of the former directors acquitted accused the SFO of trying to retrofit the case to him.[72] The lowered evidential test available to prosecutors to seek DPA approval has been a cause for concern in respect of the subsequent prosecution of implicated individuals, whereby the evidential test remains the normal Full Code Test for Crown Prosecutors. This can be evidenced in the *Tesco Stores Ltd* DPA, whereby the company agreed a DPA on the basis of an identification principle offence to which directors were thereafter personally acquitted; concerns as to whether the company should have agreed the DPA in the first place swiftly arose, including by one of the former directors.[73] One might speculate that this is perhaps why in *Güralp Systems Ltd*, Mr Justice William Davis was rushed through the process of approving a DPA prior to the imminent individuals' verdict: in order to ensure that the foundation of the identification

68 Serious Fraud Office, 'Deferred Prosecution Agreement – Statement of Facts – SFO v ICBC SB PLC' (*Serious Fraud Office*, 1 June 2016) <https://www.sfo.gov.uk/cases/standard-bank-plc/> accessed 1 March 2018, para 202.

69 *Bluu Solutions Limited and Tetris-Projects Limited* (n 63). With the opportunity to hear from counsel representing the implicated individuals. *See Director of the Serious Fraud Office v Amec Foster Wheeler Limited* [2021] Lloyd's Rep FC 353 (Crown) [5].

70 The one individual convicted was a third party to the offending companies, having received a bribe. Notably, the de-anonymised judgment was removed from the SFO website two months after its publication.

71 In former Tesco Stores Ltd director Carl Rogberg's out-of-court press interview, he stated that the process had 'enormous consequences' on his career and health – having suffered a heart attack during the first trial and ongoing illness. *See* Ben Chapman, 'Former Tesco Executive Carl Rogberg Cleared Over £250m Fraud and False Accounting Scandal' (*The Independent*, 23 January 2019) <https://www.independent.co.uk/news/business/news/carl-rogberg-tesco-executive-fraud-trial-cleared-false-accounting-scandal-court-a8741966.html> accessed 8 February 2021. *See also* BBC News, 'Tesco Fraud Trial Abandoned After Defendant's Heart Attack' (*BBC News*, 6 February 2018) <https://www.bbc.co.uk/news/business-42943382> accessed 8 February 2021. Similarly, Adrian Leek's (former head of sales and marketing of Sarclad Ltd) lawyer, Paul Haycock of Irwin Mitchell's Regulatory and Criminal Investigations group, noted the health impact of the process on his client. *See* Dave Grimshaw and David Shirt, 'Three Sarclad Execs Acquitted in 17m DPA Case' (*Irwin Mitchell*, 16 July 2019) <https://www.irwinmitchell.com/news-and-insights/newsandmedia/2019/july/three-sarclad-execs-acquitted-in-17m-dpa-case> accessed 9 February 2021.

72 Comments came from former operations director of field services within Serco, Simon Marshall. *See* Oliver Gill, 'Abolish Serious Fraud Office Says Acquitted Ex-Serco Boss' (*The Telegraph*, 8 May 2021) <https://www.telegraph.co.uk/business/2021/05/08/abolish-serious-fraud-office-says-acquitted-ex-serco-boss/> accessed 13 May 2021.

73 Former finance director Carl Rogberg went on to state that Tesco Stores had entered into the DPA on a 'completely false basis' and questioned the allegedly 'rushed' decision to enter into a DPA and pay such an enormous financial penalty. *See* BBC News, '"I Should Never Have Been Charged" – Former Tesco Director' (*BBC News*, 23 January 2019) <https://www.bbc.co.uk/news/business-46970604> accessed 8 February 2021.

principle-based DPA would not thereafter be undermined.[74] Evidence failings have undermined the SFO throughout, and in recent years the prosecutor faced huge backlash when the trial of former directors of Serco Geografix Ltd collapsed due to human error.[75] The integrity of the tool has consequently been called into question by such individuals, in disputing the accuracy of the agreed (between the prosecutor and the company) statement of facts.[76]

74 Mr Justice William Davis was rushed to make a preliminary and then final judgment approving the DPA, with only 36 hours to review the relevant papers prior to the preliminary hearing, as the trial of the individuals was imminent. Notably, 'the alleged criminal liability of [Güralp Systems Ltd was] very largely dependent upon culpability on the part of Dr Güralp'. *See Serious Fraud Office v Güralp Systems Ltd* [2020] Lloyd's Rep FC 90 (Crown) [11].

75 Private Eye, 'Trial and Error' *Private Eye* (London, 28 May to 10 June 2021) 40. The subsequent collapse of the trials against former executives of G4S C&J raised similar concerns.

76 Former Serco director Simon Marshall has claimed that the statement of facts which implicated him was 'incorrect'. *See* Gill (n 72). Prior to her Tanzanian plea agreement, former head of corporate and investment banking at Stanbic Bank Ltd Shose Sinare was reportedly suing Stanbic and Standard Bank in Tanzania in respect of misrepresentations and falsehoods within the *Standard Bank* DPA process; though the result of that potential litigation has not been reported, it will unlikely have been successful in light of Sinare's plea agreement. *See* Daily News, 'Shose Sinare Seeks 30m US Dollars Damages From Stanbic' (*Daily News*, 2 March 2016) <https://allafrica.com/stories/201603021200.html> accessed 1 February 2021.

CHAPTER 3

An introduction to D&O

3.1 A brief history of insurance

The first *known* contract of insurance dates back to the fourteenth century: a marine insurance contract devised in Genoa, Italy. As trade by marine voyage proliferated in the fourteenth and fifteenth centuries, methods of insuring did the same. Trade across the continent saw growth in insurance practices, and policies seen in England around the time were typically issued in both Italian and English. Records differ on the date of the first known insurance transaction in England: reports from the Court of Admiralty suggest it to be 1545, in the case of *Emerson v De Sallanova*,[1] whereas Guido Rossi states that Italian merchants residing in London were involved in such practices in 1426.[2] Nevertheless, the oldest known English policy extant is recorded in the 1547 case of *Broke v Maynard*.[3]

With marine insurance present in the UK in at least the 1500s, the first known life insurance policy in the UK swiftly followed in 1583.[4] Insurance grew within the jurisdiction from thereon, with the 1666 Great Fire of London provoking development of fire and property insurance in the jurisdiction, and the Industrial Revolution of the 1800s overseeing different lines of accident insurance and motor (and aviation) insurance. The 1800s further attracted vast volumes of reinsurance: the practice of insurance companies obtaining insurance.[5]

Following the Great Fire of London, the decimation of much of the City forced business into surviving coffee shops. Each coffee shop was frequented by a particular group, and it was in the shop owned by Edward Lloyd that those interested in shipping found their home (from at least 1688). Lloyd rented tables ("boxes") to businessmen seeking to arrange the sale of insurance products to passing ship owners.[6] The arrangement would involve the written recording of the sum paid for the insurance (the "premium"), the limit of liability, and an inventory of the details of the ship's voyage. Brokers, in representing their clients, approached the wealthy visitors of Lloyd's who were in the business of

1 William Vance, 'The Early History of Insurance Law' (1908) 8(1) Colum Law Rev 1, 11, citing *Emerson v De Sallanova* (1547) Select Pleas of the Admiralty SS.

2 Guido Rossi, 'England 1523–1601: The Beginnings of Marine Insurance' in AB Leonard (ed), *Marine Insurance* (Palgrave Macmillan 2016) 130–148.

3 William Holdsworth, 'The Early History of the Contract of Insurance' (1917) 17(2) Colum Law Rev 85, 96, citing *Broke v Maynard* (1547) Select Pleas of the Admiralty SS.

4 Niels Viggo Haueter, *A History of UK Insurance* (2nd edn, Swiss Re 2017) 5.

5 Özlem Gürses, *Reinsuring Clauses* (Informa Law 2010) para 1.01.

6 The Lloyd's of London building in the City still has "boxes". Underwriters take up their boxes, and brokers sit at the end of the table to discuss the needs of the client.

 DOI: 10.4324/9781003456964-4

investing in such risks in exchange for a fee. Those approached were "underwriters": individuals who would sign their name under the name of the ship in taking on a proportion of the stated limit of liability. Lloyd formalised the deals by requesting payment in exchange for the documentation of the details of each arrangement.

Following Edward Lloyd's death in 1713, the insurance business of "Lloyd's" continued to evolve. In 1771, "New Lloyd's" was founded after a number of established underwriters sought distance from those gaining unsavoury reputations, and the subscription market was formally established following the formation of a committee which intended to obtain capital from outside investors. In 1871, the Society of Lloyd's was established as a legal entity by the first Lloyd's Act, limiting the use of the "Lloyd's" name.[7] Though Lloyd's of London has undoubtedly changed over time, it remains the world's insurance marketplace, and Edward Lloyd is credited with the advent of the modern-day international insurance (and reinsurance) market.[8]

Indemnity insurance contracts as developed and popularised in the fourteenth century[9] are not all that different from those of the modern day. Fundamentally, an indemnity insurance contract is one whereby the consideration offered by the *insured* is the provision of a premium (which need not be monetary,[10] or paid in advance), in exchange for the promise of the *insurer* to provide indemnification to the insured upon the occurrence of a defined loss. The insurer thus takes on the risk previously borne by the insured, as the nature of insurance requires an inherent sense of uncertainty, such as to the event giving rise to the loss.[11] A description attempts to provide what the lack of a clear and decisive definition cannot: 'it is a concept which it is better to describe than attempt to define.'[12] Nevertheless, case law has provided useful indication – not least to regulators – which in its essence outlines the foundational pillars of exchange of premium for risk, the element of uncertainty, insurable interest,[13] and subject matter (distinguishing insurance from a mere wager).[14] Where, in liability policies, the subject matter is the liability itself,[15] exposure to the type of liability covered by the policy gives rise to insurable interest.[16]

---

7 The powers and functions of Lloyd's are now set out in the Lloyd's Act 1982, though parts of the Lloyd's Acts of 1871, 1911, and 1954 remain in force. *See* Alison Padfield, *Insurance Claims* (5th edn, Bloomsbury Professional 2021) para 1.7.

8 For the history of Lloyd's, *see* Lloyd's, 'Coffee and Commerce' (*Lloyd's*, 2023) <https://www.lloyds.com/about-lloyds/history/coffee-and-commerce> accessed 8 May 2023. *See also* Haueter (n 4) 10.

9 First said to be modelled on the maritime loan (which developed into the contract of bottomry), and later in the century an adaptation of sale, the popularity of the insurance contract saw its evolution to 'a distinct species of the large genus innomin tract' whereby the insured would provide a premium in exchange for the insurer undertaking the risk. *See* Holdsworth (n 3) 89–91.

10 Similarly, the benefit provided by the insurer need not be monetary. *See Re Digital Satellite Warranty Cover Ltd* [2011] EWHC 122 (Ch).

11 The uncertainty underpinning life insurance cases is the timeframe as to when the death will occur. In non-indemnity insurance (such as life insurance), the sum payable by the insurer is determined when the contract is ended. Thus, it is not calculated within a limit of indemnity in reference to the loss suffered, as in an indemnity insurance contract.

12 *Medical Defence Union Ltd v Department of Trade* [1980] Ch 82, 95 (Sir Robert Megarry V-C).

13 A requirement under sections 4(1)–(2) of the Marine Insurance Act 1906. A contract to provide cover irrespective of insurance interest will otherwise be void.

14 *See Prudential Insurance Co v Commissioners of Inland Revenue* [1904] 2 KB 658, 663 (Channell J).

15 *Feasey v Sun Life Assurance Company of Canada* [2003] EWCA Civ 885 [95] (Waller LJ). *See also* Franziska Arnold-Dwyer, *Insurable Interest and the Law* (Routledge 2020) 20.

16 Arnold-Dwyer (n 15) 20. Such exposure arises 'by reason of owing a legal duty or obligation to a third party'.

3.1.1 Insurance law in development

As insurance practices increased in England, particularly in the fourteenth century, resolution of disputes became a difficult task. The merchant courts arguably, given their specialty, were not best equipped to deal with insurance disputes, and litigants would reportedly on occasion bring cases already settled by merchant courts to the common law courts for resolution.[17] Merchant courts were not sanctioned by law, and thus their judgments were only enforceable to the extent agreed by the parties.[18] Admiralty courts experienced a similar lack of success. As such, a necessary statutory intervention followed in the first English insurance act of 1601.[19] The English government, alongside the Aldermen's Court of London, the Queen's Privy Council, and local institutions, collaborated in overseeing the establishment of the specialist marine insurance court. However, this was not entirely revolutionary. Reliance on the coordination of relevant institutions undermined the impact of the insurance court, which did not have exclusive jurisdiction over marine insurance disputes.[20] Thus, insurance law did not develop to any great extent for the next 150 years, until Lord Mansfield was appointed Chief Justice of the Court of King's Bench in 1756.[21] Upon Lord Mansfield's retirement from the Bench in 1788, such was his impact, it is said that 'he left a complete system of insurance law' in place,[22] and many fundamental principles remain applicable in the modern day. As a result, the common law courts became the arbiter of merchant disputes.

A number of insurance law principles developed in the 1800s remain important today. It is important to note that, whilst the consideration offered in exchange might be a premium suitably calculated, the insurer is placed in a somewhat vulnerable position in agreeing to take on the risk. In liability policies, though a definition of "Loss" will set parameters, and the limit of liability will operate as a cap, there remains an element of uncertainty as regards the potential for claims. It is established that there is an element of trust between the insurer and the insured, to the extent that the insurer relies on the insured's representation of their knowledge of the facts when presenting the risk. In this respect, as per *Carter v Boehm*, the insurance contract is one of 'good faith', which forbids either party from concealment (but not innocent silence).[23] However, as per *Pawson v Watson*, a reasoned approach is taken in considering the outcome of an incorrect representation where made on account of the representor's incorrect belief, and will not necessarily amount to an actionable misrepresentation.[24] Both cases, from 1766 and 1778 respectively, set out underpinning insurance law principles which emanate from and exemplify the long-lasting wisdom of Lord Mansfield.

---

17 Vance (n 1) 14.

18 Much like arbitration. *See* Arthur Schreiber, 'Lord Mansfield – The Father of Insurance Law' (1960) 12 Ins LJ 766, 767.

19 43 Eliz.

20 Rossi in Leonard (ed) (n 2) 130–148.

21 It is said that this can 'be considered as the date of the beginning of the development of the modern law of insurance as a part of the common law system'. Reportedly, until Lord Mansfield's appointment, reported insurance cases 'did not exceed sixty in number', and none of those decided set out any 'great principle'. *See* Vance (n 1) 16.

22 ibid 17. In describing his excellence, Vance points to Lord Mansfield's use of specialist juries in the practice of insurance, establishing 'customs and usages' in parallel with 'time-honored maritime laws of the Continent'.

23 (1766) 3 Burrow 1905 (KB) 1911 (Lord Mansfield).

24 (1778) 2 Cowp 785 (KB) 788 (Lord Mansfield).

As to statute governing the insurance contract, this area of law first developed against a backdrop of a heavily marine-led market. As such, statute followed in its name, with the Marine Insurance Acts of 1745 and 1788 responding to public concerns on moral hazard and public policy in relation to insurable interest, and the Marine Insurance Act of 1906 ("MIA 1906") introducing a more comprehensive rulebook. Such was the influence of Lloyd's at the time, that its standard marine insurance policy formed the foundation of the MIA 1906. Though the MIA 1906 codified the particularities of *marine* insurance law, its application in practice became universal. Thus, important change arrived with the passing of the Consumer Insurance (Disclosure and Representations) Act 2012 ("CIDRA 2012") and the Insurance Act 2015 ("IA 2015"), following the work of the Law Commission and the Scottish Law Commission (the "Law Commissions"). This new legislation saw divergence in statutory authority governing consumer-related insurance contracts (under the CIDRA 2012) and business-related insurance (under the IA 2015), with a more intentional consideration of the different types of insurance.

As insurance law has developed through the courts and statute books, with a focus on the insurance contract, insurance policy wording has been treated differently. It has over time been considered that, generally, the market is best placed to control policy wording (in line with the law), and thus the extent of coverage offered to insureds. Over time, therefore, the market has introduced policies covering many different types of risk. Naturally, different types of insurance have developed in turn. First party insurance arises where a party insures their own life, property, or belongings. In contrast, third party insurance arises where a party insures against their potential legal liability to another: such as in circumstances whereby a motorist damages the vehicle of another,[25] or where a company director misleads investors in misrepresenting the financial state of the company. This book focusses on directors' and officers' ("D&O") liability insurance, an insurance package which will typically predominantly cover three key risks: loss suffered by the director upon a claim made against them (where the company does not provide indemnification), sums paid by the company upon its indemnification of its directors, and the company's own liabilities.

3.2 D&O insurance

3.2.1 A brief history of D&O insurance

Professional indemnity ("professional lines") insurance (which includes errors and omissions insurance (also known as "E&O" or "professional liability")) is designed to protect a company and its professionals from third-party outsider claims, typically in respect of negligent services or advice.[26] D&O liability insurance is a variety of professional indemnity/management liability insurance which exists to provide protection to senior individuals within companies,[27] and the corporate bodies, from defined liability. Liability incurred by those senior individuals must be incurred within the capacity of director or

25 Third party motorist cover is a form of compulsory insurance in the UK. *See* Road Traffic Act 1988, pt 4.

26 Professional indemnity insurance is a requirement in some professions, at the direction of the profession regulators. For example, firms that are authorised by the Solicitors Regulation Authority.

27 Which can mean past, present, and future directors and officers, depending on policy wording. *See* Robert Merkin, *Colinvaux's Law of Insurance* (12th edn, Sweet & Maxwell 2019) para 21-258.

senior officer (if the latter is provided for within the policy), as liability incurred in a separate capacity will fall outside the D&O policy and may instead fall within the scope of professional indemnity insurance.[28] Larry Goanos, a D&O insurance expert in the US, has argued that D&O is 'undeniably, the most prominent of professional lines insurance products'.[29]

The origin of D&O insurance is not as clear as the origins of the business of Edward Lloyd's London coffee shop. According to Jonathan Mukwiri, D&O is 'effectively an American export'.[30] However, the first D&O policy written in the US is a trophy which many claim to hold. Seemingly the most probable claim is that the first D&O policy was written in the mid-1930s following the stock market crash and introduction of harsh Securities Acts[31] which prohibited corporations from indemnifying directors. In response to the restrictions introduced, Lloyd's of London in 1934 drafted the first "personal financial protection insurance" policies (now known as "D&O") for two large publicly held companies, Flintkote Corporation and Federated Department Stores.[32] Despite the introduction of the personal protection product, uptake was 'minimal'[33] as directors did not perceive their personal risk to be excessive and it was not popularised for several decades. Others have argued that the first D&O policy was written in 1962 by St Paul, following the passing of laws in America in the 1940s and 1950s which allowed companies to indemnify their directors and officers, representing the product's popularisation.[34] Reportedly, by 1965, ten percent of public companies held personal protection insurance for senior individuals.[35]

The nature of D&O policies has evolved over time in line with market fluctuation, consumer demand, competition, and developing law and regulation (amongst other influencing factors). Developments within the insurance sphere see not only fluctuations in premium costs, but also changes in the extent of coverage offered, with softer markets welcoming more insured-friendly policies and harder markets overseeing a restriction in the extent of protection insurers are willing to offer. The cycle of shifting markets is not exclusive to D&O insurance, though it has led to various transformations in the product since its inception (most likely in the 1930s).

---

28 Statements made in the promotion of the company will typically be made in the capacity of director and thus fall to be governed by D&O. *See Murray Goulburn Co-operative Co Ltd v AIG Australia Ltd* [2021] FCA 288. Statements made in an advisory capacity, for example, to company clients, will otherwise fall within professional indemnity cover. *See Channon v Ward* [2017] EWCA Civ 13.

29 Larry Goanos, *D&O 101: Understanding Directors and Officers Liability Insurance* (Wells Media Group Inc 2014) 34. Provision of D&O insurance may form part of a director's service contract, as discussed in: *TMO Renewables Ltd (In Liquidation) v Yeo Chancery Division* [2021] EWHC 2773 (Ch).

30 Jonathan Mukwuri, 'Directors' and Officers' Insurance in the UK' (2017) 28(4) EBLR 547, 548, citing Colin Baxter, 'Demystifying D&O Insurance' (1995) 15 OJLS 537, 538.

31 Securities Act of 1933 (US); Securities Act of 1934 (US); Investment Company Act of 1940 (US).

32 Robert Cavallaro, 'Corporate Buyer Beware: Deficiencies in Directors' and Officers' Insurance for Employment Practices Liability' (1997) 26(1) Hofstra Law Review 217, 221 <http://scholarlycommons.law.hofstra.edu/hlr/vol26/iss1/6> accessed 19 June 2020.

33 Kristopher Marsh, 'A Short History of D&O Insurance' (*Discover D&O*, 8 June 2015) <https://web.archive.org/web/20210127094213/https://www.discoverdando.com/a-short-history-of-dando-insurance/> accessed 19 June 2020.

34 Larry Goanos, *Claims Made and Reported: A Journey Through D&O, E&O and Other Professional Lines of Insurance* (Kindle edn, Sixth and Spring Books 2011) location 282; Goanos, *D&O 101: Understanding Directors and Officers Liability Insurance* (n 29) 28; ibid.

35 Marsh, 'A Short History of D&O Insurance' (n 33).

The original concept of "personal financial protection insurance" was likely introduced to provide personal protection to directors and senior officers of corporations following the 1929 Wall Street Crash, which led to a high-risk market and the prohibition on the protection of executives by their employer corporations (under the US Securities Acts).[36] Directors became increasingly demanding of personal protection, and this was pursued 'vigorously' by corporate officials.[37] D&O insurance became increasingly popular throughout the 1960s when executive claims became more commonplace (during a period of increased mergers and acquisitions), and individuals sought such protection where their employer corporation was unable to provide indemnification.[38] Popularisation saw more insurers enter the market and thus increased competition, which in the 1970s led to the distinct structuring of most D&O policies as comprising "Insuring Agreement A" and "Insuring Agreement B" (commonly known as "Side A" and "Side B"). Side A continues to represent the traditional D&O policy, which provides indemnification for individual directors and senior officers where their employer corporation is unable to do so (for financial or legal reasons, or where unwilling).[39] Side B insures the corporation itself, providing reimbursement where the corporation has met its indemnification obligations to its executives[40] (which would otherwise be covered by Side A). Thus, the director cannot claim under Side B.

At the end of the 1970s, the market was thriving, and 'approximately 70 percent of public companies had some form of D&O insurance in place'.[41] However, there was a steep decline by the mid-1980s when the 1987 stock market crash saw the D&O market plummet. The cost of claims increased by over 50 percent, reinsurance capacity was restricted, the majority of the top insurers left the market, and consumers saw their premium costs triple and limits of liability halve.[42] As the sector began to repair, the nature of D&O again underwent significant development with the introduction of "Insuring Agreement C" (also known as "Side C"). A US Court of Appeals ruling in the Ninth Circuit in *Nordstrom Inc v Chubb & Son Inc*[43] held that an insurer would be required to pay 100 percent of all settlements (in most cases) where the defendants were both insured individuals and the

36 Joseph Bishop, 'Sitting Ducks and Decoy Ducks: New Trends in the Indemnification of Corporate Directors and Officers' (1968) 77(6) Yale LJ 1078, 1082.

37 Joseph Monteleone and Nicholas Conca, 'Directors and Officers Indemnification and Liability Insurance: An Overview of Legal and Practical Issues' (1996) 51(3) The Business Lawyer 573, 574.

38 'However, D&O insurance is not simply a U.S. import, as is sometimes claimed: there is a European lineage also. "European" D&O developed from the separate classes of legal expenses insurance, written for managers, and professional indemnity insurance, which often covered the activities of lawyers and others as members of corporate boards.' *See* Chris Parsons, 'Directors' and Officers' Liability Insurance: A Target or a Shield?' (2000) 21(3) Comp Law 77, 78. *See also* Marsh, 'A Short History of D&O Insurance' (n 33).

39 *Some* policies feature an exclusion clause excluding liability where the company is permitted to indemnify the director (even if it refuses to do so). *See* Merkin, *Colinvaux's Law of Insurance* (n 27) para 21-249. The company will typically be the policyholder: *AXA SA v Genworth Financial International Holdings Inc* [2019] EWHC 3376 (Comm). However, where this is the case, directors are still co-insureds: *CE Heath Casualty & General Insurance Ltd v Grey* (1993) 32 NSWLR 25.

40 In *Intergraph Best (Vic) Pty Ltd v QBE Insurance Ltd* [2005] VSCA 180, the company could not recover where the directors were not personally liable for the defence costs, and the defence costs paid by the company were not paid pursuant to an indemnity provision. Since there was no legal liability by way of indemnity owed to its directors, Side B could not respond.

41 Marsh, 'A Short History of D&O Insurance' (n 33).

42 ibid.

43 54 F 3d 1424 (9th Cir 1995).

uninsured corporation (the latter for corporate liability).[44] Side C was thereafter introduced by AIG in 1995 to provide entity coverage to corporations for securities-related claims,[45] and other insurers soon followed suit.

The introduction of the Private Securities Litigation Reform Act 1995 in the US encouraged growth in the D&O insurance market, as the instrument led to a reduction in securities litigation (by 45 percent over the next two years), though the market suffered as a result of securities litigation again in 2001.[46] At its inception, insureds could purchase varying percentages of Side C cover but this has subsequently evolved to 100 percent entity cover as standard. Modern D&O policies tend to take the standard form of ABC cover (comprising all three Sides A, B, and C). However, in some policies, Side C is provided separately on account of the scope for erosion of the limit of indemnity, where shareholder actions have the potential to obliterate any protection under Side A.[47] With increased premiums having been reported in 2019 and continued uncertainty as a consequence of the 2020 COVID-19 global health pandemic,[48] the market was described as a 'difficult place to do business'.[49] Exiting the pandemic period, as the market appeared to settle, decreases in premiums were reported.[50]

3.2.2 The nature of D&O insurance

Coverage under a D&O policy will typically be provided on the following basis, subject to the limitations with the definitions (capitalised) and any exclusions: "covering an Insured from Loss arising from Claims made for (and/or alleging) Wrongful Acts during the Policy Period". "Claim" is not to be misconstrued with "claim" (note the varied capitalisation): the former refers to a policy-defined demand made against the insured by a third party, whereas the latter refers to the claim thereafter made by the insured against the insurer for coverage. A D&O policy is "Claims made", therefore responding to Claims made against the insured and notified to the insurer within the policy period. Therefore, D&O insurance does not respond on an occurrence basis: as and when events happen which may give rise to a future Claim against the insured. Though a policy

44 Goanos, *D&O 101: Understanding Directors and Officers Liability Insurance* (n 29) 93–94.

45 Michael Rossi, 'Recent Developments in D&O Insurance Law and Products in the United States' (1997) 5(4) Int ILR 101, 102–103.

46 Marsh, 'A Short History of D&O Insurance' (n 33).

47 The trend of shareholder actions 'was given a significant boost' when the House of Lords held that such a claim 'may in some cases rank equally with a claim by other unsecured creditors'. *See* Merkin, *Colinvaux's Law of Insurance* (n 27) para 21-251, citing *Soden v British and Commonwealth Holdings Plc* [1998] AC 298 (HL).

48 Jennifer Williams-Alvarez, 'Cost of Insuring Board Directors From Lawsuits Doubles in Covid Era' (*Financial Times*, 16 September 2020) <https://www.ft.com/content/fa626a0f-2806-4197-a1e8-61deb08944af> accessed 27 September 2021; Daniel Thomas, 'Cost of Liability Insurance for Company Directors Soars' (*Financial Times*, 7 February 2021) <https://www.ft.com/content/7fd09758-ac7b-469a-9096-486a707f2915> accessed 27 September 2021.

49 David Ritchie, 'News & Insights: State of the Market for Directors' & Officers'' (*Gallagher*, 2 April 2020) <https://www.ajg.com/uk/news-and-insights/2020/april/state-of-the-market-for-directors-and-officers/> accessed 19 June 2020.

50 *See for example* Marsh, 'UK Directors and Officers Liability Insurance H1 2022 Market Update' (*Marsh*, 26 August 2022) <https://www.marsh.com/ie/services/financial-professional-liability/insights/uk-directors-and-officers-liability-insurance-h1-2022-market-update.html> accessed 3 April 2023. *See also* Priya Huskins, 'Looking Ahead to 2023: A Guide for D&O Insurance Renewals' (*Woodruff Sawyer*, 20 September 2022) <https://woodruffsawyer.com/do-notebook/do-looking-ahead-guide/> accessed 3 April 2023.

may require notification of the insurer (by the insured) of Claims *and Circumstances* (something reasonably likely to give rise to a Claim), notification of Circumstances is not a trigger of cover, as a Claim must follow in order for the policy to respond.[51] Thus, a requirement for notification of Circumstances does not transform the policy from Claims made to occurrence-based.

The demand against the insured which constitutes a "Claim" may be one for monetary or non-monetary relief, but can also include civil proceedings, criminal proceedings, formal administrative or regulatory proceedings, and in some definitions also (criminal, administrative, or regulatory) investigations.[52] In essence, the definition will target the object claimed, as opposed to the cause of action.[53] The Claim against the insured will be made on the basis of a defined "Wrongful Act", which will typically include any actual, alleged, or attempted breach of duty or breach of trust, neglect, error, misstatement, misleading statement, omission, or act. Coverage may be needed where "Loss" arises from the Claim made. "Loss" will usually include (compensatory) damages (so far as the damages are insurable by law), and judgments, awards, or settlements. The "Loss" definition may include defence costs, though this may be covered by way of separate undertaking (**Section 14.3**). Interpretation of the "Insured" will depend on the applicable Side of coverage and could be an individual director or senior officer,[54] in their insured capacity as such, or the company. Under Side A, the individual director(s) is covered against liability to third parties where the company does not indemnify,[55] and serves as a source of protection for personal assets.[56] Under Side B, the company is reimbursed where it indemnifies its directors. Side C offers entity coverage, the extent of which depends on policy wording, though commonly for larger companies is restricted to securities-related claims.

A reading of the policy cannot focus on clauses and definitions purely independently, but must also be considered as a whole. Though coverage may *prima facie* be offered, an exclusion clause contained within the policy may operate to exclude liability. A key exclusion seen in D&O policies is the "Conduct exclusion" clause, which will typically operate to exclude liability on the basis of dishonest or fraudulent acts (and it may be

51 *HLB Kidsons (a firm) v Lloyd's Underwriters subscribing to Lloyd's Policy No 621/PKID00101* [2007] EWHC 1951 (Comm).

52 Allianz, 'Complete Directors & Officers: Policy Wording' (*Allianz Insurance plc*, 2020) <https://www.allianzebroker.co.uk/content/allianzebroker/en_gb/application/content/documents/commercial-products/sme/complete-directors-and-officers/complete-directors-officers-policy-wording/_jcr_content/documentProperties/currentDocument.res/complete-directors-officers-wording_acom4288.pdf> accessed 15 October 2020, 8; WR Berkley UK Limited, 'Directors and Officers Liability and Company Reimbursement Insurance Policy' (*WR Berkley*, May 2018) <https://www.brokerdirect.co.uk/wp-content/uploads/2018/08/Directors-Officers-WRB_PolicyWording_V06_MAY18.pdf> accessed 23 November 2020, 7.

53 The set of facts which may give rise to multiple Claims. 'A cause of action is simply a factual situation the existence of which entitles one person to obtain from the court a remedy against another person.' *See Letang v Cooper* [1964] 2 All ER 929 (QB) 934 (Diplock LJ).

54 There is often contention as to what a senior officer can be defined as, but an accepted definition is 'those to whom the company's directors delegate certain managerial functions and [are] usually put in charge of the practical execution of decisions taken by the board of directors'. *See* Adolfo Paolini and Deepak Nambisan, *Directors' and Officers' Liability Insurance* (Informa Law 2008) para 7.35.

55 Some policies feature an exclusion clause excluding liability where the company is permitted to indemnify the director (even if it refuses to do so). *See* Merkin, *Colinvaux's Law of Insurance* (n 27) para 21-249.

56 Such protection not only encourages individuals to take up high-risk directorship roles, but also encourages companies to invest in and provide appropriate executive protection. *See RSUI Indemnity Company v David H Murdock and Dole Food Company Inc* 2021 WL 803867, 23 (Del Mar 3 2021).

a further requirement that those acts be deliberate). Such an exclusion may therefore impact the extent to which coverage is extended in respect of criminal proceedings and/or investigations, for example. A "Contract exclusion" may also exist to preclude coverage for Claims arising from a contract and/or agreement, depending on policy wording. In addition to a number of exclusions (such as "Bodily Injury and Property Damage", "Terrorism", and so forth), other clauses may – when applied alongside exclusions – serve to restrict liability. For example, an "Interrelated Wrongful Acts" or "Related Claims" clause, when invoked, will have the effect of tying together Claims, thus imposing a single self-insured retention[57] and single limit of indemnity. An exclusion applicable to one of a number of related Claims tied together would have the effect of excluding liability for the collated Claim.

In the UK, it was not until the Companies Act of 1989[58] that the ability of the company to purchase or maintain liability insurance for its officers arose. Although section 232(1) of the CA 2006 renders void any provision (for example, within the articles of association) purporting to exempt a director from liability that would otherwise attach 'in connection with any negligence, default, breach of duty or breach of trust in relation to the company',[59] section 233 provides that a company is not prevented 'from purchasing and maintaining for a director of the company, or of an associated company, insurance against any such liability'.[60] Section 234 allows for 'qualifying third party indemnity provision'.[61] Therefore, in accordance with section 234, a company can indemnify its directors where a third party brings an action against them, with some important exceptions.

A company cannot indemnify a director for liabilities owed to the company itself or to an associated company,[62] nor defence costs incurred in civil proceedings brought successfully against the director by the (associated) company,[63] but can indemnify in respect of civil proceedings brought by third parties. Indemnification is not permitted in respect of penalties imposed by regulatory authorities.[64] In respect of criminal proceedings, indemnification is not permitted for criminal fines,[65] nor for defence costs incurred where the director is thereafter convicted (and it is the final decision in the proceedings).[66] Such an indemnity provision is typically set out within a company's articles of association, but is not (in most circumstances) contractually enforceable by the director (forming a contract

---

57 A self-insured retention is the amount of loss the insured must pay before the insurer provides coverage.

58 The Companies Act 1989, through section 137, amended the earlier Companies Act 1985, section 310, on this matter.

59 Companies Act 2006, s 232(1).

60 ibid s 233.

61 This must be included in the directors' annual financial report to the company. See ibid s 236. Premiums paid by the company must also be disclosed in the company's accounts. *See* Merkin, *Colinvaux's Law of Insurance* (n 27) para 21-247.

62 Companies Act 2006, s 234(2).

63 ibid s 234(3)(b)(ii).

64 ibid s 234(3)(a)(ii).

65 ibid s 234(3)(a)(i).

66 ibid ss 234(3)(a)(i), 234(4).

between the members (not the directors) and the company).[67] Therefore, such a provision may be set out by way of a separate contract.[68]

Where a DPA is agreed by a company, various claims may arise against a (former) director as a result. If the director is considered to have committed the underlying wrongdoing pursuant to the DPA, or to have allowed its continuation unchecked, it may be the case that criminal proceedings against that individual ensue. In the same circumstances, and perhaps where the director has permitted the agreement of a DPA and it is believed that this was the incorrect decision for the company, civil proceedings may follow (for example, for breach of directors' duties). In this respect, it is crucial to ascertain the response of D&O coverage in such circumstances, particularly in respect of the advancement (or indemnification) of defence costs, and the potential application of the Conduct exclusion clause.

3.3 D&O market response to DPAs

Since their introduction in the UK in 2014, DPAs have prompted warnings signalled throughout the D&O insurance industry. In 2017, partners at Clyde & Co LLP Mark Sutton and Karen Boto warned that increased use of DPAs would lead to further individual prosecutions and thus increased D&O claims.[69] This was further echoed by insurer Chubb in 2019 when it was outlined that the demands of corporate cooperation 'heightens the risk of subsequent individual prosecutions for associated Directors and Officers',[70] thus pointing to an inherent risk to individuals within the DPA framework. Partners in the financial and professional risks team at Browne Jacobson LLP, Jonathan Newbold and Marlene Henderson, highlighted in 2018 that continued and growing focus on individual accountability for corporate crime would lead senior individuals to seek advancement of defence costs.[71] This is a trend likely to continue in the UK as the government continues to address issues relating to corporate criminal liability.[72] Indeed, the increase in D&O claims has been cautioned by Chubb, setting out in 2019 that the number of claims based

67 LexisPSL, 'Directors and Officers Insurance Policies' (*LexisNexis*, 2021) <https://www.lexisnexis.co.uk/legal/guidance/directors-officers-insurance-policies> accessed 16 February 2021, citing The Companies (Model Articles) Regulations 2008, SI 2008/3229, reg 2, sch 1, arts 52, 53 (private companies); The Companies (Model Articles) Regulations 2008, SI 2008/3229, reg 4, sch 3, arts 85, 86 (public companies).

68 Guy Wilkes and Francis Kean, 'The Position of Individuals in Regulatory Investigations: A Changing Landscape' (2017) 1(2) Journal of Financial Compliance 172, 178. *See also TMO Renewables Ltd (In Liquidation) v Yeo Chancery Division* (n 29).

69 Mark Sutton and Karen Boto, 'Guest Post: D&O Insurance Implications as Deferred Prosecution Agreements Take Off in the U.K.' (*The D&O Diary*, 30 January 2017) <https://www.dandodiary.com/2017/01/articles/international-d-o/guest-post-insurance-implications-deferred-prosecution-agreements-take-off-u-k/> accessed 8 October 2021.

70 Chubb, 'Directors and Officers Claims are Increasing Both in Cost and Severity: Is Your Business Exposed?' (*Chubb*, 2019) <https://web.archive.org/web/20191226170511/https://www.chubb.com/uk-en/_assets/documents/final-06_18_do_claims_brochure_v2_lowres.pdf> accessed 26 June 2020, 3.

71 Jonathan Newbold and Marlene Henderson, 'Corporate Crackdown' (2018) 168(7798) NLJ 19.

72 The focus on further addressing corporate criminal liability and individuals behind it can be evidenced by discussions during the recent Law Commission Corporate Criminal Liability project. *See* Law Commission, *Corporate Criminal Liability* (Law Com 2021) paras 4.6–4.14, 8.1–8.18. *See also* Law Commission, 'Corporate Criminal Liability' (*Law Commission*, 2021) <https://www.lawcom.gov.uk/project/corporate-criminal-liability/> accessed 7 October 2021.

on regulatory proceedings had tripled for the insurer since 2012.[73] Simon Cooper, D&O insurance consultant, warned in 2014 that insurers may need to 're-examine and possibly redraft policies' to account for the 'immediate risk' presented by the then-brand new DPA framework – for example, where companies 'use guilty directors as bargaining chips'.[74]

This was further supported following the third UK DPA with Rolls-Royce, when Sutton and Boto warned that insurers may wish to 'review their policy wordings' as regards DPAs where individuals' names are omitted, and went as far as suggesting that '[t]hey may wish to consider including a new exclusion, avoiding any liability for claims that arise out of an approved DPA'.[75] A rationale for this proposal – which is somewhat extreme considering the objective of the policy (to protect directors against defined Claims arising during the policy period) – was that it would 'avoid a situation where Insurers are obliged to advance costs only to then seek to claw them back upon a conviction'.[76] In light of the fact that no successful prosecutions of directors or senior officers of DPA-agreeing companies have thus far arisen from UK DPAs, such a measure (upon reflection) seems all the more extreme.[77] However, the increase in claims cited by Chubb may signal a need for reconsideration of premiums, which would likely be unpopular.[78] The market's sensitivity to exposure caused by lack of clarity thus becomes a vulnerability ultimately shared by insureds.

Despite market consideration of harsh limitation of cover, D&O professionals Guy Wilkes and Francis Kean in 2017 attempted to opt for a more positive perspective, in stating that most D&O policies will at least be triggered to respond to 'provide protection to directors who are either the target of a regulatory investigation or who are required to attend an interview in the context of such an investigation'.[79] However, whilst a policy might respond by providing an advancement of defence costs, ultimate indemnification is a separate consideration. Furthermore, Wilkes and Kean were somewhat hesitant in their positivity and outlined that D&O insurers generally 'have no appetite to cover the full cost of regulatory investigations involving individuals',[80] which signposts the somewhat paradoxical self-protectionist position of insurers and exposures to implicated individuals.

Such lack of clarity on the position of D&O insurers in respect of DPAs and coverage of individuals undoubtedly raises a number of considerations for insureds and insurers. With such heightened risk and obscurity, insurers are likely to become inquisitorial and investigative during the underwriting stage; this is a suggestion for 'wise' insurers heralded by Sutton and Boto.[81] It may, however, be argued that this is not a new posi-

73 Chubb, 'Directors and Officers Claims are Increasing Both in Cost and Severity: Is Your Business Exposed?' (n 70) 3.

74 Simon Cooper, 'DPAs and the Implications for D&O Insurers' (*Lexology*, 15 April 2014) <https://www.lexology.com/library/detail.aspx?g=a4290a5a-bf72-4ceb-92af-bf9ea7daaa59> accessed 9 October 2023.

75 Sutton and Boto (n 69).

76 ibid.

77 This suggestion was made when only three DPAs had been agreed – there have now been 13, and therefore one has the benefit of hindsight in drawing this conclusion.

78 Though the market was deemed to have hardened between 2018 and 2021, '[t]hroughout 2022, insureds witnessed rapid premium relief'. *See* Patrick Whelan, 'What to Expect from the D&O Market in 2023' (*Beazley*, 13 February 2023) <https://www.beazley.com/en-gb/articles/what-expect-do-market-2023> accessed 19 May 2023.

79 Wilkes and Kean (n 68) 180.

80 ibid.

81 Sutton and Boto (n 69).

tion propelled by the introduction of DPAs. The IA 2015 sought to balance the position between prospective insureds and insurers by placing an increased burden on insurers to ask questions,[82] and this development is not attributed to the (then) recent implementation of DPAs. Furthermore, in a 2007 empirical study of the D&O underwriting process, it was found that insurers (certainly in the US market) would typically conduct their own investigations into corporate governance, regulatory filings, and so forth, in calculating the price of the premium.[83] This suggests that the approach by insurers may not have significantly changed. Nonetheless, the lack of clarity demonstrates the need for further attention.

Upon the introduction of DPAs, Cooper noted that the statement of facts prepared (in part) by the company would mean that 'directors and officers will struggle to defend themselves'.[84] This projected struggle was fairly assessed and has been observed as the tool has been used. Sutton, Boto (in 2017), and Kean (in 2019) have, however, previously provided some solace to insureds in setting out that cover will likely not be refused until the end of proceedings. D&O policies will, in the main, bear a "Conduct exclusion" clause which will operate to exclude liability on the basis of dishonest or fraudulent acts (and it may be a further requirement that those acts be deliberate). Typically, the clause is invoked either by admission or final adjudication (**Sections 15.2.3.1 and 15.2.3.2**). The position that refusal of cover will come at the end of proceedings is thus on the basis that an individual – '"innocent until proven guilty"' – can rely upon the final adjudication trigger of a Conduct exclusion clause to ensure interim protection.[85] Whether this is so, exposure may still arise depending on factual circumstances and policy wording where the trigger by admission arises. However, Sutton and Boto considered that implicated individuals would find some measure of protection in the fact that such an admission is made by the company itself.[86]

Back in 1988, it was considered in *International Association of Chiefs of Police v St Paul Fire and Marine Insurance Co* whether, despite an admission within a settlement agreement, coverage could attach where the Conduct exclusion clause set out: 'if a claim of dishonesty, unlawful profit, or advantage *isn't proven*, we'll cover the expenses for defending that claim' (emphasis added).[87] In this US case, an admission was deemed to constitute proof sufficient to refuse coverage, despite the fact that it was not subject to a finding of fact by the court.[88] Insurance lawyers Robert Horkovich and Alexander Hardiman have commented that this case may present an argument adopted by insurers in reliance upon admissions to refuse coverage post-DPA, though they do not specifically comment on whether this line of argument would be advanced against individual insureds (as well as

82 Disclosure required by the prospective insured is as a minimum 'disclosure which gives the insurer sufficient information to put a prudent insurer on notice *that it needs to make further enquiries* for the purpose of revealing those material circumstances' (emphasis added). *See* Insurance Act 2015, s 3(4)(b).

83 In 2008, Professor Miriam Baer, writing on insuring corporate crime, drew reference to the study conducted by Professors Tom Baker and Sean Griffith. *See* Miriam Baer, 'Insuring Corporate Crime' (2008) 83 Ind LJ 1035, 1090, citing Tom Baker and Sean Griffith, 'Predicting Corporate Governance Risk: Evidence from the Directors' & Officers' Liability Insurance Market' (2007) 74(2) U Chi L Rev 487, 511–513.

84 Cooper (n 74).

85 Francis Kean, 'Being Thrown Under the Bus: Why Directors Should Worry About Deferred Prosecution Agreements' (*LinkedIn*, 11 February 2019) <https://www.linkedin.com/pulse/being-thrown-under-bus-why-directors-should-worry-deferred-kean/> accessed 9 October 2023.

86 Sutton and Boto (n 69).

87 686 F Supp 115, 117 (D Md 1988).

88 ibid 118.

insured entities).[89] However, Wilkes and Kean in 2017 warned that insurers may seek to apply policy exclusions to an individual's claim 'by reference to facts or conduct that relate to another aspect of the insurance claim or the conduct of other insured individuals' – or by reference to the conduct of an (insured) company – in refusing cover.[90] Horkovich and Hardiman note the importance of severability provisions (clearly separating the position of each insured) in ensuring that an insured's scope of coverage is not substantially narrowed.[91] This clearly represents yet another significant exposure to insureds, which is ultimately inherent within policy wording.

89 Robert Horkovich and Alexander Hardiman, 'How the New SEC Settlement Policy Affects Your D&O Coverage' (*Risk Management*, April 2012) <https://www.andersonkill.com/webpdfext/How_the_New_SEC_Settlement_Policy_Affects_Your_D&O_Coverage.pdf> accessed 23 November 2020, 1.

90 Wilkes and Kean (n 68) 181.

91 Horkovich and Hardiman (n 89) 2.

PART II

DPAS AND DIRECTORS

As deferred prosecution agreements ("DPA(s)") in the UK are not available to individuals, Part II of the book seeks to explore the impact of the corporate agreements on related, and often implicated, individuals. The beginning of Part II, which is Chapter 4, first seeks to identify the foundation upon which UK DPAs were built. Looking to the history of DPAs in the US, and the extent of transplantation into the UK system, the original objectives of the tool and its development are considered in order to better understand its functioning. With this basis, Part II moves to consider the position of implicated (former) directors when the DPA process arises and just before that – in the pre-negotiation stage. A key theme of Part II is the balancing of the director's professional duties and personal rights. The former is dealt with first, in identifying how directors' duties owed to the company may be engaged, and possibly breached, early in the DPA process and particularly in considering any corporate self-report. Thereafter, the director's right to defence is explored, with consideration of the impact of any exercised defence on the corporate and, in reverse, the extent to which a corporate can hamper the individual's own defence. At this stage, the impact of DPA-related documentation (even where a DPA is not approved) is discussed, and Part II then moves on to deliberate the issue of naming and identifying individuals in such documentation. Having considered any avenues for redress where naming does occur, Part II concludes by exploring the extent to which a director can seek protection from prosecution in obtaining leniency measures: whether through the corporate DPA or other means.

DOI: 10.4324/9781003456964-5

CHAPTER 4

DPAs and individual availability or protection

4.1 United States

DPAs in the US can be agreed with the DoJ in respect of criminal liability, or with the Securities and Exchange Commission ("SEC") in respect of civil liability.[1] Though the DoJ has various divisions spanning both criminal and civil liability, and its guidance on DPAs (**Sections 4.1.1 and 4.1.2**) provides for civil use,[2] use of DPAs is focussed almost entirely on criminal cases. Unlike the UK, DPAs can be agreed with individuals as well as corporations. In order to assess the availability of DPAs for individuals implicated in corporate crime and/or the impact of corporate DPAs on individual defendants in the US, DPA use within the criminal context must first be explored alongside a brief history of the provision (with a focus on the position of individuals).

4.1.1 DPAs and criminal liability

The concept of deferral within criminal justice, either of certain consequences or of the offender to other systems, presents in many forms within the US. "Pretrial diversion" does not necessarily require a charge (sometimes referred to as "precharge diversion") but allows an alleged offender to submit to a 'program of supervision and services administered by the U.S. Probation Service'[3] without (or with limited) court involvement. The "pretrial diversion program" ("PDP") period (of no more than 18 months) begins upon the signing of a pretrial diversion agreement, which outlines the terms of the probation.[4] Completion of the programme will mean that the individual does not face charge, or that a charge made is dismissed, and failure to complete will mean that the individual faces prosecution. In 1982, Sharon Moyer outlined that "pretrial diversion programs" have three categories: 'deferred

1 Stephanie Brooker and others, 'Negotiating Closure of Government Investigations: NPAs, DPAs, and Beyond' (*Gibson Dunn*, 1 October 2020) <https://www.gibsondunn.com/wp-content/uploads/2020/10/WebcastSlides-Negotiating-Closure-of-Government-Investigations-NPAs-DPAs-and-Beyond-01-OCT-2020.pdf> accessed 22 March 2021.

2 *See for example* Deputy Attorney General Rod Rosenstein, 'Deputy Attorney General Rod J. Rosenstein Delivers Remarks at the American Conference Institute's 35th International Conference on the Foreign Corrupt Practices Act' (*The United States Department of Justice*, 29 November 2018) <https://www.justice.gov/opa/speech/deputy-attorney-general-rod-j-rosenstein-delivers-remarks-american-conference-institute-0> accessed 13 May 2020.

3 The United States Department of Justice, Justice Manual § 9-22.010 (2011).

4 The United States Department of Justice, Justice Manual: Criminal Resource Manual 701–799 § 712 (2020).

DOI: 10.4324/9781003456964-6

prosecution, dispute settlement and unconditional diversion programs.'[5] Notably, deferred prosecution is referred to by Moyer as 'deferred prosecution programs' and not "agreements" and the explanation given resembles the modern-day PDP. It can reasonably be observed that the concept of deferred prosecution has its roots in early examples of pretrial diversion methods; notably, the Thompson Memorandum (explored later in **Section 4.1.1**) made reference to pretrial diversion and agreements in respect of corporations.[6]

One key difference between a PDP and DPAs is that the PDP seeks to divert the case from the court and prosecutor to a rehabilitative-style programme, whereas DPAs retain some element of punitive sanction (albeit with rehabilitative measures such as compliance programmes) and require judicial approval. In a US DPA, a "criminal Information" (charge) is filed and deferred, following court approval.[7] Sprenger notes another difference to be the type of underlying offences, with an express objective of PDPs being 'to save prosecutive and judicial resources for concentration on major cases'[8] (thus suggesting their lack of availability for those considered to be major).[9]

Deferred prosecution, or pretrial diversion, in the US is said to have its roots in Chicago in the early twentieth century. First introduced in 1914 to deal with low-level criminal offences and juvenile or first-time offenders, the Chicago Boys' Court sought to take a rehabilitative approach in order to avoid the consequences of criminal conviction and entry into the criminal justice system.[10] The approach would often make provision for 'counseling, training, and job-placement programs'[11] in order to offer a second chance to offenders and to avoid persons capable of rehabilitation from becoming stuck in the system. In 1947, Charles Meyer (then Federal Probation and Parole Officer in Chicago) wrote about the use of deferred prosecution in cases of juvenile offenders in Brooklyn. In the "Brooklyn Plan", the prosecution would be deferred on an interim basis for approximately one week by a district attorney, the case referred to a probation officer for investigation and compiling of a report about the offender (as in a presentence report for the courts), and then the attorney would make a final decision as to deferral.[12] The case would therefore not necessarily ever reach the courts, and the decision-making power lay with law enforcement. Following experimentation in Brooklyn, the US Attorney General authorised all US attorneys to implement the procedure in cases of juvenile offenders.[13] In 1947 the concept

5 Sharon Moyer, 'Pretrial Diversion: An Overview' (*National Criminal Justice Reference Service*, April 1982) <https://www.ojp.gov/pdffiles1/Digitization/82890NCJRS.pdf> accessed 20 March 2021.

6 Larry Thompson, 'Principles of Federal Prosecution of Business Organizations' (*The United States Department of Justice*, 20 January 2003) <https://web.archive.org/web/20030429005746/https://www.justice.gov/dag/cftf/corporate_guidelines.htm> accessed 20 March 2021; James Anderson and Ivan Waggoner, *The Changing Role of Criminal Law in Controlling Corporate Behavior* (RAND Corporation 2014) 51.

7 Speedy Trial Act 18 USC § 3161(h)(2) (Supp IV 1974).

8 The United States Department of Justice, Justice Manual § 9-22.010 (2011).

9 Polly Sprenger, *Deferred Prosecution Agreements: The Law and Practice of Negotiated Corporate Criminal Penalties* (Sweet & Maxwell 2015) 78.

10 Benjamin Greenblum, 'What Happens to a Prosecution Deferred? Judicial Oversight of Corporate Deferred Prosecution Agreements' (Oct 2005) 105(6) Colum L Rev 1863, 1866; Peter Reilly, 'Justice Deferred is Justice Denied: We Must End Our Failed Experiment in Deferring Corporate Criminal Prosecutions' (2015) 2 BYU L Rev 307, 314–315.

11 Reilly (n 10) 315.

12 Charles Meyer, 'The "Brooklyn Plan" of Deferred Prosecution for Juvenile Offenders' (1931–1951) 37(6) JCLC 478, 478–480.

13 ibid.

was formally recognised by the Judicial Conference, with continued focus on juvenile offenders.[14]

Use of deferred prosecution for drug-related offences became prominent in 1962 following the case of *Robinson v California*[15] and increased focus on rehabilitation. Thereafter, throughout the 1970s, there was significant development in the use of the deferred prosecution or pretrial diversion concept. This followed the 1967 President's Commission Report, which highlighted the ability of prosecutors to divert offenders to 'noncriminal methods of treatment and control',[16] with focus on the increased use of community resources. Detoxification programmes and referrals to hospital, social agency, and mediation became increasingly common.[17] The 1974 Speedy Trial Act (and US Code on Crimes and Criminal Procedure) set out that provisions on timely trials do not apply where delay to prosecution occurs as a result of a deferral agreed in writing between the attorney and offender, with the approval of the court[18] – thus representing a distinct formality in DPAs distinguishable from modern-day PDPs.[19] In 1978, the Performance Standards and Goals for Pretrial Diversion by the Board of Directors of the National Association of Pretrial Services Agencies set out national standards for pretrial diversion programs.[20]

---

14 Reilly (n 10) 314.

15 370 US 660 (1962).

16 The President's Commission on Law Enforcement and Administration of Justice, 'The Challenge of Crime in a Free Society' (*United States Government Printing Office Washington DC*, February 1967) <https://assets.documentcloud.org/documents/3932081/Crimecommishreport.pdf> accessed 20 March 2021, 133–134.

17 Sally Hillsman, 'Pretrial Diversion of Youthful Adults: A Decade of Reform and Research' (Winter 1982) 7(3) Justice Syst J 361, 362.

18 Speedy Trial Act 18 USC § 3161(h) (Supp IV 1974) (US). 'Any period of delay during which prosecution is deferred by the attorney for the Government pursuant to written agreement with the defendant, *with the approval of the court*, for the purpose of allowing the defendant to demonstrate his good conduct' (emphasis added): 18 USC § 3161(h)(2). The wording of the Act has caused some conflict in interpretation in recent years. Though previously a "rubber-stamp" approach was taken, the increased use in dealing with corporate crime has led to increased judicial scrutiny. Though in *Fokker* it was argued that the first instance judge had significantly overstepped the scope of his authority in refusing a DPA which was, in his opinion, detrimental to the integrity of the court, there remains dissatisfaction with this decision. The appeal court in *Fokker* set out that the Act permitted a judge to refuse a DPA on the basis that there was some attempt of the parties to evade the Act's time limitation (70 days to reach trial). However, it has been argued (prior and since *Fokker*) that the role of the judiciary is broader in respect of the approval of DPAs. Far from violating the separation of powers, the offer of a DPA remains a prosecutorial decision, whereas the filing of the charge and accompanying Motion to Exclude Time (as per the Act) leads to a submission to the court's jurisdiction. That jurisdiction extends not only to approving a DPA not *prima facie* used to evade time limitations, but also to the inherent supervisory power to ensure the administration of justice. The exercise of such powers does not mean that the judiciary assumes the role of the prosecutor in making charging decisions, but instead acts as a check and balance to ensure that the DPA is fair and in the public interest. Such a role was envisaged by Congress in passing the Act, as the requirement for court approval was an amendment added during the lifetime of the Bill and stands out against other alternative prosecution provisions, which do not provide for such a role. *See also United States v HSBC Bank USA NA* 12-CR-763 (EDNY Jan 28 2016); *United States v Fokker Servs BV* 818 F 3d 733 (DC Cir 2016); *United States v Saena Tech Corp* 1:14-CR-00066 (DDC Oct 21 2015), 140 F Supp 3d 11; Opening Brief of the United States in *United States v Fokker Servs BV* 79 F Supp 3d 160 (DDC 2015) (No 15-3016, 15-3017); Mary Miller, 'More Than Just a Potted Plant: A Court's Authority to Review Deferred Prosecution Agreements Under the Speedy Trial Act and Under Its Inherent Supervisory Power' (2016) 115(1) Mich L Rev 135; Paola Henry, 'Individual Accountability for Corporate Crimes After the Yates Memo: Deferred Prosecution Agreements & Criminal Justice Reform' (2016) 6(1) Am Univ Bus Law Rev 153; Elizabeth Daniels, 'Getting DPA Review and Rejection Right' (2017) 16(1) Conn Pub Int LJ 101.

19 Despite conflicting opinion from Baer as to the existence of '"private"' DPAs which do not reach the court, this is actually a form of PDP. *See* Miriam Baer, 'Insuring Corporate Crime' (2008) 83 Ind LJ 1035, 1047.

20 Hillsman (n 17) 369–370.

DPAs have been used at federal level for corporations since 1992.[21] As the number of corporate DPAs has increased since the end of the twentieth century, attracting the introduction of swathes of memoranda on corporate use, use in individual cases has declined.[22] The ability for prosecutors to agree DPAs with individuals remains, though the appetite for use with individuals behind corporate crime appears to be low.

In 1999 the Holder Memorandum, a review of corporate criminal prosecution and extension of the existing US Attorney's Manual, suggested that DPAs (though not expressly mentioned) might be available to corporations deemed to have engaged in suitable cooperation. Focus on individual accountability for corporate crime was a key undertone of the Holder Memorandum, and was arguably the foundation for the normalisation of requiring corporate cooperation in prosecutorial investigations against individuals which has since followed suit.[23] The Holder Memorandum was succeeded by the Thompson Memorandum of 2003 which formally 'opened the door'[24] to the use of DPAs for corporations, though it set out that this would not substitute the prosecution of criminally culpable individuals.[25] It was set out that the use of 'joint defense agreements' between the corporation and suspected individuals on the mutual disclosure of information and assertion of privilege would be considered evidence of a lack of corporate desire to cooperate,[26] further exposing the inequality of treatment of individuals in comparison to the corporation. Building on the eight factors for prosecutorial consideration within the Holder Memorandum, the Thompson Memorandum added a ninth factor and made adherence compulsory: 'the adequacy of the prosecution of individuals responsible for the corporation's malfeasance'.[27]

The position of both individuals and corporations in respect of waiver of attorney-client privilege has changed over the years, with the 'aggressive'[28] stance of the Thompson Memorandum addressed in the McNulty Memorandum of 2006, Attorney-Client Privilege Protection Act of 2006, and Filip Memorandum of 2008 progressively affording greater protection to individuals. The developments in this period demonstrated attempts to ensure that individuals were not overwhelmingly disadvantaged by the (prosecutorial) expectation of corporations to cooperate at their expense.

The Yates Memorandum of 2015 (titled "Individual Accountability for Corporate Wrongdoing") outlined an "all-or-nothing" approach to corporate cooperation and the accountability of individuals involved in corporate wrongdoing. Under the memorandum, corporations were required to surrender information about all individuals connected with

21 Sprenger (n 9) 78.

22 'Since the early 2000s, the Department of Justice ("DOJ") has entered into several hundred DPAs and NPAs with corporate defendants, but virtually none with noncorporate individuals.' *See* Andrea Amulic, 'Humanizing the Corporation While Dehumanizing the Individual: The Misuse of Deferred-Prosecution Agreements in the United States' (2017) 116(1) Mich L Rev 123, 125. However, DPAs are still offered across the US to individuals through Circuit Courts. For example, a DPA was offered to Craig Bolz for failure to maintain a holding/septic tank, and to Jeremy Mayotte for disorderly domestic conduct. *See The Star News*, 'Circuit Court Reports' (*Central Wisconsin News*, 5 July 2023) <https://www.centralwinews.com/sports/2023/07/05/circuit-court-reports-5/?destination=star-news> accessed 17 July 2023.

23 Sharon Oded, 'Coughing up Executives or Rolling the Dice?: Individual Accountability for Corporate Corruption' (2016) 35(1) YLPR 49, 55–57.

24 Alan Vinegrad, 'Deferred Prosecution of Corporations' (2003) 230 NYLJ 72.

25 Sprenger (n 9) 13.

26 Thompson (n 6); Anderson and Waggoner (n 6) 52.

27 Thompson (n 6); Sprenger (n 9) 92.

28 Anderson and Waggoner (n 6) 51.

the wrongdoing – at whatever level – in order to receive any cooperation credit at all.[29] Without complete compliance, there would be no possibility for corporations to obtain a DPA. As a result of the stark focus on individual accountability, immunity afforded to individuals who cooperate in corporate investigations or as a condition of a DPA would only be allowed in extraordinary circumstances.[30] Though the objectives of the memorandum were to encourage transformation of corporate culture and to regain public confidence – particularly following the financial crisis of 2008 and controversial lack of individual prosecutions – it was argued that the memorandum may in reality have undermined the achievement of such objectives and led once more to the suppression of individual rights.[31]

As a result of its restrictive nature, prosecutors found themselves unable to follow the strict requirements whilst maintaining fair deliverance of justice.[32] In a speech delivered by Deputy Attorney General Rod Rosenstein in November 2018, revisions to the hard-line memorandum were announced. Pursuance of individuals in corporate wrongdoing was to remain a 'top priority';[33] however the "all-or-nothing" approach which required exhaustive information about all individuals connected with the corporate offence was amended. Prosecutors were instead instructed to focus on 'the individuals who play significant roles in setting a company on a course of criminal conduct'.[34] Corporate credit for cooperation in the pursuance of individuals would be afforded where corporations could demonstrate that they had acted in good faith in identifying those substantially involved and reported such information to the prosecutor. Revisions to the criminal approach were somewhat similar to the civil (DoJ) pursuance of individuals, whereby corporations must identify individuals substantially involved in wrongdoing and – to obtain credit – 'must identify all wrongdoing by senior officials, including members of senior management or the board of directors'.[35]

However, in 2021, the Monaco Memorandum was announced and made a clear reversion to the essence of the Yates Memorandum pre-Rosenstein's revisions.[36] The Monaco Memorandum is clear in setting out that in order 'to receive *any* consideration for cooperation, the company must identify *all* individuals involved in or responsible for the misconduct at issue, regardless of their position, status, or seniority' (emphasis added), and this includes 'individuals inside and outside of the company'; it is, however, set out that the

29 Sally Quillian Yates, 'Individual Accountability for Corporate Wrongdoing' (*The United States Department of Justice*, 9 September 2015) <https://www.justice.gov/archives/dag/file/769036/download> accessed 22 March 2021.

30 ibid; Oded (n 23) 66.

31 Oded (n 23) 53, 77.

32 Sidley Austin LLP, 'DOJ Announces Important Changes to Yates Memo' (*Sidley Austin LLP*, 30 November 2018) <https://www.sidley.com/en/insights/newsupdates/2018/11/doj-announces-important-changes-to-yates-memo> accessed 13 May 2020. It actually ended up being the case that DPAs continued to be agreed without compliance with the "all-or-nothing" approach. *See United States v Saena Tech Corp* (n 18) 41; Henry (n 18) 161.

33 Rosenstein (n 2).

34 ibid.

35 ibid.

36 'This Memorandum reinstates the prior guidance issued by this Office that to qualify for any cooperation credit, corporations must provide to the Department all relevant facts relating to the individuals responsible for the misconduct. See Memorandum from Deputy Attorney General Sally Quillian Yates, "Individual Accountability for Corporate Wrongdoing" (Sept. 9, 2015).' *See* Lisa Monaco, 'Corporate Crime Advisory Group and Initial Revisions to Corporate Criminal Enforcement Policies' (*The United States Department of Justice*, 28 October 2021) <https://www.justice.gov/d9/pages/attachments/2021/10/28/2021.10.28_dag_memo_re_corporate_enforcement.pdf> accessed 12 April 2023, 3.

information to be provided is 'all nonprivileged information'.[37] Revisions to the Monaco Memorandum set out in 2022 only further emphasise the hard-line approach. The expectations set out in the 2021 Memorandum are reiterated, but focus is given to the timely nature of cooperation by corporations in respect of individuals. This includes timely disclosures of 'all relevant, non-privileged facts and evidence about individual misconduct'.[38] The revisions acknowledge the importance of prosecutors' cross-border cooperation with international prosecuting agencies in the pursuit of individuals, and set out that – whilst the US may forego prosecution in the event that it is pursued overseas – any decision made not to prosecute must demonstrate a significant likelihood that the prosecution in the other jurisdiction will be brought and will be 'effective'.[39] As a result of the amendments in approach, the restrictions experienced in following the Yates Memorandum – which led to the Rosenstein revisions – are likely to be felt once more.

Interestingly, the 2022 Revisions to the Monaco Memorandum set out that investigations into and charges against individuals should be completed prior to the entry of a resolution against the corporation. To the extent that the corporate resolution is completed first, 'the prosecution or corporate resolution authorization memorandum must be accompanied by a memorandum that includes a discussion of all potentially culpable individuals', which includes the status of the ongoing investigation(s) and an investigative plan towards reaching resolution.[40] Though this raises concerns regarding the level of detail provided on implicated individuals within the corporate DPA (**Section 8.3.2**) – to which the individuals would likely have no input – DPAs agreed since have demonstrated attempts to anonymise individual identities.[41]

The US Justice Manual (previously known as the US Attorney's Manual), which provides advisory guidance, provides that 'in general, prosecutors should not agree to accept a corporate guilty plea in exchange for non prosecution of individuals'.[42] DPAs do not necessarily require a guilty plea, and are not plea-bargaining agreements,[43] but nonetheless this provision read in line with current memoranda is likely to set the tone for DPA availability for individuals involved in corporate crime. As discussed, the concept of deferred prosecution in cases of individual offenders was originally intended to provide an alternative to prosecution for low-level offences and first-time offenders. This was arguably a retributive and rehabilitative initiative, intended to avoid punitive sanctions where not warranted or considered proportionate. However, punitive sanction was, as outlined in 1967, to remain in necessary cases:

---

37 ibid.

38 Lisa Monaco, 'Further Revisions to Corporate Criminal Enforcement Policies Following Discussions With Corporate Crime Advisory Group' (*The United States Department of Justice*, 15 September 2022) <https://www.justice.gov/opa/speech/file/1535301/download> accessed 12 April 2023, 3.

39 ibid 4.

40 ibid 3.

41 *See for example United States of America v UOP LLC, d/b/a Honeywell UOP* 4:22-cr-00624 (SD Tex 2022) A-2-A-3.

42 Sprenger (n 9) 99. 'Provable individual criminal charges should be pursued, particularly if they implicate high-level corporate officers, even in the face of an offer of a corporate guilty plea or some other disposition of the charges against the corporation, including a deferred prosecution or non-prosecution agreement, or a civil resolution.' *See* The United States Department of Justice, '9-28.000 – Principles of Federal Prosecution of Business Organizations' (*The United States Department of Justice*, April 2023) <https://www.justice.gov/jm/jm-9-28000-principles-federal-prosecution-business-organizations> accessed 12 April 2023, 9-28.210.

43 Reilly (n 10) 312.

> Prosecutors should endeavor, to make discriminating charge decisions, assuring that offenders who merit criminal sanctions are not released and that other offenders are either released or diverted to noncriminal methods of treatment and control.[44]

An area of concern for some academics in respect of the use of DPAs in corporate cases is that the underlying offences tend to be of such a serious nature that would never have been contemplated in the twentieth-century use of the alternative tool to prosecution for individuals.[45] This concern can be somewhat addressed by acknowledging that the purpose of deferred prosecution, to ensure rehabilitation and minimisation of collateral consequences, can still be achieved in corporate cases where the corporation is no longer participating in wrongdoing (and is perhaps, for example, led by a new management team). When considering the extension of a DPA to individuals behind the corporate crime – either on the basis of a joint DPA with the corporation or separate agreement – questions once more arise as to whether the original intention of the tool can be met. Societal views and approaches evolve; however the current focus on individual accountability (particularly following the financial crisis of 2008) would arguably not be reflected in a more flexible use of individual DPAs. Permitting the director of a criminally liable corporation to obtain a DPA on the basis of their involvement and responsibility – at a criminal standard – would not reflect the original intention of the rehabilitation of low-level offenders. Corporate crime often has significant gravitas and, in current circumstances whereby individual (non-corporate-related) DPAs are low in number, an extension of DPA availability to criminally culpable individuals in such cases would be in line with neither original nor evolved intention.

Furthermore, though prosecutors remain able to agree DPAs with individuals in the US, their use with senior figures behind corporate criminal liability is increasingly unlikely. The increased focus on prosecution of individuals involved in corporate crime and identification of those individuals as part of corporate cooperation, combined with dwindling numbers of individual DPAs in comparison to corporate DPAs, suggests that this would not be a realistic proposition. In the US, individuals behind a corporate's wrongdoing *can* avoid investigation where they cooperate in the corporation's DPA, though this is rare and is likely to remain so.[46] It may be the case that lower-level employees involved in corporate

44 The President's Commission on Law Enforcement and Administration of Justice (n 16) 134.

45 Amulic (n 22) 133–134, 152; Anthony Partridge, *Legislative History of Title I of the Speedy Trial Act of 1974* (Federal Judicial Center 1980) 117.

46 Matthew Fishbein, 'Why Individuals Aren't Prosecuted for Conduct Companies Admit' (2014) 252 NYLJ 56; Oded (n 23) 66. Rarity of such instances remains the case, despite more general confusion as to the terms of high-profile corporate DPAs. In 2017, the US DoJ agreed a DPA with Boeing in relation to conduct that led to crashes of two Boeing 737 MAX aeroplanes with fatal consequences. The DPA has since been the subject of much criticism, particularly – and understandably – by bereaved family members, a number of whom have (unsuccessfully) appealed to US courts to have the DPA set aside. In an article in *The Times*, the DPA and lack of successful individual prosecutions were criticised. The article states: 'thanks to a sweetheart legal settlement struck with the federal government, not a single executive has been jailed', and further, '[the DPA] guaranteed Boeing and its top executives immunity from federal criminal persecution'. *See* Danny Fortson and Katie Gatens, 'My Child Died on Boeing's Faulty Jet. Why Have its Bosses Not Faced Justice?' (*The Times*, 16 July 2023) <https://www.thetimes.co.uk/article/my-child-died-on-boeings-faulty-jet-why-have-its-bosses-not-faced-justice-l8dkbdcsz> accessed 16 July 2023. The latter quotation in particular represents a misunderstanding of the DPA, which expressly states that it 'does not provide any protection against prosecution of any individuals, regardless of their affiliation with the Company'. *See* The United States Department of Justice, 'U.S. v. The Boeing Company – Final DPA Package' (*The United States Department of Justice*, 7 January 2021) <https://www.justice.gov/opa/press-release/file/1351336/download> accessed 16 July 2023. However, it

crime to a lesser extent will be availed the opportunity to enter a DPA with prosecutors, but it is highly unlikely that this provision will be extended to directors or senior officers in the near future.

Despite the apparent shift in focus from the impact of prosecution on individuals to that on corporations, and the seeming lack of available alternative prosecutorial options for individuals in comparison to the corporate body, some remain dissatisfied with the measures in place to ensure individual accountability for corporate crime.[47] This is where the types of offences for which settlement is permitted become polarised: individuals largely remain limited to pretrial diversion tools for low-level offences, whereas corporations are availed the opportunity to agree DPAs with prosecutors for those considered far more severe. Arguably, this takes into consideration the differing nature of individuals and corporations in respect of the capability, deservedness, and "otherwise" consequences of being rehabilitated. However, this does present concerns as to the vastly different treatment of individuals and corporate bodies within the justice system.[48] Since corporate crime is often more severe, it is arguably not necessary to separate individuals offending extra-corporately to those offending intra-corporately in terms of assessing whether either party is more generally disadvantaged. One could observe that those who may have offended intra-corporately are more exposed to being at the mercy of a corporation's desire to cooperate with prosecutors at their expense.

Similarly, the attitude of prosecutors would appear to suggest that there is an increased focus on prosecuting individuals involved in corporate crime. However, this does not mean that individuals participating in extra-corporate serious crime (such as fraud) would not be under similar scrutiny. Interestingly, Judge Jed Rakoff in 2013 stated that corporations 'almost always settle', whereas individuals 'often go to trial'.[49] Judge Rakoff references the shift in prosecutorial approach to dealing with corporate crime, from a focus on prosecuting the individuals to a more recent focus on corporations. The focus on corporations has, according to Judge Rakoff, been 'rationalized as part of an attempt to transform "corporate cultures"' but has led to a lack of accountability of the human offenders.[50] In his words, 'perhaps the happiest of all are the executives, or former executives, who actually committed the underlying misconduct, for they are left untouched'.[51] Though there has been recent desire seen within the Yates and Monaco Memoranda to hold such individuals accountable, this nonetheless demonstrates a potential void arising from the use of DPAs, which has also been observed in the UK. Arguably, the position of directors and senior officers in respect of making a potentially self-incriminating self-report is therefore very similar to those in the UK (**Section 6.2**).

is important to observe that, at times, there is a (mistaken) public perception that implicated executives are protected within the corporate DPA, where this is often not the case.

47 Judge Jed Rakoff, 'Why Have no High Level Executives Been Prosecuted in Connection With the Financial Crisis?' (*The CLS Blue Sky Blog*, 15 November 2013) <https://clsbluesky.law.columbia.edu/2013/11/15/why-have-no-high-level-executives-been-prosecuted-in-connection-with-the-financial-crisis/> accessed 19 March 2021; Elizabeth Warren, 'The Corporate Executive Accountability Act' (*Senator Elizabeth Warren*, April 2019) <https://www.warren.senate.gov/imo/media/doc/2019.4.1%20Corporate%20Executive%20Accountability%20Act%20Summary.pdf> accessed 20 April 2020.

48 Amulic (n 22) 127.

49 Rakoff (n 47).

50 ibid.

51 ibid.

4.1.2 DPAs and civil liability

The DoJ's approach to individual cases arising as a result of corporate crime appears to be clear, with it being unlikely that individual defendants (particularly those senior within the corporation) have the opportunity to agree DPAs on the basis of their own criminal liability. However, in the US, DPAs can be agreed on the basis of civil violations. The SEC Enforcement Division's Cooperation Program encourages cooperation of both corporations and individuals in respect of corporate crime, with an understanding that cooperation tools may remain available for use in individual cases.[52] The framework for assessing individual cooperation, in respect of any reflective outcome, considers the assistance provided, the importance of the underlying matter, the interest in accountability, and the profile of the individual.[53] The profile of the individual considers professional occupation and the degree to which the opportunity to commit future violations will arise, with the positions of 'officer or director of public companies' and 'member of senior management' expressly outlined.[54] Despite this, on the SEC "Spotlight on Enforcement Cooperation Program" webpage, the potential availability of DPAs to corporate directors is noted.

In 2016, Uni-Pixel Inc settled with the SEC having consented to the entry of a final judgment on the basis of misrepresentations made as to its product development status, which impacted its stock price. Former chairman of the board of directors Bernard Marren agreed to a DPA with the SEC in respect of Uni-Pixel Inc's conduct, having aided and abetted the corporation's violations (aware that the corporation's press releases were inaccurate but failing to ensure correction was made).[55] A term of Marren's DPA was to extensively cooperate with the ongoing investigation, and a failure to meet this (and any other) term could lead to an enforcement action against him for the underlying securities violation(s).[56] Marren was also required to resign from all officer and directorship positions.[57] In 2017, both former Chief Executive Officer Reed Killion and former Chief Financial Officer Jeffrey Tomz consented to the entry of a final judgment for securities violations and for aiding and abetting securities violations. Civil financial penalties were imposed and Killion was barred from serving as an officer or company director (and Tomz suspended from accountancy practice) for a period of four years.[58]

In 2016, Yu Kai Yuan agreed a DPA with the SEC in the SEC's first DPA with an individual defendant for civil charges relating to the violation of the Foreign Corrupt Practices Act. Yuan was an employee (a sales executive) of Parametric Technology (Hong Kong)

---

52 US Securities and Exchange Commission, 'Spotlight on Enforcement Cooperation Program' (*US Securities and Exchange Commission*, 20 September 2016) <https://web.archive.org/web/20190725145221/https://www.sec.gov/spotlight/enforcement-cooperation-initiative.shtmll> accessed 22 March 2021.

53 Policy Statement Concerning Cooperation by Individuals in its Investigations and Related Enforcement Actions 17 CFR § 202.12 (SEC).

54 ibid § 202.12(d)(3).

55 *Bernard Thomas Marren (SEC)* <https://www.sec.gov/litigation/complaints/2016/comp-pr2016-45-dpa.pdf> accessed 22 March 2021; US Securities and Exchange Commission, 'SEC: Tech Company Misled Investors About Key Product' Program' (*US Securities and Exchange Commission*, 9 March 2016) <https://www.sec.gov/news/pressrelease/2016-45.html> accessed 22 March 2021.

56 *Bernard Thomas Marren (SEC)* (n 55) [4], [13].

57 ibid [8(a)].

58 *Securities and Exchange Commission v Reed J Killion, Jeffrey W Tomz, and Uni-Pixel Inc* No 4:16-cv-00621 (SD Tex filed Mar 9 2016); US Securities and Exchange Commission, 'Former Executives of Tech Company Agree to Pay Penalties to Settle SEC Action' (*US Securities and Exchange Commission*, 13 October 2017) <https://www.sec.gov/litigation/litreleases/2017/lr23968.htm> accessed 22 March 2021.

Ltd and Parametric Technology (Shanghai) Software Co Ltd, which collectively as "PTC-China" agreed a non-prosecution agreement with the DoJ.[59] Yuan's DPA was based on his causing corporate securities violations, without formal admission, and the statement of facts attached (running to one paragraph and 13 subparagraphs) was focussed on the conduct of PTC China. This, according to Professor Mike Koehler, 'might be the most inconsequential legal document you will ever read'[60] due to its lack of detail regarding Yuan's precise involvement.

The aforementioned cases demonstrate the more flexible approach of the SEC to settlement with individuals by way of DPA. A framework is in place to ensure that factors such as the seniority of the offender and the severity of the offending are considered, but it appears that a DPA may be available to individuals on the basis of cooperation where the wrongdoing is more akin to facilitation of the corporate crime (an arguably lower level of offending). Though dealing with civil liability, this ensures that some level of accountability of the individual is met whilst maximising the opportunity to hold the corporation to account on the basis of promised individual cooperation. The DPA with Marren represents a use with directors, here where a director has been aware of wrongdoing and failed to act accordingly, and the DPA with Yuan represents a use with lower-level employees for causing the commission of corporate crime.

This demonstrates greater scope for individual settlement and cooperation and equalises the power imbalance created by corporate DPAs requiring the exposure of individuals. Where individual DPAs based on civil liability are agreed, corporations do not retain unreasonable control in respect of their own cooperation and the potential tactical framing of individuals. SEC DPAs are not required to be filed with the court, and their public availability is not mandatory (though typical).[61] It is not clear, therefore, whether SEC use of individual DPAs in respect of corporate violations can yet be deemed habitual, but this does not appear to have become common practice. The offences to which individual DPAs can be agreed with the SEC are unclear, though would likely be limited in the cases of senior officers and directors to lower-level offences or lower-level involvement in those considered to be more serious. This would be a reflection of the history of the intended use of DPAs, evolving attitudes in respect of individual accountability, and the SEC's framework on cooperation.

Furthermore, whilst DPAs are theoretically available for individuals, their use in reality in response to involvement in corporate crime is uncertain and will likely depend on the severity of the offence, the extent to which the individual was involved, and whether the offence raises questions of criminal or civil liability. The extent to which individuals are protected by corporate DPAs is clear: the incorporation of terms within a corporate DPA allowing for the protection from prosecution of individuals is to be avoided except in exceptional circumstances. The reality is that those exceptional circumstances are highly unlikely to permit the protection of directors or senior officers or those involved in the wrongdoing to a significant level.

59 *In Re Yu Kai Yuan (SEC)* <https://www.sec.gov/litigation/admin/2016/34-77145-dpa.pdf> accessed 22 March 2021 [6(a)].

60 Mike Koehler, 'Issues to Consider from the PTC Enforcement Action' (*FCPA Professor*, 18 February 2016) <https://fcpaprofessor.com/category/yu-kai-yuan/> accessed 22 March 2021.

61 Brooker and others (n 1).

4.2 United Kingdom

Unlike the US, which has an extensive recent history on the use of DPAs in individual cases, relevant UK provision does not allow prosecutors to offer DPAs to individuals. The first introduction of the proposal of DPAs to the House of Lords within the (then) Crime and Courts Bill (the "Bill") on 30 October 2012 saw early discussion of the applicability to individuals. The proposed provision on applicability read 'P may be a body corporate, a partnership or an unincorporated association, but may not be an individual',[62] and this wording remains the same in Schedule 17 of the CACA 2013.[63]

Lord McNally, who introduced the relevant amendment of the Bill to the House of Lords, strictly outlined that the tool would be used only to assist prosecutors in addressing corporate economic crime and would not be available to individuals: individuals engaging in economic crime would remain 'best dealt with through criminal prosecution'.[64] Lord Marks of Henley-on-Thames followed by questioning the distinction between companies and individuals. Troubled by the rationale that DPAs would apply only to companies due to their un-imprisonable nature (arguing that DPAs would not be available in such circumstances anyway), Lord Marks outlined that if DPAs were centred on the willingness of the defendant,[65] this '[could] be as easily met in the case of an individual offender'.[66] Lord Goldsmith somewhat concurred with Lord Marks, stating that 'a broader power, which was only applied appropriately' would not only address concerns about corporates buying their way out of trouble but could also benefit individuals and the greater public.[67] The fact that DPAs were not to be restricted to use for failure to prevent bribery offences (which do not require consideration of *mens rea*)[68] further supported his point.[69] Lord Woolf added that DPAs would be much more attractive to the corporate sector where availability extended to individuals, noting the inclusion of company officers, and that not doing so may prevent an agreement which would otherwise be of great public benefit.[70]

Lord Phillips of Sudbury was a strong opponent of the introduction of DPAs and cited the proposed inequality between corporate and individual offenders as one reason. Questioning whether directors and executives would be shielded from prosecution following a corporate DPA, Lord Phillips noted that this would be a failure of the regime.[71] Having heard the differing views, Lord McNally closed by reiterating that DPAs (in their proposed form) were designed to deal with corporate economic crime and the difficulties in prosecuting companies: difficulties which were said not to exist in the case of individuals for economic crime offences.[72] Lord McNally clearly set out that directors '[would] not be immune from prosecution' where a company obtains a DPA,[73] and stated that this issue

62 HL Deb 30 October 2012, vol 740, col 560.

63 Crime and Courts Act 2013, sch 17 para 4(1).

64 HL Deb 30 October 2012 (n 62) col 568.

65 Willingness to admit guilt; pay a financial penalty; cooperate in an investigation; put compliance measures in place; and the suitability of a penalty and compliance measures in respect of the offence committed. *See* ibid col 574.

66 ibid

67 ibid col 577.

68 Bribery Act 2010, s 7.

69 HL Deb 30 October 2012 (n 62) col 577.

70 ibid col 579.

71 ibid col 581.

72 ibid col 583.

73 ibid col 584.

would be discussed once more the following month (which, per Hansard, did not occur). This debate was the most extensive conversation in respect of the position of individuals, and the Bill progressed without returning to the issue of broadening the scope of the tool. Nevertheless, it is clear that there was some original support for individual DPAs.

One week prior to the aforementioned House of Lords debate, the government published its response to a consultation on DPAs which had been launched in 2012;[74] the response set out the position of respondents and the approach to be taken in introducing the provision. The consultation did not make much reference to the position of individuals, though this was addressed further in the government response. Despite the fact that 48 percent of 63 respondents supported a wider application of DPAs, not only to other types of offences but also availability to individuals, the prosecution of individuals involved in economic crime was deemed to be 'effective' and to negate the necessity to broaden the scope of the proposed provision.[75] Two responses raised concerns that an extension of the provision to individuals would adversely advantage those engaging in white-collar crime, in comparison to other offences.[76] The government clearly set out that its position was to limit the availability of DPAs and prohibit use in individual cases.

Thus, Schedule 17 of the CACA 2013 expressly excludes DPAs for individual offenders.[77] The Explanatory Notes to the CACA 2013 do not provide further explanation as to the inability of individuals to agree DPAs. However, the document does set out that a DPA with a partnership or unincorporated association must be written in its own name, and not the names of the partners or members, and penalties paid must originate from the partnership or unincorporated association's account.[78] Proceedings against culpable individuals for the same offence forming the basis of the company's DPA are not prevented by the agreement or its expiration,[79] though a DPA is not likely to be determined as in the interests of justice where a company's approach (for example in withholding material) may be prejudicial to individual criminal proceedings.[80] This provides minimal clarification in confirming that an individual offender should not be afforded protection by a company's DPA. The DPA Code is largely focussed on the position of the offending company throughout the process and similarly provides little clarity on the position of individuals. It is, however, stated that the prosecutor must remember that a self-report will incriminate individuals, and thus it will 'ordinarily be appropriate' to investigate and (where necessary) prosecute those individuals.[81] The SFO's Operational Handbook chapter on DPAs

74 Ministry of Justice, *Consultation on a New Enforcement Tool to Deal With Economic Crime Committed by Commercial Organisations: Deferred Prosecution Agreements* (Cm 8348, 2012).

75 Ministry of Justice, *Deferred Prosecution Agreements: Government Response to the Consultation on a New Enforcement Tool to Deal With Economic Crime Committed by Commercial Organisations* (Cm 8463, 2012) paras 40–47.

76 ibid para 43.

77 Crime and Courts Act 2013, sch 17 para 4(1).

78 Explanatory Notes to the Crime and Courts Act 2013, para 545.

79 ibid para 567.

80 ibid para 557.

81 Crown Prosecution Service and Serious Fraud Office, 'Deferred Prosecution Agreements Code of Practice' (*Crown Prosecution Service*, 11 February 2014) <https://www.cps.gov.uk/sites/default/files/documents/publications/dpa_cop.pdf> accessed 9 June 2020, para 2.9.1.

published in October 2020 is more explicit, and clearly sets out that a DPA 'does not provide any protection against the prosecution of linked individuals'[82] (**Section 10.2**).

The Select Committee on the Bribery Act 2010 considered the use and efficacy of DPAs in its post-legislative scrutiny report published in March 2019. Within this, the Select Committee made clear that DPAs were not an alternative to individual prosecutions but conversely made such prosecutions 'all the more important'.[83] The report was debated by the House of Lords in February 2021.[84] Lord Saville of Newdigate, chairman of the Select Committee, stressed that the extension of DPAs to individuals – or the use of DPAs 'as a means of avoiding the prosecution of the individuals' – must not occur.[85] Baroness Wheatcroft observed that DPAs were an effective means of persuading companies to take responsibility for wrongdoing, whilst 'not preventing prosecution of individuals'.[86] However, Lord Gold noted the concerning lack of *successful* prosecutions against individuals responsible for wrongdoing forming the subject of corporate DPAs and reiterated the relative importance[87] – a message supported by Lord Davidson of Glen Clova.[88] The Advocate General for Scotland Lord Steward of Dirleton emphasised that DPAs do not bar individual prosecutions, but outlined that individual prosecutions might be more generally impacted as a result of fast-track extradition arrangements provided for within the UK–EU withdrawal agreement.[89] This debate demonstrates a slight shift in opinion, with less favour for individual DPAs and increased focus on successful prosecution.

The position in the UK is thus clear: an individual cannot currently agree a DPA and cannot therefore be co-defendant of a joint DPA with a corporate body. The government position remained consistent throughout the lifetime of the Crime and Courts Bill, though did broaden the scope to allow partnerships and unincorporated associations to agree DPAs in their own (not "owner's") name. Despite differing opinion of respondents to the original consultation and of some members of the House of Lords in respect of allowing individual DPAs, this was not reflected in the CACA 2013. Supporting documentation such as the Explanatory Notes, DPA Code, and SFO Operational Handbook has served to provide greater clarity on the position of individuals, clearly setting out that individual prosecutions would not be prevented by a corporate DPA. Far from protection, these provisions have created areas of vast exposure for individuals.

82 Serious Fraud Office, 'Deferred Prosecution Agreements' (*Serious Fraud Office*, 23 October 2020) <https://www.sfo.gov.uk/publications/guidance-policy-and-protocols/sfo-operational-handbook/deferred-prosecution-agreements/> accessed 23 October 2020.

83 Select Committee on the Bribery Act 2010, *The Bribery Act 2010: Post-Legislative Scrutiny* (HL 2017–19, 303) para 315.

84 The debate of the report had faced delays as a result of elections, Brexit, and the COVID-19 health pandemic. *See* HL Deb 3 February 2021, vol 809, col 326GC.

85 ibid.

86 ibid col 345GC.

87 ibid col 332GC.

88 ibid col 356GC.

89 'These new arrangements provide stronger protections for individuals, including provisions that make it clear that a person cannot be surrendered if their fundamental rights are at risk, or extradition would be disproportionate, or they are likely to face long periods of pre-trial detention'. *See* ibid cols 360GC–361GC.

4.2.1 Pretrial diversion programmes

Though DPAs within the CACA 2013 statutory framework are not available to individuals, an initiative launched by Durham Constabulary named "Checkpoint" provides individuals the opportunity to enter a 'four-month long offender management programme' with the objective of rehabilitating the offender.[90] The offender enters into a four-month tailored contract with the Constabulary (agreed between the individual and the navigator), and will either face no further action (if there is no reoffending during the contractual period) or will face an 'alternative prosecution' upon non-compliance, whereby the details of the Checkpoint programme will be provided to the court.[91] Though use of the term "alternative prosecution" is somewhat unclear, this would appear to simply mean that the individual is ultimately prosecuted as an "alternative" to the completion of the programme (and no further action).

The programme is termed a 'deferred prosecution' by the Constabulary,[92] by lawyers,[93] in the House of Lords,[94] and in the media.[95] The programme cannot strictly be considered a DPA as, primarily, it does not fall within the statutory legal framework under Schedule 17 to the CACA 2013; nor is a prosecution actually made (subject to deferral); and, further, it does not retain an element of punitive sanction or require judicial approval. Notably, the programme has been referred to as a 'deferred prosecution scheme',[96] though this may provoke confusion.[97] The programme is akin to the modern-day US PDP, whereby an offender is dealt with by way of a rehabilitative programme without court involvement (if successful). The decision to progress the case to charge/prosecution is deferred, such that – should the individual fail to successfully complete the programme – that decision may then be taken. However, it is the *decision* that is deferred, as no prosecution is made as a basis for the contract.[98] Furthermore, as opposed to a finding by the court, contract

90 'The crime must be less than three months old and was committed in County Durham and Darlington.' *See* Durham Constabulary, 'Checkpoint' (*Durham Constabulary*, 2015) <https://web.archive.org/web/20210618185243/https://www.durham.police.uk/Services/Checkpoint/Checkpoint.aspx> accessed 8 October 2021.

91 ibid.

92 ibid. *See also* Kevin Weir and others, 'Checkpoint: An Innovative Programme to Navigate People Away From the Cycle of Reoffending – A Randomised Control Trial Evaluation' (2022) 95(3) Pol J 562, 572. Kevin Weir is a Detective Superintendent and Project Manager of the Checkpoint initiative.

93 Tori Adams and Siân Beaven, 'DPAs for the Masses: A Rehabilitative Approach' (2021) (Aug) Counsel 31, 31–33.

94 HL Deb 27 February 2020, vol 802, col 350 (Lord Keen, The Advocate General for Scotland).

95 Josh Halliday, 'Durham's Pioneering Police Scheme Slashes Reoffending Rates' (*The Guardian*, 14 February 2020) <https://www.theguardian.com/uk-news/2020/feb/14/durham-pioneering-police-scheme-slashes-reoffending-rates-rehabilitation-programme> accessed 8 October 2021.

96 Kevin Weir and others (n 92) 566.

97 Further confusion cannot be added to the concept of DPAs, as the previous Director of the SFO had undertaken measures to appeal to the public in providing clarity. *See* Lisa Osofsky, 'We're Defending the UK as a Safe Place for Business' (*The Times*, 30 June 2021) <https://www.thetimes.co.uk/article/were-defending-the-uk-as-a-safe-place-for-business-617f500fw> accessed 30 June 2021.

98 In answer to the question: 'Within the Checkpoint scheme, is it the case that the offender is prosecuted in front of the court, and *then* the court elects to defer prosecution pending completion of the Checkpoint programme?', Tracy Claughton (Diversion and Rehabilitation Team (DART) of Durham Constabulary) responded: 'No the process is to deter the court process … Should they fail then the case is passed back to the OIC and they progress to alternative disposal in the form of caution or charge.' *See* Email from Tracy Claughton to author (31 March 2023).

breach is determined by the case officer, in conjunction with information provided by the navigator working with the individual.[99]

Though DPAs as they were first introduced in the US adopted a very similar approach to "Checkpoint", and similar language, the consequent formalities introduced throughout the years have changed the nature of the US framework and created a divergence between DPAs and PDPs.[100] Furthermore, it is important to identify the difference between DPAs and PDPs in respect of individual offenders, to highlight the nature of the alternative resolution faced, and to determine the legal outcomes.

The consequences of the Durham Constabulary and similar PDP initiatives[101] are not further explored herein due to their present restrictions in territory and scope. Though "Checkpoint" is available to individuals who have engaged in 'fraud', this is limited to 'lower-level ... fraud'[102] more akin to forgery,[103] as opposed to economic crime (the latter of which being the principal target of corporate DPAs).[104] Further, a contract based on fraud offences is rare in comparison with other types of offending.[105] Therefore, it is unlikely that a (former) director implicated in a corporate DPA would be availed the opportunity to enter a "Checkpoint" programme; this is predominantly due to the level and complexity of corporate-directed economic crime.

99 Many thanks to Stephanie Kilili-Guttridge, Policy and Commissioning Officer, for clarifying these details on the Checkpoint process: Email from Stephanie Kilili-Guttridge to author (30 March 2023).

100 '[We are] in an era where the penal policy goal of rehabilitation has been abandoned in the prosecution of individuals'. *See* Federico Mazzacuva, 'Justifications and Purposes of Negotiated Justice for Corporate Offenders: Deferred and Non-Prosecution Agreements in the UK and US Systems of Criminal Justice' (2014) 78(3) J Crim L 249, 261.

101 The "Turning-Point" project in Birmingham followed a similar format. The trial hypothesis was as follows: 'Offenders who have not been previously been [sic] convicted at court, but whom the police would otherwise charge for prosecution, can be more cost effectively dealt with by police-led offender management than by prosecution, subject to a condition of the certainty of prosecution in the event of reoffending or breaking an agreed "contract" about their conduct.' *See* Jamie Hobday and Molly Slothower, 'The Turning-Point Project' (*College of Policing What Works Network*, 9 February 2021) <https://web.archive.org/web/20210727193441/https://whatworks.college.police.uk/Research/Research-Map/Pages/ResearchProject.aspx?projectid=307> accessed 8 October 2021.

102 '[Checkpoint] aims to deal with certain offences, like shoplifting, low-level assault or fraud, by giving the offender the chance to make amends rather than go to court.' *See* Durham Constabulary, 'Checkpoint is a New Scheme we are Introducing to Reduce Re-offending' (*Facebook*, 21 January 2015) <https://www.facebook.com/durhamconstabulary/photos/checkpoint-is-a-new-scheme-we-are-introducing-to-reduce-re-offendingit-aims-to-d/757832337628719/> accessed 8 October 2021 (official page).

103 The study demonstrated that as of December 2015, of 356 offenders, five 'fraud or forgery' offences were subject to a Checkpoint programme; this can be contrasted with over 50 theft offences, over 50 drunk and disorderly offences, over 30 drug possession offences, over 30 common assault offences, and so forth. *See* Gillian Routledge, 'A Protocol and Experimental Trial: The Checkpoint Desistance Programme in Durham' (Master's thesis, University of Cambridge Wolfson College 2015) 80. This Distinction-awarded thesis has been supported by Durham Constabulary. *See* Durham Constabulary, 'Checkpoint' (n 90).

104 HL Deb 30 October 2012 (n 62) col 567 (Lord McNally). It is worth noting that 'seriousness of the incident in its entirety' has been cited as a reason for refusal of entry to Checkpoint, though this was in the context of an offence against the person: *R (on the application of ABC) v Chief Constable of Durham* [2021] EWHC 2655 (Admin) [29].

105 *See* n 103.

CHAPTER 5

Before the DPA offer

5.1 Leave if implicated

The position of (particularly senior) individuals implicated in the underlying wrongdoing for which the DPA is negotiated, in respect of their ongoing position within the company, appears to be becoming clearer as the DPA provision is increasingly used. Within the DPA Code published in 2014, it was outlined that a public interest factor against prosecution (and thus in favour of DPA) would be that the company seeking a DPA 'is effectively a different entity from that which committed the offences'.[1] An example given is the complete reform of the company's management team, with a focus on how the company may have sanctioned culpable individuals: disciplinary action '*has* been taken against *all*' (emphasis added) those culpable, with dismissal in appropriate circumstances.[2] This suggests that there is not a demand upon dismissal of those culpable where disciplinary action would suffice; this is likely to depend on the extent of involvement in the wrongdoing and thus will likely also consider the seniority of the individual. Six years on, the SFO reiterated this factor against prosecution in its new SFO Operational Handbook chapter on DPAs, though with more discretionary language. It stated that the company's management team '*may* have been completely changed' and 'disciplinary action *may have* been taken against all the culpable individuals' (emphasis added).[3]

Interestingly, the Handbook states that 'case teams should ensure that any individuals authorised to represent the Company in DPA negotiations are not implicated in the matters under investigation such that they may be considered suspects'.[4] This does not suggest that those considered suspects cannot remain within the company, but does outline that there cannot be involvement of those individuals in the DPA negotiations insofar as representing the company. This may lead to the view that those under suspicion can continue to engage in lower-level negotiation-related activities, such as the compiling of information for the statement of facts. The Handbook chapter might be read as a shift away from the more seemingly strict approach set out in the DPA Code. However, it is likely that this

1 Crown Prosecution Service and Serious Fraud Office, 'Deferred Prosecution Agreements Code of Practice' (*Crown Prosecution Service*, 11 February 2014) <https://www.cps.gov.uk/sites/default/files/documents/publications/dpa_cop.pdf> accessed 9 June 2020, para 2.8.2(v).

2 ibid.

3 Serious Fraud Office, 'Deferred Prosecution Agreements' (*Serious Fraud Office*, 23 October 2020) <https://www.sfo.gov.uk/publications/guidance-policy-and-protocols/sfo-operational-handbook/deferred-prosecution-agreements/> accessed 23 October 2020.

4 ibid.

 DOI: 10.4324/9781003456964-7

more discretionary language is used to take into account lower-level employees and not to permit greater entitlement of directors to remain (within the company and involved in negotiations).

In circumstances where directors are suspected to be culpable individuals, it is likely firstly that this would be considered an appropriate ground for dismissal or serious disciplinary action, and secondly that those directors would not be permitted to have any involvement in DPA negotiations (perhaps finding that they are suspended during the period of investigation). It was noted within the *Tesco Stores Ltd* statement of facts that the board of parent company Tesco Plc had immediately suspended the three named implicated directors (of the subsidiary) upon the revelation of the underlying misconduct.[5] Where directors are suspended during the period of investigation, they will not generally be consulted on the drafting of the statement of facts as they will be considered third parties.[6]

In November 2018, Sir Leveson provided evidence to the House of Lords' Select Committee and focussed largely on the operation of DPAs. At this point, four DPAs had received judicial approval and all by Sir Leveson, who was given responsibility for the policing of the provision upon its inception and thus undertook responsibility for the first four cases.[7] Sir Leveson's stance on individuals was undoubtedly clear: implicated individuals facing prosecution cannot remain in the company. These individuals, referred to by Sir Leveson as the 'cause of the problem', must be '[rooted] out'.[8] So clear was this approach, it was expressed as being 'critical' to the corporate's ability to obtain a DPA and its demonstration of compliance and engagement in self-reporting.[9] 'Critical' it was also deemed to be to prosecute individuals, whatever their status within a company; according to Sir Leveson prosecution or 'punishment' of the senior individuals was determined to be the 'best [deterrent]'.[10]

Though deemed critical, the prosecution of individuals was not necessarily outlined to be a critical factor in favour of DPA approval (**Section 2.2**). In context, it appears that Sir Leveson was suggesting that accountability of individuals is critical in general and in respect of deterrence, and that the availability of a DPA would be considered in line with whether any of those facing prosecution remained within the company. Pinsent Mason's response in respect of DPAs and individual prosecutions was not explicitly focussed on the individuals' ability to remain within the company but instead the willingness to self-report: it was stated that the lack of formal leniency policy for individuals was a disincentive to corporate self-reporting.[11] Though this position was not directly addressed by the Select Committee, it was stated that where culpable individuals remained within the company it would be 'unlikely' that the company would obtain a DPA regardless of any self-report.[12]

5 Serious Fraud Office, 'Deferred Prosecution Agreement – Statement of Facts – SFO v Tesco Stores Ltd' (*Serious Fraud Office*, 23 January 2019) <https://www.sfo.gov.uk/download/deferred-prosecution-agreement-statement-of-facts-sfo-v-tesco-stores-ltd/> accessed 26 June 2020, para 11.

6 Serious Fraud Office, 'Deferred Prosecution Agreements' (n 3).

7 Select Committee on the Bribery Act 2010, *The Bribery Act 2010: Post Legislative Scrutiny: Evidence Session No 16* (HL 2017–19, 303) question 150.

8 ibid question 153.

9 ibid.

10 ibid.

11 Select Committee on the Bribery Act 2010, *The Bribery Act 2010: Post-Legislative Scrutiny* (HL 2017–19, 303) para 314.

12 ibid.

There does appear to be some difference in approach and opinion in respect of individuals suspected of involvement in corporate wrongdoing, regarding DPAs. In respect of "culpable" individuals, the language of the DPA Code is more explicit in stating the relevant factors in favour of or against prosecution. This wording is approached in a more discretionary manner by the SFO in its Operational Handbook. However, the DPA Code sets out the factors as considerations which prosecutors 'may' take into account and this allows for similar discretion.[13] This is reflected in Sir Leveson's preliminary judgment in the UK's first DPA, where it was stated that the company taking a different form to that which committed the offending was 'by no means a necessary requirement'.[14] There is not an outright requirement within the two aforementioned provisions that the culpable individuals cannot remain in the company at the time of DPA negotiation and/or approval, and though Sir Leveson's first judgment appears to reflect this, his later comments to the Select Committee present a juxtaposition. The Select Committee set out that culpable individuals would unlikely remain within the company, and Sir Leveson clearly expressed that those facing prosecution must not remain if the company is to be granted a DPA. Distinction may be drawn between implicated individuals and those facing prosecution, which one might consider suggests that where individuals are simply being investigated (internally or by prosecutors) and have not yet been prosecuted, they may be entitled to remain without causing detriment to the company's opportunity of obtaining a DPA.

In six of the 13 published UK DPA judgments, reference to the offending company being "effectively a different entity" (or similar) is outlined,[15] with some reference in others to changes in corporate culture and approach (or trading status).[16] This is demonstrative of the indicative nature of the factors for consideration in the DPA Code, and the discretion of the judge in approving DPAs with companies not necessarily deemed to be an entirely new creature. Interestingly, all of the 13 published DPA judgments make reference to the removal and/or replacement of culpable and/or senior individuals. Some judgments place greater focus on the fact that the management team of the company is entirely new and not a representation of that in place at the time of offending, whereas others are clearer in outlining that senior individuals were dismissed.[17] In the *Sarclad Ltd* preliminary judgment, Sir Leveson, in setting out the evolved nature of the company, stated that none of the (then)

13 Crown Prosecution Service and Serious Fraud Office, 'Deferred Prosecution Agreements Code of Practice' (n 1) para 2.

14 *Serious Fraud Office v Standard Bank Plc (now ICBC Standard Bank Plc) (Preliminary)* [2016] Lloyd's Rep FC 91 (Crown) [34].

15 *Standard Bank Plc (now ICBC Standard Bank Plc) (Preliminary)* (n 14); *Serious Fraud Office v Sarclad Limited (Serious Fraud Office v XYZ Ltd) (Preliminary)* [2016] Lexis Citation 685 (Crown) [43] (Sir Brian Leveson); *Director of the Serious Fraud Office v Airbus SE* [2021] Lloyd's Rep FC 159 (Crown) [76] (Dame Victoria Sharp); *Director of the Serious Fraud Office v Airline Services Ltd* [2021] Lloyd's Rep FC 42 (Crown) [51(c)] (Mrs Justice May DBE); *Director of the Serious Fraud Office v Amec Foster Wheeler Limited* [2021] Lloyd's Rep FC 353 (Crown) [50] (Edis LJ); *R v Entain Plc* [2023] Lexis Citation 2484 (Crown) [12] (Dame Victoria Sharp).

16 *Serious Fraud Office v Rolls-Royce Plc* [2017] Lloyd's Rep FC 249 (Crown) [51] (Sir Brian Leveson); *Serious Fraud Office v Serco Geografix Ltd* [2019] Lloyd's Rep FC 518 (Crown) [40] (William Davis J); *Serious Fraud Office v Güralp Systems Ltd* [2020] Lloyd's Rep FC 90 (Crown) [49] (William Davis J).

17 'In the period since Sarclad identified the misconduct, two senior employees have been dismissed.' *See Sarclad Limited (Serious Fraud Office v XYZ Ltd) (Preliminary)* (n 15) [43]; 'Since 2015 it has parted with sixty three of its top and senior management employees: thirty one have been dismissed, and thirty two have left voluntarily or retired.' *See also Airbus SE* (n 15) [78].

current employees or directors faced criminal charges at the time of the conclusion of the investigation.[18] Thus, it appears to be the case that individuals under investigation need not necessarily – depending on the circumstances[19] – be dismissed at the time of DPA negotiations or approval, as long as those under suspicion (particularly directors) do not have involvement in the process and have not yet been prosecuted (and that disciplinary action is taken where necessary). The company being a substantially different entity is not compulsory, but it is likely that a company's willingness to actively protect suspected individuals or reluctance to make changes in compliance or management where necessary will hamper the ability to obtain a DPA.

The consideration of individuals is a crucial concern in respect of the disparity in treatment of smaller companies and larger companies when it comes to obtaining a DPA. It is important to outline that companies used simply to effect criminal wrongdoing 'as a dishonest venture from first to last'[20] (for example, a one-man company vehicle for fraud)[21] will not be able to obtain a DPA in any event. However, in smaller companies with less numerous workforces it is likely that senior individuals will either be under increased personal scrutiny, or simply that their replacement (particularly where the company is facing criminal investigation) is likely to be more difficult.

5.2 The corporate self-report

Self-reporting is a crucial factor in respect of DPAs, focussing on the company's willingness to approach prosecutors first and take accountability for its wrongdoing. Self-reporting is not mandatory in order to obtain a DPA but is the norm, and cases in which a company has not provided a self-report will require utmost cooperation once wrongdoing is uncovered. According to the SFO Operational Handbook: 'the failure of a Company to self-report is not a bar to DPA negotiations per se but must be considered as a factor when assessing whether a DPA is in the public interest.'[22]

Self-reporting is not covered in Schedule 17 of the CACA 2013 but is a focus within the DPA Code. Public interest factors in favour of prosecution, and thus against a DPA, include failure to notify prosecutors of the wrongdoing within reasonable time of awareness of it; and giving a knowing or believed inaccurate, misleading, or incomplete report, or a report without verification of its contents.[23] A key factor in favour of obtaining a DPA is cooperation, and the definition provided within the DPA Code focusses largely on the company's self-report and management team's 'genuinely proactive approach'.[24] This approach entails the reporting of wrongdoing within a reasonable time of awareness of it;

18 *Sarclad Limited (Serious Fraud Office v XYZ Ltd) (Preliminary)* (n 15) [43].

19 In the approved judgment of the DPAs of Bluu Solutions Limited and Tetris Projects Limited, Mrs Justice May stated: 'Like Edis LJ in *Amec* I regard the replacement of management as a necessary feature here, without which I would not have been prepared to give approval.' *See Director of the Serious Fraud Office v Bluu Solutions Limited and Tetris-Projects Limited* [2023] EWHC 1976 (KB) [84].

20 Select Committee on the Bribery Act 2010, *The Bribery Act 2010: Post Legislative Scrutiny: Evidence Session No 16* (n 7) question 150.

21 *Moore Stephens (a firm) v Stone Rolls Ltd (in liquidation)* [2009] UKHL 39 [1], [92] (Lord Phillips and Lord Scott).

22 Serious Fraud Office, 'Deferred Prosecution Agreements' (n 3).

23 Crown Prosecution Service and Serious Fraud Office, 'Deferred Prosecution Agreements Code of Practice' (n 1) paras 2.8.1(v)–(vi).

24 ibid para 2.8.2(i).

ensuring the report contains sufficient detail; providing an internal investigation report and relevant documents; and taking remedial steps. Witnesses should also be identified, made available for interview on request, and their accounts and documents presented to them disclosed.[25]

Notably, the extent to which the prosecutor was already aware of the wrongdoing will likely have some impact on the assessment of cooperation: the DPA Code refers to the reporting of wrongdoing 'otherwise unknown to the prosecutor'.[26] In giving evidence to the Select Committee, Hannah von Dadelszen (Head of Fraud at the SFO) stated that whilst Rolls-Royce had not initially self-reported – as its wrongdoing had been uncovered by a whistleblower and the company was approached first by the SFO[27] – it had disclosed material that the prosecutor 'would not have uncovered in a perhaps more adversarial forum'.[28] The prosecutor will need to consider the 'totality' of the self-report when considering the weight to afford it, including whether material has been withheld in respect of implicated individuals.[29] This will also include whether the investigation into individuals has been prejudiced by the company not providing an earlier self-report, with critical assessment of the internal investigation conducted.[30] There is thus a clear focus on the company's treatment of individuals at the earliest stage, and particularly the extent to which individuals are protected by a company and, conversely, implicated.

The SFO Operational Handbook adds that a prosecutor should consider the extent to which the wrongdoing was already known and the voluntariness of the self-report, considering whether there was a 'threat of imminent disclosure by a third party or compulsion'.[31] Typically a DPA's terms will require ongoing commitments to report wrongdoing as it becomes known or occurs. Though some argue that DPAs provide a 'powerful incentive'[32] to self-report, self-reporting does not guarantee a DPA. This was seen in *Skansen Interiors Limited*[33] (**Section 1.1.5.12**), though this decision has been subject to some criticism and concern, particularly in light of the fact that the underlying wrongdoing of the *Rolls-Royce* DPA was not uncovered by self-reporting.[34] In this respect, the Select Committee set out that there must, in cases where a DPA has been

25 ibid.

26 This is also referred to in the Select Committee on the Bribery Act 2010's report published in 2019. *See* ibid; Select Committee on the Bribery Act 2010, *The Bribery Act 2010: Post-Legislative Scrutiny* (n 11) paras 312, 316.

27 Serious Fraud Office, 'Deferred Prosecution Agreement – Statement of Facts – SFO v Rolls Royce PLC' (*Serious Fraud Office*, 17 January 2017) <https://www.sfo.gov.uk/download/deferred-prosecution-agreement-statement-facts-sfo-v-rolls-royce-plc/> accessed 15 May 2020, para 9.

28 Select Committee on the Bribery Act 2010, *The Bribery Act 2010: Post-Legislative Scrutiny* (n 11) para 259.

29 Crown Prosecution Service and Serious Fraud Office, 'Deferred Prosecution Agreements Code of Practice' (n 1) para 2.9.1.

30 ibid para 2.9.3.

31 Serious Fraud Office, 'Deferred Prosecution Agreements' (n 3).

32 Select Committee on the Bribery Act 2010, *The Bribery Act 2010: Post-Legislative Scrutiny* (n 11) para 327 (PricewaterhouseCoopers).

33 (Southwark Crown Court, 21 February 2018).

34 Investigation into Rolls-Royce followed internet postings, which then ultimately spurred an internal corporate investigation: *Rolls-Royce Plc* (n 15) [16]. *See also* Select Committee on the Bribery Act 2010, *The Bribery Act 2010: Post-Legislative Scrutiny* (n 11) para 277.

agreed, be a distinction in the financial penalty discount where a company has made an initial self-report and where it has not.[35]

The focus on self-reporting is not simply to assist the negotiation and agreement of the corporate's DPA but is also designed to impact individuals implicated within it. The DPA Code sets out that the self-report of wrongdoing will be based on the actions of individuals within the company, and as such their investigation and (possibly) prosecution will ordinarily be appropriate.[36] In accessing information that would otherwise be 'impossible or impractical' to obtain, prosecutors are more likely to achieve the 'best possible deterrent' in pursuing the implicated individuals.[37] Baker McKenzie, in evidence to the Select Committee, set out that a corporate self-report not only 'increases the likelihood of individual prosecutions' but actually '*forces* companies to provide information and co-operate with the prosecutor in relation to the prosecution of individuals' (emphasis added).[38] Use of such terminology is interesting: a company is not "forced" to make a self-report from a more general perspective, but will be required to cooperate with prosecutors (and that may include the making of a self-report) in order to avail itself of the opportunity of being offered a DPA. However, this does highlight the onus on a company to separate itself from the implicated individuals, and even to go further in acting against their interests.

Though it was argued during the consultation process that the objective of DPAs and self-reporting was cost saving, as opposed to pursuing individuals,[39] it appears that there remains in practice a great onus on companies to assist prosecutors in the latter instance. In respect of the cooperation expected of a company during negotiations, it was outlined within the Select Committee's report (of conclusions and recommendations) that this '*must* include provision of *all* available evidence which might implicate any individuals, however senior'[40] (emphasis added). Over recent years, the approach to corporate cooperation in the US has emulated a similar tone (**Section 4.1.1**). In fact, Susan Hawley, Policy Director at Corruption Watch and witness for the Select Committee, referred to the approach taken in the US and the onus on companies to surrender individuals for prosecution.[41] Whilst US Deputy Attorney General Rod Rosenstein's amendments to the Yates Memorandum in 2018 backtracked somewhat on the "all-or-nothing" stance within the Yates Memorandum, the gentler approach was somewhat short-lived.[42]

35 Select Committee on the Bribery Act 2010, *The Bribery Act 2010: Post-Legislative Scrutiny* (n 11) para 309.

36 Crown Prosecution Service and Serious Fraud Office, 'Deferred Prosecution Agreements Code of Practice' (n 1) para 2.9.1.

37 Select Committee on the Bribery Act 2010, *The Bribery Act 2010: Post-Legislative Scrutiny* (n 11) paras 312–313.

38 ibid para 312.

39 Ministry of Justice, *Deferred Prosecution Agreements: Government Response to the Consultation on a New Enforcement Tool to Deal With Economic Crime Committed by Commercial Organisations* (Cm 8463, 2012) para 208.

40 Select Committee on the Bribery Act 2010, *The Bribery Act 2010: Post-Legislative Scrutiny* (n 11) para 317.

41 ibid para 311.

42 Pursuant to Rosenstein's amendments, exhaustive information about every involved individual (at whatever level within the corporation) was no longer compulsory, but focus remained on senior figures. Cooperation credit would be afforded where corporations could demonstrate that they had acted in good faith in identifying those substantially involved and reported such information to the prosecutor, and prosecutors were to remain focussed on those playing 'significant roles' in the wrongdoing. *See* Deputy Attorney General Rod Rosenstein,

This demonstrates a shared focus of both UK and US prosecutors in requiring companies to cease protection of individuals implicated in the underlying wrongdoing in order for a DPA to be considered. It is not simply enough to self-report, or cooperate to a reasonable extent following whistleblower exposure, as companies will be expected to actively provide all evidence relevant to implicated individuals (and in a timely fashion). Though the US briefly moved away from the consuming requirement entailing the provision of evidence of misconduct committed by *all* implicated individuals (drawing its focus to those significantly involved), the Monaco Memorandum restored this approach, and the Select Committee recommends that this tough approach be taken in the UK. This presents a power imbalance between the company and individuals, as the company has significant control over the incrimination of the individual, and an inequality in treatment as the company is rewarded for participating in such an imbalance whilst the individual is not afforded the opportunity of any involvement in the process.

Individuals cannot agree DPAs in the UK and cannot be protected from prosecution within the terms of a corporate DPA.[43] According to Pinsent Masons, this 'lack of a formal leniency policy' for individuals is a 'major disincentive to self-report'.[44] Pinsent Masons suggested that a leniency policy benefitting those party to the decision-making of whether to self-report would see an increase in corporate accountability.[45] This is a difficult position to reconcile: firstly, it is not enough (according to Sir Leveson) for a company to self-report where the individuals considered to be the 'cause of the problem' are not 'root[ed] out'.[46] Therefore, the introduction of leniency provisions would *prima facie* be counter-intuitive and would lead companies down a path of self-reporting with no prospect of DPA approval. Secondly, as individuals suspected of being involved in the wrongdoing of the company are not permitted to be involved in the DPA negotiation process,[47] it is unlikely that DPA negotiations would be offered by the prosecutor where the decision-makers remain those implicated. Thirdly, the suggestion of a formal leniency policy or process for directors in tandem with the DPA provision suggests the need for some level of protection or mitigation in respect of personal accountability for wrongdoing. This would be contrary to the intention behind the DPA provision (in its current form) and would move further from achieving the aforementioned "best deterrent" from engaging in corporate crime – punishing the individuals involved. It may be the case that leniency can be facilitated within the scope of existing provisions, such as the Serious Organised Crime and Police Act 2005 and Sentencing Act 2020, though this would likely have limited impact on the ability of a director to remain part of the negotiations and potentially part of the company (**Section 10.1**).

Leniency policy or process might not necessarily constitute a means of alternative to prosecution in the same form as DPAs, but might instead arise in the form of implementing

---

'Deputy Attorney General Rod J. Rosenstein Delivers Remarks at the American Conference Institute's 35th International Conference on the Foreign Corrupt Practices Act' (*The United States Department of Justice*, 29 November 2018) <https://www.justice.gov/opa/speech/deputy-attorney-general-rod-j-rosenstein-delivers-remarks-american-conference-institute-0> accessed 13 May 2020.

43 Serious Fraud Office, 'Deferred Prosecution Agreements' (n 3).

44 Select Committee on the Bribery Act 2010, *The Bribery Act 2010: Post-Legislative Scrutiny* (n 11) para 314.

45 ibid.

46 ibid para 313.

47 Serious Fraud Office, 'Deferred Prosecution Agreements' (n 3).

safeguards to protect the individual's right to defence. This would, however, likely impact the individual's position within the company. Increased prosecutions, as noted by Baker McKenzie, arguably stem not only from the prosecutor's increased awareness of the extent of individual involvement but also the ability to use certain documentation against the individual. The position of individuals in respect of the use of information by prosecutors and their ability to exercise privilege must therefore be explored further (**Sections 7.1, 7.2, and 7.3**).

CHAPTER 6

Directors' duties

6.1 General duties under the Companies Act 2006

Directors' duties must be considered in respect of the interaction with DPAs, and particularly in relation to the increased onus on self-reporting. The Companies Act 2006 ("CA 2006") codified directors' duties into statutory provisions, which can be found through sections 171 to 177. Duties within the CA 2006 are not mutually exclusive.[1] According to the (then) Department of Trade and Industry's guidance document published in 2007, these provisions are 'essentially the same as the existing duties established by case law' and equitable principles,[2] with the notable exception being procedures for dealing with conflicts of interest.[3] Codification followed recommendation of The Company Law Review Steering Group to provide clarity in the area and promote good business practice and responsibility.[4] "Director" for the purpose of owing duties is defined under section 250 as 'any person occupying the position of director, by whatever name called' thus bearing a wide scope inclusive of name and function. A de facto director, a person who acts as and potentially goes by the title of director without having been validly appointed as such, may therefore owe directors' duties in respect of certain actions.[5] A de facto director will owe duties in respect of managerial tasks below board level, and where participating at board level in corporate governance.[6] A shadow director – 'a person in accordance with whose directions or instructions the directors of the company are accustomed to act'[7] but often not referred to by the title of director – owes directors' duties where and when those duties are capable of applying.[8]

1 Companies Act 2006, s 179.

2 ibid s 170(3).

3 Department of Trade and Industry, 'Companies Act 2006: Duties of Company Directors' (*GOV.UK*, June 2007) <https://webarchive.nationalarchives.gov.uk/20090609024504/http://www.berr.gov.uk/files/file40139.pdf> accessed 5 April 2021.

4 The Company Law Review Steering Group, 'Modern Company Law for a Competitive Economy: Final Report' (*Department of Trade and Industry*, 2001) <https://webarchive.nationalarchives.gov.uk/20060215135312/http://www.dti.gov.uk/cld/final_report/prelims.pdf> accessed 22 April 2021, 17.

5 Explanatory Notes to the Companies Act 2006, para 308.

6 Andrea Lista, 'Directors' Duties in the UK' in Adolfo Paolini (ed), *Research Handbook on Directors' Duties* (Edward Elgar Publishing 2016) 73–74.

7 Companies Act 2006, s 251(1).

8 'The general duties apply to a shadow director of a company where and to the extent that they are capable of so applying.' *See* ibid s 170(5); Small Business, Enterprise and Employment Act 2015, s 89(1). 'Where the [common law] rule or [equitable] principle does not apply to a shadow director, the statutory duty replacing that rule or principle will not apply either.' *See* Explanatory Notes to the Companies Act 2006, para 310.

 DOI: 10.4324/9781003456964-8

Section 170 sets out the scope and nature of the duties, with subsection (1) outlining that duties are owed to the company; this demonstrates the separate legal nature of the company.[9] However, there are circumstances where a director may owe duties to others, such as to creditors upon insolvency.[10] The first duty under section 171 is the duty to act within powers, which entails acting within the company's constitution (section 171(a)) and exercising powers only for the purposes for which they are conferred (section 171(b)). Section 171(a) thus sets out the importance of the company's articles of association and directors' adherence to them,[11] and section 171(b) provides that such adherence will be considered against the proper purpose rule.[12] Linked with the proper purpose rule is the duty to act in the best interest of the company, which has been somewhat modified in codification into section 172.[13]

Section 172 entitled 'duty to promote the success of the company' requires a director to act in a way which they in good faith consider (subjectively) 'would be most likely to promote the success of the company for the benefit of its members as a whole'.[14] Six matters in which the director must have regard in discharging this duty are the likely long-term consequences of a decision, employee interests, the need to foster business relationships, the wider impact of the company's operations (community and environment noted), the desirability of maintaining a reputation for high standards of business conduct, and the need to act fairly as between members of the company.[15] These factors are not exhaustive[16] and are of equal weight, though circumstances may lead to differing levels of relevance.[17] Having regard to the factors will likely encompass the duty under section 174 to exercise reasonable care, skill, and diligence,[18] which expands the previous common law obligation to exercise reasonable care and skill.[19] The care, skill, and diligence falling within the scope of the duty is that which would be exercised by a reasonably diligent person: bearing the general knowledge, skill, and experience that may reasonably be expected of a person carrying out the same corporate functions as the director; and with the general knowledge, skill, and experience of the director in question.[20]

Section 173 outlines the duty to exercise independent judgment: the codified version of the obligation not to fetter discretion.[21] Under section 173(2)(a), the duty is not breached where a director acts in accordance with company authority set out in any prior agreement

9 Lista in Paolini (ed) (n 6) 76.

10 Or prior to the inevitability of insolvency: *BTI 2014 LLC v Sequana SA* [2022] UKSC 25. *See also* Explanatory Notes to the Companies Act 2006, para 332; *Kinsela v Russell Kinsela Pty Ltd* (1986) 4 NSWLR 722; *West Mercia Safetywear Ltd v Dodd* [1988] BCLC 250 (CA); *Re Pantone 485 Ltd* [2002] 1 BCLC 266 (Ch); Lista in Paolini (ed) (n 6) 77.

11 Constitution is defined under: Companies Act 2006, s 257; Explanatory Notes to the Companies Act 2006, para 324.

12 Explanatory Notes to the Companies Act 2006, para 323; Lista in Paolini (ed) (n 6) 78–80.

13 Lista in Paolini (ed) (n 6) 82.

14 Companies Act 2006, s 172(1).

15 ibid.

16 Explanatory Notes to the Companies Act 2006, para 326; HL Deb 9 May 2006, vol 681, col 846 (Lord Goldsmith).

17 Tristan Hall and Andrew Milne, 'United Kingdom' in Edward Smerdon (ed), *Directors' Liability and Indemnification* (3rd edn, Gomer Press 2016) 662.

18 Explanatory Notes to the Companies Act 2006, para 328.

19 Tahir Ashraf, 'Directors' Duties With a Particular Focus on the Companies Act 2006' (2012) 54(2) Int JLM 125, 129.

20 Companies Act 2006, s 174(2); *Norman v Theodore Goddard (a firm)* [1991] BCLC 1028 (Ch) 1031.

21 Explanatory Notes to the Companies Act 2006, para 334; Lista in Paolini (ed) (n 6) 90.

restricting directors' discretion. This judgment may not necessarily mirror the wishes of the members,[22] but will not – under section 173(2)(b) – constitute a breach where exercised within the company's constitution.

A broad duty to avoid conflicts of interest is set out within section 175. A director must avoid a situation which gives rise to, or can give rise to, a direct or indirect interest which conflicts, or may conflict, with the company's interests.[23] Specified situations include use of property, information, or opportunity in an exploitative manner, irrespective of whether the company could have taken any advantage from those situations.[24] The duty to avoid conflicts of interest, in respect of the exploitation of any property, information, or opportunity of which a person became aware at a time when they were a director, will continue when that person ceases to be a director.[25] The duty is not breached if the situation cannot reasonably be regarded as giving rise to a conflict,[26] if it relates to a transaction or arrangement with the company itself,[27] or where the matter has been authorised by the directors.[28] Section 176 sets out the duty not to accept benefits from third parties,[29] with benefits being those incurred as a result of directorship.[30] This duty is somewhat interlinked with section 175: section 176 is not breached where 'the benefit cannot reasonably be regarded as likely to give rise to a conflict of interest',[31] and both duties have some element of continuing application when a person ceases to be a director. The duty under section 176 continues to apply in respect of acts or omissions committed by the director prior to the director's ceasing to hold the position.[32]

Section 177 entitled 'duty to declare interest in proposed transaction or arrangement' sets out that a director must declare to the other directors the nature and extent of any direct or indirect interest relating to or arising out of a proposed transaction or arrangement with the company,[33] before the company enters into the transaction or arrangement.[34] Declaration of an interest of which the director is not aware, or in relation to a transaction or arrangement of which the director is not aware, will not be required. Here, a director is "aware" where they 'ought reasonably to be aware'.[35] Like section 176, this duty is somewhat interlinked with section 175: a director need not make a declaration where the interest cannot reasonably be regarded as likely to give rise to a conflict of interests.[36] A

22 Ashraf (n 19) 129.

23 Companies Act 2006, s 175(1).

24 ibid s 175(2).

25 ibid s 170(2)(a).

26 ibid s 175(4)(a).

27 ibid s 175(3).

28 ibid s 175(4)(b). Such authorisation can only be given in private companies where the constitution does not invalidate the action and in public companies where the constitution positively enables such authorisation: ibid s 175(5). Authorisation is effective where the relevant meeting's quorum requirement is met without counting the relevant director or any other interested director, and authorisation was agreed without their voting (or would have been should their votes be subtracted): ibid s 175(6).

29 'A "third party" means a person other than the company, an associated body corporate or a person acting on behalf of the company or an associated body corporate.' *See* ibid s 176(2).

30 ibid s 176(1).

31 ibid s 176(4).

32 ibid s 170(2)(b).

33 ibid s 177(1).

34 ibid s 177(4).

35 ibid s 177(5).

36 ibid s 177(6)(a). Other circumstances in which a declaration need not be made include where the other directors are already aware of it (deemed to be so where they ought reasonably be aware), and/or the interest

declaration which later becomes or is proved to be inaccurate or incomplete will require a further declaration.[37]

6.2 A duty to self-report?

Whilst a prosecuted director will not (realistically) be able to remain with the company for DPA negotiations to be successful, there is no clear requirement that an implicated director cannot be involved in the earlier self-reporting stage. Notably, however, they would not be able to participate in the negotiations thereafter if themselves a suspect, and negotiations may not arise if the implicated individual seeks to hinder the process.[38]

6.2.1 Section 172

Under section 172, a director owes a duty to the company to act in a way in which they in good faith consider 'would be most likely to promote the success of the company for the benefit of its members as a whole'.[39] Prior to its codification, the duty under section 172 took the form of an obligation to act *bona fide* in a manner in which the director considered to be in the company's interests and not for any collateral purpose.[40] Thus, the test remains subjective.[41] The duty is not invokable as a defence for noncompliance with another duty,[42] and applies in respect of the company and not the wider corporate group.[43] Where there is no distinct evidence of the consideration of the promotion of the success of the company, the test to be applied is 'whether an intelligent and honest man in the position of a director of the company concerned, could, in the whole of the existing circumstances, have reasonably believed that the transactions were for the benefit of the company'.[44] The difference in wording between the latter 1970 test which requires that the director "believe", and the codified duty which requires the director "consider" that a decision is for the corporate benefit, raised some concern after the implementation of the CA 2006,[45] but the 1970 test has continued to be considered.[46] If the purposes of the company (and thus its success) include those other than for the benefit of its members, the

concerns terms of the director's contract, which have been or are to be considered by a directors' meeting or relevant committee: ibid s 177(6).

37 ibid s 177(3).

38 Serious Fraud Office, 'Deferred Prosecution Agreements' (*Serious Fraud Office*, 23 October 2020) <https://www.sfo.gov.uk/publications/guidance-policy-and-protocols/sfo-operational-handbook/deferred-prosecution-agreements/> accessed 23 October 2020; Select Committee on the Bribery Act 2010, *The Bribery Act 2010: Post-Legislative Scrutiny* (HL 2017–19, 303) para 314.

39 Companies Act 2006, s 172(1).

40 *Re Smith & Fawcett Ltd* [1942] Ch 304 (CA) 306 (Lord Greene MR); *Halsbury's Laws* (5th edn, 2016) vol 14, para 584.

41 *Regentcrest Plc (In Liquidation) v Cohen* [2001] 2 BCLC 80 (Ch) [120] (Jonathan Parker J). This test remains subjective under section 172: *Birdi v Specsavers Optical Group Ltd* [2015] EWHC 2870 (Ch) [61].

42 Explanatory Notes to the Companies Act 2006, para 313.

43 *Charterbridge Corporation Ltd v Lloyds Bank Ltd* [1970] Ch 62 (Ch) 74 (Pennycuick J); *Extrasure Travel Insurances Ltd v Scattergood* [2002] EWHC 3093 (Ch) [91]; *Halsbury's Laws* (n 40) para 584.

44 *Charterbridge Corporation Ltd v Lloyds Bank Ltd* (n 43) 74 (Pennycuick J); *Colin Gwyer & Associates Ltd v London Wharf (Limehouse) Ltd* [2002] EWHC 2748 (Ch) [73]; *Halsbury's Laws* (n 40) para 584. Cited in a case in relation to concerns as to the conduct of a fellow director, and the extent to which a director should document such concerns and seek advice: *Atkinson & Mummery v Kingsley and Smith* [2020] EWHC 2913 (Ch).

45 Alistair Alcock, 'An Accidental Change to Directors' Duties?' (2009) 30(12) Comp Law 362, 366–367.

46 *Madoff Securities International Ltd (in liquidation) v Raven* [2013] EWHC 3147 (Comm) [194].

duty continues to have effect as if referring to those purposes.[47] Section 172 is a fiduciary duty, and one of the directors' duties most frequently articulated.[48]

In respect of dealing with the knowledge of suspected wrongdoing within a reasonable time within the company, the director(s) will need to bear in mind their professional duty to promote the success of the company, in good faith. Regulated companies in the financial services sector have a positive duty to notify regulators in certain circumstances, such as the notification of 'matters having a serious regulatory impact'[49] to the Financial Conduct Authority ("FCA"). Where a positive duty to notify regulators arises, a company needs to be wary of onward disclosure of wrongdoing to prosecutors.[50] If a company wishes to avail itself of the opportunity of negotiating a DPA, a self-report to the prosecutor will in most cases be necessary, and departure from this general principle will tend only to occur where a company cooperates extensively following the uncovering of wrongdoing.[51] DPAs may be approved in cases with whistleblower involvement,[52] but generally a prosecutor will not consider a perceived attempt to avoid accountability until the corporate hand is forced to constitute true proactivity nor cooperation.[53] Thus, the director must consider the risk of any onward disclosure to prosecutors materialising into prosecution, and whether the company would wish to negotiate a DPA at some point in the future. Where no regulatory notification obligations arise, the director will still be required to consider the risk of exposure of known wrongdoing to prosecutors and the desirability of entering DPA negotiations, should the option arise.

A director must 'have regard ... to',[54] or 'give proper consideration to', the factors set out under section 172(1), and the extent to which this is practised in making decisions will

47 Companies Act 2006, s 172(2). A "member" for whose benefit the director must act is a subscriber of a company's memorandum of association, and every other person who agrees to become a member and whose name is entered in the register of members: Companies Act 2006, ss 112(1)–(2).

48 Lista in Paolini (ed) (n 6) 82.

49 More specifically defined within the FCA Handbook. *See* FCA, 'FCA Handbook' (*Financial Conduct Authority*, 7 March 2016) <https://www.handbook.fca.org.uk/handbook/SUP/15/?view=chapter> accessed 6 April 2021, SUP 15.3.1R.

50 For example, the Financial Reporting Council and SFO have a Memorandum of Understanding which provides for information sharing. *See* Serious Fraud Office and Financial Reporting Council, 'Memorandum of Understanding between the Serious Fraud Office and the Financial Reporting Council' (*Financial Reporting Council*, May 2016) <https://www.frc.org.uk/getattachment/c41c0866-6496-4c9e-9228-f9de2086ff7e/Memorandum-of-Understanding-between-the-FRC-and-the-Serious-Fraud-Office-pdf.pdf> accessed 14 May 2021.

51 'Even if the prosecuting authorities became aware of the relevant conduct by the actions of a third party, if subsequent self-reporting or co-operation overall, is of a high quality and brings significant wrongdoing to light that would not otherwise have come to the attention of the authorities, this will be a significant factor in favour of a DPA: see Rolls Royce para 22 of the final judgment and Sarclad at paras 37 to 38 of the preliminary judgment. To that extent, there is no necessary bright line between self-reporting and co-operation.' *See Director of the Serious Fraud Office v Airbus SE* [2021] Lloyd's Rep FC 159 (Crown) [68]. *See Serious Fraud Office v Rolls-Royce Plc* [2017] Lloyd's Rep FC 249 (Crown) [22]; *Serious Fraud Office v Sarclad Limited (Serious Fraud Office v XYZ Ltd) (Preliminary)* [2016] Lexis Citation 685 (Crown) [37]–[38].

52 *Rolls-Royce Plc* (n 51) [16]–[18].

53 'Considerable weight may be given to a genuinely proactive approach adopted by P's management team when the offending is brought to their notice, involving within a reasonable time of the offending coming to light reporting P's offending otherwise unknown to the prosecutor'. *See* Crown Prosecution Service and Serious Fraud Office, 'Deferred Prosecution Agreements Code of Practice' (*Crown Prosecution Service*, 11 February 2014) <https://www.cps.gov.uk/sites/default/files/documents/publications/dpa_cop.pdf> accessed 9 June 2020, para 2.8.2(i).

54 Companies Act 2006, s 172(1).

be a 'matter for [their] good faith judg[e]ment'.[55] In considering whether to self-report wrongdoing to prosecutors, the director has a duty under section 172(1)(a) to have regard to 'the likely consequences of any decision in the long term'. A decision not to self-report or to provide an incomplete and/or disingenuous self-report would be very likely to impact the company's prospects of being invited to enter DPA negotiations or obtaining DPA approval. Self-reporting presents potential benefits which many directors would consider to promote the success of the company, and increases the likelihood of a company being invited to enter into DPA negotiations. Upon DPA approval, a company will avoid conviction and thus debarment,[56] will benefit from enhanced compliance measures, and will obtain a lesser fine as a result of a reduction imposed for cooperation (insofar as the DPA terms are complied with).

The director must have regard to the company's desirability for 'maintaining a reputation for high standards of business conduct', under section 172(1)(e), which will likely comprise the importance of accountability for wrongdoing and willingness to cooperate in effecting reform and enhanced compliance. Furthermore, this may also entail efforts to avoid conviction and debarment which may follow, with the effect of restricting business and impacting commercial reputation. Proper self-reporting and cooperation may also avail a company the opportunity to negotiate settlements, such as DPAs, with prosecutors in overseas jurisdictions in respect of the same or connected conduct. Where a DPA is not agreed or approved, the integrity of a company's self-report and willingness to cooperate in ensuring self-accountability will likely be reflected upon in mitigation in any criminal proceedings which ensue.[57] 'The impact of the company's operations on the community', to which the director must have regard under section 172(1)(d), may also include the company's contribution to greater corporate accountability and justice irrespective of whether a DPA results from a self-report.

Though there are many benefits of self-reporting and the opportunity to negotiate and agree a DPA, there are also many risk exposures which a director will need to have regard

---

55 HC Deb 17 October 2006, vol 450, col 789 (Margaret Hodge).

56 A 2020 government Green Paper proposed the inclusion of an explicit discretionary exclusion ground covering DPAs to allow contracting authorities to exclude organisations which are subject to DPAs from procurements where appropriate (and not disproportionate or detrimental to the ability of prosecutors to negotiate future DPAs). *See* Cabinet Office, *Transforming Public Procurement* (CP 353, 2020) 112–115. However, this was ultimately not pursued: 'A specific exclusion ground for DPAs is … not justified or appropriate … In order to provide clarity on DPAs, we will instead set out in guidance that the circumstances leading to a DPA should be considered in the context of the discretionary exclusion grounds … and that commitments made under a DPA should be considered as part of the assessment of evidence of self-cleaning. Contracting authorities should examine the specific conditions of the DPA in order to reach a considered view.' *See* Cabinet Office, 'Consultation outcome: Transforming Public Procurement – Government Response to Consultation' (*UK Government*, 6 December 2021) <https://www.gov.uk/government/consultations/green-paper-transforming-public-procurement/outcome/transforming-public-procurement-government-response-to-consultation#contents> accessed 8 June 2023, Q20. Thus, '[a] DPA will not trigger mandatory debarment under the EU Public Procurement Regime, since it is not a criminal offence.' *See* Qingxiu Bu, 'The Viability of Deferred Prosecution Agreements (DPAs) in the UK: The Impact on Global Anti-Bribery Compliance' (2021) 22 EBOR 173, 178.

57 'Corporation co-operated with investigation, made early admissions and/or voluntarily reported offending' is a factor 'reducing seriousness or reflecting mitigation' set out in the Sentencing Council Guidelines. *See* Sentencing Council, 'Corporate Offenders: Fraud, Bribery and Money Laundering' (*Sentencing Council*, 1 October 2014) <https://www.sentencingcouncil.org.uk/offences/crown-court/item/corporate-offenders-fraud-bribery-and-money-laundering/> accessed 15 May 2021.

to as 'the likely consequences of any decision in the long term'.[58] It may be the case that a director oversees a self-report in the hope of obtaining a DPA (this being what they in good faith consider to promote the success of the company in the circumstances), but a DPA is not offered or approved. Despite the making of a self-report, a DPA is not guaranteed.[59] Whilst it may be that a DPA is not offered on the basis of limited evidence of criminal wrongdoing to support the prosecution's case, it may alternatively be that prosecutors simply elect to pursue prosecution.[60] If prosecution leads to criminal liability, the company may be significantly disadvantaged by debarment, impact on commercial reputation, financial position, and so forth; this would thus be contrary to some of the factors noted under section 172(1). A self-report to prosecutors may also lead to civil liability (the impact of DPA-related documentation on civil claims is notable: **Section 7.3.4**),[61] likely to impact a company's 'reputation for high standards of business conduct'.[62] This will particularly be the case where a DPA or prosecution is reached, thus publicising the extent of the corporate's accepted wrongdoing, and third parties elect to claim against the company for any losses incurred in relation to the underlying wrongdoing. Civil liability may extend to a civil settlement with prosecutors where neither a DPA nor prosecution materialises.[63]

Irrespective of whether a DPA is offered and approved in the UK, it remains possible that a company could incur criminal liability in overseas jurisdictions. Though in recent years there has been a greater effort by international prosecuting agencies to coordinate in investigation and settlement, this is not guaranteed. This also means that provisions for information sharing may be enhanced,[64] subject to relevant legal restrictions, as prosecutors establish joint approaches such as that seen in the *Airbus SE* case.[65] In some jurisdictions, such as the US, limited waivers of privilege are not recognised.[66] Thus, where

58 Companies Act 2006, s 172(1)(a).

59 *Skansen Interiors Limited* (Southwark Crown Court, 21 February 2018). *See also* Select Committee on the Bribery Act 2010, *The Bribery Act 2010: post-legislative scrutiny* (HL 2017–19, 303) para 278.

60 For example, where the company does not satisfy the prosecutor that it meets the public interest factors against prosecution set out within the DPA Code. *See* Crown Prosecution Service and Serious Fraud Office, 'Deferred Prosecution Agreements Code of Practice' (n 53) para 2.

61 Ruth Cowley and others, 'Self-Reporting Bribery: The Ongoing Dilemma' (*Norton Rose Fulbright*, August 2018) <https://www.nortonrosefulbright.com/en-gb/knowledge/publications/37889dc7/self-reporting-bribery-the-ongoing-dilemma> accessed 30 March 2021.

62 Companies Act 2006, s 172(1)(e).

63 'In cases where neither limb of the evidential stage can be met by the conclusion of any DPA negotiations and it is not considered appropriate to continue the criminal investigation, the prosecutor should consider whether a Civil Recovery Order is appropriate.' *See* Crown Prosecution Service and Serious Fraud Office, 'Deferred Prosecution Agreements Code of Practice' (n 53) para 1.7.

64 Speaking about the SFO's work with the US, then-Director of the SFO Lisa Osofsky said: 'There are so many avenues for cooperation there, including shared use of important intelligence information that can, especially in a white collar case, really crack open our cases'. *See* ParliamentLive.TV, 'Justice Committee 18 December 2018, Witnesses: Lisa Osofsky, Director, Serious Fraud Office' (*ParliamentLive.TV*, 18 December 2018) <https://parliamentlive.tv/event/index/756b77d2-3d1d-4f13-8f9b-1e5a46be2d24?in=10:07:02> accessed 6 May 2021, [10:11]. There is no available Hansard from the evidence, though it can be viewed by video.

65 'On 31 January 2017 the SFO and the PNF entered into a Joint Investigation Team ("JIT") Agreement' in order to investigate the wider Airbus group. *See* Serious Fraud Office, 'R v Airbus – Statement of Facts Amended' (*Serious Fraud Office*, 28 February 2020) <https://www.sfo.gov.uk/download/airbus-se-deferred-prosecution-agreement-statement-of-facts/> accessed 11 February 2021, para 37.

66 'Under New York law … disclosure of a privileged document, even for a limited purpose, gives rise to a loss of privilege': Kit Jarvis, 'Cross-Border Privilege Issues Facing Financial Institutions' (2008) 23(4) JIBFL 179.

a company has made a self-report featuring limited waivers on certain documentation, such as interview notes, this may lead to loss of privilege. Any loss of privilege exposes the company to a greater risk of liability, and may encourage increased third-party civil claims (**Section 7.3.4**).

In deciding whether to make a self-report, a director will also need to consider the timing in doing so. A belated report of wrongdoing (for example, some time following whistleblower exposure or notification of an investigation (or pre-investigation)) is less likely to be considered sufficient cooperation for the purpose of being offered a DPA. Similarly, an incomplete self-report will be less likely to be viewed as constituting sufficient cooperation.[67] Self-reporting wrongdoing has been referred to as a 'business decision',[68] and 'commercial decisions are often made at speed'.[69] Some may dispute whether reporting can truly constitute a commercial decision, particularly in respect of the extent to which directors' duties may in some circumstances essentially remove the element of choice (where, for example, self-reporting would undoubtedly promote the success of the company long-term thus giving rise to the section 172 duty, or where required by the company's constitution). However, it remains the case that the decision to self-report – if reporting with hopes of negotiating a DPA – requires a prompt approach. In considering the 'likely consequences of any decision in the long term',[70] it will be crucial for directors to consider the company's objective in self-reporting so as to determine the importance of timing.

Once alerted to potential wrongdoing, a company may wish to conduct an internal investigation as a scoping measure in order to determine the extent of the underlying situation. This will most likely precede a self-report, to enable the company to familiarise itself with the circumstances to report and the appropriate body to report to. For regulated companies in the financial services sector, notification to the FCA is required 'immediately [the company] becomes aware, or has information which reasonably suggests' that a matter having a serious regulatory impact 'has occurred, may have occurred or may occur in the foreseeable future'.[71] In the regulatory sphere there is great focus on the timing of notification of suspected wrongdoing, even where suspicions are not yet founded on material proof (note the use of the term "may"). Notifications, in some circumstances, can be made orally and followed with written notification to ensure promptness where appropriate.[72]

The desirability of making a notification to a prosecutor, where not under a strict corporate duty to notify (this does not refer to the directors' general duties), would likely depend on the circumstances. Where wrongdoing is mooted as having potentially occurred but the company has little information or evidence to substantiate the claim, it may be wary of making a blind notification-style report to prosecutors in the event that it later elects not to self-report fully. However, a company intending to make a self-report but delayed

67 A key factor in favour of obtaining a DPA is cooperation, and the definition provided within the DPA Code focusses largely on the company's self-report and management team's 'genuinely proactive approach': Crown Prosecution Service and Serious Fraud Office, 'Deferred Prosecution Agreements Code of Practice' (n 53) para 2.8.2(i).

68 Cowley and others (n 61).

69 Lisa Linklater, 'Codifying Directors' Duties: Better in Principle Than in Practice?' (2002) 23(9) Comp Law 261, 261.

70 Companies Act 2006, s 172(1)(a).

71 FCA, 'FCA Handbook' (n 49) SUP 15.3.1R.

72 ibid SUP 15.7.2G.

in ensuring that the internal investigation is being properly conducted, and the report as complete as possible, may wish to make a notification-style report to the prosecutor to alert the prosecutor to the fact that a self-report should be expected within a certain period. This happened in the case of *Sarclad Ltd*, whereby the company's law firm conducting an investigation orally informed the SFO that an unidentified client might be making a self-report, and a month later revealed the identity, at which point a date was agreed upon for the self-report to be submitted.[73] As long as it can be demonstrated that the delay between the notification and self-report was not used in order to obstruct the following investigation, for example to conceal or destroy evidence or to conduct privileged interviews without consultation, this may be considered by the prosecutor as a clear early indication of willingness to cooperate and to do so thoroughly. A company may not necessarily need to consider pre-self-report notification, particularly where any early internal investigation is not likely to be unduly time or resource consuming, but it may be a consideration where wrongdoing is more extensive and substantial (for example, rooted throughout a corporate group).

6.2.1.1 Individual liability

A further risk exposure of self-reporting is that individual liability may arise. This may be a particular risk to the director(s) personally where they have been involved in the underlying wrongdoing. Where the making of a self-report would promote the success of the company and the director in good faith recognises that to be the case, the director will be required to honour their duty to the company irrespective of their personal interests: this is explored further in the analysis of section 175 (**Section 6.2.2**). Within the scope of the section 172 duty, a wrongdoing director *may* need to disclose such wrongdoing and/or relevant information to their principal (the company, and in this context the board).[74] The director is required to disclose to the company any information which is acquired as a result of directorship, and which is relevant for the company to know and would be of interest to it.[75] To promote the success of the company and its best interests, the director will be required to risk personal liability in order to comply with their directors' duties either in making a self-report or assisting the company by providing the relevant information in order to allow it to do so (where a self-report is deemed to be desirable). Personal liability arising as a result may be criminal: for example, where the company's suspected offence is based upon the identification principle. The reality of UK DPAs based on identification principle offences and the successful prosecution of individuals is another matter (**Section 8.3.1.1**), but even where conviction does not materialise financial liability may be incurred.[76] Liability may also be civil: for example, where the involvement in the wrongdoing is deemed to have constituted a breach of the director's duties under the CA 2006.

73 *Sarclad Limited (Serious Fraud Office v XYZ Ltd) (Preliminary)* (n 51) [24].

74 *Item Software (UK) Ltd v Fassihi* [2004] EWCA Civ 1244 [41] (Arden LJ); *Stobart Group Ltd v Tinkler* [2019] EWHC 258 (Comm) [393]; *Butterworths Corporate Law Service*, paras CL10.19–10.20.

75 *Bhullar v Bhullar* [2003] EWCA Civ 424 [41] (Jonathan Parker LJ); *Halsbury's Laws* (n 40) para 584.

76 The impact has the potential to be far-reaching – individuals who have been subjects of unsuccessful post-DPA approval prosecutions have noted the burden on their careers and health. *See* Ben Chapman, 'Former Tesco Executive Carl Rogberg Cleared Over £250m Fraud and False Accounting Scandal' (*The Independent*, 23 January 2019) <https://www.independent.co.uk/news/business/news/carl-rogberg-tesco-executive-fraud-trial-cleared-false-accounting-scandal-court-a8741966.html> accessed 8 February 2021. *See also* Oliver Gill, 'Abolish Serious Fraud Office Says Acquitted Ex-Serco Boss' (*The Telegraph*, 8 May 2021) <https://www

6.2.1.2 Barclays

The exposures associated with cooperation in a criminal investigation can be seen in the wider context of Barclays. An investigation into 'Barclays Bank' was launched by the SFO in August 2012 in respect of commercial arrangements made in 2008 with 'Qatar Holdings'.[77] Criminal proceedings were initiated in July 2017 against Barclays PLC and four individuals, whereby all were charged with conspiracy to commit fraud and the provision of unlawful financial assistance; Barclays Bank PLC (a wholly owned subsidiary of Barclays PLC) was also charged with unlawful financial assistance in February 2018.[78] Following an application by Barclays PLC and Barclays Bank PLC, charges against both were dismissed in May 2018,[79] and an application made by the SFO to the High Court to reinstate charges was thereafter dismissed.[80] Reporting restrictions were placed on the latter judgment until 28 February 2020, with both aforementioned judgments making explicit reference to the individuals involved.

In April 2019 there was an application by the individuals to dismiss the case on the ground of there being no case to answer: this was allowed for John Varley (Barclays Group Chief Executive and director of Barclays) but the trials of Roger Jenkins (Barclays Capital Executive Chairman of Investment Management in the Middle East and North Africa), Tom Kalaris (Barclays Wealth Management Chief Executive Officer), Richard Boath (Barclays Capital Head of European Financial Institutions Group), and Chris Lucas (Barclays Group Finance Director) were permitted to proceed.[81] The SFO appealed the decision in respect of Varley, but was unsuccessful.[82] Due to ill health, Lucas was not charged and tried.[83] The trial of Jenkins, Boath, and Kalaris spanned five months, and the jury took fewer than six hours to acquit on 28 February 2020.[84] As a result, no convictions materialised from the SFO's seven-year investigation into Barclays.

It was reported in July 2015 that the SFO had 'asked [Barclays] to consider a [DPA]'.[85] Sky News reported that, according to people close to the matter, the SFO had written to Barclays 'to propose such a move' but there was suggestion that 'some bank directors were lukewarm about the idea of signing a DPA'.[86] The SFO did not comment, but Barclays stated: '"We are not in a position to comment on an ongoing legal matter, save to clarify

.telegraph.co.uk/business/2021/05/08/abolish-serious-fraud-office-says-acquitted-ex-serco-boss/> accessed 13 May 2021.

77 Serious Fraud Office, 'Barclays Bank and Qatar' (*Serious Fraud Office*, 30 August 2012) <http://web.archive.org/web/20120922112157/https://www.sfo.gov.uk/our-work/our-cases/case-progress/barclays-bank-and-qatar.aspx> accessed 8 April 2021.

78 Serious Fraud Office, 'Barclays PLC and Qatar Holding LLC' (*Serious Fraud Office*, 28 February 2020) <https://www.sfo.gov.uk/cases/barclays-qatar-holding/> accessed 22 February 2021.

79 *The Queen v Barclays PLC and Barclays Bank PLC* [2020] Lloyd's Rep FC 325 (Crown) [6].

80 *Serious Fraud Office v Barclays plc* [2018] EWHC 3055 (QB) [3].

81 *R v Varley* [2019] EWCA Crim 1074 [627]. For the positions of the individuals, *see Barclays PLC and Barclays Bank PLC* (n 79) [9].

82 *Varley* (n 81).

83 Serious Fraud Office, 'Former Barclays Executives Acquitted of Conspiracy to Commit Fraud' (*Serious Fraud Office*, 28 February 2020) <https://www.sfo.gov.uk/2020/02/28/former-barclays-executives-acquitted-of-conspiracy-to-commit-fraud/> accessed 8 April 2021.

84 Jemma Slingo, 'SFO on Rack After Barclays Blow' (2020) (10) LS Gaz.

85 'The [SFO] has asked the bank to consider a deferred prosecution agreement as its three-year probe continues, Sky News learns.' *See* Mark Kleinman, 'SFO Offers Barclays Deal Amid Qatar Probe' (*Sky News*, 21 July 2015) <https://web.archive.org/web/20150724174826/https://news.sky.com/story/1522666/sfo-offers-barclays-deal-amid-qatar-probe> accessed 8 April 2021.

86 ibid.

that there has been no offer made of a DPA.'"[87] An offer of a DPA would have suggested that negotiations had reached a later stage, as the invitation to enter DPA negotiations and the offer of a DPA 'at the conclusion of the discussions'[88] are distinct: negotiations do not guarantee an offer.[89] If negotiations had started between the SFO and Barclays, both parties would have signed an undertaking as to the confidentiality of the DPA negotiations, and thus Barclays would likely not have been in a position to confirm any offer in any event.[90]

In respect of other wrongdoing, Barclays Bank PLC entered into a DPA with the US DoJ in June 2012 for a period of two years.[91] Cooperation in the US investigation was deemed to have been 'extraordinary and extensive' and the agreement was partly reached on the basis of the company's 'commitment to future cooperation with the Fraud Section and other government authorities in the United States and United Kingdom'.[92] Irrespective of whether a DPA was offered or negotiated by the SFO, it would appear that there was some level of cooperation with the prosecutor in its investigation. It is unclear whether Barclays elected to self-report to the SFO; however it is known that Barclays satisfied disclosure obligations to the Financial Services Authority ("FSA", now known as the FCA) and the FSA then passed information to the SFO.[93] Barclays made a limited waiver of privilege to the SFO in respect of certain documentation with use permitted 'for the purpose of its investigation, prosecution and SFO related criminal proceedings and to disclose them to a third party in accordance with its statutory functions'.[94] This limited waiver included interview transcripts, some of which were referred to 'in open court at trial and cross-examining Mr Jenkins in particular'.[95] Despite privilege in those documents being lost, later requests by third-party claimants for their disclosure in civil proceedings were nonetheless met by redactions,[96] until disclosure of the unredacted documents was ordered.[97] This waiver demonstrates some level of cooperation by Barclays, but also the risk of civil proceedings arising as a result of doing so.

Ultimately the companies were not convicted, nor were the individuals, but all were at some stage charged and will have incurred varying financial liabilities in defence throughout the seven-year period. In the event that Barclays was not offered a DPA, one questions why. It may be that Barclays was not deemed to have engaged in sufficient cooperation,

---

87 ibid.

88 Crown Prosecution Service and Serious Fraud Office, 'Deferred Prosecution Agreements Code of Practice' (n 53) para 2.1.

89 ibid.

90 ibid para 3.6(i). Unless negotiations reach such a stage whereby disclosure is required, as a listed company, in order to uphold the interest of market integrity (**Section 1.1.3.1**).

91 The United States Department of Justice, 'Agreement: Barclays Bank PLC' (*The United States Department of Justice*, 26 June 2012) <https://www.justice.gov/iso/opa/resources/337201271017335469822.pdf> accessed 8 April 2021.

92 ibid.

93 Jill Treanor, 'Barclays Investigation Details Given to Serious Fraud Office' (*The Guardian*, 9 August 2012) <https://www.theguardian.com/business/2012/aug/09/barclays-investigation-serious-fraud-office?newsfeed=true> accessed 8 April 2021; Simon Goodley, 'Serious Fraud Office Investigating Barclays Pyments to Qatar' (*The Guardian*, 30 August 2012) <https://www.theguardian.com/business/2012/aug/29/sfo-investigation-barclays-qatar> accessed 8 April 2021.

94 *PCP Capital Partners LLP v Barclays Bank Plc* [2020] EWHC 1393 (Comm) [10].

95 ibid [11].

96 The claimants in the proceedings were PCP Capital Partners LLP and PCP International Finance Limited. *See* ibid [11]–[12].

97 ibid [120], [128].

and there may not have been a self-report around the time disclosure obligations to regulators were met. If directors, presented with a DPA offer or not, were 'lukewarm about the idea of signing a DPA',[98] this may suggest that a DPA was not perceived to promote the success of the company(ies). Where conduct is wrong but not criminal, a DPA giving rise to potential criminal proceedings upon any breach would not promote the success of the company. One may argue that a DPA would not be agreed in such circumstances, but questions have arisen as to whether previously agreed DPAs have a true basis of criminal liability.[99]

A director faced with a matter requiring notification to regulators but which is not perceived, in good faith, to be criminal should pay serious consideration and caution to the making of a self-report. A self-report made may not lead to corporate criminal prosecution (or DPA) and may not significantly impact the prospect of civil liability arising, particularly where a regulatory investigation and/or proceedings are already underway. In this respect, a company may self-report as a precautionary measure in the event that conduct is determined to be criminal (should a criminal investigation arise). If conduct is determined to be criminal and a company is not deemed to have been forthcoming in self-reporting, or is not wholly cooperative thereafter, the company will be severely restricting its chances of entering DPA negotiations. There will thus be a fine line to be drawn and will ultimately be dependent on the circumstances. Directors facing similar circumstances should be advised to consider the type of offending, the prospect of criminal liability arising, and the benefits and exposures of making a self-report in order to assess whether the decision to self-report would promote the success of the company.

Any decision made in good faith (and evidentially proven to be so) will not give rise to a breach of duty, even where that decision leads to a position contrary to the factors set out under section 172(1).[100] As the decision to offer a DPA lies solely with the prosecutor, and the decision to approve a DPA lies with the judge, the company can only influence those decisions so far in the cooperation offered in the circumstances. The benefit of the section 172 duty is that it is determined subjectively. However, this does not mean that a director can use the subjective notion of good faith as a defence for all decisions, as evidence will be needed to support any claims of having made decisions in this way,[101] and thus a director will need to disregard personal interests when making decisions on self-reporting.

---

98 Kleinman (n 85).

99 Max Walters, 'News: DPAs in the Spotlight Following Failed Tesco Prosecutions' (2019) (3) LS Gaz; Maria Cronin and Craig Hogg, 'Legal Update – White Collar Crime: Time to Rethink DPAs After Tesco Failures' (2019) (7) LS Gaz.

100 '[It] is unlikely that the court will doubt the director's honesty and professed support for the company's best interests unless substantial detriment to the company has resulted from his act or omission': *Stobart Group Ltd v Tinkler* (n 74) [396]. *See also Regentcrest Plc (In Liquidation) v Cohen* (n 41) [120] (Jonathan Parker J); *Birdi v Specsavers Optical Group Ltd* (n 41) [61].

101 The evidential burden (unless shifted) is on the party asserting the breach: *Stobart Group Ltd v Tinkler* (n 74) [397]; *Charles Forte Investments v Amanda* [1964] Ch 240 (CA) 260–261. 'Where his decision is one that no reasonable director could have considered to be in the best interests of the company then reliance upon his own suggested contrary belief will not avoid a finding of breach.' *See Stobart Group Ltd v Tinkler* (n 74) [397]. *See also Re Southern Counties Fresh Foods Ltd* [2008] EWHC 2810 (Ch) [53].

6.2.2 Section 175

Under section 175 of the CA 2006, a director has a duty to avoid conflicts of interest. A director must avoid actual or potential conflicts with the company's interests in situations which give rise to actual or potential direct or indirect personal interests.[102] This duty applies not only to conflict of interest but also conflict of duty, which means that the director must prioritise duties owed to the company over their personal interests.[103] In deciding whether to self-report, a director involved to some extent in the underlying wrongdoing will likely consider the impact of doing so on their personal interests. For example, a director may not yet have considered their potential culpability and course of action and may not be ready or willing to approach prosecutors in a manner which may potentially be self-incriminating. Ultimately, a self-report will need to be sufficiently extensive and complete, and thus omitted details of individual involvement would likely leave the company more exposed. A self-report could be used against the company at trial and,[104] as prosecutors are focussing even more on individual criminal accountability, this would be a likely eventuality where a DPA is not offered.

As discussed within the scope of section 172 (**Section 6.2.1**), a director involved in wrongdoing or with knowledge of it *may* need to disclose such relevant information to their principal.[105] Required to disclose information acquired as a result of directorship, and that relevant for the company to know and of interest to it,[106] a director has a duty to promote the success and best interests of the company. In this respect, the section 172 duty is reinforced by section 175, which provides that the director cannot elevate their personal interests so as to escape their duty to avoid conflicts of interest. A director will thus not be able to elect to avoid making a self-report or disclosing relevant information in exercising their personal interests where the company's interests require otherwise. Where a director is required by virtue of section 172 either to disclose relevant information so as to allow the company to self-report, or to coordinate the making of a self-report, but finds that this presents a conflict with their personal interests as prohibited under section 175, the 'immediate course of action is disclosure or resignation'.[107]

Under section 175(2), the duty to avoid conflicts of interest particularly applies to the 'exploitation of any property, information or opportunity', irrespective of any profit or advantage the company may have (or not have) incurred from that property, information, or opportunity. This is a continuing duty even where a person ceases to be a director, in regard to any property, information, or opportunity which the director became aware of during their directorship.[108] The continuing duty upon resignation, provided for under section 170(2), takes a slightly reduced form: the duty under section 175 encompasses a "no conflict" and "no profit" rule, whereas the continuing duty encompasses only a "no profit"

102 Companies Act 2006, s 175(1).

103 Lista in Paolini (ed) (n 6) 94.

104 Where a DPA is not offered. *See* Crown Prosecution Service and Serious Fraud Office, 'Deferred Prosecution Agreements Code of Practice' (n 53) para 4.6(ii).

105 *Item Software (UK) Ltd v Fassihi* (n 74) [41] (Arden LJ); *Stobart Group Ltd v Tinkler* (n 74) [393]; *Butterworths Corporate Law Service*, paras CL10.19–10.20.

106 *Bhullar* (n 75) [41] (Jonathan Parker LJ); *Halsbury's Laws* (n 40) para 584.

107 Lista in Paolini (ed) (n 6) 96, citing *Industrial Development Consultants Ltd v Cooley* [1972] 2 All ER 162 (Assizes).

108 Companies Act 2006, s 170(2).

rule.[109] Any information relating to the wrongdoing cannot therefore be exploited by the director for their personal interests in order to gain a profit (for example, in withholding it from the company); this is the case even where the company may not have obtained an advantage (for example, a DPA as opposed to prosecution) from its use.

If a self-report and/or DPA is commercially perceived as a 'business decision',[110] a director may also be in breach of the section 175 duty where that business opportunity is exploited (for example, an incomplete self-report is made) for their personal interests. Here, the company need not be able to take a guaranteed advantage in order for a breach to arise. As such, one may read this section as including not only typical business opportunities[111] – such as contracts for sales of goods – but also opportunities to avoid incurring greater liability than may otherwise arise, even where those endeavours prove unsuccessful. This may also mean that any information, confidential or otherwise,[112] cannot be exploited by a former (or present) director in forming their own defence in personal proceedings, where the business opportunity of a DPA arises and that defence would lead to a profit as prohibited under section 170(2) (or section 175). Thus, exploitation of privileged information may give rise to a breach of the section 175 duty (**Section 7.1**).

Section 175 sets out that a director must avoid situations which may give rise to a conflict with the company's interests, and to that extent it is self-evident that the director has a duty to avoid criminal wrongdoing which may ultimately benefit them. Prior to the CA 2006 codification of duties, there was greater reliance on the 'engagements' entered into by directors in which personal interests may arise to conflict with 'those whom he is bound to protect'.[113] Codification has set out a broader scope, from "engagements" to "situations", which addresses a key point set out within the CA 2006 Explanatory Notes: 'the possibility that a director may put his own or other interests ahead of those of the company'.[114] Under section 175(4)(a), the duty to avoid conflicts of interest is not breached 'if the situation cannot reasonably be regarded as likely to give rise to a conflict of interest'. Criminal wrongdoing to which a director is involved (by virtue of their directorship) would likely be considered a situation giving rise to a conflict. Likewise, a decision not to self-report as a result of that wrongdoing, in order to protect personal interests, would likely be considered a situation giving rise to a conflict. Although the 'concept of reasonableness ... avoids a very harsh test',[115] the decision as to whether to self-report even where not involved in wrongdoing could reasonably be regarded as likely to give rise to a conflict of interests, where the director is personally concerned about share value or

109 '[The] object of the "no conflict rule" is to prevent the fiduciary from being swayed by considerations of his personal interests ... If he has no powers to exercise, then the foundation for the rule has been undermined and the rule will not apply.' *See Ultraframe (UK) Ltd v Fielding* [2005] EWHC 1638 (Ch) [1308] (Lewison J); *Chan v Zacharia* [1985] LRC (Comm) 709 (HCA) 726 (Deane J); *Halsbury's Laws* (n 40) para 590.

110 Cowley and others (n 61).

111 *Bhullar* (n 75).

112 *Berryland Books Ltd v BK Books Ltd* [2009] EWHC 1877 (Ch) [23]; *Berryland Books v Baldwin* [2010] EWCA Civ 1440; *Halsbury's Laws* (n 40) para 590.

113 '[I]t is a rule of universal application that no one having such duties to discharge shall be allowed to enter into engagements in which he has or can have a personal interest conflicting or which possibly may conflict with the interests of those whom he is bound to protect.' *See Aberdeen Ry Co v Blaikie Brothers* [1843–60] All ER Rep 249 (HL) 252 (Lord Cranworth LC); *Boardman v Phipps* [1966] 3 All ER 721 (HL) 745.

114 Explanatory Notes to the Companies Act 2006, para 298.

115 HL Deb 6 February 2006, vol 678, col GC293 (Lord Goldsmith).

other directorships,[116] for example. There are numerous circumstances in which the duty to avoid conflicts of interest is capable of applying, but application will only occur where appropriate:[117] 'flexibility of application is of the essence of the rule'.[118] In reality, where there is suspected involvement in criminal wrongdoing by a director, to the detriment of the company, this is likely to apply.

The duty is not breached where 'the matter has been authorised by the directors'[119] in accordance with the requirements set out under section 175(4)(b).[120] Directors granting such authorisation remain obliged to comply with their own directors' duties and will need to consider whether such authorisation promotes the success of the company.[121] As such authorisation is made in advance, discretion in self-reporting may be authorised in order to allow for differing circumstances, but the interests of the company will remain paramount and any resulting benefit to directors will be inadvertent. The CA 2006 Explanatory Notes suggest that authorisation can occur in relation to 'most conflicts of interest arising from *third party dealings* by the director'[122] (emphasis added), and it is likely that this emphasis is unrestrictive and authorisation for the 'matter'[123] remains as broad as section 175 in general. Authorisation to allow directors to commit criminal acts as a result of their directorship would not correspond with the authorising directors' other general duties, nor would it be valid.

6.2.3 Section 171

A company's directors manage the business and do so by exercising powers conferred upon them by the company's constitution.[124] Under section 171(1)(b), the director can only exercise those powers for the purposes for which they are conferred, and this emulates the proper purpose rule. This is somewhat interlinked with other general duties, as the proper purpose rule requires that the director act in the company's interests.[125] A director has powers for the benefit of the company and not themselves.[126] Some actions nullify a director's actual authority – authority conferred expressly by the principal – such

116 '[I]f a director wishes to take on a directorship in another company which could possibly put them in a position of conflict with the company, they are free to seek the consent of the independent directors.' *See* Simon Witney, 'Duties Owed by Shadow Directors: Closing in on the Puppet Masters?' (2016) 4 JBL 311, 320.

117 ibid.

118 *Bhullar* (n 75) [28] (Jonathan Parker LJ). *See also Boardman v Phipps* (n 113) 752; ibid 320.

119 Companies Act 2006, s 175(4)(b). Such authorisation can only be given in private companies where the constitution does not invalidate the action and in public companies where the constitution positively enables such authorisation: Companies Act 2006, s 175(5). Authorisation is effective where the relevant meeting's quorum requirement is met without counting the relevant director or any other interested director, and authorisation was agreed without their voting (or would have been should their votes be subtracted): Companies Act 2006, s 175(6).

120 ibid ss 175(5)–(6).

121 ibid s 172(1); HL Deb 9 February 2006, vol 678, col GC326 (Lord Goldsmith).

122 Explanatory Notes to the Companies Act 2006, para 302.

123 Companies Act 2006, s 175(4)(b).

124 ibid s 171; The Companies (Model Articles) Regulations 2008, SI 2008/3229, sch 1 art 3, sch 2 art 3, sch 3 art 3; The Companies (Tables A to F) Regulations 1985, SI 1985/805, table A art 70; *Halsbury's Laws* (n 40) para 581; *John Shaw & Sons (Salford) Ltd v Shaw* [1935] 2 KB 113 (CA) (Greer LJ); *Stobart Group Ltd v Tinkler* (n 74) [395].

125 *Re Smith & Fawcett Ltd* (n 40) 306 (Lord Greene MR); *Howard Smith Ltd v Ampol Petroleum Ltd* [1974] AC 821 (PC) 834; Lista in Paolini (ed) (n 6) 78.

126 Ashraf (n 19) 127.

as acting fraudulently or acting in the director's own interests.[127] Though this does not nullify the director's apparent authority in respect of the principal being bound by the director's actions,[128] this does give rise to a breach of the duty under section 171 for acting outside of its scope.

In order to determine whether a director has acted for a proper purpose, it will first be determined what the relevant power is; the proper purpose for which it was conferred; the substantial purpose for which it was exercised; and then whether that exercising was proper.[129] In *West Coast Capital (Lios) Limited*, the purpose for the director's exercising of their powers was interpreted as looking at the director's motivation, a subjective test which could be determined by objective assessment of the conduct and circumstances.[130] Dispute as to the purpose for a decision (for example, where there are multiple purposes arising) will, according to *Howard Smith Ltd v Ampol Petroleum Ltd*, entitle the court to assess objectively 'how critical or pressing or substantial an alleged requirement may have been'.[131] In *Eclairs Group Ltd v JKX Oil & Gas plc*, Lord Sumption expressed the view that a director has a duty to exercise powers "only" for the purpose for which those powers are conferred, thus giving rise to a breach of the duty wherever a director is influenced by an improper purpose, and preferred a causation analysis as opposed to determination of a single purpose.[132] Despite this, Lord Sumption stated that where the power was exercised for some proper purpose, and would have been so exercised even in the absence of any coexisting improper purpose, justice may not require that decision to be set aside.[133] Lord Sumption's causation point was a minority view and *obiter dicta*, and for now the approach in *Howard Smith Ltd* remains.[134]

The director's decision will only be set aside where made under the influence of personal interest or dishonest considerations, or where the primary or dominant purpose for which it was made was improper.[135] In respect of involvement in the underlying criminal wrongdoing, where effected by the use of powers conferred, this would fall outside the scope of authority and give rise to a breach of the section 171 duty. The decision whether to self-report will be determined by the scope of the powers conferred, but any decision made cannot be influenced by personal interests if to be considered made with a proper purpose. It may remain the case that a decision inadvertently benefits a director in respect of their personal culpability, but the governing consideration will be the interests of the company and achieving the objects of it.[136] Any decision made in this respect must not be

127 *Halsbury's Laws* (n 40) para 583.

128 *Macmillan Inc v Bishopsgate Investment Trust plc (No 3)* [1995] 3 All ER 747 (Ch) 753; *Hopkins v TL Dallas Group Ltd* [2004] EWHC 1379 (Ch) [89]; William Bowstead and others, *Bowstead & Reynolds on Agency* (17th edn, Sweet & Maxwell 2001).

129 *Halsbury's Laws* (n 40) para 583; *Howard Smith Ltd v Ampol Petroleum Ltd* (n 125); *Extrasure Travel Insurances Ltd v Scattergood* (n 43) [92]; *Quob Park Estate Ltd* [2017] EWHC 2621 (Ch).

130 [2008] CSOH 72 [21]. However, in respect of the claimant not needing to prove dishonesty or pursuit of a collateral purpose by the director, the test is objective. *See Extrasure Travel Insurances Ltd v Scattergood* (n 43) [92] (Jonathan Crow).

131 *Howard Smith Ltd v Ampol Petroleum Ltd* (n 125) 822.

132 [2015] UKSC 71 [21] (Lord Sumption).

133 ibid.

134 Adam Shaw-Mellors, 'Directors' Duties and the Proper Purpose Rule' (2016) 3 JBL 241, 245–246.

135 *Eclairs Group Ltd v JKX Oil & Gas plc* (n 132) [17] (Lord Sumption). In respect of court intervention, 'the presence of an alien purpose will not lead the court to act upon a breach of this duty unless it substantially motivated the exercise of the power'. *See Stobart Group Ltd v Tinkler* (n 74) [427].

136 Ashraf (n 19) 127.

made with the improper purpose of achieving or assisting personal interests, or under the influence of those personal interests. In this respect, a director could not answer an alleged breach by stating that they were acting in the best interests of the company.[137]

6.2.4 Section 173

The obligation not to fetter discretion prohibits a director from restricting their future ability from exercising independent judgement:[138] for example, by irreversibly transferring their managemental decision-making role to others. This is the case except where provided for by the company's constitution,[139] and does not prohibit a director from making an agreement as to the exercising of their powers.[140] The duty does not render a director unable to seek any advice; a director may be required to obtain external advice, but doing so does not absolve them from the section 173 duty and their final judgement is their own responsibility.[141] Though independence of judgement is the tone of the duty, this does not entitle a director to act for their own personal and thus independent interests. When making decisions, a director has a duty to exercise independent judgement 'in the context of him operating as a member of the board of directors' and does not therefore have a 'licence' to act independently of the board in management:[142] the duty exists in order to support the board.[143] Simply put, a director should not go behind the back of the board and thus other directors.[144]

Self-reporting to a regulator or prosecutor will be a critical decision for a company and thus unlikely a decision to be made and enforced by one member of the board alone, except where authorised. Within a smaller company whereby there is perhaps one director, that director's independent judgement will remain so as judgements made in the company's interests will be independent from any personal interests, which must be set aside. Legal advice as to self-reporting and the conducting of any internal investigation may be necessary, but directors must ensure that their independent judgement in the context of their membership of the board is central to any decision-making. Where legal advice is obtained, a director must therefore be clear in determining whether that advice is given in respect of their personal or professional capacity.

6.2.5 Section 174

Though separate duties, questions arising as to adherence with the section 172 duty in respect of decisions made (irrespective of determined breach) may also lead to questions as to whether a director exercised reasonable care, skill, and diligence under section

137 *Regentcrest Plc (In Liquidation) v Cohen* (n 41) [123] (Jonathan Parker J); *Stobart Group Ltd v Tinkler* (n 74) [428].

138 *Clark v Workman* [1920] 1 IR 107 (Ch); *Ryanair Ltd v Aer Lingus Group plc* [2011] 3 IR 69 [18]; *Halsbury's Laws* (n 40) para 587.

139 Companies Act 2006, s 173(2)(b); Explanatory Notes to the Companies Act 2006, para 316.

140 Companies Act 2006, s 173(2)(a); *Thorby v Goldberg* [1964] HCA 41; *Fulham Football Club Ltd v Cabra Estates plc* [1994] 1 BCLC 363 (CA) 392 (Neill LJ); *Halsbury's Laws* (n 40) para 587.

141 HL Deb 6 February 2006 (n 115) col GC282 (Lord Goldsmith).

142 *Stobart Group Ltd v Tinkler* (n 74) [413].

143 ibid [413]–[414].

144 *Minmar (929) Ltd v Khalatschi* [2011] EWHC 1159 (Ch); *Re Assured Logistics Solutions Ltd* [2011] EWHC 3029 (Ch) [32]; ibid [405(iii)].

174(1).[145] The standard of care expected under section 174 reflects that under section 214(4) of the Insolvency Act 1986,[146] which was followed prior to the implementation of the CA 2006.[147] This sets out both an objective and subjective test,[148] to determine the general knowledge, skill, and experience to be reasonably expected of a person in the director's position, and the director's own general knowledge, skill, and experience.[149] A director has a continuing duty to 'acquire and maintain a sufficient knowledge and understanding of the company's business'[150] even where delegating authority to others.[151] In this respect, directors must adequately monitor and supervise those to whom they have delegated authority.[152] A director may be required to obtain external advice irrespective of the duty under section 173 to exercise independent judgement, and this may be the case in exercising the duty under section 174.[153]

When considering whether to self-report, how extensive a self-report should be, and the conducting of an internal investigation, a director may be required to obtain legal advice in order to sufficiently satisfy prosecutors and/or regulators – this will particularly be the case where self-reporting in the hope of entering DPA negotiations. In such circumstances, a director cannot simply accept advice or information without question and should take a critical and probing viewpoint;[154] care should also be taken to understand the capacity in which such advice is provided (personal or professional). The director's own knowledge may influence their continuing involvement in the investigative and reporting process and decision making, and this may thus impact the director's ability to comply with section 174 where not duly considered. It was set out in *Cohen v Selby*[155] that there must be a sufficient causal link between the breach of duty and loss, which will have relevance not only where directors are involved in the underlying wrongdoing, but also where there is a failure to meet the expectations of prosecutors and/or regulators.

6.3 Directors' liability

6.3.1 Breach of directors' general duties

Breach or threatened breach of the general duties under the CA 2006 bears the same consequences as the corresponding common law rule or equitable principle.[156] Each duty, except that under section 174, is enforceable as a fiduciary duty owed by a director to the

145 Explanatory Notes to the Companies Act 2006, para 328; Hall and Milne in Smerdon (ed) (n 17) 663.

146 'I want to emphasise the point that it is not making a change from what is already the common law.' *See* HL Deb 6 February 2006 (n 115) col GC284 (Lord Goldsmith).

147 *Norman v Theodore Goddard (a firm)* (n 20); *Re D'Jan of London Ltd* [1994] 1 BCLC 561 (Ch) 563 (Hoffmann LJ).

148 *Re D'Jan of London Ltd* (n 147) 563 (Hoffmann LJ).

149 Companies Act 2006, s 174(2). '[The] intention is to ensure that a minimum standard of conduct is required of all directors.' *See* Hall and Milne in Smerdon (ed) (n 17) 664.

150 *Re Barings plc (No 5)* [1999] 1 BCLC 433 (Ch) 436 (Parker J).

151 The Companies (Model Articles) Regulations 2008, SI 2008/3229, art 5.

152 Involving a non-executive director: *Equitable Life Assurance Society v Bowley* [2003] EWHC 2263 (Comm).

153 *Hedger (Liquidator of Pro4sport Ltd) v Adams* [2015] EWHC 2540 (Ch) [46].

154 *Weavering Capital (UK) Ltd (In Liquidation) v Peterson* [2013] EWCA Civ 71 [34] (McCombe LJ).

155 [2001] 1 BCLC 176 (CA) 182; *Halsbury's Laws* (n 40) para 588.

156 Companies Act 2006, s 178(1).

company.[157] The consequence of a breach of the duty under section 174 is damages.[158] In respect of the fiduciary duties,[159] the CA 2006 Explanatory Notes set out some examples of the consequences of breach: payment of damages or compensation upon corporate loss, restoration of corporate property, account of profits, and contract recission (where failure to disclose interest arises).[160] Claims for breach of a fiduciary duty are subject to the six-year limitation period set out in the Limitation Act 1980, except where related to fraud or recovery of company property or profits from it.[161] Conduct constituting a breach of duty may be treated otherwise where prior authorisation is obtained. The duty to avoid conflicts of interest (and conflicts of duties)[162] under section 175 may be authorised in accordance with the company's constitution,[163] and requirements as to quorum and voting are met.[164] Where authorisation occurs, the underlying transaction need not be set aside.[165] A director will not be in breach of the section 175 duty where acting in accordance with the company's articles of association,[166] and shareholders may be able to provide the necessary authorisation.[167]

Where already committed, section 239 of the CA 2006 permits ratification of conduct (amounting to negligence, default, breach of duty, or breach of trust)[168] by shareholder resolution.[169] The concerned director and persons connected to the director are not eligible members in respect of voting in favour of the resolution,[170] and ratification will render the relevant conduct free from future claims by the company.[171] Alternatively, on application to court by a director, the court may relieve the director wholly or in part from liability (existing or which may arise) for breach of duty (or negligence, default, or breach of trust) where the director is determined to have acted honestly and reasonably, and ought fairly

157 ibid s 178(2); Explanatory Notes to the Companies Act 2006, para 305.

158 *Brown v Bashir* [2021] EWHC 337 (Ch) [31].

159 A company director is a fiduciary in respect of the company: *Bristol and West Building Society v Mothew* [1998] Ch 1 (CA) 16. *See also Girardet v Crease & Co* (1987) 11 BCLR (2d) 361, 362 (Southin J); *Henderson v Merrett Syndicates Ltd (No 1)* [1995] 2 AC 145 (HL) 205 (Lord Browne-Wilkinson).

160 Explanatory Notes to the Companies Act 2006, para 322.

161 Breach of fiduciary duty claims are typically covered by the limitation period as under: Limitation Act 1980, s 21; *Gwembe Valley Development Co Ltd v Koshy (No 3)* [2003] EWCA Civ 1048. No limitation period under section 21 applies to actions in respect of 'any fraud or fraudulent breach of trust to which the trustee was a party or privy', including deliberate and dishonest concealment of profits: Limitation Act 1980, s 21(1)(a); *Gwembe Valley Development Co Ltd v Koshy (No 3)* [2003] EWCA Civ 1048. No limitation period under section 21 applies to actions to recover company property or proceeds from it: Limitation Act 1980, s 21(1)(b); *JJ Harrison (Properties) Ltd v Harrison* [2001] EWCA Civ 1467; *Burnden Holdings (UK) v Fielding* [2018] UKSC 14. *See also Halsbury's Laws* (n 40) para 599.

162 Companies Act 2006, s 175(7).

163 In private companies where nothing in the constitution invalidates such authorisation, and in public companies where the constitution provides for such authorisation. *See* ibid s 175(5).

164 Requirement as to the quorum at the relevant meeting must be met without counting the concerned director or other interested directors, and the matter must be agreed to without the aforementioned parties having voted (or would have been agreed if their votes had not been counted). *See* ibid s 175(6).

165 ibid s 180(1).

166 ibid s 180(4)(b); Explanatory Notes to the Companies Act 2006, para 316.

167 Subject to any rule of law. *See* Companies Act 2006, s 180(4)(a); Explanatory Notes to the Companies Act 2006, para 316.

168 Companies Act 2006, s 239(1).

169 ibid s 239(2).

170 ibid ss 239(3)–(4).

171 Relating to claims brought by the company itself or by way of derivative action. *See* Hall and Milne in Smerdon (ed) (n 17) 664.

to be excused having regard to all the circumstances of the case.[172] It has been argued that this is more likely to occur where the consequences of personal liability 'would be unduly harsh, and disproportionate'.[173] This is unlikely to occur in circumstances whereby a director has been involved in criminal wrongdoing or where a director has dishonestly acted for personal interests in leading or contributing to decisions based on self-reporting.

6.3.2 Claims for breach of duty

As duties under the CA 2006 are owed to the company, it follows that only the company can enforce them.[174] According to Hall and Milne, the unitary board system of the UK means that claims are rarely brought by companies against their current directors. More likely than such inward claims are claims by a company against former directors (which become increasingly likely where implicated directors are ousted in pursuit of a DPA).[175] Former directors may also be subject to claims brought by liquidators and administrators where the company is insolvent;[176] a liquidator may conduct an inquiry into directors' conduct and has powers to compel presence at interview in order to do so.[177] It may be that information is thereafter disclosed by insolvency practitioners where criminal liability is suspected.[178] A derivative claim (also known as derivative action) may be brought by one or more shareholders against a director (or former director)[179] to enforce a right vested in the company and in seeking relief on its behalf,[180] in respect of negligence, default, breach of duty, or breach of trust (actual or proposed).[181] Permission of the court must be granted in order to make a derivative claim[182] and will not be granted where the conduct has been authorised or ratified by the company,[183] where a person acting under section 172 would not proceed with the claim,[184] and where the claim is made for a political point.[185]

---

172 Companies Act 2006, s 1157.

173 Hall and Milne in Smerdon (ed) (n 17) 665.

174 Companies Act 2006, s 170(1); Explanatory Notes to the Companies Act 2006, para 307.

175 Hall and Milne in Smerdon (ed) (n 17) 665. The enforceability of a duty upon alleged breach or threatened breach will often depend on the circumstances, and this remains the case for former or current directors and for shadow directors. A minority shareholder may petition the court under section 994 for some order of restraint against the company where it considers that its interests have been unfairly prejudiced, and this claim may involve a director by virtue of their position as director or shareholder (where applicable), but such a claim would not be against a director personally for breach of duty. *See* Companies Act 2006, s 994.

176 For breach of duty, claims may be brought against a director by a liquidator or administrator as if brought by the company under: Insolvency Act 1986, s 212(1). *See also* Insolvency Act 1986, ss 213–214; Small Business, Enterprise and Employment Act 2015, s 117; Hall and Milne in Smerdon (ed) (n 17) 666.

177 Insolvency Act 1986, s 236.

178 'It is common practice for insolvency practitioners to report suspected criminal offences and thereafter to provide relevant documentation supporting this.' *See* The Insolvency Service, '16. Insolvency Practitioners Providing Support in Criminal Investigations and Proceedings' (*The Insolvency Service*, 2021) <https://www.insolvencydirect.bis.gov.uk/insolvencyprofessionandlegislation/dearip/dearipmill/chapter20.htm> accessed 15 May 2021. 'In any type of liquidation, the liquidator must report any criminal offences apparently committed in relation to the company by any past or present officers or members': Sarah Worthington, *Sealy and Worthington's Texts, Cases and Materials in Company Law* (11th edn, Oxford University Press 2016) 871. *See also* Insolvency Act 1986, s 218.

179 Companies Act 2006, s 260(5)(a).

180 ibid s 260(1); Explanatory Notes to the Companies Act 2006, para 483.

181 Companies Act 2006, s 260(3).

182 ibid s 261(1).

183 ibid ss 263(2)(b)–(c).

184 ibid s 263(2)(a).

185 Hall and Milne in Smerdon (ed) (n 17) 667–668.

6.3.3 *Related claims*

In respect of conduct which may be regarded as a breach of the general duties under the CA 2006, other liability may arise: compliance or otherwise with the duties does not extinguish the requirement to abide by all other laws.[186] Of the individual prosecutions arising from UK DPAs, offences relating to corruption and bribery (conspiracy to commit the relevant wrongdoing) and fraud have been prevalent. As yet, no individual prosecution of an implicated director within a DPA-agreeing company has produced a conviction, but financial liabilities in defence still arise. However, where convicted of an offence in relation to the running of the company, a director may face disqualification under the Company Directors Disqualification Act 1986 for a period of up to 15 years.[187] Actions by regulators may also arise.[188] Notably, a company director will not typically be liable to third parties whilst acting in their capacity of director, as the company is a separate legal person at law.[189] However, in circumstances where the corporate veil is lifted/pierced and where the company is no longer considered to be a separate legal person, the director may incur personal liability.[190] A director may also incur personal liability to a third party when they act in a personal capacity by way of an assumption of responsibility.[191]

186 Explanatory Notes to the Companies Act 2006, para 314.

187 'The court may make a disqualification order against a person where he is convicted of an indictable offence (whether on indictment or summarily) in connection with the promotion, formation, management, liquidation or striking off of a company'. *See* Company Directors Disqualification Act 1986, s 2(1).

188 A director of an FCA regulated company as an FCA Approved Person will be required to adhere to the FCA's Principles for Approved Persons. *See* FCA, 'FCA Handbook' (*Financial Conduct Authority*, 9 September 2005) <https://www.handbook.fca.org.uk/handbook/SIFA/7/7.html?date=2006-08-30> accessed 19 April 2021, SIFA 7.7.

189 '[T]he company is ex hypothesi a distinct legal persona.' *See Salomon v A Salomon & Co Ltd* [1897] AC 22 (HL) 42 (Lord Herschell).

190 *Gilford Motor Ltd v Horne* [1933] Ch 935 (CA) has long been considered a pinpoint in the introduction of the veil of incorporation as a metaphor for the separate legal personality principle which can, in certain circumstances, be circumvented (or "lifted") to attribute liability to individuals and 'disregard the legal ownership of the business'. *See* Gregory Allan, 'To Pierce or Not to Pierce? A Doctrinal Reappraisal of Judicial Responses to Improper Exploitation of the Corporate Form' [2018] JBL 559, 572.

191 *Williams v Natural Life Health Foods Ltd* [1998] 1 WLR 830 (HL) 835–837 (Lord Steyn); Christian Witting, 'Justifying Liability to Third Parties for Negligent Misstatements' (2000) 20(4) OJLS 615, 625–626; Financial Services and Markets Act 2000, s 90; Harry Edwards and Jon Ford, 'The Securities Litigation Review: United Kingdom – England & Wales' (*Herbert Smith Freehills LLP*, 4 June 2020) <https://thelawreviews.co.uk/title/the-securities-litigation-review/united-kingdom-england--wales> accessed 15 May 2021.

CHAPTER 7

Right to defence

When DPA negotiations arise, an implicated individual at such a senior level as director is likely to be required to leave the company (even if not legally: practically and realistically), particularly if that individual is facing prosecution. Where an implicated director is able to remain and the company is able to obtain a DPA, a director facing prosecution would be in a difficult position in respect of their own defence. A common term in all UK DPAs is that public statements made by the company and its employees (as authorised by the company) which are contrary to the DPA (including the statement of facts) may constitute a breach of the agreement. Crucially, the term states that this does not extend to 'any present or former director … in the course of any criminal or civil proceedings instituted against or by the said individual'.[1] However, more recent DPAs have gone further to include the caveat: 'unless such individual is speaking on behalf of [the company]'.[2] In this respect, the decision whether the public statement made by an individual should be imputed to the company, for the purpose of determining breach of the DPA, remains at the 'sole discretion' of the prosecutor.[3]

Prima facie, a director would be able to put forward a full defence without prejudice to the company. However, it remains at the prosecutor's discretion to determine whether that individual is speaking on their own behalf or on behalf of the company. This becomes more complicated in respect of directors, 'the directing mind and will'[4] of the company, in comparison to lower-level employees. This could, therefore, mean that a director in the defence of their own prosecution could expose the company to DPA breach proceedings and follow-on litigation, as well as exposing themselves to the follow-on litigation which may personally ensue from such circumstances (for example, for breach of directors'

1 *See for example* Serious Fraud Office, 'Deferred Prosecution Agreement – SFO v ICBC SB PLC' (*Serious Fraud Office*, 3 September 2019) <https://www.sfo.gov.uk/download/deferred-prosecution-agreement-sfo-v-icbc-sb-plc/?wpdmdl=7600> accessed 15 May 2020, para 36.

2 Serious Fraud Office, 'Airline Services Limited Deferred Prosecution Agreement: ASL Signed DPA (Without Indictment)' (*Serious Fraud Office*, 30 October 2020) <https://www.sfo.gov.uk/download/airline-services-limited-deferred-prosecution-agreement/> accessed 2 November 2020, para 29. Alternatively, if the company is deemed to authorise the contradictory statement. *See* Serious Fraud Office, 'Amec Foster Wheeler Energy Limited – Deferred Prosecution Agreement' (*Serious Fraud Office*, 2 July 2021) <https://www.sfo.gov.uk/download/amec-foster-wheeler-energy-limited-deferred-prosecution-agreement/> accessed 2 July 2021, para 48.

3 Serious Fraud Office, 'Airline Services Limited Deferred Prosecution Agreement: ASL Signed DPA (Without Indictment)' (n 2) para 29.

4 *Tesco Supermarkets Ltd v Nattrass* [1972] AC 153 (HL) 180; *HL Bolton (Engineering) Co Ltd v TJ Graham & Sons Ltd* [1957] 1 QB 159 (CA) 172 (Denning LJ); *Lennard's Carrying Co Ltd v Asiatic Petroleum Co Ltd* [1915] AC 705 (HL) 713 (Viscount Haldane LC).

DOI: 10.4324/9781003456964-9

duties). Whilst a DPA-specific formal leniency policy does not exist in respect of individuals implicated in a corporate DPA (or in the preceding investigation), the extent of an individual's protection will largely be governed by their ability to put forward a defence in their own proceedings. As a starting point, the term of the DPA regarding contrary statements will not apply where the individual is no longer an employee of the company, unless deemed to be authorised by the company.[5] However, exposures may remain.

7.1 Legal professional privilege

A key potential obstruction to both a company's ability to negotiate a DPA and an individual's ability to present a good defence in their respective cases is a claim of "legal professional privilege" ("LPP"). Privilege may, depending on the circumstances, be claimed by the party under investigation or by a third party. LPP encompasses both legal advice privilege and litigation privilege.[6]

7.1.1 An individual's access to defence

A company may assert LPP over certain confidential communications and/or documentation created prior to or during DPA negotiations, which may impact an individual's defence in their own criminal proceedings. The rationale for the company's decision may be to avoid further litigation against it, such as civil claims. Where documentation is brought in front of the court, privilege is often lost and thus third-party litigants may be empowered to bring claims on the basis of that further evidence, and overseas prosecutors or regulators may elect to pursue proceedings. Under "legal advice privilege", privilege can be asserted over communication between a client and lawyer where the dominant purpose of that communication is seeking or obtaining legal advice. "Litigation privilege" is more encompassing and can be claimed over communications between not only clients and lawyers but also third parties, where that communication arises for the dominant purpose of obtaining legal advice or information in respect of litigation.[7] Such litigation must be adversarial (not investigative or inquisitorial) and in reasonable contemplation or in progress at the time of the communication. DPA negotiations would likely be considered adversarial as negotiations take place with no guarantee of approval and on the basis that the alternative avenue will likely be prosecution, thus placing prosecution (deferred or otherwise) in reasonable contemplation.[8] Privileged communications can be shared with

5 'If the SFO determines that a public statement by AFWEL or by any person it believes to be authorised by AFWEL contradicts in whole or in part a matter described in the Statement of Facts, the SFO shall so notify AFWEL. If AFWEL publicly repudiates such statement(s) within five (5) Business Days after notification by the SFO, no breach of the Agreement will have occurred. If AFWEL does not so publicly repudiate such statement(s), the SFO may act in accordance with [the paragraphs relating to breach of the agreement].' *See* Serious Fraud Office, 'Amec Foster Wheeler Energy Limited – Deferred Prosecution Agreement' (n 2) para 48.

6 Legal advice privilege and litigation privilege are limbs of the same privilege: legal professional privilege. *See R (on the application of Jet2.com Ltd) v Civil Aviation Authority (Law Society of England and Wales intervening)* [2020] EWCA Civ 35 [71], [95].

7 *Three Rivers District Council v Governor and Company of the Bank of England (No 6)* [2004] UKHL 48 [27].

8 '[W]e are not sure that every SFO manifestation of concern would properly be regarded as adversarial litigation, but when the SFO specifically makes clear to the company the prospect of its criminal prosecution … and legal advisers are engaged to deal with that situation, as in the present case, there is a clear ground for

a third party within a "limited waiver", allowing information sharing without a loss of privilege against the wider world,[9] though can cause wider issues where overseas jurisdictions do not recognise the concept.[10]

The case of *R (on the application of AL) v Serious Fraud Office*[11] ("*AL*"), brought on behalf of former Sarclad executives (with some as interested parties), focussed on privilege and DPA investigations and negotiations. Comments made in this respect were *obiter*, as the High Court was not deemed to be the appropriate forum for dispute, but nonetheless give useful and extensive indication. In determining whether to self-report, Sarclad (previously known as "XYZ Ltd") instructed an external law firm to conduct an internal investigation, during which time interviews were held with four senior executives and notes of the interviews were taken.[12] These notes formed the basis of the decision to self-report to the SFO, but Sarclad claimed privilege over the notes when they were thereafter sought by the prosecutor. Sarclad instead agreed that the external law firm would provide an "oral proffer" of the interview notes, amounting to an oral summary. The SFO was able to take notes and disclose those notes to the implicated individuals under criminal investigation. The individuals then sought disclosure of the original interview notes and did so through the SFO. However, when the SFO again approached Sarclad, it met a maintained claim of privilege.

Mr Justice Green in *AL* opined that the oral proffer constituted a waiver of the interview notes which would have thus allowed their disclosure to the SFO and further to the individuals; it is thus likely that such an approach of refusal will not be allowed in future cases. Two lines of argument were provided as to why Sarclad would not have a proper claim of privilege in the circumstances. Firstly, even if a limited waiver of the interview notes was made in respect of the SFO alone, there was a real possibility that there would be onward disclosure to the individuals and that those individuals were facing prosecution. Secondly, a waiver for a limited purpose would have included the onward disclosure to the individuals on the basis of this being an integral part of the process and squarely in contemplation.[13] The waiver could be implied on the basis of there existing a sufficiently close nexus.[14]

Where a company engages in DPA negotiations with a prosecutor, or cooperates in an investigation in the hope that a DPA may be offered, an inherent part of the process is the understanding that implicated individuals will also be subject to criminal investigation and (where appropriate) prosecution in a personal capacity. The company's 'genuinely proactive' approach to cooperation will be considered in line with its assistance in respect

contending that criminal prosecution is in reasonable contemplation.' *See Director of the Serious Fraud Office v Eurasian Natural Resources Corporation Ltd (Law Society intervening)* [2018] EWCA Civ 2006 [96].

9 *Property Alliance Group Ltd v Royal Bank of Scotland plc* [2015] EWHC 1557 (Ch).

10 'Under New York law ... disclosure of a privileged document, even for a limited purpose, gives rise to a loss of privilege': Kit Jarvis, 'Cross-Border Privilege Issues Facing Financial Institutions' (2008) 23(4) JIBFL 179.

11 [2018] EWHC 856 (Admin).

12 ibid [3].

13 ibid [117].

14 *Belhaj v Director of Public Prosecutions* [2018] EWHC 513 (Admin) [31]–[32]; Laura Ford and Shabaz Ahmed, 'Regulatory Enforcement and Privilege – Waiver, Content, Cherry-Picking' (*DLA Piper*, 7 October 2020) <https://www.dlapiper.com/en/us/insights/publications/2020/10/regulatory-enforcement-and-privilege/> accessed 28 March 2021.

of the investigation into individuals.[15] Thus, the DPA Code sets out that a 'strong' factor in favour of prosecution over DPA (in respect of a self-report) is 'withhold[ing] material that would jeopardise an effective investigation and where appropriate prosecution of those individuals'.[16] The terms of negotiations will set out disclosure obligations under the Criminal Procedure and Investigations Act ("CPIA") 1996 in respect of implicated individuals. Further, within the company's pre-negotiation confidentiality undertaking with the prosecutor (which forms the basis of the DPA negotiations), there is a mutual understanding that the fact of DPA negotiations and information and material exchanged remains confidential, with one exception being disclosure required by law.[17] The company will thereafter agree within the approved DPA terms to cooperate in the investigation into and prosecution of relevant individuals.

There is a clear understanding that individuals will be investigated, and companies will be required to cooperate in assisting such investigations. It is also clear that any information disclosed by the company during an investigation (in anticipation of DPA negotiations) and/or DPA negotiations – even under a limited waiver to the prosecutor alone – is disclosed subject to a recognition of the prosecutor's duty of onward disclosure to implicated individuals (thus falling within the scope of the limited waiver). A company would thus be unlikely to be able to obstruct the prosecutor's disclosure obligations by making a claim of privilege, as in *AL*. The prosecutor cannot force a company to make a waiver and directly penalise the company's decision not to do so. However, such enforcement would not be necessary in these circumstances since the company's limited waiver will have been made with onward disclosure 'squarely in contemplation'[18] and in recognition of those disclosure obligations (within the terms of negotiations and/or pre-negotiation confidentiality undertaking).

Corporate obstruction of the prosecutor's disclosure obligations may be considered an insufficient claim to privilege (since the scope of the limited waiver entails such circumstance), and also a breach of the pre-negotiation confidentiality undertaking. As the latter undertaking is contractual in nature (**Section 18.4.1.3**), between the company and the prosecutor, the prosecutor could in theory bring an action against the company for specific performance to ensure that disclosure obligations to the individual are met, within the parameters of the limited waiver. The individual would be able to make use of the material in support of their own defence, which may impact the company's privilege as it may be lost when appearing in open court.[19] Whilst a company cannot be refused a DPA or be

15 'Co-operation will include identifying relevant witnesses, disclosing their accounts and the documents shown to them. Where practicable it will involve making the witnesses available for interview when requested. It will further include providing a report in respect of any internal investigation including source documents.' *See* Crown Prosecution Service and Serious Fraud Office, 'Deferred Prosecution Agreements Code of Practice' (*Crown Prosecution Service*, 11 February 2014) <https://www.cps.gov.uk/sites/default/files/documents/publications/dpa_cop.pdf> accessed 9 June 2020, para 2.8.2(i).

16 ibid para 2.9.1.

17 ibid para 3.9.1; Serious Fraud Office, 'Deferred Prosecution Agreements' (*Serious Fraud Office*, 23 October 2020) <https://www.sfo.gov.uk/publications/guidance-policy-and-protocols/sfo-operational-handbook/deferred-prosecution-agreements/> accessed 23 October 2020.

18 *R (on the application of AL) v Serious Fraud Office* (n 11) [117].

19 The saving of time and costs is an inherent part of DPAs, and the lack of jury trial means that evidence is not presented to the court in the same way. Instead, the company and prosecutor negotiate a statement of facts which forms part of the application to court for DPA approval. That statement of facts may contain references to or excerpts from evidence gathered during the criminal investigation, which may include material disclosed to the prosecutor under a limited waiver. The extent to which that privilege is impacted by the subsequent

held to be in breach of the terms of a DPA for a decision not to waive privilege, it may be the case that a DPA is refused or determined to be breached on the basis of the adverse implications and consequences arising from that decision.[20]

In respect of documentation created in reasonable contemplation of litigation and disclosed on the basis of a limited waiver by a company to a prosecutor (which would likely include documentation created in anticipation of a self-report and/or DPA negotiations), an individual would likely be able to seek disclosure of such documentation within the parameters of that limited waiver and the prosecutor's disclosure obligations. This would include documentation which would assist the individual's defence and/or undermine the prosecution's case against it,[21] and could therefore include internal interview notes, internal investigation and self-reports, evidence passed to prosecutors, and so forth. In reverse, a (former) director may be able to assert LPP to obstruct the company's disclosure of certain documentation to the prosecutor, which will be analysed hereon.

7.1.2 The company's ability to obtain a DPA

Where a company and its director(s) instruct a lawyer under a joint retainer, or where the company and director share a joint interest in the subject matter of the communication (of either one or both parties with a lawyer) at the time of its creation (and that communication arises in furtherance of the joint purpose or interest), "joint privilege" may arise.[22] Where joint privilege arises, all parties must consent to a waiver. That joint privilege sits 'within the ambit of legal professional privilege'.[23] In cases of a joint retainer, joint privilege will arise where the director has dealt with the lawyer in a personal capacity, and not as a representative of the company.[24] Where a joint retainer does not arise, the director will need to evidentially establish that communication made with the lawyer in seeking advice was done in a personal capacity (not as a representative of the company); the individual made their seeking advice in a personal capacity clear to the lawyer, and the lawyer knew or ought to have appreciated that they were communicating in the director's personal capacity; those with whom the joint privilege was claimed knew or ought to have appreciated the legal position; and the communication was confidential.[25]

---

publication of the statement of facts and reference to it in open court in the final hearing depends on the extent to which the privileged material is assimilated into the statement of facts. A purely narrative reference to legal advice, such as a simple statement that legal advice was sought or obtained, does not constitute a waiver. *See PCP Capital Partners LLP v Barclays Bank Plc* [2020] EWHC 1393 (Comm) [49]. Similarly, where a document is referred to in open court, its confidentiality is not necessarily lost where that reference does not sufficiently constitute an 'exposure of the document to the public' warranting loss of the confidentiality of the document as a whole. *See SL Claimants v Tesco PLC* [2019] EWHC 3315 (Ch) [42].

20 'An organisation that does not waive privilege and provide witness accounts does not attain the corresponding factor against prosecution that is found in the DPA Code [para 2.8.2(1)] but will not be penalised by the SFO.' *See* Serious Fraud Office, 'SFO Operational Handbook: Corporate Co-Operation Guidance' (*Serious Fraud Office*, 16 August 2019) <https://www.sfo.gov.uk/publications/guidance-policy-and-protocols/sfo-operational-handbook/corporate-co-operation-guidance/> accessed 10 August 2020, 5. *See also Eurasian Natural Resources Corporation Ltd* (n 8) [117].

21 Criminal Procedure and Investigations Act 1996, ss 3(1), 7A(2).

22 *R (on the application of Ford) v Financial Services Authority* [2011] EWHC 2583 (Admin) [16].

23 *Hellenic Mutual War Risks Association (Bermuda) Ltd v Harrison (The Sagheera)* [1997] 1 Lloyd's Rep 160 (QB); ibid [17].

24 *R (on the application of Ford) v Financial Services Authority* (n 22) [40].

25 ibid [40]. Joint privilege shared between a company and its director(s) may arise where an internal lawyer is engaged. In such cases, it will be necessary to determine the role performed by the internal lawyer

A director or former director may claim that certain documentation is privileged in order to prevent the company from making certain disclosures to a prosecutor. In doing so, a (former) director may protect their own interests but find that the company's ability to self-report or negotiate a DPA is significantly reduced. Waiver of privilege is not a requirement in order to successfully negotiate a DPA but is a clear indicator of cooperation, and the adverse implication of not doing so may mean that the prosecutor is unable to identify the full extent of the offending as required under the DPA Code.[26] Waiver of privilege was not made in the first two UK DPAs (nor in the sixth)[27] of the 13 so far agreed and published; however the adverse impact will naturally differ from case to case. Where a refusal to waive privilege does lead to a failure to negotiate a DPA (albeit indirectly) and that refusal was at the instruction of a director in furtherance of their own interests, the (serving) director may be deemed to have acted in breach of their directors' duties.

Under the iniquity exception, a claim to LPP will be overridden where a lawyer is instructed for the purpose of furthering or concealing an "iniquity".[28] That iniquity might be a crime (the exception is sometimes referred to as the "fraud" exception),[29] or simply conduct which has gone 'beyond ... a civil wrong'.[30] In the recent case of *Barrowfen Properties Ltd v Patel*, the scope of the exception was confirmed to apply to alleged breaches of directors' duties where those allegations 'involve fraud, dishonesty, bad faith or sharp practice or where the director consciously or deliberately prefers his or her own interests over the interests of the company and does so "under a cloak of secrecy"'.[31] The iniquity exception applies regardless of whether the lawyer is aware of the wrongful purpose.[32] Where it is determined that a (former) director has instructed a lawyer in order to further or conceal the original criminal wrongdoing forming the subject of DPA negotiations, or in order to obstruct the internal investigation, self-reporting, or DPA negotiation process in breach of their directors' duties, the iniquity exception may be triggered in order to override the individual's claim of privilege. This will mean that the company will be entitled to waive the "joint" privilege during the investigation/negotiations without obtaining that director's consent. However, if the privilege is shared with others, their consent will remain necessary prior to any waiver.

---

in respect of the advice and/or documentation in which privilege is claimed. An internal lawyer acting as a "rubber stamp" on communications or recorder of discussions, for example, will not necessarily give rise to a claim of privilege. The internal lawyer will need to play an active role in providing legal advice, not simply commercial advice, in order for privilege to arise.

26 Crown Prosecution Service and Serious Fraud Office, 'Deferred Prosecution Agreements Code of Practice' (n 15) para 2.2(ii).

27 The first, second, and sixth DPAs are with Standard Bank, Sarclad Ltd, and Güralp Systems Ltd, respectively. It is unclear whether a waiver was made in the thirteenth (with Entain plc), but the existing documentation does not appear to suggest so.

28 *Ventouris v Mountain* [1991] 1 WLR 607 (CA) 611 (Bingham LJ).

29 *Kuwait Airways Corpn v Iraqi Airways Co (No 6)* [2005] EWCA Civ 286 [14] (Longmore LJ).

30 *BBGP Managing General Partner Ltd v Babcock & Brown Global Partners* [2010] EWHC 2176 (Ch) [62]; *Barrowfen Properties Ltd v Patel* [2020] EWHC 2536 (Ch) [33].

31 The iniquity exception applied in defeating the defendants' claim to LPP and thus forced disclosure, where five allegations of breach of directors' duties were deemed to have a (very) strong *prima facie* case. *See Barrowfen Properties Ltd v Patel* (n 30) [35].

32 ibid [24].

7.1.3 Company obstructing the individual's case

Where joint privilege arises, a company may similarly be able to obstruct an individual's waiver of relevant documentation in order to formulate their defence. This will be particularly relevant to documentation not disclosed to the prosecutor during DPA negotiations. Such an obstruction may be in the company's perceived interests where there is a threat of civil or regulatory proceedings, or criminal proceedings overseas. There is increasing expectation of companies to be fully transparent and cooperative throughout the DPA process and, though waiver of privilege cannot be forced by prosecutors, a decision not to do so may be considered a breach of the terms of a DPA or DPA negotiations where the adverse impact is that those terms are not met.[33] Under the standard terms of a DPA, a company will be required to cooperate in the investigation into and (where appropriate) prosecution of individuals, and such actions may be deemed as irreconcilable with this obligation.

Typically, disclosures made by the SFO to the company will be for the purpose of allowing the company to obtain legal advice: principally as to the desirability of entering DPA negotiations or entering a DPA.[34] As such, despite the SFO being a legal professional, it is highly unlikely that the legal advice will come from the prosecutor, so as to attract LPP. Such disclosures and information exchanged between the prosecutor and company will fall within the scope of the confidentiality undertaking signed pre-negotiations, thus attracting confidentiality by other means.

7.2 Privilege against self-incrimination

The Human Rights Act ("HRA") 1998 incorporates the European Convention on Human Rights ("ECHR") into UK law and the right to have a hearing that corresponds with the principles of fairness – the right to a fair trial – can be found under Article 6.[35] The right to a fair trial encompasses the privilege against self-incrimination and the right to silence, which are to be distinguished from each other. Both concern the right of an individual to refuse to speak and, as a result, avoid self-incrimination. The adverse effects of each right differ: the right to silence concerns the inferences drawn at trial from an individual's choice to remain silent during interview or the trial process, whereas the privilege against self-incrimination concerns situations where an individual is legally compelled to provide answers or material that may incriminate them.[36] The right to silence has been somewhat qualified as being confined to questioning, by Lord Mustill in *R v Director of Serious Fraud Office, ex p Smith*.[37] The privilege against self-incrimination remains more general: one is not obliged to act in a way that may self-incriminate.[38]

The long-standing privilege against self-incrimination has been ascribed two well-known common law definitions: 'a person is not bound to answer a question which may

33 The decision to pursue a company for breach may involve a 'a multifactorial and complex judgment call'. *See R (on the application of AL) v Serious Fraud Office* (n 11) [45].

34 Serious Fraud Office, 'Deferred Prosecution Agreements' (n 17).

35 Human Rights Act 1998, sch 1 pt 1 art 6.

36 Ian Dennis, *The Law of Evidence* (6th edn, Sweet & Maxwell 2017) 154.

37 [1993] AC 1 (HL) 30–32 (Lord Mustill).

38 Dennis (n 36) 156–157.

render him liable to punishment, penalty or forfeiture',[39] and 'a man is not bound to provide evidence against himself by being forced to answer questions or produce documents'.[40] The common law privilege encompasses both civil and criminal law. The landmark case of *ex p Smith* concerned the removal of the privilege in pre-trial criminal investigations (including after the individual has been charged) where compulsive powers are invoked by the SFO in order to compel an individual to act in a way which may be contrary to the privilege.[41] Where the privilege is removed during pre-trial criminal investigations, the question of admissibility of material disclosed under the compulsive power is raised – considering whether the operation of the compulsive power has consequential adverse effects on an individual forced to surrender their privilege against self-incrimination.

Section 2 of the Criminal Justice Act 1987 ("CJA 1987") confers powers ("section 2 powers") on the SFO to compel individuals to 'answer questions or otherwise furnish information'[42] under interview or 'produce … any specified documents'[43] on issues surrounding serious or complex fraud, and that individual need not be the person under investigation. Crucially, section 2 powers cannot be used to compel a person to waive LPP.[44] Use of section 2 powers may be to expedite the investigative process or to ensure that all necessary information is exposed: both undoubtedly saving valuable time and money. As section 2 makes cooperation with the SFO's requests compulsory during the investigative stage, refusal of an individual to comply will be considered an act of contempt of court and dealt with accordingly.[45] Any compulsion forced on an individual by law tends to raise human rights concerns; where an individual is forced to speak under interview, the privilege against self-incrimination and encompassing right to a fair trial appear to be at risk. This impact of section 2 powers is addressed in the consequences of their use rather than the compulsion itself, predominantly within admissibility provisions.

The admissibility of statements or material provided under compulsion by law ultimately depends on the construction of the statute from which the compulsive power derives, particularly where the statute does not expressly outline the intended use.[46] *Saunders v United Kingdom*[47] paved the way for development and clarity on the admissibility of statements given under compulsion. In this case, statements made under compulsion to inspectors from the Department of Trade and Industry were handed to prosecutors

39 *Rio Tinto Zinc Corporation v Westinghouse Electric Corporation* [1978] AC 547 (HL) 563 (Lord Denning MR).

40 *Tate Access Floors Inc v Boswell* [1991] Ch 512 (Ch) 529 (Sir Nicolas Browne-Wilkinson VC).

41 Criminal Justice Act 1987, s 2; Dennis (n 36) 161–162.

42 Criminal Justice Act 1987, s 2(2).

43 ibid s 2(3).

44 'A person shall not under this section be required to disclose any information or produce any document which he would be entitled to refuse to disclose or produce on grounds of legal professional privilege in proceedings in the High Court, except that a lawyer may be required to furnish the name and address of his client.' *See* ibid s 2(9). Communications between a lawyer and their client within the scope of the professional relationship fall within the scope of Article 8 of the ECHR: 'A person's communication with a lawyer in the context of legal assistance falls within the scope of private life … whether in the context of assistance for civil or criminal litigation or in the context of seeking general legal advice, individuals who consult a lawyer can reasonably expect that their communication is private and confidential.' *See Altay v Turkey (No 2)* App no 11236/09 (ECtHR, 9 April 2019), para 49.

45 *ex p Smith* (n 37) 40.

46 *See Commissioners of Customs and Excise v Harz* [1967] 1 AC 760 (HL) 816. *See also* Peter Mirfield, *Silence, Confessions and Improperly Obtained Evidence* (Oxford University Press 1997) 230.

47 App no 19187/91 (ECtHR, 17 December 1996).

and subsequently used against their maker at trial, which was considered to be an abuse of the maker's right to a fair trial.[48] Section 59 and Schedule 3 of the Youth Justice and Criminal Evidence Act 1999 were introduced in response, to outline the admissibility of forced statements. Paragraph 20 of Schedule 3 inserts a subsection into the CJA 1987, at section 2(8AA), which prevents the admissibility of forced statements except where the maker or someone on their behalf raises the statement or asks a question in relation to it in the proceedings arising out of the prosecution.[49] Statements forced under section 2 are also admissible where the maker knowingly or recklessly makes a false or misleading statement and where, during a prosecution for a separate offence, the maker makes a statement inconsistent with that made under section 2.[50]

Strict limitations exist to preserve a person's privilege against self-incrimination where information is compulsorily surrendered as a result of section 2 powers. Despite these limitations, information provided in response to section 2 powers may be disclosable in civil proceedings.[51] Further, section 3(5)(c) of the CJA 1987 provides for the use of statements against third parties and allows the SFO to disclose any information obtained through the use of its section 2 powers 'for the purposes of any criminal investigation or criminal proceedings'.[52] In the background to the case of *Omers Administration Corp v Tesco Plc*, the SFO had obtained information from third parties which included interview transcripts and witness statements: some made under section 2 compulsion and others in circumstances giving rise to the reasonable expectation of confidentiality.[53] Within the scope of the pre-negotiation confidentiality undertaking which disallowed onward disclosure, that information was disclosed to Tesco Stores Ltd and its parent company Tesco Plc on two occasions in order to allow the companies to take advice as to the desirability of entering into DPA negotiations and of entering into the proposed DPA,[54] in line with section 3(5)(c) of the CJA 1987.[55] Disclosure of that information was thereafter sought by claimants in civil proceedings against Tesco Plc, which were based upon the same wrongdoing as the DPA. The third parties from whom the documentation had been obtained were alerted to the risk of disclosure and permitted to make objections.[56] However, the judge ultimately decided that disclosure was permitted, subject to it being made within a 'confidentiality club'.[57]

According to the SFO's Operational Handbook chapter titled "Section 2 Notices", a section 2 notice made to explore a corporate's affairs 'should' be issued to an individual, and not in the corporate's name, so as to ensure that the individual is personally responsible for

48 Dennis (n 36) 164.

49 Youth Justice and Criminal Evidence Act 1999, sch 3 para 20; Criminal Justice Act 1987, s 2(8AA).

50 Criminal Justice Act 1987, ss 2(8), 2(14).

51 *Omers Administration Corp v Tesco Plc* [2019] EWHC 109 (Ch).

52 Criminal Justice Act 1987, s 3(5)(c).

53 Such documentation was not subject to legal professional privilege. *See Omers Administration Corp v Tesco Plc* (n 51) [10], [14], [105].

54 ibid [18]–[21].

55 Where disclosure is made, the individual(s) who made the statements under section 2 compulsion are required to be notified by the SFO and have the right to make objections; a lack of consent from the individual would require judicial consideration of the issue of onward disclosure. Where it is not appropriate or practicable to notify the individual (in time or more generally), the SFO will need to consider whether the individual should be notified of the disclosure thereafter, if at all. *See* ibid [39]; *R (on the application of Kent Pharmaceuticals Ltd) v Serious Fraud Office* [2004] EWCA Civ 1494.

56 *Omers Administration Corp v Tesco Plc* (n 51) [26].

57 ibid [85], [111].

compliance and liable for non-compliance.[58] Information obtained from a company's former or current employees, including its directors and senior officers, will thus be obtained from that individual in their personal capacity and will be disclosable to the company – or to other individuals – where required 'for the purposes of any criminal investigation or criminal proceedings',[59] including in DPA negotiations.[60] The original intention of the section 2 interview forming the background of *ex p Smith* was to interview a director as to the suspected activities of their company; the persons under investigation were 'the applicant, together with 13 companies and trusts'.[61] The use of statements made under section 2 against others had been outlined: '"if a prosecution is brought against anyone else as a result of this investigation you may be asked to make a formal witness statement in the normal way."'[62]

In the case of a (former) director called to furnish information in respect of wrongdoing of the company within which they are implicated, the risk of statements made under section 2 becoming admissible increases; the director might find that statements made in their defence in personal proceedings are inconsistent with those made under section 2 in respect of the company, thus giving rise to their admissibility.[63] In order to comply with section 2 and exercise the privilege against self-incrimination in such circumstances, the individual would be best advised to give a full and frank account during their section 2 interview, as required by law, and then be mindful of the submissions they make in their own proceedings,[64] with strong consideration of invoking their privilege against self-incrimination to avoid making contrasting statements. Though the SFO does have the power to issue section 2 notices against an individual whilst their trial is ongoing, such powers exist outside the courtroom and remain inadmissible against the individual except where the individual allows them to become so.[65] In any event, exercising of the power in such a way is unlikely.[66]

Applying the literal rule of statutory interpretation: where the prosecutory proceedings are for the offence which *was* the subject of the section 2 interview and investigative proceedings, the individual should be able to make statements during those proceedings which are inconsistent with those previously made under their section 2 interview. Section 2(8)(b) outlines that

> a statement by a person in response to a requirement imposed by virtue of this section may only be used in evidence against him … on a prosecution for some *other* offence where in giving evidence he makes a statement inconsistent with it[67] (emphasis added).

58 Serious Fraud Office, 'Section 2 Powers' (*Serious Fraud Office*, 18 May 2020) <https://web.archive.org/web/20210208222222/https://www.sfo.gov.uk/download/section-2-powers/> accessed 26 February 2021, 5.

59 Criminal Justice Act 1987, s 3(5)(c).

60 *Omers Administration Corp v Tesco Plc* (n 51).

61 *ex p Smith* (n 37) 26.

62 This statement refers to the making of a witness statement in compliance with section 9 of the Criminal Justice Act 1967. *See* ibid 11.

63 Criminal Justice Act 1987, s 2(8)(b).

64 In prosecutory proceedings for an offence other than that which is the subject of the section 2 interview. *See* ibid.

65 Youth Justice and Criminal Evidence Act 1999, sch 3 para 20; ibid ss 8, 9.

66 *ex p Smith* (n 37) 43.

67 Criminal Justice Act 1987, s 2(8)(b).

This suggests that, during the prosecutory proceedings for an offence which *was* the subject of the section 2 investigation, an individual is entitled to make inconsistent statements without risk of their original statements becoming admissible against them. This, however, is clearly a risky approach for an individual to choose to adopt. Were the purposive approach of statutory interpretation to be taken, regard would be had to the original intention of the provision – which was set out by The Earl of Caithness as being: 'so that suspects cannot play games with the SFO or the court, and to preserve the general safeguard against admissibility of statements made to the SFO by the accused'.[68] Furthermore, it may be deemed that such an approach taken by an individual would allow for admissibility to arise.

The only other way that statements made under section 2 compulsion could become admissible against their maker during prosecutory proceedings for the offence investigated would be where that individual (or someone on their behalf) raises them or asks a question in relation to them.[69] Therefore, it can be strongly advised that the individual in question never draws reference to the interview in any way. Should they choose to do so, the individual must understand that they effectively admit the self-incriminating evidence surrendered by compulsion contrary to their own privilege of self-incrimination into their own proceedings, withdrawing any protection the CJA 1987 had afforded them (by virtue of their privilege against self-incrimination in the prosecutory proceedings). If the individual takes care to acknowledge the protection afforded by the CJA 1987 during the prosecutory stage, in theory they are able to exercise compliance with section 2 requirements and their privilege against self-incrimination. Though the two may not be exercised simultaneously, the privilege against self-incrimination being withdrawn during the investigative stage cannot have actual adverse consequences until the prosecutory stage, whereby the individual is then able to exercise the privilege once more.

A further difficulty arises when the execution of a section 2 interview leads the SFO to finding extrinsic evidence, which is then admissible.[70] In these circumstances, the privilege against self-incrimination continues to be preserved throughout the prosecutory proceedings of the individual, but their ability to defend themselves is somewhat reduced. It does not matter in such circumstances how rigidly an individual follows advice, as extrinsic evidence is admissible and an unfortunate by-product, for the individual, of being called for interview under section 2 powers. This is, in reality, the only way that the SFO is able to benefit from the use of a section 2 interview conducted in the investigation of an individual against that individual, where admissibility does not become possible by virtue of the individual's own doing.[71] Individuals should ensure that they strictly answer the questions asked under section 2 interview and do not give information beyond that required, particularly information which may lead to the finding of damning extrinsic evidence.

68 HL Deb 12 May 1987, vol 487, col 578.

69 Youth Justice and Criminal Evidence Act 1999, sch 3 para 20; Criminal Justice Act 1987, s 2(8AA).

70 For example, in the tracing of funds. *See ex p Smith* (n 37) 41. *See also* Sandeep Savla, 'Serious Fraud Office Powers Under Section 2 of the Criminal Justice Act 1987 and Police and Criminal Evidence Act 1984' (1997) 4(3) JFC 223, 226.

71 Savla (n 70) 230.

7.2.1 The SFO's section 2 powers and a self-report in the interests of all

It will likely be the case that those known to be implicated will not be able to engage in DPA negotiations. However, an implicated director may still elect to make a corporate self-report (prior to any offer to enter negotiations) in order to adhere to their directors' duties (**Section 6.2**). In such circumstances, there may not be any concern that their own involvement would give rise to criminal liability, or the director may simply hope that the act of self-reporting will provide some mitigation in their personal circumstances. In doing so, the director will likely be considering the potential personal impact of any information contained within the self-report.

For a director attempting somewhat paradoxically to ensure that professional duties and personal interests are met, compliance with section 2 may be a saving grace. If a director can make the SFO aware of potential fraud within their employer company and the SFO thereafter elects to use its section 2 powers to investigate the company (and potentially affiliated individuals), the director can fulfil their duty to self-report in the best interests of the company by abiding by the requirements of section 2 and giving a full and frank account in their interview, which is held in their personal capacity. The information disclosed within their section 2 interview can then be used "against" the company without admissibility issues, 'for the purposes of any criminal investigation or criminal proceedings',[72] but not against the individual. Compliance with section 2 alone does not appear to be too risky for the director, except where statements made direct the SFO to personally incriminating extrinsic evidence. One might reasonably suggest that compliance with section 2 allows the director to fulfil their "duty" to self-report as a scapegoat from the pre-existing expectation to make a professional admission or acceptance of wrongdoing which could personally self-incriminate, such that statements then made under section 2 which do self-incriminate cannot be used against the director. This would thus afford greater protection, with unharmed privilege against self-incrimination during the prosecutory stage.

Requiring directors to make disclosures about their company under section 2 is a highly effective way of gathering important information about the company's affairs, and could lead to increased chances of prosecution of the company and related individuals (as opposed to where section 2 is not deployed). Whilst use of the power may undermine the ability to prosecute a wrongdoing director complicit in the company's criminality, the disclosed information may lead to the finding of valuable evidence, and the director may be required to make witness statements against the company at trial,[73] increasing the prospect of prosecution. This may be considered to be in the greater interests of justice: without the use of section 2, it may be the case that both the company and director escape conviction, and prosecution of a company will likely be in the greater interests of third

72 Criminal Justice Act 1987, s 3(5)(c).

73 Though a witness statement forced by compulsion under section 20(2)(j) of the Health and Safety at Work Act 1974 cannot be used against its maker (similar to the admissibility of statements made under section 2 of the Criminal Justice Act 1987), it has been held that the exercising of the privilege against self-incrimination is limited to the maker of the statement: a director cannot claim privilege against self-incrimination to avoid incriminating its "employer" company, or vice versa. *See* Health and Safety Executive, 'Witness Statements' (*HSE*, 2019) <http://www.hse.gov.uk/enforce/enforcementguide/investigation/witness-witness.htm#fn7> accessed 20 September 2019, paras 36–38. *See also R v Hertfordshire County Council, ex p Green Environmental Industries Ltd* [2000] 2 AC 412 (HL); *Walkers Snack Foods Ltd v Coventry City Council* [1998] 3 All ER 163 (QB).

parties than the prosecution of an individual alone. Furthermore, where multiple individuals are interviewed (particularly multiple directors, in the case of larger companies), the admissibility of their statements against each other may increase the prospect of individual prosecutions. Arguably, aside from the ability to pinpoint evidence which could be used against suspects as a result of disclosures made under section 2 interview,[74] the admissibility of statements against third parties allows the purpose of the provision to be fulfilled.[75]

In the highly unlikely, but not impossible, situation whereby a director remains with the company beyond the point of the self-report and DPA negotiations, the director may find that their ability to exercise the privilege against self-incrimination becomes more difficult. An approved DPA will, as a standard term, require the full cooperation of the company in the investigation into and (where appropriate) prosecution of individuals. Therefore, where a director exercises their privilege against self-incrimination in personal proceedings which follow DPA approval, this may be considered a breach of the DPA term as not constituting full cooperation with the prosecution of implicated individuals. Further, where a director makes a statement inconsistent with the DPA's statement of facts during their own proceedings, this may also constitute a breach of a standard DPA term (where considered to be made on behalf of the company: **Section 7**).[76] A director's section 2 statements may thereafter become admissible against them where statements made in proceedings are inconsistent with those under section 2.

A breach of a DPA will likely constitute a breach of directors' duties, as the director would no longer be acting in the best interests of and promoting the success of the company under section 172 of the CA 2006.[77] Therefore, a director may be able to comply with section 2 and fulfil their duty to self-report in order to obtain a corporate DPA, but at the point in which the terms of the DPA are agreed, the privilege against self-incrimination is effectively withdrawn in ensuring compliance with the DPA alongside their directorship duties (which are considered to be of greater importance). Though not explicitly withdrawn, it would not be possible for a remaining director to comply with the terms of the DPA (which if broken, can lead to the "deferred" prosecution being reinstated) and act within the best interests of the company in doing so, and simultaneously exercise their privilege against self-incrimination.

Prohibiting or inhibiting the full investigation into the individuals implicated in the DPA wrongdoing, including the director themselves, would be contrary to the DPA terms.

---

74 For example, in the tracing of funds. *See ex p Smith* (n 37) 41. *See also* Savla (n 70) 226.

75 The Criminal Justice Act 1987 was introduced in response to the Fraud Trials' Committee Report (the "Roskill Report") of 1986, which identified the need for a new organisation to deal with serious fraud matters following a period of public unsettlement on the authorities' dealing with such issues. The Criminal Justice Act 1987 created the Serious Fraud Office, and section 2 specifically outlined its 'primary investigative tools' – designed to better approach the prosecution of serious or complex fraud. *See* Serious Fraud Office, 'SFO Historical Background and Powers' (*Serious Fraud Office*, July 2019) <https://www.sfo.gov.uk/publications/corporate-information/sfo-historical-background-powers/> accessed 28 July 2019.

76 Serious Fraud Office, 'Airline Services Limited Deferred Prosecution Agreement: ASL Signed DPA (Without Indictment)' (n 2) para 29. This is more likely in the case of statements made by present directors, in contrast with lower-level employees, as the former may make up the 'the directing mind and will' of the company. *See Tesco Supermarkets Ltd v Nattrass* (n 4) 180.

77 This is assessed subjectively, though '[where] his decision is one that no reasonable director could have considered to be in the best interests of the company then reliance upon his own suggested contrary belief will not avoid a finding of breach'. *See Stobart Group Ltd v Tinkler* [2019] EWHC 258 (Comm) [397]. *See also Re Southern Counties Fresh Foods Ltd* [2008] EWHC 2810 (Ch) [53].

This has recently been seen in the US as Telefonaktiebolaget LM Ericsson, a corporation that agreed a DPA with the DoJ in 2019, breached the terms of its DPA. According to the case before the court and the DoJ press release, breach of the DPA (which is determined at the sole discretion of the DoJ) arose due to a failure of Ericsson to cooperate in investigations into individuals, through disclosure failures, which prevented the US from charging those implicated individuals.[78] On this basis, a plea agreement was posed to the court (Ericsson pleaded guilty to the original charges deferred by the DPA), accompanied by a request to accept to proceed to sentencing.

It is highly unlikely that an implicated remaining director would be able to exercise their privilege against self-incrimination during the period of DPA negotiations and remain part of those negotiations, as doing so would likely constitute a failure to be 'genuinely proactive'[79] in cooperation, and their remaining within the company would likely be sufficient in itself to collapse negotiations. This position may differ slightly where a company has undertaken not to finalise disciplinary action against implicated individuals at the request of the prosecutor, but in such circumstances the (potentially suspended) director would not be able to play an active role in the DPA negotiations in any event.

7.2.2 Sweett Group PLC

Sweett Group PLC ("Sweett") pleaded guilty in 2016 to one count of failure to prevent bribery, contrary to section 7 of the Bribery Act 2010. Sweett Group PLC self-reported following a *Wall Street Journal* article which uncovered the wrongdoing of its subsidiary Cyril Sweett International Limited ("CSIL") in respect of a design contract of a Moroccan hospital.[80] Sweett was refused a DPA by the SFO on the basis of its cooperation being dogged with 'shortcomings'.[81] Sweett's first self-report was followed by a second made a year later, and cooperation was blighted with refusal to disclose certain documentation and the exercising of LPP, which collectively created an 'antagonistic' relationship between the company's legal representation and the SFO.[82] Having made a market announcement to the effect that it was fully cooperating with the SFO, Sweett was forced to retract the statement and followed by stating that it was 'reasonably' cooperating whilst exercising

78 *United States v Telefonaktiebolaget LM Ericsson* 19 Cr 884 (LTS) 1, A-13, A-14; The United States Department of Justice, 'Ericsson to Plead Guilty and Pay Over $206M Following Breach of 2019 FCPA Deferred Prosecution Agreement' (*The United States Department of Justice*, 2 March 2023) <https://www.justice.gov/opa/pr/ericsson-plead-guilty-and-pay-over-206m-following-breach-2019-fcpa-deferred-prosecution> accessed 26 March 2023; Ericsson, 'U.S. Department of Justice Resolves 2019 Deferred Prosecution Agreement Breaches With Ericsson' (*Ericsson*, 2 March 2023) <https://www.ericsson.com/en/press-releases/2023/3/u.s.-department-of-justice-resolves-2019-deferred-prosecution-agreement-breaches-with-ericsson> accessed 26 March 2023.

79 Crown Prosecution Service and Serious Fraud Office, 'Deferred Prosecution Agreements Code of Practice' (n 15) para 2.8.2(i).

80 Joe Palazzolo and Christopher Matthews, 'Inside a Bribery Probe at Storied Architecture Firm HLW' (*The Wall Street Journal*, 21 June 2013) <https://www.wsj.com/articles/SB10001424127887323300004578557190292596654> accessed 24 February 2021.

81 Calum Macdonald, 'Lessons From the First s7 UK Bribery Act Case' (*Allen & Overy*, 14 April 2016) <https://www.allenovery.com/en-gb/global/news-and-insights/publications/lessons-from-the-first-s7-uk-briberyact-case> accessed 31 August 2020.

82 ibid.

its LPP.[83] Despite a decision to replace its legal representation, Sweett was not availed the opportunity to agree a DPA; ultimately, His Honour Judge Beddoe stated that the company was responsible for decisions taken.[84]

In relation to a separate investigation into suspected corruption in Iraq, former managing director of CSIL Richard Kingston was convicted in 2016 for two counts of destruction of evidence, contrary to section 2(16) of the CJA 1987. Kingston was not liable for the destruction of evidence in respect of the offence to which Sweett was convicted. However, it is unclear the connection between the alleged Iraq corruption, Kingston, and any potential involvement (or otherwise) of the Sweett group of companies. According to the SFO website, the investigation into Kingston in respect of his June 2015 arrest is ongoing, for purposes unstated.[85] Kingston's conviction for destruction offences in response to section 2 powers may be seen as an example of the conflict faced by directors. There is *no suggestion* by the SFO that Kingston was involved in the alleged corruption in relation to Iraq by virtue of his position as managing director of the subsidiary. However, a conflict does arise when directors are so implicated, and consequences can arise upon destruction of evidence to preserve personal interests. This would amount to a conflict with professional duties owed to the company, to act in its best interests,[86] and such actions of a director (where remaining within the company) could lead to the lack of an opportunity for a company to negotiate or agree a DPA.

7.3 Use of materials against individuals

Before considering the impact on individuals, it is prudent to understand the extent to which DPA-related material can be used against the company in the event of its prosecution. The nature of a DPA means that, upon agreement between the company and prosecutor, and approval of the judge, proceedings are instituted against the company and then automatically suspended.[87] The effect of this process is that the prosecution of the company is deferred. Deferral is based upon the fulfilment of various terms contained within the DPA, and the company may be prosecuted where it does not comply with those terms.[88] Where the company is prosecuted for the underlying offence of the approved DPA – on the basis of a DPA breach – the statement of facts will be used against the company as a formal admission of liability pursuant to section 10 of the CJA 1967.[89] However, where

83 'Sweett Group believes that it is doing all that it reasonably can to cooperate with the SFO investigation while at the same time exercising its fundamental right to legal professional privilege in fulfilling its corporate and regulatory requirements.' *See* Iain Withers, 'Sweett "Not Co-Operating" With Serious Fraud Office investigation' (*Building*, 11 November 2014) <https://www.building.co.uk/news/sweett-not-co-operating-with-serious-fraud-office-investigation/5072057.article> accessed 9 October 2023.

84 Macdonald (n 81).

85 Serious Fraud Office, 'Individual Charged With Destruction of Evidence' (*Serious Fraud Office*, 9 November 2015) <https://www.sfo.gov.uk/2015/11/09/individual-charged-with-destruction-of-evidence/> accessed 24 February 2021; Serious Fraud Office, 'Richard Kingston Convicted and Sentenced for Destroying Bribery and Corruption Evidence' (*Serious Fraud Office*, 21 December 2016) <https://www.sfo.gov.uk/2016/12/21/richard-kingston-convicted-sentenced-destroying-bribery-corruption-evidence/> accessed 16 June 2023.

86 Companies Act 2006, ss 172, 175.

87 Crime and Courts Act 2013, sch 17 para 2.

88 Crown Prosecution Service and Serious Fraud Office, 'Deferred Prosecution Agreements Code of Practice' (n 15) para 12.7.

89 Crime and Courts Act 2013, sch 17 para 13(2).

a DPA is negotiated but does not receive judicial approval (and thus does not come into force), the prosecution is limited in its use of material against the company.

Any material referring to the fact that negotiations once took place, including any draft DPA or statement of facts (or material created for the sole purpose of preparing those drafts),[90] or statements indicating the entering of negotiations,[91] cannot be used against the company except in two exceptional circumstances. Firstly, where the company is prosecuted for an offence consisting of the provision of inaccurate, misleading, or incomplete information;[92] and secondly, where the company is prosecuted for some other offence and makes a statement inconsistent with the material whilst giving evidence.[93] In the latter instance, such material will only be used against the company where evidence relating to it 'is adduced, or a question relating to it is asked, by or on behalf of [the company] in the proceedings arising out of the prosecution'.[94] This means that the aforementioned material would not be admissible evidence against the company for the offence(s) for which the DPA was originally negotiated, though (subject to the rules of evidence) there is 'no limitation' on the use of other information obtained by the prosecutor during negotiations.[95]

Therefore, though there is reliance upon the fact that an approved DPA's statement of facts will constitute an admission of the company upon DPA breach, there is some level of protection to a company where negotiations collapse due to the limited circumstances in which any draft DPA documentation or the fact of those negotiations can be used against it. The purpose of this limitation was to provide like protection which would be afforded to documents obtained under compulsion.[96]

7.3.1 DPA approved

Where the company's DPA is approved by a judge, the statement of facts pursuant to that agreement may constitute admissible hearsay evidence against an individual and thus a (former) director.[97] However, there may be instances where the statement of facts to an approved DPA is not published. When an individual is the subject of ongoing criminal proceedings in relation to the wrongdoing within the DPA, the fact of the company's DPA might be announced but further details made subject to reporting restrictions by way of an order under section 4(2) of the Contempt of Court Act 1981. This was seen, for example, following the *G4S C&J* DPA. That order requires the postponement of the publication of the preliminary and final written applications for DPA approval and any reporting which

90 ibid sch 17 para 6(b).
91 ibid sch 17 para 6(a).
92 ibid sch 17 para 13(4)(a).
93 ibid sch 17 para 13(4)(b).
94 ibid sch 17 para 13(5).
95 Crown Prosecution Service and Serious Fraud Office, 'Deferred Prosecution Agreements Code of Practice' (n 15) para 4.5.
96 Ministry of Justice, *Deferred Prosecution Agreements: Government Response to the Consultation on a New Enforcement Tool to Deal With Economic Crime Committed by Commercial Organisations* (Cm 8463, 2012) para 154.
97 ibid para 164; Michael Bisgrove and Mark Weekes, 'Deferred Prosecution Agreements: A Practical Consideration' (2014) 6 Crim LR 416, 424. Hearsay evidence is defined under section 114(1) of the Criminal Justice Act 2003 as 'a statement not made in oral evidence in the proceedings [which] is admissible as evidence of any matter stated', and under Rule 33.1(a) of the CPR as 'a statement made, otherwise than by a person while giving oral evidence in proceedings, which is tendered as evidence of the matters stated'. *See* Criminal Justice Act 2003, s 144(1); CPR 33.1(a).

would identify individuals referred to in the application and final hearing proceedings. Any reports made in relation to the final hearing, DPA approval, and reasons for approval must outline that the DPA relates only to the criminal wrongdoing of the company and does not address the liability of any individuals.[98] Furthermore, an order may be made under paragraph 12 of Schedule 17 of the CACA 2013 to postpone the prosecutor's publication of certain DPA documentation,[99] as was the case in *G4S C&J*.[100] In the *G4S C&J* case, the orders made remained in place until the conclusion of the criminal proceedings against individuals previously employed by the company (though may in some cases be until further order).

Publication restrictions are put in place where there is deemed to be a substantial risk of prejudice to the administration of justice in ongoing or future proceedings.[101] This does not necessarily refer to the use of the material in evidence against an individual, but might refer to public reaction and/or consideration of the jury of extrinsic evidence (if it, or parts of it, is not admitted as evidence). Where under paragraph 8(7) it states that 'the prosecutor must publish'[102] certain materials upon DPA approval (subject to an order under paragraph 12), 'publish' is not defined. Publication is also not defined within the CACA 2013 Explanatory Notes. In this instance, it would appear that publication simply means the act of making public certain documentation. This is in line with the importance placed on the transparency of the process during the debating stage of the statutory provision. In its first extensive introduction to the House of Lords, Lord McNally set out that:

> Public scrutiny of the DPA process is very important to ensure that its operation is transparent and that justice is done and seen to be done. A DPA will be approved in open court and published by the prosecutor. This will make sure that the details of the organisation's alleged wrongdoings and the sanctions provided for in the agreement will always be in the public domain.[103]

This original intention of the provision is represented within the DPA Code, which reads:

> Transparency remains a key aspect of the success and proper operation of DPAs, and accordingly Schedule 17 of the Act requires in prescribed circumstances the prosecutor to publish on its website orders made by the court or decisions made by the prosecutor.[104]

98 Mr Justice William Davis, 'Serious Fraud Office v G4S Care & Justice Services (UK) Limited: Order Made Under Section 4(2) of the Contempt of Court Act 1981' (*Courts and Tribunals Judiciary*, 17 July 2020) <https://www.judiciary.uk/wp-content/uploads/2020/07/Revised-Draft-CCA-Order-for-final-DPA-hearing-15.07.20-2-1.pdf> 12 February 2021.

99 The SFO Operational Handbook outlines that this postponement will typically only apply to the statement of facts. *See* Serious Fraud Office, 'Deferred Prosecution Agreements' (n 17).

100 Mr Justice William Davis, 'Serious Fraud Office v G4S Care & Justice Services (UK) Limited: Order Made Under Paragraph 12 of Schedule 17 of the Crime and Courts Act 2003' (*Courts and Tribunals Judiciary*, 17 July 2020) <https://www.judiciary.uk/wp-content/uploads/2020/07/Tab-B-Postponement-Order-G4S-1.pdf> 12 February 2021.

101 Crime and Courts Act 2013, sch 17 para 12(1); Explanatory Notes to the Crime and Courts Act 2013, para 570; Contempt of Court Act 1981, s 4(2).

102 Crime and Courts Act 2013, sch 17 para 8(7).

103 HL Deb 30 October 2012, vol 740, col 583 (Lord McNally).

104 Crown Prosecution Service and Serious Fraud Office, 'Deferred Prosecution Agreements Code of Practice' (n 15) para 16.1.

The subsequent paragraph of the DPA Code sets out that these requirements are subject to paragraph 12 of the CACA 2013 and any postponement orders made.[105] Interestingly, this part of the DPA Code – which sits under heading 16 titled "Publishing decisions and postponement" – specifies the mode of the prosecutor's publication as being to its website. The publication of 'orders made by the court or decisions made by the prosecutor' may not, under this particular paragraph of the DPA Code, include the prosecutor's publication requirements under paragraph 8(7) of the CACA 2013 (including the DPA and thus statement of facts)[106] but is nonetheless indicative of the continued intention of publication and preferred forum. As a former director would not be involved in the DPA negotiations and will thus be part of the wider public, this may mean that a paragraph 12 order postponing publication would restrict the admissibility of the statement of facts against them as hearsay evidence. On the other hand, the statement of facts may still constitute admissible hearsay evidence against the individual where it is not published to the website and made available for wider public consumption, if effected on the basis of further reporting restrictions or mechanisms put in place to ensure compliance with the relevant orders.[107]

Regardless of whether the statement of facts is deemed to be admissible as hearsay evidence against the individual, 'other information' gathered during the period of DPA negotiations can be used against the individual with 'no limitation' (subject to the rules of evidence).[108] This may lead to circumstances where the foundational evidential basis of the statement of facts is admissible, in any event. "Other evidence" admissible against the individual may include pre-existing documentation (such as emails), the corporate self-report or internal investigation reports to the prosecutor prior to negotiations (likely to include further evidence),[109] interview notes or witness statements obtained by the company and disclosed to the prosecutor, any third-party documentation obtained by the prosecutor, and information obtained by the prosecutor after enquiries made following the company's disclosures to it.[110] These examples are provided in the DPA Code as a non-exhaustive list of evidence which may be admissible against the company (where the DPA is not approved). However, this list serves as a useful example of "other evidence" which may be used against individuals whether or not the DPA is approved.

Where the DPA is approved, the company will have agreed to various terms relating to cooperation. The requirement of the company to cooperate in the investigation into

105 'All requirements to publish under this section are subject to any enactment or order of the court under paragraph 12 of Schedule 17 to the Act preventing such publication from being made.' *See* ibid para 16.2.

106 Publication of the DPA is required under paragraph 8(7)(a) of Schedule 17 of the Crime and Courts Act 2013. This can be taken to include the statement of facts, which is 'contain[ed]' within the DPA, as per paragraph 5(1) of Schedule 17. The Act's Explanatory Notes, under paragraph 571, state that: 'Where a DPA has been entered into (subject to any necessary publication restrictions to avoid prejudice to future prosecutions) the final Agreement, including the statement of facts, will be a matter of public record.' *See* Explanatory Notes to the Crime and Courts Act 2013, para 571; Crime and Courts Act 2013, sch 17.

107 This might include the holding of the trial in private due to reporting restrictions and the introduction of hearsay evidence. *See* CrimPR 6.6(3)(c)(i)–6.6(3)(c)(iii).

108 Crown Prosecution Service and Serious Fraud Office, 'Deferred Prosecution Agreements Code of Practice' (n 15) para 4.5; Serious Fraud Office, 'Deferred Prosecution Agreements' (n 17).

109 'All supporting evidence including, but not limited to emails, banking evidence and witness accounts, must be provided to the SFO's Intelligence Unit as part of the self-reporting process.' *See* Serious Fraud Office, 'Corporate Self-Reporting' (*Serious Fraud Office*, October 2012) <https://www.sfo.gov.uk/publications/guidance-policy-and-protocols/guidance-for-corporates/corporate-self-reporting/> accessed 16 May 2021.

110 Crown Prosecution Service and Serious Fraud Office, 'Deferred Prosecution Agreements Code of Practice' (n 15) para 4.6.

and prosecution of relevant individuals is a subject of utmost priority.[111] This cooperation may extend to the provision of further evidence, the responsibility for holding certain evidence, and its best efforts to make individuals available for interview. Though not yet expressly outlined, it may be considered a necessary form of cooperation in line with these obligations for the company to make representatives available as prosecution witnesses in the trial of individuals. Thus, whilst in circumstances whereby the statement of facts is inadmissible against an individual one might consider this loss to effectively amount to evidence of the company's acceptance of liability,[112] representatives within the company called as prosecution witnesses may be considered to have comparable effect.[113]

The extent to which such "other evidence" obtained, which may well have been sufficient as a basis to enter a DPA with the company, is sufficient to lead to the conviction of an individual director, is a topic which has sparked debate. This is particularly controversial where the company's DPA offence is one which requires the establishment of the identification principle. In the *Tesco Stores Ltd* case, for example, the company entered into such a DPA but three directors – named within the DPA documentation – were subsequently acquitted on the basis of there being no case to answer or evidence put forward by the SFO.[114] Nonetheless, in future cases, that evidence might produce a different result. Indeed, one of the potential reasons that can be attributed to the SFO's lack of successful prosecutions in the cases of the Tesco Stores Ltd directors was the lack of expert witness,[115] which cannot be reflected upon as an isolated incident.[116]

Use of the statement of facts as hearsay evidence against a director might lead to further criticism of the prosecutor where that individual's prosecution does not lead to conviction. Criticism has already occurred where a statement of facts, and thus the acceptance of liability of the company, is based upon the agreed guilty mind of the director(s) and that guilty mind is not established on trial of the director(s).[117] The submission of that statement of facts as evidence in the trial of the director might exacerbate the focus on flaws within this evolved concept of companies accepting liability on the basis of unproven or non-existent intentions.

111 Serious Fraud Office, 'Deferred Prosecution Agreements' (n 17); Select Committee on the Bribery Act 2010, *The Bribery Act 2010: Post-Legislative Scrutiny* (HL 2017–19, 303) para 315.

112 'There is no requirement for formal admissions of guilt in respect of the offences charged by the indictment though it will be necessary for [the company] to admit the contents and meaning of key documents referred to in the statement of facts.' *See* Crown Prosecution Service and Serious Fraud Office, 'Deferred Prosecution Agreements Code of Practice' (n 15) para 6.3.

113 Though the prosecutor's selection of witnesses will be crucial. In the case against the former Tesco Stores Ltd directors, chief prosecution witness Mr Amit Soni's position undermined the prosecution's case. *See R v Bush* [2019] EWCA Crim 29 [52], [111], [121], [126].

114 Select Committee on the Bribery Act 2010, *The Bribery Act 2010: Post-Legislative Scrutiny* (n 111) paras 318–319.

115 *Bush* (n 113) [59], [125].

116 Individuals prosecuted following both the *Serco Geografix Ltd* and *G4S C&J* DPAs were also acquitted at trial, despite the companies having agreed DPAs on the basis of identification principle offences which had relied upon the conduct of the respective individuals. The lack of success in the individual prosecutions has, however, largely been attributed to evidence failings of the SFO. *See* Kate Beioley, 'Serious Fraud Office Abandons Case Against Former G4S Executives' (*Financial Times*, 10 March 2023) <https://www.ft.com/content/93323263-6617-48c4-8567-ad8c32ba0f1f> accessed 16 March 2023.

117 Max Walters, 'News: DPAs in the Spotlight Following Failed Tesco Prosecutions' (2019) (3) LS Gaz; Maria Cronin and Craig Hogg, 'Legal Update – White Collar Crime: Time to Rethink DPAs After Tesco Failures' (2019) (7) LS Gaz.

Furthermore, the prosecutor will continue to be bound by its duty of disclosure to individual defendants despite any confidentiality obligations owed to the company and regardless of whether a DPA is approved. Under section 3(1)(a) of the CPIA 1996, any material identified by the prosecutor which 'might reasonably be considered capable of undermining the case for the prosecution against the accused or of assisting the case for the accused' should be disclosed to the accused. Disclosure obligations under CPIA 1996 do not apply in respect of the company, as the DPA Code sets out a specific disclosure framework, but remain in place in respect of relevant individuals.[118] Prior to the case of *AL*, a former Sarclad senior executive had sought disclosure from the SFO of the full records and notes of interviews conducted by Sarclad (through external lawyers) prior to its self-report. Sarclad had, during its own SFO investigation, refused to provide the SFO with the full interview notes on the basis of privilege and instead gave an "oral proffer", which constituted an oral summary of the notes. When the executive later sought disclosure of the documentation through the SFO, Sarclad again refused such requests. After the Crown Court refused an application to require the SFO to make such disclosures, on the basis that the prosecutor was not in possession of the documentation and thus the CPIA 1996 did not apply, the senior executive applied for judicial review of the SFO's decision not to pursue the company further.[119]

Though it was ultimately determined that the High Court was not the correct forum for dispute, Mr Justice Green highlighted concerns at the SFO's decision not to pursue Sarclad for what appeared to be a breach of the terms of cooperation within its DPA, in failing to make such disclosures.[120] This judgment demonstrates (in *obiter*) that an individual prosecuted following a DPA could seek disclosure of internal investigation first interview notes and that these would not be privileged.[121] Read in line with the subsequent case of *Director of the Serious Fraud Office v Eurasian Natural Resources Corporation Ltd*,[122] communications – including interviews – between an individual within a company and the company's lawyers would not attract legal advice privilege, except where those conversations were based on such advice.[123] However, interview notes created by lawyers during such communications might attract litigation privilege where the dominant purpose of their creation was to resist or avoid contemplated criminal proceedings (**Section 7.1.2**).[124]

118 It is worth noting that the collapse of the cases against Nicholas Woods and Simon Marshall, former Serco executives, on the basis of disclosure failings, prompted the SFO to commission Sir Brian Altman KC to conduct a review into the matter. The review focussed on disclosure failures only and set out 18 recommendations, all of which the SFO accepted. The recommendations focussed on the SFO's disclosure practices, rather than the law relating to disclosure. *See* Brian Altman and Rebecca Chalkley, 'Report to the Serious Fraud Office: The Collapse of *R V. Woods & Marshall* on 26 April 2021' (*Serious Fraud Office*, July 2022) <https://www.sfo.gov.uk/download/review-of-r-v-woods-marshall-by-brian-altman-qc/> accessed 8 February 2023; Serious Fraud Office, 'Implementation Update – May 2023: Altman Review' (*Serious Fraud Office*, 24 May 2023) <https://www.sfo.gov.uk/download/implementation-update-may-2023-altman-review/> accessed 3 June 2023.

119 *R (on the application of AL) v Serious Fraud Office* (n 11) [2]–[7].

120 These concerns were shared by HHJ Testar in the application to the Crown Court to require the SFO to seek disclosure. *See* ibid [38].

121 ibid [105]; *Three Rivers District Council v Governor and Company of the Bank of England (No 6)* (n 7) [102]; *Three Rivers District Council v Bank of England (No 5)* [2003] QB 1556 (CA) [93].

122 *Eurasian Natural Resources Corporation Ltd* (n 8).

123 ibid [123].

124 ibid [136].

Though the DPA Code sets out that the law on LPP is not altered by DPAs,[125] it is considered to be one of the SFO's indicators of cooperation.[126] Whilst a lack of waiver might not *prima facie* be deemed "uncooperative", this will likely depend on the legitimacy of the privilege claims, and any later determination of unfounded privilege claims may be perceived as uncooperative. Whilst many companies might elect to waive privilege, this might not always be possible or desirable; waiver can expose a company to further criminal proceedings overseas and to civil proceedings, which may also impact implicated individuals. If joint interest privilege applies – for example, where the company and former director retain a lawyer to provide both advice in the same matter but in individual capacities,[127] or where the two parties simply have a joint interest in the subject matter of a communication – this may enable a former director to obtain relevant documentation, as the company will not be able to claim privilege to refuse to do so.[128] However, this will not apply where the parties become involved in hostile proceedings.[129]

Any evidence against an implicated individual may be disclosed to the company under DPA disclosure rules;[130] this may ultimately support the company's case against the former director for breach of duty.

7.3.2 DPA not approved

Where the company's DPA is not approved, any draft DPA or statement of facts will not be admissible against an individual, nor will the fact of negotiations having taken place or documentation pertaining to that fact. This can be traced back to the House of Lords' early debates on the DPA tool, where it was stated that confidentiality of the negotiation discussions would be protected to avoid prejudice to the company prosecuted and to other criminal proceedings.[131] However, the aforementioned (**Section 7.3.1**) "other evidence" obtained by the prosecutor during DPA negotiations will remain admissible without limitation (subject to the rules of evidence) against an individual.[132] Where the DPA is not approved, this will mean that the company is not bound by the terms of cooperation within it and thus will not be under an obligation – by virtue of a DPA – to assist in the investigation and prosecution of individuals. This will likely mean that companies will be more inclined to claim privilege over documentation, and may impact the prosecutor's ability to access evidence it would otherwise wish to use against individuals.

125 Crown Prosecution Service and Serious Fraud Office, 'Deferred Prosecution Agreements Code of Practice' (n 15) para 3.3.

126 Serious Fraud Office, 'Deferred Prosecution Agreements' (n 17).

127 *R (on the application of Ford) v Financial Services Authority* (n 22).

128 LexisPSL, 'Privilege – Joint and Common Interest Privilege' (*LexisNexis*, 2021) <https://www.lexisnexis.co.uk/legal/guidance/privilege-joint-common-interest-privilege> accessed 16 February 2021.

129 *Re Hydrosan Ltd* [1991] BCLC 418 (Ch) 421.

130 Serious Fraud Office, 'Deferred Prosecution Agreements' (n 17).

131 HL Deb 30 October 2012 (n 103) col 569 (Lord McNally).

132 Crown Prosecution Service and Serious Fraud Office, 'Deferred Prosecution Agreements Code of Practice' (n 15) para 4.5; Serious Fraud Office, 'Deferred Prosecution Agreements' (n 17).

7.3.3 Can the statement of facts be imputed to a (former) director?

The identification principle has traditionally been referred to as a 'restrictive method of attribution'.[133] Under this principle, the *mens rea* of the directing mind and will of the company – typically the board of directors or those with delegated power from the board[134] – is imputed/attributed to the company for the purpose of establishing corporate criminal liability.[135] This has recently been expanded, so as to extend the *mens rea* to encompass senior managers.[136] In the circumstances of a DPA agreed for an identification principle offence, a company will accept (and possibly admit) liability on the basis of what essentially amounts to an attribution of liability from the directing mind and will. This will often occur prior to any determination of liability of the relevant individual(s), and therefore the question arises as to whether the company's acceptance of liability can be attributed back to the individual for the purpose of constituting the individual's own account and/or admission.

In such circumstances, the company – though liable by virtue of the adopted *mens rea* of its directing mind and will – is liable for the "identification principle offence" in its own right. The company by nature has 'no mind or morals'[137] and will thus inevitably be reliant upon the acts and/or minds of human persons in order to function and incur liability. Though a separate legal personality, there is no separate legal mind born by the incorporation of a company by which decisions or admissions can be made. On the other hand, a company director is capable of making conscious decisions and admissions, and thus there is no need to adopt the *mens rea* of another in order to establish liability; the *mens rea* of the director is their own. Where a director commits a criminal offence, whether in a personal or professional capacity, that director is ultimately also liable in their own right. As such, the statement of facts and any acceptance and/or admission of liability within it will not be imputed to the director so as to be considered their own account. This principle was outlined in the government's response to consultation on DPAs in 2012, where it was stated that:

> Should criminal proceedings subsequently be taken against an individual, admissions made during DPA negotiations should not be capable of being relied upon during those proceedings. It would be unfair to rely upon this information in the criminal prosecution of an individual as such information could not be treated as an admission by the individual.[138]

133 Russell Hopkins, 'Corporate Directing Mind and Will in Civil Cases' (*Lexology*, 26 February 2019) <https://www.lexology.com/library/detail.aspx?g=33e9c623-c8e6-4786-9600-56b5eb569ab8> accessed 7 March 2021.

134 *Bilta (UK) Ltd (in liquidation) v Nazir* [2015] UKSC 23 [67] (Lord Sumption); Andrew de Mestre, 'Company Directors – When Will Companies be Responsible for the Things They Do?' (Chancery Bar Association Jersey Conference, Jersey, 7 November 2019) <https://www.chba.org.uk/for-members/library/overseas-seminars/company-directors-attribution> accessed 7 March 2021, paras 7–10.

135 *Tesco Supermarkets Ltd v Nattrass* (n 4); *Lennard's Carrying Co Ltd v Asiatic Petroleum Co Ltd* (n 4); Crown Prosecution Service, 'Corporate Prosecutions' (*Crown Prosecution Service*, 2021) <https://www.cps.gov.uk/legal-guidance/corporate-prosecutions> accessed 7 March 2021.

136 Economic Crime and Corporate Transparency Act 2023, s 196(1).

137 Bisgrove and Weekes (n 97) 419.

138 Ministry of Justice, *Deferred Prosecution Agreements: Government Response to the Consultation on a New Enforcement Tool to Deal With Economic Crime Committed by Commercial Organisations* (n 96) para 164.

Where the *mens rea* of a director is adopted in order to establish corporate criminal liability, the subsequent account of the company need not be attributed back to that director in order to establish the director's own liability; the *mens rea* of the director already purportedly exists. However, any position taken by the company might be persuasive in reaching a determination of that director's personal liability. The statement of facts would be admissible (rules of evidence permitting) as hearsay evidence against the individual.

This area becomes slightly more complicated when considering the position of smaller companies, and particularly "one-man" companies. Dealing first with one-man companies whereby the leader of the company and alleged engineer of the corporate's criminal wrongdoing remains director: it is a near-impossible prospect that such a company would obtain a DPA. This would not be in line with the common themes of corporate reform or the principles of justice.[139] Hypothetically, for the purpose of the director's criminal prosecution, the company's statement of facts would not be imputed to the director as constituting the director's own formal admission. Within the scope of criminal law, there would be no need to disregard the veil of incorporation and separate legal personality where the company had accepted criminal liability in a DPA and an individual director had been prosecuted. The evidence which would stem from that statement of facts – in terms of "other evidence" and the statement of facts as hearsay – would likely negate the need for such imputation, in any event. Where the director pleads their personal innocence, this would likely constitute a breach of the DPA as it would be considered that the company, by virtue of an imputation from its director, would be making statements contrary to the DPA.[140] Where the one-man company no longer bears the same wrongdoing director, it would remain highly unlikely that the company would be able to obtain a DPA unless significant corporate reform could be established. In such situations, the possibility of an imputed account of the company to the former director would become even further removed.

The issue with "identification principle offence" DPAs is that a company often reaches a premature position on the basis of a *mens rea* which may not have existed.[141] The statement of facts may be persuasive as hearsay evidence against a director but, if ultimately made prematurely and without the foundational basis of an existing *mens rea*, cannot be on its own determinative of liability. The starting point for determining a (former) director's *mens rea* in their own criminal proceedings should ultimately be in assessing the director and not solely the account of those leading a reformed corporate structure, for which that director once served. The use of "other evidence" should provide a suitable collection of evidence from the company, itself having informed the statement of facts;[142] if that evidence is not suitable, one might question whether the DPA itself was appropriate.

139 Sir Brian Leveson stated: ""I cannot contemplate agreeing a DPA if the people who were responsible for the corrupt payments or other criminality remained in the company."' *See* Select Committee on the Bribery Act 2010, *The Bribery Act 2010: Post-Legislative Scrutiny* (n 111) para 313.

140 Serious Fraud Office, 'Airline Services Limited Deferred Prosecution Agreement: ASL Signed DPA (Without Indictment)' (n 2) para 29

141 "Premature" in respect of the fact that the evidential stage in the Full Code Test (in the Code for Crown Prosecutors) need not be established – a DPA can instead be applied for on the basis of a reasonable suspicion based upon admissible evidence, and the reasonable grounds for believing that further admissible evidence would be obtained within a reasonable time, and would be capable of establishing a realistic prospect of conviction in accordance with the Test. *See* Crown Prosecution Service and Serious Fraud Office, 'Deferred Prosecution Agreements Code of Practice' (n 15) para 1.3.

142 Which the implicated director is highly unlikely to have had any involvement in.

7.3.4 Civil proceedings

Schedule 17 of the CACA 2013 deals with the use of DPA material in criminal proceedings, under paragraph 13, though as discussed this considers use against the company and not individuals, and does not cover use in civil proceedings. The DPA Code is also silent on this, but the 2012 government response to consultation sets out when DPA material can be used in civil proceedings against the company. Where the DPA has been approved, the DPA and statement of facts 'should be capable of being treated as hearsay evidence' but claimants would not be able to obtain the aforementioned "other evidence" (**Section 7.3.1**) 'other than in accordance with the existing legal framework'.[143] Where the DPA has not been approved, the confidentiality of the negotiations will mean that a third party is unlikely to know of them. In the event that the fact becomes known, disclosure of material provided by the company to the prosecutor during those negotiations will not be made, except where the prosecutor is under a legal obligation to do so.[144]

Prior to *Omers*, documentation had been obtained by compulsion by the SFO from third parties during DPA negotiations (which led to DPA approval) with Tesco Stores Ltd. This documentation (which included interview transcripts and witness statements) was provided by the SFO to Tesco Stores Ltd and its parent company Tesco PLC during negotiations for legal advice purposes and was,[145] in this case, determined to be disclosable by the companies in ongoing civil proceedings despite confidentiality obligations to the SFO.[146] The claimants in this case were split into two groups and represented investors in Tesco Plc shares.[147] In this case, both parties were parties to the ongoing civil proceedings and therefore 'relevance [was] the *prima facie* test'.[148] Whilst there was consideration of confidentiality, this did not on its own offer protection: if the 'overriding objective of dealing with the case justly and at proportionate cost' could not be achieved without disclosure, then disregarding confidentiality should be of 'litigious advantage'.[149] There was consideration of the impact on third-party individuals within the judgment, with discussion of a confidentiality club and invitation by the judge for suggestions in mitigating the consequences of disclosure.[150] The approach to individuals in relation to civil proceedings is not clarified, but will not differ significantly from proceedings against the company.

In *Libyan Investment Authority v Credit Suisse International*,[151] an application for permission to serve a claim outside of the jurisdiction was made in relation to a claim by the Libyan Investment Authority ("LIA") against Credit Suisse. The dispute arose in relation to an alleged bribe paid by Credit Suisse to "Mr Giahmi" (also a defendant) in exchange for him exerting corrupt influence over LIA officers and employees

143 Ministry of Justice, *Deferred Prosecution Agreements: Government Response to the Consultation on a New Enforcement Tool to Deal With Economic Crime Committed by Commercial Organisations* (n 96) para 166.

144 ibid paras 169–170.

145 *Omers Administration Corp v Tesco Plc* (n 51) [20].

146 ibid [1], [10], [112]–[113].

147 ibid [8].

148 ibid [79].

149 ibid [79].

150 ibid [111]–[114].

151 [2020] EWHC 1387 (Comm).

(regarding investment in original and restricted notes).[152] It was noted within the judgment that Giahmi had always maintained that he 'acted as an honest and legitimate businessman, providing legitimate intermediary and deal making services for which he was entitled to remuneration'.[153] For permission to serve to be granted, it was necessary for the claimant to demonstrate that there was a serious issue to be tried (a real as opposed to fanciful prospect of success); that there was a good arguable case that the claim fell within at least one of the heads of jurisdiction; and that in all the circumstances England and Wales was clearly or distinctly the most appropriate forum for the trial of the dispute.[154]

The principal area of dispute in this case was whether there existed a serious issue to be tried, in essence an "arguable claim".[155] Amongst other matters leading Mr Justice Foxton to the conclusion that there was an arguable claim, one was the admissions of bribery made by Societe Generale in DPAs with US and French authorities (the French DPA equivalent being the *convention judiciaire d'intérêt public* ("CJIP")) in relation to trades involving Giahmi. Though, notably, those were outlined *not* to be admissions of Giahmi personally. It was stated within the judgment that in one of those DPAs (or equivalent), Societe Generale admitted that it was aware of an individual paying bribes to Libyan government officials.[156] However, the published DPA and CJIP do not refer to the implicated individual by name and instead simply refer to the conduct which an anonymous party is *alleged* to have committed, and Societe Generale's awareness of it.[157] Expressed clearly by Mr Justice Foxton was the fact that the allegations against the defendants (including Giahmi) were 'strongly denied', and would likely be greatly contested at trial, but that this did not detract from their demonstrativeness of a serious issue to be tried.[158]

Ultimately permission was granted,[159] demonstrating the potential use of corporate admissions or statements made within DPAs (internationally), which implicate individuals, to form a basis of permitting a claim to be made against an individual in the UK. The DPA had previously been raised in a separate application by LIA for permission to serve out of the jurisdiction, which was granted and thereafter challenged by Giahmi on the basis that there was no real prospect of success as a result of the underlying claims being time-barred and due to the failure of LIA to comply with its disclosure obligations.[160] Though this particular claim related to alleged fraud and not bribery, the US DPA was referred to in outlining that Societe Generale had admitted to engaging an individual in a bribery scheme, though there was anonymisation within the DPA.[161] It was ultimately

152 ibid [1]–[6].
153 ibid [7].
154 ibid [8]; *AK Investments CJSC v Kyrgyz Mobil Telecom Limited* [2011] UKPC 7 (Lord Collins).
155 *Libyan Investment Authority v Credit Suisse International* (n 151) [11].
156 ibid [13(5)].
157 *United States of America v Societe Generale SA* (Case 18-CR-253 (DLI)); *Le Procureur de la Republique Financier et Societe Generale SA* (Cour d'appel de Paris, Mai 24 2018, PNF-15 254 000 424); ibid [13(5)].
158 *Libyan Investment Authority v Credit Suisse International* (n 151) [14].
159 ibid [44].
160 ibid [2].
161 ibid [11]; *United States of America v Societe Generale SA* (n 157) A-7.

determined in this case that there was no real prospect of success, on the basis of the time limitation and disclosure failures.[162]

In the case of *ECU Group Plc v HSBC Bank Plc*,[163] the extent to which a DPA can be used to draw inference of third-party wrongdoing was considered (though in a limited sense), so as to determine whether a claimant had sufficient knowledge at an earlier time to plead a claim (whilst within the limitation period). The facts of the case did not lead to the permission of inference to be drawn, as the '"historic misconduct"'[164] referred to was in relation to alleged wrongdoing committed outside the time period of the DPA wrongdoing.[165] Furthermore, it was briefly acknowledged that the DPA constitutes a 'consensual agreement',[166] though this was not expanded upon. It would appear that the unparalleled time periods and consequent decision that the DPA would not be used to draw inference somewhat restricted the extent of analysis on this particular point within the judgment. The case does, however, suggest that a corporate negotiated DPA (here agreed in a foreign jurisdiction: the US) may be considered in evidence, as drawing an inference of individual wrongdoing, in permitting third-party civil proceedings, as the possibility was not outrightly excluded.

As it has been set out that admissions or statements made by a company within a DPA can form the basis of setting out a serious issue to be tried (supporting a case against an individual, even if just allowing the claim/proceedings against the individual to be made), and are capable of being treated as hearsay evidence,[167] it follows that they may be raised in evidence against an individual during civil proceedings.[168] In *Shagang Shipping Company Ltd (in liquidation) v HNA Group Company Ltd*,[169] it was reiterated that admissibility of hearsay evidence in civil proceedings would not be based upon a fact-finding rule; the court is instead required to have regard to 'any circumstances from which any inference can reasonably be drawn as to the reliability or otherwise of the evidence'.[170] The negotiated nature of the admissions will be assessed in respect of their credibility, but nevertheless represent an account agreed upon by a company and prosecutor typically following many years of investigation and negotiation, and put to the court by the prosecutor on the basis that they understand them to be accurate.[171] The DPA and/or statement of facts would, therefore, be admissible hearsay evidence in civil proceedings, but any drafts made pursuant to unsuccessful negotiations would most likely not. In accordance with

162 *Libyan Investment Authority v JP Morgan Markets Ltd* [2019] EWHC 1452 (Comm) [194]. Civil claims have similarly arisen following a DPA revealing otherwise unknown wrongdoing. *See Allianz Global Investors GmbH v G4S Limited (formerly known as GS4 PLC)* [2022] EWHC 1081 (Ch) [21] (Mr Justice Miles). *See also Various Claimants v G4S Limited (formerly G4S PLC)* [2022] EWHC 1742 (Ch); *Various Claimants v Serco Group plc* [2022] EWHC 2052 (Ch).

163 [2021] EWHC 2875 (Comm).

164 ibid [418.3].

165 ibid [400]–[419], [620]–[623] (Moulder J).

166 ibid [16] (Moulder J).

167 '[A] statement made otherwise than by a person while giving oral evidence in the proceedings which is tendered as evidence of the matters stated'. *See* Civil Evidence Act 1995, s 1(2)(a).

168 'In civil proceedings evidence shall not be excluded on the ground that it is hearsay.' *See* ibid s 1(1).

169 [2020] UKSC 34.

170 Civil Evidence Act 1995, s 4(1); ibid [96]; *Re B (Children) (Care Proceedings: Standard of Proof) (CAFCASS intervening)* [2008] UKHL 35.

171 *Director of the Serious Fraud Office v Amec Foster Wheeler Limited* [2021] Lloyd's Rep FC 353 (Crown) [11]–[12] (Edis LJ); Crown Prosecution Service and Serious Fraud Office, 'Deferred Prosecution Agreements Code of Practice' (n 15) para 6.2.

Omers, "other evidence" arising from DPA negotiations may be obtainable by claimants in civil proceedings,[172] but this case will not be a "one size fits all" decision and disclosure may depend on a balancing of factors such as confidentiality, private or public interest, and relevance. Nevertheless, disclosure and admissibility as hearsay evidence against individuals following DPA negotiation remain possible.

172 A self-report may ultimately be used against an individual: directly or indirectly. A statement of facts and/or "other evidence" would likely have more value, forming an indirect use of the corporate self-report (the statement of facts and other evidence likely arising from the self-report). The extent to which a self-report becomes admissible may depend on the breadth of privilege and any limited waiver. Where a self-report has been disclosed to an individual and used in evidence in their own criminal proceedings, such use may lead to privilege being lost and open up use for third parties in civil proceedings thereafter. *See PCP Capital Partners LLP v Barclays Bank Plc* (n 19) [106]. *See also* Ministry of Justice, *Consultation on a New Enforcement Tool to Deal With Economic Crime Committed by Commercial Organisations: Deferred Prosecution Agreements* (Cm 8348, 2012) 121.

CHAPTER 8

Naming in documentation

8.1 Relevant statute and guidance

DPAs in their novelty in the UK, as an alternative to prosecution for companies and not individuals, were introduced with little provision addressing the adverse impact on individuals. Though there is some guidance within the DPA Code on the use of certain material against individuals[1] (**Section 7.3**), and provision in relevant documentation on postponement of publication to avoid prejudice to individual proceedings,[2] there was no guidance on the *naming* of individuals within documentation until late 2020. The SFO Operational Handbook chapter on DPAs, published on 23 October 2020, finally set out guidance on the naming of individuals, though arguably came too late. The Handbook appears to separate the statement of facts' drafting stage and publication stage, in respect of the provision of guidance on naming individuals. Regarding the naming of individuals during the drafting of the statement of facts and negotiation stage, it is set out within the Handbook that:

> Consideration must be given to the necessity for and impact of the identities of third parties being published and whether this would be compliant with the Data Protection Act 2018 and the European Convention on Human Rights. In some cases anonymization of the identity of third parties in the statement of facts may be appropriate prior to publication.[3]

In respect of the publication of the statement of facts, postponement where necessary to avoid the risk of prejudice to linked proceedings is set out, though:

> Ordinarily such delayed publication should only apply to the statement of facts since the DPA itself and the court's judgment will probably not include information tending to identify individuals.[4]

It is outlined that the risk of prejudice in the naming of individuals may be addressed by way of the publication of 'a redacted or (further) anonymised statement of facts'; application for an order for reporting restrictions under section 4(2) of the Contempt of Court

1 Crown Prosecution Service and Serious Fraud Office, 'Deferred Prosecution Agreements Code of Practice' (*Crown Prosecution Service*, 11 February 2014) <https://www.cps.gov.uk/sites/default/files/documents/publications/dpa_cop.pdf> accessed 9 June 2020, para 4.5.

2 Explanatory Notes to the Crime and Courts Act 2013, para 570.

3 Serious Fraud Office, 'Deferred Prosecution Agreements' (*Serious Fraud Office*, 23 October 2020) <https://www.sfo.gov.uk/publications/guidance-policy-and-protocols/sfo-operational-handbook/deferred-prosecution-agreements/> accessed 23 October 2020.

4 ibid.

 DOI: 10.4324/9781003456964-10

Act 1981; and consideration of risks posed by human rights issues in other jurisdictions.[5] Notably, these options precede the conclusion of cases against individuals.

By the time the Handbook chapter was published, eight UK DPAs had been approved (all agreed by the SFO). One of those eight DPAs named individuals within the actual DPA document (*Standard Bank*), and three of those eight named individuals within the judgment (*Standard Bank*, *Tesco Stores Ltd*, and *Güralp Systems Ltd*). Therefore, Handbook commentary tending to suggest that a DPA and/or judgment will 'probably not include information tending to identify individuals'[6] cannot be deemed reflective of previous practice, but instead guidance for the SFO position going forward. Though this guidance may be adhered to by the SFO in respect of DPA drafting, ultimately the drafting of the judgment is at the discretion of the judge. Of the eight approved DPAs at the time, six statements of facts had been published and four of those six (two-thirds) had expressly named individuals (*Standard Bank*, *Sarclad Ltd*, *Tesco Stores Ltd*, and *Güralp Systems Ltd*). The latter three all resulted in the criminal prosecution of individuals named within the UK, with no resulting convictions. Though there was no UK criminal prosecution of the individuals named in the *Standard Bank* DPA, individuals were prosecuted in Tanzania and entered a plea agreement there.[7]

8.2 Naming "unindicted co-conspirators"

8.2.1 US approach

In the US, the naming and accusing of an individual in a criminal case to which the individual is not a defendant has been the subject of much disapproval.[8] In *United States v Briggs*,[9] the naming of 'unindicted co-conspirators'[10] in a grand jury indictment (of others) was in violation of due process. In the case of *In re Smith*,[11] the naming of an individual as an unindicted co-conspirator in a factual resume read in open court and filed in a criminal case – prepared in furtherance of a plea hearing – was in violation of the individual's liberty and property rights, as afforded by the Fifth Amendment of the US Constitution. In both cases there was focus on the lack of forum for vindication available

5 ibid. This was addressed in the *Rolls-Royce* approved judgment, in relation to punishment for corruption and bribery and in consideration of Article 3 of the European Convention on Human Rights. *See Serious Fraud Office v Rolls-Royce Plc* [2017] Lloyd's Rep FC 249 (Crown) [32].

6 Serious Fraud Office, 'Deferred Prosecution Agreements' (n 3).

7 Ofisi ya Taifa ya Mashtaka, 'Tweet' (*Twitter*, 28 August 2020) <https://twitter.com/OMashtaka/status/1299305655996690432?s=20> accessed 4 January 2021; Basel Institute on Governance, 'From the UK's First Deferred Prosecution Agreement to a Plea Bargain in Tanzania' (*Basel Institute on Governance*, 9 September 2020) <https://baselgovernance.org/news/uks-first-deferred-prosecution-agreement-plea-bargain-tanzania> accessed 2 February 2021.

8 *United States v Briggs* 514 F 2d 794 (5th Cir 1975); *In re Smith* 656 F 2d 1101 (5th Cir 1981); *United States of America v Holy Land Foundation for Relief and Development and others* CR No 3:04-CR-240-G (ND Tex Dec 8 2006).

9 *United States v Briggs* (n 8).

10 'Any person who allegedly "agreed with others to violate the law but who is not being charged with an offense and who, consequently, will not be tried or sentenced for his criminal conduct."' *See* United States Senate Committee on the Judiciary and Subcommittee on the Constitution, Federalism, and Property Rights, *Impeachment Or Indictment: Is a Sitting President Subject to the Compulsory Criminal Process?* (Serial no J-105-119, US Government Printing Office 1999) 225. *See also* Ira Robbins, 'Guilty Without Charge: Assessing the Due Process Rights of Unindicted Co-Conspirators' (2004) 1 Fed Cts L Rev 1, 6.

11 *In re Smith* (n 8).

to those named as unindicted co-conspirators.[12] Since the DPA process is designed to avoid the necessity of a criminal trial, and thus removes a forum for vindication of individuals named within the company's statement of facts, implicated individuals should not be named within DPA-related documentation. Even where individuals are later prosecuted and thus arguably afforded some forum for vindication, this does not remove their right to protection at a prior stage.[13] There has been some distinction between the identification of unindicted co-conspirators pre-trial and at trial (of others): identification at trial (typically in evidence against another) 'does not allow for the reasonable inference that they are criminals', whereas identification within pre-trial documentation does.[14] Though *In re Smith* outlined that the naming of an individual was not done for the purpose of determining factual bases for the defendants' guilty pleas,[15] it remains the case that this was pre-trial and the same outcome could have been achieved by adopting an anonymous or pseudonymous approach.

This approach has been translated into the US DoJ's Justice Manual (Criminal) where it is stated that 'ordinarily, there is no need to name a person as an unindicted co-conspirator in an indictment in order to fulfill any legitimate prosecutorial interest or duty' and any descriptors should be generic and non-specific.[16] However, this is discretionary, and federal prosecutors may depart from the advice where it is considered that there is 'significant justification'[17] in doing so. It has been posed that attitudes against the identification of unindicted co-conspirators have led to increased use of anonymity tools (such as the reference to individuals by number or by "John Doe"), though the discretion in specificity in relation to the extent of those individuals' involvement in wrongdoing may nevertheless render those individuals identifiable as a result.[18] Though this area has not been addressed by the US Supreme Court, and the naming of unindicted co-conspirators may still occur,[19] it is not taken to be general practice.

It has been argued that whilst prosecutors in the US may opt to name unindicted co-conspirators so as to allow for a hearsay exception in evidence at trial,[20] this will not necessarily result where plea-bargain agreements are obtained, and thus may not be necessary pre-trial.[21] Significant justification is required in order to identify unindicted third-party wrongdoers by name, or in order to use unnecessarily specific descriptors (such as initials) during plea proceedings of another.[22] Tayed suggests that the use of plea-bargaining would

12 *United States v Briggs* (n 8) 804; ibid 1107.

13 *In re Smith* (n 8) 1107; Raeed Tayed, 'Implicated but not Charged: Improving Due Process for Unindicted Co-Conspirators' (2014) 47(2) Akron L Rev 551, 563.

14 *United States v Anderson* 55 F Supp 2d 1163, 1169–1170 (D Kan 1999).

15 *In re Smith* (n 8) 1106.

16 The United States Department of Justice, 'Justice Manual > 9-11.130 – Limitation on Naming Persons as Unindicted Co-Conspirators' (*The United States Department of Justice*, April 2018) <https://www.justice.gov/jm/jm-9-11000-grand-jury#9-11.130> accessed 2 February 2021.

17 ibid.

18 'By failing to impose limits on the level of specificity used in describing unindicted co-conspirators in indictments, the [US Attorneys' Manual] opens the door to undue specificity whose effect is equivalent to naming such individuals.' *See* Tayed (n 13) 562.

19 ibid 552.

20 *United States v Anderson* (n 14) 1169; The United States Department of Justice, 'Justice Manual > 9-11.130 – Limitation on Naming Persons as Unindicted Co-Conspirators' (n 16).

21 Tayed (n 13) 584–585.

22 The United States Department of Justice, 'Justice Manual > 9-16.500 – Identifying Uncharged Third-Parties During Plea and Sentencing Proceedings' (*The United States Department of Justice*, December 2014)

promote the approach of filing under seal.[23] Filing pre-trial documentation under seal would mean that such documentation would not be publicly accessible. This approach, for reasons explored in **Section 8.2.3**, would not be adoptable in the UK as a means of permanent restriction (considered contrary to the principle of open justice), though reporting restrictions may instead be of use as an interim safeguard.

8.2.2 European Court of Human Rights approach

The case of *Vicent del Campo v Spain*[24] concerns the extent to which an unindicted individual named in judicial proceedings (to which they have no involvement), and therein described as having engaged in criminal conduct, is protected under Article 8 of the ECHR. Vicent Del Campo had been accused of harassment in the workplace (a public school), but allegations against him personally were not pursued by the alleged victim.[25] The alleged victim instituted judicial proceedings against the Regional Administration of Castilla-Léon ("the Administration") in respect of the harassment, the Department of Education being aware of it, and the failure to take effective measures to ensure its cessation.[26] In its judgment, ruling against the Administration, the High Court of Justice of Castilla-Léon frequently identified Del Campo by full name and other personal data and – going beyond the determination of strict liability of the Administration – outlined that Del Campo's conduct had amounted to harassment. Del Campo had not been aware of the judicial proceedings, having understood the matter to have ceased upon an understanding that the alleged victim would not pursue criminal charges against him, and learnt of the judgment as a result of a newspaper report.[27] Del Campo, on application to the court, was granted access to the case file but was not permitted to be a party to the proceedings, on the basis of him not being an interested party.[28] An *amparo* appeal (regarding protection of constitutional rights) was lodged with the domestic Constitutional Court, and upon a declaration of inadmissibility the matter was brought to the European Court of Human Rights ("ECtHR").[29]

In respect of Del Campo's right to respect for private and family life in accordance with Article 8 of the ECHR, it was unanimously determined that the right had been violated.[30] Del Campo was not a party to the underlying proceedings and did not have the opportunity to participate in them, though the domestic courts had set out the opportunity to defend allegations in a recovery action.[31] A recovery action would allow Del Campo to contest liability of the Administration,[32] including any acts attributed to him personally.[33]

<https://www.justice.gov/jm/jm-9-16000-pleas-federal-rule-criminal-procedure-11#9-16.500> accessed 2 February 2021.

23 FRE R 801(d)(2)(E); Tayed (n 13) 584–585.

24 App no 25527/13 (ECtHR, 6 November 2018).

25 ibid para 3.

26 ibid para 10.

27 ibid para 11.

28 ibid para 12.

29 ibid para 14.

30 ibid para 56.

31 ibid para 39.

32 *Ley 30/1992, de 26 de noviembre, de Régimen Jurídico de las Administraciones Públicas y del Procedimiento Administrativo Común* (Spain).

33 *Vicent Del Campo v Spain* (n 24) para 13.

The naming of Del Campo and conclusions as to the nature of his conduct were held to be capable of adversely affecting his enjoyment of private and family life, with Article 8 encompassing the right to protection of reputation[34] (which includes a person's honour).[35] Article 8 cannot be relied upon in respect of loss of reputation amounting to the foreseeable consequence of one's own actions (with the example given of 'the commission of a criminal offence'); however it was determined that Del Campo could not have foreseen the consequences as he was not aware of nor a party to the proceedings, he understood the original complaint to have been dismissed, and he had never been charged with or proven to have committed an offence.[36]

Though the interference was deemed to have been in accordance with the law,[37] it was not justified under Article 8(2) as the High Court's actions were 'disproportionate to the legitimate aims pursued'[38] and not necessary in a democratic society. The High Court had gone beyond declaring liability of the Administration, in drawing conclusions as to the nature of Del Campo's conduct and by identifying him by name and other relevant data,[39] which 'stigmatised' him and was capable of having a major impact on his personal and professional life.[40] Though there is 'public interest in ensuring transparency of court proceedings',[41] 'protection of personal data is of fundamental importance' under Article 8, and disclosure of name and conclusions as to his actions 'was not supported by any cogent reasons'.[42] The alleged violation of Article 6(1) (and Article 13)[43] of the ECHR in *Vicent del Campo* was not examined as a result of the findings in respect of Article 8.[44]

8.2.3 UK approach

According to *The New York Times* reporting in 2013, 22 individuals were notified by the SFO that they were being investigated when the prosecutor alerted them to the fact that they had been named in court papers relating to the indictment of Tom Hayes, Terry Farr and James Gilmour (in relation to London Interbank Offered Rate ("LIBOR") manipulation), and that their names may be released by the court within a week. None of those 22 individuals had at the time been charged, and some had not been interviewed, even upon volunteering to do so.[45] Prior to publication by the court, anticipated on the Monday, the High Court issued an injunction prohibiting reporting of the names following an article

34 ibid para 36; *Axel Springer AG v Germany* App no 39954/08 (ECtHR, 7 February 2012), para 83.
35 *Vicent Del Campo v Spain* (n 24) para 36; *A v Norway* App no 28070/06 (ECtHR, 9 April 2009), para 63.
36 *Vicent Del Campo v Spain* (n 24) para 41; *Axel Springer AG v Germany* (n 34) para 83.
37 *Vicent Del Campo v Spain* (n 24) para 44.
38 ibid para 56.
39 ibid para 47.
40 ibid para 48.
41 ibid para 45.
42 ibid para 49.
43 'Everyone whose rights and freedoms as set forth in this Convention are violated shall have an effective remedy before a national authority notwithstanding that the violation has been committed by persons acting in an official capacity.' *See* Convention for the Protection of Human Rights and Fundamental Freedoms (European Convention on Human Rights, as amended) (ECHR) art 13.
44 *Vicent Del Campo v Spain* (n 24) para 60.
45 Chad Bray, '22 Under Investigation in Libor Case in Britain' (*The New York Times*, 21 October 2013) <https://dealbook.nytimes.com/2013/10/21/22-named-as-co-conspirators-in-libor-case-in-britain/> accessed 27 April 2021.

posted on *The Wall Street Journal* website.[46] On the Monday, Justice Jeremy Cooke permitted removal of the names of the unindicted third parties from two of the draft indictments and thus refrained from publishing the names, after representatives of the individuals (whom they referred to as "Mr X" or "Y") refuted their naming on the public record. Names remained on one indictment.[47] The injunction was lifted, as it was opined that the individuals would not be harmed at that stage (as action by the SFO would arise in the future), though *The Wall Street Journal* was cautioned against reporting the names where improperly obtained.[48] Ultimately six of the 22 individuals were prosecuted and acquitted of all charges,[49] but names of others unindicted remain publicly available.[50]

The 2017 Supreme Court judgment in *Khuja v Times Newspapers Limited*[51] considered the naming of unindicted persons at trial. As opposed to economic crime, this case concerned the naming of an individual (known as "PNM") in evidence in a trial relating to sexual offences against minors. PNM had been named by one victim in their statements to the police and was arrested, released on bail with the condition of surrendering his passport, and de-arrested.[52] The victim had referred to a person sharing the same first name as PNM, and PNM was thereafter mentioned during the trial (for example, one police officer noted that he had not been identified by the victim during an identity parade) and was identified by his full name.[53] The question facing the Supreme Court was whether the media could identify PNM in their reports on the matter. Multiple orders had been made in respect of the reporting of information identifying or tending to identify PNM, and an order under section 4(2) of the Contempt of Court Act 1981 was in place to prohibit such reporting in anticipation of a charge. Upon notification that a charge would not be made, *The Times* and *Oxford Mail* applied to the court to lift the order.[54] A draft ruling proposing to lift the order was never formalised as the matter moved to the High Court when PNM applied for an interim injunction.[55] PNM argued that the necessity for the High Court order was twofold: to protect against the tort of misuse of private information; and to protect against infringement of the right to private and family life under Article 8 of the ECHR. PNM was ultimately unsuccessful: the order was revoked, and PNM named in the Supreme Court judgment as Tariq Khuja.[56]

---

46 The court order was thereafter published by *The Wall Street Journal*. *See The Wall Street Journal Editor*, 'In the Matter of R v Tom Hayes, Terry Farr and James Gilmour' (*The Wall Street Journal*, 21 October 2013) <http://online.wsj.com/public/resources/documents/injunction20131017.pdf> accessed 27 April 2021. *See also* David Enrich and Jenny Strasburg, 'U.K. Expected to Name Alleged Co-Conspirators in Libor Scandal' (*The Wall Street Journal*, 21 October 2013) <https://www.wsj.com/articles/SB10001424052702304864504579141350746645742> accessed 27 April 2021; Bray (n 45).

47 Enrich and Strasburg (n 46); Bray (n 45).

48 Bray (n 45); Cassell Bryan-Low and Jenny Strasburg, 'Judge Allows Publication of Names in Libor Case' (*The Wall Street Journal*, 21 October 2013) <https://www.wsj.com/articles/SB10001424052702304402104579149500282467112> accessed 27 April 2021.

49 Serious Fraud Office, 'LIBOR Defendants Acquitted' (*Serious Fraud Office*, 28 January 2016) <https://www.sfo.gov.uk/2016/01/27/libor-defendants-aquitted/> accessed 27 April 2021.

50 Enrich and Strasburg (n 46).

51 [2017] UKSC 49.

52 ibid [4].

53 ibid [7].

54 ibid [10].

55 So as to restrain publication of information identifying PNM as a person connected with the investigation, the subject of the section 4(2) orders, or the claimant in the present proceedings. *See* ibid [11].

56 The application was dismissed in reserved judgment, and an appeal was dismissed by the Court of Appeal, though the status quo was preserved by the continuation of the original order. The order under s 4(2) of

It was outlined by Lord Sumption – with whom Lord Neuberger, Lady Hale, Lord Clarke, and Lord Reed agreed – that the reporting of matters discussed at a public trial were not matters in which Khuja could have had any reasonable expectation of privacy, in respect of giving rise to the tort of misuse of private information.[57] The matters discussed did not relate to Khuja's family, and neither he nor his family participated in the trial, and thus any impact on his family life as per Article 8 of the ECHR would be indirect and incidental; using the same authority to protect reputation cannot be established where there is no reasonable expectation of privacy.[58] Speaking to the privileged right to produce a fair and accurate report of legal proceedings, as per Article 10 of the ECHR:

> the collateral impact that this process has on those affected is part of the price to be paid for open justice and the freedom of the press to report fairly and accurately on judicial proceedings held in public.[59]

As such, any defamation claim in respect of adverse impact on family life as an indirect result of reputational harm would not result in an injunction against reporting.[60] However, Lord Kerr and Lord Wilson (in dissent) would have allowed the appeal.[61] In dissent, it was outlined that Lord Rodger in *Re Guardian News and Media Ltd*[62] had stated a legal presumption that the wider public believe that an individual charged with an offence is innocent until proven guilty, but had done so without supporting evidence or authority. As the application was only for an interim injunction, it was set out that at interim inquiry Lord Kerr and Lord Wilson were of the view that Khuja would have been able to establish his right to an injunction in accordance with his Article 8 right. Khuja not being a defendant in the relevant trial removed any opportunity for him to clear his name where the media was confined to fair, accurate, and contemporaneous reporting,[63] also removing the opportunity to 'vindicate his reputation' in civil proceedings.[64] In concluding, Lord Kerr and Lord Wilson outlined that the court needed to recognise that identification carried a risk of generating widespread public belief of guilt and perceived evasion of punishment, in considering the impact on Khuja's Article 8 right (particularly without forum for vindication), despite the fact that in law there exists a presumption of innocence.[65]

Though not a case of naming of unindicted persons at trial, the 2017 Supreme Court judgment in *Financial Conduct Authority v Macris*[66] demonstrates the objection to the identification of individuals in the issuing of a public regulatory notice against a corporate body. The FCA had issued a notice to JP Morgan Chase Bank NA and referred

---

the Contempt of Court Act 1981 was revoked by the Supreme Court and the appeal dismissed, with the defendant named in the judgment. *See* ibid [11], [36].

57 ibid [34(1)]; *Campbell v Mirror Group Newspapers Ltd* [2004] UKHL 22 [14] (Lord Nicholls).

58 *Khuja v Times Newspapers Limited* (n 51) [34(3)].

59 ibid [34(2)].

60 ibid [34(3)].

61 ibid [37].

62 [2010] UKSC 1 [66] (Lord Rodger).

63 Defamation Act 1996, s 14(1); *PNM v Times Newspapers Ltd* [2013] EWHC 3177 (QB) [76] (Tugendhat J); *Khuja v Times Newspapers Limited* (n 51) [32] (Lord Sumption).

64 Defamation Act 1996, s 14(1); *Khuja v Times Newspapers Limited* (n 51) [34(2)] (Lord Sumption); UKSupremeCourt, 'Khuja v Times Newspapers Limited and Others' (*YouTube*, 19 July 2017) <https://www.youtube.com/watch?v=QSQQfYYB9yo> accessed 27 April 2021, [05:31]–[05:43].

65 *Khuja v Times Newspapers Limited* (n 51) [58] (Lord Kerr and Lord Wilson).

66 [2017] UKSC 19.

to the conduct of the 'CIO London management'.[67] The litigation in question arose as a consequence of one individual, Achilles Macris – at the time of the notice, the Bank's International Chief Investment Officer (and head of a unit of the Bank in London called the "Chief Investment Office") – disputing that the wording used had identified him, thus giving rise to the protections set out within section 393 of the Financial Services and Markets Act 2000, as amended by the Financial Services Act 2012. Such protections provide an individual, where identified, with the opportunity to make representations to the regulator, upon the provision of adequate notice. Macris was not provided such notice and thus did not have the opportunity to make representations. The issue facing the Supreme Court was whether Macris was in fact "identified" within the regulatory notice, so as to give rise to such procedure.

There was argument within the case that Macris was not the only manager in CIO International in London; however, uncontested witness statements were provided to the extent that those within the markets would have known/believed the notice to refer to him.[68] In the leading judgment by Lord Sumption, it was set out that:

> [A] person is identified in a notice under section 393 if he is identified by name or by a synonym for him, such as his office or job title. In the case of a synonym, it must be apparent from the notice itself that it could apply to only one person and that person must be identifiable from information which is either in the notice or publicly available elsewhere.[69]

However, Lord Sumption – with whom Lord Neuberger and Lord Hodge agreed – held that Macris was not a third party for the purpose of triggering section 393, considering a specific test of 'whether the terms of the notice itself would have conveyed to a reasonable member of the public *without* extrinsic information that any of these terms was a synonym for [the individual]' (emphasis added).[70] Lord Mance agreed with Lord Wilson (in dissent) on the point of law but ultimately reached the same outcome as Lord Sumption in allowing the appeal.[71] Lord Wilson, in dissent, raised issue with the decision of the court, and questioned whether the point raised by the appeal would have 'significant implications for individuals wrongly criticised in warning and decision notices given by the [FCA] to others'.[72] Lord Wilson criticised the attitude towards the consideration of extrinsic evidence, and acknowledged the realities of jigsaw identification by the 'ordinary market operator'[73] upon reading such a notice. In this respect, Lord Wilson set out an alternative test, which ultimately was not followed by the majority:

> Are the words in the notice such as would reasonably lead an operator in the same sector of the market who is not personally acquainted with the applicant, by reference only to information in the public domain to which he would have ready access, to conclude that the individual referred to in the notice is the applicant?[74]

67 ibid [8].
68 ibid.
69 ibid [11] (Lord Sumption).
70 ibid [17] (Lord Sumption).
71 'A notice will, in my view, only identify an individual if it does so to persons operating in that world, unacquainted with the particular individual or his company, though familiar with information generally available publicly to operators in that world.' *See* ibid [37] (Lord Mance).
72 ibid [46] (Lord Wilson).
73 ibid [66] (Lord Wilson).
74 ibid [63] (Lord Wilson).

Where synonyms can give rise to identification, the approach proposed by Lord Wilson aligns more clearly with the objectives of the section 393 protections, which in the words of Lord Sumption are 'for protecting them against unfair prejudice'.[75] In any event, despite any criticism of the Supreme Court in its interpretation of "identification", it is interesting to note that the Financial Services and Markets Act 2000, as amended by the Financial Services Act 2012, provides such protection (though arguably flawed) through the statutory framework – an option arguably overlooked in the development of the CACA 2013.[76]

8.3 Naming individuals in DPA documentation

8.3.1 Anonymising the statement of facts and judgment

Where there is discretion to anonymise the statement of facts and/or judgment, as there is in UK DPA cases, that discretion should be exercised except where the implicated individual has been convicted of the offence referred to. Such discretion lies with the prosecutor and the judge. The prosecutor has the discretion to draft the statement of facts in an anonymised manner,[77] as has been previously exercised. The judge has the discretion not only to anonymise the judgment handed down, but also to direct that the statement of facts be suitably anonymised.[78] The judge cannot, however, adjudicate on factual differences or conduct a fact-finding trial.[79]

Reporting restrictions ordered during DPA proceedings provide an interim safeguard in protecting an implicated individual's right to a fair trial as under Article 6 of the ECHR, but the protecting of their Article 8 right (including protection of reputation) requires earlier attention in the drafting stage of the statement of facts. In *Vicent del Campo* it was determined that the domestic High Court had discretion in respect of naming or allowing the identification of Del Campo within the judgment (a practice followed by the domestic Constitutional Court),[80] and in respect of reporting in line with ECHR and public policy considerations.[81] The High Court had the ability to anonymise Del Campo, and the ECtHR set out that it may have elected to do so by use of initials.[82] As there is precedent for this practice in respect of UK DPAs, there is no reason why – as the ECtHR determined with the Spanish High Court – the court should not '[adopt] appropriate measures to protect

75 ibid [6] (Lord Sumption).

76 Amanda Pinto, 'Right to Anonymity: Fallout from DPAs on Third Parties' (*The Times*, 10 December 2015) <https://www.thetimes.co.uk/article/right-to-anonymity-fallout-from-dpas-on-third-parties-7v6kb-f6gk67> accessed 25 September 2023.

77 Serious Fraud Office, 'Deferred Prosecution Agreements' (n 3).

78 'Sir Brian Leveson told us that in one of the four cases to date he had not approved the application on the first occasion: "I made a number of points to the SFO and to the company concerned. In effect, I told them to go away and think again … They did think again. Then the parties came back and I was prepared to be satisfied." Since the hearing was in private, we do not know the reason why Sir Leveson did not approve the application on the first occasion'. *See* Select Committee on the Bribery Act 2010, *The Bribery Act 2010: Post-Legislative Scrutiny* (HL 2017–19, 303) para 290. *See also Director of the Serious Fraud Office v Amec Foster Wheeler Limited* [2021] Lloyd's Rep FC 353 (Crown) [4]-[5] (Edis LJ); *Director of the Serious Fraud Office v AB Ltd and another* [2021] Lexis Citation 1385 (Crown) [20] (Mrs Justice May DBE).

79 Crown Prosecution Service and Serious Fraud Office, 'Deferred Prosecution Agreements Code of Practice' (n 1) para 6.2.

80 *Vicent Del Campo v Spain* (n 24) paras 24, 52.

81 ibid para 50.

82 ibid para 51.

[the individuals'] right to respect for private life in drafting the judgment'[83] and in giving direction as to the appropriateness of the drafting of the statement of facts (albeit not in amending the presented facts).

In assessing the naming of unindicted third parties in legal proceedings, it is not sufficient to simply consider the typical approach taken in criminal trials. A criminal trial will, in accordance with the principle of open justice, generally be held in open court, and evidence communicated will thus be done so publicly.[84] The trial referred to in the case of *Khuja* was an open and public trial, one in which Khuja was named but not an involved party. Khuja was not able to give evidence in his own defence, though evidence was given in reference to him and in support of his presumed innocence.[85] That trial being public in nature meant that Khuja was not determined to have had a reasonable expectation of privacy, in respect of giving rise to the tort of misuse of private information,[86] and that the press were entitled to make a fair and accurate report of the legal proceedings (in fact, they were under a duty to do so).[87] Sir Igor Judge set out the importance of reporting criminal trials in *Re Trinity Mirror plc*,[88] with focus on those convicted and their expected consequences of criminal wrongdoing, particularly in resulting reports and public scrutiny. Arguably *Khuja* goes further than this, in setting out that reporting the identity of persons mentioned at trial but not themselves indicted ascribes to the principle of open justice. Notably, however, the importance of reporting in this argument centres on criminal trials and ensuring the right to a fair trial of those indicted.

In contrast, the DPA process is conducted very differently. The principle of open justice is not absolute and is somewhat restricted in the DPA process by the CACA 2013,[89] but remains capable of being adhered to despite its private elements. Though it has been

---

83 ibid para 55.

84 *A-G v Leveller Magazine Ltd* [1979] AC 440 (HL) 450 (Lord Diplock); Paul Wragg, 'Open Justice and Privacy' (2017) 22(3) CL 89, 89; C Edwin Baker, *Human Liberty and Freedom of Speech* (Oxford University Press 1989) 68.

85 *Khuja v Times Newspapers Limited* (n 51) [57].

86 ibid [34(1)]; *Campbell v Mirror Group Newspapers Ltd* (n 57) [14] (Lord Nicholls).

87 'Whilst it must not overstep the bounds set, inter alia, in the "interests of national security" or for "maintaining the authority of the judiciary", it is nevertheless incumbent on it to impart information and ideas on matters of public interest. Not only does the press have the task of imparting such information and ideas: the public also has a right to receive them. Were it otherwise, the press would be unable to play its vital role of "public watchdog"'. *See The Sunday Times v The United Kingdom* App no 13166/87 (ECtHR, 26 November 1991), para 50(c). *See also The Observer and The Guardian v The United Kingdom* App no 13585/88 (ECtHR, 26 November 1991), para 59(b); *Campbell v Mirror Group Newspapers Ltd* (n 57) [107] (Lord Hope); Convention for the Protection of Human Rights and Fundamental Freedoms (European Convention on Human Rights, as amended) (ECHR) art 10.

88 '[I]t is impossible to over-emphasise the importance to be attached to the ability of the media to report criminal trials. In simple terms this represents the embodiment of the principle of open justice in a free country. An important aspect of the public interest in the administration of criminal justice is that the identity of those convicted and sentenced for criminal offices should not be concealed. Uncomfortable though it may frequently be for the defendant that is a normal consequence of his crime. Moreover the principle protects his interests too, by helping to secure the fair trial … From time to time occasions will arise where restrictions on this principle are considered appropriate, but they depend on express legislation, and, where the court is vested with a discretion to exercise such powers, on the absolute necessity for doing so in the individual case.' *See* [2008] EWCA Crim 50 [32] (Sir Igor Judge P).

89 The preliminary hearing must be held in private, and the final hearing may be held in private. *See* Crime and Courts Act 2013, sch 17 paras 7(4), 8(5). *See also* Edward Craven and Alex Bailin, 'Publicity: The UK Perspective' (*Global Investigations Review*, 3 January 2020) <https://globalinvestigationsreview.com/guide/the-practitioners-guide-global-investigations/2020/article/publicity-the-uk-perspective> accessed 1 May 2021.

outlined that a hearing *in camera*, such as a DPA preliminary hearing, involves a departure from the principle of open justice (not natural justice),[90] a public final hearing and/or ultimate publication (following removal of reporting restrictions) of DPA documentation (including the statement of facts) into the public domain constitutes a 'relatively modest [interference]'.[91]

The statement of facts pursuant to the DPA is negotiated in private, and the facts are not adjudicated upon by the judge.[92] The statement of facts as evidence, and its treatment and verifiability, is therefore not open to public scrutiny in the same way, nor immediately subscribed to the principle of open justice (though later published and publicly available).[93] The statement of facts is agreed between the wrongdoer company and prosecutor – and thus can be taken to represent the prosecutor's position on and understanding as to the matter – and is approved by the judge (albeit holistically) as forming part of the DPA. An implicated individual is not permitted to be involved in the drafting of the statement of facts, and though the prosecutor is required to make a written declaration to the court that the information is not known to be inaccurate, misleading, or incomplete,[94] the account is ultimately that agreed between the prosecutor and company alone.[95] The ECtHR in *Vicent del Campo* reiterated the position of the domestic Constitutional Court, that 'neither the reasoning nor the statement of facts' in the proceedings against the Administration had 'the force of *res judicata*' in respect of subsequent proceedings against the individual.[96] Irrespective of this point, the adverse impact of the statement of facts (and/or judgment) continues to be a matter of wider concern.[97]

Although there is no scope for public scrutiny of the negotiations and private (preliminary) hearing conducted prior to final approval, the State may have a positive duty to ensure that individuals' rights under Article 8 are protected.[98] Article 8 includes the right to protection of reputation,[99] protected also within Article 10(2),[100] and this is particularly crucial where an individual is wholly restricted from any forum to clear their name. The DPA process is inherently confidential and, as previously set out, it is unlikely that individuals implicated in wrongdoing would either know of negotiations or know of their progress. The preliminary

---

90 *Guardian News and Media Ltd v Incedal* [2014] EWCA Crim 1861 [12].

91 'The extent of interference with the principle of open justice occasioned by a private hearing was, in this case, relatively modest given that all parties agreed that my judgment should be public.' *See R (on the application of Grace Bay II Holdings Sarl) v Pensions Regulator* [2017] EWHC 7 (Admin) [7]. '[T]he open justice principle may well require some information about proceedings which are quite properly taking place in private being put into the public domain, depending on all the circumstances.' *See R (on the application of DSD) v Parole Board of England and Wales* [2018] EWHC 694 (Admin) [175].

92 Crown Prosecution Service and Serious Fraud Office, 'Deferred Prosecution Agreements Code of Practice' (n 1) para 6.2.

93 'The open justice principle applies equally to the publication of the proceedings themselves as it does to evidence communicated to the court, at least in criminal proceedings': Wragg (n 84) 89.

94 Crown Prosecution Service and Serious Fraud Office, 'Deferred Prosecution Agreements Code of Practice' (n 1) para 5.5.

95 Serious Fraud Office, 'Deferred Prosecution Agreements' (n 3).

96 *Vicent Del Campo v Spain* (n 24) para 39.

97 Despite the presumption of innocence at law, identification of unindicted individuals at trial may nonetheless generate a widespread public belief of guilt and perceived evasion of punishment, as per Lord Kerr and Lord Wilson (in *obiter*). *See Khuja v Times Newspapers Limited* (n 51) [58] (Lord Kerr and Lord Wilson).

98 *Vicent Del Campo v Spain* (n 24) para 37; *X and Y v The Netherlands* App no 8978/80 (ECtHR, 26 March 1985), para 23.

99 *Axel Springer AG v Germany* (n 34) para 83; *Vicent Del Campo v Spain* (n 24) para 36.

100 *Campbell v Mirror Group Newspapers Ltd* (n 57) [139] (Baroness Hale).

hearing is held in private,[101] which would mean that an individual implicated in the underlying wrongdoing would not know of the formal DPA hearings until the DPA's final approval at final hearing.[102] The final hearing is typically held in public and documentation is published except where subject to reporting restrictions. This would likely mean that, as with Del Campo, implicated individuals would be deprived of the opportunity to request nondisclosure of their identity within the statement of facts prior to final judgment.[103] Though reporting restrictions may protect the Article 6 right, there would be no scope for the individual to request nondisclosure to ensure continued Article 8 protection upon the lifting of those restrictions, unless invited by the court to do so (which is not guaranteed).[104] Drawing comparison to *Vicent del Campo*, it is difficult to see how there could be deemed to exist effective and adequate safeguards to protect an individual's Article 8 right in such circumstances.[105]

Though the naming of an individual in the trial of another, to which the individual had no forum for dispute, was a matter of concern in *Khuja*, this can arguably be observed as a case focussed more on the principle of open justice than on misuse of private information, with consideration of the importance of public scrutiny.[106] It has been argued that whilst in misuse of private information claims neither Article 8 nor Article 10 is treated as having presumptive priority,[107] this position is 'indefensible' in misuse of private information claims which also bear the issue of the principle of open justice, due to the principle's constitutional importance.[108] In respect of the content of the statement of facts and judgment, specifically in terms of reference to implicated individuals, the issue centres more on misuse of private information as the openness of the DPA process is largely settled. Though, in respect of involved parties to a dispute, anonymity may be considered 'a departure from the principle of open justice',[109] and this may well also be the case in respect of unindicted individuals named in public criminal trials,[110] the position in respect of the DPA process can be distinguished. Despite the State's margin of appreciation in cases concerning Article 8,[111] where there is no scope for such public scrutiny the positive duty continues (and cannot be deemed to be at an imbalance to Article 10).

---

101 Crime and Courts Act 2013, sch 17 para 7(4).

102 The SFO had previously published press releases following the approval of a "DPA in principle" at the preliminary hearing, though this does not appear to be reflected in recent practice. *See* Serious Fraud Office, 'SFO Announces DPA in Principle with Serco Geografix Ltd' (*Serious Fraud Office*, 3 July 2019) <https://www.sfo.gov.uk/2019/07/03/sfo-announces-dpa-in-principle-with-serco-geografix-ltd/> accessed 3 May 2021.

103 *Vicent Del Campo v Spain* (n 24) para 53.

104 'Paragraph 12 of Schedule 17 says that the court may order that the publication of information by the prosecutor under paragraph 8(7) be postponed for such period as the court considers necessary if it appears to the court that postponement is necessary for avoiding a substantial risk of prejudice to the administration of justice in any legal proceedings. *I have heard submissions from counsel on behalf of some individuals and have decided that such an order is necessary.* There are to be charging decisions within three months and if there are any prosecutions of individuals then it is necessary in the interests of justice that reporting of these proceedings should be controlled' (emphasis added). *See Amec Foster Wheeler Limited* (n 78) [4] (Edis LJ).

105 *Vicent Del Campo v Spain* (n 24) para 53.

106 *Khuja v Times Newspapers Limited* (n 51) [12]; *Scott v Scott* [1913] AC 417 (HL) 463 (Lord Atkinson).

107 *Campbell v Mirror Group Newspapers Ltd* (n 57) [138] (Baroness Hale); *Re S (a child) (identification: restriction on publication)* [2004] UKHL 47 [17] (Lord Steyn).

108 Wragg (n 84) 92.

109 *Yassin v General Medical Council* [2015] EWHC 2955 (Admin) [59].

110 *Khuja v Times Newspapers Limited* (n 51).

111 *Axel Springer AG v Germany* (n 34) para 61; *A v Norway* (n 35) para 66. Notably, this margin of appreciation means that the ECtHR has a review function over such relevant decisions (regarding the conflict between Article 8 and Article 10) and not a re-assessment function. *See Axel Springer AG v Germany* (n 34) para 86.

In reality, Article 10 need not be impacted significantly more than the CACA 2013 already provides, when considering the naming (or otherwise) of individuals in DPA documentation. Under Article 10, the press has the right to inform, and the public has the right to be informed.[112] Where an individual is prosecuted, the right of the press to report on those proceedings will remain and, upon the verdict, comparisons to the DPA and/or surrounding observations may be made. Reference to the DPA will not typically be permitted during the period of the individual's trial, where reporting restrictions are imposed, so as to preserve the individual's Article 6 right to a fair trial. The press will thus ultimately have the opportunity to report on the extent of the individual's own liability. Where an individual is not prosecuted, it follows that a prosecutor's agreeing to name the individual as being involved in criminal wrongdoing and the reporting of it would, in any event, be contrary to the duty to ensure the protection of a person's reputation under Article 10(2).[113] As the issue of naming relates to misuse of private information and not open justice, and in that respect neither Article 8 nor Article 10 have presumptive priority, a balance must be met in observing both rights. If the naming of individuals (or otherwise) does not serve as an affront to the Article 10 right, it is entirely proportionate to respect an individual's Article 8 right in anonymising their identity. This is particularly prudent in acknowledging that the departure from the principle of open justice in respect of DPA negotiations (including the preliminary hearing) does not provide a forum for vindication.

There is no pressing need or legal requirement, in the DPA provisions or within Article 10, for individuals to be named within DPA documentation.[114] Indeed, there is precedent for the anonymisation of UK DPA statement of facts and avoidance of identification within approved judgments. Article 10 is not impacted in this respect as the press remains able to report on the DPA final hearing and documentation, and the individual's trial where prosecuted, and to thereafter make comparisons between the two (upon the conclusion of the individual's trial). Anonymisation within the DPA documentation serves as a safeguard to ensure the protection of the reputation of individuals insofar as their identity is not explicitly set out and ascribed to the wrongdoing described. This is an appropriate measure to protect the reputation of those thereafter acquitted of criminal wrongdoing, and does not detract from the punishment of those ultimately convicted as their own conviction would become a matter of public record.

It is not vital that corporate accountability within a DPA exhaustively identifies all implicated parties where justice can be served in doing so independently (where such liability is deemed to have arisen). The identification of unindicted individuals in the

112 European Court of Human Rights, 'Guide on Article 10 of the European Convention on Human Rights – Freedom of Expression' (*Council of Europe*, 31 August 2020) <https://www.echr.coe.int/Documents/Guide_Art_10_ENG.pdf> accessed 29 April 2021.

113 'The exercise of these freedoms, since it carries with it duties and responsibilities, may be subject to such formalities, conditions, restrictions or penalties as are prescribed by law and are necessary in a democratic society … for the protection of the reputation or rights of others'. *See* Convention for the Protection of Human Rights and Fundamental Freedoms (European Convention on Human Rights, as amended) (ECHR) art 10(2).

114 'The Statement of Facts required by paragraph 5(1) of Schedule 17 in a version which anonymises the names of the individuals and some of the corporations involved is incorporated into this judgment. I was supplied with a version which contains that information. Similarly, the Indictment is attached to this judgment in a form which omits the names of the persons with whom it is alleged that FWEL jointly committed the 10 offences. Again, I have seen a version of the Indictment which contains that information. There is no obligation in the 2013 Act which requires the publication of these full versions, which I do not make part of this judgment.' *See Amec Foster Wheeler Limited* (n 78) [5] (Edis LJ).

purported factual account agreed by a prosecutor and approved by a judge (without *factual* adjudication) as a matter of public record is not proportionate to identification in evidence presented in an open and public trial with the benefit of scrutinisation. Further, it is not in the interests of justice to allow an agreement between a prosecutor and a purported criminal (agreed voluntarily and to the latter's benefit, and without scrutiny as to verifiability of the underlying alleged facts), to hold another uninvolved, unaware, and unindicted party out to have engaged in criminal wrongdoing on public record (outlined by the prosecutor and approved by the judge, albeit by some level of oversight).

A DPA being a voluntary and agreed sanction restricts the element of public scrutiny throughout the process (until approval), but does not necessarily restrict the approving (or otherwise) judge in their ability to measure the interests of justice and fairness, reasonableness, and proportionality of the agreement.[115] It may be deemed necessary in making such an assessment to identify implicated individuals, for the purpose of understanding the scale of corporate wrongdoing. Obvious identifiers need not be incorporated into the statement of facts to allow for this inquiry, and may be discussed during the private preliminary hearing in order to assist the decision.[116] The requirement upon the judge to deliver an approved judgment with reasons for approval serves as a protective measure of the Article 10 right (including the public's right to be informed and scrutinise) and the company's Article 6 right to a fair hearing, whilst anonymity in drafting allows for the protection of the implicated individuals' Article 6 and Article 8 rights. In the event that it is deemed necessary to refer to an implicated individual at final (public) hearing, the court has the discretionary benefit of invoking section 11 of the Contempt of Court Act 1981 to allow their identity to be withheld from the public in those proceedings, and in prohibiting publication of the identity where necessary for the purpose for which it was withheld. The court is able to use its case management powers to ensure that the various rights arising are protected and to ensure the administration of justice.

Where an individual is prosecuted following the corporate DPA (or is still awaiting trial upon its approval), one may see the individual's own criminal proceedings as an opportunity to clear their name where the corporate's statement of facts has identified them. This may be the case, albeit indirectly and not within the DPA proceedings, but the opportunity to achieve full vindication is ultimately reliant upon the ability to seek amendment of the statement of facts (**Section 9.1.4**).

In his inquiry presented to Parliament on the culture, practices and ethics of the press in 2012, Sir Brian Leveson set out that:

> [Save] in exceptional and clearly identified circumstances (for example, where there may be an immediate risk to the public), the names or identifying details of those who are arrested or suspected of a crime should not be released to the press nor the public.[117]

---

115 Crime and Courts Act 2013, sch 17 paras 7(1), 8(1).

116 'I ought to add that the identities and positions of employees within Rolls-Royce referred to in the Statement of Facts have been made known to me so that I have been able to assess their comparative seniority and, thus, the responsibility of Rolls-Royce but, given the continued criminal investigation into individuals, to go further than the Statement of Facts or my summary and identify the employees or others by name, would be to prejudice potential criminal proceedings.' *See Rolls-Royce Plc* (n 5) [32].

117 The Right Honourable Lord Justice Leveson, *An Inquiry Into the Culture, Practices and Ethics of the Press* (HC-2012, 780-II) para G2.39. The inquiry is referred to in Lord Kerr and Lord Wilson's dissenting judgment in *Khuja v Times Newspapers Limited* (n 51) [49]. *See also Scott v Scott* (n 106) 463.

With focus on both the Article 6 and Article 8 rights of individuals, Sir Leveson recommended that guidance in this area be strengthened.[118] Ultimately it was deemed in the government's response in 2018 that the overall position may have moved on, and the Independent Press Standards Organisation ("IPSO") was deemed to be an appropriate regulator of relevant issues.[119] Interestingly, within the IPSO Editor's Code of Practice provision on the reporting of crime, no mention is made of the identification of suspects.[120]

Sir Leveson's position is prudent in respect of DPAs not only as he approved the first four cases to face the court, but also because he took responsibility for the implementation or 'policing of the scheme'.[121] Interestingly, of the four DPAs Sir Leveson approved, three named implicated individuals. Reporting restrictions were imposed in two of those three cases, pending the outcome of the implicated individuals' own cases within the jurisdiction, but were not imposed on the first (*Standard Bank*) as the individuals involved could not be prosecuted within the jurisdiction. The publication of the latter did, however, still have the potential to impact their position overseas.[122]

In *Sarclad Ltd*, the company was anonymised pending the outcome of the proceedings against individuals. In *Tesco Stores Ltd*, the company was not anonymised, which allowed inferences to be drawn by the public as to the position of the Tesco Stores Ltd directors who had already been prosecuted, albeit that reporting restrictions were imposed so as to avoid reporting such comparisons until a verdict was reached. Despite the fact that reporting restrictions were imposed in both cases, the lifting of those restrictions upon conclusion of the respective individuals' trials ultimately led to the revelation of their naming within the DPA documentation – perversely, despite their personal acquittal. This, particularly in the case of the *Tesco Stores Ltd* directors, became the subject of much criticism and highlighted a flaw within the current approach to drafting the company's bill of indictment,[123] the statement of facts,[124] DPA, and judgment.[125]

---

118 The Right Honourable Lord Justice Leveson, *An Inquiry Into the Culture, Practices and Ethics of the Press* (n 117) para G2.39.

119 HC Deb 1 March 2018, vol 636, cols 966–967 (Matt Hancock).

120 Independent Press Standards Organisation, 'Editor's Code of Practice' (*IPSO*, 2021) <https://www.ipso.co.uk/editors-code-of-practice/#ReportingOfCrime> accessed 30 April 2021.

121 Select Committee on the Bribery Act 2010, *The Bribery Act 2010: Post-Legislative Scrutiny: Evidence Session No 16* (HL 2017–19, 303) question 150.

122 Further, it arguably did so. Following the publication of the UK DPA, overseas investigations were launched and some parties named within the DPA went on to agree plea agreements. *See* Basel Institute on Governance (n 7).

123 In *United States v Briggs* (n 8), the naming of an unindicted individual in a grand jury indictment was determined to be a violation of due process. However, unindicted individuals have been named in a bill of indictment preferred following consent of the Crown Court judge pursuant to DPA approval in the UK. *See* Serious Fraud Office, 'Deferred Prosecution Agreement – SFO v ICBC SB PLC' (*Serious Fraud Office*, 3 September 2019) <https://www.sfo.gov.uk/download/deferred-prosecution-agreement-sfo-v-icbc-sb-plc/?wpdmdl=7600> accessed 15 May 2020, para 1. *See also* Crime and Courts Act 2013, sch 17 para 2(1).

124 In *In re Smith* (n 8), the naming of an individual as an unindicted co-conspirator in a factual resume read in open court and filed in a criminal case (pursuant to a plea hearing) was in violation of the individual's liberty and property rights, as afforded by the Fifth Amendment of the US Constitution. In *Standard Bank, Sarclad Ltd, Tesco Stores Ltd* and *Güralp Systems Ltd*, individuals were named in the statement of facts pursuant to a company's DPA (some were facing trial, though not in all cases).

125 In *Vicent Del Campo v Spain* (n 24), the naming of an unindicted individual in a court judgment was in breach of the individual's Article 8 of the ECHR right. In *Khuja v Times Newspapers Limited* (n 51) [34(2)], this was considered a collateral impact of open justice and freedom of the press. In *Standard Bank*, individuals were named in the DPA judgments (preliminary and final) despite the fact that neither was facing prosecution within the jurisdiction (nor, at the time, had they been prosecuted outside the jurisdiction). *See Serious Fraud Office*

In the case of *In re Smith*,[126] the naming of an individual as an unindicted co-conspirator in a factual resume read in open court and filed in a criminal case – prepared in furtherance of a plea hearing – was in violation of the individual's liberty and property rights as afforded by the Fifth Amendment of the US Constitution. In this case, and *United States v Briggs*, there was focus on the lack of forum for vindication available to those named as unindicted co-conspirators.[127]

The three DPAs approved by Sir Leveson which name individuals spanned a time period of 2015 to 2017. It was in 2012 that Sir Leveson made his recommendation to Parliament that names or identifying details of individuals suspected of criminal wrongdoing should not be released to the press or public.[128] One may argue that reporting restrictions ensured that the identity of the implicated individuals were not exposed in direct correlation with the DPA prior to the outcome of their respective trials, but that was only the case in relation to domestic proceedings and those facing sanction elsewhere (those implicated in *Standard Bank*) did not receive the same protection. Indeed, the third DPA approved by Sir Leveson (*Rolls-Royce*) did anonymise individuals in order to safeguard against potential human rights violations faced elsewhere – in respect of punishment for economic crime.[129] However, if his own criteria were to be applied in respect of naming more generally (and no reporting restrictions), it is difficult to determine the applicable 'exceptional and clearly identified circumstances' for doing so: there does not appear to have been, for example, an 'immediate risk to the public' requiring their exposure.[130]

One might perceive the four DPAs naming individuals implicated *within* the DPA-agreeing company (and additionally the DPA with *Güralp Systems Ltd* approved by Mr Justice William Davis (the sixth UK DPA to be agreed)) to be evidence of a new tool in its infancy and suffering as a result of inadequacy in the lack of provision as to the position of individuals. It had appeared from the approach taken since (in the reported cases post-*Güralp Systems Ltd* and one before it)[131] that anonymisation of individuals was becoming standard practice. The tenth DPA with *AFWEL* signalled some development in respect of providing clarity in this area, with the following paragraph imposed at the top of each published DPA-related document:

---

v Standard Bank Plc (now ICBC Standard Bank Plc) (Preliminary) [2016] Lloyd's Rep FC 91 (Crown) (named throughout in respect of the underlying wrongdoing); *Serious Fraud Office v Standard Bank Plc (now ICBC Standard Bank Plc) (Final)* [2016] Lloyd's Rep FC 102 (Crown) [10] (in respect of the particulars of offence). In *Tesco Stores Ltd* and *Güralp Systems Ltd*, individuals were named within the respective DPA judgments but were facing trial at the time the judgment was drafted (not published, due to reporting restrictions). *See Serious Fraud Office v Tesco Stores Ltd* [2019] Lloyd's Rep FC 283 (Crown) [114] (in respect of the order under section 4(2) of the Contempt of Court Act 1981); *Serious Fraud Office v Güralp Systems Ltd* [2020] Lloyd's Rep FC 90 (Crown) (named throughout in respect of the underlying wrongdoing).

126 *In re Smith* (n 8).

127 *United States v Briggs* (n 8) 804; ibid 1107.

128 The Right Honourable Lord Justice Leveson, *An Inquiry Into the Culture, Practices and Ethics of the Pess* (n 117) para G2.39.

129 '[T]o name the recipients of corrupt payments or bribes, in relation to certain countries, could lead to action or the imposition of a penalty which, in this country, we would regard as contravening Article 3 of the European Convention on Human Rights. In the circumstances, none are identified.' *See Rolls-Royce Plc* (n 5) [32] (Sir Brian Leveson).

130 The Right Honourable Lord Justice Leveson, *An Inquiry Into the Culture, Practices and Ethics of the Press* (n 117) para G2.39.

131 Further, by references made to an anonymised statement of facts (currently subject to reporting restrictions) within the tenth DPA. *See Amec Foster Wheeler Limited* (n 78) [4] (Edis LJ).

> Upon determining the issue of approval of the DPA, the Court did not make findings of fact. No process took place by which the culpability of individual people was determined or assessed. The Court observed that companies act through individuals, and it was necessary to consider some individual conduct for that reason, but the Court did not hear from any individuals or call upon them for their side of the story. The judgment in the DPA solely dealt with the culpability of the company Amec Foster Wheeler Energy Limited and not that of any individual person. No findings of any kind were made against any individual.[132]

Further to this, the approved judgment is also clear in outlining that the statement of facts is anonymised.[133] A similar approach had been taken in the more recent DPAs with *Bluu Solutions Limited* and *Tetris Projects Limited*,[134] approved by Mrs Justice May, upon initial publication of the agreements. Whilst reporting restrictions were in place by way of court order, the press made such a disclaimer when reporting.[135] The statement of facts pursuant to the *Bluu Solutions Limited* and *Tetris Projects Limited* DPAs is not entirely anonymous: one party is referred to explicitly by name. Though the statement of facts does not name the therein allegedly implicated directors of the DPA-agreeing companies, the name of one of two alleged agents (external to the DPA companies) is provided. Notably, the statement of facts became publicly available only after the lifting of reporting restrictions on 2 March 2023, which were said to have been in place in order to protect those awaiting trial.[136] By this date, the named agent – Roger Dewhirst – had entered a guilty plea in respect of receiving of bribes. The SFO website, in March 2023, stated as follows:

> The DPA Statement of Facts and Judgment contain anonymised names of individuals subsequently acquitted at trial. These individuals are subject to an anonymisation order and cannot be named.[137]

This represented progress, but such progress was significantly impacted when the DPAs with the two companies expired in July 2023. Upon publication of the notice of discontinuance pursuant to the two DPAs, the 'de-anonymised judgment'[138] was released.

132 *See for example* Serious Fraud Office, 'Amec Foster Wheeler Energy Limited – Deferred Prosecution Agreement' (*Serious Fraud Office*, 2 July 2021) <https://www.sfo.gov.uk/download/amec-foster-wheeler-energy-limited-deferred-prosecution-agreement/> accessed 2 July 2021. 'The Notice should be seen in the context of the growing list of cases where individuals have been exonerated following the conclusion of DPAs based on the attribution of their culpability to a company.' *See* Robin Lööf, 'DPAs – Judicial Oversight Restated' (2021) 7 Arch Rev 4, 5.

133 *Amec Foster Wheeler Limited* (n 78) [4] (Edis LJ).

134 *AB Ltd and another* (n 78) [16] (Mrs Justice May DBE).

135 'The DPAs only relate to the potential criminal liability of the companies and do not address whether liability of any sort attaches to any current or former employee or agent of the companies. Upon determining the issue of approval of the DPAs, the Court did not make findings of fact. No process took place by which the culpability of individual people was determined or assessed. (Note: Any further reporting of the matters in this press release must also include this full disclaimer.)' *See* Serious Fraud Office, 'SFO Secures Two DPAs With Companies for Bribery Act Offences' (*Serious Fraud Office*, 20 July 2021) <https://www.sfo.gov.uk/2021/07/20/sfo-secures-two-dpas-with-companies-for-bribery-act-offences/> accessed 2 October 2021.

136 Ruby Hamid and others, 'The DPA Challenge – The SFO's First DPA-Related Conviction of an Individual Bucks the Trend' (*Ashurst*, 10 March 2023) <https://www.ashurst.com/en/news-and-insights/legal-updates/the-dpa-challenge---the-sfos-first-dpa-related-conviction/> accessed 28 March 2023.

137 Serious Fraud Office, 'R v Bluu Solutions Limited and Tetris Projects Limited' (*Serious Fraud Office*, 9 March 2023) <https://www.sfo.gov.uk/cases/r-v-bluu-solutions-limited-and-tetris-projects-limited/> accessed 28 March 2023.

138 Serious Fraud Office, 'R v Bluu Solutions Limited and Tetris Projects Limited' (*Serious Fraud Office*, 28 July 2023) <https://www.sfo.gov.uk/cases/r-v-bluu-solutions-limited-and-tetris-projects-limited/> accessed 28 July 2023. It is important to acknowledge that there is no requirement to publish a subsequent de-anonymised judgment in order to identify individuals, where an anonymised approving judgment has

Previously, the "anonymised" judgment – like the statement of facts – had only named Roger Dewhirst. However, the de-anonymised version further identifies by name and job position three individuals.[139] The judgment goes into detail on the alleged offending, in respect of each count, implicating each named individual by reference to their own alleged conduct. Mrs Justice May does set out within the de-anonymised judgment that the agreed "facts" between the SFO and the DPA-agreeing companies were not agreed by the individuals referred to, 'nor [had] they been asked for their comments'.[140] Mrs Justice May further expresses that 'I am making no findings of fact concerning [the individuals]'.[141] However, given the progress seemingly made in the identification of individuals, the publication of the de-anonymised judgment is particularly perplexing due to the fact that – at the time of its publication – the three freshly identified individuals had all been *acquitted* of the relevant charges made against them personally,[142] and the judgment makes no reference to that fact.[143]

The original anonymised version of the judgment was said to have been anonymised pending the completion of criminal proceedings against the implicated (and unidentified) individuals. At the end of the de-anonymised judgment, a 'post-judgment' note is provided in italics, and states that: '[t]hose proceedings having now concluded, and having had no objection from the parties, anonymisation is now lifted and this judgment may be published'.[144] It is unclear what forum (if any) was made available to the respective parties in order to object to their identification in the subsequently published de-anonymised judgment. However, it is crucial to outline that the judgment does *not* make any reference to the fact that the individuals were acquitted of the charges made against them, even in the post-judgment note. In October 2023, the relevant page on the SFO website, once bearing an attachment to the de-anonymised judgment, was "re-anonymised". Possibly a consequence of challenge of the decision to de-anonymise, though without judgment on the issue, the de-anonymised judgment and details identifying the acquitted individuals by name on the SFO page are no longer available.[145] Accordingly, those individuals are

already been published. When the *Sarclad Ltd* DPA was approved, a redacted judgment was first published. *See Serious Fraud Office v XYZ Limited* [2016] Lloyd's Rep FC 509 (Crown). When the full version of the judgment was later published, individuals were not named (though arguably reference made to them by their job position was not a necessary step, and could contribute to jigsaw identification). *See Serious Fraud Office v Sarclad Limited (Serious Fraud Office v XYZ Ltd) (Final)* [2016] Lexis Citation 686 (Crown). If it is deemed necessary to publish a subsequent de-anonymised judgment in order to identify the corporate defendant by name, that is appropriate, but individuals need not be identified by name if acquitted.

139 *Director of the Serious Fraud Office v Bluu Solutions Limited and Tetris-Projects Limited* [2023] EWHC 1976 (KB).

140 ibid [16] (Mrs Justice May).

141 ibid.

142 Serious Fraud Office, 'R v Bluu Solutions Limited and Tetris Projects Limited' (n 138).

143 The part of the judgment that refers to the individuals' own proceedings has not been updated, in comparison to the anonymised version, and continues to state that: 'I understand that criminal proceedings have already been commenced against certain of the individuals concerned in this case. It is vitally important that nothing should prejudice the fairness of those proceedings.' It is only in the post-judgment note that the completion of those proceedings is acknowledged, though with no mention of the outcome: 'Those proceedings having now concluded'. *See Bluu Solutions Limited and Tetris-Projects Limited* (n 139) [17] (Mrs Justice May).

144 ibid.

145 As of 2 October 2023. *See* Serious Fraud Office, 'R v Bluu Solutions Limited and Tetris Projects Limited' (*Serious Fraud Office*, 2 October 2023) <https://www.sfo.gov.uk/cases/r-v-bluu-solutions-limited-and-tetris-projects-limited/> accessed 2 October 2023.

anonymised herein on the basis that this recent decision to de-anonymise may be subject to challenge.

Prior to the publication of this de-anonymised judgment, it was clear that the issue of naming had not been fully resolved and had remained a possibility. Though the *AFWEL* statement of facts is currently anonymised, Lord Justice Edis – in approving the DPA – was open to the option of later supplementing the statement of facts with the names '[o]nce decisions have been taken about which individuals, if any, will be *prosecuted* as a result of their involvement in this case' (emphasis added).[146] The DPA is due to expire in July 2024, and it is integral that such naming *only* occurs following *conviction* of the individuals set to be named. As the *AFWEL* DPA was approved, and judgment published, prior to the DPAs with *Bluu Solutions Limited* and *Tetris Projects Limited*, it may be the case that Lord Justice Edis' comment was a catalyst for Mrs Justice May's decision to de-anonymise. However, individuals had been prosecuted when the original anonymised judgment was published, and it remains the case that their subsequent acquittals should not have triggered the decision to de-anonymise.

With the benefit now of increased guidance in this area provided by the SFO Operational Handbook, it had appeared that greater consideration was being paid to the appropriateness of naming (or otherwise). However, it must be noted that the Handbook is an internal guide and is not binding on the judiciary. Thus, there must be a responsibility upon the judiciary to avoid the practice of naming acquitted individuals in DPA documentation. This is also of particular importance in regard to the position of individuals not yet prosecuted or tried. Where an individual is convicted prior to the corporate DPA, naming them may not be such an issue, providing that the content is accurate – as the individual will not have the opportunity to contribute to it. Where the individual is prosecuted and acquitted prior to the corporate DPA, or prior to its expiry, the DPA documentation should be anonymised accordingly.

8.3.1.1 Types of offences

Table 8.1 demonstrates that there has been no distinction in the approach to naming individuals in respect of different types of offences: DPAs have been successfully agreed and approved in cases where individuals have not been named, and strict liability (on at least four occasions) and/or identification principle (on at least three occasions) offences form the underlying basis of the agreement. Individuals have been named in respect of both strict liability offences (on five occasions (counting the *Bluu Solutions Limited* and *Tetris Projects Limited* DPAs separately)) and identification principle offences (on five occasions), demonstrating no elevated necessity in either case in order to facilitate DPA approval.

Table 8.2, in the final two rows, demonstrates that in the most recent DPAs agreed between the SFO and *Bluu Solutions Limited* and *Tetris Projects Limited*, individuals were named in the DPA documentation and one individual was later successfully prosecuted to conviction.[147] However, an asterisk (*) is denoted, to draw attention to the fact that the individual convicted was a third party to the companies that ultimately agreed the DPA. The offences for which the companies agreed the DPA relate to bribery, and the

146 *Amec Foster Wheeler Limited* (n 78) [5] (Edis LJ).

147 Serious Fraud Office, 'R v Bluu Solutions Limited and Tetris Projects Limited' (n 137).

Table 8.1 Demonstrating the 13 UK DPAs, underlying offence(s) and its type, and whether any individual(s) is named in the DPA documentation (statement of facts, DPA, or judgment) in respect of the offence.

Company with agreed DPA	*Offence forming basis of DPA (parentheses signal number of counts)*	*Type of offence*	*Individual named in DPA documentation in respect of the offence?*
Standard Bank	Failure to prevent bribery	Strict liability	Yes
Sarclad Ltd	Conspiracy to corrupt	Identification principle	Yes
	Conspiracy to bribe	Identification principle	Yes
	Failure to prevent bribery	Strict liability	Yes
Rolls-Royce	Conspiracy to corrupt (6)	Identification principle	No
	Failure to prevent bribery (5)	Strict liability	No
	False accounting	Identification principle	No
Tesco Stores Ltd	False accounting	Identification principle	Yes
Serco Geografix Ltd	Fraud (3)	Identification principle	No
	False accounting (2)	Identification principle	No
Güralp Systems Ltd	Conspiracy to make corrupt payments	Identification principle	Yes
	Failure to prevent bribery	Strict liability	Yes
Airbus SE	Failure to prevent bribery (5)	Strict liability	No
G4S C&J	Fraud (3)	Identification principle	No
Airline Services Ltd	Failure to prevent bribery (3)	Strict liability	No
Amec Foster Wheeler Energy Limited	Conspiracy to make corrupt payments (9)	Identification principle	No[1]
	Failure to prevent bribery (1)	Strict liability	No[2]
Bluu Solutions Limited	Bribing another person (4)	Identification principle (section 1 offence)[3]	Yes
	Failure to prevent bribery (1)	Strict liability	
Tetris Projects Limited	Failure to prevent bribery (1)	Strict liability	
Entain Plc	Failure to prevent bribery (4)	Strict liability	No

1 Whilst the publication of the statement of facts was restricted, the approved judgment outlined that it was drafted in an anonymous form. *See Amec Foster Wheeler Limited* (n 78) [4] (Edis LJ). Upon its publication, this remained the case (though see **Section 9.1.4** for more discussion on this).

2 ibid.

3 The section 1 offence refers to the bribing of another person, whereby the defendant 'offers, promises or gives a financial or other advantage to another person' and either 'intends the advantage … to induce a person to perform improperly a relevant function or activity, or to reward a person for the improper performance of such a function or activity', or 'knows or believes that the acceptance of the advantage would itself constitute the improper performance of a relevant function or activity'. *See* Bribery Act 2010, ss 1(2)–(3).

individual convicted was a third-party recipient of those bribe payments. Further, there cannot be said to be any convictions of implicated individuals from *within* the wrongdoing companies.

In all of the cases denoted in Table 8.2, individuals named were directors or senior officers of the wrongdoing company ("intra-corporate individuals") that agreed the respective

DPA. In the final two cases, two former directors of Tetris Projects Limited, though not Bluu Solutions Limited, were named (in addition to the convicted extra-corporate third party). Thus, Table 8.2 demonstrates that the naming of intra-corporate individuals in DPA documentation and their later prosecution for offences based on the same conduct did *not* impact the prospects of success of that prosecution, with no difference in result for those corresponding to identification principle or strict liability corporate offences. Taking Table 8.1 and Table 8.2 into account, it cannot reasonably be argued that it is in the interests of ensuring the administration of justice (in order to obtain a DPA and/or in order to obtain individual convictions) to name implicated intra-corporate individuals within the DPA documentation in either type of corporate offence. In respect of any argument put forward in favour of naming individuals in order to obtain individual convictions, on the basis of the outcome of the singular conviction following the *Bluu Solutions Limited* and

Table 8.2 Demonstrating the UK DPAs in which individuals were named in the DPA documentation (statement of facts, DPA, or judgment), whether the individuals were prosecuted, for what offence, and whether an individual conviction resulted.

Company with agreed DPA	*Offence forming basis of DPA*	*Type of offence*	*Individual named in DPA documentation in respect of the offence?*	*Individual prosecuted in the UK?*	*Individual convicted in the UK?*
Standard Bank	Failure to prevent bribery	Strict liability	Yes	No	N/A
Sarclad Ltd	Conspiracy to corrupt	Identification principle	Yes	Yes	No
	Conspiracy to bribe	Identification principle	Yes	Yes	No
	Failure to prevent bribery	Strict liability	Yes	Yes (conspiracy to bribe, row above)	No
Tesco Stores Ltd	False accounting	Identification principle	Yes	Yes	No
Güralp Systems Ltd	Conspiracy to make corrupt payments	Identification principle	Yes	Yes	No
	Failure to prevent bribery	Strict liability	Yes	Yes (conspiracy to corrupt, row above)	No
Bluu Solutions Limited	Bribing another person	Identification principle	Yes*	Yes*	Yes*
	Failure to prevent bribery	Strict liability	Yes*	Yes*	Yes*
Tetris Projects Limited	Failure to prevent bribery	Strict liability	Yes*	Yes*	Yes*

Tetris Projects Limited DPAs, it must be noted that the naming of the convicted individual within the statement of facts – prior to the publication of the de-anonymised judgment (which named acquitted individuals) – was at the time effected solely for the reason that the individual had already been convicted. At this point in time, those who had been *acquitted* were seemingly intentionally anonymised (albeit by name only) by way of an 'anonymisation order',[148] and should have remained that way following expiry of the DPAs.

8.3.2 Sufficient level of anonymity

As a starting point, unindicted individuals should not be identified within DPA documentation by name. It may be the case that reference to the conduct of individuals remains a necessity: for example, where setting out the basis for an agreement based on an identification principle offence. The ECtHR has suggested that a court with discretion to anonymise individuals may elect to do so in appropriate cases by use of initials.[149] However, this carries a disproportionate risk of identification in circumstances where other types of identifiers are just as usable.

Identification principle offences have, in the UK, formed the basis of DPAs where individuals are referred to as "[Company] Employee" or "[Company] Senior Employee" within the documentation,[150] sometimes accompanied by numbers to enable differentiation. In making reference to a more specific job title such as "Finance Director", it is prudent to consider the necessity and appropriateness of vast discussion tending to lead to identification (such as employment history),[151] and particular care will need to be taken in cases relating to smaller organisations (or) where the job title can be easily cross-referenced to Companies House.[152] In the US, DoJ guidance sets out that descriptors should be generic and non-specific.[153] This is discretionary, but 'significant justification' is required in order to identify unindicted third-party wrongdoers 'by name or unnecessarily-specific description' (such as initials) during plea proceedings of another.[154] Use of initials poses an unnecessary risk of jigsaw identification, particularly where related proceedings are ongoing domestically or overseas.

---

148 ibid.

149 *Vicent Del Campo v Spain* (n 24) para 51.

150 Serious Fraud Office, 'Deferred Prosecution Agreement – Statement of Facts – SFO v Rolls Royce PLC' (*Serious Fraud Office*, 17 January 2017) <https://www.sfo.gov.uk/download/deferred-prosecution-agreement-statement-facts-sfo-v-rolls-royce-plc/> accessed 15 May 2020; Serious Fraud Office, 'R v Airbus – Statement of Facts Amended' (*Serious Fraud Office*, 28 February 2020) <https://www.sfo.gov.uk/download/airbus-se-deferred-prosecution-agreement-statement-of-facts/> accessed 11 February 2021.

151 Serious Fraud Office, 'Deferred Prosecution Agreement – Serco Geografix Ltd & SFO: Serco DPA SOF for Publication' (*Serious Fraud Office*, 28 April 2021) <https://www.sfo.gov.uk/download/deferred-prosecution-agreement-serco-geografix-ltd-sfo/> accessed 28 April 2021, paras 6–7.

152 For example, in the shared statement of facts pursuant to the *Bluu Solutions Limited* and *Tetris Projects Limited* DPAs, the second alleged agent is anonymised, known only as "Agent 2", yet the company 'founded by Agent 2 on 21 February 2013' is identified by name. With this level of identifying information, it takes no more than two minutes to check Companies House and retrieve names. *See* Serious Fraud Office, 'Statement of Facts' (*Serious Fraud Office*, 2 March 2023) <https://www.sfo.gov.uk/download/r-v-bluu-solutions-limited-and-tetris-projects-limited/> accessed 28 March 2023, para 38.

153 The United States Department of Justice, 'Justice Manual > 9-11.130 – Limitation on Naming Persons as Unindicted Co-Conspirators' (n 16).

154 The United States Department of Justice, 'Justice Manual > 9-16.500 – Identifying Uncharged Third-Parties During Plea and Sentencing Proceedings' (n 22).

Jigsaw identification occurs 'whereby anonymisation may be undermined by correctly identifying someone as a result of relating separate snippets of information'.[155] In taking measures to avoid jigsaw identification, judges should be wary of transposing large parts of the statement of facts into the judgment where not strictly necessary in setting out the reasons for approval,[156] if the judgment does not fall within the realm of reporting restrictions imposed.[157] Where reporting restrictions are imposed, this is inevitably done over only some aspects of the process which can fuel interest and attempts to fill informational gaps.[158] Whilst this may be the case, a decision not to impose reporting restrictions could ultimately lead to substantial prejudice to the administration of justice in individuals' own proceedings. Reporting restrictions therefore remain of paramount importance. Whilst this serves as an interim safeguard to protect an individual's Article 6 right to a fair trial, the safeguarding of an individual's Article 8 right (particularly in cases where the individual is acquitted) continues to require consideration of anonymity in the drafting stages. The case of *AL*[159] arose in the period between the company's DPA (within which individuals were named in the statement of facts, albeit subject to reporting restrictions) and the conclusion of the individuals' trial, and use of the individuals' own initials throughout has made the parties easily identifiable for those familiar with the wider case, particularly for users of the SFO website (as a result of their news releases).

In *JIH v News Group Newspapers Ltd*,[160] it was submitted by counsel for the claimant that an injunction to restrict publication of private information should either seek to anonymise the parties or alternatively restrict publication of the underlying facts, and that it would be in the public interest to outline the facts in order to provide reason for decisions made.[161] The tone of this approach can be considered in DPA cases, in informing the public as to the facts and reasons for DPA approval (thus protecting the press and public's right under Article 10), whilst continuing to protect the rights of unindicted individuals. Knowing that it is possible and there is precedent for anonymising DPA documentation, whilst allowing the judge to be notified of the identities and positions of implicated individuals in order to facilitate the approval decision,[162] it is arguably inappropriate to provide unnecessarily specific description such as personal initials or employment history.

155 *Donald v Ntuli* [2010] EWCA Civ 1276 [55] (Maurice Kay LJ); Rebecca Moosavian, 'Jigsaws and Curiosities: The Unintended Consequences of Misuse of Private Information Injunctions' (2016) 21(4) CL 104.

156 Crime and Courts Act 2013, sch 17 para 8(4).

157 Moosavian (n 155) 107.

158 ibid 108.

159 *R (on the application of AL) v Serious Fraud Office* [2018] EWHC 856 (Admin).

160 Ultimately the nature of the case led the judge to the conclusion that '[the] only real choice is to allow the public to know the Claimant's identity or to allow them to know nothing at all about the action'. *See JIH v News Group Newspapers Ltd* [2010] EWHC 2818 [8], [48], [63]. In the Court of Appeal, it was outlined that '[whilst] [counsel's submission] is not an unfair assessment in the present case, in other cases the position will sometimes be a little less stark'. *See JIH v News Group Newspapers Ltd* [2011] EWCA Civ 42 [25] (Neuberger MR).

161 Moosavian (n 155) 108.

162 *Rolls-Royce Plc* (n 5) [32]; *AB Ltd and another* (n 78) [22].

CHAPTER 9

Avenues for redress

9.1 Avenues for redress

Though the case of *Financial Conduct Authority v Macris* focusses on the avenues for third-party protection where those third parties are mentioned within regulatory notices, the statutory provision providing for such protection under section 393 of the Financial Services and Markets Act 2000, as amended by the Financial Services Act 2012, is not replicated within the CACA 2013. As such, the ability for identified third parties (by name or synonym) to provide representations in their own defence is not available through statutory provision, but only if incorporated in the DPA process by the involved parties (for example, the judiciary or the prosecutor). Whilst Schedule 17 of the CACA 2013 remains silent in this regard, consideration must be afforded to alternative potential avenues of redress where individuals are identified within DPA documentation.

9.1.1 Misuse of private information

Where the DPA documentation is not anonymised, this may give rise to a claim for misuse of private information. The tort of misuse of private information was set out in *Campbell v Mirror Group Newspapers Ltd*[1] by Lord Nicholls and requires a twofold determinative approach: firstly, whether the claimant had a reasonable expectation of privacy, and secondly, whether the claimant's Article 8 right outweighs the defendant's right protected under Article 10. In comparison to the ECtHR approach to Article 8, the consideration of a reasonable expectation of privacy appears to have become somewhat convoluted. There was a difference in opinion in *Re an application by JR38 for Judicial Review (Northern Ireland)*,[2] as the majority posed the view that reasonable expectation of privacy was the touchstone of the Article 8 right, whereas the minority – in line with the ECtHR[3] – deemed it to be a significant factor in determining Article 8's applicability.[4] There has been criticism that the approach taken in considering the claimant's reasonable expectation of privacy has thus become a consideration of whether the Article 8(1) right arises, as

1 [2004] UKHL 22 [14] (Lord Nicholls).

2 [2015] UKSC 42.

3 '[Reasonable] expectation as to privacy may be a significant, though not necessarily conclusive factor.' *See PG and JH v United Kingdom* App no 44787/98 (ECtHR, 25 September 2001). *See also* Joe Purshouse, 'The Reasonable Expectation of Privacy and the Criminal Suspect' (2016) 79(5) Mod L Rev 871, 874.

4 Purshouse (n 4) 879.

DOI: 10.4324/9781003456964-11

opposed to a consideration in line with whether justification arises for departure from it as provided under Article 8(2).[5]

Ultimately, it has been clearly set out that a reasonable expectation of privacy does not arise 'in relation to proceedings in open court'.[6] In line with the discussion in **Section 8.2.3**, open court criminal proceedings cannot reasonably be compared to DPA proceedings, and this is particularly so in respect of the position of unindicted implicated individuals. The DPA process requires that the negotiations and preliminary hearing be conducted in private and confidentially. Judicial approval of the DPA – that the DPA is in the interests of justice and that the terms are fair, reasonable, and proportionate[7] – with reasons for approval,[8] is held in open court,[9] though the final hearing can be held in private.[10] There is no requirement or expectation that individuals be named, and no opportunity for their involvement unless invited (though this invitation would relate only to the hearings, and not negotiations). It is in this respect that it may be argued that individuals implicated in the corporate wrongdoing have a reasonable expectation of privacy in relation to their identification within the statement of facts and/or approved judgment, where those documents are drafted prior to their own prosecution or conviction. Weighed against Article 10, there is no violation of this right where anonymisation tools are used within the DPA.[11] Although arguably considered a matter of public interest, reports on the DPA and reports on any individual prosecution are likely to remain permitted, albeit subject to reporting restrictions: for example, that no reference be made to the DPA in reporting on the individual's case during the period of their trial.

9.1.2 Defamation

An individual may wish to make a claim in defamation in respect of protection of reputation.[12] It has been argued that in order to avoid an abuse of process, misuse of private information and defamation claims should not be brought as parallel proceedings.[13] An

5 ibid 880–881.

6 *Khuja v Times Newspapers Limited* [2017] UKSC 49 [34(3)].

7 Crime and Courts Act 2013, sch 17 para 8(1).

8 ibid sch 17 para 8(4).

9 ibid sch 17 para 8(6).

10 ibid sch 17 para 8(5). 'Paragraph 8(5) provides that the final hearing may be held in private: this is to allow the final proposed DPA to be set out before the judge and any final issues to be resolved in a free and frank environment. But if the court decides to approve the DPA and make a declaration, the court must do so in open court, giving reasons for its decision (paragraph 8(6)).' *See* Explanatory Notes to the Crime and Courts Act 2013, para 559.

11 'It is unlawful for a public authority to act in a way which is incompatible with a Convention right.' *See* Human Rights Act 1998, s 6(1). "Public authority" includes 'a court or tribunal'. *See* Human Rights Act 1998, s 6(3)(a).

12 The common law definition of defamation has followed the dictum of Lord Atkin, who set forth the test: 'would the words tend to lower the plaintiff in the estimation of right-thinking members of society generally?' *See Sim v Stretch* [1936] 2 All ER 1237 (HL) 1240. The test was not intended to have universal application, but has generally been so followed, save for a substitution of "right-thinking members of society" to the relevant group where required. The statement may be defamatory if 'it tends to make the plaintiff be shunned and avoided'. *See Youssoupoff v Metro-Goldwyn-Mayer Pictures Ltd* (1934) 50 TLR 581 (CA) 587 (Slesser LJ). According to the Defamation Act 2013, s 1(1), the statement must cause or be likely to cause 'serious harm to the reputation of the claimant'.

13 Sarah Gale, 'Defamation and the Misuse of Private Information: A Comparative Analysis' (2018) 26 Tort L Rev 38 <https://openaccess.city.ac.uk/id/eprint/20872/f> accessed 30 April 2021.

individual may wish to seek redress in respect of claims made about them within the statement of facts and/or judgment which are felt to have caused or be likely to cause serious harm to their reputation.[14] A defamatory action cannot arise in respect of statements made by a judge (orally or written) or any other party in the course of court proceedings, nor in respect of documentation brought into existence for the purpose of those court proceedings.[15] This also extends to statements made during a criminal investigation and thus would cover those made within DPA negotiations.[16] Therefore, the statement of facts published by the prosecutor pursuant to the direction of the court and the publication of the judgment in relation to the DPA will be absolutely privileged, and thus afforded immunity from defamation claims.

Repetition of defamatory statements is treated as a defamation in its own right.[17] In respect of news reports made in relation to the DPA proceedings (ultimately referring only to a public final hearing, due to the private nature of the prior stages), the fair and accurate report of public court proceedings is absolutely privileged where published contemporaneously with those proceedings,[18] except where done with malice.[19] Where reporting restrictions are imposed on certain elements – for example, on reporting in relation to the statement of facts – publication will be treated as contemporaneous where published as soon as practicable after those restrictions are lifted.[20] It may be that disputes arise where the media considers there is a legitimate interest in publishing non-contemporaneous reports, for example, where comparisons are made in respect of the DPA proceedings and completed individual proceedings (depending on timing), though publication may be made with the risk of liability nonetheless.[21] In *Khuja* it was acknowledged that the protection of absolute privilege would leave unindicted but named individuals with no means of clearing their name, though such a consequence would be the collateral impact of open justice and afree press.[22] Furthermore, the media may advance the public interest defence in any event.[23]

---

14 Defamation Act 2013, s 1(1).

15 'The absolute privilege which covers proceedings in or before a court of justice can be divided into three categories. The first category covers all matters that are done coram judice. This extends to everything that is said in the course of proceedings by judges, parties, counsel and witnesses, and includes the contents of documents put in as evidence. The second covers everything that is done from the inception of the proceedings onwards and extends to all pleadings and other documents brought into existence for the purpose of the proceedings and starting with the writ or other document which institutes the proceedings.' The third category described refers to 'the privilege attaching to evidence which a witness gave coram judice extended to the precognition or proof of that evidence taken by a solicitor'. *See Lincoln v Daniels* [1962] 1 QB 237 (CA) 257–258 (Devlin LJ). *See also Watson v McEwan* [1905] AC 480 (HL).

16 *Taylor v Serious Fraud Office* [1998] 4 All ER 801 (HL) 802.

17 '[R]epeating someone else's libellous statement is just as bad as making the statement directly'. *See Rubber Improvement Ltd v Daily Telegraph Ltd* [1964] AC 234 (HL) 260 (Lord Reid).

18 Defamation Act 1996, s 14(1).

19 ibid s 15(1), sch 1 para 2.

20 ibid s 14(2).

21 'The invariable rule since the decision in *Bonnard v Perryman* [1891] 2 Ch 269 has been that even where absolute privilege is not available or its availability is in dispute, the court will not grant an interlocutory injunction in advance of publication if the defendant asserts that he will plead justification, unless, exceptionally, the court is satisfied that the defence is bound to fail … in its modern form, its function is to balance the freedom of the press and the right of the claimant to protect his reputation, by confining the plaintiff to the post-publication remedies to which he may prove himself entitled at a trial.' *See Khuja v Times Newspapers Limited* (n 6) [19].

22 ibid [32], [34(2)].

23 Defamation Act 2013, s 4.

9.1.3 Data protection

The Data Protection Act 2018 implements the General Data Protection Regulation[24] into UK law and governs the processing of 'personal data',[25] which may include identifying a person by name.[26] Under Part 3 of the Data Protection Act 2018, entitled "Law Enforcement Processing", a 'competent authority'[27] may process data for 'law enforcement purposes'.[28] Personal data can lawfully be processed where it is necessary for the performance of a task carried out by the law enforcement authority:[29] for example, in preparing and publishing the statement of facts pursuant to the DPA.[30] Judiciary UK has set out that the public interest of the administration of justice[31] (and principle of open justice) may necessitate publication of personal data within judgments.[32] However, where 'strictly necessary in the interests of the administration of justice', restrictions may be placed on the publication of an individual's name within a judgment and, in addition, legal proceedings may be held in private.[33]

Use of the unindicted individual's name must be lawful and fair,[34] '[constituting] a necessary and proportionate measure in a democratic society with due regard for the legitimate interests of the natural person concerned'.[35] Doing so is a 'distinct notion'[36] from the Article 6 right to a fair trial. Naming unindicted individuals within the statement of facts – and judgment – is arguably not a 'necessary'[37] aspect of the preparing and publishing of the document for the purpose of the administration of justice,[38] nor is it a requirement in law.[39] As Table 8.2 (**Section 8.3.1.1**) demonstrates, there is no correlation between naming and the ability to obtain DPA approval. Neither can it be considered proportionate: the individual is not a defendant or an involved party in the DPA process, which is inherently different from a criminal trial, and is ultimately based on an agreed account between the company and the prosecutor. The long-term publication on public record cannot be said to be in the legitimate interests of the unindicted individual. Circumstances may differ where an individual has been prosecuted and/or convicted (particularly in the latter

24 Regulation (EU) 2016/679 of the European Parliament and of the Council of 27 April 2016 on the protection of natural persons with regard to the processing of personal data and on the free movement of such data, and repealing Directive 95/46/EC (General Data Protection Regulation) [2016] OJ L119/1.

25 'Any information relating to an identified or identifiable living individual'. *See* Data Protection Act 2018, s 3(2).

26 ibid s 3(a).

27 Including the Director of the SFO and Director of Public Prosecutions, and a court or tribunal: ibid s 30, sch 7.

28 'Purposes of the prevention, investigation, detection or prosecution of criminal offences or the execution of criminal penalties, including the safeguarding against and the prevention of threats to public security.' *See* ibid s 31.

29 ibid s 35(2)(b).

30 Crime and Courts Act 2013, sch 17 para 8(7).

31 Data Protection Act 2018, s 8(a).

32 Lord Chief Justice of England and Wales and Senior President of Tribunals, 'Judiciary and Data Protection: Privacy Notice' (*Courts and Tribunals Judiciary*, 2021) <https://www.judiciary.uk/about-the-judiciary/judiciary-and-data-protection-privacy-notice/> accessed 1 May 2021.

33 ibid.

34 Data Protection Act 2018, s 35(1).

35 Explanatory Notes to the Data Protection Act 2018, para 182.

36 ibid.

37 Data Protection Act 2018, s 35(2)(b).

38 ibid s 8(a).

39 ibid s 8(c).

circumstance), but unindicted individuals may argue that their naming is contrary to the data protection provisions.

In respect of information provided by the company during DPA negotiations, this may be disclosed by the SFO (or CPS) where required by law, as an exception to any confidentiality undertakings governing the negotiations. This may be required to fulfil disclosure obligations to other regulatory or prosecution agencies under section 3(5) of the CJA 1987, or under the Data Protection Act 2018.[40]

Under section 38(1) of the Data Protection Act 2018, data must be accurate, and erased or rectified without delay where determined to be inaccurate: "inaccurate" is defined as 'incorrect or misleading as to any matter of fact'.[41] Whilst this may on first view appear to provide an avenue for redress, in rectifying any inaccuracies in respect of the inclusion of a name within a statement of facts,[42] 'misleading as to any matter of fact' does not apply to the content of a statement but instead to the fact that the statement has been made.[43] In giving the example of an individual's conviction overturned on appeal, it is outlined within the Explanatory Notes to the Data Protection Act 2018 that whilst the individual's personal record on the police database would be amended, the content of a witness statement found at appeal to be unreliable could not be.[44] It would, therefore, appear to be the case that the data protection provision would not provide a forum for the amendment of the statement of facts upon later determination that the content relating to a named individual is inaccurate.[45]

9.1.4 Amending the statement of facts

The ability to amend the statement of facts post-DPA approval has been the subject of some concern. The statement of facts forms part of the DPA – it is 'contain[ed]'[46] within it. According to the CACA 2013 and the Criminal Procedure Rules, a DPA can only be varied on an application on breach of the agreement[47] (where the court has invited the parties to agree to remedy the breach),[48] or where variation is necessary to avoid a failure of the defendant to comply with the terms in circumstances that were not, and could not have been, foreseen by the parties at the time the agreement was made.[49] This therefore places a condition of breach or avoidance of breach in order for any amendment to be made. Issues arise where the statement of facts ascribes a person's name to the criminal wrongdoing forming the underlying basis of the corporate DPA, and that individual is thereafter personally acquitted of criminal liability in relation to such wrongdoing.

40 Serious Fraud Office, 'Deferred Prosecution Agreements' (*Serious Fraud Office*, 23 October 2020) <https://www.sfo.gov.uk/publications/guidance-policy-and-protocols/sfo-operational-handbook/deferred-prosecution-agreements/> accessed 23 October 2020; Crown Prosecution Service and Serious Fraud Office, 'Deferred Prosecution Agreements Code of Practice' (*Crown Prosecution Service*, 11 February 2014) <https://www.cps.gov.uk/sites/default/files/documents/publications/dpa_cop.pdf> accessed 9 June 2020, para 3.7.

41 Data Protection Act 2018, s 205.

42 Rectification defined as 'corrected'. *See* Explanatory Notes to the Data Protection Act 2018, para 199.

43 ibid para 187.

44 ibid.

45 Crime and Courts Act 2013, sch 17 paras 11(3), 13(4).

46 'A DPA must contain a statement of facts relating to the alleged offence': ibid sch 17 para 5(1).

47 ibid sch 17 para 9(3)(a); CrimPR 11.5.

48 Crime and Courts Act 2013, sch 17 para 10(1)(a); CrimPR 11.6(1)(a).

49 Crime and Courts Act 2013, sch 17 para 10(1)(b); CrimPR 11.6(1)(b).

When the *Tesco Stores Ltd* DPA was agreed, criminal proceedings against three former directors were pending[50] and reporting restrictions were imposed so as to restrict publication of the DPA, statement of facts, and that said during the public final hearing.[51] According to Sir Leveson, such restrictions were imposed following representations made by the former directors (suggesting their potential knowledge of negotiations).[52] In the *Tesco Stores Ltd* case, the SFO on 28 March 2017 confirmed that a DPA had been agreed in principle (at the preliminary hearing) following a Regulatory News Service announcement by Tesco Plc;[53] the approved DPA was then announced on 10 April 2017.[54] Upon the acquittal of the three former directors, counsel on their behalf submitted that 'there is an inherent unfairness in the juxtaposition of the acquittals and the Statement of Facts which ascribes wrongdoing to them' and suggested by skeleton argument that the statement of facts be redacted or made the subject of an addendum.[55] This was opposed by counsel for the SFO and Tesco Stores Ltd, who both challenged the locus of the individuals to intervene or seek to alter the concluded 'DPA *or* Statement of Facts'[56] (emphasis added), as the statement of facts could in future be considered a formal admission by the company under section 10 of the CJA 1967.[57] The press also challenged any amendment on the grounds that it would offend the principle of open justice, 'potentially limiting the ability to comment fully on the DPA and its background all of which is and has been a matter of real public interest'.[58] In his judgment, Sir Leveson permitted the reporting restrictions to come to an end,[59] stating:

> I have no doubt that I have no jurisdiction now to alter or modify either the terms of the DPA or its supporting Statement of Facts; having approved the agreement, the role of the Court is limited to enforcing its terms. As a consequence of the statutory scheme, however, it was always common ground that the defendants were not involved in or parties to any agreement in relation to the DPA or Statement of Facts.[60]

Sir Leveson went on to outline that reporting on the DPA during the period of reporting restrictions had been clear in stating that the DPA addressed the criminal liability of Tesco Stores Ltd alone and 'did not address whether liability of any sort attached' to individuals, and that 'that remains the case'.[61]

The position in respect of amendments to a DPA's statement of facts would thus appear to be clear: statute provides only for amendment to the DPA (read as containing

50 The three individuals had been charged on 9 September 2016, six months prior to the "DPA in principle" announcement. *See* Serious Fraud Office, 'Charges in Tesco Investigation' (*Serious Fraud Office*, 9 September 2016) <https://www.sfo.gov.uk/2016/09/09/charges-tesco-investigation/> accessed 3 May 2021.

51 *Serious Fraud Office v Tesco Stores Ltd* [2019] EW Misc 1 (Crown) [1].

52 ibid.

53 Serious Fraud Office, 'SFO Confirms DPA in Principle With Tesco' (*Serious Fraud Office*, 28 March 2017) <https://www.sfo.gov.uk/2017/03/28/sfo-confirms-dpa-principle-tesco/> accessed 3 May 2021.

54 Serious Fraud Office, 'SFO Agrees Deferred Prosecution Agreement With Tesco' (*Serious Fraud Office*, 10 April 2017) <https://www.sfo.gov.uk/2017/04/10/sfo-agrees-deferred-prosecution-agreement-with-tesco/> accessed 3 May 2021.

55 *Serious Fraud Office v Tesco Stores Ltd* (n 51) [2].

56 ibid [3].

57 ibid; Crime and Courts Act 2013, sch 17 para 13(2).

58 *Serious Fraud Office v Tesco Stores Ltd* (n 51) [3].

59 ibid [5].

60 ibid [4] (Sir Brian Leveson).

61 ibid.

the statement of facts)[62] where there is a breach of the agreement or in order to avoid a breach which was not and could not have been foreseen,[63] and the court is otherwise restricted to enforcement of its terms without scope for alteration or modification.[64] This position is further supported by academic literature.[65] This, however, is inconsistent with the *Airbus SE* DPA (approved on 31 January 2020), to which an amendment was made to the statement of facts on 28 February 2020 and addendum added on 25 September 2020.[66] Interestingly, there was a distinction between 'DPA *or* Statement of Facts'[67] (emphasis added) in the judgment relating to the former Tesco directors' aforementioned application. In regard to *Airbus SE*, the amendment to the statement of facts corrected a dating error in respect of a market share agreement.[68] The addendum outlines that it 'corrects an error in respect of amounts referred to at paragraphs 170, 180 and 196'.[69] However, the amendments are not solely numerical but instead change the nature of the language and appear to remove certain terms in respect of the conduct of anonymised individuals. For example, the original statement of facts at paragraph 170 read:

> A number of Airbus employees *made or* promised success based commission payments of approximately €5 million to Intermediary 5.[70] (emphasis added)

This was amended to read:

> A number of Airbus employees promised success based commission payments of approximately €4.68 million to Intermediary 5.[71]

Additionally, the original statement of facts at paragraph 196 read: 'Between 10 April 2012 and 31 July 2013 Intermediary 8 paid €3,850,115 to Company D. Intermediary 8 retained about €60,000.'[72] The amended version removed the latter sentence and reworded the remainder.[73] This is evidence of removal of language from the statement of facts which tended to refer to conduct by anonymised individuals. The amendments within the

---

62 'A DPA must contain a statement of facts relating to the alleged offence': Crime and Courts Act 2013, sch 17 para 5(1).

63 ibid sch 17 para 10(1); CrimPR 11.6(1).

64 *Serious Fraud Office v Tesco Stores Ltd* (n 51) [4].

65 '[T]here is no provision for a judgment or statement of facts to be revised to remove references to individuals.' *See* Colin King and Nicholas Lord, 'Deferred Prosecution Agreements in England and Wales: Castles Made of Sand?' (2020) (Apr) PL 307, 326. *See also* Karl Laird, 'Deferred Prosecution Agreements: The Latest Developments' (2021) 4 Crim LR 283, 297. *See also* Robin Lööf, 'DPAs – Judicial Oversight Restated' (2021) 7 Arch Rev 45.

66 Serious Fraud Office, 'R v Airbus SE – Deferred Prosecution Agreement' (Serious Fraud Office, 2023) <https://www.sfo.gov.uk/download/airbus-se-deferred-prosecution-agreement-statement-of-facts/> accessed 12 April 2023.

67 *Serious Fraud Office v Tesco Stores Ltd* (n 51) [3].

68 'Please note that on 28 February 2020 a minor amendment was made to paragraph 91 (page 20) of the Statement of Facts to change the date of the market share agreement referred to therein from 30 October 2015 to 29 March 2013.' *See* Serious Fraud Office, 'R v Airbus SE – Deferred Prosecution Agreement' (n 66).

69 Serious Fraud Office, 'R v Airbus – Addendum to Statement of Facts 25/09/2020' (*Serious Fraud Office*, 25 September 2020) <https://www.sfo.gov.uk/download/airbus-se-deferred-prosecution-agreement-statement-of-facts/> accessed 11 February 2021, para 1.

70 ibid para 2(i).

71 ibid para 3(i).

72 ibid para 2(iii).

73 'Between March 2012 and February 2014, Airbus paid Intermediary 8 a total of €3,909,756. At least €3,534,323 of this sum related to the Ghana campaign, a sum in excess of the agreed commission amount as per the ECA declaration (€3,001,718.15). Between 10 April 2012 and 31 July 2013 Intermediary 8 paid €2,752,422 to Company D.' *See* ibid para 4.

addendum were agreed by the SFO and Airbus SE[74] and presented on a court document with the case number, but with no accompanying comments or judgment to provide further explanation. It would thus appear possible to both amend a statement of facts from an approved DPA and/or make it the subject of an addendum, and there is precedent for doing so. The question arises as to why a statement of facts can be amended in respect of the purported conduct of an anonymised individual, but not in respect of the purported conduct of a named individual acquitted of criminal wrongdoing, where that alleged wrongdoing was based upon the same purported conduct outlined within the DPA's statement of facts. Referring back to Sir Leveson's judgment, it would appear that there *is* in fact scope to alter or modify the statement of facts and that the court is not simply limited to enforcement of DPA terms.[75] This is the case despite the fact that the statement of facts may in future be deemed a formal admission by the company.[76]

An argument for the differentiation between the *Tesco Stores Ltd* and *Airbus SE* cases may be that the latter remained anonymous in respect of individuals throughout, whereas the anonymisation of individuals within the former's statement of facts may be contrary to the principle of open justice and restrict the ability to report on the background of a DPA which forms a matter of real public interest.[77] However, any amendment or addendum would be reported by the SFO (or CPS) and would not itself be subject to reporting restrictions, and would – if the *Airbus SE* case serves as precedent – clearly outline the previous and updated versions. It follows that the press would not be restricted from reporting on the background of the DPA and the individual's subsequent acquittal, and would nevertheless be required to set out that the DPA does not address whether liability of any sort attached to the individuals in any event.

One may argue that it is more in line with the principles of natural justice, to which the principle of open justice is a part, to allow the correction of documentation held on public record ascribing a person to criminal wrongdoing for which they have subsequently been determined – via the justice system – to not be criminally liable. It is crucial in this respect to be minded that the statement of facts forms an agreed account between the company and the prosecutor. Although the prosecutor must give a written statement to the court to the effect that the account is not known to be 'inaccurate, misleading or incomplete',[78] the statement of facts is not exposed to open court and adjudged on its integrity in the same way as evidence presented at trial.[79] In the *Tesco Stores Ltd* case, the statement of facts in the corporate DPA named individuals as having been involved in the criminal wrongdoing but the individuals' own trials collapsed on lack of evidence-related issues.[80] Furthermore,

---

74 ibid para 3.

75 *Serious Fraud Office v Tesco Stores Ltd* (n 51) [4].

76 ibid [3]; Crime and Courts Act 2013, sch 17 para 13(2); Criminal Justice Act 1967, s 10.

77 *Serious Fraud Office v Tesco Stores Ltd* (n 51) [3].

78 Crown Prosecution Service and Serious Fraud Office, 'Deferred Prosecution Agreements Code of Practice' (n 40) para 5.5.

79 Though Lööf considered the extent of judicial involvement in respect of the statement of facts (with regard to previous judgments), he ultimately stated that 'the DPA procedure in reality does not put the court in a position to provide independent and objective scrutiny of the agreed evidential basis'. *See* Lööf (n 65) 5.

80 In the proceedings against Bush and Scouler there was a finding of no case to answer, and the SFO elected not to offer evidence at Rogberg's trial. *See R v Bush* [2019] EWCA Crim 29 [2]–[4]. *See also* Serious Fraud Office, 'Deferred Prosecution Agreement Between the SFO and Tesco Published' (*Serious Fraud Office*, 23 January 2019) <https://www.sfo.gov.uk/2019/01/23/deferred-prosecution-agreement-between-the-sfo-and-tesco-published/> accessed 3 May 2021.

arguably it is in line with the principles of natural justice (and thus in the interests of justice) to allow for correction, in order to recognise the discrepancies in process between DPAs and criminal trials, to recognise the position and rights of individuals, and to allow the public to be accurately informed. This maintains the interests of individuals protected under Article 8 (protection of reputation) and the interests of the press and wider public under Article 10 (to inform and to be informed), whilst also preserving the individual's Article 6 right in respect of any civil proceedings which may arise as a result of the DPA and statement of facts.

Within the approved judgment of the *AFWEL* DPA, it is set out that the statement of facts (which at the time of publication of the judgment was itself unpublished due to reporting restrictions, following submissions by counsel representing the individuals)[81] and the indictment are anonymised – despite the fact that the company and individual(s) were said to have jointly committed the offences set out – though Lord Justice Edis had the benefit of seeing identifiable versions of both documents.[82] Lord Justice Edis, having considered the individuals' right to a fair trial, stated the following:

> Once decisions have been taken about which individuals, if any, will be prosecuted as a result of their involvement in this case, I will hold a further hearing in order to receive submissions about whether these reasons should be supplemented by the substituted statement of facts and Indictment containing names which have presently been omitted. I expect that hearing to take place before the end of this year.[83]

This contradicts the position taken by Sir Leveson as regards the *Tesco Stores Ltd* DPA statement of facts, and continues to adopt a similar approach to that taken in *Airbus SE*. However, rather than an amendment and addendum to the documentation, it is suggested within *AFWEL* that it would be possible to substitute the statement of facts and the indictment altogether. This may be considered adequate due to the fact that the approving judge clearly gave DPA approval in light of both the anonymised and identifiable versions. However, such an action would go far beyond 'enforcing [the DPA's] terms'.[84] If considering the CACA 2013 and Criminal Procedure Rules, such substitution of DPA documentation post-approval – and prior to any breach proceedings – is beyond the statutory scope of judicial power in respect of DPAs. However, it may be the case that the DPA tool is left to the judiciary to develop within the common law, as has been the case in respect of the approach taken to the publication of the preliminary judgments (for example).[85]

The dictum provided by Lord Justice Edis, regarding substitution of statement of facts, is nonetheless troubling as it does not provide clarification or limitation as to when a statement of facts and/or indictment may be substituted so as to name individuals. The decision of the court in respect of any amendment to the DPA would not be subject to a right of appeal by the individual, and therefore an individual would be limited in scope

81 *Director of the Serious Fraud Office v Amec Foster Wheeler Limited* [2021] Lloyd's Rep FC 353 (Crown) [4] (Edis LJ).

82 ibid [5] (Edis LJ).

83 ibid.

84 *Serious Fraud Office v Tesco Stores Ltd* (n 51) [4].

85 There is no requirement within Schedule 17 to the Crime and Courts Act 2013 to publish preliminary judgments; however, some judges have elected to do so. *See for example Serious Fraud Office v Standard Bank Plc (now ICBC Standard Bank Plc) (Preliminary)* [2016] Lloyd's Rep FC 91 (Crown).

to judicial review.[86] DPAs are effected through the Crown Court,[87] the decisions of which may be subject to judicial review by the High Court 'other than its jurisdiction in matters relating to trial on indictment'.[88] Taking a literal interpretative approach, a DPA does not feature a trial but instead a suspension of proceedings following the preferring of a bill of indictment;[89] therefore, a decision in respect of an approved DPA – particularly where breach proceedings have not arisen – should be permitted to be subject to judicial review. If this were the case, a decision to substitute the statement of facts (or anonymised judgment) may be challenged on the basis of there being an error of law,[90] contradiction to natural justice, or breach of human rights,[91] in seeking to set aside the decision.[92] Taking a purposive approach, considering the objective of review in circumstances other than those excluded, a matter following DPA approval would likely be considered an 'integral part of the … process'[93] and thus subject to the exclusion.[94] The decision would not be considered to bind an individual, but instead simply to impact the individual by implication, and therefore would unlikely be considered reviewable.[95] Alternatively, the decision of the prosecutor may be challenged by judicial review;[96] however – from Lord Justice Edis' words – the decision would ultimately be one made by the judge.

Bluu Solutions Limited and *Tetris Projects Limited* demonstrate another approach. Though two separate DPAs, there is a shared statement of facts and one approved judgment covering both cases. In these cases, reporting restrictions had (at the time of DPA approval) been imposed pending the outcome of the cases against implicated individuals.[97] Upon the lifting of these restrictions, it became clear that the statement of facts had – subsequent to DPA approval – been altered in respect of the identification of individuals, pursuant to an anonymisation order.[98] The DPA approval was announced on 20 July 2021, and reporting restrictions were lifted on 2 March 2023. The cases against the implicated executives ceased, with acquittals of all, in January 2023.[99] The case against one implicated agent, Roger Dewhirst, concluded shortly before the DPA reporting restrictions were

86 This is the case in the UK, though it is the subject of recent dispute in the US (**Section 1.1.3.4**).

87 Crime and Courts Act 2013, sch 17 para 2(3).

88 Senior Courts Act 1981, s 29(3).

89 Crime and Courts Act 2013, sch 17 para 2.

90 *Anisminic Ltd v Foreign Compensation Commission* [1969] 2 AC 147 (HL).

91 *R v Secretary of State for the Home Department, ex p Simms* [2000] 2 AC 115 (HL).

92 *Halsbury's Laws* (5th edn, 2018) vol 61A, paras 1, 30.

93 *R v Crown Court at Manchester, ex p DPP* [1993] 1 WLR 1524 (HL) 1528, citing *Re Sampson* [1987] 1 WLR 194 (HL).

94 Senior Courts Act 1981, s 29(3).

95 *Crown Court at Manchester, ex p DPP* (n 93) 1530, citing *R v Inner London Crown Court, ex p Benjamin* (1986) 85 Cr App R 267.

96 *R (on the application of AL) v Serious Fraud Office* [2018] EWHC 856 (Admin).

97 Ruby Hamid and others, 'The DPA Challenge – The SFO's First DPA-Related Conviction of an Individual Bucks the Trend' (*Ashurst*, 10 March 2023) <https://www.ashurst.com/en/news-and-insights/legal-updates/the-dpa-challenge---the-sfos-first-dpa-related-conviction/> accessed 28 March 2023.

98 'The DPA Statement of Facts and Judgment contain anonymised names of individuals subsequently acquitted at trial. These individuals are subject to an anonymisation order and cannot be named.' *See* Serious Fraud Office, 'R v Bluu Solutions Limited and Tetris Projects Limited' (*Serious Fraud Office*, 9 March 2023) <https://www.sfo.gov.uk/cases/r-v-bluu-solutions-limited-and-tetris-projects-limited/> accessed 28 March 2023.

99 Adrian Darbishire and Tom Doble, 'SFO Tetris Bluu Bribery Trial Concludes With Not Guilty Verdicts' (*QEB Hollis Whiteman*, January 2023) <https://www.qebholliswhiteman.co.uk/site/library/recent-cases/sfo-ttris-bluu-bribery-trial-concludes-with-not-guilty-verdicts> accessed 28 March 2023.

lifted, after the defendant entered a guilty plea.[100] This demonstrates that, where reporting restrictions are placed on the statement of facts pending the outcome of cases against implicated individuals, there is an opportunity to amend such documentation pursuant to an anonymity order prior to their publication. This, in the recent cases, did not amount to a change in the presentation of facts, but simply to the identification of individuals. Notably, where the de-anonymised version of the approving judgment was published in July 2023, upon expiry of the two DPAs, the original anonymised judgment was not amended at source (like the statement of facts), but a new judgment issued.

Notably, anonymity within the documentation does not remove the possibility of jigsaw identification in order to ascribe an identity to the individuals behind the frank and scathing account of the statement of facts, due to the substantial amount of information given. The details on the former directors (identified by position) are vast, not only in identifying information, but also in allegations made against them. Under paragraph 160 of the statement of facts, it states: '[i]n their management roles at [Tetris Projects Limited], Director 1 and Director 2 did not demonstrate their commitment to preventing bribery by persons associated with [Tetris Projects Limited]'.[101] Such a statement – which must be read in light of the acquittals for related offences – could have great implications in respect of follow-on claims, and in particular in respect of directors' duties (not least considering the subsequent identification of those individuals in the subsequently issued de-anonymised judgment).

One may argue that the amendment and addendum to the *Airbus SE* statement of facts were made in order to correct errors, both numerical and in respect of conduct. If the statement of facts in referring to a named individual made an error as to their conduct, this would suggest that corrections *could* be made. However, the language presented under paragraph 160 of the *Bluu Solutions Limited* and *Tetris Projects Limited* statement of facts (above) demonstrates that there was no reflection upon the "facts" presented within the statement of facts (agreed between the companies and SFO) despite acquittals of the individuals on the basis of the alleged conduct. This therefore demonstrates that whilst the statement of facts could be altered by way of anonymisation prior to publication, there was no intention to amend in respect of the alleged conduct of individuals. If substitution is to be made, as suggested in *AFWEL*, it should not significantly alter the factual account in relation to the corporate offending, nor the offences upon which the DPA is based; if a significant change must be made, this may be effected by way of variation of the DPA (including the attached statement of facts).[102] This may provide clarity on efforts made in *Bluu Solutions Limited* and *Tetris Projects Limited* not to amend the statement of facts in respect of the individuals' alleged conduct: in the case of *Bluu Solutions Limited*, identification principle offences make up four of the five counts which often refer to the implicated *acquitted* individuals explicitly (albeit anonymously). To make such an amendment

100 Hamid and others (n 97).

101 Serious Fraud Office, 'Statement of Facts' (*Serious Fraud Office*, 2 March 2023) <https://www.sfo.gov.uk/download/r-v-bluu-solutions-limited-and-tetris-projects-limited/> accessed 28 March 2023, para 160.

102 For example, where the company is deemed to have breached the DPA in respect of the common term that the company 'agrees that the Statement of Facts … is true and accurate to the best of its knowledge and belief'. *See for example* Serious Fraud Office, 'Amec Foster Wheeler Energy Limited – Deferred Prosecution Agreement' (*Serious Fraud Office*, 2 July 2021) <https://www.sfo.gov.uk/download/amec-foster-wheeler-energy-limited-deferred-prosecution-agreement/> accessed 2 July 2021, para 2.

would require variation, but could undermine the DPA and call into question the rationale for its agreement in the first place.

Even where errors are not made in respect of the underlying conduct – for example, the authorisation of a payment – it may be the case that precise language requires correction where, for example, it is outlined that the conduct was performed 'dishonestly';[103] if the individual is subsequently determined in their own criminal proceedings to have behaved honestly, this would also constitute a revisable error.[104] In respect of a subsequent effort to identify individuals, naming following a decision not to prosecute, or an unsuccessful prosecution, must not occur: it must only be where an individual is convicted that their name thereafter is identified in respect of the DPA.[105] To do so otherwise may be possible, when considering *Airbus SE*, but would be contrary to the individual's rights.

103 The *Tesco Stores Ltd* DPA's statement of facts expressly outlined that the three named former directors had acted dishonestly, whereas this was found not to be the case in the trial of two of them where there was no case to answer (and in the third the prosecution offered no evidence, and the jury was instructed to acquit). *See* Serious Fraud Office, 'Deferred Prosecution Agreement – Statement of Facts – SFO v Tesco Stores Ltd' (*Serious Fraud Office*, 23 January 2019) <https://www.sfo.gov.uk/download/deferred-prosecution-agreement-statement-of-facts-sfo-v-tesco-stores-ltd/> accessed 26 June 2020, para 9. *See also Bush* (n 80) [121]–[131].

104 Though it may continue to draw speculation as to whether the DPA should have been agreed if the predicate offence required dishonesty.

105 As seen in the case of *Director of the Serious Fraud Office v AB Ltd and another* [2021] Lexis Citation 1385 (Crown) with the naming of an implicated convicted third-party agent.

CHAPTER 10

Protection from prosecution

10.1 Cooperation agreements as an "assisting offender"

A director who is also a suspect in relation to corporate criminal wrongdoing will not be availed the opportunity to agree a DPA in the UK but may find some measure of protection within the provisions set out under sections 71 and 72 of the Serious Organised Crime and Police Act ("SOCPA") 2005, and sections 74 and 387–388 of the Sentencing Act 2020 ("SA 2020") (which repeal and replace sections 73 and 74 of SOCPA 2005). The statutory frameworks sit alongside the pre-existing common law provision known as "King's Evidence" (previously "Queen's Evidence"), though sections 387–388 of the SA 2020 (previously section 74 of the SOCPA 2005) represent a new addition.[1] The provisions include immunity from prosecution,[2] undertakings as to restricted use of evidence,[3] reduction in sentence,[4] and sentence review.[5] Where such measures are taken, the individual is referred to as an 'assisting offender'[6] (to be distinguished from "assisting *an* offender").

According to CPS guidance, typically the leniency written notice/agreement will be signed by the individual following interview under caution, whereby the individual provides an initial version of information. It may, however, be that signature can be obtained following a scoping interview (prior to interview under caution). Discussion regarding potential leniency can be raised by either the prosecutor or the individual, and a confidential scoping interview will be an opportunity for the prosecutor to determine the reason for cooperation, the extent to which the individual may be able to assist, and the extent of the underlying offending.[7] The scoping interview will be preceded by a proffer letter which will outline the purpose of the interview, including the fact that it will not be used

1 *R v Blackburn* [2007] EWCA Crim 2290 [25], [29].
2 Serious Organised Crime and Police Act 2005, s 71.
3 ibid s 72.
4 Sentencing Act 2020, s 74.
5 ibid ss 387–8.
6 Crown Prosecution Service, 'King's Evidence – Immunities, Undertakings and Agreements Under the Serious Organised Crime and Police Act 2005' (*Crown Prosecution Service*, 9 September 2022) <https://www.cps.gov.uk/legal-guidance/kings-evidence-immunities-undertakings-and-agreements-under-serious-organised-crime> accessed 12 April 2023.
7 Crown Prosecution Service, 'SOCPA Agreements: Note for Those Representing Assisting Offenders' (*Crown Prosecution Service*, April 2016) <https://web.archive.org/web/20210625040215/https://www.cps.gov.uk/legal-guidance/socpa-agreements-note-those-representing-assisting-offenders> accessed 5 May 2021.

DOI: 10.4324/9781003456964-12

to obtain admissions, but neither the letter nor the interview can be taken to represent any guarantee as to whether leniency will be adopted.[8]

Prior to any arrangement, there must be an element of cleansing whereby the individual – themselves a suspect – fully admits their involvement in criminal activity (specific to the investigation and on a more general level), discloses all available information in relation to the investigation, and agrees to continue providing complete cooperation until the conclusion of proceedings arising from the investigation.[9] Depending on the circumstances of the case, an individual may be asked whether they would be prepared to waive LPP as part of the cleansing process, in order to assist the prosecutor in assessing the appropriateness of offering leniency. Refusal to waive privilege does not necessarily mean that the individual will not be offered leniency and, crucially, waiver does not guarantee leniency.[10] The process of cleansing has therefore been described as 'highly risky',[11] and bears similarities to the process of DPA negotiation which is also based on no guarantee of approval.

In cases where a company is engaging cooperatively with the prosecutor (for example, where a self-report has been made with ongoing investigative support, and/or where DPA negotiations are underway), the prospect of offering leniency to an individual under the frameworks may be less attractive to prosecutors. Where an individual will likely be able to find support for leniency in such circumstances will be where the prosecutor is looking to prosecute other implicated individuals, or where the company's cooperation is not producing sufficient results in respect of building an evidential basis for a DPA. In order to obtain a DPA, there is some expectation that the company will be a new entity with a new management team – a wholly reformed version of its former criminal "self" – and that implicated directors will, therefore, leave (particularly where personally prosecuted and/or the cause of the problem).[12] In becoming this reformed character, it may be the case that integral sources of knowledge and information as to the criminal wrongdoing (such as former directors) are lost. In order to make an application to the court for a DPA, a prosecutor must be able to set out that the evidential test is met, or at least that there are reasonable grounds to believe that it would be met upon further investigation.[13] It may be the case that, despite extensive cooperation from the "new entity", this standard and thus corporate accountability for previous wrongdoing can only be obtained with the cooperation of former employees, and notably directors.

---

8 ibid.

9 ibid.

10 Crown Prosecution Service, 'King's Evidence – Immunities, Undertakings and Agreements Under the Serious Organised Crime and Police Act 2005' (n 6).

11 Ilana Baines, 'SOCPA Agreements: What are They All About?' (*Lawyer Monthly*, 4 September 2019) <https://www.lawyer-monthly.com/2019/09/socpa-agreements-what-are-they-all-about/> accessed 5 May 2021.

12 Crown Prosecution Service and Serious Fraud Office, 'Deferred Prosecution Agreements Code of Practice' (*Crown Prosecution Service*, 11 February 2014) <https://www.cps.gov.uk/sites/default/files/documents/publications/dpa_cop.pdf> accessed 9 June 2020, para 2.8.2(v); Select Committee on the Bribery Act 2010, *The Bribery Act 2010: post- legislative scrutiny: Evidence Session No 16* (HL 2017–19, 303) question 153.

13 Relating to the evidential stage of the Full Code Test in the Code for Crown Prosecutors. *See* Crown Prosecution Service and Serious Fraud Office, 'Deferred Prosecution Agreements Code of Practice' (n 12) para 1.2.

There is currently great attention around and criticism of the lack of criminal convictions of individuals implicated in the criminality forming the basis of corporate DPAs, with a perceived sense of lack of accountability and measure of untouchability. In this respect, leniency agreements may not be a prosecutor's first port of call in facilitating the obtaining of a DPA. The SFO has compulsive powers under section 2 of the CJA 1987, but (as discussed under **Section 7.2**) those powers render anything disclosed as a result inadmissible against their maker (with some exceptions).[14] It is in this respect that the SFO is heavily reliant on extrinsic evidence found, in order to effectively make use of the powers and continue the pursuit of individual criminal accountability. With the inherent issues posed by section 2 in their use against suspects targeted with a view to prosecution, it may be that the SFO resorts to SOCPA 2005 and the SA 2020.

SOCPA 2005 and SA 2020 leniency provisions are used sparingly. The most recent CPS data show that between May 2021 and April 2022, neither immunity nor restricted use undertakings were deployed, though there were four cases in which a reduction in sentence was used and one case in which sentencing was reviewed.[15] The data from the year prior demonstrate a very similar trend: between May 2020 and April 2021, neither immunity nor restricted use undertakings were deployed, though there were three cases in which a reduction in sentence was used and three cases in which sentencing was reviewed.[16] In the year before that, neither immunity nor restricted use undertakings were used, though there was one case in which a reduction in sentence was used and five cases in which sentencing was reviewed.[17]

Due to its smaller caseload, the SFO does not publish similar yearly use statistics as publication has been deemed by it, and the Information Commissioner's Office, to pose a likelihood of prejudice. With a high risk of jigsaw identification, it is considered that publication would serve as a deterrent to cooperation (with particular mention of economic crime),[18] and ultimately weigh against the public interest in disclosure.[19] However, on some occasions (where confidentiality is not a basis of the leniency deal) the SFO has

---

14 A statement made in response to section 2 powers can only be used against the maker in a prosecution for knowingly or recklessly making a false or misleading statement whilst purporting to comply with the provision, or where on a prosecution for some other offence the statement maker makes another statement inconsistent with it. In the latter case, the statement can only be used where evidence relating to it is adduced, or a question relating to it is asked, by or on behalf of that person in the proceedings arising out of the prosecution. *See* Criminal Justice Act 1987, ss 2(8)–(8AA).

15 Director of Public Prosecutions, 'Letter from the DPP to the Attorney General on Agreements Made Under Sections 71 to 74 of SOCPA 2005 and the Sentencing Act 2020, Covering the Period 1 May 2021 to 30 April 2022' (*Crown Prosecution Service*, 18 October 2022) <https://www.cps.gov.uk/publication/letter-dpp-attorney-general-agreements-made-under-sections-71-74-socpa-2005-and> accessed 3 April 2023.

16 Director of Public Prosecutions, 'Letter from the DPP to the Attorney General on Agreements Made Under Sections 71 to 74 of SOCPA 2005 Covering the Period 1 May 2020 to 30 April 2021' (*Crown Prosecution Service*, 9 July 2021) <https://www.cps.gov.uk/publication/letter-dpp-attorney-general-agreements-made-under-sections-71-74-socpa-2005-covering-2> accessed 2 October 2021.

17 Director of Public Prosecutions, 'Letter from the DPP to the Attorney General on Agreements Made Under Sections 71 to 74 of SOCPA 2005 Covering the Period 1 May 2019 to 30 April 2020' (*Crown Prosecution Service*, 2 October 2020) <https://www.cps.gov.uk/publication/letter-dpp-attorney-general-agreements-made-under-sections-71-74-socpa-2005-covering-1> accessed 6 May 2021.

18 Carolyn Howes, 'Freedom of Information Act 2000 (FOIA) Decision Notice: Reference: FS50908836' (*Information Commissioner's Office*, 8 July 2020) <https://ico.org.uk/media/action-weve-taken/decision-notices/2020/2618014/fs50908836.pdf> accessed 5 May 2021, para 26.

19 ibid paras 29–33, 41–43.

disclosed whether SOCPA 2005 has been deployed in reporting on case outcome.[20] One may consider the relatively small numbers within the CPS's data to pose a similar risk of jigsaw identification, though circumstances such as the nature of the underlying offences[21] and anonymity may differ.

In December 2018 (pre-SA 2020, when all provisions were contained within the SOCPA 2005), then-Director of the SFO Lisa Osofsky (2018–2023), in evidence to the Justice Committee, offered a view on the use of leniency provisions. When asked about dealing with the notoriously slow pace of SFO conclusion of cases, Osofsky set out that the use of cooperators under the SOCPA 2005 provisions would provide assistance in '[obtaining] insiders to help us wade through what can otherwise be a morass of documents'.[22] Osofsky also mentioned the use of cooperators in respect of an alliance with the US in multijurisdictional cases to 'really crack open our cases' and assist the prosecutor(s) in understanding the nature of the criminality, the 'really relevant documents', and bringing life to trial evidence.[23] At the Global Investigations Review's Women in Investigations Conference in May 2019, Osofsky again pointed to the increased use of SOCPA 2005 provisions, particularly in giving evidence *against* senior individuals involved in corporate crime.[24] With vast experience of plea deals, as a former US prosecutor, it is clear that Osofsky saw great value in the use of cooperative tools during her time as Director of the SFO. However, if the focus is largely on (successfully) prosecuting senior individuals, former directors may find it difficult to set out their case for SOCPA 2005 and SA 2020 leniency. It will likely be that the value will be larger where the cooperator's assistance supports not only the prosecution of fellow senior individuals, but also the foundational evidential basis of the corporate DPA. This may lead to an imbalance whereby former directors of larger companies, with a more numerous board, are availed a greater opportunity to pursue leniency than those from smaller companies.

10.1.1 Restricted use of evidence

Under section 72 of the SOCPA 2005, a prosecutor may offer an individual an undertaking that information (of any specified description) will not be used against that individual in criminal proceedings[25] (brought against that individual),[26] where it is deemed to be appropriate for the purposes of the investigation or prosecution of an offence.[27] The

20 *R v Clay and Clark* (Southwark Crown Court, 12 October 2015); Serious Fraud Office, 'Arck LLP: Two Sentenced to a Total of 12 Years and 10 Months' (*Serious Fraud Office*, 12 October 2015) <https://www.sfo.gov.uk/2015/10/12/arck-llp-two-sentenced-to-a-total-of-12-years-and-10-months/> accessed 5 May 2021.

21 Relating to homicide and drug-related offences: *Blackburn* (n 1).

22 There is no available Hansard from the evidence, though it can be viewed by video: ParliamentLive.TV, 'Justice Committee 18 December 2018, Witnesses: Lisa Osofsky, Director, Serious Fraud Office' (*ParliamentLive.TV*, 18 December 2018) <https://parliamentlive.tv/event/index/756b77d2-3d1d-4f13-8f9b-1e5a46be2d24?in=10:07:02> accessed 6 May 2021, [10:38].

23 ibid [10:11].

24 Baines (n 11); Neill Blundell and Max Hobbs, 'Legal Inoculation: The Director of the SFO Raises the Prospect of "Immunity Deals"' (*Macfarlanes LLP*, 13 June 2019) <https://blog.macfarlanes.com/post/102fm03/legal-inoculation-the-director-of-the-sfo-raises-the-prospect-of-immunity-deals> accessed 5 May 2021.

25 Serious Organised Crime and Police Act 2005, s 72(2)(a).

26 Within England, Wales, or Northern Ireland. *See* ibid s 72(3). *See also* Explanatory Notes to the Serious Organised Crime and Police Act 2005, para 173.

27 Serious Organised Crime and Police Act 2005, s 72(1).

'restricted use undertaking'[28] ceases to have effect if the individual fails to comply with its conditions,[29] and in this respect it is a 'conditional undertaking'.[30] The use of section 72 may *prima facie* be regarded as producing similar outcomes in respect of admissibility of evidence to the use of section 2 powers under the CJA 1987: information disclosed in response to use of section 2 powers is (generally) inadmissible against its discloser, and section 72 of the SOCPA 2005 may be invoked to conditionally restrict the use of similar or the same evidence.

It may be in the SFO's (and CPS's)[31] interests to first approach the relevant individual with the offer to discuss the use of a section 72 restricted use undertaking. This may avoid hostility and provide an individual with a greater sense of control, whilst maintaining the ability to gain valuable evidence against the company and other individuals. The prosecutor (notably the SFO, when comparing to the use of section 2) will also have greater freedom in drafting the conditions within the restricted use undertaking, in respect of circumstances that may trigger a breach and render the information disclosed to be admissible (conditions should be fair, so as to avoid an abuse of process). In a statement to the House of Commons in 1981, the Attorney General set out that where other (extrinsic) evidence arises, proceedings may still be brought,[32] thus in a similar vein to the CJA 1987. On balance, the use of section 2 powers provides an element of compulsion and carries a punitive element beyond prosecution for the underlying criminal offence, itself setting out a separate offence relating to the falsification, concealment, destruction, or disposal of evidence.[33]

10.1.2 Immunity

Under section 71 of the SOCPA 2005, a prosecutor (including the Director of Public Prosecutions (CPS) and Director of the SFO) may offer a person an 'immunity notice' where it is appropriate to do so for the purposes of the investigation or prosecution of an offence.[34] The immunity notice must be in writing[35] and will outline that no proceedings will be brought against the individual for an offence specified within.[36] It will cease to have effect where the individual fails to comply with its conditions,[37] and is to that extent 'conditional immunity'.[38] Immunity will only be offered in 'the most exceptional cases',[39] and the Attorney General must be consulted prior to any offer of immunity under section

28 ibid.

29 ibid s 72(4).

30 Explanatory Notes to the Serious Organised Crime and Police Act 2005, para 173.

31 The CPS does not have use of section 2 powers under the Criminal Justice Act 1987.

32 HC Deb 9 November 1981, vol 12, col 12 (Attorney General). It is set out within CPS guidance that this extrinsic evidence may be obtained directly or indirectly as a result of disclosures made under the restricted use undertaking. *See* Crown Prosecution Service, 'King's Evidence – Immunities, Undertakings and Agreements Under the Serious Organised Crime and Police Act 2005' (n 6). The finding of extrinsic evidence led to the prosecution of a cooperator of other offences in *Blackburn* (n 1) [9].

33 Criminal Justice Act 1987, s 2(16).

34 Serious Organised Crime and Police Act 2005, s 71(1).

35 ibid; Explanatory Notes to the Serious Organised Crime and Police Act 2005, para 172.

36 Serious Organised Crime and Police Act 2005, s 71(2).

37 ibid s 71(3).

38 Explanatory Notes to the Serious Organised Crime and Police Act 2005, para 172.

39 Crown Prosecution Service, 'King's Evidence – Immunities, Undertakings and Agreements Under the Serious Organised Crime and Police Act 2005' (n 6).

71 (though notably their approval is not a requirement).[40] There are no statutory rules setting out circumstances deemed to be appropriate in offering immunity, but the Attorney General in 1981 set out a ('non-exhaustive')[41] criteria to apply:

(i) whether in the *interests of justice* it is of more value to have a suspected person as a witness for the Crown than as a possible defendant;
(ii) whether in the interests of public safety and security the obtaining of information about the extent and nature of criminal activities is of greater importance than the possible conviction of an individual;
(iii) whether it is *very* unlikely that *any* information could be obtained without an offer of immunity and whether it is also very unlikely that any prosecution could be launched against the person to whom the immunity is offered.[42] (emphasis added)

The first criterion may be approached as a balancing exercise to consider the benefits of building a stronger foundation for a corporate DPA and whether prosecutions of other individuals may arise, weighed against the (potentially) alternative benefit of pursuing the relevant individual. This will be a difficult consideration, particularly with growing criticism as to the lack of accountability of individuals involved in DPA-related criminality. In this respect, potential assistance in the prosecution of other individuals may prove a greater incentive to prosecutors in employing SOCPA 2005 provisions (for example, where prosecutions may be in greater numbers). DPAs were introduced to incentivise cooperation as a result of difficulties faced in successfully prosecuting corporate crime and, where similar concerns arise in respect of the successful prosecution of individuals behind that crime, it may ultimately be in the interests of justice to pursue leniency in appropriate cases. Though Lord McNally, in introducing the relevant amendment of the Crime and Courts Bill (later the CACA 2013) to the House of Lords, was clear that directors would not be immune from prosecution where the company agrees a DPA,[43] the SOCPA 2005 provisions had already been in place for some time and used to afford leniency to directors.

The third criterion will likely be where former directors of now "new" entities present great value, and can be split into two parts. The first part considers whether it would be "very" unlikely that without immunity "any" information could be obtained, and can itself be viewed in two ways. If the requirement is that it must be "very" unlikely that "any" information be otherwise obtained, the inherent cooperative nature of DPAs might suggest that there would be little scope for immunity of an individual, as the company would likely be able to disclose *something*. Alternatively, this may be read as being more closely aligned with the specific information prosecutors seek to obtain,[44] in which case former directors may be able to provide information which the "new entity" cannot. Knowing that immunity is rare and permitted only in exceptional circumstances, it is

40 ibid.

41 ibid.

42 HC Deb 9 November 1981 (n 32) col 12 (Attorney General).

43 'Individual directors of companies will not be immune from prosecution if their company is part of a plea bargain.' *See* HL Deb 30 October 2012, vol 740, col 584 (Lord McNally).

44 Lisa Osofsky, then-Director of the SFO, said in 2018 that use of cooperators would help the prosecutor to understand 'what are the really relevant documents'. *See* ParliamentLive.TV, 'Justice Committee 18 December 2018, Witnesses: Lisa Osofsky, Director, Serious Fraud Office' (n 22) [10:11].

likely that this part of the criterion will be read quite inflexibly, though when read in line with the first criterion may provide some scope for a wider reading where in the interests of justice.

The second part of the third criterion considers whether it would be "very" unlikely that any prosecution could be brought against the individual concerned. This relates back to the complexity of corporate crime but interestingly focusses not on conviction but on prosecution. In the 13 UK DPA cases thus far, it is known that individuals have been prosecuted as a result of seven cases (where counting *Bluu Solutions Limited* and *Tetris Projects Limited* separately). Therefore, this threshold may also pose some difficulty unless read in line with the first criterion.

10.1.3 Reduction in sentence

Reduction in sentence, previously provided for under section 73 of the SOCPA 2005, can now be found under section 74 of the SA 2020. However, the nature of the provision has not changed, and therefore existing case law interpreting section 73 of the SOCPA 2005 remains relevant.[45] Whilst there are no Explanatory Notes to the SA 2020, the Explanatory Notes to the SOCPA 2005 had set out that the reduction in sentence provision may be used by the court 'in exceptional circumstances'.[46]

Under section 74 of the SA 2020, a court may impose a reduction in sentence[47] where a defendant pleads guilty to an offence and – in accordance with a written agreement with a prosecutor – has assisted or offered to assist the prosecutor or investigator in relation to an offence.[48] Section 73 of the SOCPA 2005, as it was, had been drafted in such a way as to preserve the separation of powers,[49] allowing prosecutors to reach an agreement with an individual but ultimately leaving sentencing power and discretion to the courts;[50] notably, the drafting remains the same in the SA 2020. Thus, the agreement does not form a guarantee or a right to a reduced sentence. This poses some risk to the individual concerned, as a guilty plea must be entered in order to qualify for judicial consideration of the content of the agreement.[51] Ultimately, this is not too far removed from the concept

45 The guidance on the provision issued by the CPS has not changed in nature whatsoever, except in reference to the relevant section of the relevant Act. *See* Crown Prosecution Service, 'King's Evidence – Immunities, Undertakings and Agreements Under the Serious Organised Crime and Police Act 2005' (n 6). *See also* Crown Prosecution Service, 'Assisting Offenders (Immunity, Undertakings and Agreements)' (*Crown Prosecution Service*, 2 August 2022) <https://www.cps.gov.uk/legal-guidance/assisting-offenders-immunity-undertakings-and-agreements> accessed 3 April 2023.

46 Explanatory Notes to the Serious Organised Crime and Police Act 2005, para 174.

47 Sentencing Act 2020, s 74.

48 ibid s 74(1).

49 The court outlined that an agreement between a prosecutor and defendant 'for the court's acquiescence' would be contrary to the principle of justice. *See R v Dougall* [2010] EWCA Crim 1048 [19].

50 'But the essential feature of that process is that the judge is expressing his view. It is also open to the parties to reach an agreement about the factual basis on which the Defendant will plead guilty. This is often known as the "agreed basis of plea". However the agreed basis of plea is always subject to the approval of the court, and the judge is not bound by the agreement'. *See* ibid [22], citing Practice Direction (Criminal Proceedings: Consolidation) [2002] 1 WLR 2070, paras IV.45.10–IV.45.12.

51 In the unreported case of *R v Hall*, defendant Bruce Hall testified against his co-accused Victor Dahdelah in accordance with a section 73 agreement with the SFO. Following his evidence, the SFO's case against Dahdelah collapsed and the prosecutor argued that Hall should not benefit from the section 73 agreement. This was not a position shared by the sentencing judge who afforded a discount but refused to suspend the sentence due to the egregious nature of his criminality (Hall had received millions of pounds sterling in

of a DPA whereby a prosecutor and offending company form an agreement which is then subject to judicial approval; the DPA defers prosecution, which cannot occur in the individual's case as per the guilty plea required but a suspended sentence may be imposed.[52] A company negotiating a DPA will be aware that one of two eventualities will occur, that it obtains a DPA[53] or does not, whereas an individual pleading guilty following agreement with a prosecutor will face greater unclarity (though certain that conviction will result) in respect of the sentence imposed.

Section 74(3) sets out that where a judge imposes a sentence less than it would have been, but for the assistance given or offered, the judge must (unless not in the public interest to do so)[54] state in open court that this is the case and outline what the sentence would otherwise have been. However, no provision is made as to the reduction itself.[55] *R v Blackburn*[56] set out that no specific rules could apply to what ultimately should be regarded as a fact-specific and not a mathematical decision, though did outline some factors for consideration, including the defendant's criminality, the quality and quantity of material provided, convictions obtained as a result, personal risks and consequences incurred, circumstances under which the guilty plea was given, and whether cooperation was offered at the first available opportunity.[57] It was clearly set out that there were no envisaged circumstances under which a defendant would not serve any sentence where the underlying offence was 'serious'; exceptionally, a reduction may exceed three-quarters of the original intended sentence but the normal reduction range would be between one-half to two-thirds.[58]

R v Dougall[59] focussed further on the potential for a suspended sentence following a (then) SOCPA 2005 'plea agreement'.[60] The defendant was a former director of DePuy International Ltd[61] and had pleaded guilty to conspiracy to corrupt, conspiring with DePuy International Ltd (a wholly owned subsidiary of DePuy Inc of which both were owned by the Johnson & Johnson group)[62] in 'substantial international corruption'.[63] Dougall had entered into a (then) section 73 agreement with the SFO which required his cooperation in UK and US corruption investigations, including those against the companies and/or individuals, and signed a witness statement with the promise to give evidence at trial should it become necessary to do so.[64] Unlike *Blackburn*, it was determined that a suspended

bribes). Interestingly, this meant that Hall's cooperative approach left him in a worse position than that of his co-accused, who was acquitted. *See* Serious Fraud Office, 'Victor Dahdelah and Bruce Hall' (*Serious Fraud Office*, 15 February 2021) <https://web.archive.org/web/20210507191000/https://www.sfo.gov.uk/cases/victor-dahdaleh-bruce-hall//> accessed 6 May 2021; David Corker, 'SOCPA: Immunity, Leniency and White Collar Criminals' (*Corker Binning*, 3 February 2016) <https://www.corkerbinning.com/socpa-immunity-leniency-and-white-collar-criminals/> accessed 5 May 2021. *See also* Sentencing Act 2020, s 74(1)(a).

52 *Dougall* (n 49) [36].

53 On the basis of settled terms. *See* CrimPR 11.4(2)(a).

54 Sentencing Act 2020, s 74(4).

55 *Blackburn* (n 1) [37].

56 ibid.

57 ibid [38]–[39].

58 ibid [41].

59 *Dougall* (n 49).

60 ibid [1]–[4].

61 Dougall sat on the board but was never a statutory director. *See* ibid [13], [15].

62 ibid [9].

63 ibid [8].

64 ibid [15]–[17].

sentence could be imposed following reflection upon a (then) section 73 agreement, based upon cooperation in assisting the investigation into white-collar crime where the original sentence would have been 12 months' imprisonment or less.[65]

In *R v Ford*,[66] the defendant had entered into a (then) section 73 agreement with the SFO and given evidence in the trial against another. Ford appealed his sentence on the basis that the judge had failed to pay appropriate attention to the *Dougall* decision regarding sentencing.[67] The court was keen to distinguish between the facts of both cases and set out that whilst Ford's assistance was 'doubtless valuable', the defendant in *Dougall* provided incomparable assistance in multijurisdictional investigations.[68] Additionally, the defendant in *Dougall* was a director within a multinational group, whereas in *Ford* the defendant acted 'at the behest of senior management'.[69] As such, there were not deemed to be 'exceptional circumstances'[70] warranting a suspended sentence, though a further reduction was granted. In *Serious Fraud Office v Papachristos*,[71] former sales and marketing director David Turner, despite 'prolonged, cynical and serious corruption of public officials',[72] received a suspended sentence in circumstances where the original sentence would have been over 12 months' imprisonment, a surpassing of the parameters set out in *Dougall.*

In *R v Clay and Clark*,[73] Kathryn Clark pursuant to a (then) section 73 agreement entered a guilty plea for her part in a 'pernicious fraud'[74] as a joint operator of Arck LLP, which was said to encourage her co-accused Richard Clay to do the same months later.[75] Whilst the Insolvency Service disqualified both Clark and Clay from serving as directors for 14 and 15 years respectively, the difference in sentence – reflecting upon Clark's section 73 agreement – was notable. Clark was given a two-year suspended sentence with 300 hours of unpaid work, and Clay was sentenced to just under 11 years' imprisonment.[76] Interestingly, in *R v Snee*[77] former managing director of Franklin Hodge Industries Ltd, Nigel Snee, cooperated with the Competition and Markets Authority ("CMA") by pleading guilty to a cartel offence and giving evidence as a witness in a trial against two individuals, who were acquitted. Though the CMA operates under the continuing common law leniency provisions, a similar sentencing approach was taken, and notably the CMA did not invite the court to disqualify Snee from being a director.[78]

---

65 ibid [36].

66 [2011] EWCA Crim 473.

67 ibid [16].

68 ibid [21].

69 ibid [19].

70 ibid [23].

71 [2014] EWCA Crim 1863.

72 ibid [78].

73 *Clay and Clark* (n 20).

74 'Their elaborate scam, which involved both defendants operating joint control over Arck LLP and its accounts, defrauded investors of their money, in some cases their pension funds and life savings.' *See* Serious Fraud Office, 'Arck LLP: Two Sentenced to a Total of 12 Years and 10 Months' (n 20).

75 Corker (n 51).

76 Clark was also given a serious crime prevention order to span five years. *See* Serious Fraud Office, 'Arck LLP: Two Sentenced to a Total of 12 Years and 10 Months' (n 20).

77 (Southwark Crown Court, 14 September 2015).

78 GOV.UK, 'Director Sentenced to 6 Months for Criminal Cartel' (*GOV.UK*, 14 September 2015) <https://www.gov.uk/government/news/director-sentenced-to-6-months-for-criminal-cartel> accessed 6 May 2021; Corker (n 51).

Under section 388 of the SA 2020 (previously section 74 of the SOCPA 2005), where an individual has been convicted of an offence and thereafter, pursuant to a written agreement, provides or offers to provide assistance to a prosecutor or investigator, their sentence may be referred back to the court for review (for decrease) where considered by the prosecutor to be in the interests of justice to do so.[79] Under section 74 of the SOCPA 2005, it was outlined that a sentence may also be referred for review (for decrease) where an individual had previously received a discounted sentence pursuant to a written agreement to provide assistance (as seen under (then) section 73 of the SOCPA 2005), but thereafter entered into another agreement regarding further assistance;[80] though this is not explicitly set out in the SA 2020 in the same way, the option is not excluded. Where an individual enters into a written agreement to provide assistance and receives a discount on reflection of the agreement, but thereafter knowingly fails to do so, the sentence may be referred for review of an increase.[81]

10.1.4 Reduction in sentence in the context of multijurisdictional investigations

It is clear from the multijurisdictional assistance provided by the defendant in *Blackburn* and from Osofsky's comments that the use of assisting offenders is not only to their benefit, but can also vastly assist prosecutors in seeking resolution of cross-border cases. This will no doubt be increasingly valuable as the consequences of Brexit for cross-border investigations become better known.[82] However, there remains a risk to defendants pleading guilty as, even where a reduction in sentence is awarded in the Crown Court, section 74 of the SA 2020 agreement does not apply to or bind other prosecutors. Though nationally double jeopardy would prevent another prosecutor from pursuing an individual for the same crime, risk remains where international double jeopardy is not recognised by overseas jurisdictions.[83] In relation to the *Dougall* case, Johnson & Johnson had agreed a DPA with the US DoJ in 2011 (prior to the introduction of UK DPAs),[84] which prevented the SFO from pursuing prosecution within the UK. The SFO stated that the DPA with DePuy International Ltd's ultimate parent company meant that the principles of double

79 Sentencing Act 2020, s 388. Previously, this had been set out within the Serious Organised Crime and Police Act 2005, s 74(2)(c); Explanatory Notes to the Serious Organised Crime and Police Act 2005, para 175. This is not an appeal, but a separate process: *Blackburn* (n 1) [33].

80 Serious Organised Crime and Police Act 2005, s 74(2)(b).

81 Sentencing Act 2020, s 387(1).

82 In 2021, Associate General Counsel at the SFO Rebecca Dix stated that it was 'business as usual' for the SFO in respect of cross-border investigations post-Brexit, with continued use of cooperation agreements and mutual legal assistance. Dix's comments were made in an event hosted by Rahman Ravelli online due to COVID-19 restrictions: Rahman Ravelli, 'Challenges Facing the SFO' (online, Rahman Ravelli 6 May 2021). However, as time passes, the true impact remains to be seen. On cross-border law enforcement: 'It is possible to conclude that Brexit has brought changes to international law enforcement cooperation, most significantly where this involves judicial matters … In short, whereas the United Kingdom once had greater harmonisation with differing legal systems, Brexit has caused an increase in bureaucracy and a decrease in trust.' *See* Matthew Shellaker, Stephen Tong and Paul Swallow, 'UK–EU Law Enforcement Cooperation Post-Brexit: A UK Law Enforcement Practitioner Perspective' [2023] Criminology & Criminal Justice <https://journals.sagepub.com/doi/10.1177/17488958231162520> accessed 22 June 2023.

83 Qingxiu Bu, 'The Viability of Deferred Prosecution Agreements (DPAs) in the UK: The Impact on Global Anti-Bribery Compliance' (2021) 22 EBOR 173, 191; Blundell and Hobbs (n 24).

84 *United States of America v (Johnson & Johnson) DePuy Inc* (Case 1:11-cr-00099-JDB).

jeopardy would apply,[85] as the DPA '[had] the legal character of a formally concluded prosecution and punishes the same conduct',[86] and instead agreed a civil recovery order with the subsidiary.

It has since been the case that coordinated settlements have been made between a company and multiple prosecutors, allowing for multiple DPAs, such as that seen in *Airbus SE*. However, in such cases, each prosecutor pursues a designated aspect of the underlying wrongdoing, most relevant to its own jurisdiction, and in this respect, the differing specific facts are able to lead to multiple DPAs.[87] Were prosecutors to agree DPAs for conduct relating to the same underlying facts, companies would incur punitive sanction within the terms of each DPA and face potential prosecution across multiple jurisdictions upon breach. The relatively settled approach of prosecutors, to prosecution following multijurisdictional investigations, appears to reduce the risk to companies and would likely also be followed in respect of implicated individuals. Though criminal prosecution for offences based on the same facts is unlikely to arise in jurisdictions such as the US and France where section 74 agreements are agreed (in the UK),[88] this is not a guarantee in these nor other jurisdictions, and a guilty plea within the UK may – as ever – lead to follow-on civil claims within and/or outside the jurisdiction.

An individual's assistance provided pursuant to a section 74 agreement may be kept confidential[89] where it is in the public interest not to disclose the sentence reduction.[90] Previously, DPAs have been anonymised to ensure that the right of individuals as protected under Article 3 of the ECHR is not prejudiced.[91] In this respect, a confidential section 74 agreement may be in the public interest where overseas prosecution of the relevant individual would be likely upon a guilty plea made within the UK, if punishment resulting from prosecution in that overseas territory would be considered contrary to Article 3 of the ECHR.

10.1.5 Restricted by the Companies Act 2006?

10.1.5.1 Section 232

Section 232 of the CA 2006 succeeded the now repealed section 310 of the Companies Act 1985. Section 232 of the CA 2006 sets out that:

---

85 The DPA was agreed between US DoJ and 'Johnson & Johnson, its subsidiaries, and its operating companies (collectively, "J&J")' on the basis of criminal conduct committed by members of the corporate group ('certain J&J operating companies and subsidiaries'). *See* ibid 1.

86 Serious Fraud Office, 'DePuy International Limited Ordered to Pay £4.829 million in Civil Recovery Order' (*Serious Fraud Office*, 8 April 2011) <https://web.archive.org/web/20151019162730/http://www.sfo.gov.uk/press-room/press-release-archive/press-releases-2011/depuy-international-limited-ordered-to-pay-4829-million-in-civil-recovery-order.aspx> accessed 7 May 2021.

87 This approach was seen in a non-DPA context in *Kulibaba v United States*, whereby US prosecutors prosecuted defendants despite their convictions in the UK, as different victims were identified in different transactions. *See Kulibaba v United States* [2014] EWHC 176 (Admin) [30]. *See also* Bu (n 83) 192.

88 Bu (n 83) 191–192.

89 Howes (n 18) para 17.

90 Sentencing Act 2020, s 74(4); Crown Prosecution Service, 'King's Evidence – Immunities, Undertakings and Agreements Under the Serious Organised Crime and Police Act 2005' (n 6).

91 'No one shall be subjected to torture or to inhuman or degrading treatment or punishment.' *See* Convention for the Protection of Human Rights and Fundamental Freedoms (European Convention on Human Rights, as amended) (ECHR) art 3. *See also Serious Fraud Office v Rolls-Royce Plc* [2017] Lloyd's Rep FC 249 (Crown) [32].

> *Any provision* that purports to exempt a director of a company (*to any extent*) from any liability that would otherwise attach to him *in connection with* any negligence, default, breach of duty or breach of trust in relation to the company is void.[92] (emphasis added)

Applying the literal rule of statutory interpretation, this provision would *prima facie* suggest that any provision, including those set out under the SOCPA 2005 and SA 2020, purporting to exempt a director (not necessarily wholly, for example, by way of an immunity notice under section 71 of the SOCPA 2005) from liability arising in connection with any of the types of liability set out (for example, criminal liability also constituting a breach of duty) would be void. This strict interpretation is at odds with case law whereby directors have benefitted from SOCPA 2005 leniency. Paragraph 427 of the CA 2006 Explanatory Notes provides further guidance and outlines that:

> Any provision, whether in the company's articles, in a contract or *otherwise*, attempting to exempt … a director in breach of this section is void.[93] (emphasis added)

This can be read in line with the previous interpretation of section 310 of the Companies Act 1985, which bore similar wording.[94] In *Burgoine v London Borough of Waltham Forest*[95] it was noted by Justice Neuberger that "or otherwise" may be construed as having a wide application. "Or otherwise" was, as a result of the words preceding it, not to be interpreted as including any arrangement to which the company is not a party.[96] Furthermore, section 232 does not automatically render leniency proposed by a prosecutor under the SOCPA 2005 or SA 2020 void. Even where the company is itself cooperating with prosecutors in negotiating a DPA, it could not be said that the company would be a party to any personal arrangement between a former director and the prosecutor in respect of the individual obtaining leniency provisions under the SOCPA 2005 or SA 2020.

As to agreements made after a director's liability has been raised, section 232 would appear to continue to apply irrespective of timing. 'This section prohibits a company from exempting a director from, or indemnifying him against, any liability'[97] in relation to those matters set out within the provision, and should be considered in line with paragraph 427 of the Explanatory Notes. The inclusion of the company's articles and contracts, as examples of provisions attempting to exempt liability, by nature encompasses action which may be taken after the issue of liability is raised. The exception to this is 'lawful provisions in the articles for dealing with conflicts of interest',[98] which demonstrates an acknowledgement of just one specific type of action that may be taken afterwards, to be expressly excluded. Although any provision (such as an alteration to the company's

92 Companies Act 2006, s 232(1).

93 Explanatory Notes to the Companies Act 2006, para 427.

94 '[Any] provision, whether contained in a company's articles or in any contract with the company or otherwise, for exempting' a director from liability for the same types of liability would be void. *See* Companies Act 1985, ss 310(1)–(2).

95 [1997] 2 BCLC 612 (Ch).

96 'I consider that the words "or otherwise" in s 310(1) are to be construed eiusdem generis with the preceding words "whether contained in a company's articles or in any contract with the company". After all, the company's articles of association are, at least in a sense, contractual provisions between the company and its members. In those circumstances, it can be said with force that there is a genus, namely an arrangement to which the company is party, which restricts what might otherwise be said to be a very wide meaning of the words "or otherwise".' *See* ibid 626–627 (Neuberger J).

97 Explanatory Notes to the Companies Act 2006, para 426.

98 ibid para 427.

articles) which purports to exempt a director from liability might be beneficial to the director's insurer, save in the case of self-controlled one-man companies, it is likely that such a provision would be opposed by shareholders (which may in any event give rise to liability). In line with the spirit of company law, the company cannot be *ex post facto* precluded from making a claim in such circumstances.

10.1.5.2 Sections 170(2) and 175

It may however be the case that a former director, in agreeing to a leniency provision, finds that liability arises for a breach of their ongoing duty to avoid conflicts of interest.[99] Information obtained during directorship cannot be exploited by a former director for their personal interests, and it may be deemed that agreeing to a restricted use undertaking under section 72 of the SOCPA 2005 would constitute such exploitation. Ultimately, the former director will benefit in respect of conditional protection from admissibility of the information, which may positively impact their own prospects of success in defending their own prosecution. The duty to avoid conflicts of interest applies irrespective of whether the company would have obtained an advantage (for example, a DPA as opposed to prosecution) from the use of the information.[100] Thus, it does not *prima facie* matter if the director's own contribution – pursuant to the restricted use undertaking – assisted the company in obtaining a DPA, though it may be reflected upon in any contemplated action for breach. In the case of a former director, the duty to avoid conflicts of interests continues in respect of the "no profit" rule (and not the "no conflict" rule), and thus a financial profit gained will need to be determined in order to establish a breach (**Section 6.2.2**).[101]

10.2 Protection by virtue of the corporate DPA?

Though joint DPAs can be agreed, a DPA with a company is not intended to protect (present or former) individuals within the company from liability. The wording of some judgments approving DPAs in this respect has set out some potential inconsistency. The approved judgment to the *Standard Bank* DPA was a foundational moment in outlining the judicial approach to DPAs thereafter, and at paragraph 12 reads:

> Conditions include the absence of any protection against prosecution of any present or former officer, employee or agent or against Standard Bank *for conduct not disclosed by it* prior to the date of the agreement (or any future criminal conduct) and provisions if the Bank were to have provided information to the SFO which it knew or ought to have known was inaccurate, misleading or incomplete.[102] (emphasis added)

Read literally, this would appear to suggest that where conduct *is* disclosed by the company to prosecutors prior to the DPA date (likely within the self-report or period of

99 Companies Act 2006, ss 170(2), 175.

100 ibid s 175(2).

101 '[The] object of the "no conflict rule" is to prevent the fiduciary from being swayed by considerations of his personal interests ... If he has no powers to exercise, then the foundation for the rule has been undermined and the rule will not apply.' *See Ultraframe (UK) Ltd v Fielding* [2005] EWHC 1638 (Ch) [1308] (Lewison J). *See also Chan v Zacharia* [1985] LRC (Comm) 709 (HCA) 726 (Deane J); *Halsbury's Laws* (5th edn, 2016) vol 14, para 590.

102 *Serious Fraud Office v Standard Bank Plc (now ICBC Standard Bank Plc) (Final)* [2016] Lloyd's Rep FC 102 (Crown) [12].

negotiations), such disclosure will allow for protection against prosecution of any present or former officer. One might suggest that the paragraph should be read more incrementally, such as:

> Conditions include the absence of any protection:
> (a) against prosecution of any present or former officer, employee or agent or
> (b) against Standard Bank for conduct not disclosed by it prior to the date of the agreement (or any future criminal conduct)

The approved judgment does not clearly separate the applicability of 'absence of protection … for conduct not disclosed by it prior to the date of the agreement' from the individuals and the company, which *prima facie* appears to therefore provide some level of protection to the individuals. However, this would appear to be a matter of drafting and can be read in line with the DPA itself in order to determine the position:

> These terms do not provide any protection against prosecution for conduct not disclosed by Standard Bank prior to the date on which the Agreement comes into force nor does it provide protection against prosecution for any future criminal conduct committed by Standard Bank. *In addition* these terms do not provide any protection against prosecution of any present or former officer, director, employee or agent of Standard Bank.[103] (emphasis added)

The DPA clearly separates the wording in respect of the company and its protection from prosecution, and the individual (and their lack of protection) by using "in addition" to present such a distinction. Ultimately the DPA itself would have more weight in respect of the attempted enforcement of any purported provision tending to protect individuals from liability, as comments made in the judgment are referring to an original document in order to provide clarification and appear simply to be an example of unfortunate drafting. In any event, the DPA is not enforceable by individuals, and the judgment's *obiter dicta* could not be read to confer protection upon them.

Though the *Standard Bank* DPA was the first to be approved in the UK, it is not the only DPA case to have brought about this inconsistency. The approved judgments of *Sarclad Ltd* and *Rolls-Royce* adopted similar wording to that in *Standard Bank* (notably all approved by Sir Leveson),[104] whilst their DPA counterparts were also clearer in separating wording in respect of the company and any individuals. In the *Rolls-Royce* judgment, however (and also that of *Güralp Systems Ltd*), the DPA tool was introduced in opening paragraphs as not covering 'nor does it protect from prosecution'[105] individuals. In the *Tesco Stores Ltd* judgment, the last DPA to be approved by Sir Leveson, more precise wording was adopted: the level of protection of the company was addressed first, and then it proceeded

103 Serious Fraud Office, 'Deferred Prosecution Agreement – Statement of Facts – SFO v ICBC SB PLC' (*Serious Fraud Office*, 1 June 2016) <https://www.sfo.gov.uk/cases/standard-bank-plc/> accessed 1 March 2018, para 5.

104 'Conditions include the provision that there is no protection against prosecution of any present or former officer, employee or agent or, indeed, of Sarclad for conduct not disclosed by it prior to the date of the agreement (or any future criminal conduct)'. *See Serious Fraud Office v Sarclad Limited (Serious Fraud Office v XYZ Ltd) (Final)* [2016] Lexis Citation 686 (Crown) [13]. 'Other conditions include the absence of any protection against prosecution of any present or former officer, employee or agent or against Rolls-Royce or RRESI for conduct not disclosed by them prior to the date of the agreement (or any future criminal conduct).' *See Rolls-Royce Plc* (n 91) [66].

105 *Rolls-Royce Plc* (n 91) [6]; *Serious Fraud Office v Güralp Systems Ltd* [2020] Lloyd's Rep FC 90 (Crown) [8].

to state 'neither is there protection from prosecution of any [individuals]'.[106] Thus, any lack of clarity may be ascribed to particulars in drafting during the early stages of a tool introduced without provision or guidance on how to approach the position of individuals (protected from prosecution or otherwise).

Any lack of clarity within the judgments can be read alongside DPA wording which, in the 12 SFO cases agreed, has taken a clearer and more cohesive approach. Every DPA has adopted similar wording (with only marginal and insignificant differences) to that found within the *Standard Bank* DPA, with wording relating to protection from prosecution of companies separated from that relating to individuals using the "in addition" drafting distinction. The DPAs of *Airbus SE, G4S C&J, Bluu Solutions Limited*, and *Tetris Projects Limited* go even further, by separating each respective part by distinct paragraphs.[107] Further, any argument that individuals are protected from prosecution by virtue of the DPA documentation alone would not be successful. The relatively recent *AFWEL* DPA does not devote a distinct paragraph within its terms, but is nonetheless clear within the relevant paragraph as to the lack of protection against prosecution of individuals.[108] The first CPS DPA agreed, with Entain plc, provides greater clarity by taking an incremental approach, as suggested above. Thus, it is clear that '[t]he terms of the DPA do not provide any protection against the prosecution of: [...]any present or former director, officer, employee or agent of Entain'.[109]

---

106 *Serious Fraud Office v Tesco Stores Ltd* [2019] Lloyd's Rep FC 283 (Crown) [70].

107 Serious Fraud Office, 'Deferred Prosecution Agreement Airbus 31.01.20' (*Serious Fraud Office*, 28 February 2020) <https://www.sfo.gov.uk/download/airbus-se-deferred-prosecution-agreement-statement-of-facts/> accessed 11 February 2021, para 10; Courts and Tribunal Judiciary, 'SFO -v- G4S: Tab C – SFO v G4S Care Justice Services (UK) Limited Deferred Prosecution Agreement' (*Courts and Tribunal Judiciary*, 17 July 2020) <https://www.judiciary.uk/judgments/sfo-v-g4s/> accessed 18 July 2020, para 10; Serious Fraud Office, 'Deferred Prosecution Agreement Bluu Solutions Limited' (*Serious Fraud Office*, 2 March 2023) <https://www.sfo.gov.uk/download/r-v-bluu-solutions-limited-and-tetris-projects-limited/> accessed 28 March 2023, para 10; Serious Fraud Office, 'Deferred Prosecution Agreement Tetris Projects Limited' (*Serious Fraud Office*, 2 March 2023) <https://www.sfo.gov.uk/download/r-v-bluu-solutions-limited-and-tetris-projects-limited/> accessed 28 March 2023, para 10.

108 '[T]his Agreement does not provide any protection against prosecution of: (i) any present or former officer, director or employee of AFWEL, or of any persons who perform or performed services for or on behalf of AFWEL (together, the "AFWEL Associated Persons")'. *See* Serious Fraud Office, 'Amec Foster Wheeler Energy Limited – Deferred Prosecution Agreement' (*Serious Fraud Office*, 2 July 2021) <https://www.sfo.gov.uk/download/amec-foster-wheeler-energy-limited-deferred-prosecution-agreement/> accessed 2 July 2021, para 6.

109 Crown Prosecution Service, 'Deferred Prosecution Agreements: R v Entain DPA' (*Crown Prosecution Service*, 5 December 2023) accessed 13 December 2023, para 51.3.

PART III

DIRECTORS' D&O INSURANCE COVERAGE

Considering the impact of deferred prosecution agreements ("DPA(s)") on directors' liability, without further considering the impact on directors' and officers' ("D&O") liability insurance, would be a real oversight. Part III of the book thus focusses on the extent to which directors can find meaningful protection under Side A of the traditional D&O policy and any more recent developing products. In order to safeguard directors' access to coverage as much as possible, the process of obtaining insurance and thereafter seeking coverage by way of a claim against the insurer is considered. In doing so, the book explores a variety of policy wording. Part III begins by discussing the precontractual obligations on the part of prospective insureds, and notable aspects of the D&O policy to consider in first obtaining insurance. Thereafter, Part III moves to the claims process and discusses the "Claims made (and reported)" nature of D&O insurance and the respective conditions to cover. A key theme of Part III is ensuring protection of (former) directors, and thus the nature of a typical ABC policy covering directors and the company is analysed in order to highlight exposures to cover. Indemnification for civil claims and criminal proceedings is explored, before moving to the advancement of defence costs and the obligations of both the insured and insurer in the process: arguably the most important aspect of the insurance analysis.

DOI: 10.4324/9781003456964-13

CHAPTER 11

Precontractual obligations

As the potential risks to liability become more greatly exposed, it is imperative to consider the extent to which directors can find protection against such liabilities. There are many aspects of the insurance process that require attention when considering the impact of DPAs on coverage pursuant to an *existing* contract of insurance. However, consideration of coverage alone is not sufficient in determining the true extent of the impact of DPAs on directors' (and corporate) liability and exposure. Given the nature of ABC D&O policies, which cover both individual directors and the corporate body(ies), it is also crucial to consider the process of arranging contracts of insurance, and thus obtaining coverage. Before considering the claims process, it is pertinent to set out the backdrop upon which precontractual obligations arise.

11.1 Fair presentation of risk

Prior to formal agreement to the contract of insurance and inception of D&O policy coverage, a prospective insured faces disclosure obligations in ensuring that the insurer is given a fair presentation of the risk before assuming risk. A company director engaged in wrongdoing, with knowledge of past or present wrongdoing, conducting an internal investigation, considering self-reporting, or engaged in DPA negotiations on behalf of the company, may (where material)[1] be required to make relevant disclosures to the insurer. Failure to do so could impact multiple insureds.

The Insurance Act 2015 ("IA 2015") came into force in August 2016, following a joint report by the English and Scottish Law Commissions in 2014 (hereafter "the Law Commissions' 2014 Report"),[2] and applies to commercial insurance. D&O insurance would thus fall to be governed by the IA 2015, insofar as the insureds are insured within their professional capacity.[3] This point was confirmed in *R (on the application of Bluefin Insurance Ltd) v Financial Ombudsman Service Ltd*,[4] in which a director had purported

1 'A circumstance or representation is material if it would influence the judgement of a prudent insurer in determining whether to take the risk and, if so, on what terms.' *See* Insurance Act 2015, s 7(3).

2 Law Commission, *Insurance Contract Law: Business Disclosure; Warranties; Insurers' Remedies for Fraudulent Claims; and Late Payment* (Law Com No 353, 2014).

3 Questions may arise as to whether an insurance contract within a D&O policy is (also) governed by the Consumer Insurance (Disclosure and Representations) Act 2012 where an insured is covered within a personal capacity (for example, a spouse). *See R (on the application of Bluefin Insurance Ltd) v Financial Ombudsman Service Ltd* [2014] EWHC 3413 (Admin) [127] (Wilkie J).

4 ibid.

DOI: 10.4324/9781003456964-14

to notify details of a potential claim to the broker, who had not relayed such a notification to the insurer, thus rendering the director without cover. Following the triggering of an investigation by the Financial Ombudsman Service, which identified the director as an 'eligible complainant' (under section 226 of the Financial Services and Markets Act 2000, as a 'consumer' under DISP 2.7.3R), the broker sought judicial review of this conclusion. The High Court held that liability incurred in the capacity of director was in the course of 'trade, business or profession' (outside the definition of 'consumer'), and thus the incurring of personal losses in such circumstances did not place the director under the definition of 'consumer'.[5] Consequently, this decision in effect negates the jurisdiction of the Financial Ombudsman Service in such disputes. Crucially, being business-related, this would fall within the scope of the IA 2015.

Previously, sections 18 and 20 of the Marine Insurance Act 1906 ("MIA 1906") governed the precontractual obligations of "assureds"[6] in respect of disclosure and representations. Under section 18(1), an assured was required to disclose all material facts (those which would influence the judgment of a prudent underwriter),[7] and under section 20(1) the assured was required to not misrepresent material facts. Both sections are repealed by the IA 2015,[8] though 'much of the old law is re-enacted'[9] and such relevant obligations can be found under section 3. The duty of fair presentation (of risk), under section 3, thus retains the duty of disclosure and subsumes failure to disclose and misrepresentation.[10]

In respect of representation, a fair presentation is deemed to be made where 'every material representation as to a matter of fact is substantially correct'.[11] This arguably imposes a lesser burden on insureds – 'not requiring every single detail to be correct'[12] – as the word "substantially" represents a new qualifying addition in comparison to section 20 of the MIA 1906. A material representation is deemed to be "substantially correct" 'if a prudent insurer would not consider the difference between what is represented and what is actually correct to be material'.[13] A fair presentation is also deemed to be made where

5 ibid [124]–[127] (Wilkie J).

6 The terms "assured" and "insured" relating to the beneficiary under a policy are often used interchangeably. *See Connecticut Mutual Life Ins Co* 108 US 498, 504 (1883), 2 Sup Ct 949: 'The contention of the plaintiff is that the words "the assured" in the policy apply to the person for whose benefit the policy was effected, that is, Luchs, and not to the party whose life was insured. There are undoubtedly instances where this distinction between the terms "assured" and "insured" is observed, though we do not find any judicial consideration of it. The application of either term to the party for whose benefit the insurance is effected, or to the party whose life is insured, has generally depended upon its collocation and context in the policy. We are of opinion that, reading the policy here in connection with the declaration and the answers of Luchs, which form a part of it, and indicate the object of procuring it, the term "assured" must be held as applicable to him, for whose benefit it was effected.'

7 Marine Insurance Act 1906, s 18(2). Material facts in the presentation of the risk include activities conducted by the assured/insured. *See Blakeley v CGU Insurance Ltd* [2017] VSCA 378. *See also* Robert Merkin, *Colinvaux's Law of Insurance* (12th edn, Sweet & Maxwell 2019) para 21-053.

8 Insurance Act 2015, s 21(2).

9 Rob Merkin and Özlem Gürses, 'The Insurance Act 2015: Rebalancing the Interests of Insurer and Assured' (2015) 78(6) MLR 1004, 1010.

10 John Birds and Katie Richards, *Birds' Modern Insurance Law* (12th edn, Sweet & Maxwell 2022) para 7-16.

11 Insurance Act 2015, s 3(3)(c).

12 Birds and Richards (n 10) para 7-17.

13 Insurance Act 2015, s 7(5).

'every material representation as to a matter of expectation or belief is made in good faith',[14] which reflects sections 20(3) and 20(5) of the MIA 1906.[15]

As far as disclosure,[16] an insured is required to disclose 'every material circumstance which the insured knows or ought to know',[17] or to make such a disclosure 'which gives the insurer sufficient information to put a prudent insurer on notice that it needs to make further enquiries for the purpose of revealing those material circumstances'.[18] That disclosure must be made 'in a manner which would be reasonably clear and accessible to a prudent insurer'.[19] A recent example of a material circumstance which required disclosure at policy renewal, in *Berkshire Assets (West London) Ltd v AXA Insurance UK plc*,[20] was criminal charges imposed on one of the company's directors. It was held that the insurer, pursuant to its standard position under its underwriting practice note, would have declined the risk upon disclosure. This demonstrates the importance of adhering to disclosure requirements where DPA-related circumstances arise, particularly at policy renewal. In respect of disclosure obligations throughout the insurance contract, as well as notification obligations, policies will often include an "Increase of risk" clause;[21] such a clause will require disclosure of 'permanent and habitual' but not temporary increases (unless otherwise expressed).[22]

Knowledge of the insured is covered under section 4 of the IA 2015. An individual insured is deemed only to know what is known to the individual, and to one or more of the individuals responsible for the insured's insurance.[23] Section 4(3) covers knowledge of an insured who is not an individual: in this instance, the insured 'knows only what is known to one or more of the individuals who are part of the insured's senior management, or responsible for the insured's insurance'.[24] The relevant parties are further defined:[25]

14 ibid s 3(3)(c).

15 'A representation may be either a representation as to a matter of fact, or as to a matter of expectation or belief.' *See* Marine Insurance Act 1906, s 20(3). 'A representation as to a matter of expectation or belief is true if it be made in good faith.' *See* Marine Insurance Act 1906, s 20(5). This IA 2015 provision 'will no doubt be construed in accordance with the decision in *Economides v Commercial Union Assurance Plc*'. *See* Birds and Richards (n 10) para 7-17, citing *Economides v Commercial Union Assurance Co Plc* [1997] 3 All ER 636 (CA) (in which there was deemed to be good faith in the presentation by the insured, but in relying upon a misrepresentation made by his father). '[W]hile there had to be some basis for the belief which was honestly held, there was no requirement that the insured had to carry out specific inquiries in order to establish an objectively reasonable basis for that belief. Accordingly, the sole obligation on the insured was that of honesty when he represented to the insurer on renewal that he believed the accuracy of his valuation.' *See Economides v Commercial Union Assurance Co Plc* [1997] 3 All ER 636 (CA) 636–637.

16 Insurance Act 2015, s 3(3)(a).

17 ibid s 3(4)(a).

18 ibid s 3(4)(b).

19 ibid s 3(3)(b). The Law Commission was keen to avoid disclosures by way of 'data dumping' of overwhelming amounts of information; such a method of disclosure, if taken now, may be considered a reckless breach of the duty of fair presentation. *See* Law Commission, *Insurance Contract Law: Business Disclosure; Warranties; Insurers' Remedies for Fraudulent Claims; and Late Payment* (n 2) paras 5.28–5.29, 11.46.

20 [2021] EWHC 2689 (Comm).

21 Robert Merkin and Özlem Gürses, 'Insurance Contracts After the Insurance Act 2015' (2016) 132(Jul) LQR 445, 445.

22 Birds and Richards (n 10) para 7-38, citing *Forrest & Sons Ltd v CGU Insurance Plc* [2006] Lloyd's Rep IR 113 (QB) (evidencing an Increase of risk clause); *Glen v Lewis* (1853) 8 Ex 607 (regarding expressly requiring notification of temporary increase of risk).

23 Insurance Act 2015, s 4(2).

24 ibid s 4(3).

25 'An individual is responsible for the insured's insurance if the individual participates on behalf of the insured in the process of procuring the insured's insurance (whether the individual does so as the insured's employee or agent, as an employee of the insured's agent or in any other capacity)'. *See* ibid s 8(b).

crucially individuals part of the insured's senior management are those 'who play significant roles in the making of decisions about how the insured's activities are to be managed or organised'.[26] This will include members of the board of directors, which 'replicates the directing mind and will test',[27] but may also include individuals not on the board 'depending on the structure and management arrangements of the insured'.[28]

In respect of knowledge of directors, and the extent to which this may be imputed to the company, the Law Commissions' 2014 Report considers the applicability of the *Re Hampshire Land Co (No 2)*[29] exception.[30] This exception sets out that knowledge of fraud (or potentially of breach of duty)[31] will not be imputed to the company in certain circumstances whereby it finds itself a victim (directly or indirectly) of that misconduct. The wider interpretation is focussed on the indirect victimisation of the company, whereby the company is a secondary victim of a fraud directed at a third party due to consequential losses it thereafter suffers.[32] The wider interpretation does not apply to restrict knowledge provisions within the IA 2015.[33] The narrower interpretation considers a more direct victimisation, whereby the principal (the company) is the primary victim of a fraud perpetrated directly against it.[34] This rule is preserved by the IA 2015, under section 6(2)(a) which preserves 'any rule of law' in this regard.[35] In *Group Josi Re v Walbrook Insurance Co Ltd*,[36] Lord Justice Saville clearly set out, in considering the application of section 18 of the MIA 1906, that any position outlining that a principal (in this case a reinsurer) ought to know of a fraud committed against it 'simply offends common sense' and such knowledge would infer that the principal was not defrauded.[37]

11.1.1 Utmost good faith

The contract of insurance[38] is unique in that since (at least)[39] the eighteenth century it has been classed as a contract of good faith, bestowing such duties on both the insurer and the

26 ibid s 8(c).

27 Law Commission, *Insurance Contract Law: Business Disclosure; Warranties; Insurers' Remedies for Fraudulent Claims; and Late Payment* (n 2) para 8.55.

28 Explanatory Notes to the Insurance Act 2015, para 54; Merkin and Gürses, 'The Insurance Act 2015: Rebalancing the Interests of Insurer and Assured' (n 9) 1012; Birds and Richards (n 10) para 7-18.

29 *Re Hampshire Land Co (No 2)* [1896] 2 Ch 743 (Ch).

30 Law Commission, *Insurance Contract Law: Business Disclosure; Warranties; Insurers' Remedies for Fraudulent Claims; and Late Payment* (n 2) para 8.67.

31 *Bilta (UK) Ltd (in liquidation) v Nazir* [2015] UKSC 23 [89] (Lord Sumption).

32 *Arab Bank plc v Zurich Insurance Co* [1998] All ER (D) 273 (Comm); Law Commission, *Insurance Contract Law: Business Disclosure; Warranties; Insurers' Remedies for Fraudulent Claims; and Late Payment* (n 2) para 8.69.

33 Law Commission, *Insurance Contract Law: Business Disclosure; Warranties; Insurers' Remedies for Fraudulent Claims; and Late Payment* (n 2) para 8.70.

34 ibid para 8.69.

35 ibid paras 8.75–8.76; *Halsbury's Laws* (5th edn, 2018) vol 60, para 36.

36 [1996] 1 WLR 1152 (CA).

37 ibid 1168 (Saville LJ).

38 The "contract of insurance" is to be distinguished from the "contract for insurance": the former is commonly used to describe the original insurance contract, and the latter to describe reinsurance. *See* Adolfo Paolini and Deepak Nambisan, *Directors' and Officers' Liability Insurance* (Informa Law 2008) para 9.12, citing Nicholas Legh-Jones and others, *MacGillivray on Insurance Law* (10th edn, Sweet & Maxwell 2003) 955; *HIH Casualty and General Insurance v Chase Manhattan* [2001] 1 All ER (Comm) 719 (QB) [1] (Aikens J).

39 'Howard Bennett suggests that its origins lie in the middle ages with the law merchant. This was a "body of transnational commercial law generated by the largely autonomous mercantile community and administered

insured. In *Carter v Boehm*,[40] Lord Mansfield, in setting out the rationale for the duty of disclosure, outlined that such a rule would 'encourage good faith'.[41] Nineteenth-century cases referred to the duty of utmost good faith in respect of both the precontractual and contractual relationships.[42] This principle was codified by section 17 of the MIA 1906, which set out under the heading "Insurance is uberrimae fidei": 'A contract of marine insurance is a contract based upon the utmost good faith and, if the utmost good faith be not observed by either party, the contract may be avoided by either party.' Despite expressly referring to marine insurance, section 17 '[reflected] the common law for all types of insurance'.[43] Though in repealing sections 18 to 20 of the MIA 1906 the precontractual obligation of utmost good faith owed on the part of the insured was *prima facie* 'dispensed' by section 21(2) of the IA 2015, and replaced by the duty of fair presentation,[44] the concept of good faith is not lost.[45] Section 17 was amended by the IA 2015, though only to the extent that the second half of the sentence regarding the remedy was removed.[46] To this extent, contracts of insurance[47] remain contracts based on utmost good faith,[48] a duty that applies 'symmetrically'[49] between insurer and insured, and good faith remains a 'general interpretative principle'.[50]

---

by specialist tribunals".' *See* Law Commission, *Insurance Contract Law Issues Paper 6 Damages for Late Payment and the Insurer's Duty of Good Faith* (Law Com IP 6, 2014) para 4.5, citing Howard Bennett, 'Mapping the Doctrine of Utmost Good Faith in Insurance Contract Law' [1999] Lloyd's Maritime and Commercial Law Quarterly 165, 186.

40 *Carter v Boehm* (1766) 3 Burrow 1905 (KB).

41 ibid 1911 (Lord Mansfield); Özlem Gürses, 'What Does "Utmost Good Faith" Mean?' (2016) King's College London, 2 <https://kclpure.kcl.ac.uk/portal/en/publications/what-does-utmost-good-faith-mean(02d45557-e695-41c8-8f20-97f1d07b5675).html> accessed 25 June 2021.

42 *Brownlie v Campbell* (1880) 5 App Cas 925 (HL); *Rozanes v Bowen* (1928) 32 Ll L Rep 98 (CA); *Britton v The Royal Insurance Company* (1866) 4 F & F 905 (Assizes) 909. *See also* Gürses (n 41) 2.

43 Law Commission, *Insurance Contract Law: Business Disclosure; Warranties; Insurers' Remedies for Fraudulent Claims; and Late Payment* (n 2) para 30.2, citing *Pan Atlantic Insurance Co Ltd v Pine Top Insurance Co Ltd* [1995] 1 AC 501 (HL) 518 (Lord Mustill); *Banque Keyser Ullmann SA v Skandia (UK) Insurance Co Ltd* [1990] 1 QB 665 (CA) 701 (Steyn J).

44 Merkin and Gürses, 'The Insurance Act 2015: Rebalancing the Interests of Insurer and Assured' (n 9) 1010.

45 For example, in regard to certain representations. *See* Insurance Act 2015, s 3(c).

46 Insurance Act 2015, s 14(3)(a). Section 17 of the MIA 1906 now reads: 'A contract of marine insurance is a contract based upon the utmost good faith.' *See* Marine Insurance Act 1906, s 17.

47 It remains the case that (despite wording) contracts of insurance of all types are governed by this provision: 'The common law mirrors this provision in relation to non-marine insurance.' *See* Explanatory Notes to the Insurance Act 2015, para 113.

48 'The intention of section 14 is that good faith will remain an interpretative principle, with section 17 of the 1906 Act and the common law continuing to provide that insurance contracts are contracts of good faith.' *See* Explanatory Notes to the Insurance Act 2015, para 116. *See also* Peter MacDonald Eggers and Simon Picken, *Good Faith and Insurance* (4th edn, Informa Law 2018) para 1.21; Bariş Soyer and Andrew Tettenborn, 'Mapping (Utmost) Good Faith in Insurance Law – Future Conditional?' (2016) 132(Oct) LQR 618.

49 '[T]he duty of utmost good faith applies equally to the insurer and to the insured. Indeed, it has long been recognised that the duty of utmost good faith applies symmetrically to both parties to an insurance contract.' *See Allianz Australia Insurance Ltd v Delor Vue Apartments CTS 39788* [2022] HCA 38 [93] (Kiefel CJ, Edelman, Steward and Gleeson JJ). On the matter of reciprocity, *see also Diamond World Jewellers Pty Ltd v Catlin Australia Pty Ltd* [2021] NSWSC 1431; *Catlin Australia Pty Ltd v Diamond World Jewellers Pty Ltd* [2022] NSWCA 282.

50 Law Commission, *Insurance Contract Law: Business Disclosure; Warranties; Insurers' Remedies for Fraudulent Claims; and Late Payment* (n 2) para 30.5. Though broader at the precontractual stage, the duty of good faith continues once the contract is formed. *See* Law Commission, *Insurance Contract Law: Business Disclosure; Warranties; Insurers' Remedies for Fraudulent Claims; and Late Payment* (n 2) paras 30.9–30.10, citing *Manifest Shipping Co Ltd v Uni-Polaris Insurance Co Ltd (The Star Sea)* [2001] UKHL 1.

11.1.2 Consequences

In removing the remedial expression in section 17 of the MIA 1906, the 'all or nothing'[51] remedy for the insurer of contract avoidance (*ab initio*) for breach of disclosure or representation obligations, based on a breach of the duty of utmost good faith, is removed.[52] In respect of breach of the duty of fair presentation, avoidance remains a possible remedy to insurers where the insured's breach is deemed a deliberate or reckless 'qualifying breach'[53] (and the insurer need not return any premiums paid);[54] or where the qualifying breach is not deliberate or reckless but, in the absence of it, the insurer would not have entered into the contract on any terms (the insurer will be required to return the premiums paid).[55] If the qualifying breach is neither deliberate nor reckless and the insurer would have entered into the contract on different terms (not relating to the premium), the contract is instead treated as if it had been entered into on those terms:[56] this position 'follows the consumer model'.[57]

11.2 The D&O policy

11.2.1 Policy construction and (imputed) knowledge

As directors are typically covered under a D&O policy by a separate contract of insurance to their co-assureds (**Section 13.1**), their exposure in respect of a perceived breach of the duty of fair presentation is somewhat reduced. The D&O policy is usually taken out by the company, and the relevant knowledge of the insured[58] as regards Side B and Side C – which *prima facie* provide indemnification (directly) to the company – will adhere to the provisions set out within section 4(3) of the IA 2015 (knowledge of an insured who is not an individual). In respect of section 4(3)(a) of the IA 2015, which provides that '[a]n insured who is not an individual knows only what is known to one or more of the individuals who are … part of the insured's senior management', the definition of 'senior management' during the debating of the Insurance Bill was extensive. In particular, there was concern that the definition set out in the Bill differentiated from that within the Explanatory Notes.[59] The central question was whether the definition should be narrow – referring to the board of directors (with concern of the Lloyd's Market Association that this would be *too* narrow)[60] – or broader. Ultimately, upon consultation of stakeholders,

51 Merkin and Gürses, 'The Insurance Act 2015: Rebalancing the Interests of Insurer and Assured' (n 9) 1014–1015.

52 Soyer and Tettenborn (n 48) 618–619.

53 Insurance Act 2015, s 8(3).

54 ibid s 8, sch 1 para 2.

55 ibid s 8, sch 1 paras 3–4.

56 'If the insurer would have entered into the contract (whether the terms relating to matters other than the premium would have been the same or different), but would have charged a higher premium, the insurer may reduce proportionately the amount to be paid on a claim.' *See* ibid s 8, sch 1 paras 5–6.

57 Merkin and Gürses, 'The Insurance Act 2015: Rebalancing the Interests of Insurer and Assured' (n 9) 1015.

58 Insurance Act 2015, s 4.

59 The Special Public Bill Committee inquiry on Insurance Bill, *Evidence Session No 2* (HL 2014) question 17 (Lord Newby).

60 Insurance Bill Deb 26 January 2015, col 8.

it was determined (and the IA 2015 reflects)[61] that whilst 'senior management' will likely include the board, it 'can also go beyond it, depending on the corporate structure of the relevant policyholder'.[62]

The knowledge of the individuals insured within the separate contracts of insurance under Side A will fall within section 4(2) of the IA 2015 (knowledge of an individual insured).[63] An individual insured remains somewhat exposed as regards disclosure obligations within the duty of fair presentation, even though under section 4(3)(a) imputing the knowledge of another member of senior management would not *prima facie* apply. Firstly, and perhaps most obviously, exposure arises where an individual insured outrightly declines to disclose matters known by them. Secondly, where the individual fails to conduct a 'reasonable search' of information in discovering what the insured 'ought to know'.[64] The concept of the 'reasonable search' was also the subject of debate as to definition during the debating stages of the Insurance Bill. It was suggested by David Hertzell of the Law Commission that the use of the term 'reasonable', which carries with it an 'inherent uncertainty', was necessary to allow it to 'be matched to the different level of entity'.[65] Further to the type of entity, this would also consider the type of cover sought and the wide variety of insurance policies on the market.[66] In the conducting of such a search, the individual may make enquiries with other members of the company's senior management.[67] However, where the other member(s) fails to disclose information or makes a misrepresentation to the individual and such information is thereafter passed by the individual to the insurer, the other member(s) of senior management as the source of such misrepresented knowledge will be liable.[68]

Thirdly, and arguably the most risky to the director, knowledge of an individual responsible for the director's insurance will be considered knowledge of the director for the purpose of section 4(2)(b).[69] Section 4(2) is clear in outlining that this relates to an 'individual' responsible for the insured's insurance and does not use the terminology 'person', which might otherwise have raised questions regarding whether the company's knowledge (as a legal person) could be considered to be that of the director, where the company is responsible for undertaking the director's D&O insurance. Instead, this can be narrowed to the individual(s) responsible (though risks remain). Particularly in small to medium enter-

---

61 '"[S]enior management" means those individuals who play significant roles in the making of decisions about how the insured's activities are to be managed or organised.' *See* Insurance Act 2015, s 4(8)(c). *See also* Explanatory Notes to the Insurance Act 2015, para 54: 'In a corporate context, this is likely to include members of the board of directors but may extend beyond this, depending on the structure and management arrangements of the insured.'

62 Insurance Bill Deb 26 January 2015, col 8.

63 Peter MacDonald Eggers, 'For One or For All: Joint and Composite Insurance Policies' (2017) 130(2) BILA J 1, 7–8.

64 Insurance Act 2015, s 4(6).

65 The Special Public Bill Committee inquiry on Insurance Bill, *Evidence Session No 1* (HL 2014) question 9 (David Hertzell).

66 HL Deb 8 January 2015, vol 758, col 545 (Lord Newby).

67 'In subsection (6) "information" includes information held within the insured's organisation or by any other person (such as the insured's agent or a person for whom cover is provided by the contract of insurance).' *See* ibid s 4(7).

68 *The National Exchange Company of Glasgow v Drew* (1855) 2 Macq 102, 145; *Cargill v Bower (No 2)* (1878) 10 Ch D 502, 513–514. *See also* MacDonald Eggers (n 63) 8.

69 Should a co-insured sign on behalf of all co-insureds, this will be deemed valid and the statements made will be those by all co-insureds. *See Suez Fortune Investments Ltd v Talbot Underwriting Ltd (The Brilliante Virtuoso)* [2019] EWHC 2599 (Comm). *See also* Merkin (n 7) para 15-058.

prises ("SMEs"), where the person(s) responsible for the company's insurance is likely to be either a director or at least part of the senior management,[70] there is less separation between the IA 2015 obligations and definition of "knowledge of an insured" than there might be in larger companies, whereby the role of the person responsible for insurance is more clearly defined and distinct. This will minimise risk for directors responsible for their own insurance (for example, companies with a sole director) but may exacerbate the risk for individuals whose insurance is coordinated/arranged by a fellow director, who would likely bear greater knowledge than an employee with such responsibility.

Although the individual director forms a member of the company's senior management, section 4(3)(a) does not apply as regards the individual's knowledge as an insured within their *own* contract of insurance. This means that any attribution to the company of knowledge of wrongdoing of another director will not impact the innocent insured director (in a composite policy). Where a company is a primary victim of fraud (or breach of duty) perpetrated directly against it, the common law rules relating to attribution remain in place so as to ensure that the company is not deemed to have held the requisite knowledge of such wrongdoing.[71] However, the common law rules in respect of a fraud perpetrated against a third party by someone within the company, rendering the company a secondary victim having suffered consequential losses, do not apply as regards the IA 2015. Therefore, the company may be deemed to have held the requisite knowledge of the wrongdoing so as to allow an insurer to seek a remedy.

If nondisclosure of the wrongdoing is considered to be deliberate or reckless, the insurer may seek to avoid the insurance contract altogether. This will likely impact Side C coverage the most, as the typical composite construction of D&O policies will ensure that other insured parties remain protected. A remedy against one insured will not automatically arise against a co-insured protected by a composite policy.[72] However, risks arise in rare joint policies whereby nondisclosure of one co-insured would be considered that of all. Where the wrongdoing has been approved by the board, the directors may themselves face coverage disputes, though this will not be by virtue of the non-inclusion of the wider interpretation of the *Re Hampshire Land* exception to the knowledge provisions in the IA 2015 and will more likely be focussed on the directors' own misconduct.

Most D&O policies contain a "Severability of Application" clause, which expressly sets out that the knowledge of one insured will not be imputed to another for the purpose of challenging that other insured's coverage.[73] Some policies are more explicit in setting out that the application/proposal for cover will be deemed a separate application/proposal by each individual insured.[74] In this instance, there may be greater obligation on the indi-

70 Insurance Act 2015, s 4(3).

71 ibid s 6(2)(a).

72 'Accordingly, under the Insurance Act 2015, if one co-assured under a composite policy is guilty of a non-disclosure or misrepresentation, inducing the insurer to agree to the insurance contract, the insurer has a remedy against that co-assured, but not against any other co-assured if that other co-assured is innocent of that non-disclosure or misrepresentation.' *See* MacDonald Eggers (n 63) 10.

73 Chubb, 'ForeFront Plus Insurance Policy' (*Chubb*, 2012) <https://web.archive.org/web/20140327013738/https://www.chubb.com/international/uk/csi/chubb15097.pdf> accessed 23 November 2020, para 2.13; Markel (UK) Limited, 'Revised D&O Wording' (*Markel International*, March 2016) <http://www.markelinternational.com/Documents/UK/Resources/Specimen%20wordings/Specimen%20wording%20-%20IT%20Consultants.pdf> accessed 24 June 2020, 12.

74 Hiscox, 'Management Liability – Directors' and Officers' Liability: Policy Wording' (*Hiscox*, 2017) <https://www.hiscox.co.uk/sites/uk/files/documents/2017-03/6757-directors-and-officers-liability-wording

vidual insured during the precontractual stage as regards responsibility for disclosure obligations, though this may minimise the risk of imputation of knowledge of another individual responsible for the insured's insurance to the insured should a dispute arise. In this respect, many D&O policies already emulate the likely interpretation of the IA 2015 knowledge provisions in respect of composite policies.

11.2.2 The example of the self-report

The matter of a self-report made or impending would be considered material: the nature of a self-report and likely ensuing investigation into the company (and its directors), and its potential consequences, would influence the judgement of a prudent insurer in determining whether to take on the risk.[75] Such a self-report, particularly if already delivered to prosecutors, would constitute a material circumstance invoking a requirement to disclose.[76] To be made in a manner reasonably clear and accessible to the insurer,[77] this may require deliverance of the self-report to the insurer in full. Notably, representations made within a self-report delivered to a prospective insurer would not be required to be exhaustively correct as long as they are made in good faith.[78] This may be advantageous to a company making an early self-report in respect of any later established minor discrepancies,[79] but may prove disadvantageous to the extent of persuading insurers to take on the risk. A self-report not yet formally made will still need to be presented to the prospective insurer on the same basis. In respect of breach of the duty of fair presentation, the director is required to disclose 'every material circumstance which the insured knows or ought to know',[80] and a self-report of potentially criminal wrongdoing would likely – circumstances depending[81] – be considered a circumstance a director ought to know. Furthermore, directors insured under Side A must be mindful that – under section 4(2)(b) – the knowledge of an individual responsible for their insurance will be considered their own knowledge; this presents risks in respect of matters represented/disclosed or which are omitted during the presentation of risk.

11.2.3 Prior Claims and Circumstances

A D&O policy is written on a "Claims made" basis, which means that cover is provided for Claims arising during the policy period (and any agreed extension) *or* for Circumstances (matters which may give rise to a Claim) notified to the insurer during the currency of

.pdf> accessed 23 November 2020, 5; Zurich, 'D&O Corporate Directors' and Officers' Liability: Policy Document' (*Zurich Insurance plc*, April 2020) <https://www.zurich.co.uk/business/-/media/Business/Documents/Specialty-lines/710008.pdf> accessed 22 January 2021, para 6.1.

75 Insurance Act 2015, s 7(3).

76 ibid s 3(4)(a).

77 ibid s 3(4)(b).

78 ibid s 3(4)(c).

79 On minor discrepancies, it is worth noting that a material representation is still deemed to be "substantially correct" 'if a prudent insurer would not consider the difference between what is represented and what is actually correct to be material'. *See* ibid s 7(5).

80 ibid s 3(4)(a).

81 Circumstances such as, for example, the size of the company and the director's continuing position within the company (for example, whether they have been suspended pending disciplinary investigation/proceedings), may have an impact on what the director ought to know.

the policy.[82] Pursuant to the exclusion clause commonly referred to as the "Prior Claims and Circumstances" exclusion, coverage will be excluded (depending on policy wording) where a Claim or Loss arises from (or in consequence of) a Circumstance (or fact, matter or occurrence): notified under any previous policy; disclosed in the proposal for the relevant policy;[83] or, if not reported/disclosed, which was or ought to have been known to the insured prior to the inception of the relevant policy.[84] Depending on policy wording, the extent of the exclusion clause may vary and the latter part relating to knowledge of the insured may be specific or more general – referring to 'any insured'.[85] In the latter instance, it appears that coverage for a Claim arising from a Circumstance not reported/disclosed, which was or ought to have been known to *any* insured prior to the inception of the relevant policy, may be precluded even in a policy also bearing a Severability of Application clause or being composite in nature.[86]

In the US, a similar approach is broadly taken across the states in respect of the Prior Claims and Circumstances exclusion clause. Even where Claims arise from known and disclosed information, coverage may be precluded where the exclusion clause so provides.[87] Where Claims arise from information known to the insured but undisclosed to the insurer, the insurer will be similarly afforded rights of remedy as regards the contract and, where misstatements, omissions in the application, or misrepresentations are made, rescission is a common avenue for recourse.[88] In *National Union Fire Ins Co of Pittsburgh Pa v Federal Deposit Insurance Corp*,[89] in an application for D&O insurance, a bank president signed and stated that 'to the best of his knowledge, no director or officer had "knowledge or information of any act, error, or omission which gives rise to a claim under

82 Though the "Claims made" nature of most D&O policies and the common Prior Claims and Circumstances exclusion may lead one to believe that disclosure is of less importance than in occurrence policies, due to a perceived lack of coverage in respect of the matters disclosed in any event, such a view would not reflect the objective of the duty of fair presentation. This objective, which can arguably be traced back to Lord Mansfield's judgment in *Carter v Boehm*, is 'to prevent fraud, and to encourage good faith'. This is a basis upon which the commercial world of insurance operates and is crucial in allowing the insurer to make a fair assessment as to risk and its willingness to assume such risk. Moreover, one must consider the flexibility in language of policies composed in an environment largely governed by the sector. *See Carter v Boehm* (n 40) 1911 (Lord Mansfield).

83 *HLB Kidsons (a firm) v Lloyd's Underwriters subscribing to Lloyd's policy No 621/PK1D00101* [2008] EWCA Civ 1206 [131] (Toulson LJ).

84 Zurich, 'D&O Corporate Directors' and Officers' Liability: Policy Document' (n 74) para 4.9; Hiscox, 'Management Liability – Directors' and Officers' Liability: Policy Wording' (n 74) 4. *See also National Employers Mutual General Insurance Association Ltd v Haydon* [1980] 2 Lloyd's Rep 149 (CA) 153 (Stephenson LJ). A Prior Claims and Circumstances exclusion, in respect of known Claims and Circumstances, may extend to circumstances a reasonable person would have thought might give rise to a Claim. *See CGU Insurance Ltd v Porthouse* [2008] HCA 30. *See also* Merkin (n 7) para 21-055.

85 Zurich, 'D&O Corporate Directors' and Officers' Liability: Policy Document' (n 74) para 4.9.

86 ibid paras 4.9, 6.1. This may depend to some extent on the manner in which "any Insured" is interpreted under the policy: whether by contract of insurance, by Sides, or by the policy in general. This may be determinable by policy drafting, in respect of inclusion under separate Insuring Agreements or under general policy conditions.

87 *Clark School for Creative Learning Inc v Philadelphia Indemnity Ins Co* 734 F 3d 51 (1st Cir 2013); Katelin O'Rourke Gorman and Timothy Kevane, 'Policy Issuance' in Martin J O'Leary (ed), *Directors & Officers Liability Insurance Deskbook* (American Bar Association 2020) 4.

88 *In re Healthsouth Corp Insurance Litigation* 308 F Supp 2d 1253 (ND Ala 2004); *LA Sound USA Inc v St Paul Fire & Marine Ins Co* 67 Cal Rptr 3d 917 (Cal Ct App 2007); O'Rourke Gorman and Kevane in O'Leary (ed) (n 87) 5–6.

89 No 03A01-9405-CH-00179, 1995 WL 48462 (Tenn Ct App Feb 8 1995); O'Rourke Gorman and Kevane in O'Leary (ed) (n 87) 5.

the proposed policy"'.[90] Having represented that inquiries had been made into the truthfulness of all statements, and because many of the directors and officers actually knew of facts giving rise to a later claim, the bank president had made a misrepresentation on the bank's behalf. The 'application excluded any claim about which any director or officer had knowledge or information',[91] and thus the relevant claim was precluded from coverage in any event.

Considering *National Union Fire Ins Co of Pittsburgh Pa* alongside an interpretation of the IA 2015 (thus, were it to be decided in the UK), the misrepresentation by the bank president would not – on its own – have been imputed to the individual insureds under a composite D&O policy, had the statement not been made on behalf of all insureds (for example, if it had just been made in respect of their own insurance). However, as the bank president was an individual responsible for the insureds' insurance, the insurer would be entitled to avoid the contract of insurance with the relevant individual(s) insured on the basis that the person responsible for their insurance (thus an individual falling within the knowledge provisions of section 4(2)(a) of the IA 2015) 'ought to have known' such information, had they conducted a reasonable search of information, and thus the nondisclosure, or misrepresentation, was reckless. Furthermore, policy wording may provide that such knowledge would impact all co-insureds.

The impact of nondisclosure and misrepresentation by an insured during the precontractual stage may be set out in express detail: some policies explicitly replicate the position set out in the IA 2015 by way of a "Disclosure clause" (or similar).[92] In some policies the matter is addressed more specifically, and where fraudulent or dishonest conduct is not disclosed and Loss arises from a Claim based upon such conduct, that Loss will not be covered (it may also be necessary that the nondisclosure (or conduct itself) renders a statement or information in the application to be untrue or inaccurate).[93] This may provide greater protection to an insured director than the IA 2015, particularly where the nondisclosure may have been deliberate and thus would otherwise have entitled the insurer to avoid the contract.[94]

90 O'Rourke Gorman and Kevane in O'Leary (ed) (n 87) 5.
91 ibid.
92 Markel (UK) Limited, 'Revised D&O Wording' (n 73) 12.
93 Chubb, 'ForeFront Plus Insurance Policy' (n 73) paras 2.13(b), 5.8(c).
94 Insurance Act 2015, s 8, sch 1 para 2.

CHAPTER 12

Notification of Claims and Circumstances

12.1 "Claim"

The word "Claim" bearing a capitalisation is to be distinguished from "claim" without such capitalisation: "Claim" in capitalised form refers to a specific policy definition relating to a "Claim" made against the insured, whereas "claim" in lowercase form refers to the claim thereafter made by the insured against the insurer for coverage.[1] The definition of Claim within a liability policy will point to the object claimed and not the cause of action[2] (the set of facts which may give rise to multiple Claims).[3] In *Thorman v New Hampshire Insurance Co (UK) Ltd*,[4] a Claim under the relevant Claims made policy was deemed to be 'the assertion by a third party against the insured of a right to some relief'.[5] However, D&O policy wording will provide a specific definition for Claim(s) and may open up broader coverage or be more restrictive.

A D&O Claim definition will typically include a written demand against the insured for monetary or non-monetary relief, civil proceedings, criminal proceedings, formal administrative or regulatory proceedings, and in some definitions also (criminal, administrative, or regulatory) investigations.[6] Some policy wording provides greater specificity in outlining the above following a 'formal notice' or 'service of a claim form or similar'.[7] In a liability policy, a Claim is not "made" against the insured until it is communicated

1 'I use a capital letter to denote a third party "Claim" as opposed to a claim by an Insured under the policy.' *See Euro Pools plc (in administration) v Royal & Sun Alliance Insurance plc* [2019] EWCA Civ 808 [48] (Dame Elizabeth Gloster). '"Claim" with a capital "C" refers to a claim by a third party such as a customer against the insured.' *See Euro Pools plc (in administration) v Royal & Sun Alliance Insurance plc* [2019] EWCA Civ 808 [93] (Males LJ).

2 'A cause of action is simply a factual situation the existence of which entitles one person to obtain from the court a remedy against another person.' *See Letang v Cooper* [1964] 2 All ER 929 (QB) 934 (Diplock LJ).

3 *West Wake Price & Co v Ching* [1957] 1 WLR 45 (QB) 55 (Devlin J).

4 [1988] 1 Lloyd's Rep 7 (CA).

5 ibid 11 (Sir John Donaldson MR). *See also* Robert Merkin, 'Liability Insurance: Recent Developments in Liability Law' (1989) 69(6) BILA J 46.

6 Allianz, 'Complete Directors & Officers: Policy Wording' (*Allianz Insurance plc*, 2020) <https://www.allianzebroker.co.uk/content/allianzebroker/en_gb/application/content/documents/commercial-products/sme/complete-directors-and-officers/complete-directors-officers-policy-wording/_jcr_content/documentProperties/currentDocument.res/complete-directors-officers-wording_acom4288.pdf> accessed 15 October 2020, 8; WR Berkley UK Limited, 'Directors and Officers Liability and Company Reimbursement Insurance Policy' (*WR Berkley*, May 2018) <https://www.brokerdirect.co.uk/wp-content/uploads/2018/08/Directors-Officers-WRB_PolicyWording_V06_MAY18.pdf> accessed 23 November 2020, 7.

7 Zurich, 'D&O Corporate Directors' and Officers' Liability: Policy Document' (*Zurich Insurance plc*, April 2020) <https://www.zurich.co.uk/business/-/media/Business/Documents/Specialty-lines/710008.pdf> accessed 22 January 2021, 9.

DOI: 10.4324/9781003456964-15

to the insured.[8] Thus, a writ issued but not served upon the insured, or legal proceedings instituted but not communicated to the insured, will not constitute a Claim.[9] In any event, notification of a Claim under a "Claims made" policy is typically a condition precedent to the extension of cover;[10] the policy to respond will be that under which the notification was made. Claims made policies require 'particular [consideration]' in respect of notification provisions and typically also feature provisions requiring notification of "Circumstances" which may or are likely to give rise to a Claim.[11]

12.2 "Circumstance"

A notified Circumstance may include notification of receipt of notice of an intention to make a Claim against the insured. Should the Claim later arise, it will be deemed to have been made during the policy period within which the notification was made.[12] A Circumstance requiring notification will typically be one which "may" or is "(reasonably) likely" to give rise to a Claim against the insured, and of which the insured was aware.[13] Where policy wording requires the notification of Circumstances which "may" give rise to a Claim, the materiality test is deemed to be weak,[14] low, and undemanding, and there only need be a possibility of claims in the future.[15] In such an instance, addition of the word "reasonably" to the clause ("may reasonably give rise to a Claim") does not affect the low materiality threshold.[16] In order to determine whether a Circumstance may (reasonably) give rise to a future Claim, 'a degree of crystal ball gazing, an estimation of the likelihood of a claim'[17] will be required. Where policy wording requires notification of a Circumstance "which is likely to give rise to a Claim",[18] there must be at least a 50 percent chance of a Claim arising from such Circumstances, which is assessed at the time

8 *J Rothschild Assurance Plc v Collyear* [1998] All ER (D) 431 (QB) (Rix J). In a recent Australian decision, involving a policy that provided a grace period of 30 days to notify after the end of the policy period, it was held that the insured need not have *actual knowledge* of the Claim within the policy period. *See Hakea Holdings Pty Ltd v Neon Underwriting Limited* [2023] FCAFC 34.

9 *Robert Irving & Burns v Stone* [1997] CLC 1593 (CA). *See also J Rothschild Assurance Plc v Collyear* (n 8) (Rix J); Alison Padfield, *Insurance Claims* (5th edn, Bloomsbury Professional 2021) para 7.7. In a recent Australian case, the requirement for written notice was interpreted as having been put in the director's possession. *See Hakea Holdings Pty Ltd v Neon Underwriting Limited* (n 8).

10 *J Rothschild Assurance Plc v Collyear* (n 8).

11 Padfield (n 9) paras 7.7–7.8. *See also McManus v European Risk Insurance Co* [2013] EWHC 18 (Ch) [8] (Ms Vivien Rose), citing *Friends Provident Life and Pensions Ltd v Sirius International Insurance Corp* [2004] EWHC 1799 (Comm) [13] (Moore-Bick J).

12 *Thorman v New Hampshire Insurance Co (UK) Ltd* (n 4) 9–10 (Sir John Donaldson MR); *Euro Pools plc (in administration) v Royal & Sun Alliance Insurance plc* (n 1) [32] (Dame Elizabeth Gloster), citing *Kajima UK Engineering Ltd v Underwriter Insurance Company Ltd* [2008] EWHC 83 (TCC) [99] (Akenhead J). *See also* Padfield (n 9) para 7.8.

13 Rix LJ set out these two factors to consider in a typical case in *HLB Kidsons (a firm) v Lloyd's Underwriters subscribing to Lloyd's policy No 621/PK1D00101* [2008] EWCA Civ 1206 [72] (Rix LJ).

14 *J Rothschild Assurance Plc v Collyear* (n 8) (Rix J). A communication stating that there is a 'chance of a claim' will likely be inadequate to constitute a notification of Circumstances: *Esined No 9 Pty Ltd v Moylan Retirement Solutions Pty Ltd (No 2)* [2020] NSWSC 359.

15 *Euro Pools plc (in administration) v Royal & Sun Alliance Insurance plc* (n 1) [39] (Dame Elizabeth Gloster), citing *J Rothschild Assurance Plc v Collyear* (n 8) (Rix J).

16 *Euro Pools plc (in administration) v Royal & Sun Alliance Insurance plc* (n 1) [39] (Dame Elizabeth Gloster).

17 *HLB Kidsons (a firm) v Lloyd's Underwriters subscribing to Lloyd's policy No 621/PK1D00101* [2008] EWCA (n 13) [135], [138] (Toulson LJ).

18 *J Rothschild Assurance Plc v Collyear* (n 8) (Rix J).

of the relevant occurrence.[19] If notification of Circumstances "which might reasonably be expected to give rise to a Claim" is required, no finite definition of such qualifying Circumstances can be given, except to note that Claims arising need not be "probable".[20]

In some cases, the obligation to notify will be so obvious that any reasonable person would recognise a real risk of a claim; where this is the case, the insured may be 'duty bound' to notify the insurer.[21] In the precontractual stage, there will also be a duty to inform the prospective insurer (in adhering to the duty of fair presentation), of matters which will be of particular importance in regard to historical misconduct.[22] Awareness of the insured is a 'pure matter of fact'.[23] Circumstances must have come to the attention of the insured (during the policy period) so that the insured can be said to be aware of them,[24] as only Circumstances of which the insured is actually aware can be the subject matter of a notification.[25] Such awareness of Circumstances triggers the duty to notify the insurer.[26]

Notification of Circumstances, like the notification of a Claim, is a condition precedent to the right to indemnity; the policy to respond will be that under which the notification was made.[27] Where a Claim arises from a notification of Circumstance(s) made in a different year, three broad questions arise: firstly, as to the scope of the circumstances notified; secondly, whether the necessary causal link exists; and thirdly, whether there is liability under the policy. The matter notified must have a sufficient factual basis so as to amount to a Circumstance,[28] a substratum of underlying external fact over and above the insured's mere concerns.[29] As such, mere concern as to having potentially made a mistake will likely not be enough.[30] In order for the notified Circumstance to be sufficient to trigger coverage upon a later Claim made against the insured, there must be a causal – not just coincidental – link between the notified Circumstance and the Claim.[31] Therefore, a historical continuum of investigation may not be sufficient where matters revealed by

19 *Layher Ltd v Lowe* (1996) 58 ConLR 42 (CA) 44 (Saville LJ); Adolfo Paolini and Deepak Nambisan, *Directors' and Officers' Liability Insurance* (Informa Law 2008) para 2.75.

20 *Kajima UK Engineering Ltd v Underwriter Insurance Company Ltd* (n 12) [99] (Akenhead J).

21 *Euro Pools plc (in administration) v Royal & Sun Alliance Insurance plc* (n 1) [43] (Dame Elizabeth Gloster), citing *HLB Kidsons (a firm) v Lloyd's Underwriters subscribing to Lloyd's policy No 621/PK1D00101* [2008] EWCA (n 13) [141] (Toulson LJ). As a result, in some cases, where Circumstances should have been notified under a previous policy, an emanating Claim may be refused: *Aldridge v Liberty Mutual Insurance Europe Ltd* [2016] EWHC 3037 (Comm).

22 ibid.

23 *HLB Kidsons (a firm) v Lloyd's Underwriters subscribing to Lloyd's policy No 621/PK1D00101* [2008] EWCA (n 13) [135] (Toulson LJ).

24 ibid [72] (Rix LJ); *McManus v European Risk Insurance Co* (n 11) [9].

25 *Kajima UK Engineering Ltd v Underwriter Insurance Company Ltd* (n 12) [99] (Akenhead J); *HLB Kidsons (a firm) v Lloyd's Underwriters subscribing to Lloyd's Policy No 621/PKID00101* [2007] EWHC 1951 (Comm) [77] (Gloster J).

26 *Euro Pools plc (in administration) v Royal & Sun Alliance Insurance plc* (n 1) [95] (Males LJ).

27 ibid [93] (Males LJ).

28 ibid [43] (Dame Elizabeth Gloster).

29 *HLB Kidsons (a firm) v Lloyd's Underwriters subscribing to Lloyd's policy No 621/PK1D00101* [2008] EWCA (n 13) [74] (Rix LJ); *McManus v European Risk Insurance Co* (n 11) [56].

30 *HLB Kidsons (a firm) v Lloyd's Underwriters subscribing to Lloyd's policy No 621/PK1D00101* [2008] EWCA (n 13) [73] (Rix LJ).

31 '[The] claim must be one "to which [the notified] circumstance has given rise". This requires that the loss or claim should be sufficiently causally related to the fact, event, happening or condition which comprises the notified circumstance, such that it can be fairly said to have arisen out of it.' *See HLB Kidsons (a firm) v Lloyd's Underwriters subscribing to Lloyd's Policy No 621/PKID00101* [2007] EWHC (n 25) [224]. *See also Kajima UK Engineering Ltd v Underwriter Insurance Company Ltd* (n 12) [99] (Akenhead J); *Euro Pools plc (in administration) v Royal & Sun Alliance Insurance plc* (n 1) [39] (Dame Elizabeth Gloster).

the investigation have nothing to do with the notified Circumstance. As such, there will likely be a continuing need to notify of Circumstances throughout an evolving investigation.[32] Where issues arise regarding the limits of Circumstances notified and potential later Claims arising, such issues are to be determined if/when a Claim arises and no declaratory relief is to be granted.[33]

In a DPA-related scenario, a notifiable Circumstance may include investigations (for example: internal, criminal, or regulatory) where not included within the Claim definition, and it will be prudent to make further notifications as the investigation develops to avoid a loss of causal link to a later notified Claim. Notification of Circumstances will be of particular importance due to the risk of a director being discharged from their role following the uncovering of wrongdoing. The Claims made nature of D&O would – without notification of Circumstances having been made under a previous policy – require the former director to continue to maintain their own Side A coverage or ensure that the company continues to purchase cover insuring former directors, in order to remain covered for risks arising which would otherwise constitute a newly notifiable Claim/Circumstance. Issues may arise, however, as regards the extent of knowledge of the Circumstances and confidentiality.

12.2.1 Blanket notifications

It is possible for an insured to make a notification of a problem (constituting a "Circumstance", rather than a "Claim") where the exact scale and consequences of that problem are, at the time of notification, unknown.[34] The cause of the problem also need not necessarily be known.[35] Such a notification is known as a "blanket notification"[36] – sometimes referred to in case law as a "hornets' nest" or "can of worms" notification.[37] Two factors to be considered in a typical case, set out by Lord Justice Rix in *HLB Kidsons (a firm) v Lloyd's Underwriters subscribing to Lloyd's policy No 621/PK1D00101*, continue to apply to blanket notifications: whether the insured is aware of the Circumstances, and whether the Circumstances are such that they "may" (depending on policy wording) give rise to a Claim.[38] A 'state of affairs' can be notified as a Circumstance where the insured is

32 *Kajima UK Engineering Ltd v Underwriter Insurance Company Ltd* (n 12) [111] (Akenhead J).

33 *McManus v European Risk Insurance Co* (n 11) [61]–[62].

34 *Euro Pools plc (in administration) v Royal & Sun Alliance Insurance plc* (n 1) [39] (Dame Elizabeth Gloster).

35 ibid [39] (Dame Elizabeth Gloster).

36 *J Rothschild Assurance Plc v Collyear* (n 8); *McManus v European Risk Insurance Co* (n 11).

37 *HLB Kidsons (a firm) v Lloyd's Underwriters subscribing to Lloyd's Policy No 621/PK1D00101* [2007] EWHC (n 25) [76]; *Kajima UK Engineering Ltd v Underwriter Insurance Company Ltd* (n 12); *Euro Pools plc (in administration) v Royal & Sun Alliance Insurance plc* (n 1). Seen also more recently in the Australian case of *Uniting Church in Australia Property Trust (NSW) v Allianz Australia Insurance Limited (Liability Judgment)* [2023] FCA 190, setting out that such a notification would attract the protections of section 40(3) of the Insurance Contracts Act 1984 (Cth) (Australia), which provides: 'Where the insured gave notice in writing to the insurer of facts that might give rise to a claim against the insured as soon as was reasonably practicable after the insured became aware of those facts but before the insurance cover provided by the contract expired, the insurer is not relieved of liability under the contract in respect of the claim, when made, by reason only that it was made after the expiration of the period of the insurance cover provided by the contract.'

38 n 13.

aware of it,[39] and this is possible provided the Circumstance notified is something which might reasonably be expected to produce a Claim.[40]

Blanket notifications may give rise to greater dispute as to whether there is a causal link between the Circumstance(s) notified and the later Claim. Though *prima facie* a wider notification of Circumstance(s) should give rise to a broader inclusion of Claims, the link must be causal and not just coincidental. Nonetheless, the 'extent and ambit of the notification' and Claims covered (or otherwise) ultimately depend 'on the particular facts and terms of the notification'.[41] A Claim can still be deemed to have arisen from a blanket notification of Circumstances even where the notification does not point to a specific event or established defect within such an event.[42]

In *J Rothschild Assurance Plc v Collyear*, the 'leading case on blanket notifications',[43] it was deemed legitimate to test a view of what the future might bring against what happened in due course – in respect of the justification of notification of Circumstances – 'where the prediction had to be not of what would be but only of what might be'.[44] In this case, a prediction based on objective evidence (as to whether a notification of Circumstances "may" give rise to a Claim) which had been scrutinised by independent professionals, and on the concern of regulatory authorities, was not 'invalid and unjustified merely because there was much other evidence which was not yet to hand' irrespective of the relevance of that evidence.[45]

Where wrongdoing (particularly historic misconduct) is unveiled, a blanket notification may be a wise approach where the nature or extent of such wrongdoing is not yet appreciated (for example, whether such wrongdoing is inactionable, or constitutes criminal or civil misconduct); the insured will be aware of the wrongdoing, and it may (or might reasonably be expected to) give rise to a later Claim.[46] A DPA is never guaranteed, though from an individual perspective there is an increasing focus on individual accountability for corporate misconduct, and thus it could be anticipated that an investigation (which may fall within the definition of Claim) or action may arise.

12.3 Confidential information

An insured might find notification problematic where faced with breaching confidentiality arrangements or risking a loss of privilege. In respect of the duty of fair presentation pre-contract, and continuing disclosure obligations as regards notification during the policy period, the IA 2015 does not change the rules relating to privilege. Privilege continues

39 ibid.

40 *Kajima UK Engineering Ltd v Underwriter Insurance Company Ltd* (n 12) [99] (Akenhead J).

41 *HLB Kidsons (a firm) v Lloyd's Underwriters subscribing to Lloyd's Policy No 621/PKID00101* [2007] EWHC (n 25) [76].

42 *McManus v European Risk Insurance Co* (n 11) [43] (Ms Vivien Rose); *Euro Pools plc (in administration) v Royal & Sun Alliance Insurance plc* (n 1) [39] (Dame Elizabeth Gloster).

43 *McManus v European Risk Insurance Co* (n 11) [39] (Ms Vivien Rose).

44 '[I]t is legitimate to test a view of what the future may bring, where that view has been contemporaneously and prophetically expressed, against what happened in due course. I do not mean, of course, that hindsight can be used to justify an unreasonable position.' *See J Rothschild Assurance Plc v Collyear* (n 8) (Rix J).

45 *J Rothschild Assurance Plc v Collyear* (n 8) (Rix J).

46 *HLB Kidsons (a firm) v Lloyd's Underwriters subscribing to Lloyd's policy No 621/PKID00101* [2008] EWCA (n 13) [72] (Rix LJ); *Kajima UK Engineering Ltd v Underwriter Insurance Company Ltd* (n 12) [99] (Akenhead J).

to apply to documentation and communications which describe facts or Circumstances worthy of notification (or disclosure), but the facts themselves remain notifiable as a Circumstance in an appropriate way.[47] Similarly, during insurance litigation (between the insurer and insured), 'privilege does not relieve a party of the obligation to make disclosure, but protects a document from inspection'.[48]

In respect of confidential but not necessarily privileged information, the duty of fair presentation (thus, disclosure) is not overridden by such confidentiality.[49] Similarly, notification obligations remain during the policy period as far as possible. The insured – irrespective of notification obligations set out within policy wording – must act in good faith to the insurer during the currency of the policy. In *Quinn Direct Insurance Ltd v Law Society*,[50] Sir Andrew Morritt outlined that failure to disclose by way of concealment of a material matter could not be justified on the basis of privilege, 'nor, perhaps, on the ground that the information he failed to disclose was confidential'.[51] In *Blackburn, Low & Co v Haslam*,[52] it was set out that an insurer's legal rights could not be affected or lessened by the fact that the relevant information was confidential, and to hold otherwise 'would cut down to an important extent the rule as to good faith'.[53] The latter was a case that referred to precontractual disclosure; however the noted impact on duty of good faith (a concept underpinning the contract) arguably embraces a more wide-ranging scope and thus continues throughout the policy period and into notification provisions.

The 'obligation'[54] to act in good faith post-contract (i.e., after the precontractual stage) – as per an express or implied duty, or even as an interpretative principle[55] – embraces the continued assistance of the insurer in minimising the risk, exemplified by the notification provisions and the Increase of risk clause. Though a failure to notify confidential information arising during the contractual period would not constitute a nondisclosure (as under the duty of fair presentation), it will mean that the condition precedent for coverage is not triggered. The obligation of good faith must be followed to the fullest extent possible, and therefore a blanket notification in circumstances restricted by confidentiality may be optimal (to be followed by a thorough notification of a Claim or Circumstances when confidentiality restrictions thereafter permit).[56]

---

47 Marsh, 'Insurance Act 2015: Frequently Asked Questions (FAQs)' (*Marsh & McLennan*, 24 November 2016) <https://www.marsh.com/content/dam/marsh/Documents/PDF/UK-en/Insurance%20Act%202015%20Frequently%20Asked%20Questions%20(FAQs).pdf> accessed 21 June 2021.

48 Padfield (n 9) para 9.21, citing CPR 31.19(3). As regards confidential documents, the importance of disclosure is evident in the fact that such documents are not protected from disclosure to the court during insurance litigation by reason of confidentiality alone. *See Science Research Council v Nasse* [1980] AC 1028 (HL).

49 Marsh, 'Insurance Act 2015: Frequently Asked Questions (FAQs)' (n 47).

50 [2010] EWCA Civ 805.

51 ibid [24] (Sir Andrew Morritt C). *See also McManus v European Risk Insurance Co* (n 11) [61].

52 (1888) 21 QBD 144.

53 ibid 153–154 (Pollock B).

54 Malcolm Clarke and Bariş Soyer, *The Insurance Act 2015: A New Regime for Commercial and Marine Insurance Law* (Informa Law 2017) 46.

55 It may be expressly provided that the insurance contract is one of good faith. It may be considered that notification is subject to an implied contractual term of good faith: *Manifest Shipping Co Ltd v Uni-Polaris Insurance Co Ltd (The Star Sea)* [2001] UKHL 1 [48]–[50] (Lord Hobhouse). It may simply be considered that good faith is a 'general interpretative principle': Law Commission, *Insurance Contract Law: Business Disclosure; Warranties; Insurers' Remedies for Fraudulent Claims; and Late Payment* (Law Com No 353, 2014) para 30.5.

56 According to Neil McCarthy of MPR Underwriting, '[m]ost policies … have provisions around prevention of notification because of confidentiality agreements, and … this is accommodated or taken into account'.

Confidentiality is a key part of DPA negotiations and thus a consideration when notifying insurers. In respect of the precontractual duty of fair presentation, under section 4(4) of the IA 2015 (regarding knowledge of the insured), a person responsible for the insured's insurance[57] will not be deemed to know confidential information if they are (or are the employee of) the insured's agent, and the information was acquired by them 'through a business relationship with a person who is not connected with *the* contract of insurance' (emphasis added). Undertaking a literal interpretation of the statute, this would suggest that a person (for example, a risk manager)[58] representing multiple insureds under a composite D&O policy would not be taken to know of DPA negotiations engaged in by the company when procuring the extension of potential insurance coverage to a director. This applies as regards section 4(2)(b) (regarding knowledge of an individual insured) and section 4(3)(b) (regarding knowledge of an insured who is not an individual).[59] It is highly likely to be the case that a serving director would know of ongoing DPA negotiations – albeit that it is unlikely that a director having engaged in the wrongdoing leading to the negotiations would still be in office. If the director themselves bears such knowledge, then they will be obliged to disclose or to notify their (prospective) insurer.[60]

In respect of negotiations arising during the contractual period, issues may arise as regards a serving director's ability to notify where the company is bound by a pre-negotiation confidentiality undertaking. Though this is not signed by the director personally, the director represents the 'directing mind and will'[61] of the company and would be bound by it (there would also exist a duty of confidence by virtue of their position).[62] In such circumstances, the director may elect to make a blanket notification. Though DPA negotiations could not be considered to constitute a Claim against the director, as the negotiations will be in respect of the corporate position, this would constitute a notifiable Circumstance (comprehensive or blanket) as the wider investigation may lead to Claims being made against the director in future. In the case of a director without such knowledge of ongoing negotiations (for example, under suspension or discharged), section 4(4) may ultimately mean that the individual responsible for their insurance is not taken to know of the negotiations either.

See Neil McCarthy, 'Deferred Prosecution Agreements' (*MPR Underwriting*, 2017) <https://www.mprunderwriting.com/deferred-prosecution-agreements/> accessed 23 September 2021.

57 The Law Commissions' 2014 Report does not make any suggestion that this should include the insured person themselves. *See* Law Commission, *Insurance Contract Law: Business Disclosure; Warranties; Insurers' Remedies for Fraudulent Claims; and Late Payment* (n 55) paras 8.61–8.66.

58 ibid para 8.64.

59 Insurance Act 2015, s 4(4).

60 In *Amec Foster Wheeler Energy (UK) Limited*, counsel for the individuals implicated were permitted to give representations prior to approval. 'Paragraph 12 of Schedule 17 says that the court may order that the publication of information by the prosecutor under paragraph 8(7) be postponed for such period as the court considers necessary if it appears to the court that postponement is necessary for avoiding a substantial risk of prejudice to the administration of justice in any legal proceedings. I have heard submissions from counsel on behalf of some individuals and have decided that such an order is necessary.' *See Director of the Serious Fraud Office v Amec Foster Wheeler Limited* [2021] Lloyd's Rep FC 353 (Crown) [4] (Edis LJ).

61 *Tesco Supermarkets Ltd v Nattrass* [1972] AC 153 (HL) 180; *HL Bolton (Engineering) Co Ltd v TJ Graham & Sons Ltd* [1957] 1 QB 159 (CA) 172 (Denning LJ); *Lennard's Carrying Co Ltd v Asiatic Petroleum Co Ltd* [1915] AC 705 (HL) 713 (Viscount Haldane LC).

62 A duty of confidence is imposed 'whenever a person receives information he knows or ought to know is fairly and reasonably to be regarded as confidential'. *See Campbell v Mirror Group Newspapers Ltd* [2004] UKHL 22 [14] (Lord Nicholls).

A "Claims cooperation" ("Cooperation") clause will typically provide that the insured 'shall give the Insurer such information and cooperation as the Insurer may reasonabl[y] require'[63] in the event of a Claim made against the insured or Circumstances notified by the insured. The "Notice and claims procedure" clause relevant to the case of *Quinn* (which effectively operated as a Cooperation clause) required the insured to 'give all such information and assistance as the company may require' upon the occurrence (and, ultimately, notification) of a Circumstance.[64] *Quinn* related to the (non)disclosure of third-party confidential information (solicitors' clients), and as such the insurer had no contractual claim to production of the privileged documents on the basis of the relevant clause (or any other policy provision) unless third-party consent was obtained.[65] This demonstrates that where an insurer seeks disclosure of privileged information and the policy wording so allows, the insurer may have a contractual claim against the insured to ensure its production.

Any dispute as to disclosure of privileged material should be resolved as soon as possible in a well-managed way, as loss of privilege may arise should the dispute be brought to court for resolution.[66] It may be the case that fewer disputes arise in a duty to defend policy (**Section 15.1.1**), but this will ultimately be reliant upon compliance of the insured. As noted in *Gan Insurance Co Ltd v Tai Ping Insurance Co Ltd (No 3)*, such a clause 'must at least extend to the determination of the nature, scope and amount of any loss and whether it fell within the policy cover'[67] and also in claims handling 'whether the loss involved any breach of any policy term or warranty'.[68] This demonstrates the cruciality of the clause in empowering the insurer's investigation upon notification of Claims and Circumstances, though it may ultimately lead to a determination that coverage should not be extended. Notably, however, the obligation of good faith will require some reflection of both parties of their respective positions.

Where a director claims LPP during a criminal investigation (for example, in order to prevent the company from making disclosures which may be detrimental to their personal position), a wholesale approach to privilege assertion will most likely be taken, and this will therefore impact notification obligations under the policy. Though privilege may apply to certain documentation and communications, the underlying facts remain notifiable as a Circumstance in an appropriate way.[69] Furthermore, a Cooperation clause may impose a contractual right of production upon insurers. In any event, such an assertion of privilege may be overridden where the individual's lawyer is instructed for the purpose of furthering or concealing an iniquity (for example, a criminal act, or in some

63 WR Berkley UK Limited, 'Directors and Officers Liability and Company Reimbursement Insurance Policy' (n 6) para 8.3.1.

64 Policy wording in this instance opted for the word "occurrence" over "circumstance". *See Quinn Direct Insurance Ltd v Law Society* (n 50) [2].

65 Such consent could be given expressly or by implication from its claim against the solicitors' firm. *See* ibid [21] (Sir Andrew Morritt C).

66 This will depend on the extent to which the material is referred to. Where a document is referred to in open court, its confidentiality is not necessarily lost where that reference does not sufficiently constitute an 'exposure of the document to the public' warranting loss of the confidentiality of the document as a whole. *See SL Claimants v Tesco PLC* [2019] EWHC 3315 (Ch) [42].

67 This case focussed on reinsurance, and the relevant "Claims cooperation clause" provided: 'The Reinsured shall co-operate with Reinsurers and/or their Appointed Representatives subscribing to this Policy in the investigation and assessment of any loss and/or circumstances giving rise to a loss.' *See* [2002] EWCA Civ 248 [6], [37].

68 ibid [37].

69 Marsh, 'Insurance Act 2015: Frequently Asked Questions (FAQs)' (n 47).

circumstances a breach of directors' duties),[70] which may therefore give rise to a requirement to notify. However, in cases of joint privilege shared with the company, this will be dependent on consent of the company. This is likely to arise in duty to indemnify policies, as the legal representation appointed in a duty to defend policy will be at the direction of the insurer.

Although there are restrictions as to the admissibility of information disclosed to prosecutors under section 2 of the CJA 1987 against the interviewed individual,[71] such admissions may be utilised by an insurer in order to refuse the individual's coverage. Section 2 does not require a waiver of LPP, and therefore this would not ordinarily be an avenue in which privileged information could be exhumed. However, through the "real evidence exception", privilege against self-incrimination does not apply to documents disclosed under section 2 if those documents are deemed to have an independent existence of the will of the discloser.[72] Information disclosed under such powers has been treated as confidential in some proceedings[73] (though confidentiality may be lost in some circumstances, for example where the information is admitted against the individual in open civil proceedings), and confidential information is not wholly excused from notification obligations (for example, by an individual treating their own information as such, with no duty owed to a third party in this respect).

There are several ways in which the insurer may become aware of the content of information disclosed. Firstly, under a duty to defend policy whereby the insurer takes over the defence of the insured. However, representation is often not permitted in section 2 interviews[74] which may leave an insurer, in such circumstances, in the same position as one under a duty to indemnify policy. Within a Cooperation clause, the insured is bound by the requirement to disclose information to the insurer, and this will likely include matters disclosed to prosecutors during interview. Furthermore, the insured will likely (under policy conditions) be required to obtain the consent of the insurer to incur or admit liability. The right to withhold consent must be exercised in good faith and not arbitrarily,[75]

70 *BBGP Managing General Partner Ltd v Babcock & Brown Global Partners* [2010] EWHC 2176 (Ch) [62]; *Barrowfen Properties Ltd v Patel* [2020] EWHC 2536 (Ch) [33]–[35].

71 Criminal Justice Act 1987, ss 8, 8(AA).

72 Serious Fraud Office, 'SFO Operational Handbook: Section 2 Notices' (*Serious Fraud Office*, 18 May 2020) <https://web.archive.org/web/20201203083617/https://www.sfo.gov.uk/publications/guidance-policy-and-protocols/sfo-operational-handbook/section-2-powers/> accessed 10 August 2020, 7, citing *Saunders v United Kingdom* App no 19187/91 (ECtHR, 17 December 1996).

73 Disclosures made under section 2 were shareable with certain third parties, subject to it being effected within a 'confidentiality club'. *See Omers Administration Corp v Tesco Plc* [2019] EWHC 109 (Ch) [85], [111].

74 There is 'no unfettered right to an interviewee to have present the solicitor of his or her own choice during the [section 2] interview'. Therefore, '[a] degree of flexibility in terms of excluding a solicitor from an interview is permissible'. *See R (Lord) v Director of the Serious Fraud Office* [2015] EWHC 865 (Admin) [18] (Davis LJ). Since this case, the entitlement to have a solicitor present has been clearly set out and curtailed within SFO publications. The criteria for representation, which must be requested in advance, are: 'If [the lawyer] believe[s] that the presence of a particular lawyer in the interview will assist the purpose of the interview and/or investigation, or that the lawyer concerned will provide essential assistance to the interviewee by way of legal advice or pastoral support.' *See* Serious Fraud Office, 'Presence of Interviewee's Legal Adviser at a Section 2 Interview – Guidance for Lawyers' (*Serious Fraud Office*, 28 February 2019) <https://www.sfo.gov.uk/download/sfo-operational-guidance-presence-interviewees-legal-adviser-section-2-interview-guidance-lawyers/> accessed 23 September 2021, para 8.

75 *Gan Insurance Co Ltd v Tai Ping Insurance Co Ltd (No 2)* [2001] EWCA Civ 1047 [54] (Mance LJ). *See also Equitas Insurance Ltd v Municipal Mutual Insurance Ltd* [2019] EWCA Civ 718 [109] (Males LJ); *Distillers-Bio-Chemicals (Australia) Property Ltd v Ajax Insurance Co Ltd* [1974] HCA 3 [42] (Stephen J).

and therefore this condition will likely be treated with flexibility as regards section 2 interviews, in light of their compulsive nature and the consequences of failure to comply.[76] However, the seeking of such consent would alert insurers to the underlying matter. Finally, an insurer may become aware by notification of either a Claim (where, for example, the definition includes investigations) or Circumstance, as despite restrictions as to admissibility, liability may (or is reasonably likely to) arise in future (for example, as regards extrinsic evidence thereafter found). If a Claim is deemed to be made, the Conduct exclusion clause may be invoked on the basis of an admission of excluded conduct (if applicable in the circumstances).

Under a policy where the lawyers instructed act on behalf of both the insured and the insurer (most likely duty to defend policies, or under a joint retainer), the lawyers will have an obligation to inform the insurers of matters which may suggest fraud on the part of the insured (despite any duties of confidence owed to the insured).[77] In respect of a joint retainer, the insurer and insured "'retain no confidence as against one another'"[78] except in relation to reports on the coverage issue.[79] Thus, such information could be used against the insured to refuse coverage.[80] This highlights the importance of the typical duty to indemnify form of D&O policies, and of separate representation not only to the company but also the insurer.

12.4 Notification

The notification requirement under a D&O Claims made policy has led many to take the view that such a policy is, in fact, "Claims made and reported".[81] Notification (or "report") of a Claim/Circumstance must be made by the insured, though policy wording may specify whether this applies to the insured company or insured person. Where a policy provides that only the insured person is able to make a notification as a condition precedent to their own coverage, it follows that a notification made by the company or another insured person will not suffice (for the relevant insured). In any event, it is crucial that the notification provision under the relevant policy is complied with, as it is a condition precedent to the extension of cover.[82] This will include not only ensuring the proper insured makes the notification, but also ensuring compliance with any particulars required by the provision (for example, the manner in which the company or insured person first became aware of the Claim or Circumstance).[83] Timing is also a condition precedent and, as such,

76 Under subsection (13), failure to comply without reasonable excuse is a criminal offence. Under subsection (14), '[a] person who, in purported compliance … (a) makes a statement which he knows to be false or misleading in a material particular; or (b) recklessly makes a statement which is false or misleading in a material particular, shall be guilty of an offence'. *See* Criminal Justice Act 1987, ss 2(13)–(14).

77 Charles Phipps, 'Three's a Crowd: Confidentiality Between Insurer, Insured and Lawyer' (2008) 116(4) BILA 29, 32–34.

78 ibid 35, citing *Hellenic Mutual War Risks Association (Bermuda) Ltd v Harrison (The Sagheera)* [1997] 1 Lloyd's Rep 160 (QB) 164 (Rix J).

79 *Goddard v Nationwide Building Society* [1987] QB 670 (CA). *See also* Phipps (n 77) 37.

80 *Brown v Guardian Royal Exchange Assurance plc* [1994] 2 Lloyd's Rep 325 (CA); *TSB Bank plc v Robert Irving & Burns* [2000] 2 All ER 826 (CA). *See also* Phipps (n 77) 39–40.

81 Paolini and Nambisan (n 19) para 2.64; Larry Goanos, *D&O 101: Understanding Directors and Officers Liability Insurance* (Wells Media Group Inc 2014) 39–40.

82 *J Rothschild Assurance Plc v Collyear* (n 8); *Euro Pools plc (in administration) v Royal & Sun Alliance Insurance plc* (n 1) [93] (Males LJ).

83 Zurich, 'D&O Corporate Directors' and Officers' Liability: Policy Document' (n 7) para 6.6.

timing specifications set out within the notification provision must be adhered to; this will typically be 'as soon as practicable'.[84] If a particular situation renders the ability to notify 'impossible or extremely onerous', the insured will for as long as that situation continues be regarded as 'temporarily discharged from the obligation' to notify; this temporary discharge will cease and the duty to notify will reactivate upon a return to a 'normal' situation.[85] Notably, a situation being confidential does not render notification impossible, but may lead to adverse consequences and further liability.

84 Paolini and Nambisan (n 19) para 2.65; *HLB Kidsons (a firm) v Lloyd's Underwriters subscribing to Lloyd's Policy No 621/PKID00101* [2007] EWHC (n 25) [32] (Gloster J). This requirement may be modified where there is a continuation of cover: *ARC Capital Partners Ltd v Brit Syndicates Ltd* [2016] EWHC 141 (Comm).

85 Paolini and Nambisan (n 19) para 2.66.

CHAPTER 13

Severability

The concept of severability can be seen in operation in differing aspects within a D&O policy and is crucial in preserving the interests and protection of each insured. Perhaps the most obvious example is the common "Severability in exclusions" clause, a specific expression of the fact that exclusions – where invoked against one insured – will not be imputed to other insureds under the policy. A "Severability in application" clause may also provide that knowledge in the policy proposal form will not be imputed to other insureds.[1]

13.1 Policy construction

Policy construction may have the effect of ensuring severability. A policy may be composite or joint. In a joint policy, the parties insured have indistinguishable rights: insurable interests are indivisible.[2] Thus, where one insured is unable to claim, the same bar applies to all other joint insureds.[3] As discussed (**Section 11.2.1**), the more likely construction of a D&O policy and generally accepted form within the market is composite.[4] Two types of composite construction were set out in *Arab Bank plc v Zurich Insurance Co*.[5] Firstly,

1 The clause is said to have originated in the US, though 'acquired popularity' in 2008 and continues to do so. *See* Frank Stadermann and Chris Banis, 'From "Severability Clause" to "Innocent Directors Clause" in Dutch D&O Policies' (2008) 116(3) BILA J 19, 22.

2 *North Atlantic Insurance Co Ltd v Nationwide General Insurance Co* [2003] EWHC 449 (Comm). *See also* Adolfo Paolini and Deepak Nambisan, *Directors' and Officers' Liability Insurance* (Informa Law 2008) paras 3.63–3.64.

3 'Joint policies are policies of insurance which insure two or more assureds, whose interests are "joint", that is whose interests are "inseparably connected so that a loss or gain necessarily affects" all of the co-assureds in the same way and to the same extent.' *See* Peter MacDonald Eggers, 'For One or For All: Joint and Composite Insurance Policies' (2017) 130(2) BILA J 1, 2, 7, citing *General Accident Fire & Life Assurance Corp Ltd v Midland Bank Ltd* [1940] 2 KB 388 (CA) 404–406.

4 Paolini and Nambisan (n 2) para 3.64.

5 *Arab Bank plc v Zurich Insurance Co* [1998] All ER (D) 273 (Comm). This case was criticised in a relatively recent New Zealand case for misinterpreting or misciting *New Hampshire Insurance Company v MGN Ltd* [1997] LRLR 24 in respect of the different types of composite policies, though the outcome itself was not criticised. *See New Zealand Fire Service Commission v Insurance Brokers Association of New Zealand* [2015] NZSC 59 [128]–[132]. The interpretation of *New Hampshire Insurance Company* made by Rix J in *Arab Bank plc* was that: 'It seems to me that the court of appeal were saying that in the typical case of a composite policy where there are several assureds with separate interests, the single policy is indeed a bundle of separate contracts. That is the prima facie position under a composite policy'. The New Zealand Supreme Court, on this point, noted at paragraph 32: 'Where all this leads is to a conclusion that the decision in *Arab Bank* is based on a mischaracterisation of the decision in *MGN* … The fact that *MGN* did not determine the point does not mean Rix J's conclusion is necessarily wrong. There is nothing in *MGN* that is contrary to the proposition that, at

DOI: 10.4324/9781003456964-16

the 'single but composite contract of insurance' under which distinct obligations are taken by the insurer in respect to the multiple insureds.[6] Secondly the 'composite policy' which forms a single document but contains two or more entirely separate contracts; it is a 'bundle of parallel bilateral contracts'.[7] The latter was seen in *J Rothschild*,[8] and is the most typical example within the D&O sphere.

'Separate or several interests'[9] mean that a composite insured is not prejudiced by its co-insureds; the insurer has separate defences against each insured (just as the insured has a separate claim against the insurer).[10] As such, an exclusion clause applied to preclude coverage for one composite insured will not be invoked against another simply on the basis of the co-insured's exclusion: dishonesty of one insured will not prejudice another innocent insured, provided that the other is not a *joint* insured.[11] Furthermore, an otherwise innocent composite insured's coverage will not be prejudiced by a co-insured's breach of the duty of disclosure or failure to adhere to disclosure obligations.[12] A composite policy will be crucial to a director insured under Side A in a DPA-related scenario, as questions regarding historic wrongdoing may raise disclosure concerns and any exclusions invoked against a fellow director or the company insured under Side C could prove fatal to coverage. If detrimental coverage decisions are made prior to the director's pursuit of coverage for their own liability, it may be the case that even defence costs are not advanced.

13.2 Interrelated Wrongful Acts and Related Claims

The intent of the "Interrelated Wrongful Acts" and "Related Claims" clauses is the same, but the process undertaken to reach the outcome differs.[13] Quite the opposite of severance, each clause operates to provide a measure of grouping of defined Wrongful Acts or Claims into a single Claim.[14] An Interrelated Wrongful Acts or Related Claims clause, when invoked, will have the effect of imposing a single self-insured retention

least in some circumstances, a composite policy can be characterised as a bundle of separate contracts.' *See also* Robert Merkin, *Colinvaux's Law of Insurance* (12th edn, Sweet & Maxwell 2019) para 15-056.

6 *Arab Bank plc v Zurich Insurance Co* (n 5) (Rix J).

7 Paolini and Nambisan (n 2) para 3.63. *See also* MacDonald Eggers (n 3) 4, citing *General Accident Fire and Life Assurance Corporation Ltd v Tanter (The Zephyr)* [1984] 1 Lloyd's Rep 58 (QB) 72 (Hobhouse J): 'The slip at all times remains a document which purports to be a composite bundle of contracts between each of the assured (or reassured) on the one side and each of the insurers (or reinsurers) on the other side.'

8 *J Rothschild Assurance Plc v Collyear* [1998] All ER (D) 431 (QB) (Rix J).

9 MacDonald Eggers (n 3) 4.

10 Paolini and Nambisan (n 2) para 3.63.

11 *Arab Bank plc v Zurich Insurance Co* (n 5) (Rix J), citing *P Samuel & Company Limited v Dumas* [1924] AC 431 (HL).

12 '[Where] an independent interest is separately insured, there can be no question of avoiding the policy for non-disclosure quoad that interest unless the person so insured was privy to the non-disclosure.' *See New Hampshire Insurance Company v MGN Ltd* (n 5) 42–43 (Potter J), 57–58 (Staughton LJ). *See also* MacDonald Eggers (n 3) 5, 7.

13 Larry Goanos, *D&O 101: Understanding Directors and Officers Liability Insurance* (Wells Media Group Inc 2014) 61.

14 This remains "Claim", rather than "claim". *See WC and AN Miller Development Co v Continental Casualty Co* No GHJ-14-00425 (D Md Nov 7 2014).

("SIR")[15] and thus a single limit of indemnity on the (now) single Claim.[16] Though Side A coverage does not typically require payment of a SIR, this is not the case under Side B or Side C.[17]

An Interrelated Wrongful Acts clause ties together Claims arising from related Wrongful Acts so as to treat them as a single Claim.[18] Depending on policy wording, a Claim need not be covered in order to invoke the Interrelated Wrongful Acts clause and be grouped as a single Claim.[19] However, a Claim must have arisen (and have been notified).[20] Further, the nature of the Claims arising from the Wrongful Acts may differ. As per the US case of *Feldman v Illinois Union Insurance Co*, new facts, defendants, and causes of actions may arise but will be considered to be Interrelated Wrongful Acts where they all pertain to the same underlying allegations.[21] The provision may be 'coverage-granting'.[22] However, where one Wrongful Act is precluded under a policy – for example, where an exclusion clause is invoked[23] – all Claims arising from an Interrelated Wrongful Act related to it will be excluded. Somewhat similar to a Prior Claims and Circumstances clause (but more specific to Wrongful Acts), a "Retroactive clause" excludes Claims against the insured for Wrongful Acts committed prior to the agreed date (often the policy inception date).[24] The Retroactive clause would thus serve to exclude all Claims where the Interrelated Wrongful Acts exclusion also applies, as the now single Claim will be deemed to have been first made on the date of the filing of the earliest.[25]

---

15 A SIR is the amount of loss the insured must pay before the insurer provides coverage (for example, where a claim is made under a policy with a £1,000,000 limit of indemnity and a SIR of £100,000, the insured will pay the £100,000 SIR and the insurer will then pay within its £1,000,000 limit). *See* Goanos, *D&O 101: Understanding Directors and Officers Liability Insurance* (n 13) 43–44, 63.

16 Katelin O'Rourke Gorman and Sarah Rogers Sepe, 'Policy Limits and Retentions' in Martin J O'Leary (ed), *Directors & Officers Liability Insurance Deskbook* (American Bar Association 2020) 135.

17 Goanos, *D&O 101: Understanding Directors and Officers Liability Insurance* (n 13) 43.

18 ibid 61. To be contrasted with *Haydon v Lo & Lo* [1997] 1 Lloyd's Rep 336 (PC) [13]–[16], where 43 incidences of theft nevertheless were deemed to amount to one demand on the insured, giving rise to one Claim.

19 It was specified that 'to be treated as a single "Claim" all that is required is for the triggering events to be "Claims" and "Interrelated Wrongful Acts," as those terms are defined in the Policy'. *See WC and AN Miller Development Co v Continental Casualty Co* (n 14); Ralph Guirgis and Sean Simpson, 'Trigger of Coverage' in Martin J O'Leary (ed), *Directors & Officers Liability Insurance Deskbook* (American Bar Association 2020) 59.

20 *WC and AN Miller Development Co v Continental Casualty Co* (n 14); Paolini and Nambisan (n 2) para 2.51.

21 198 Cal App 4th 1495 (Cal Ct App 2011).

22 *Northrop Grumman Innovation Systems Inc v Zurich American Insurance Company and others* CA No N18C-09-210, 29 (Del Super Ct Feb 2 2021).

23 Though a Claim was precluded by virtue of the Contract Exclusion clause, there was still deemed to be a Wrongful Act: *WC and AN Miller Development Co v Continental Casualty Co* (n 14).

24 'The intent is to underwrite the risk for wrongful acts on a going-forward basis only.' *See* Martin O'Leary and Kimberly Forrester, 'Policy Exclusions' in Martin J O'Leary (ed), *Directors & Officers Liability Insurance Deskbook* (American Bar Association 2020) 181. Notably this chapter subheading refers to '"Prior Acts" Exclusion' but appears to refer to the Retroactive clause; Professor Adolfo Paolini has suggested that the phrase "prior acts" 'is apt to cause confusion', but sets out that '[t]he "prior acts" exclusion refers to *claims made* before the inception of insurance and not to potentially wrongful acts which later may develop into a claim'. *See* Paolini and Nambisan (n 2) para 4.45 (emphasis added). The Retroactive clause, if used to exclude coverage for a Claim, requires a causal link between that Claim and the underlying act; the scope of the causal test will depend on the wording of the exclusion clause: *ARC Capital Partners Ltd v Brit Syndicates Ltd* [2016] EWHC 141 (Comm). *See also* Merkin (n 5) para 21-012.

25 *Connect America Holdings LLC v Arch Insurance* 174 F Supp 3d 894, 901 (ED Pa 2016); Goanos, *D&O 101: Understanding Directors and Officers Liability Insurance* (n 13) 61.

A Related Claims clause operates to tie together Claims from the same or related facts/events/circumstances in order to classify them as a single Claim. The manner in which the assessment as to relatedness is made may depend on policy wording. In the absence of clear policy wording, New York courts have applied a "sufficient factual nexus test":[26] this arises where Claims arise from common facts which demonstrate a factual nexus.[27] Where policy wording is particularly restrictive, this could lead to many Claims being grouped together. Where one Claim is excluded, all related Claims will be excluded; this particular provision is likely to apply only to related Claims made against the particular insured, and severability provisions would intervene to protect the interests and continue to allow coverage to others. 'Insurers only exclude from coverage new claims that are related to prior claims',[28] and therefore such a clause applies only where the prior Claims have been duly notified under the same or a previous policy.[29] Where a Related Claims clause features within a policy, the now single Claim will be deemed to have been made when the first Claim was made and therefore may fall outside the policy period. A Related Claims clause coupled with a "Prior Claims and Circumstances" exclusion would exclude coverage for related Claims where the first Claim was made prior to the inception date of the policy.[30]

It will be crucial in a DPA scenario to understand the impact of such clauses on coverage to insureds. In respect of Interrelated Wrongful Acts, an individual engaged in numerous instances of wrongdoing over an extended period could be exposed where a Retroactive clause dates the collectivised Wrongful Acts back to a policy which does not provide coverage. As regards Related Claims, an individual could face a multitude of actions: for example, former directors of Tesco Stores Ltd post-DPA faced criminal prosecution, privilege disputes, and employment tribunal hearings.[31] Such grouping could lead to considerable exposure to lack of coverage where an exclusion clause applies to one Claim and therefore presides over the collectivised single Claim. Though it is likely that such clauses will apply to particular insureds, a policy lacking sufficient severability

26 *Weaver v Axis Surplus Insurance Co* No 13-CV-7374 (SJF)(ARL), at 24 (EDNY Oct 30 2014); O'Rourke Gorman and Rogers Sepe in O'Leary (ed) (n 16) 138–139.

27 'This exists where the claims are neither factually nor legally distinct, but instead arise from common facts and where the logically connected facts and circumstances demonstrate a factual nexus among the claims.' *See* Guirgis and Simpson in O'Leary (ed) (n 19) 59.

28 '[This] is a higher standard (and better for the insured) than just tying the exclusion back to prior Interrelated Wrongful Acts.' *See* Goanos, *D&O 101: Understanding Directors and Officers Liability Insurance* (n 13) 62.

29 In paragraph 2.51, reference to "Interrelated Wrongful Acts" appears to refer also to Related Claims, and can in any event apply as such. *See* Paolini and Nambisan (n 2) para 2.51.

30 In respect of Interrelated Wrongful Acts: conversely, '[if] the prior Interrelated Wrongful Acts didn't give rise to an actual claim before the starting date for covered acts, then the new claim would be eligible for coverage'. *See* Goanos, *D&O 101: Understanding Directors and Officers Liability Insurance* (n 13) 62–63. cf *WC and AN Miller Development Co v Continental Casualty Co* (n 14), which sets out that a Claim must have been made, but need not be covered.

31 *R v Bush* [2019] EWCA Crim 29 (prosecution challenging the ruling of "no case to answer" at trial, unsuccessfully); *Serious Fraud Office v Tesco Stores Ltd* [2019] EW Misc 1 (Crown) (representatives of individuals implicated by name in the statement of facts applying to amend the document, unsuccessfully); *Omers Administration Corp v Tesco Plc* [2019] EWHC 109 (Ch) (third parties applying for disclosure of information disclosed under section 2 interviews to the SFO, successfully); *Tesco Plc, Tesco Stores Ltd v Mr C Bush, Mr C Rogberg* (2020) UKEAT/0069/20/AT (former directors challenging case management decisions made by the Employment Tribunal, unsuccessfully).

language could be detrimental to co-insureds where a DPA is agreed. DPAs commonly relate to historic and egregious conduct,[32] likely to invoke the Interrelated Wrongful Acts clause, and would likely lead to follow-on actions which may give rise to the application of the Related Claims provision. Where undermined by an exclusion, this could be fatal in respect of policy response.

32 *Serious Fraud Office v Rolls-Royce Plc* [2017] Lloyd's Rep FC 249 (Crown) [61].

CHAPTER 14

Indemnification

This chapter covers ultimate indemnification and not advancement of defence costs. Following a corporate DPA, a (former) director may face multiple causes of action which may give rise to Claims under their D&O policy. This may be the case where the (former) director has participated in the wrongdoing which forms the underlying offence to the DPA (and/) or where the director has been involved in the negotiations. In either of the aforementioned events, the director may face a civil claim for breach of their directors' duties.[1]

14.1 Civil claims for breach of directors' duties

The company may undertake a civil claim against the director in respect of the director's breach of their general duties owed to the company.[2] In such circumstances, Side A will be vital as the company will not be permitted to indemnify the director.[3] Civil proceedings (and a written demand for compensation, monetary damages, or non-monetary relief) will typically be included within the definition of Claim under a D&O policy, therefore once made against the insured triggering the obligation to notify the insurer as a condition precedent to coverage. The definition of Wrongful Act will also typically include any actual, alleged, or attempted breach of duty or breach of trust. Loss, also sometimes termed "Financial Loss", under a policy will usually include (compensatory) damages (so far as the damages are insurable by law)[4] and judgments, awards, or settlements. Therefore, a director liable for common law damages for breach of sections 171 or 174 of

1 Companies Act 2006.

2 Most likely, in the circumstances, at the direction of the company's directors or by derivative action (individual members pursuing interests of the company for the company); very unlikely to be by a liquidator where the company has just agreed a DPA, as the company needs to remain "alive" even where liabilities within the DPA are met by a parent company. *See* Sarah Worthington, *Sealy and Worthington's Texts, Cases and Materials in Company Law* (11th edn, Oxford University Press 2016) 665.

3 Companies Act 2006, s 234(2).

4 Exemplary damages and punitive damages are not necessarily uninsurable in the UK, but public policy will be crucial. *See Lancashire County Council v Municipal Mutual Insurance Limited* [1995] LRLR 293 (QB). *See also* Law Commission, *Aggravated, Exemplary and Restitutionary Damages* (Law Com No 247, 1997); James Scoville, Clare Swirski and Benjamin Lyon, 'Insurance and Reinsurance in the UK (England and Wales): Overview' (*Thomson Reuters Practical Law*, 1 November 2020) <https://uk.practicallaw.thomsonreuters.com/0-501-2031?transitionType=Default&contextData=(sc.Default)> accessed 1 November 2021. In the US, punitive damages may be uninsurable in some states: public policy in respect of insurability of punitive damages will be balanced against the relevant state's consideration as to upholding freedom of contract. *See Continental Casualty Co v Kinsey* 499 NW 2d 574 (ND 1993).

 DOI: 10.4324/9781003456964-17

the CA 2006, or for equitable compensation for breach of sections 171–173 of the CA 2006 may be covered in this respect.[5] Loss will not typically cover costs incurred in complying with injunctive relief, a remedy available for the (generally threatened) breach of sections 171–177 of the CA 2006.

The insurer may, where provided for within policy wording, be entitled to refuse coverage in respect of the entire claim where the policy contains an Illegal Profits exclusion clause (often combined with the Conduct exclusion). The Illegal Profits exclusion will generally operate to exclude coverage for Loss in connection with any Claim "based upon, arising out of or attributable to" the insured gaining any profit or advantage to which they were not legally entitled, and will be invoked upon admission by the insured or final adjudication.[6] Such an exclusion would render a Claim against a director for breach of section 175 or 176 of the CA 2006 non-covered where an account of profits or disgorgement of profits is ordered.[7]

In circumstances where a director faces a financial penalty imposed by the court, the question has arisen as to whether the court can demand and utilise the director's D&O policy in fixing the penalty imposed.[8] The question as to the extent to which provision of insurance and consequent ability to meet the obligation to pay the financial penalty should be considered is as yet undetermined. Although arguably financial penalties are set according to prescribed structures, this issue raises questions as to means-testing, and any precedent against imposing a financial penalty where a wrongdoer director lacks insurance coverage may impact the deterrent effect against such wrongdoing. Rather than averting a financial penalty altogether in such circumstances, the court might instead consider an approach to payment.

A director may also face civil claims brought by the company's shareholders on its behalf, by way of a derivative claim. This will typically be within the statutory framework, under section 260 of the CA 2006, supplemented by the Civil Procedure Rules.[9] However, in exceptional circumstances where section 260 does not respond, a derivative claim may be brought under the old common law rules; the most likely circumstance in which this might take place in respect of DPA-related actions is where a member of the company brings proceedings (most likely a member of the parent company of its wronged subsidiary).[10] Section 260(3) allows for the bringing of a derivative claim in respect of a cause of action from an actual or proposed act or omission involving breach of duty or breach of trust by

5 'The orthodox view is that equitable compensation is not available for breach of "fiduciary duties" strictly labelled – that is, the equitable no conflict and no profit rules.' *See* Worthington (n 2) 431–434.

6 WR Berkley UK Limited, 'Directors and Officers Liability and Company Reimbursement Insurance Policy' (*WR Berkley*, May 2018) <https://www.brokerdirect.co.uk/wp-content/uploads/2018/08/Directors-Officers-WRB_PolicyWording_V06_MAY18.pdf> accessed 23 November 2020, para 5.5.2; GB Underwriting, 'Management Liability (D&O) and Company Reimbursement Policy Wording' (*GB Underwriting Ltd*, July 2014) <https://web.archive.org/web/20160413182237/http://www.gbunderwriting.co.uk/downloads/> accessed 17 December 2020, para 5.5.2.

7 In respect of section 175 of the CA 2006, a director will only be liable for profits made as a result of their disloyalty. In respect of section 176 of the CA 2006, such profits are held on constructive trust. *See Warman International Ltd v Dwyer* [1995] HCA 18; *FHR European Ventures LLP and others v Cedar Capital Partners LLC* [2014] UKSC 45. *See also* Worthington (n 2) 431–434.

8 *BOS International (Australia) Ltd v Babcock & Brown International Pty Ltd* [2011] NSWSC 1382.

9 CPR 19.9–19.9F.

10 *Final Appeal Waddington Ltd v Chan Choo Hoo Thomas* [2009] 2 BCLC 82 (HK). *See also* Worthington (n 2) 695

a director.[11] If another remedy is available the action will not proceed,[12] and where the majority (excluding the wrongdoers) do not wish for the claim to proceed it will cease.[13] The application of the Claim, Loss, and Wrongful Acts definitions will be largely the same for a civil claim for breach of directors' duties as the analysis above (in respect of a civil claim made by the company, as opposed to the shareholders acting on its behalf).

14.1.1 Impact of the Insured vs Insured exclusion

The "Insured vs Insured" exclusion clause was originally introduced to prevent the extension of coverage for collusive claims.[14] However, its existence may impact a director's ability to obtain indemnification where the company (or shareholders on the company's behalf) makes a legitimate claim against it. Where coverage is precluded for the director under Side A, the operation of the clause (if applicable throughout all Sides of the policy) will also serve to preclude coverage to the company under Side C. Common exceptions/carvebacks to the exclusion include derivative claims, though there may be specificity within the exception as to the form of the action.[15]

A company is not necessarily legally precluded from claiming against a (former) director for the director's breach of duty, even if the company agrees a DPA on the basis of the same underlying conduct (as committed by the director). Clarified in *Bilta v Nazir*, the maxim *ex turpi causa non oritur actio* would not apply in such circumstances.[16] However, aside from any lack of coverage set out by an Insured vs Insured exclusion, the company's recovery (under Side C) may in any event be limited where it is perceived that the company is attempting to recover a criminal fine imposed within the DPA, based on intentional or negligent conduct; in such circumstances, it is crucial to look at the true basis of the claim.

Irrespective of whether the Claim against the director is brought by the company or by way of a derivative claim, the director will not be covered where the Claim is "based upon, arising out of or attributable to any actual dishonest or fraudulent act"; this wording is typical of the "Conduct exclusion" clause, also sometimes termed the "Deliberate acts" exclusion. The types of conduct featured within the clause may be expanded, depending on policy wording, and may (for example) expressly exclude "malicious" acts. Explored more later, the Conduct exclusion clause is typically invoked upon admission by the insured or final adjudication or judgment by a court or tribunal (**Sections 15.2.3.1 and 15.2.3.2**).

In respect of defence costs incurred in civil proceedings 'brought by the company, or an associated company', corporate indemnification will not be possible where judgment

---

11 'A derivative claim under this Chapter may be brought only in respect of a cause of action arising from an actual or proposed act or omission involving negligence, default, breach of duty or breach of trust by a director of the company.' *See* Companies Act 2006, s 260(3).

12 *Prudential Assurance Co Ltd v Newman Industries Ltd (No 2)* [1982] Ch 204 (CA).

13 *Smith v Croft (No 2)* [1988] Ch 114 (Ch).

14 Martin O'Leary and Kimberly Forrester, 'Policy Exclusions' in Martin J O'Leary (ed), *Directors & Officers Liability Insurance Deskbook* (American Bar Association 2020) 166.

15 For example, an 'independent shareholder derivative claim'. *See* ibid. *See also* Larry Goanos, *D&O 101: Understanding Directors and Officers Liability Insurance* (Wells Media Group Inc 2014) 81.

16 'It would be a remarkable paradox if the mere breach of those duties by doing an illegal act adverse to the company's interest was enough to make the duty unenforceable at the suit of the company to whom it is owed ... In that situation it is in reality the dishonest directors who are relying on their own dishonesty to found a defence. The company's culpability is wholly derived from them, which is the very matter of which complaint is made.' *See Bilta (UK) Ltd (in liquidation) v Nazir* [2015] UKSC 23 [89] (Lord Sumption).

is given against the director,[17] and judgment will be considered to be the final decision in the underlying proceedings.[18] With some Insured vs Insured exclusions drafted with carvebacks to allow for defence costs cover, a Side A policy providing such cover will be crucial.

14.2 A director convicted of a criminal offence

Where a corporate DPA is approved by the court, it is highly likely that the prosecutor will look to target the prosecution of individuals connected with the underlying DPA offence. Though none of the individual prosecutions of company directors connected with corporate DPAs have thus far been successful in the UK, it remains possible that an individual – particularly a (former) director – may be convicted of a criminal offence. Criminal proceedings are likely to fall within the policy definition of Claim, though some more restrictive policies may not include this feature. Loss as defined within the policy will not include fines imposed within criminal proceedings, as they are uninsurable as a matter of law and public policy.[19] Whether defence costs are subsumed by the definition of Loss or covered as a separate undertaking will depend on policy wording. A typical exclusion clause will be prefaced by setting out that its application will render the insurer not liable for Loss "in connection with any Claim", and the following terminology (as to the precise exclusion) will vary depending on policy wording.[20]

In connection with the liability insurance principle that only actual liability is indemnified, in respect of defence costs this would suggest that it must be established that the insured is under an actual legal liability, or that the Claim falls within the scope of the policy.[21] This can be contractually disclaimed,[22] and D&O defence costs cover tends to operate in such a way, particularly as regards allegations and successful defence (**Section 14.3**). If the liability principle were to apply (for example, without a contractual refutation), a criminal conviction established beyond all reasonable doubt would raise minimal issues as regards liability incurred.[23] This would be more contentious where conviction arises following an SA 2020 agreement under section 74 (previously section 73 of the

17 Companies Act 2006, s 234(3)(b)(ii).

18 ibid s 234(4). Where not appealed against: s 234(5)(a)(i), or where the appeal is disposed of: s 234(5)(a)(ii).

19 *Beresford v Royal Insurance Co* [1938] AC 586 (HL) 590, 603, citing *Cleaver v Mutual Reserve Fund Life Association* [1892] 1 QB 147 (CA) (Fry LJ); *Gray v Barr* [1971] 2 QB 554 (CA).

20 As such, it is crucial to determine whether defence costs sit within the definition of Loss so as to establish whether the indemnification for defence costs will be impacted by the fate of the overarching claim. This is a more relevant consideration where the director is acquitted, or the proceedings are not considered to be final (for example, where under appeal).

21 *AstraZeneca Insurance Co Ltd v XL Insurance (Bermuda) Ltd* [2013] EWHC 349 (Comm) [96] (Flaux J); *JCS Cost Management Ltd v QBE Insurance (International) Ltd* [2015] NZCA 524 [42] (Courtney and Clifford JJ), citing Robert Merkin, *Colinvaux's Law of Insurance* (10th edn, Sweet & Maxwell 2014) para 20-086; *Post Office v Norwich Union Fire Insurance Society Ltd* [1967] 2 QB 363 (CA) 373–376.

22 *See for example Legg v Sterte Garage Ltd* [2016] EWCA Civ 97: costs incurred '"in connection with any event which is or may be the subject of indemnity"'.

23 *AstraZeneca Insurance Co Ltd v XL Insurance (Bermuda) Ltd* sets out that a judgment (or settlement) will not necessarily establish actual legal liability, though may be strong evidence of it; an insured must be able to prove on the balance of probabilities that they were actually liable. *See AstraZeneca Insurance Co Ltd v XL Insurance (Bermuda) Ltd* [2013] EWHC (n 21) [96] (Flaux J).

SOCPA 2005),[24] as *prima facie* this may be considered a settlement with prosecutors. However, the agreement[25] reached between the prosecutor and the individual represents an acceptance of both parties as to how the case may be finalised without their objection and, as discretion resides with the judiciary in terms of its enforcement *in effectum*, it could not be considered a basis upon which to refuse coverage in respect of there being no actual legal liability.

In any event, costs incurred in the defence of criminal proceedings (whether within the definition of Loss or otherwise) in which the director is convicted are not recoverable as a matter of law and public policy. Even if this were not the case, most D&O policies require an insured to seek the insurer's consent prior to admittance of liability (**Section 18.4.2.1**), and thus coverage may be precluded where such consent is not given or sought and a guilty plea is entered.[26] The section 74 process requires an admission as to all wrongdoing,[27] not necessarily just the underlying offence being investigated (which may invoke the Conduct exclusion clause), and therefore consent will be crucial; even where coverage is not applied in respect of the criminal proceedings, third-party claims may thereafter arise and there may be questions as to coverage. The insurer's right to withhold consent to incur liability must be exercised in good faith and not arbitrarily, nor 'with reference to considerations wholly extraneous to the subject matter of the particular claim'.[28] Consideration of the corporate DPA statement of facts in related proceedings against the individual would be unlikely to be considered to be wholly extraneous, though the insurer may reflect upon the fact that no successful prosecutions have yet arisen following UK corporate DPAs.

A Claim made against an insured must relate to a defined Wrongful Act, which will typically include 'any actual or alleged breach of duty, neglect, error, misstatement, misleading statement, omission or act',[29] and will likely also include breach of trust. The Wrongful Act must be committed by the insured person in their capacity as such, which is often noted within the definition terminology.[30] The inclusion of "omission or act" broadens the scope of the definition. Notably, the definition does not encompass specifically criminal acts, which are often expressly excluded. Though an insurer is

24 An individual will agree to plead guilty, pursuant to a written agreement, having assisted or offered to assist the prosecutor or investigation in relation to an offence: Sentencing Act 2020, s 74(1). However, judicial discretion remains in respect of sentencing and whether a reduction is imposed: *R v Dougall* [2010] EWCA Crim 1048 [22], citing Practice Direction (Criminal Proceedings: Consolidation) [2002] 1 WLR 2070, paras IV.45.10–IV.45.12.

25 Though referred to as a 'plea agreement', it can be distinguished from the types of plea bargains which may be seen in other jurisdictions. *See Dougall* (n 24) [1]–[4].

26 Adolfo Paolini and Deepak Nambisan, *Directors' and Officers' Liability Insurance* (Informa Law 2008) para 8.34.

27 Crown Prosecution Service, 'SOCPA Agreements: Note for Those Representing Assisting Offenders' (*Crown Prosecution Service*, April 2016) <https://web.archive.org/web/20210625040215/https://www.cps.gov.uk/legal-guidance/socpa-agreements-note-those-representing-assisting-offenders> accessed 5 May 2021.

28 *Gan Insurance Co Ltd v Tai Ping Insurance Co Ltd (No 2)* [2001] EWCA Civ 1047 [54] (Mance LJ). *See also Equitas Insurance Ltd v Municipal Mutual Insurance Ltd* [2019] EWCA Civ 718 [109] (Males LJ); *Distillers-Bio-Chemicals (Australia) Property Ltd v Ajax Insurance Co Ltd* [1974] HCA 3 [42] (Stephen J).

29 Goanos, *D&O 101: Understanding Directors and Officers Liability Insurance* (n 15) 69. *See also for example* Zurich, 'D&O Corporate Directors' and Officers' Liability: Policy Document' (*Zurich Insurance plc*, April 2020) <https://www.zurich.co.uk/business/-/media/Business/Documents/Specialty-lines/710008.pdf> accessed 22 January 2021, 13.

30 Goanos, *D&O 101: Understanding Directors and Officers Liability Insurance* (n 15) 69.

entitled to go beyond the particulars of the claim and establish the true nature of liability,[31] this is unlikely to occur where a director is seeking coverage on the basis of a criminal conviction by virtue of the clear exclusion of liability.

A Claim against an insured may *prima facie*, when considering the policy definitions, be covered. However, exclusion clauses within a policy will serve to preclude coverage. As aforementioned (**Section 14.1.1**), a Conduct exclusion clause operates to exclude certain types of misconduct; typically, the clause will exclude coverage for dishonest or fraudulent acts, and it may be a further requirement that those acts be deliberate (depending on policy wording).[32] Many Conduct exclusion clauses also provide that the gaining of a personal profit, remuneration, or advantage to which the insured was not legally entitled will invoke the clause. Criminal misconduct may feature within the clause, but if not expressly mentioned will be precluded on public policy grounds and the maxim *ex turpi causa non oritur actio*. The latter prevents a legal person who commits an unlawful act from seeking indemnity against the liability which resulted from that act,[33] where in the public interest and necessary to uphold the integrity of the legal system.[34] In any event, a criminal act will fall within the Conduct exclusion clause where the act otherwise falls within the scope of its wording (for example, where the act was dishonest). Most Conduct exclusion clauses are prefaced with the words "the Insurer shall not be liable for any Loss arising out of, based upon or attributable to" (or similar), which vastly restricts the clause for the insured and allows for many more circumstances in which the clause might be invoked in order to preclude coverage.

A final adjudication or admission of the insured will usually be required to trigger the clause, and a conviction will generally be considered a final adjudication unless under appeal. An admission will typically be required in written form, and some clauses may go further to require that the admission be "formal", though the exact formalities in which the admission must be made to trigger the clause are typically undefined. For example, it is not prescribed that the written admission be addressed to the insurer. It may be prescribed that the admission must be made "by the Insured Person" (**Section 15.2.3.1**). Some Conduct exclusion clauses may also allow coverage to be precluded where there is an 'acknowledgement'[35] by the insured (as opposed to an admission), which provides an even lower threshold for insurers and significantly restricts coverage to the insured.

31 '[U]nderwriters' liability depends upon the true facts and not simply upon the way in which the claimant chooses to put its case.' *See MDIS Ltd (formerly McDonnell Information Systems Ltd) v Swinbank* [1999] All ER (D) 815 (CA) [22] (Clarke LJ).

32 One cannot be indemnified as a result of their deliberate criminal act; this may be despite the fact that the person was aware that they were committing the action, but unaware that it was criminal. *See Burrows v Rhodes* [1899] 1 QB 816; *Beresford v Royal Insurance Co* (n 19); *Haseldine v Hosken* [1933] 1 KB 822 (CA) 833 (Scrutton LJ). *See also* Paolini and Nambisan (n 26) para 4.04.

33 Furthermore, the clause may also exclude coverage for an intentional regulatory or statutory breach. There must be protection from moral hazards. *See* Samet Caliskan, 'Mitigating Risk Through D&O Insurance: Assessing the Role of Illegality Defence and Corporate Attribution' (2019) 132 BILA J 1.

34 'In assessing whether the public interest would be harmed in that way, it is necessary (a) to consider the underlying purpose of the prohibition which has been transgressed and whether that purpose will be enhanced by denial of the claim, (b) to consider any other relevant public policy on which the denial of the claim may have an impact and (c) to consider whether denial of the claim would be a proportionate response to the illegality, bearing in mind that punishment is a matter for the criminal courts.' This is known as the "range of factors" test. *See Patel v Mirza* [2016] UKSC 42 [120] (Lord Toulson).

35 AXA, 'Directors and Officers Liability Insurance (D&O)' (*AXA Insurance Ltd*, 2019) <https://www.axa.ch/servlets/external/docstoredocument?accesscode=afklo> accessed 28 July 2020, para DI.1.3.

Where a director enters into an agreement with a prosecutor pursuant to section 74 of the SA 2020, the signing of the agreement may be considered a (formal) admission or acknowledgement, as would the entering of a guilty plea without such agreement. A Conduct exclusion clause will typically be drafted so as to preclude all coverage, including defence costs, and therefore may impact advancement provisions (explored under **Section 15.2.3.1 and 15.2.3.2**) particularly where invoked earlier on in the process by way of admission.

A Contract exclusion clause will typically preclude coverage for liability arising from contracts[36] and sometimes 'agreements'.[37] Exactly what constitutes an "agreement" for the purpose of invoking the clause is not clearly defined, though is most likely to be considered to be any agreement giving rise to liability (albeit not contractual). Policy wording may exclude an "express oral or written contract or agreement" or simply a "contract or agreement". Like the Conduct exclusion, a Contract exclusion clause will often be prefaced with the words "the Insurer shall not be liable for any Loss arising out of, based upon or attributable to" (or similar), which has the potential to heavily restrict coverage – particularly where "agreement" is a feature of the clause.[38]

An agreement between a prosecutor and director pursuant to section 74 of the SA 2020 is unlikely to be considered a contract. Legal 500-recommended lawyer Siobhain Egan, who instructed Kalyani Kaul KC and Dee Connolly in representing former director of Arck LLP Kathryn Clark, in a case which included a section 73 of the SOCPA 2005 agreement (now section 74 of the SA 2020), warns that a prosecutor can withdraw from such an agreement 'at any time and for any reason'.[39] However, it would qualify as an agreement for the purpose of invoking the Contract exclusion clause where wording so permits. Most Contract exclusion clauses will allow for defence costs coverage, which is not typically included within the Conduct exclusion clause. In some policies a Contract exclusion clause may allow further coverage, disapplying the Contract exclusion clause where liability would have arisen but for the contract/agreement. In respect of a section 74 agreement, arguably criminal liability would have arisen anyway, though this may depend on the circumstances. In any event, both aforementioned eventualities will not apply where a criminal conviction has been given in the underlying Claim.

14.3 A director acquitted of a criminal offence

Considering the record of UK DPAs and ensuing individual prosecutions, it is currently far more likely that a director in such a position would be acquitted than convicted. Nevertheless, costs may be incurred in the defence of such proceedings. It is crucial to

36 *Omega Proteins Ltd v Aspen Insurance UK Ltd* [2010] EWHC 2280 (Comm); *MDIS Ltd (formerly McDonnell Information Systems Ltd) v Swinbank* (n 31).

37 AIG PrivateEdge, 'D&O Coverage Section' (*AIG*, 2016) <https://www.aig.co.uk/content/dam/aig/emea/united-kingdom/documents/Financial-lines/PrivateEdge/privateedge-do-2016.pdf> accessed 23 November 2020, para 5.11; Allianz Broker, 'Directors & Officers Liability Section' (*Allianz*, 2020) <https://www.allianz.co.uk/content/dam/onemarketing/azuk/allianzcouk/broker/docs/policy-wording/LD0008-directors-and-officers-liability-section-policies-incepted-prior-to-310717.pdf> accessed 22 October 2020, 19.

38 Such wording has the potential to restrict not only claims in contract but also in tort.

39 Siobhain Egan, 'What Is a SOCPA Agreement and How Can It Help Me? – By Siobhain Egan' (*Lewis Nedas*, 19 July 2019) <https://lewisnedas.co.uk/newsroom/blog/corporate-commercial/what-is-a-socpa-agreement-how-can-it-help-me-by-siobhain-egan.html> accessed 7 July 2021.

establish whether defence costs are provided within the policy's definition of Loss, or by a separate undertaking. Where defence costs are subsumed by the definition of Loss, there is *prima facie* considerable exposure for an insured, particularly where the Loss definition is prefaced with the words "which the insured is legally liable to pay on account of a Claim".[40] Such wording is connected with the principle of liability insurance that an insured must demonstrate that they have incurred actual legal liability in order to recover under their insurance policy.[41] Therefore, this would suggest that where defence costs are included within the definition of Loss and thus the main insuring clause,[42] the insured's recovery is subject to this principle. Actual legal liability does not include an insured's liability to pay defence costs,[43] and therefore an insured could only obtain indemnification for defence costs where they are actually liable in the underlying Claim.[44] This would lead to a perverse outcome, whereby in the context of criminal proceedings an insured could only seek indemnification costs upon conviction, which would ultimately (as discussed under **Section 14.2**) be excluded.

Despite this general principle, in respect of defence costs provided within Loss – which inherently respond to allegations – actual legal liability need not be determined (such a requirement would be contrary to commercial sense). Instead, it need only be established that the Claim against the insured for which defence costs are incurred would fall within the scope of the policy ("the scope test" hereafter).[45] The common inclusion of criminal proceedings within the Claim definition avails the possibility of indemnification of such defence costs,[46] and therefore appears to satisfy the scope test. However, in respect of a

40 *AstraZeneca Insurance Co Ltd v XL Insurance (Bermuda) Ltd* [2013] EWHC (n 21) [68] (Flaux J), citing *Structural Polymer Systems Ltd v Brown (The Baltic Universal)* [1999] CLC 268 (QB).

41 '[I]n my judgment there is a consistent and well-established line of authority that, in the absence of clear contrary wording in the contract of liability insurance, under English law (i) the insured has to establish that it was under an actual legal liability, not just an alleged liability, to the third party before it is entitled to an indemnity under the contract and (ii) the ascertainment of loss by a judgment or settlement does not automatically establish such actual legal liability (although a judgment against the insured may be strong evidence of such liability). It is still open to the insurer to challenge that there was an actual legal liability, in which case it is for the insured to prove that there was.' *See AstraZeneca Insurance Co Ltd v XL Insurance (Bermuda) Ltd* [2013] EWHC (n 21) [96] (Flaux J). *See also AstraZeneca Insurance Co Ltd v XL Insurance (Bermuda) Ltd* [2013] EWCA Civ 1660 [21] (Clarke LJ). This has been neatly set out in *Australasian Correctional Services Pty Ltd v AIG Australia Ltd* [2018] FCA 2043 [15] (Allsop CJ): 'The primary liability in the insuring clause to indemnify for "all amounts which the Insured shall become legally liable to pay" is to be interpreted as indemnity for legal liability ascertained by judgment, award, or settlement: *Distillers Co Biochemicals (Aust) Pty Ltd v Ajax Insurance Co Ltd* (1974) 130 CLR 1 at 25–26; *Post Office v Norwich Union Fire Insurance Society Ltd* [1967] 2 QB 363 at 373–74 and 377–78; *Vero Insurance Ltd v Baycorp Advantage Ltd* [2004] NSWCA 390; 13 ANZ Insurance Cases 61-630 at [1], [48] and [89]; *Allianz Australia Insurance Ltd v Bluescope Steel Ltd* [2014] NSWCA 276; 87 NSWLR 332 at 349 [78], 381 [267]–[270].'

42 *American Casualty Co v Rahn* 854 F Supp 492 (WD Mich 1994). *See also* Paolini and Nambisan (n 26) para 8.18.

43 'Your own costs of defending a claim can never be something you are obligated to pay by reason of judgment or settlement'. *See AstraZeneca Insurance Co Ltd v XL Insurance (Bermuda) Ltd* [2013] EWHC (n 21) [138] (Flaux J). *See also AstraZeneca Insurance Co Ltd v XL Insurance (Bermuda) Ltd* [2013] EWCA (n 41) [76] (Clarke LJ).

44 *AstraZeneca Insurance Co Ltd v XL Insurance (Bermuda) Ltd* [2013] EWHC (n 21) [137]–[145] (Flaux J).

45 Due to the different nature of defence costs cover, as compared to other substantive cover. *See JCS Cost Management Ltd v QBE Insurance (International) Ltd* (n 21) [42] (Courtney and Clifford JJ), citing Merkin, *Colinvaux's Law of Insurance* (n 259) para 20-086. *See also Post Office v Norwich Union Fire Insurance Society Ltd* (n 21); *Bradley v Eagle Star Insurance Co Ltd* [1989] AC 957 (HL); *Omega Proteins Ltd v Aspen Insurance UK Ltd* (n 36); *Rathbone Brothers plc v Novae Corporate Underwriting Ltd* [2014] EWCA Civ 1464 [64] (Elias LJ); Alison Padfield, *Insurance Claims* (5th edn, Bloomsbury Professional 2021) para 8.11.

46 Provided criminal liability is not ultimately established, as defence costs would then be excluded.

Claim *successfully defended*, determination as to indemnification for defence costs is said in *JCS Cost Management Ltd v QBE Insurance (International) Ltd* (a New Zealand Court of Appeal case) to raise two questions: the factual and legal basis upon which the insured would have been held liable had the Claim against them succeeded, and whether the true nature of the Claim would have been covered by the policy.[47] Following this interpretation, the Claim *and* the application of exclusions are to be considered in accordance with a wider and more comprehensive interpretation of the policy. Criminal liability would not be covered by a D&O policy, and this would therefore suggest that a director would not be entitled to indemnification of defence costs incurred against a successfully defended Claim unless the factual circumstances point to a covered true liability (for example, negligence). As the two *JCS Cost Management Ltd* scope test interpretative questions remain based on a consideration of liability (actual, or "but for" a successful defence), the approach to the interpretation of criminal defence costs cover essentially renders such costs incurred in a successful defence a loan, and not an indemnity.

The actual legal liability insurance principle and the scope test can be disclaimed by contractual expression,[48] and intrinsically the provision of defence costs within a D&O policy (particularly where inclusive of criminal proceedings)[49] operates in such a way. Professor Robert Merkin KC states '[a] D&O policy stripped of defence costs cover ... is not worth the paper that it is written on'[50] and, as such, defence costs cover within D&O policies cannot be subject to such restrictive interpretation of insurance principles if it is to function. To retain the policy's value and the commercial purpose to provide protection against allegations as well as liability (unless excluded within the policy), the defence costs provision is instead subject to contractual principles.[51] In adopting a contractual interpretation, the test of business efficacy will be utilised to give effect to the intention of the parties in providing the scope of coverage envisaged upon purchasing a policy with such cover, and to make a policy bearing such a provision workable.[52] Were a policy bearing defence costs cover to be interpreted in accordance with insurance principles, in relation to criminal proceedings, a defendant convicted would be precluded coverage as a result of the Conduct exclusion clause and a defendant acquitted would be precluded coverage on the basis of the analysis above.[53] Clearly, this renders the intention of the

47 *JCS Cost Management Ltd v QBE Insurance (International) Ltd* (n 21) [51] (Courtney and Clifford JJ).

48 The actual legal liability principle can be contractually disclaimed as regards no established liability, and the scope test can be contractually disclaimed as regards no covered liability. According to Professor Adolfo Paolini and Deepak Nambisan, it is 'rare' in D&O insurance that 'the contract [will] require that, for defence costs to be payable, the insured's liability to a third party in respect of an insured risk has actually been established': Paolini and Nambisan (n 26) para 1.27.

49 Particularly where criminal proceedings are included within the Claim definition, as otherwise the interpretation of the scope test (considering the application of the Conduct exclusion and general principles relating to indemnification of criminal actions) would leave very limited circumstances whereby defence costs incurred in a successful defence would be indemnified.

50 Robert Merkin, 'Directors' and Officers' Insurance and the Global Financial Crisis' (2009) 118(2) BILA J 2, 10.

51 '[A] term will only be implied if it satisfies the test of business necessity'. *See Marks and Spencer plc v BNP Paribas Securities Services Trust Company (Jersey) Limited* [2015] UKSC 72 [17] (Lord Neuberger).

52 *Mediterranean Salvage & Towage Ltd v Seamar Trading & Commerce Inc* [2009] EWCA Civ 531 [18] (Lord Clarke), citing *Philips Electronique Grand Public SA v British Sky Broadcasting Ltd* [1995] EMLR 472 (CA) 480–482 (Sir Bingham MR).

53 Though this sort of issue was highlighted, no solution was offered in *AstraZeneca Insurance Co Ltd v XL Insurance (Bermuda) Ltd* [2013] EWCA (n 41) [80] (Clarke LJ): 'This means that AZ does not recover if it successfully defends a claim. This is surprising and from the point of view of AZ, profoundly unsatisfactory. It

provision practically illusory,[54] and 'the court will lean against a construction which would defeat this intention or make it substantially ineffective'.[55]

Interpretation of defence costs cover must be based upon policy wording *and* objective, and not be influenced by considerations as to underlying liability: in this respect, the insured is to be entitled to indemnification for successfully defended Claims as per the contractual provision. Defence costs cover which forms part of the definition of Loss is in any event 'an accessory to the main insuring clause and therefore follows the fortunes of that clause',[56] thus bound by the fate of any exclusions invoked[57] and part of the total aggregate limit of liability.[58] Exclusion clauses are not therefore redundant as regards defence costs cover interpreted alongside contractual principles, but the nature of the insurer's obligation may impact their application (for example, whether mandatory or discretionary (**Section 15.1.2**)). In any event, advancement will be made subject to the insurer's right of recoupment.

Essentially, therefore, the scope test applied to determine indemnification of defence costs can be reframed in determining whether the defence costs cover itself is triggered simply as a result of a *Claim* made,[59] and not *liability* incurred (or which would have occurred had the Claim against the insured succeeded). To this extent, defence costs can *bona fide* be included within the Loss definition, as it is simply the interpretative indemnification principle which can be distinguished from the remainder of the clause to give effect to it, and the cover otherwise remains subject to the fate of the claim. The scope test may still be applicable insofar as it permits the determination of the true nature of the Claim.[60] Such a term of interpretation and application must be implied to ensure the commercial and practical coherence.[61] If criminal proceedings are not included within the Claim definition, any provision for defence costs in such circumstances will be reliant

is, however, as it seems to me, the result of having defense costs only catered for, and then maladroitly, by way of treating them *as an addition to and an element of damages*' (emphasis added).

54 '[T]he contract must not be construed so as to defeat that object, nor so as to render it practically illusory.' *See Cornish v Accident Insurance Co Ltd* (1889) 23 QBD 453 (CA) 456 (Lindley LJ).

55 '[W]here it is plain that the parties were intending to effect a contract of insurance or an insurance of a particular kind, the court will lean against a construction which would defeat this intention or make it substantially ineffective': *Halsbury's Laws* (5th edn, 2018) vol 60, para 83.

56 Paolini and Nambisan (n 26) para 8.19.

57 *Silbermann v CGU Insurance Ltd* [2003] NSWCA 203; *Wilkie v Gordian Runoff Ltd* [2003] NSWSC 1059. *See also* ibid para 8.20.

58 *Helfand v National Union Fire Ins Co* 10 Cal App 4th 869 (1992). *See also* Paolini and Nambisan (n 26) para 8.18.

59 Irrespective of it being a liability policy. *See AstraZeneca Insurance Co Ltd v XL Insurance (Bermuda) Ltd* [2013] EWCA (n 41) [19] (Clarke LJ).

60 *JCS Cost Management Ltd v QBE Insurance (International) Ltd* (n 21) [51] (Courtney and Clifford JJ). This is a typical approach: 'The insurers could go behind the form of the claim in the pleading and look at the true nature of the claim to see the real underlying basis for the insured's liability.' *See AstraZeneca Insurance Co Ltd v XL Insurance (Bermuda) Ltd* [2013] EWHC (n 21) [53], citing *McDonnell Information Systems Ltd v Swinbank* [1998] All ER (D) 410 (QB) (Mance J); *MDIS Ltd (formerly McDonnell Information Systems Ltd) v Swinbank* (n 31) (Peter Gibson, Judge and Clarke LJJ), citing *West Wake Price & Co v Ching* (n 124).

61 'The business efficacy test does not require "absolute necessity"; a term may only be implied if, without it, the contract would lack commercial or practical coherence'. *See Halsbury's Laws* (5th edn, 2019) vol 22, para 169, citing *Marks and Spencer plc v BNP Paribas Securities Services Trust Company (Jersey) Limited* (n 289) [21] (Lord Neuberger).

upon a freestanding and broader defence costs cover but will remain limited to indemnification for successful defences only.[62]

To embed the cover further, the insurer and insured may also agree the inclusion of a "KC clause" (previously "QC clause") or other form of contingency insurance.[63] A "KC clause" is said to offer 'additional cover'[64] to an insured. Typically, this clause provides that the insurer will indemnify the insured without proof of actual loss where a King's Counsel determines that it is more likely than not that there will be a loss.[65] Where cover is acknowledged, this provides coverage to the insured where 'no defence can conscientiously be advanced' in the underlying Claim.[66] This may be problematic in current times, as prosecutions of intra-corporate individuals following DPAs have been wholly unsuccessful, but may provide an extra element of protection as such cases increase.

If defence costs are covered as a separate undertaking, this will typically mean that they are not provided for within the main insuring clause and do not contribute to the limit of indemnity (instead provided in addition).[67] This is uncommon, and the default position is that defence costs are *not* provided as a separate undertaking.[68] Such a policy was seen in *Poole Harbour Yacht Club Marina Ltd v Excess Insurance Co*,[69] whereby defence costs were provided for as a separate undertaking – a 'wholly independent form of cover'[70] within the policy – and exclusion clauses had even been drafted in terms which meant that they did not apply to the defence costs provision.[71] If therefore provided outside of the Loss definition and thus the main insuring clause, the scope test will not apply in any event as regards questions of covered liability,[72] but the insured will have the benefit of preserving the policy's limit should related Claims and Loss arise. The cover, unique in its response to alleged liability, will be interpreted alongside contractual principles. Whether provided under the definition of Loss or a separate undertaking, such cover will inevitably be subject to the condition precedent to indemnity that the insured obtains the insurer's consent to incur defence costs.[73]

62 As even a freestanding defence costs agreement cannot indemnify for defence costs incurred in proceedings resulting in a conviction.

63 *AstraZeneca Insurance Co Ltd v XL Insurance (Bermuda) Ltd* [2013] EWHC (n 21) [76] (Flaux J), citing *Thornton Springer v NEM Insurance Co Ltd* [2000] CLC 975 (QB) 986 (Colman J), citing *West Wake Price & Co v Ching* (n 124); *Post Office v Norwich Union Fire Insurance Society Ltd* (n 21); *Bradley v Eagle Star Insurance Co Ltd* (n 283) 964–966 (Lord Brandon). *See also* Jesse Crozier, 'What Price Success: AstraZeneca in the Court of Appeal' (2014) 127 BILA J 1, 8.

64 *AstraZeneca Insurance Co Ltd v XL Insurance (Bermuda) Ltd* [2013] EWHC (n 21) [44] (Flaux J), citing *West Wake Price & Co v Ching* (n 124) 49 (Devlin J).

65 *AstraZeneca Insurance Co Ltd v XL Insurance (Bermuda) Ltd* [2013] EWHC (n 21) [45] (Flaux J), citing *West Wake Price & Co v Ching* (n 124) 50 (Devlin J).

66 *Channon v Ward* [2017] EWCA Civ 13 [43] (Tomlinson LJ).

67 Paolini and Nambisan (n 26) para 8.17.

68 *Wyeth & Brothers Ltd v Cigna Insurance Co of Europe SA-NV* [2001] EWCA Civ 175. *See also* ibid para 8.07.

69 [2001] Lloyd's Rep IR 580 (QB).

70 Paolini and Nambisan (n 26) para 8.13.

71 ibid paras 8.11–8.13.

72 If outside of the Loss definition and provided as a separate undertaking, defence costs need not be linked to a Claim covered under the policy. *See Rathbone Brothers plc v Novae Corporate Underwriting Ltd* (n 45) [63]–[64] (Elias LJ).

73 Which cannot be unreasonably withheld. *See Poole Harbour Yacht Club Marina Ltd v Excess Insurance Co* (n 69). *See also* Paolini and Nambisan (n 26) para 8.37.

Furthermore, it is crucial for directors to ensure that their D&O policy wording is broad enough to include indemnification for defence costs following acquittal in cases relating to a corporate DPA. With a default contractual interpretation, the onus will be on ensuring that the provision does not expressly restrict its own application. As the prospect of individual acquittal, as opposed to conviction, is currently more likely following a corporate DPA, it is vital to ensure that such costs are covered under the policy so as to uphold its value. Following the DPA agreed by Serco Geografix Ltd, two former directors Nicholas Woods and Simon Marshall were prosecuted but ultimately acquitted of offences relating to the corporate DPA. Following issues relating to the disclosure of evidence, the SFO accepted liability for (defence) costs which totalled £2.7 million.[74] It is suggested that this acceptance of liability arose due to the SFO's 'significant failings',[75] and may not be applicable in every DPA-related individual prosecution which collapses or leads to acquittal. Thus, whilst not every individual will be so "fortunate",[76] it is crucial to ensure directors are adequately protected.

The alleged act or omission may fall within the scope of the Wrongful Act definition, albeit that a Conduct exclusion clause would likely exist to preclude coverage where the act or omission is criminal in nature (which may be deemed deliberate, dishonest, fraudulent, or as otherwise prescribed within the clause wording). Where a director is ultimately acquitted within criminal proceedings, it is crucial that the Wrongful Act definition encompasses not just actual Wrongful Acts, but also alleged Wrongful Acts in order to give effect to the above interpretation (as regards alleged, and not just actual, liability). In this respect, where only actual Wrongful Acts are covered, the policy wording may in effect be too narrow as to extend coverage to an acquitted director.[77] It is in practice common for the Wrongful Act definition to encompass "actual, alleged or attempted" defined acts. In order for the Conduct exclusion clause to be invoked, it is probable that either a final adjudication or admission will be required. The acquittal of the director in the underlying proceedings will mean that an adjudication as to liability has not been reached, though the insurer may bring an action against the insured to determine liability.[78] Thus, it is more likely that the insurer will seek to identify an admission.

---

74 'The SFO paid £2.7 million in full and final settlement of any claim by or on behalf of Mr Woods and/or Mr Marshall against the SFO for costs incurred in connection with, or arising out of, the trial, the charges and/ or the investigation. When applying for an adjournment of the trial on 26 April 2021, the SFO had accepted liability for reasonably incurred wasted costs in respect of the trial. The SFO has not accepted liability for any non-trial related costs.' *See* Email from A Abed to author (30 September 2021). This email was a response to a Freedom of Information request made under the Freedom of Information Act 2000 by the author to the Serious Fraud Office on 2 September 2021 (Case FOI2021-111). A Abed is the Information Officer from the Public Relations & Information Team who responded.

75 Jonathan Ames, 'SFO's Serco Fraud Trial Collapses' (*The Times*, 27 April 2021) <https://www.thetimes.co.uk/article/ex-serco-executives-cleared-of-hiding-profits-from-electronic-tagging-contracts-wsx2x3sq9> accessed 27 April 2021.

76 Interestingly, the SFO may become further liable to pay the defence costs of former G4S executives. The SFO chose not to proceed with the trial against three individuals, and in its Annual Report and Accounts of 2022–23 set out that: 'the defendants in the G4S case submitted orders for all recoverable costs incurred by their defence. Hearings and settlement negotiations have not yet taken place'. Though a fixed sum was not set out in the accounts, '[d]ue to the uncertainty on both timing and quantum', it appears that the agency has set aside approximately £6 million. *See* Serious Fraud Office, *Annual Report and Accounts 2022–23* (2023, HC 1473) 34.

77 Unless in separate proceedings it is established that the true nature of the act is not criminal, and instead falls within the definition.

78 An insurer may elect to seek a declaratory judgment, though it will be required to do so in good faith.

Though not technically an acquittal, where a director is granted an immunity notice by prosecutors pursuant to section 71 of the SOCPA 2005, it may be considered that an admission or acknowledgement of wrongdoing excluded by virtue of the Conduct exclusion clause has occurred. The effect of this would be to preclude coverage for defence costs incurred prior to the point at which the immunity notice was served. In such circumstances, whilst it would remain pertinent for the insured to ensure that the provision of defence costs is dependent on alleged (and not just actual) liability (in the event that exclusions do not apply), a Conduct exclusion clause may impact recovery. In order for an immunity notice to be granted, the Attorney General must be consulted, and this process involves comprehensive supporting documentation and consideration of whether the cleansing process has taken place; the cleansing process will require the individual to fully admit their involvement in criminal activity (generally) and may lead to requests to waive LPP.[79] In such circumstances, any costs incurred would likely be excluded by the Conduct exclusion clause, insofar as the policy includes criminal investigations within the Claims definition, and the investigation is into the insured.

An analysis of the Contract exclusion clause would likely follow the same direction as that discussed above in respect of section 74 of the SA 2020. However, section 71 differs from section 74 in that an immunity notice does not require a written agreement between the prosecutor and individual; instead, the individual is offered a written notice, though the individual's compliance is still a requirement. Insofar as this may be deemed at least an agreement, a broadly constructed Contract exclusion may exclude coverage.

14.4 Subrogation

The insurer's rights of subrogation is a general principle of insurance (though it does not arise as a right in co-insurance). However, it is commonplace that such rights are provided for by express terms, and the application of the rights of subrogation 'can be modified, excluded or extended by contract'.[80] Particularly where provided for by express contractual provision, an insurer exercising rights of subrogation must act in good faith.[81] Subrogation applies in relation to contracts of indemnity alone,[82] and ensures that the insured is never more than fully indemnified.[83] The insurer's rights of subrogation arise when the insurer has fully indemnified the insured[84] – which means indemnification in

79 Crown Prosecution Service, 'SOCPA Agreements: Note for Those Representing Assisting Offenders' (n 27).

80 John Birds and Katie Richards, *Birds' Modern Insurance Law* (12th edn, Sweet & Maxwell 2022) para 17-03.

81 ibid para 8-04.

82 A liability insurance policy is a contract of indemnity. *See British Cash and Parcel Conveyors Ltd v Lamson Store Service Company Ltd* [1908] 1 KB 1006 (CA).

83 *Castellain v Preston* (1883) 11 QBD 380 (CA) 386 (Brett LJ). *See also* Padfield (n 45) para 12.1.

'[I]f insurers have paid on a claim and compensation is later paid to the insured, the insurers can recoup their payment by a common law action for money had and received. It is clear that the insurers also have an equitable interest in the compensation itself.' *See* Robert Merkin, *Insurance Law: Doctrines and Principles* (4th edn, Hart Publishing 2022) 355, citing *Lord Napier and Ettrick v Hunter* [1993] AC 713 (HL). Therefore, if the director was to go on to receive payments made in respect of losses incurred as a shareholder, the insurer would be entitled to be subrogated to the rights of the insured to the extent that the benefits relate to a covered loss.

84 Marine Insurance Act 1906, s 79. *See also Castellain v Preston* (n 83) 388 (Brett LJ); *John Edwards & Co v Motor Union Insurance Co Ltd* [1922] 2 KB 249, 254 (McCardie J). To the extent required under the policy: *Lord Napier and Ettrick v Hunter* (n 83).

relation to all claims arising out of the same facts under a single policy[85] – and entitles the insurer to step into the insured's shoes in pursuing any right of action in the insured's name against a third party (which may diminish the loss insured against).[86]

Where the insurer exercises its rights of subrogation on behalf of an insured individual in challenging the company's agreement to a DPA,[87] and likely also the content of the statement of facts, issues may arise in relation to the DPA's terms. A common term amongst all UK DPAs is that the company and representatives of it (where authorised by the company) cannot contest the DPA, nor make statements contradicting its content.[88] In most circumstances, a director accused of committing (or assisting) the corporate wrongdoing which forms the basis of the DPA will not remain with the company; if the director were to remain, the likelihood of the company agreeing the DPA would be very low. Therefore, an insurer exercising the rights of subrogation on behalf of an insured former director would not be considered a breach of the DPA's terms. Two exceptions may arise: firstly, where the director remains with the company; and secondly, where the insurer also insures the company within an ABC policy which provides broader entity coverage under Side C.

In the former instance, should an insurer under a duty to defend policy take over the defence of an insured director who remains with the company (even if thereafter demoted from the directorship role and now an employee),[89] thus representing the individual, the insurer's exercising of its rights of subrogation may be considered to be a breach of the DPA.[90] This will similarly be the case within a duty to indemnify policy, as an insurer exercising its rights of subrogation does so in the insured's name, and with the insured's consent.[91] Breach will be considered if the company is deemed to have authorised the individual's contest of the DPA contents, which may arise whereby the company expressly

85 *Page v Scottish Insurance Corporation Ltd* (1929) 33 Ll L Rep 134 (CA). *See also* Padfield (n 45) para 12.3.

86 Not provided for by section 79 of the Marine Insurance Act 1906 but demanded by equity: Rob Merkin and Aybüke Naz Durmuş, 'Subrogation of Maritime Claims' (2022) NUS Law Working Paper 2022/018, 6 <https://papers.ssrn.com/sol3/papers.cfm?abstract_id=4257360> accessed 27 March 2023. 'The insurer and the insured are one': *Mason v Sainsbury* (1782) 3 Doug 61, 65 (Buller J). The European Court of Justice has set out that the subrogated insurer possesses the same rights as the insured whose shoes it has stepped within, and thus the law which governs the action is, in principle, that of the country in which that damage occurs: Case C-264/22 *Fonds de Garantie des Victimes des Actes de Terrorisme and d'Autres Infractions v Victoria Seguros SA* [2023] Lloyd's Rep IR Plus 24. As a side note, an insurer may pursue the individual insured for recoupment where payment is made (for example, by advancement of defence costs) for losses which transpire to be non-covered.

87 '[B]y indemnifying the insured, the insurer retains the right to proceed against … any third party whose conduct has wrongfully caused the insured to incur insured defence costs.' *See* Paolini and Nambisan (n 26) para 1.34.

88 *See for example* Serious Fraud Office, 'Amec Foster Wheeler Energy Limited – Deferred Prosecution Agreement' (*Serious Fraud Office*, 2 July 2021) <https://www.sfo.gov.uk/download/amec-foster-wheeler-energy-limited-deferred-prosecution-agreement/> accessed 2 July 2021, para 48.

89 If the individual is demoted to such a level that they would no longer be covered for new Claims under a D&O policy, the "Claims made" nature of D&O (and any notifications previously made) will mean that coverage is not necessarily outrightly excluded.

90 This may also apply in a duty to indemnify policy where the insured director complies with its (typically agreed) obligation to assist the insurer in exercising its rights of subrogation.

91 Unless compelled by the court, which is the subject of some debate but principally in respect of an employer's right of action being subrogated to the insurer as against an employee. In any event, where compelled by the court, this will not be considered to be authorised by the company if publicly repudiated. *See Morris v Ford Motor Co* [1973] 1 QB 792 (CA) 801; *Lister v Romford Ice and Cold Storage Co Ltd* [1957] AC 555 (HL).

permits such contest, or where the company fails to publicly repudiate the individual's position.[92]

The insurer is under an obligation to act in good faith (and, certainly in a duty to defend policy, in the insured's best interests in defence),[93] and therefore there may be some consideration as to the impact of the exercising of the rights of subrogation. For example, where the individual remains a director of the company and the consequence of the insurer's exercising of the rights of subrogation is DPA breach, this may be considered to constitute a breach of the director's duties to the company (such as the duty to act in a way in which they in good faith consider 'would be most likely to promote the success of the company for the benefit of its members as a whole', though subjective)[94] and therefore adverse to the director's best interests (particularly where acquitted in criminal proceedings). To this extent, the insurer's rights of subrogation in DPA-related circumstances can be considered to be restricted.

In respect of the second exception referenced, rights of subrogation are impacted by co-insurance. The manner in which such rights are impacted has been the subject of debate for some time. This was first considered to be on the basis of circuity of action, where a co-insured receives indemnification for a covered loss under a policy and then, by virtue of a right of action that co-insured holds against another co-insured, the insurer exercises its rights of subrogation in a claim under which that latter co-insured would also be entitled to indemnification.[95] Further cases sought to rely not upon circuity of action, with situations arising whereby the issue of circuity might not arise (for example, where multiple co-insureds incur liability but only one co-insured incurs an insured loss), but instead upon the basis of an exclusion of such rights by way of an implied term in the insurance contract or policy.[96] The fundamental basis for the implied term is an understanding between co-insureds that, should liabilities arise between them, the right of action will not be exercised amongst co-insureds. The prospect of such exercised claims, thus necessitating the implied term, was by Lord Bingham (in *obiter*) observed as an 'obvious absurdity'.[97] Lord Justice Elias observed that such an implied term would '[make] express what the parties must have intended'.[98]

Later cases have looked to the intention of the parties in respect of the liability to one another as co-insureds, on the basis of the construction of the contract (thus not

92 *See for example* Serious Fraud Office, 'Amec Foster Wheeler Energy Limited – Deferred Prosecution Agreement' (n 88) para 48.

93 *Travelers Insurance Co Ltd v XYZ* [2019] UKSC 48; *Groom v Crocker* [1939] 1 KB 194 (CA); *K/S Merc-Scandia XXXXII v Certain Lloyd's Underwriters (The Mercandian Continent)* [2001] EWCA Civ 1275. *See also* Malcolm Clarke and Bariş Soyer, *The Insurance Act 2015: A New Regime for Commercial and Marine Insurance Law* (Informa Law 2017) 48; Padfield (n 45) para 9.13; Birds and Richards (n 80) para 8-04.

94 If, for example, the director is readily compliant with the insurer's exercising of its rights of subrogation. *See* Companies Act 2006, s 172(1).

95 *Siebe Gorman & Co Ltd v Barclays Bank Ltd (The Yasin)* [1979] 2 Lloyd's Rep 45. *See also Petrofina Ltd v Magnaload Ltd* [1984] 1 QB 127, 139–140. This has since been criticised in *Gard Marine & Energy Ltd v China National Chartering Co Ltd (The Ocean Victory)* [2015] EWCA Civ 1464.

96 *Stone Vickers Ltd v Appledore Ferguson Shipbuilders Ltd* [1991] 2 Lloyd's Rep 288; *National Oilwell (UK) v Davy Offshore Ltd* [1993] 2 Lloyd's Rep 582 (CA).

97 *Co-Operative Retail Services Limited v Taylor Young Partnership* [2002] UKHL 17 [7] (Lord Bingham). *See also* Özlem Gürses, *Marine Insurance Law* (2nd edn, Routledge 2017) 290.

98 *Rathbone Brothers plc v Novae Corporate Underwriting Ltd* (n 45) [85].

necessitating in all cases an implied term).[99] A contractual interpretation approach has been adopted, and 'an implied term cannot withstand express language to the contrary':[100] if the underlying contract provides for liability between co-insureds, this will take precedence over such an implied term. The general principle is that, contractual expression aside, an insurer cannot exercise subrogation rights in respect of a policy taken out for the benefit of joint insureds.[101]

Furthermore, (contractual expression aside) any implied term restricting actions between co-insureds would apply in respect of disputes arising for insured losses, and consequently would *not* negate rights of subrogation in respect of those *not* insured. According to the general principle that, by the operation of subrogation, a co-insured is precluded from claiming against another co-insured, it is important to observe that this does not encompass claims that fall outside of the scope of the policy (for example, those excluded by virtue of public policy,[102] or a Conduct exclusion clause).[103] Whilst acknowledging the advancement in approach since, in respect of subrogation and co-insurance, this position can be somewhat reconciled with the rationale of the theoretical concept of circuity of action, as well as the subsequently considered implied term. Thus, where loss is incurred but falls outside of the scope of the policy (and thus the insurer is not liable for the loss), a right of action of one co-insured arising against another co-insured will not restrict the insurer's rights of subrogation.

Furthermore, whether an insurer can exercise its subrogation rights in claiming against the co-insured company or another co-insured director, in respect of the corporate DPA underlying offending, will depend on whether a right of action of the insured against the co-insured arises,[104] and whether the loss incurred was caused by excluded misconduct by that co-insured or, if not, the rights of subrogation are permitted by the underlying contract. Where the corporate agrees a DPA on the basis of such criminal conduct, the insurer may then exercise its rights of subrogation in claiming against it where the co-insured would have a cause of action (for example, where it is suggested that the company misled the prosecution and court in its statement of facts). Most D&O policies will contain a term outlining the insurer's rights of subrogation in express form.[105] Such a term may

99 An intention to allow for such liability would mean that there would be no implied term to the effect of excluding rights of subrogation.

100 *Gard Marine & Energy Ltd v China National Chartering Co Ltd (The Ocean Victory)* [2017] UKSC 35. *See also Co-Operative Retail Services Limited v Taylor Young Partnership* (n 97); *Tyco Fire & Integrated Solutions (UK) Ltd v Rolls Royce Motor Cars Ltd* [2008] EWCA Civ 286 [77] (Rix LJ). An implied term excluding rights of subrogation was made in the case of *Rathbone Brothers plc v Novae Corporate Underwriting Ltd* (n 45), though this can be attributed to the particulars of the facts of the case, and the principle set out by Rix LJ was not criticised.

101 The determinative question is whether the policy was taken out for the benefit of the co-insured against whom the insurer wishes to exercise its rights of subrogation of the part of the insured. *See Mark Rowlands Ltd v Berni Inns* [1986] QB 211 (CA); cf *Lister v Romford Ice and Cold Storage Co Ltd* (n 91). *See also Cape Distribution Limited v Cape Intermediate Holdings Plc* [2016] EWHC 1119 (QB) [174]–[181] (Picken J).

102 *Burrows v Rhodes* (n 32). *See also Beresford v Royal Insurance Co* (n 19). *See also* Paolini and Nambisan (n 26) para 4.04.

103 *National Oilwell (UK) Ltd v Davy Offshore Ltd* (n 96) 614–616 (Colman J); *Netherlands v Youell* [1997] 2 Lloyd's Rep 440 (QB) 450–451 (Rix J). *See also* Padfield (n 45) para 12.4.

104 The right arises where a third party is liable for the loss. *See MH Smith (Plant Hire) Ltd v DL Mainwaring (t/a Inshore)* [1986] 2 Lloyd's Rep 244 (CA) 246 (Kerr LJ). This also includes benefits received by the insured that relate to the loss, including compensation.

105 Most policies will also bear an Insured vs Insured exclusion, which limits the insured's ability to adversely impact the insurer's rights of subrogation. *See Tyco Fire & Integrated Solutions (UK) Ltd v Rolls*

exclude or modify some of the common law principles, and the correct approach is to first consider the parties' contractual rights, and thereafter to revert to general subrogation principles only upon the construing of a term which is ambiguous or not all-embracing.[106] Issues of co-insurance and subrogation will not arise where the director obtains Side A coverage independently of an ABC policy, nor where the company obtains Side C coverage independently.[107]

Royce Motor Cars Ltd (n 100) [18] (Rix LJ): in joint insurance there is an implied term that co-insureds will not claim against each other in respect of losses covered under the joint policy, '"however, the position might be different if on the express terms of their contract, one party might be liable to indemnify the other for its breach, default or negligence"'.

106 *Lucas v Exports Credit Guarantee Department* [1974] 1 WLR 909 (HL). *See also* Birds and Richards (n 80).

107 Despite the fact that the company may have purchased the director's Side A coverage. *See CSE Aviation Ltd v Cardale Doors Ltd* (QBD (Comm), 13 April 2000): 'Subrogation does not look to the person who paid the premium, it identifies the assured upon whose shoulders liability rests and on whose behalf the compensation payments have been made.'

CHAPTER 15

Advancement of defence costs

15.1 Policy construction

15.1.1 Duty to defend

Where there is a duty upon the insurer to defend the insured ("duty to defend"), the preclusion of coverage at the stage of defence is very unlikely. The general principle is that duty to defend policies, being broader than duty to indemnify (also known as "non-duty to defend") policies, require the insurer to defend *potentially* covered claims, though this does not extend to *non*-covered claims.[1] An advancement will not be necessary in duty to defend policies, since the insurer is in charge of the defence. This is effected by a "Claims control" clause (or similar wording) with mandatory wording (thus imposing the duty). This form of compulsory agency requires that the insurer directs any litigation in the insured's interests and not the insurer's;[2] in defending an insured, the insurer must act in good faith.[3]

An insured will be required to cooperate with their defence and thus to comply with any requests made by the insurer for information and documentation relevant to the Claim or Circumstance notified.[4] The disclosure will be that which is 'reasonably required' by the insurer in the particular circumstances of the case.[5] An insured is not, therefore, entitled to interfere with the conduct of proceedings.[6] Notably, an invoked Insured vs Insured exclusion will likely disclaim the insurer's duty to defend.[7] In practice, D&O policies

1 *Montrose Chemical Corp v Superior Court* 6 Cal 4th 287, 295 (Cal 1993); *Buss v Superior Court* 16 Cal 4th 35, 47–48 (Cal 1997); *S Cal Pizza Co v Certain Underwriters at Lloyd's* 40 Cal App 5th 140, 252 Cal Rptr 3d 639, 639–640 (Cal Ct App 2019); *Wyeth & Brothers Ltd v Cigna Insurance Co of Europe SA-NV* [2001] EWCA Civ 175.

2 *Travelers Insurance Co Ltd v XYZ* [2019] UKSC 48. *See also* Alison Padfield, *Insurance Claims* (5th edn, Bloomsbury Professional 2021) para 9.13.

3 *Groom v Crocker* [1939] 1 KB 194 (CA); *K/S Merc-Scandia XXXXII v Certain Lloyd's Underwriters (The Mercandian Continent)* [2001] EWCA Civ 1275. *See also* Malcolm Clarke and Bariş Soyer, *The Insurance Act 2015: A New Regime for Commercial and Marine Insurance Law* (Informa Law 2017).

4 *Denso Manufacturing UK Ltd v Great Lakes Reinsurance (UK) plc* [2017] EWHC 391 (Comm) [45]–[48]; *Parker v National Farmers Union Mutual Insurance Society Ltd* [2012] EWHC 2156 (Comm) [189] (Teare J). *See also* Padfield (n 2) para 9.13.

5 *Ted Baker plc v AXA Insurance UK plc (No 2)* [2014] EWHC 3548 (Comm) [108] (Eder J).

6 *Groom v Crocker* (n 3) 202–203 (Lord Greene MR).

7 cf *Chartrand v Illinois Union Insurance Co* 2009 WL 2776484 (ND Cal Aug 28 2009).

DOI: 10.4324/9781003456964-18

rarely include a duty to defend,[8] particularly in respect of public companies.[9] Unlike New York law,[10] there exists no duty to defend within UK law unless contractually expressed.[11]

15.1.2 Duty to indemnify

Duty to indemnify policies typically provide that the insurer is able to participate in the settlement of the claim ("right to defend"), but only *covered* defence costs must be advanced.[12] Where *potentially* covered defence costs are advanced in duty to indemnify policies,[13] a later determination that the costs are *non*-covered will require their repayment to the insurer.[14] In duty to indemnify policies, the insured must obtain the consent of the insurer prior to incurring defence costs, and this consent shall not be unreasonably withheld/delayed by the insurer.[15] Where consent is not obtained prior to incurring defence costs, the insurer will not be required to pay the amount.[16] Furthermore, defence costs will usually be considered "reasonable and necessary fees, costs and expenses" (or similar) and the insurer will be required to pay them within a reasonable time.[17]

The provision for advancement of defence costs within a duty to indemnify policy may be mandatory or discretionary. Whether mandatory or discretionary, a Claim must have been made against the insured so as to trigger coverage under the policy, and the insurer remains able to refuse advancement on other grounds (for example, nondisclosure) unless expressly stated.[18] Furthermore, any defence costs advanced remain subject to the

8 '"[D&O] policies generally do not obligate the carrier to provide the insured with a defense."' *See US Telepacific Corp v US Specialty Insurance Co* No CV 18-5083-DMG (AGRx), at 3 (9th Cir July 19 2019), citing *Helfand v National Union Fire Ins Co* 10 Cal App 4th 869 (1992) 879. *See also* Larry Goanos, *D&O 101: Understanding Directors and Officers Liability Insurance* (Wells Media Group Inc 2014) 104.

9 'While duty to defend policies are somewhat common among private companies, public companies typically have a non-duty to defend policies.' *See* Lawrence Trautman and Kara Altenbaumer-Price, 'D&O Insurance: A Primer' (2012) 1(2) AUBLR 337, 351.

10 In addition, under Californian law: 'the duty to defend is a creature of contract—if a given insurance policy disclaims it, no such duty will be imposed on the insurer.' *See US Telepacific Corp v US Specialty Insurance Co* (n 8) 3, citing *Buss v Superior Court* (n 1) 47.

11 *AstraZeneca Insurance Co Ltd v XL Insurance (Bermuda) Ltd* [2013] EWHC 349 (Comm) [28] (Flaux J).

12 *Hulton & Co v Mountain* (1929) 28 LILR 249 (CA); *Wilkie v Gordian Runoff Ltd* [2005] HCA 17. *See also* Adolfo Paolini and Deepak Nambisan, *Directors' and Officers' Liability Insurance* (Informa Law 2008) para 1.31. In *Newcastle Resources Pty Ltd (formerly known as SCE Resources Pty Ltd) v Certain Underwriters at Lloyd's Syndicate CVS 1919* [2022] NSWSC 1485, the insurer had originally taken on the defence of the insured (though was not under a duty to defend), and later ceased doing so, which prompted the insured to seek a declaration that the insurer was required to pay defence costs. It was held that the insured was only entitled to defence costs for covered claims. However, as the clause stated that the insurer 'will pay' defence costs 'incurred', the insurer was obliged to pay defence costs contemporaneously, subject to the right of recoupment.

13 Likely, where contractually provided for. *See US Telepacific Corp v US Specialty Insurance Co* (n 8) 4.

14 In a 2020 US decision, policy wording allowed for the advancement of defence costs for only covered claims, and thus did not include 'potentially covered claims'. *See US Telepacific Corp v US Specialty Insurance Company* No 19-55828, at 2 (9th Cir Jun 17 2020).

15 *Poole Harbour Yacht Club Marina Ltd v Excess Insurance Co* [2001] Lloyd's Rep IR 580 (QB). *See also* Paolini and Nambisan (n 12) para 8.37.

16 *Antico v Fielding Australia Pty Ltd* [1997] HCA 35. *See also* Paolini and Nambisan (n 12) para 8.42.

17 'It is an implied term of every contract of insurance that if the insured makes a claim under the contract, the insurer must pay any sums due in respect of the claim within a reasonable time.' *See* Insurance Act 2015, s 13A(1).

18 *Onley v Catlin Syndicate Ltd as the Underwriting Member of Lloyd's Syndicate 2003* [2018] FCAFC 119 [52].

insurer's right of recoupment (if, for example, it later transpires that coverage was to be precluded for the underlying Claim *and including* defence costs).[19]

Where advancement is mandatory, costs are advanced as incurred by the insured: this has been termed the "contemporaneous advancement principle".[20] Though a mandatory obligation on the insurer, this may be departed from where an exclusion clause is triggered.[21] However, the exclusion must *actually* be triggered. In *Wilkie v Gordian RunOff Ltd*,[22] a Conduct exclusion requiring a determination "in fact" could not be invoked to refuse advancement where such a determination had not occurred.[23] This was due to the fact that the advancement provision was set out by way of extension to the main insuring clause. As the advancement provision was a separate undertaking and therefore not provided for within the definition of Loss, the provision was not *prima facie* therefore bound by the fate of the exclusions applicable to the main insuring clause.[24] Though the advancement provision outlined a right of recoupment to the insurer upon a later determination that the Claim was not covered – which may well have been based upon the Conduct exclusion clause – the Conduct exclusion clause was 'insusceptible of a notional anticipatory and completed operation to disengage'[25] the extension at the point of advancement. Notably, the Conduct exclusion clause was the sole basis upon which the insurer refused to advance defence costs and no argument was made as to nondisclosure.[26]

Where advancement is discretionary, costs are advanced at the insurer's discretion or (depending on policy wording) when not in dispute between the insurer and insured.[27] In *Silbermann v CGU Insurance Ltd*,[28] the court held by a 2:1 majority that a discretionary obligation permitted the insurer to refuse advancement on the basis of an allegation of dishonesty/fraud made against the insured, despite the fact that the relevant Conduct exclusion clause required that such conduct be established by judgment or final adjudication in order to be invoked.[29] However, the discretion in this case was limited as the court held that it 'could only be exercised where there were realistic grounds to believe that the directors had acted dishonestly',[30] such was the requirement of the policy's "Dishonesty exclusion". In line with the principle of utmost good faith (implied into the contract by the Insurance Contracts Act 1984 (Cth)), any defence by the insurer would need to be based on reasonable grounds.[31]

Notably, the provision for advancement of defence costs in *Silbermann* was an extension of the main insuring clause. Justice of Appeal Hodgson in dissent held that the inclusion of defence costs within the definition of Loss in the main insuring clause meant that

19 Where defence costs are incurred in criminal proceedings and the director is ultimately convicted (for example).

20 The concept of contemporaneous advancement/payment was discussed in *Little v MGIC Indem Corp* 836 F 2d 789 (3d Cir 1987).

21 Some Contract exclusion clauses permit defence costs cover; however an invoked Conduct exclusion will not typically do so.

22 *Wilkie v Gordian Runoff Ltd* (n 12).

23 ibid; Paolini and Nambisan (n 12) paras 8.28–8.30.

24 *Wilkie v Gordian Runoff Ltd* (n 12) [19], [23]–[25], [32]–[34], [42].

25 ibid [44].

26 ibid [10].

27 *US Telepacific Corp v US Specialty Insurance Company* (n 14) 3.

28 *Silbermann v CGU Insurance Ltd* [2003] NSWCA 203.

29 ibid; Paolini and Nambisan (n 12) para 8.26.

30 Paolini and Nambisan (n 12) para 8.26.

31 *Silbermann v CGU Insurance Ltd* (n 28) [51], [78].

the insurer only had discretion as to timing of payment.[32] Whereas, the majority held that the extension of indemnity provided for by the advancement provision was a discretionary obligation on the insurer *irrespective* of any underlying dispute as to indemnity within the main insuring clause.[33] A crucial difference between *Wilkie* and *Silbermann* is that, though in both policies the provision for advancement of defence costs was by way of extension to the main insuring clause, the *Wilkie* provision imposed a mandatory obligation of advancement on the insurer, whereas the *Silbermann* provision imposed only a discretionary obligation. Unlike the contemporaneous advancement principle seen in cases of mandatory advancement, *Silbermann* set out that the discretionary obligation did not intend that coverage must be provided upfront:[34] advancement of defence costs was at the insurer's discretion, though any indicated confirmation to indemnify would need to be honoured. Such a discretionary obligation entitled the insurer to refuse advancement, and the insurer would be permitted to seek judgment against the insured in order to refuse coverage.[35] Any advancement made would be subject to the insurer's right to recoupment.

15.2 Refusal of advancement

15.2.1 Defence costs provision

The provision for "Defence Costs" is 'generally regarded as ancillary to the main insuring clause',[36] that is, defence costs cover typically accompanies the main insuring clause by forming part of the definition of Loss. A provision for "Advancement of Defence Costs" is typically provided for by extension to the main insuring clause (irrespective of whether "Defence Costs" are provided by way of separate undertaking),[37] and thus will be subject to certain definitions and exclusions within it. Foremost, a Claim must be made against the insured and notified so as to trigger coverage. It may also be that allocation of defence costs forms a precondition to cover, thus to be agreed prior to advancement. Other restrictions may apply to the advancement provision: for example, the company may be first required to advance, with the insurer providing a "back up" role where this is not effected.[38]

In respect of the insurer's ability to rely upon an exclusion clause within the policy to refuse an advancement of defence costs, this will depend on policy wording. Though not strictly concerning an advancement, an exclusion actually invoked in respect of coverage under a duty to defend policy may disclaim the insurer's duty; the insurer is required to defend *potentially* covered claims, but not *non*-covered claims.[39] Under a duty to indemnify policy, it will be crucial to determine whether the insurer's obligation to advance

32 ibid [49] (Hodgson JA).

33 ibid [69]–[70] (Tobias JA).

34 ibid [77] (Tobias JA).

35 ibid.

36 Paolini and Nambisan (n 12) para 8.21.

37 The default position is that defence costs are *not* provided as a separate undertaking. *See* ibid para 8.07, citing *Wyeth & Brothers Ltd v Cigna Insurance Co of Europe SA-NV* (n 1).

38 Paolini and Nambisan (n 12) para 8.21, citing Rosenberg, Sigelko and Miller, *D&O Liability Insurance – Coverage, Liability and Advice Issues* (American Bar Association 1996) 18.

39 *Montrose Chemical Corp v Superior Court* (n 1) 295; *Buss v Superior Court* (n 1) 47–48; *S Cal Pizza Co v Certain Underwriters at Lloyd's* (n 1) 639–640. *See also Australasian Correctional Services Pty Ltd v AIG Australia Ltd* [2018] FCA 2043 [35] (Allsop CJ): 'The contractual responsibility is, however, to defend the suit, reinforced by the contractual obligation to pay **all** expenses incurred by the **insurer** in undertaking defence of the suit. This obligation to defend the suit will arise if a claim in the suit could come within the cover and, on

defence costs is mandatory or discretionary. In any event, an insured will be in a better position if the relevant exclusion (focussing predominantly here on the Conduct exclusion) requires only a final adjudication to be invoked, and is not so broad as to encompass admissions/acknowledgements by the insured.

A policy imposing mandatory advancement obligations on the insurer will require any exclusion sought to be relied upon in defence to be *actually* invoked.[40] In *Wilkie*, an adjudication was necessary to invoke the Conduct exclusion clause. This will typically mean, particularly where only an adjudication is sought, that the underlying Claim will have concluded prior to dispute regarding indemnification of defence costs (thus, the dispute is more likely to arise in regard to *repayment* by the insured, than contemporaneous payment by the insurer).[41] A limitation on the ability to refuse advancement on the basis of an exclusion clause will not usually limit the insurer's entitlement to raise a separate defence, for example, in refusing advancement on the basis of the insured's nondisclosure, unless expressly agreed.[42] A policy imposing discretionary advancement obligations on the insured may empower the insurer to refuse advancements based upon allegations of Wrongful Acts (where constituting a notified Claim), without requiring a final adjudication or admission. In *Silbermann*, it was set out that the insurer could refuse advancement where it had reasonable grounds to do so, with realistic grounds to believe that the basis of the exclusion would apply (for example, realistic grounds to believe that the insured had been dishonest, within such a worded Conduct exclusion).

Thus, it can be observed that a discretionary advancement obligation poses a significantly exacerbated risk upon the insured where a corporate DPA has already been agreed, and especially so where its published contents are particularly damaging as regards the insured. A DPA statement of facts referring to an insured by name and setting out purported misconduct committed by the insured may provide a basis upon which the insurer elects to refuse advancement in the insured's own related proceedings, likely with self-considered reasonable grounds for doing so. The statement of facts is unlikely to be verified by the insured accused of wrongdoing within it (**Section 8.3.1**),[43] and is not subject to the same evidential scrutiny as may be seen in a jury trial (however, it remains subject to a reduced prosecutorial evidential test[44] and judicial approval (though the facts are

the plain words, must extend to the whole suit.' *See also* Robert Merkin, *Colinvaux's Law of Insurance* (12th edn, Sweet & Maxwell 2019) para 21-172.

40 *Evolution Precast Systems Pty Ltd v Chubb Insurance Australia Ltd* [2020] FCA 1690 [70] (Derrington J).

41 Where required in the underlying Claim.

42 *Onley v Catlin Syndicate Ltd as the Underwriting Member of Lloyd's Syndicate 2003* (n 18) [52].

43 A director suspected of implication within the wrongdoing will likely not be permitted to remain within the company in order for DPA negotiations to be effective, and would certainly not be able to participate actively in such negotiations. *See* Serious Fraud Office, 'Deferred Prosecution Agreements' (*Serious Fraud Office*, 23 October 2020) <https://www.sfo.gov.uk/publications/guidance-policy-and-protocols/sfo-operational-handbook/deferred-prosecution-agreements/> accessed 23 October 2020.

44 Either the Full Code Test in the Code for Crown Prosecutors, or '[p]rosecutors must be satisfied and record that … upon some admissible evidence that P has committed the offence, and there are reasonable grounds for believing that a continued investigation would provide further admissible evidence within a reasonable period of time, so that all the evidence together would be capable of establishing a realistic prospect of conviction in accordance with the Full Code Test'. *See* Crown Prosecution Service and Serious Fraud Office, 'Deferred Prosecution Agreements Code of Practice' (*Crown Prosecution Service*, 11 February 2014) <https://www.cps.gov.uk/sites/default/files/documents/publications/dpa_cop.pdf> accessed 9 June 2020, para 1.2(i).

not verified by the judge)).[45] This not only highlights the far-reaching harm of naming (or identification) within corporate DPAs, but also the need for insureds in such circumstances to ensure that the Advancement of Defence Costs provision is sufficiently robust.

15.2.2 Insurer's ability to conduct its own investigation

The insurer is entitled to conduct its own investigation into a claim by way of 'investigation into the facts on which [it is] based',[46] 'and look at the true nature of the claim to see the real underlying basis for the insured's liability'.[47] An insurer, where the corporate DPA has been approved and documentation published, may look to the DPA and particularly the statement of facts in order to determine whether there is a basis upon which to refuse an advancement of defence costs to the insured. Where a Claim would otherwise be covered, an insurer will likely seek to rely upon an exclusion clause in order to decline an advancement.

Where an insurer seeks to refuse an advancement on the basis that it has purportedly looked at the true nature of the claim and root of the insured's liability, the insured individual may in certain circumstances counter this point; this will particularly be the case where an insurer is under a mandatory obligation to advance. For example, where an insurer seeks to determine the insured's liability prior to conclusion of criminal proceedings against the insured themselves, the insured may argue that the root of their liability does not amount to criminal misconduct (which would ultimately, upon sufficient judicial determination, be non-covered) or dishonesty, but instead equates to negligence or another covered form of civil liability. When the former directors of Tesco Stores Ltd faced trial post-corporate DPA, it was determined that the disputed accounting practices were not criminal in nature, but were improper.[48] In similar cases, conduct may be deemed negligent or in breach of the directors' duties (as opposed to criminal), but in such instances defence costs would likely be covered under a typical D&O policy. Thus, whilst the insurer may seek to rely upon the corporate DPA statement of facts, the insured may have reasonable grounds for refuting any attempted declination of advancement.

45 'The parties should resolve any factual issues necessary to allow the court to agree terms of the DPA on a clear, fair and accurate basis. The court does not have the power to adjudicate upon factual differences in DPA proceedings.' *See* ibid para 6.2. *See also Director of the Serious Fraud Office v Amec Foster Wheeler Limited* [2021] Lloyd's Rep FC 353 (Crown) [11]. 'My approval of the DPA is simply a confirmation of those facts, the facts being admitted by [the defendant]'. *See Serious Fraud Office v Serco Geografix Ltd* [2019] Lloyd's Rep FC 518 (Crown) [29].

46 *AstraZeneca Insurance Co Ltd v XL Insurance (Bermuda) Ltd* [2013] EWHC (n 11) [43].

47 '[T]he insurers could go behind the form of the claim in the pleading and look at the true nature of the claim to see the real underlying basis for the insured's liability.' *See* ibid [53], citing *McDonnell Information Systems Ltd v Swinbank* [1998] All ER (D) 410 (QB) (Mance J); *MDIS Ltd (formerly McDonnell Information Systems Ltd) v Swinbank* [1999] All ER (D) 815 (CA) (Peter Gibson, Judge and Clarke LJJ), citing *West Wake Price & Co v Ching* [1957] 1 WLR 45 (QB). *See also* Vanessa Finch, 'Personal Accountability and Corporate Control: The Role of Directors' and Officers' Liability Insurance' (1994) 57(6) Mod L Rev 880, 889.

48 'Thus, some of the income may have been "improperly recognised" on the basis that it was commercially unwise, was not in accordance with best accounting practice or failed to meet company policy but was not necessarily unlawfully recognised … importantly, all [witnesses] were clear that they were not aware of any unlawfully booked income or the use of false documentation at the relevant time.' *See R v Bush* [2019] EWCA Crim 29 [125] (Lady Justice Hallett DBE).

15.2.3 Use of DPA statement of facts

Individual prosecutions tend to follow the corporate DPA. As a result, the DPA and related documentation – including the statement of facts – are often publicly available by the time the proceedings arise. There has been a greater shift more recently in imposing reporting restrictions on certain parts of the DPA and in (temporarily, in some cases)[49] anonymising the attached statement of facts. However, there is no clear precedent requiring such anonymisation and, with relatively few cases to consider (only 13 UK DPAs agreed thus far), it remains possible that the statement of facts may – as they have before – be published in a manner which identifies implicated individuals prior to the individuals' trial (**Section 8.3**).[50] Where this occurs, an insurer may seek to rely upon the statement of facts, or the DPA itself, to refuse an advancement of defence costs to an insured individual.

Most Conduct exclusion clauses are prefaced with the words "the Insurer shall not be liable for any Loss arising out of, based upon or attributable to" (or similar), which vastly restricts coverage for the insured and broadens the scope of the clause. Furthermore, it will be in the insured's interests to ensure that the exclusion is not invoked.

15.2.3.1 Conduct exclusion – admission

The primary means by which an insurer is likely to refuse advancement to an insured director is by invoking the Conduct exclusion clause. The Conduct exclusion clause almost always relies upon a "final adjudication or judgment" in order to be triggered, but many also allow for an "admission" or "acknowledgement" of the precluded wrongdoing. At the point in which an advancement in respect of criminal proceedings is sought, a final adjudication is unlikely to be relied upon (at least, in the underlying proceedings). It may be the case that an adverse judgment in civil proceedings based upon the same misconduct provides sufficient basis for an insurer to refuse coverage on the basis of the Conduct exclusion; most Conduct exclusions are broadly worded in respect of the final adjudication requirement and do not specifically require a final adjudication in the underlying

---

49 'Paragraph 12 of Schedule 17 says that the court may order that the publication of information by the prosecutor under paragraph 8(7) be postponed for such period as the court considers necessary if it appears to the court that postponement is necessary for avoiding a substantial risk of prejudice to the administration of justice in any legal proceedings … I will hear submissions as to the extent of that order from the parties when they have seen what is deployed in open court. In particular, I will hear submissions about the anonymised Statement of Facts once counsel for the individuals have read it. For now, it is covered by the reporting restriction order, and must not be published by the SFO in pursuance of its statutory duty until further order.' *See Amec Foster Wheeler Limited* (n 45) [4] (Edis LJ).

50 This occurred in the Standard Bank DPA (2015). Although the individuals were in other jurisdictions and their own proceedings would not be heard in the UK, policy concerns remain. Following the Standard Bank DPA, an investigation by the Tanzanian Prevention and Combating of Corruption Bureau led to the arrest of five individuals (three of whom were mentioned within the UK DPA by name). Following the amendment of Tanzanian legislation in September 2019 which permitted plea bargain agreements, such agreements were negotiated and agreed between the Director of Public Prosecutions and the five individuals. However, in 2016, it had been reported that Shose Sinare (one of those named in the UK DPA) was suing Stanbic Bank and Standard Bank in Tanzania in regard to misrepresentations and falsehoods within the DPA process, which is presumed to have been an action in defamation. There is no reported result of the action, though Sinare's subsequent plea bargain agreement would suggest that this would not have presented a successful result. *See* Basel Institute on Governance, 'From the UK's First Deferred Prosecution Agreement to a Plea Bargain in Tanzania' (*Basel Institute on Governance*, 9 September 2020) <https://baselgovernance.org/news/uks-first-deferred-prosecution-agreement-plea-bargain-tanzania> accessed 2 February 2021; Daily News, 'Shose Sinare Seeks 30m US Dollars Damages from Stanbic' (*Daily News*, 2 March 2016) <https://allafrica.com/stories/201603021200.html> accessed 1 February 2021.

proceedings. Should the clause require a "final adjudication or judgment", it may also be the case that the insurer seeks a declaratory judgment against the insured in order to invoke the exclusion, though doing so may come at some reputational price in respect of the insurer's willingness to protect its insureds. Where a final adjudication has not been obtained, it is likely that the insurer will look to establish an admission in order to trigger the exclusion clause. The wording of the exclusion clause will be crucial in respect of the protection extended to the insured following a corporate DPA.

Insureds will need to take forensic notice of the root of the admission and determine whether an admission "by any Insured", "by the Insured", or "by the Insured Person" (for example) is required, as each may be interpreted as bearing different meanings. Where the phrase "by any Insured" is used, it is likely that the clause will be read as bearing a broad scope, and therefore any admission to the wrongdoing by any insured under the policy may suffice. In these circumstances, the DPA statement of facts may be relied upon to preclude coverage to the insured individual, particularly where the policy is not composite. Part of the DPA negotiation process (in which the individual will most likely have no, or very little, involvement) will be the drafting of the statement of facts, an extensive document outlining details of the wrongdoing which forms part of the DPA. There is no adjudication or assessment of the facts during the court proceedings which form part of the DPA process, and therefore the prosecutor and company must agree on the content within the statement of facts.[51] The statement of facts does not require formal admission of wrongdoing by the company, but the company 'must admit the contents and meaning of key documents referred to in the statement of facts'.[52] Further, the statement of facts is considered an admission by the company under section 10 of the CJA 1967 in criminal proceedings brought against it for the relevant offence (for example, should a DPA not be agreed).[53]

On the basis that the statement of facts in its entirety is often deemed to be an "admission" and is likely to be so by the insurer, coverage extended to the company (under Side C) may be precluded irrespective of whether the insurer has seen its full contents.[54] In respect of an individual insured, coverage may be precluded where the statement of facts is anonymised but individuals remain identifiable as a result of jigsaw identification. On the basis that there is a written admission by *an* insured – where the company is insured under the D&O policy – the exclusion clause may be invoked to refuse coverage to any insured on the basis of the same underlying excluded conduct. Where the director's prosecution relates to the corporate DPA, it is likely that the basis will be the same underlying conduct and the director may even represent the "directing mind and will" with which the corporate's offence was established (if it is an identification principle offence, such as fraud). An individual insured's exposure will be further increased where the exclusion clause can also be established by "acknowledgement" of any insured of excluded conduct.

51 *Amec Foster Wheeler Limited* (n 45) [11]–[12] (Edis LJ).

52 Serious Fraud Office, 'Deferred Prosecution Agreements' (n 43).

53 Crown Prosecution Service and Serious Fraud Office, 'Deferred Prosecution Agreements Code of Practice' (n 44) para 6.4; Crime and Courts Act 2013, sch 17 para 13(2).

54 An admission may be 'evidence (for instance of a written nature) being non-covered supporting the contention that the alleged acts took place'. *See* AIC, 'Directors' and Officers' Insurance: AIC Guide' (*Thomson Reuters Practical Law*, 26 August 2010) <https://uk.practicallaw.thomsonreuters.com/0-503-1690?transitionType=Default&contextData=(sc.Default)&firstPage=true&OWSessionId=2adf19263cf448e4913ed9ed3525deff&skipAnonymous=true> accessed 10 October 2023.

Where the clause wording enables its establishment by way of an admission "by the Insured" or "by the Insured Person", interpretation is likely to be construed more narrowly, and it will likely be a requirement that the admission be made by the insured individual. Though it may be the case under Side C that an admission by a company director could be deemed that of the company itself, thus "by the Insured", such corporate attribution principles would not apply in reverse.[55] Whether the corporate statement of facts can be determined an admission by an insured individual may *prima facie* appear to be answered in the negative, though may in reality depend on the extent to which the individual was involved in its drafting. It is likely that an implicated individual will not be permitted to have any involvement in the DPA negotiation or drafting process. However, should an individual be regarded as having contributed somewhat to the statement of facts – for example, by providing evidence to the company or having made statements in internal interviews which are ultimately included within the document – it may be considered that the statement of facts itself *contains* admissions by the insured individual (as opposed to it, in its entirety, representing an admission).

The extent to which such contribution may be sufficient in triggering the Conduct exclusion clause may depend on a number of factors. Policy wording will be one such factor: an admission will typically be required in written form (as a statement of facts is always drafted), and some clauses may go further to require that the admission be "formal", though the exact formalities in which the admission must be made to trigger the clause are not defined. For example, it is not typically prescribed that the written admission be addressed to the insurer, however such a requirement may impact the extent to which an individual's "contribution" to the statement of facts could be relied upon. Furthermore, the individual's position within the company may be considered: if the individual remains with the company, or remained with the company during the DPA preparatory/negotiation period, it may be considered that the contribution to the statement of facts goes beyond an incidental inclusion of third-party material, such that it can more reasonably be deemed to "contain" an admission.

It may also be the case that the publication of a statement of facts tending to identify individuals is postponed pending the outcome of the individuals' own criminal proceedings. Nonetheless, the identifying document is published upon completion of those proceedings, despite the verdict.[56] Though this is unlikely to impact any advancement of defence costs in respect of the criminal proceedings, a dispute may arise when reporting restrictions are lifted and there is deemed to be a perceived basis for refusal of indemnification, and demand for recoupment. Where convicted, the individual will not be indemnifiable in any event, though costs incurred in a successful criminal defence will not (policy wording providing) be subject to repayment unless an exclusion is invoked. This may arise in circumstances where the insurer seeks an adverse judgment against the insured following an acquittal on a backdrop of procedural errors (for example, where the case against the individual collapses on evidential issues as in the trial of the Serco Geografix

55 Unless perhaps the company is operating the individual's defence (in which case Side A is not likely to respond).

56 This happened in the *Tesco Stores Ltd* case, whereby reporting restrictions lifted upon the acquittal of directors unveiled a statement of facts which implicated those acquitted by name. Efforts to apply to amend the statement of facts following publication were unsuccessful. *See Serious Fraud Office v Tesco Stores Ltd* [2019] EW Misc 1 (Crown).

Ltd individuals). Ultimately, irrespective of whether criminal misconduct is expressly featured within the Conduct exclusion, the maxim *ex turpi causa non oritur actio* and public policy would prevent ultimate indemnification for deliberate unlawful acts in any event.[57]

Where a guilty plea is entered, this will be deemed an admission (or acknowledgement) for the purpose of invoking the Conduct exclusion clause. Where a director enters into an agreement with a prosecutor pursuant to section 74 of the SA 2020, the signing of the agreement may be considered a (formal) admission; where the director goes on to enter a guilty plea, this would also be considered a (formal) admission. Policy wording will bear some reflection in the extent to which defence costs can be advanced for the negotiations of such an agreement. Defence costs are not necessarily advanced based on an understanding that the insured is innocent, and therefore may not (though are likely to) be precluded until the signing of an agreement. The signing of an agreement will not, however, constitute a final adjudication until a conviction and reduced sentence are imposed and no appeals are pending; nor will signing the agreement constitute a final judgment until the conviction and sentence are imposed.

The Beazley Side A difference-in-conditions policy (**Section 16.3**), which offers broader coverage than traditional Side A, outlines that '[f]ormal written admission by the company in a deferred prosecution agreement statement of fact does not constitute formal written admission by an insured person'[58] in respect of the Conduct exclusion clause. Though this does not signal an example of Side A policy wording, it does demonstrate an interpretation of the statement of facts and the position of the individual in a policy designed to offer broader cover.

15.2.3.2 Conduct exclusion – final adjudication or judgment

An insurer seeking to rely upon a "final adjudication or judgment" in order to invoke the Conduct exclusion clause, so as to avoid advancement of defence costs prior to the completion of the individual's own proceedings, will likely need to do so on the basis of an adverse judgment in civil proceedings based upon the same misconduct, or by seeking a declaratory judgment against the insured. It may not be possible for the insurer to rely upon the corporate DPA as a "final adjudication". When a prosecution is deferred, the criminal proceedings are not "final" until the expiration of the DPA. The proceedings can be reinstituted at any point and are effectively paused pending the fulfilment of the obligations within the DPA.[59] Once the DPA has expired and is complete, the prosecutor gives notice to the court that it does not want proceedings to continue; no notice of discontinuance is then needed where the court terminates the DPA.[60] Upon this termination, the insurer would be able to argue that a "final adjudication or judgment" has been made

57 Deliberate and fraudulent acts fall outside the scope of a liability policy. *See Total Graphics Ltd v AGF Insurance Ltd* [1997] 1 Lloyd's Rep 599.

58 Beazley, 'Side A DIC Policy' (*Beazley*) <https://web.archive.org/web/20220421213351/https://www.beazley.com/documents/Wordings/Side%20A%20DIC.pdf> accessed 7 September 2021, 3.

59 Proceedings must have concluded, including any appeals: *Stein v Axis Insurance Co* 10 Cal App 5th 673 (Cal Ct App 2017). This can be contrasted with the New York approach which considers finality to be upon sentencing, irrespective of pending appeals (though this approach does not appear to be typical of the market): *Dupree v Scottsdale Insurance Company* 129 AD 3d 586 (NY App Div 2015). *See also* Kevin LaCroix, 'D&O Insurance: A "Final" Analysis' (*The D&O Diary*, 28 June 2015) <https://www.dandodiary.com/2015/06/articles/d-o-insurance/do-insurance-a-final-analysis/> accessed 23 October 2020.

60 Crime and Courts Act 2013, sch 17 para 11.

for the purposes of refusing coverage or seeking reimbursement for any indemnification already advanced.

The issue as to whether a DPA can be considered a final adjudication was considered for the first time in the recent US case of *Rochester Drug Co-Operative Inc v Hiscox Ins Co*.[61] Dividing the analysis by looking at the words "final" and "adjudication" separately, a similar position was adopted in respect of finality: a DPA following approval (in the US, pursuant to the Speedy Trial Act) will not be final as 'the court must either rule on dismissal of the charges or, in the event of a breach of the deferred prosecution agreement, preside over the prosecution of the case'.[62] In respect of "adjudication", the court adopted the view that since *Black's Law Dictionary* defines "adjudication" as "'[t]he legal process of resolving a dispute; the process of judicially deciding a case'",[63] a DPA could not fall within such a definition. The rationale was twofold: firstly, that 'courts should not substantively review [DPAs]',[64] and secondly, that '[DPAs] do not resolve the underlying dispute because the agreement is contingent upon the defendant complying with its terms'.[65]

The *Rochester* interpretation as regards finality can be considered applicable within the US and UK in respect of DPAs, whilst the DPA is ongoing. Once the DPA period has expired, it will be considered final.[66] The interpretation as regards adjudication may differ, not in respect of the compliance required in order to reach a point of ultimate resolution (expiration), but instead due to the increased judicial involvement in approving UK DPAs. In any event, it has generally been accepted that settlements do not constitute "adjudications" within the context of insurance exclusions.[67] DPAs are commonly referred to as negotiated 'settlements',[68] albeit within the criminal sphere, and thus would unlikely be considered an adjudication. This will particularly be the case whilst the DPA is ongoing and, upon its expiration (where no breach has occurred), a lack of conviction would likely see no change in approach.

It may be the case that a clause requiring a "final adjudication or judgment" would embrace a DPA within the UK, by virtue of the fact that the court must provide an approved judgment upon DPA approval. However, the extent to which the clause could be invoked will likely rest on whether the word "final" applies to "judgment" as well as "adjudication", in which case the DPA period will need to have expired. The *Rochester* analysis of

61 466 F Supp 3d 337 (WDNY 2020).

62 ibid 354.

63 ibid, citing Brian A Garner, *Black's Law Dictionary* (11th edn, Thomson Reuters 2019).

64 *Rochester Drug Co-Operative Inc v Hiscox Ins Co* (n 61) 354, citing *United States v HSBC Bank USA NA* 863 F 3d 125, 138 (2d Cir 2017).

65 *Rochester Drug Co-Operative Inc v Hiscox Ins Co* (n 61) 354, citing *First Mercury Ins Co v Law Office of Kenneth B Schwartz* No CV171763SJFAKT, at 16 (EDNY Mar 1 2019): '(finding conditional plea agreement was not a final adjudication for purposes of an illegal conduct exclusion where charge based on criminal, dishonest, fraudulent, or malicious conduct was withdrawn at sentencing).'

66 This must be the case due to the doctrine of double jeopardy.

67 *US Bank National Association v Indian Harbor Insurance Co* 2014 WL 3012969 (D Minn 2014); *JP Morgan Sec Inc v Vigilant Ins Co* 126 AD 3d 76 (NY App Div 2015).

68 DPAs have frequently been referred to in the UK as "settlements". *See Director of the Serious Fraud Office v Airbus SE* [2021] Lloyd's Rep FC 159 (Crown) [4] (Dame Victoria Sharp); Select Committee on the Bribery Act 2010, *The Bribery Act 2010: Post-Legislative Scrutiny* (HL 2017–19, 303) para 303; Lisa Osofsky, 'We're Defending the UK as a Safe Place for Business' (*The Times*, 30 June 2021) <https://www.thetimes.co.uk/article/were-defending-the-uk-as-a-safe-place-for-business-617f500fw> accessed 30 June 2021 (by the then-Director of the SFO); Colin King and Nicholas Lord, 'Deferred Prosecution Agreements in England and Wales: Castles Made of Sand?' (2020) (Apr) PL 307, 326 (by academics).

"adjudication" appears to require judicial resolution, whereas "judgment" as per *Black's Law Dictionary* instead simply relates to a court decision.[69] US cases have deliberated the "final adjudication or judgment" policy wording and determined that the phrase is disjunctive, placing emphasis on the "or" connector to separate the two eventualities.[70] "Final adjudication" has borne a more resolution-focussed interpretation, thus becoming final only upon completion of the case and any appeals. "Final judgment" has borne a more specific interpretation, such that a case facing the court is considered final once judicial decision is given, irrespective of any pending appeals. Though a UK DPA cannot be appealed, an adjudication would not be deemed to have occurred upon its approval, due to the ongoing DPA period prior to its expiration. However, a DPA approved by the court pursuant to an approved judgment would likely be considered a judgment. In each case, it is most likely that neither an adjudication nor judgment would be deemed to be final until the expiration of the DPA, as no ultimate determination of liability is reached until that point (for example, no conviction has occurred).[71]

Furthermore, whether the DPA – upon expiration – could be relied upon as a "final adjudication or judgment" in order to refuse advancement of defence costs to an individual, pursuant to proceedings based upon the same underlying conduct, will likely depend upon the scope of the clause. The fact that a DPA's statement of facts may contain admissions by the company does not automatically render the DPA a final adjudication.[72] However, should the DPA expire before individual proceedings are brought or complete, the admissions contained within it may provide a basis for an insurer to refuse coverage – potentially reliant upon the admission, or on the "final adjudication *or judgment*" – in order to refuse an advancement of defence costs. Some clauses are drafted using restrictive language, requiring a final adjudication or judgment in the underlying proceedings and/or against the insured.[73] However, many clauses are broader in scope and provide only for a final adjudication or judgment, without further specifying against whom the final adjudication or judgment must be made, and whether it must be made in the underlying action. An insured in such circumstances will be better protected where the more restrictive wording is adopted, particularly where the corporate DPA has already expired.

15.2.3.3 Policy construction and severability

A Severability clause will be of great importance to an insured where a corporate DPA is agreed, and particularly where the statement of facts identifies an insured individual or may otherwise be deemed to contain admissions by them. A standard "Severability in exclusions" clause will expressly provide that an exclusion invoked against one insured will not thereafter be invoked against another (purely by virtue of the fact that the parties are co-insureds). However, just as a "Severability in application" clause operates to ensure that the knowledge of one prospective insured will not be imputed to another as regards

69 Mick Woodley (ed), *Osborn's Concise Law Dictionary* (12th edn, Sweet & Maxwell 2013); Daniel Greenberg (ed), *Jowitt's Dictionary of English Law* (5th edn, Sweet & Maxwell 2019).

70 *Stein v Axis Insurance Co* (n 59), citing *Unencumbered Assets v Great Am Ins Co* 817 F Supp 2d 1014 (SD Ohio 2011), citing *Chubb Custom Ins Co v Triumph Capital Group Inc* No 04–1893–BLS2, at 3 (MassSuperCt Feb 9 2007).

71 *Unencumbered Assets v Great Am Ins Co* (n 71), citing *Chubb Custom Ins Co v Triumph Capital Group Inc* (n 71) 3.

72 *Rochester Drug Co-Operative Inc v Hiscox Ins Co* (n 61) 354.

73 *Stein v Axis Insurance Co* (n 59).

the policy proposal, a comprehensive Severability clause may provide that knowledge and/or admission of one insured will not be imputed to a co-insured in relation to Claims (or Circumstances) alleging Wrongful Acts arising during the policy period. Such a provision will be pertinent to insured individuals where a corporate DPA has been agreed, and would be read in line with policy exclusions to ensure that the admissions by the company would not automatically be deemed those of the individual, unless expressly otherwise stated.[74]

Exclusion clauses may be applicable to the insured entity under Side C, though notably the extent to which an insured individual's coverage (under Side A) may be impacted will depend somewhat on the policy construction. Should an exclusion apply to preclude coverage to the insured entity under a composite policy, the same exclusion will not automatically apply to preclude coverage to the insured individual. However, where the policy is joint in nature, any exclusion clause invoked against one insured (including the entity) will apply to other co-insureds (thus including the individual).[75]

15.2.4 The internal investigation and self-report

A director may seek an advancement of defence costs during an internal investigation, which may ultimately include the making of a corporate self-report. Whether such coverage would arise largely depends on the inclusion of internal investigations within the definition of Claim, as defence costs cover will not be triggered upon the notification of Circumstances alone. During the internal investigation stage, it is unlikely that a director would be bound by confidentiality requirements, which in any event may not impact the notification obligations within the policy. If the internal investigation is included within the Claim definition, the insurer reserves its right of recoupment should – for example – it be later determined that the director has committed criminal wrongdoing and the Conduct exclusion clause be invoked.

The Conduct exclusion clause is unlikely to be invoked at the stage of the investigation, which is inherently inconclusive during the process and is corporate-focussed; further, no DPA will yet have arisen or is likely to have been discussed with prosecutors. To the extent that a corporate self-report could be relied upon by an insurer to invoke the Conduct exclusion against an individual, this will largely involve similar considerations to the DPA statement of facts. However, a self-report compiled by the company may not be so readily available to the insurer as it will not often be published. Nevertheless, it is unlikely – unless interviews or significant individual contributions are relied upon – that the exclusion will be triggered, particularly where wording requires either a final adjudication or a more formal admission (for example, to the insurer in writing).

The position may change where a serving director elects to direct or participate in the making of a personally damning corporate self-report in the hope that such an action may be considered in mitigation against them personally for the relevant underlying wrongdoing reported. In such circumstances, the director may need to seek consent from the

74 Where an exclusion clause is ambiguous, it will ordinarily be construed in favour of coverage and against the insurer: *Rochester Drug Co-Operative Inc v Hiscox Ins Co* (n 61) 352, citing *Andy Warhol Found for Visual Arts Inc v Fed Ins Co* 189 F 3d 208, 215 (2d Cir 1999).

75 *Arab Bank plc v Zurich Insurance Co* [1998] All ER (D) 273 (Comm) (Rix J), citing *P Samuel & Company Limited v Dumas* [1924] AC 431 (HL).

insurer to admit liability (under Side A). This will be required if a Claim is deemed to have arisen against the insured individual, which may be the case if – for example – the prosecutor's investigation into the company is parallel to an investigation into the individual and the Claim definition includes investigations. A failure to obtain such consent, if the self-report is considered to be particularly personally incriminating, may lead to a relinquishing of liability by the insurer and the Conduct exclusion clause may be invoked on the basis of such admission.

15.2.5 Failure of insured to disclose

Where an exclusion clause cannot be invoked in order to refuse an advancement of defence costs to an individual following a corporate DPA – for example, where the Conduct exclusion requires a final adjudication and this is not deemed to have occurred[76] – an insurer may still refuse advancement on the basis of pre-policy nondisclosure (where applicable in the circumstances). In the Australian case of *Onley v Catlin Syndicate Ltd as the Underwriting Member of Lloyd's Syndicate 2003*,[77] it was determined that an advancement provision would not prevent an insurer from avoiding a policy on the basis of a pre-policy nondisclosure, unless the insurer's precontractual rights were expressly or impliedly waived.[78] Thus, the insured could be refused an advancement where an 'operative ground for refusal, such as avoidance',[79] arises, even where no exclusion clauses within the policy are triggered. In respect of the requisite proof of nondisclosure an insurer must establish in order to decline advancement, *Onley* set out that only a 'real or substantial ground' for alleging nondisclosure was required and not necessarily 'all necessary proof of the insured's conduct'. This was denoted to be 'consistent with [the insurer's] obligation of utmost good faith'.[80]

As such, an insured may be at a disadvantage where the company implicates them within the corporate DPA. The insurer may interpret the statement of facts and rely upon it as suggesting a nondisclosure by the relevant individual of the stated misconduct during the precontractual stage. In this or a similar situation, whereby the insurer agrees to advance defence costs until the invoking of an exclusion clause, but then avoids doing so on the basis of nondisclosure instead, it may be argued that this is an attempt at undercutting

76 '[T]he extent of any limitation on an insurer arising from an agreement to advance defence costs, will be limited to the obligations contained in the extension and by its terms.' *See Onley v Catlin Syndicate Ltd as the Underwriting Member of Lloyd's Syndicate 2003* (n 18) [52].

77 *Onley v Catlin Syndicate Ltd as the Underwriting Member of Lloyd's Syndicate 2003* (n 18).

78 ibid [52], [72].

79 ibid [51], citing Desmond Herrington and Ronald Shaw Ashton, *The Law of Liability Insurance* (3rd edn, LexisNexis Butterworths 2013) para 8-583, citing *Intergraph Best (Vic) Pty Ltd v QBE Insurance Ltd* [2005] VSCA 180; *Rich v CGU Insurance Limited* [2005] HCA 16; *Wilkie v Gordian Runoff Ltd* (n 12); *Silbermann v CGU Insurance Ltd* (n 28). Avoidance remains a remedy for breach of the duty of fair presentation under section 3 of the Insurance Act 2015: Insurance Act 2015, sch 1.

80 Within section 13(1) of the Insurance Contracts Act 1984 (Cth) (Australia). *See Onley v Catlin Syndicate Ltd as the Underwriting Member of Lloyd's Syndicate 2003* (n 18) [7].

the coverage. The insurer must prove the allegation of (fraudulent)[81] nondisclosure, but an advancement would not be necessary in the meantime, for public policy reasons.[82]

Where there is a failure to notify the insurer during the policy period, the condition precedent trigger for coverage under the policy simply does not arise so as to avail the insured the opportunity to obtain an advancement of defence costs.

15.3 Good faith of the insurer and payment within a reasonable time

As detailed in **Section 11.1.1**, section 17 of the MIA 1906 setting out that '[a] contract of marine insurance is a contract based upon the utmost good faith'[83] was amended by the IA 2015, though only to the extent that the second half of the sentence regarding the remedy was removed.[84] To this extent, all contracts of insurance[85] remain contracts based on utmost good faith,[86] and good faith according to the Law Commissions remains a 'general interpretative principle'.[87] It can also be said that the insurance contract (post-contract) remains subject to an implied contractual term of good faith with limited but nonetheless some flexibility in application in different situations, and thus subject to contract law remedies where implied.[88] The post-contractual "duty" (also referred to as an 'obligation')[89] upon the insurer is one of good faith, and not "utmost good faith",[90] and focusses more

81 Implying a promise that the insurer would cover a wrongly undisclosed risk (by virtue of the indirect terms of limitation on refusal to advance costs) was stretching the principles of implication, irrespective of whether the nondisclosure was fraudulent. However, in respect of fraudulent disclosure, public policy further supported the court's conclusion. *See Onley v Catlin Syndicate Ltd as the Underwriting Member of Lloyd's Syndicate 2003* (n 18) [49]–[50], [79].

82 *Onley v Catlin Syndicate Ltd as the Underwriting Member of Lloyd's Syndicate 2003* (n 18) [74], [76].

83 Referring to cases in the nineteenth century: '[they] expressed that the parties are subject to the duty of good faith throughout their contractual relationship.' *See* Özlem Gürses, 'What Does "Utmost Good Faith" Mean?' (2016) King's College London, 2 <https://kclpure.kcl.ac.uk/portal/en/publications/what-does-utmost-good-faith-mean(02d45557-e695-41c8-8f20-97f1d07b5675).html> accessed 25 June 2021, citing *Britton v The Royal Insurance Company* (1866) 4 F & F 905 (Assizes) 909.

84 Section 17 now reads: 'A contract of marine insurance is a contract based upon the utmost good faith.' *See* Marine Insurance Act 1906, s 17.

85 It remains the case that (despite wording) contracts of insurance of all types are governed by this provision: 'The common law mirrors this provision in relation to non-marine insurance.' *See* Explanatory Notes to the Insurance Act 2015, para 113.

86 'The intention of section 14 is that good faith will remain an interpretative principle, with section 17 of the 1906 Act and the common law continuing to provide that insurance contracts are contracts of good faith.' *See* ibid para 116. *See also* Peter MacDonald Eggers and Simon Picken, *Good Faith and Insurance* (4th edn, Informa Law 2018) para 1.21; Bariş Soyer and Andrew Tettenborn, 'Mapping (Utmost) Good Faith in Insurance Law – Future Conditional?' (2016) 132(Oct) LQR 618.

87 Law Commission, *Insurance Contract Law: Business Disclosure; Warranties; Insurers' Remedies for Fraudulent Claims; and Late Payment* (Law Com No 353, 2014) para 30.5. Though broader at the precontractual stage, the duty of good faith continues once the contract is formed. *See Manifest Shipping Co Ltd v Uni-Polaris Insurance Co Ltd (The Star Sea)* [2001] UKHL 1.

88 *The Star Sea* (n 87) [18]–[50] (Lord Hobhouse); *Versloot Dredging BV v HDI Gerling Industrie Versicherung AG* [2016] UKSC 45 [8] (Lord Sumption). This is not by virtue of a general duty of good faith imposed within contract law, a concept which has been rejected by the Supreme Court: *Pakistan International Airline Corporation v Times Travel (UK) Ltd* [2021] UKSC 40 [95] (Lord Burrows).

89 Clarke and Soyer (n 3) 46.

90 Law Commission, *Insurance Contract Law Issues Paper 6 Damages for Late Payment and the Insurer's Duty of Good Faith* (Law Com IP 6, 2014) para 4.17. Although it has been noted that the word "utmost" 'does not add much to the duty': Gürses (n 83) 9.

on failure to act in such a way, rather than by imposition of positive obligations.[91] In this respect, it is widely recognised that the duty 'encompasses notions of "fairness, reasonableness and community standards of decency and fair dealing"'.[92]

Reliance upon an insurer acting in good faith is arguably all the more crucial to an insured director during the advancement stage, as access to a defence will be important not only in minimising potential criminal or civil liability, but also financial liability arising for any Claims which may thereafter be made against them and be non-covered under their policy. It has been observed that whilst a general duty does not exist upon insurers to act in good faith when assessing and paying claims, the statutory remedy of damages for late payment as under section 13A(5) of the IA 2015 continues to provide some protection to the insured.[93] When considering use of the terminology "claims" in this regard, the correct interpretation is to be a claim made by the insured under the insurance policy (thus, against the insurer). An insurer is bound within the contract of insurance by the implied term 'that if the insured makes a claim under the contract, the insurer must pay any sums due in respect of the claim within a reasonable time',[94] as under section 13A(1). Section 13A of the IA 2015 falls within Part 4A headed "Late payment of claims", a new addition to the Act inserted by section 28 of the Enterprise Act 2016. As such, this implied term requiring timely payment of claims can be considered alongside the 'general interpretative principle'[95] of good faith; according to the Law Commissions, the insurer's duty of good faith is not to be considered an implied term in isolation in this respect.[96]

In respect of a D&O policy with provision for advancement of defence costs (or, for provision of a defence under a duty to defend policy), it can be considered that there is an implied term on the basis of business efficacy that such advancements (or paid services) will be made where no exclusion applies.[97] It has been set out within US precedent that where no breach of contract has occurred, there is no breach of good faith (for example, regarding advancement).[98] However, in the UK, 'post-contractual breach of the duty of utmost good faith … may arise without a contractual breach'.[99] In this respect, it remains clear that an insurer must only refuse advancement within the terms of the policy and the context of the insurance contract (for example, on the basis of an exclusion clause or non-disclosure), but also that the insurer must not act in bad faith. As regards duty to defend

91 Law Commission, *Reforming Insurance Contract Law: Issues Paper 7: The Insured's Post-Contract Duty of Good Faith* (Law Com IP 7, 2010) para 7.15. Within the scope of the contract and liabilities therein, per recent Australian caselaw: *Allianz Australia Insurance Limited v Delor Vue Apartments CTS 39788* [2022] HCA 38.

92 Gürses (n 83) 7, citing *CGU Insurance Ltd v AMP Financial Planning Pty Ltd* [2007] HCA 36 [15] (Gleeson CJ and Crennan J).

93 John Birds and Katie Richards, *Birds' Modern Insurance Law* (12th edn, Sweet & Maxwell 2022) para 8-04.

94 Insurance Act 2015, s 13A(1).

95 Law Commission, *Insurance Contract Law: Business Disclosure; Warranties; Insurers' Remedies for Fraudulent Claims; and Late Payment* (n 87) para 30.5. Though broader at the precontractual stage, the duty of good faith continues once the contract is formed. *See The Star Sea* (n 87).

96 Law Commission, *Insurance Contract Law Issues Paper 6 Damages for Late Payment and the Insurer's Duty of Good Faith* (n 90) paras 4.48–4.51.

97 Law Commission, *Insurance Contract Law: Business Disclosure; Warranties; Insurers' Remedies for Fraudulent Claims; and Late Payment* (n 87) paras 30.23, 30.57–30.58.

98 *US Telepacific Corp v US Specialty Insurance Co* (n 8).

99 Gürses (n 83) 6, citing *Drake Insurance Plc (In Provisional Liquidation) v Provident Insurance Plc* [2003] EWCA Civ 1834.

policies, the insurer is under an obligation to act in good faith when doing so;[100] though duty to defend forms are relatively rare in D&O.[101] In Australia, it has also been clearly set out within case law that the insurer, as a consequence of (utmost) good faith, may be required to act 'with due regard to the legitimate interests of an assured'.[102]

In the US and Australia, an insurer is bound by the duty of good faith in paying valid claims promptly.[103] Both *Wilkie* and *Silbermann* were decided in the context of Australian law and thus applying the Insurance Contracts Act 1984 (Cth), which under sections 13 and 14 requires the parties to act (by way of implied term in a contract of insurance) with utmost good faith. It can be observed that in the context of claims made under a UK D&O policy (for example, as regards advancement), the duty of good faith upon the insurer continues to apply. As aforementioned, section 13A(1) of the IA 2015 implies a term into every contract of insurance that an insurer must pay sums due in respect of a claim within a reasonable time.[104] This "reasonable" timeframe includes reasonable time to investigate and assess the claim made by the insured against the insurer.[105] However, the concept of "reasonableness" depends on 'all the relevant circumstances'.[106] Section 13A(3) of the IA 2015 denotes some examples of matters to take into account when determining reasonableness, including for example 'the size and complexity of the claim'.[107]

A defence is available to the insurer, found under section 13A(4) of the IA 2015, 'where it had reasonable grounds for disputing the validity or quantum of a claim'.[108] Section 13A(4) provides that where there is a demonstration by the insurer of such reasonable grounds for dispute, the insurer will not be in breach of the implied term by failing to make payment whilst the dispute is ongoing.[109] Reasonable grounds for dispute are to be judged objectively.[110] However, this defence is qualified, as the insurer's conduct in handling the claim may still be a relevant factor in determining breach.[111] Consideration of the insurer's conduct means that even where the grounds for dispute (or further investigation) are reasonable, an insurer may still be in breach of the implied term where its actions during the process are unreasonable. Within the Explanatory Notes to the Enterprise Act 2016, the

100 'In *The Mercandian Continent*, Lord Justice Longmore stated that good faith would be required where the insurer takes over the insured's defence of a claim.' *See* Law Commission, *Insurance Contract Law: Business Disclosure; Warranties; Insurers" Remedies for Fraudulent Claims; and Late Payment* (n 87) para 30.58, citing *The Mercandian Continent* (n 3) [22], [27]. *See also Groom v Crocker* (n 3).

101 '"[D&O] policies generally do not obligate the carrier to provide the insured with a defense."' *See US Telepacific Corp v US Specialty Insurance Co* (n 8) 3, citing *Helfand v National Union Fire Ins Co* (n 8) 879. *See also* Goanos, *D&O 101: Understanding Directors and Officers Liability Insurance* (n 8) 104.

102 Gürses (n 83) 7, citing *CGU Insurance Ltd v AMP Financial Planning Pty Ltd* (n 92) [15] (Gleeson CJ and Crennan J).

103 Law Commission, *Insurance Contract Law Issues Paper 6 Damages for Late Payment and the Insurer's Duty of Good Faith* (n 90) para 7.5. *See also CGU Insurance Ltd v AMP Financial Planning Pty Ltd* (n 92); Gürses (n 83) 6.

104 Insurance Act 2015, s 13A(1).

105 ibid s 13A(2).

106 ibid s 13A(3).

107 ibid s 13A(3)(b).

108 Explanatory Notes to the Enterprise Act 2016, para 269.

109 Insurance Act 2015, s 13A(4)(a). This was observed in *Quadra Commodities SA v XL Insurance Company SE* [2022] EWHC 431 (Comm), where although there were unnecessary delays on the part of the insurer, the implied term was not breached as such delays occurred within a reasonable time for payment of the claim, having regard to the fact that there were reasonable grounds for disputing the claim within the relevant time period.

110 Explanatory Notes to the Enterprise Act 2016, para 269.

111 Insurance Act 2015, s 13A(4)(b).

examples of an unreasonably slow investigation, and unreasonably slow change in position following further evidence arising in support of the claim's validity, are given.[112]

Furthermore, it can be appreciated that an insurer facing a claim by an insured for an advancement of defence costs – or requiring the insurer to act upon its duty to defend – is bound by an implied term within the contract of insurance requiring timely payment. The insurer is bound by contractual obligations to adhere to the policy, underpinned by good faith, and has an obligation not to act in bad faith in delaying payment.[113] Where an insurer has a reasonable and legitimate ground for delaying payment pending further investigation of the claim, or for refusing payment altogether, the insurer will not be considered to have breached the implied term under section 13A of the IA 2015 unless it acted unreasonably during the course of the process. As such, an insured could anticipate that whilst an investigation may be entered into by the insurer, such an investigation will be carried out within a reasonable timeframe. Where a director seeks an advancement of defence costs pursuant to an action against them, following a corporate DPA, it could reasonably be expected that the insurer will investigate the claim for advancement under the policy. However, if there is no exclusion clause or other ground (for example, nondisclosure) upon which the insurer can dispute liability, the insured should receive an advancement within a reasonable time. Any advancement of defence costs made which later transpires to be non-covered under the policy will be subject to the insurer's right of recoupment.

15.4 Right of recoupment

The right of insurers to recoup defence costs in duty to defend policies has recently become a contentious area, with now conflicting decisions in various jurisdictions across the US. Previously, it was generally the case that an insurer could seek recoupment of defence costs where it was determined that the underlying claim was not covered, and where the policy expressly provided for such a right of recoupment (often referred to by way of a "Reservation of rights" clause). This approach is still taken in some jurisdictions, where the underlying claim is not covered and thus the insurer is not deemed to owe a duty to defend.[114] The interpretation in *Buss v Superior Court*[115] set out that an insurer has the right to recoupment where the underlying claim was never covered, but not where the claim was potentially covered (and later determined not to be so).[116] Some distinction might be made between a duty to defend covered and potentially covered claims, and an even broader duty to defend *all* claims. In either event, the insurer will be contractually bound by the policy wording used. The recent case of *American Western Home Ins Co v Gjonaj Realty & Management Co*[117] declined to follow precedent in this area, and the insurer was not entitled to recoup defence costs – despite the fact that the insurer was acknowledged not to owe a duty to defend in the underlying claim – to avoid the risk of

112 Explanatory Notes to the Enterprise Act 2016, para 270.

113 *Fargnoli v GA Bonus plc* [1997] CLC 653, 670–671. *See also* Clarke and Soyer (n 3) 47.

114 *Nautilus Insurance Company v Access Medical LLC* 2021 WL 936076 (Nev Mar 11 2021).

115 *Buss v Superior Court* (n 1).

116 ibid 46 (Mosk J); Alec Boyd, 'Defense Obligations' in Martin J O'Leary (ed), *Directors & Officers Liability Insurance Deskbook* (American Bar Association 2020) 130.

117 192 AD 3d 28 (2d Dept 2020).

eroding the broader nature of duty to defend policies, and because there was no express contractual provision to bestow such a right.[118]

Requirement for provision on recoupment in order for the right to arise bears some logic in respect of defence costs, if it is accepted that the provision is not subject to the general liability principle (**Section 14.3**).[119] In *Fitzpatrick v American Honda Motor Co*,[120] it was set out that the duty to defend is a contractual obligation upon the insured, and permitting recoupment without contractual provision 'would allow duty to defend to become coextensive with duty to indemnify'.[121] Recoupment in such circumstances has been termed 'inappropriate'.[122] With conflicting decisions in the US and without clear precedent in the UK, an insured director should be cautious in ensuring that their duty to defend policy does not contain restrictive recoupment language, particularly if the purpose of taking out the policy is to obtain defence coverage irrespective of the ultimate result (law and public policy permitting).

Within a duty to indemnify policy, any defence costs advanced will generally be subject to a right of recoupment by the insurer, as such policy language is very common. In *Onley*, it was set out that the advancement extension in the requisite policy would apply to the defence costs in the relevant proceedings (but for the issue of nondisclosure), but subject to the right of recoupment should it ultimately be established that the claim was not covered under the policy.[123] As the provision for advancement is typically an extension to and thus bound by the fate of the main insuring clause, any costs advanced in a non-covered claim within a policy which does not bear recoupment provision may nonetheless be recoverable by the insurer.

The insurer may argue that there is a right of recoupment due to there being an implied contractual term. The argument of an implied contract (created by a reservation of rights letter) did not succeed in *American Western Home Ins Co*;[124] however this was principally due to the fact that the relevant policy was duty to defend, and not duty to indemnify. Pursuant to this argument, an insurer may argue that the policy provides coverage for claims covered within its terms and conditions, and therefore any costs paid in respect of non-covered claims would be recoverable by the insurer as a result of the lack of consideration provided for this additional offering. It may be argued that this analogy conforms to the liability insurance principle requiring actual liability and does not consider the commercial purpose of defence costs cover; however the ultimate indemnification of defence costs and provision for advancement of defence costs can be distinguished.

118 Michael Zigelman and others, 'Jurisdictions Continue to be Split Over Insurer's Right to Recoup Defense Costs' (*Reuters*, 29 June 2021) <https://www.reuters.com/legal/legalindustry/jurisdictions-continue-be-split-over-insurers-right-recoup-defense-costs-2021-06-29/> accessed 18 August 2021.

119 *AstraZeneca Insurance Co Ltd v XL Insurance (Bermuda) Ltd* [2013] EWHC (n 11); *AstraZeneca Insurance Co Ltd v XL Insurance (Bermuda) Ltd* [2013] EWCA Civ 1660.

120 78 NY 2d 61, 65 (1991).

121 Jonathan Dachs, 'The Insurer's Right to Recoupment of Defence Costs' (*New York Law Journal*, 16 March 2021) <https://www.law.com/newyorklawjournal/2021/03/16/the-insurers-right-to-recoupment-of-defense-costs/> accessed 18 August 2021. 'The conclusion we reach here flows naturally from the fact that the duty to defend derives, in the first instance, not from the complaint drafted by a third party, but rather from the insurer's own contract with the insured'. *See* ibid 68 (Titone J).

122 *Crescent Beach Club v Indian Harbor Ins Co* 468 F Supp 3d 515, 554 (EDNY 2020), citing *Century Sur Co v Vas & Sons Corp* No 17-CV-5392 (DLI) (RLM) (EDNY Aug 31 2018), report and recommendation adopted 2018 WL 4804656 (EDNY Sept 30 2018).

123 *Onley v Catlin Syndicate Ltd as the Underwriting Member of Lloyd's Syndicate 2003* (n 18) [17].

124 *American Western Home Ins Co v Gjonaj Realty & Management Co* (n 117).

Where defence costs are provided for by way of separate undertaking, the provision for recoupment may differ in scope. In any event, a Claim considered to fall within the *scope* of the policy definition would need to arise and be notified in order for defence costs cover to be triggered. The success of this argument will depend on the extent to which the advancement provision is bound by the main insuring clause and policy wording.

From a practical and realistic perspective, though policies frequently bear recoupment language, 'this provision is seldom invoked'.[125] It may be that insureds do not have the financial wherewithal to make repayments and, according to industry specialist Larry Goanos, there may also be some element of reputation preservation within the relatively small D&O insurance community.[126] If this is the case, it is all the more unlikely that insurers will habitually pursue insureds under duty to defend policies for costs paid by the insurer in funding their defence.

In a duty to indemnify policy, it is usually a requirement of the insureds to obtain the insurer's consent prior to incurring defence costs. Where the insured fails to do so, it may be liable for the costs (or a portion of them).[127] Where consent is given, the insured may be required to sign a guarantee essentially outlining their commitment to repay the defence costs advanced should the policy require.[128] The policyholders may be considered to be jointly and severally liable (policy wording permitting) for the repayment of costs to the insurer, and some policies will determine that the aggregate limit of indemnity is reduced by the owed amount until such repayment is made.[129]

15.5 Allocation of defence costs

Agreement as to allocation may be a precondition to advancement of defence costs (and settlement), and any lack of agreement may allow the insurer to take a discretionary approach to advancement.[130] Professor Adolfo Paolini and Deepak Nambisan note four scenarios which may lead to allocation disputes, including dispute as to the apportionment of liability between the D&O insurer and the company's insurer (if applicable), or the company itself; when the underlying Claim against the insured features other uninsured defendants; when the director acts in more than one capacity; and where the insured incurs liability for insured and uninsured perils.[131]

An interpretation of the 'Reasonably Related Defence Costs Test'[132] in allocation of defence costs, where a director is prosecuted concurrent with a corporate DPA, will likely

125 Goanos, *D&O 101: Understanding Directors and Officers Liability Insurance* (n 8) 102.

126 ibid 102–103.

127 Thomas H Bentz, 'A Buyer's Guide to Obtaining Comprehensive D&O Insurance Coverage' (*Holland & Knight*, 2014) <https://issuu.com/hollandknight/docs/holland-knight-d_o-insurance-covera> accessed 3 November 2020, 16.

128 ibid 17.

129 GB Underwriting, 'Management Liability (D&O) and Company Reimbursement Policy Wording' (*GB Underwriting Ltd*, July 2014) <https://web.archive.org/web/20160413182237/http://www.gbunderwriting.co.uk/downloads/> accessed 17 December 2020, para 8.5.

130 Paolini and Nambisan (n 12) para 8.22.

131 ibid para 8.47.

132 '[D]efence costs are regarded as "reasonably related" to the defence of covered claims if those costs would have been incurred had it been the case that only insured claims against the officers and directors had been alleged in the relevant proceedings. If this is the case, then insurers are liable to pay 100% of defence costs even if these result in benefiting both insured and uninsured claims.' *See* ibid para 8.53.

be advantageous to the director in respect of certainty provided where one party is not insured under the policy (for example, the company), and/or where there are covered and non-covered related claims. Where 'directors' and officers' liability is concurrent with that of the [uninsured] company, there should not be any allocation as between them'.[133] Often, the prosecution of directors is dealt with separately from the corporate DPA, and it is likely that the directors will seek separate representation. In the US decision of *Safeway Stores Inc v National Union Fire Insurance Corp*,[134] there was still deemed to be concurrency despite some separation in the cases relating to the corporation and the directors.[135]

The same approach can be taken in respect of a claim involving insured and uninsured directors. The reasonably related test may incidentally benefit uninsured directors, particularly where efforts are made in case management to streamline the dealing with related proceedings. In the case of the Tesco Stores Ltd former directors, following the *Tesco Stores Ltd* DPA, the directors were originally on trial simultaneously (though the trial of one of the three was severed due to ill health), and two of the directors have since made efforts to have their employment tribunal cases heard together.[136] The test, applied in the New Zealand case of *New Zealand Forest Products Limited v The New Zealand Insurance Company Limited*,[137] has been applied in England in *Wyeth & Brothers Ltd v Cigna Insurance Co of Europe SA-NV*[138] and its principle followed in other jurisdictions.[139] Though this approach provides a level of certainty, a policy offering defence costs cover within the limit of indemnity may be expeditiously exhausted in a DPA scenario, particularly where the defence costs of an uninsured company are considered to be reasonably related. The inclusion of entity coverage under Side C with clearly defined separate limits will serve to remove such a risk of depreciation of directors' cover under Side A, though exposure may remain where a particular peril is non-covered under Side C.

Where multiple Claims are made against a director, there will be an advancement of defence costs for all where the reasonably related test is successfully applied, and it is deemed that at least one Claim is covered under the policy. To avoid this, an insurer will need to prove that defence costs for Claims made against the insured are completely unrelated.[140] Where no allocation clause exists, there will be reliance on the perceived nature of the claim in determining whether it is covered, potentially covered, or non-covered when considering whether there is an obligation to defend or to advance defence costs. Where allocation is not a precondition to advancement, dispute surrounding the coverage of a claim may mean that advancement is not made based on the allocation issue;[141] this is

133 ibid para 8.58, citing *Coronation Insurance Co v Clearly Canadian Beverage Corp* (1999) 117 BCAC 22 (CA).

134 64 F 3d 1282 (9th Cir 1995).

135 Paolini and Nambisan (n 12) para 8.56.

136 *Tesco Plc, Tesco Stores Ltd v Mr C Bush, Mr C Rogberg* (2020) UKEAT/0069/20/AT.

137 [1997] UKPC 37. *See also Zurich Insurance Plc UK Branch v International Energy Group Ltd* [2016] AC 509; *Financial Conduct Authority v Arch Insurance* [2021] UKSC 1.

138 *Wyeth & Brothers Ltd v Cigna Insurance Co of Europe SA-NV* (n 1).

139 *Safeway Stores Inc v National Union Fire Insurance Corp* (n 134); *Coronation Insurance Co v Clearly Canadian Beverage Corp* (n 133). *See also* Paolini and Nambisan (n 12) paras 8.55–8.58.

140 Paolini and Nambisan (n 12) para 8.53.

141 This is particularly so where defence costs (and their advancement) are included within the total limit of indemnity, as the 'defence costs cover complements the core insuring clause … and therefore follows the fortunes of that clause'. Thus, if cover is to be excluded for the underlying liability, cover for the defence of that liability would be excluded in the same respect. *See* ibid para 8.19.

an increasing risk should DPA-related claims become more frequent in number and more frequently determined to be non-covered. Despite this, even when there are disputes as to whether the claim is covered/non-covered, some US policies pay 100% defence costs in a mixed claim.[142] This approach may be imported into UK policies, and it may be the case that allocation clauses do not cover investigation and defence costs, thus allowing some extension of coverage at an insured director's vulnerable time (this will be policy wording dependent).[143]

The US case of *Chartrand v Illinois Union Insurance Co*[144] illustrates that a policy bearing an Insured vs Insured exclusion will not operate to preclude all coverage where at least one Claim is made by an uninsured party, due to the ability to allocate defence costs,[145] which may be a relevant consideration should follow-on actions arise post-DPA.

15.5.1 The larger settlement rule

The larger settlement rule, as laid down in the US case of *Nordstrom Inc v Chubb & Son Inc*,[146] will apply where the director and company are part of a settlement to which one of the parties is uninsured, and that uninsured party's acts are determined to have increased the settlement (if provided within policy wording).[147] A joint DPA cannot be agreed with prosecutors by both the company and the director as co-defendants in the UK, as the latter is not availed the opportunity to agree a DPA.[148] Thus, should a DPA be considered a settlement for the purpose of applying this rule, this rule will not be applied so as to allocate away to the company (if uninsured) the director's defence costs. This may, however, apply in respect of consequential civil claims which arise against the company and (former) director. Notably, 'no allocation is necessary if the insured executive's liability was coterminous with that of the uninsured companies', and has not increased due to an uninsured person/company.[149]

142 Francis Kean, 'Allocation Clauses in D&O Polices: What You Need to Know' (*Willis Towers Watson*, 5 October 2018) <https://web.archive.org/web/20210126160701/https://www.willistowerswatson.com/en-GB/Insights/2018/10/allocation-clauses-in-do-polices-what-you-need-to-know> accessed 18 December 2020.

143 ibid.

144 *Chartrand v Illinois Union Insurance Co* (n 7).

145 Martin O'Leary and Kimberly Forrester, 'Policy Exclusions' in Martin J O'Leary (ed), *Directors & Officers Liability Insurance Deskbook* (American Bar Association 2020) 169.

146 *Nordstrom Inc v Chubb & Son Inc* 54 F 3d 1424 (9th Cir 1995).

147 *RSUI Indemnity Company v David H Murdock and Dole Food Company Inc* 2021 WL 803867, 41–42 (Del Mar 3 2021), citing *Nordstrom Inc v Chubb & Son Inc* (n 146) 1432, citing *Harbor Ins Co v Continental Bank Corp* 922 F 2d 357, 358 (7th Cir 1990); *Caterpillar Inc v Great Am Ins Co* 864 F Supp 849, 853 (CD Ill 1994). *See also* Goanos, *D&O 101: Understanding Directors and Officers Liability Insurance* (n 8) 93–94.

148 This may, however, be possible in the UK.

149 *Level 3 Communications Inc v Federal Insurance Co* 1999 WL 675295 (ND Ill Aug 18 1999). *See also* Martin O'Leary and Kimberly Forrester, 'Allocation' in Martin J O'Leary (ed), *Directors & Officers Liability Insurance Deskbook* (American Bar Association 2020) 225.

CHAPTER 16

Preservation of directors' protection

16.1 Order of Payments

An ABC D&O policy will typically bear an "Order/Priority of Payments" clause, which will follow the order of coverage from Side A to Side B and then to Side C.[1] Where each Side has its own tower of coverage, as D&O policies are "Claims made", the order of payments will be based on the chronological order in which Claims against parties falling within that tower were made.[2] Where Claims are deemed to have been made against multiple co-insureds under one Side at the same time, the allocation clause will respond. If the policy limit is likely to be exhausted by the indemnification, and the co-insureds are entitled to indemnification at the same point, it is likely that an equitable approach will be taken; the IA 2015, which requires the insurer to pay any sums due within a reasonable time,[3] will likely be considered the most reasonable approach. As elaborated in the case of *Teal Assurance Co Ltd v WR Berkley Insurance (Europe) Ltd*,[4] an insured cannot decide the order in which claims will be paid by the insurer.[5]

16.2 Preservation of the limit of indemnity

Where individual and corporate wrongdoing – and certainly accountability for wrongdoing – is so closely connected, various exposures arise as regards directors' protection under Side A. Policy composition where the director and company are co-insureds, and allocation of defence costs where questions as to coverage or insurability arise, are two examples of scenarios whereby the aggregate limit of indemnity within a D&O policy could face exhaustion, due to the colossal costs involved in corporate DPAs. This was previously warned by Chubb in 2019, when a claims example was given of a company entering into a DPA with a UK, US, and another regulator whereby allegedly almost 100 individuals were called to participate in the investigation, and Chubb advanced millions of

1 Larry Goanos, *D&O 101: Understanding Directors and Officers Liability Insurance* (Wells Media Group Inc 2014) 115; *In re TierOne Corp* 2012 WL 4513554 (Bankr D Neb Oct 2 2012).

2 *Teal Assurance Co Ltd v WR Berkley Insurance (Europe) Ltd* [2013] UKSC 57.

3 Insurance Act 2015, s 13A(1).

4 *Teal Assurance Co Ltd v WR Berkley Insurance (Europe) Ltd* (n 2).

5 In this case, the insured was not entitled to choose which claims had priority and thus fell within certain layers of the policy tower. The decisions of the lower courts were upheld: *Teal Assurance Co Ltd v WR Berkley Insurance (Europe) Ltd* [2011] EWHC 91 (Comm); *Teal Assurance Company Limited v WR Berkley Insurance (Europe) Limited* [2011] EWCA Civ 1570. *See Teal Assurance Co Ltd v WR Berkley Insurance (Europe) Ltd* (n 2) [2].

DOI: 10.4324/9781003456964-19

pounds in payments to their client, which was anticipated to most likely exhaust their primary limit under their policy.[6] For further context, the scale of the *Airbus SE* investigation meant that 'more than 1,750 entities were investigated globally as part of the case, spanning a database of more than 30 million documents';[7] the lawyers involved made 29 'subject matter presentations' to the SFO and French Parquet National Financier, whereby all key documents and related individuals were identified;[8] and the process involved numerous legal experts of various different law firms in the UK, France, and US, organised into a 'virtual law firm structure', which will all have come at a significant financial cost.[9] The UK DPA (which was part of a tri-country global settlement) contained a term requiring Airbus SE to pay the reasonable costs incurred by the SFO in its investigation, which totalled €6,989,401.[10]

Following the collapse of the trial of former Serco directors Nicholas Woods and Simon Marshall, the SFO agreed to pay the individuals £2.7 million in full and final settlement of any claim 'for costs incurred in connection with, or arising out of, the trial, the charges and/or the investigation'.[11] Whilst on this occasion the SFO bore the expense, this can be considered a rare circumstance; the trial collapsed due to 'significant failings'[12] by the prosecutor in respect of evidence. It was not possible for the SFO to determine how the £2.7 million sum could be apportioned to each former director when asked to do so by way of Freedom of Information request.[13] However, the exorbitant sum demonstrates the clear need for policy response under Side A, in cases where the costs would not be borne by

6 Chubb, 'Directors and Officers Claims are Increasing Both in Cost and Severity: Is Your Business Exposed?' (*Chubb*, 2019) <https://web.archive.org/web/20191226170511/https://www.chubb.com/uk-en/_assets/documents/final-06_18_do_claims_brochure_v2_lowres.pdf> accessed 26 June 2020, 3. It is not clear whether this claims example refers to a real client. However, real examples of internationally coordinated settlements have been observed since UK DPA introduction. In 2017, the *Rolls-Royce* UK DPA accompanied a US DPA and a settlement with the Brazilian Ministério Público Federal, and the investigation included hundreds of employees' data. *See Serious Fraud Office v Rolls-Royce Plc* [2017] Lloyd's Rep FC 249 (Crown); Serious Fraud Office, 'Deferred Prosecution Agreement – Statement of Facts – SFO v Rolls Royce PLC' (*Serious Fraud Office*, 17 January 2017) <https://www.sfo.gov.uk/download/deferred-prosecution-agreement-statement-facts-sfo-v-rolls-royce-plc/> accessed 15 May 2020.

7 Cristiano Dalla Bona, 'How Dechert Helped Airbus Reach the World's Largest Bribery Settlement' (*The Lawyer*, 23 October 2020) <https://www.thelawyer.com/how-dechert-helped-airbus-reach-the-worlds-largest-bribery-settlement/> accessed 16 December 2020.

8 ibid.

9 This included, though was not limited to, lawyers within Dechert, Clifford Chance, August Debouzy, Paul Hastings, and Arnold & Porter. The process also drew on the expertise of Hugo Keith KC of Three Raymond Buildings, Ben FitzGerald of QEB Hollis Whiteman (counsel to Airbus), and Tony Shaw KC of Red Lion Chambers (assisting Dechert). The Forensic Risk Alliance contributed e-discovery and accounting expertise. This was alongside the work of Airbus SE's internal legal team and general counsel John Harrison. *See* ibid.

10 *Director of the Serious Fraud Office v Airbus SE* [2021] Lloyd's Rep FC 159 (Crown) [88].

11 Email from A Abed to author (30 September 2021). This email was a response to a Freedom of Information request made under the Freedom of Information Act 2000 by the author to the Serious Fraud Office on 2 September 2021 (Case FOI2021-111). A Abed is the Information Officer from the Public Relations & Information Team who responded.

12 Jonathan Ames, 'SFO's Serco Fraud Trial Collapses' (*The Times*, 27 April 2021) <https://www.thetimes.co.uk/article/ex-serco-executives-cleared-of-hiding-profits-from-electronic-tagging-contracts-wsx2x3sq9> accessed 27 April 2021. It is worth bearing in mind that the SFO's decision not to bring former G4S executives to trial, years into the case, has left the agency awaiting the outcome of hearings and negotiations in respect of their liability for the defence costs of those individuals. The SFO is understood to have set aside approximately £6 million. *See* Serious Fraud Office, *Annual Report and Accounts 2022–23* (2023, HC 1473) 34.

13 'It is not possible to precisely apportion the £2.7million payment between each defendant.' *See* Email from A Abed to author (n 11).

the prosecutor. Lack of coverage to an individual when faced with such financial liability could be life-altering, life-changing, or even life-ruining.

It is crucial that Side A cover, particularly as regards defence costs, is ringfenced to ensure that the aggregate limit of indemnity is not consumed by corporate losses. This may be achieved by: (a) the provision of a separate tower for Side A with a separate limit, whilst ensuring composite policy composition; (b) providing directors' defence costs as a separate undertaking, not bound by the fortunes of the main insuring clause(s); or (c) the inclusion of a rigorous Order/Priority of Payments clause, and sufficient allocation provision. Such protective measures must be ensured particularly where the DPA case and individual prosecution are concurrent.

16.2.1 The potential for joint DPAs

In the US, where DPAs can be agreed with individuals, the possibility of a joint DPA with both a corporate and individual defendant arises. This remains somewhat unlikely considering the increased and continuing focus on the prosecution of individuals behind corporate crime, but nevertheless not impossible. In such circumstances, the consideration of whether the statement of facts would constitute an admission by the insured for the purpose of invoking the Conduct exclusion clause would be the same in the case of both parties: the statement of facts will constitute an admission by the parties jointly and severally. In the UK, shared statement of facts has now been seen in the *Bluu Solutions Limited* and *Tetris Projects Limited* DPAs.[14]

If individual DPAs were to be implemented in the UK, the interpretation would be the same, except where – for example – a particular part was drafted by one defendant without the other(s), and it is that part which the insurer intends to rely upon to invoke the exclusion against the uninvolved party. If the statement of facts were to expressly state elements of exclusive contribution, it could not be argued that the individual's agreement to the penalty would amount to an implied acceptance of wrongdoing exclusively admitted by co-defendants (due to the clear and purposeful disclaimer). Where the statement of facts is to be considered an admission of guilt upon breach (under section 10 of the CJA 1967, in the UK),[15] there would need to be some reflection upon its drafting. A jointly drafted statement of facts would be considered an admission by each in its entirety, whereas a statement of facts which is compartmentalised (in sections of contribution by separate parties alone) would be considered an admission to the relevant offence, but excluding admissions made exclusively by other parties in respect of their own conduct. It is likely in such circumstances that two separate statement of facts would attach to one DPA concurrently, which is not precluded by Schedule 17 to the CACA 2013.[16]

Were a joint DPA to arise with corporate and individual co-defendants, allocation issues may arise where the company (for example) is uninsured. Where the reasonably

14 Serious Fraud Office, 'Statement of Facts' (*Serious Fraud Office*, 2 March 2023) <https://www.sfo.gov.uk/download/r-v-bluu-solutions-limited-and-tetris-projects-limited/> accessed 28 March 2023.

15 Crime and Courts Act 2013, sch 17 para 13(2).

16 'A DPA must contain *a* statement of facts relating to the alleged offence, which may include admissions made by P' (emphasis added). Though a singular "a" is adopted in the language of the provision, this is not exclusive (for example, it does not specify "one") and could instead be interpreted as setting out a minimum. *See* ibid sch 17 para 5(1).

related test applies, or even in ABC policies whereby the company is insured but there is insufficient severability in respect of policy limits, this could see dramatic exhaustion in the aggregate limit of indemnity, particularly if Side A is not ringfenced. Greater costs will inevitably be incurred despite any simultaneous investigation into the co-defendants. This can be evidenced by considering the costs incurred by the SFO in the investigations relating to the *Serco Geografix Ltd* DPA, whereby the investigation into the company cost £3,723,679, and the investigations into the two former directors Simon Marshall and Nicholas Woods cost £3,130,277 in respect of each individual.[17] Payment of the prosecutor's reasonable investigation costs tends to comprise part of the penalty within a DPA, and would not ultimately be indemnifiable due to *ex turpi causa non oritur actio* and the consideration of the public interest and integrity of the justice system.[18] However, these figures, alongside those noted above in respect of the SFO's settlement of individual costs, represent the exorbitant costs associated with DPAs and threat to limits particularly where coverage disputes arise.[19] Therefore, it will be crucial to ensure that the company is insured under Side C, and that the measures suggested above are adopted.

16.3 Side A DIC and developing products

A Side A difference-in-conditions ("DIC") policy operates as a drop-down to provide coverage where the core traditional Side A policy will not or cannot do so, therefore 'filling the coverage gaps'.[20] DIC is useful as a tool to circumvent the restrictive exclusion clauses present in standard Side A cover. Generally, the only exclusion that remains is the Conduct exclusion,[21] thus rendering DIC useful as a comfort blanket of protection to provide coverage where the primary insurer wrongfully denies cover,[22] or does not provide cover for other reasons (policy wording relevant here).[23] The Beazley DIC policy, in respect of its Conduct exclusion clause, expressly outlines that a company's statement of facts pursuant to a DPA 'does not constitute formal written admission by an insured person'.[24] This demonstrates some movement towards recognition of the implications surrounding corporate statement of facts and coverage disputes, and will positively impact a director's ability to obtain an advancement of defence costs in criminal proceedings post-DPA. Advancement

17 Email from A Abed to author (n 11).

18 *Patel v Mirza* [2016] UKSC 42 [120] (Lord Toulson).

19 This would be further exacerbated if DPAs were to be expanded in the UK to civil violations, as they are in the US.

20 GB&A, 'Understanding The Many Facets Of Side A DIC D&O' (*GB&A*, 2019) <https://www.gbainsurance.com/facets_side_a_dic_918> accessed 16 September 2019.

21 Marsh, 'FINPRO Coverage Considerations: Why a Company Should Consider Buying Side A Difference in Conditions ("Side A DIC") Coverage' (*Marsh*, 2019) <https://www.marsh.com/us/insights/research/finpro-coverage-considerations-why-a-company-should-consider-buying-side-a-difference-in-conditions-coverage.html> accessed 16 September 2019.

22 Willis HRH, 'A-Side D&O FAQ' (*Willis*, June 2009) <https://www.willis.com/Documents/Publications/Services/Executive_Risks/2009/Executive_Risks_Alert_-_0609_-_A-Side_FAQs.pdf> accessed 28 August 2019.

23 Chubb, 'Side A Claim Payments' (*Chubb*, September 2017) <https://www.gbainsurance.com/sites/default/files/2018-09/D%26O%20-%20Side%20A%20Claim%20Payments%20Chubb%20Whitepaper.pdf> accessed 16 September 2019, 10.

24 Beazley, 'Side A DIC Policy' (*Beazley*) <https://web.archive.org/web/20220421213351/https://www.beazley.com/documents/Wordings/Side%20A%20DIC.pdf> accessed 7 September 2021, 3.

will be offered as part of the DIC coverage where the company and primary insurer fail to advance and the DIC policy terms permit response.

The Beazley DIC policy covers Loss which is not indemnified by the company or the primary insurer which the insurer 'would be *contractually* required to pay or advance'[25] (emphasis added), subject to the DIC policy Conduct exclusion. Where the underlying Side A policy does not contractually provide for defence costs cover in criminal proceedings (for example), the Beazley DIC policy would not respond, irrespective of the fact that the Conduct exclusion clause may not be invoked. The Berkshire Hathaway specimen DIC policy is not as restrictive as that provided by Beazley. Berkshire Hathaway provides coverage for 'all Loss'[26] where the company or the primary insurer does not respond, subject to the DIC policy's Conduct exclusion clause. Although the Loss must arise from a Claim alleging a Wrongful Act as per the first policy's definitions (subject to any amendment within the DIC policy's definitions), there is no express specification that the Loss indemnified by way of "DIC" will only be that which the primary insurer is legally or contractually required to pay but for the Conduct exclusion.

If the primary policy provides for defence costs, the same coverage will be extended under DIC (unless otherwise stated); where this is not the case, DIC policies providing additional defence costs cover (beyond the primary policy) will be interpreted alongside contractual principles, providing that the trigger for cover has arisen. However, a DIC policy omitting such a provision would not serve to provide coverage where the Side A policy does not respond on the same basis. If the Side A policy was to respond, the value of DIC would be its application where Side A does not provide coverage for another reason, or its broader terms. This demonstrates the importance to directors of the inclusion of defence costs within the underlying policy, or as an express addition to coverage provided under DIC.

In the US, many corporations include, as a condition of a senior executive employment contract, that protection be extended by the corporation in circumstances where the executive is the subject of a criminal allegation or that of a similar nature.[27] Such conditions may be further protected by the state requiring adherence to corporate bylaws. This contractual condition is viewed as a necessity of employment by many executives and is offered alongside D&O insurance, which may also be a condition of the executive's protection package. Whilst it is the case that corporations can agree to mandatory advancement of defence costs, in most American local jurisdictions the individual protected must show an entitlement to ultimate indemnification and therefore will be required to repay any defence costs advanced by the company if not so entitled.[28] D&O protection remains vital even where corporations promise advancement of defence costs as part of

25 If it were not for an invoked exclusion by the primary insurer, or denial to pay for defence costs incurred unnecessarily, or denial to pay on the basis of late notification. *See* ibid.

26 Berkshire Hathaway Specialty Insurance, 'Executive First Side A DIC Directors & Officers Liability Policy' (*Berkshire Hathaway*, 2015) <https://www.bhspecialty.com/wp-content/uploads/2016/02/EP-DIC-001-02-2015-SIDE-A-DIC-POLICY-FORM.pdf> accessed 9 September 2021.

27 James Wing and Andrew Oringer, 'Discipline Involving Multiple Disciplines—Protecting Innocent Executives in the Age of "Cooperation"' (2015) 70(4) The Business Lawyer 1123, 1127.

28 'In most cases, indemnification is permitted only if executives can show that the conduct questioned in the underlying civil or criminal litigation was in good faith and that they reasonably believed that it was not contrary to the corporation's interests and was not illegal (state law formulations of this principle vary).' *See* ibid 1128.

an employment package, as a later reluctance or refusal to cover such costs will leave an individual without solid protection.

With the current ‘“cooperation revolution”’[29] requiring corporations in the US to cooperate in conflict with their own individuals, against their best interests and the promises once extended, it is increasingly crucial to ensure individuals are sufficiently protected. DIC coverage is particularly important in the US as it offers greater protection regarding the advancement of defence costs, often beyond that of state and corporate bylaws and promises, and provides the individuals with a protected separate limit. In the US, DIC policies will also protect the individual's right to exercise their Fifth Amendment privilege,[30] which may be compromised by the corporation, particularly with an increasing focus in internal investigation and cooperation with authorities.[31] Individual protection is increasingly important, separate from the interests or influence of the corporation itself.

Other products have entered the market in recent years in attempts to broaden the scope of directors' protection and to remedy the negatives that can arise within an ABC policy. For example, the ‘Side-A Match Edge (SAME)℠ Endorsement’ extends the breadth of a Side A policy to the DIC coverage when purchased together through AIG, with the DIC policy offering broader advancement and pre-Claim investigations coverage.[32] Willis Towers Watson offer ‘Directors’ All Risk Cover (DARCstar)’, which operates on an “all risks” basis whereby ‘the assumption is that the risk is covered unless excluded’, also offering internal and external investigations cover and advancement of all costs where allocation disputes arise.[33]

The introduction of such products could be perceived as demonstrating two shifts within D&O: the devaluation of Side A since its inception, and/or the increasing risk and thus need for directors to obtain coverage of ever-widening scope. In respect of a perceived devaluation, the introduction of Side C – though intended to protect Side A[34] – has weakened many ABC policies, particularly where the aggregate limit of indemnity is communal (not divided by Sides), where allocation provisions are unclear and trigger disputes, and where severability provisions are weak. For some time there was a greater focus on ensuring corporate responsibility for criminal activity, and this is evidenced by the proliferation of DPAs for corporations in the US over the past few decades and the relatively recent introduction of the tool in the UK (and subsequent jurisdictions).[35] Whilst

29 ibid 1123.

30 The privilege against self-incrimination, which can be exercised in legal proceedings and investigations. *See United States v Balsys* 524 US 666, 672 (1998).

31 Wing and Oringer (n 27) 1138.

32 AIG, ‘A New Standard for Side-A Directors and Officers Liability’ (*American International Group Inc*, 2014) <https://web.archive.org/web/20211004043442/https://www.aig.com/content/dam/aig/america-canada/us/documents/business/management-liability/sidea-external-final-brochure.pdf> accessed 17 September 2021.

33 Willis Towers Watson, ‘Directors’ & Officers’ Insurance’ (*Willis Towers Watson*, 1 September 2020) <https://www.willistowerswatson.com/-/media/WTW/Insights/2020/09/directors-and-officers-insurance.pdf?modified=20200901122754> accessed 17 December 2020, 9.

34 Following the decision in *Nordstrom Inc v Chubb & Son Inc* 54 F 3d 1424 (9th Cir 1995).

35 Introduced in Singapore in March 2018 by the Criminal Justice Reform Act. Since September 2018, available in Canada under the Criminal Code of Canada, RSC 1985, c C-46, Schedule to Part XXII.1. Available in France, known as “*Convention Judiciaire d'Intérêt Public*”, since December 2019 under Article 22 of *loi n° 2016-1691 du 9 décembre 2016 relative à la transparence, à la lutte contre la corruption et à la modernisation de la vie économique (1)* (“Sapin II”). Introduced in the States of Jersey in December 2022 by the Criminal Justice (Deferred Prosecution Agreements) (Jersey) Law 2023. Support, based on the UK model, demonstrated in the Law Reform Commission of Ireland's report on regulatory powers and corporate offences. *See*

this focus undoubtedly remains, particularly in the UK, the gravitating spotlight to individuals behind corporate crime is exposing such individuals to (particularly criminal) accountability.

With risk increasing, and increasing encouragement and incentivisation of corporate cooperation in ensuring individual accountability, it is crucial for directors to ensure that their D&O cover does not leave them exposed. Hence, such products as those offered by AIG and Willis Towers Watson are becoming all the more crucial if the adequate scope of primary Side A cover cannot be obtained. In cases where Side A DIC or other products offering broader coverage cannot be obtained (for example, due to financial difficulties), it is pertinent that directors ensure their primary Side A cover is rigorous enough to adequately protect in the current corporate '"cooperation revolution"'[36] climate.

16.4 Former directors

Former directors may be exposed where the company continues to purchase D&O insurance on a Claims made basis (as is typical) but without sufficient cover to extend to former directors. It will be crucial for former directors to stay informed as to their level of protection, and, though uncommon, it may be prudent for the individual to purchase their own Side A cover.[37] As DPA offences have commonly been predicated on historic wrongdoing, it will be vital for former directors to remain protected. Legal representation will likely be required during the lengthy investigations, as soul-searching missions to find the individuals responsible, and during any criminal (or civil) proceedings against the individuals which may thereafter arise.

16.5 The danger of the Related Claims clause

Though a director cannot be a co-defendant in a UK DPA, as DPAs are not available to individuals, it may be detrimental to an insured director if they face civil proceedings as co-defendants with the company whilst their own criminal proceedings are ongoing.[38] In such circumstances, the consequences of the civil proceedings may impact the insurance claim relating to the criminal proceedings where a Related Claims clause is invoked (**Section 13.2**). An Allianz sample Related Claim definition reads:

Law Reform Commission of Ireland, *Regulatory Powers and Corporate Offences: Volume I* (LRC 119-2018, 2018) 219–279. Support demonstrated in the Australian Law Reform Commission's final report on corporate criminal responsibility in 2020. *See* Australian Law Reform Commission, *Final Report: Corporate Criminal Responsibility* (ALRC Report 136, 2020). Support demonstrated in the Zondo Commission's report in South Africa in 2022. *See* Judicial Commission of Inquiry into allegations of State Capture, 'Corruption and Fraud in the Public Sector, Judicial Commission of Inquiry into State Capture Report: Part 1: Vol. 1: South African Airways and its Associated Companies' (*South African Government*, 4 January 2022) <https://www.gov.za/documents/judicial-commission-enquiry-state-capture-report-part-1-4-jan-2022-0000> accessed 12 April 2023, 852. Reportedly under consideration by the Malaysian Anti-Corruption Commission. *See* The Star, 'Azam: DPA Being Assessed' (*The Star*, 2 October 2023) <https://www.thestar.com.my/news/nation/2023/10/02/azam-dpa-being-assessed> accessed 3 October 2023.

36 Wing and Oringer (n 27) 1123.

37 Guy Wilkes and Francis Kean, 'The Position of Individuals in Regulatory Investigations: A Changing Landscape' (2017) 1(2) Journal of Financial Compliance 172, 181.

38 *RSUI Indemnity Company v David H Murdock and Dole Food Company Inc* 2021 WL 803867, 6–8 (Del Mar 3 2021). Here, a stockholder action and federal securities class action named the company and a number of executives as co-defendants, and the D&O insurer joined them as a single Claim.

> Any and all Claims and/or Investigations and or Self Report Investigations (whether made or commenced before, during or after the Period of Insurance) arising out of, based upon or attributable to the same source or cause.[39]

Joinder of Claims by the same source or cause to constitute one single "Related Claim"[40] (subject to the same treatment as the Claim definition) presents great risk to an insured director, drafted in such broad terms. This sample clause also demonstrates – conversely to the positives of the potential for cover – the exposures arising where investigations are included within the policy. The relevant Allianz policy includes investigations within the Claim definition, but nevertheless explicitly outlines investigations as a separate matter for joinder under a Related Claims clause. For an individual insured to obtain optimum coverage, the Related Claims clause should not feature within the policy. However, this is unlikely. It may be the case that the policy condition relating to Related Claims sets out that the Claims will be deemed a single matter where made against the insured as a sole defendant only. This is similarly extremely unlikely, as the clause is designed to limit the insurer's scope of liability and therefore may be subject to limited negotiation at the policy application stage.

Furthermore, it is not only civil proceedings relating to DPAs which may see the director become a co-defendant, as individuals have also been prosecuted as co-defendants in DPA-related cases.[41] Where possible, the director should seek severance of proceedings and may rely upon prejudice to their own proceedings,[42] for example in respect of access to a defence (via defence costs cover).[43] Where the Related Claims clause is applied in such circumstances, despite severability provisions under a policy, an insured director may find that cover is greatly diminished. If the co-defendant company is uninsured and the applicable allocation provisions do not provide for the allocation of the costs away from the policy, the limit of indemnity could also be expeditiously reduced.[44]

39 Allianz, 'Complete Directors & Officers: Policy Wording' (*Allianz Insurance plc*, 2020) <https://www.allianzebroker.co.uk/content/allianzebroker/en_gb/application/content/documents/commercial-products/sme/complete-directors-and-officers/complete-directors-officers-policy-wording/_jcr_content/documentProperties/currentDocument.res/complete-directors-officers-wording_acom4288.pdf> accessed 15 October 2020, 13.

40 'All Related Claims shall be deemed to be one single matter and deemed to be made at the same time as the first of such Related Claims was made or is deemed to have been made.' *See* ibid 22.

41 This has been the case following the *Sarclad Ltd, Tesco Stores Ltd, Serco Geografix Ltd, Güralp Systems Ltd, G4S C&J, Bluu Solutions Limited,* and *Tetris Projects Limited* DPAs. Further, in the US, DPAs are available to individuals.

42 In respect of the UK, *see* Indictment Act 1921, s 5(3). *See also* Criminal Justice Act 1987, s 7(1)(e).

43 This may fall within the scope of the right to a fair trial. *See* Human Rights Act 1998, sch 1 pt 1 arts 6(3)(b)–(c); Convention for the Protection of Human Rights and Fundamental Freedoms (European Convention on Human Rights, as amended) (ECHR) arts 6(3)(b)–(c).

Tesco Supermarkets Ltd v Nattrass [1972] AC 153 (HL) 180.

44 Under the larger settlement rule, 'no allocation is necessary if the insured executive's liability was coterminous with that of the uninsured companies', and has not increased due to an uninsured person/company. *See Level 3 Communications Inc v Federal Insurance Co* 1999 WL 675295 (ND Ill Aug 18 1999). Under the reasonably related test, exhaustion of the limit will be a consideration where the defence costs of an uninsured company are considered to be reasonably related, as there will not be allocation between them, thus supporting the value of Side C. *See Coronation Insurance Co v Clearly Canadian Beverage Corp* (1999) 117 BCAC 22 (CA).

PART IV

COMPANIES' D&O INSURANCE COVERAGE

Recognising the importance of considering the impact of deferred prosecution agreements ("DPA(s)") on directors' liability, and consequently directors' coverage under Side A of a directors' and officers' ("D&O") liability insurance policy, is alone insufficient in painting a fuller picture. Part IV thus considers the response of Side B and Side C of a D&O policy: Side B providing indemnification to a corporate body where it meets its own indemnification obligations to its directors, and Side C amounting to varying levels of entity coverage. Combining the three Sides of coverage in the traditional ABC D&O policy may be convenient, but can carry with it various exposures to those insured. Vulnerabilities arise where coverage afforded to entities exhausts the policy limit of indemnity, where exclusions applied to preclude coverage against one insured consequently apply to other co-insureds, and where knowledge of co-insureds is deemed to be shared. Providing just a few examples gives an idea of the collateral damage that can result where an ABC policy responds (or otherwise) in DPA-related circumstances. Thus, Part IV seeks to identify the issues arising under Side B and Side C in such circumstances and highlights the consequential impact on individual co-insureds.

DOI: 10.4324/9781003456964-20

CHAPTER 17

Coverage under Side B

A company is permitted to indemnify its directors by virtue of section 234 of the CA 2006 as regards third-party actions (with some exceptions) (**Section 3.2.2**). Such indemnification is not a legal requirement,[1] but a company may opt to offer such a provision in order to ameliorate the directorship role and thus facilitate recruitment. Where offered, a company may seek cover under Side B in order to transfer its liability through insurance and obtain its own indemnification for indemnifying its director(s).[2] Side B is commonly referred to within a policy as "company reimbursement cover" and operates in practice as a form of balance sheet protection. It is thus the "Side" of D&O coverage which most commonly responds.

17.1 The position of Side B in DPA-related circumstances

In DPA-related cases, indemnification of directors has great value. However, the company is limited in its ability to indemnify, and this position may vary depending on the DPA stage. A common term amongst UK DPAs requires the company to cooperate in the prosecution of individuals and will typically be worded as follows: 'shall cooperate fully and honestly with any and all SFO pre-investigations, investigations and prosecutions … subject to applicable law and regulations.'[3] Wording may vary, and it may be specified that the cooperation requirement spans the term of the agreement[4] (or even beyond the term),[5] or that cooperation will include specified actions such as retention of material.[6]

1 Explanatory Notes to the Companies Act 2006, para 429.

2 It is the company that is insured. *See Porter v GIO* [2003] NSWSC 668.

3 Serious Fraud Office, 'Amec Foster Wheeler Energy Limited – Deferred Prosecution Agreement' (*Serious Fraud Office*, 2 July 2021) <https://www.sfo.gov.uk/download/amec-foster-wheeler-energy-limited-deferred-prosecution-agreement/> accessed 2 July 2021, para 11.

4 Courts and Tribunal Judiciary, 'SFO -v- G4S: Tab C – SFO v G4S Care Justice Services (UK) Limited Deferred Prosecution Agreement' (*Courts and Tribunal Judiciary*, 17 July 2020) <https://www.judiciary.uk/judgments/sfo-v-g4s/> accessed 18 July 2020, para 12. cf ibid para 11 (which has no timing specification).

5 For example, where a parent company agrees an undertaking attached to the subsidiary's DPA: 'This undertaking affords a considerable benefit to the interests of justice by ensuring cooperation throughout any prosecution, even if proceedings continue beyond 2 years.' *See Director of the Serious Fraud Office v Bluu Solutions Limited and Tetris-Projects Limited* [2023] EWHC 1976 (KB) [93] (Mrs Justice May DBE).

6 Serious Fraud Office, 'Deferred Prosecution Agreement, Statement of Facts, Approved Judgment – SFO v Güralp Systems Ltd: Deferred Prosecution Agreement' (*Serious Fraud Office*, 20 December 2019) <https://www.sfo.gov.uk/download/deferred-prosecution-agreement-statement-of-facts-approved-judgment-sfo-v-guralp-systems-ltd/> accessed 9 February 2021, para 9.

DOI: 10.4324/9781003456964-21

Nonetheless, such terms are typically broad in scope. There will also commonly be a term requiring the company to:

> cooperate fully and honestly with any other domestic or foreign law enforcement and regulatory authorities and agencies in any investigation or prosecution of any of its present or former officers, directors, employees, agents, and consultants, or any third party, in any and all matters relating to the conduct which is the subject of the Indictment and described in the Statement of Facts, subject to applicable laws and regulations.[7]

Language of the given example may differ between DPAs but will typically require the same scope and nature of cooperation. Considering that a DPA requires the company to cooperate fully with prosecutors in the investigation into and/or prosecution of directors, arguably the company's provision of a defence to such individuals would be contrary to its terms.[8] This will likely particularly be the case where the company is facilitating a defence which in essence contests the basis or content of the DPA, as it may be considered that such an action constitutes a contradiction of the agreement. The company is expressly disallowed from raising a defence or making or authorising public statements to be made which contradict the statement of facts.[9] Though the defence restriction appears to apply to the company's raising its own defence, this is not specified, and in any event the funding of a contesting director's defence may constitute the authorisation of a contradictory public statement.[10] It is therefore unlikely that a company with an active DPA will indemnify its (former) directors, and Side B is consequently likely to be less prominent in DPA-related circumstances.

The approach as regards the corporate indemnification of directors may *prima facie* be less restrictive where the company has not yet agreed a DPA. However, this will likely in turn restrict the company's ability to reach such an agreement. With increasing focus on self-reporting, the price of a DPA is often the surrendering of (former) individuals. Whilst prosecutors may recognise that a company providing such indemnification is doing so in line with its obligations, the public perception of this juxtaposing corporate position may be a factor in opting not to offer a DPA.[11] As a result, the company may elect not to indemnify its directors if it wishes to avail itself of the opportunity to successfully negotiate,

---

7 Serious Fraud Office, 'Deferred Prosecution Agreement Airbus 31.01.20' (*Serious Fraud Office*, 28 February 2020) <https://www.sfo.gov.uk/download/airbus-se-deferred-prosecution-agreement-statement-of-facts/> accessed 11 February 2021, para 13.

8 This would also arguably be contrary to any clause within the Side B policy requiring cooperation with the insurer in respect of mitigation of costs.

9 This is a common term throughout all UK DPAs. *See for example* Serious Fraud Office, 'Deferred Prosecution Agreement Airbus 31.01.20' (n 7) para 15: 'Nothing in paragraphs 11 through 14 [regarding cooperation] is intended to derogate from Airbus' legal rights to raise any defences or assert affirmative claims in criminal, civil, and regulatory proceedings in other fora or jurisdictions relating to the matters set out in the Statement of Facts, provided such defences and claims do not contradict, in whole or in part, a statement contained in the Statement of Facts or otherwise violate paragraphs 35 through 37 below [regarding public statements].'

10 'Airbus agrees that it shall not make, *and it shall not authorise* its present or future lawyers, officers, directors, employees, agents or shareholders, or any other person authorised to speak on Airbus' behalf to make any public statement contradicting the matters described in the Statement of Facts' (emphasis added). *See* ibid para 35.

11 The public interest must be considered by prosecutors before offering a DPA. *See* Crown Prosecution Service and Serious Fraud Office, 'Deferred Prosecution Agreements Code of Practice' (*Crown Prosecution Service*, 11 February 2014) <https://www.cps.gov.uk/sites/default/files/documents/publications/dpa_cop.pdf> accessed 9 June 2020, para 1.2(ii).

and Side B has considerably less pertinence where a company wishes to or is negotiating a DPA.

This issue was litigated in the US between 2006 and 2008, following a DPA entered into by KPMG with prosecutors.[12] In background to the case of *US v Stein I*,[13] KPMG had been prevented from advancing legal costs to its directors, officers, and employees by virtue of its DPA. The case arises against the backdrop of US memoranda and their implementation by the government. The 1999 Holder Memorandum set out that 'willingness to cooperate in the investigation of its agents' would be a consideration in deciding whether to prosecute a corporation, alongside 'whether the corporation appears to be protecting its culpable employees and agents'. This was followed by the example: 'through the advancing of attorneys [sic] fees … [which] may be considered by the prosecutor in weighing the extent and value of a corporation's cooperation'.[14] There was a footnote to the memorandum which noted that where a state requires such payment to be made, prior to a determination of guilt, this adherence to the law 'should not be considered a failure to cooperate'.[15]

Under the Holder Memorandum, an advancement made except where required by law would thus be considered as protectionist and may be a factor weighed against the corporation.[16] The 2003 Thompson Memorandum which followed differed in that it was binding on all federal prosecutors, but the aforementioned provisions regarding advancement remained wholly unchanged.[17] This was thus a consideration of prosecutors in the investigation into KPMG, and was taken by KPMG to be determinative on the basis of representations made by chief counsel to the United States Attorney.[18]

On the understanding that it did not have a binding legal obligation to advance legal fees, KPMG implemented a policy whereby it capped fees at $400,000 (US). Payment of fees was conditional on full cooperation by the individual concerned with KPMG and the government, which entailed not invoking the privilege against self-incrimination (under the Fifth Amendment). Further, advancement would cease upon charging with a criminal offence.[19] The government worked with KPMG in ensuring that the messages circulated

12 The United States Department of Justice, 'KPMG to Pay $456 Million for Criminal Violations in Relation to Largest-Ever Tax Shelter Fraud Case' (*The United States Department of Justice*, 29 August 2005) <https://www.justice.gov/archive/opa/pr/2005/August/05_ag_433.html> accessed 9 October 2021.

13 435 F Supp 2d 330 (SDNY 2006).

14 The Deputy Attorney General, 'Bringing Criminal Charges Against Corporations' (*The United States Department of Justice*, 16 June 1999) <https://www.justice.gov/sites/default/files/criminal-fraud/legacy/2010/04/11/charging-corps.PDF> accessed 21 March 2021.

15 ibid.

16 *US v Stein I* (n 13) 337.

17 Larry Thompson, 'Principles of Federal Prosecution of Business Organizations' (*The United States Department of Justice*, 20 January 2003) <https://web.archive.org/web/20030429005746/https://www.justice.gov/dag/cftf/corporate_guidelines.htm> accessed 20 March 2021. 'Thus, all United States Attorneys now are obliged to consider the advancing of legal fees by business entities, except such advances as are required by law, as at least possibly indicative of an attempt to protect culpable employees and as a factor weighing in favor of indictment of the entity.' *See US v Stein I* (n 13) 337–338.

18 'In sum, Ms. Neiman's comment that "misconduct" cannot or should not "be rewarded" under "federal guidelines," whatever went through her mind when she said it, was understood by both KPMG and government representatives as a reminder that payment of legal fees by KPMG, beyond any that it might legally be obligated to pay, could well count against KPMG in the government's decision whether to indict the firm … Thus, while the [US Attorney's Office] did not say in so many words that it did not want KPMG to pay legal fees, no one at the meeting could have failed to draw that conclusion.' *See US v Stein I* (n 13) 342–344.

19 ibid 344–346.

amongst its personnel encouraged interviews without counsel.[20] This hostile environment led to multiple occasions whereby the government would notify KPMG of a lack of individual cooperation, which ultimately led to the removal of legal fee advancement.[21] Problematically, in Stein's case, KPMG had not followed the $400,000 cap, and the government grew increasingly unimpressed with the corporation's cooperation, thus leading to a complete cessation of payment of Stein's fees and severance agreement.[22] This ultimately led to the KPMG DPA, which continued to require cooperation into the investigations into and prosecutions/proceedings against individuals; failure to do so would 'almost certainly … result in the criminal conviction … as the admissions that KPMG … made would foreclose a successful defense'.[23]

Individuals indicted by the government on the same day as the DPA,[24] known as the "KPMG Defendants", thereafter 'moved to dismiss the indictment or for other relief on the ground that the government had interfered improperly with the advancement of attorneys' fees by KPMG in violation of their constitutional and other rights'.[25] It was ultimately determined that the KPMG Defendants' Fifth and Sixth US Constitutional rights had been violated. The Thompson Memorandum – as regards advancement – did not pass the test of scrutiny and was deemed to violate due process and 'excessively the constitutional rights of the individuals … to defend themselves'; '[t]he actions of the [US Attorney's Office] in this case compounded the problem that the Thompson Memorandum created' by way of reinforcement of the threat posed by and inherent within the memorandum and also failed against scrutiny.[26] Though it was KPMG's decision to cease advancement upon individual indictment, this was a 'direct consequence of the pressure applied by the Thompson Memorandum and the [US Attorney's Office]',[27] as the government 'held the proverbial gun to its head'.[28] Irrespective of state law on corporate advancement, the Thompson Memorandum and the government's threatening to take into account corporate advancement were held to have 'interfered with the rights of such employees to a fair trial and to the effective assistance of counsel',[29] without justification of such interference (and irrespective of prejudice).[30] The government could not seek to influence the KPMG Defendants' defences[31] and, pertinently, it was also outlined (briefly) that 'the

20 ibid 347.

21 ibid.

22 ibid 347–348.

23 ibid 349–350.

24 *US v Stein II* 541 F 3d 130, 139–140 (2d Cir 2008).

25 *US v Stein I* (n 13) 350.

26 The test of strict scrutiny under the Due Process Clause. *See* ibid 364–365.

27 ibid 353.

28 ibid 336.

29 ibid 382.

30 '[T]his guarantees more than the mere presence of a lawyer at a criminal trial. It protects, among other things, an individual's right to choose the lawyer or lawyers he or she desires and to use one's own funds to mount the defense that one wishes to present.' *See* ibid 365–366, 369, 372, citing *Caplin Drysdale Chartered v United States* 491 US 617, 624 (1989).

31 'A defendant is guaranteed also "the right to be represented by an otherwise qualified attorney whom that defendant can afford to hire" — in other words, to use his or her own assets to defend the case, free of government regulation.' *See US v Stein I* (n 13) 357, citing *Caplin Drysdale Chartered v United States* (n 30) 624.

prosecution may not conceal exculpatory evidence or plea agreements with key government witnesses'.[32]

Judge Kaplan outlined that a corporation could cooperate with the government and pay the defence costs of its (former) employees simultaneously, with 'no necessary inconsistency'.[33] Furthermore, on the basis of the government's representation that the advancement of defence costs would not be considered in determining DPA compliance, and that it had no objection to KPMG doing so,[34] Judge Kaplan directed that the government 'shall adhere to its representation'.[35] In considering remedial action, Judge Kaplan determined that the violation could be resolved by advancement (by KPMG voluntarily or by government urgence within the power of the DPA cooperation clause), or by the KPMG Defendants obtaining an advancement order via summary proceeding.[36] However, thereafter in *US v Stein IV*,[37] Judge Kaplan dismissed the indictment against the defendants as no other remedy could put the KPMG Defendants in the position that they would otherwise have been in.[38]

In the appeal case of *US v Stein II*,[39] against this dismissal, it was held that the 'government … unjustifiably interfered with defendants' relationship with counsel and their ability to mount a defense, in violation of the Sixth Amendment', but the court did not rule on the district court's Fifth Amendment finding.[40] It was established that Judge Kaplan's findings of fact were not 'clearly erroneous' and thus were undisturbed.[41] However, the government contested that dismissal of the indictment was incorrect as it had cured any violation by stating that KPMG could '"exercise its business judgment"'.[42] This was unsuccessful, and dismissal of the indictment was 'required'.[43] Though the Sixth Amendment right to counsel was deprived by KPMG, this was deemed to have amounted to state action in the circumstances as the government became '(in effect) paymaster' of the relevant fees policy.[44] Most of the state action relevant to the consideration of the Sixth Amendment right occurred prior to the indictments, thus before the paymaster effectively directed cessation of advancement.[45] However, 'the government's pre-indictment conduct was of a kind that

32 *US v Stein I* (n 13) 358–359, citing *Giglio v United States* 405 US 150 (1972); *Brady v Maryland* 373 US 83, 87 (1963); *United States v Agurs* 427 US 97, 112 (1976).

33 *US v Stein I* (n 13) 364.

34 ibid 351.

35 ibid 382.

36 It was mooted that the government's substantial influence and power over KPMG by virtue of the DPA could be exerted in compelling KPMG to advance defence costs. *See* ibid 380.

37 495 F Supp 2d 390 (SDNY 2007).

38 ibid 419–428; *US v Stein II* (n 24) 142.

39 *US v Stein II* (n 24).

40 ibid 134.

41 ibid 143–144.

42 ibid 145; *US v Stein I* (n 13) 351.

43 'The prosecutor's isolated and ambiguous statement in a proceeding to which KPMG was not a party (and the nearly 16-month period of legal limbo that ensued) did not restore defendants to the status quo ante … Having assumed a supine position in the DPA — under which KPMG must continue to cooperate fully with the government — it is not all that likely that the firm would feel free to reverse course.' *See US v Stein II* (n 24) 145–146.

44 ibid 146–151.

45 By way of indictments. *See* ibid 150, 152.

would have post-indictment effects of Sixth Amendment significance, and did' and therefore such conduct was not 'immune from scrutiny'.[46]

Irrespective of the fact that the KPMG Defendants were not necessarily entitled to advancement by law, the Sixth Amendment prohibits government interference with defence resources without justification, which the government could not establish.[47] Though some of the KPMG Defendants were deprived of their right to counsel of choice, and others were not so deprived of choice (but instead faced unjustifiable interference by the government in their relationship with counsel and ability to defend themselves), in both instances the Sixth Amendment was violated. Notably, since the *Stein I* case, the McNulty Memorandum had been implemented, which set out that prosecutors may 'in extremely rare circumstances' consider advancement policies only where they are 'intended to impede a criminal investigation', and with the approval of the Deputy Attorney General.[48]

Drawing upon the *Stein* decisions in considering a UK director in a similar position, it would *prima facie* appear that similar reasoning could be applied in setting out that a prosecutor cannot interfere with an individual's defence, and thus the funding of it.[49] Therefore, an expectation of corporate cooperation within a DPA term – or factor in favour of offering a DPA – which restricts a corporate's indemnification of its directors (expressly or de facto as a result of the power imbalance, as in *Stein*) may be considered to be contrary to an individual's right to a fair trial.

This becomes problematic when considering the DPA term which disallows a company from making or authorising statements which contradict the DPA and statement of facts. A serving director (as the continuing 'directing mind and will')[50] exercising their right to defence in such circumstances may expose the company to DPA breach, which effectively compels the company to withdraw from providing any assistance in defence. DPAs will not realistically be amended to omit this term,[51] and therefore this will be a remaining

46 'Although defendants' Sixth Amendment rights attached only upon indictment, the district court properly considered pre-indictment state action that affected defendants post-indictment. When the government acts prior to indictment so as to impair the suspect's relationship with counsel post- indictment, the pre-indictment actions ripen into cognizable Sixth Amendment deprivations upon indictment.' *See* ibid 154.

47 ibid 156, citing *Stein v KPMG LLP* 486 F 3d 753, 762 (2d Cir 2007).

48 Paul McNulty, 'Principles of Federal Prosecution of Business Organizations' (*The United States Department of Justice*, 5 July 2007) <https://www.justice.gov/sites/default/files/dag/legacy/2007/07/05/mcnulty_memo.pdf> accessed 9 October 2021.

49 Article 6 of ECHR, implemented in Article 6 of the HRA 1998, sets out the right to a fair trial, which includes the right 'to have adequate time and facilities for the preparation of his defence' and the right 'to defend himself in person or through legal assistance of his own choosing'. *See* Convention for the Protection of Human Rights and Fundamental Freedoms (European Convention on Human Rights, as amended) (ECHR) arts 6(3)(b)–(c); Human Rights Act 1998, sch 1 pt 1 arts 6(3)(b)–(c). An individual has a right to counsel, implicit within the right to a fair trial, and the conducting of the defence is a matter between the defendant and their counsel. That right arises irrespective of funding of counsel, except in cases of failure by legal aid counsel to provide effective representation. *See Kamasinski v Austria* App no 9783/82 (ECtHR, 19 December 1989), para 65; *Stanford v United Kingdom* App no 16757/90 (ECtHR, 23 February 1994), para 28.

50 *Tesco Supermarkets Ltd v Nattrass* [1972] AC 153 (HL) 180.

51 Following a US DPA with Standard Chartered Bank, the chairman Sir John Peace in a press call contradicted the DPA's statement of facts by stating that the bank had not deliberately engaged in misconduct (notably, the statement of facts was based upon *wilful* misconduct). The chairman was thereafter forced to make an announcement through the Stock Exchange retreating on these claims, which were 'legally and factually incorrect'. The US Department of Justice told *The Times* that '"[i]n denying that Standard Chartered acted wilfully, Mr Peace blatantly contradicted the bank's acceptance of responsibility for its crimes. Under the terms of our agreement, Standard Chartered was required to retract the statement or be subject to prosecution"'. This demonstrates the foundational importance of such a term within US DPAs, which has been imported into UK

exposure. It is most likely that a director considered to have been involved in the criminality will no longer be part of the company, in order for the company to have obtained a DPA, and therefore a company would be able to publicly repudiate the former director's statements. However, the continued indemnification by the company of the individual's defence costs may still be considered an authorisation of such statements being made.

It is most likely that the corporate's agreement to indemnify the (former) director will be contractual,[52] and therefore failure to adhere to the agreement may give rise to an action against the company in contract.[53] Ultimately, though a DPA drafted in such a way that existing contractual agreements are disregarded may be considered 'improper',[54] resolution of this conflict in the interests of all parties whilst the allegedly wrongdoing director (in the very unlikely circumstances) remains with the company is unlikely and may be considered a risk of trying to benefit from all possible avenues (i.e., by obtaining a DPA, whilst being indemnified by the company). If the *Stein* interpretation of funding of defence is to be considered somewhat influential in the UK (as the importer of the model and its vast history), the corporate indemnification of former directors in adherence to contractual obligations whilst publicly repudiating statements made may be permissible in respect of corporate cooperation. However, the real issue is likely to remain in respect of remaining (allegedly) wrongdoing directors. Nevertheless, this demonstrates the potentially unlikely response of Side B and highlights the pressing need for sufficient Side A coverage of directors and former directors in such circumstances.

In the event that a company is permitted to honour its indemnification obligations during negotiations, or indemnification takes place during an earlier stage, the company can advance defence costs to a director but cannot indemnify for defence costs incurred in criminal proceedings in which the director is convicted.[55] Advancement could therefore be crucial where the director's Side A policy will not respond (for example, due to an exhausted limit). Though the company cannot indemnify the director for liabilities owed to the company itself, or for defence costs incurred in such civil litigation, indemnification is possible (with some exceptions) for third-party claims, and these may relate to actions which have also led to punitive sanctions imposed upon the company (for example, a

DPAs. *See* Patrick Hosking, 'Sir John Peace Apologises for Standard Chartered Press Call Gaffe' (*The Times*, 22 March 2013) <https://www.thetimes.co.uk/article/sir-john-peace-apologises-for-standard-chartered-press-call-gaffe-tgfw8gkl6h9> accessed 9 October 2021. Reportedly, Southern District Attorney Polly Greenberg tells a story about turning up on Peace's doorstep and threatening breach proceedings, which led to the relinquished position. This account was given by Polly Sprenger, former SFO lawyer, whose comments were made in an event hosted by the Institute of Advanced Legal Studies (School of Advanced Study University of London) online due to COVID-19 restrictions: The Centre for Financial Law, Regulation and Compliance, 'Deferred Prosecution Agreements' (online, Institute of Advanced Legal Studies 10 December 2020).

52 Guy Wilkes and Francis Kean, 'The Position of Individuals in Regulatory Investigations: A Changing Landscape' (2017) 1(2) Journal of Financial Compliance 172, 178.

53 The matter of contractual requirement to advance was not ruled upon in *Stein*, though the following was set out: 'All of the KPMG Defendants therefore had, at a minimum, every reason to expect that KPMG would pay their legal expenses … it appears quite possible that all had contractual and other legal rights to indemnification and advancement of defense costs, although the Court declines to decide that in this ruling … All of the defendants save Stein, who has an express contract with KPMG, arguably are protected by a contract, implied in fact from KPMG's uniform past practice and the circumstances of the business, pursuant to which they are entitled to have their defense costs paid by KPMG.' *See US v Stein I* (n 13) 356.

54 Candace Zierdt and Ellen S Podgor, 'Corporate Deferred Prosecutions Through the Looking Glass of Contract Policing' (2007) 96(1) KY LJ 1, 19.

55 Companies Act 2006, s 234(3)(b)(i).

DPA).[56] The extent to which the company can then be indemnified under Side B for its indemnification of the director(s) in such circumstances will depend on the policy's composition and wording.

The Side B clause is typically expressed in the following form, though nuances may differ depending on policy wording: "The [Insurer] shall pay, on behalf of the Insured Company, Loss *to the extent that its Insured Persons are Indemnifiable for that Loss*" (emphasis added). A company may indemnify its director(s) for liabilities which are not excluded under the CA 2006 but are also not indemnifiable under a D&O policy: for example, where the company wishes to avoid reputational harm and indemnifies the director for an otherwise non-covered claim. The italicised extract generally refers to the concept of "indemnifiable" in a legal context,[57] and not as regards the policy provisions for indemnification. However, policy wording may specify that Side B responds only where the company has indemnified an insured director for a Claim made against the director, as per the policy's "Claim" definition.[58]

Side B in any event follows the principle of liability insurance that actual legal liability must be incurred in order to be indemnified,[59] and will not serve to cover *ex gratia* payments[60] unless contractually expressed. As Side B covers the company (though indirectly benefits the director, too), it is the liability of the company in meeting its indemnification obligations that will be considered, and thus any varying interpretations as regards the liability principle will not apply.[61] Where such italicised wording in the sample clause is not present, the coverage will nonetheless be provided within the main insuring clause and will therefore be subject to its definitions and exclusions, and in accordance with the liability principle (discussed in **Section 14.3**).

17.2 Policy structure

As D&O policies are typically composite in nature, Side A and Side B are sufficiently separate that a lack of coverage under Side A would not impact Side B.[62] An issue is presented with policy wording within exclusions clauses which preface the subject matter excluded with "Claims arising out of, based upon or attributable to", which is broad in scope and increases exposure to the insured. An exclusion clause is typically applied in respect of "Loss arising from any Claim", though may differ in wording slightly (for example, "Loss in connection with any Claim"). Under a composite policy, an exclusion

56 Though, as noted, this will be unlikely and will largely depend on whether the DPA period is ongoing, and timing specifications of terms noted within the agreement.

57 Chubb, 'ForeFront Plus Insurance Policy' (*Chubb*, 2012) <https://web.archive.org/web/20140327013738/https://www.chubb.com/international/uk/csi/chubb15097.pdf> accessed 23 November 2020, 12.

58 Zurich, 'D&O Corporate Directors' and Officers' Liability: Policy Document' (*Zurich Insurance plc*, April 2020) <https://www.zurich.co.uk/business/-/media/Business/Documents/Specialty-lines/710008.pdf> accessed 22 January 2021, 14.

59 *AstraZeneca Insurance Co Ltd v XL Insurance (Bermuda) Ltd* [2013] EWHC 349 (Comm) [96] (Flaux J). *See also* Alison Padfield, *Insurance Claims* (5th edn, Bloomsbury Professional 2021) para 8.11.

60 Adolfo Paolini and Deepak Nambisan, *Directors' and Officers' Liability Insurance* (Informa Law 2008) para 3.67. *See also Cruise and Maritime Services International Ltd v Navigators Underwriting Agency Ltd (The Marco Polo)* [2017] EWHC 843 (Comm); *Marketform Managing Agency Ltd v Amashaw Pty Ltd* [2018] NSWCA 70.

61 Such as those relating to the interpretation of defence costs cover.

62 '[T]here is no link between Side A and Side B of the cover, so that Side B may be relied upon by the company even if Side A is inapplicable in the circumstances.' *See* Paolini and Nambisan (n 60) para 3.68.

clause invoked against a director under Side A would not automatically be invoked under Side B,[63] and as "Claim" is generally defined as being against an insured (or, sometimes, "any Insured"), the exclusion would not be applicable due to the severability provided by the policy's composite nature (and often an additional "Severability in exclusions" clause). Where a policy is not composite and instead joint in nature, this may *prima facie* expose the risk of lack of coverage to a company under Side B where the generalised wording of "Claims arising out of, based upon or attributable to" can be interpreted as applicable to Claims made against "any Insured" under the policy.

However, as the wording of Side B tends to focus on the coverability of the Claim made against the insured director, when considering whether indemnification can be made to the insured company, the definitions and exclusions as regards that Claim are therefore not interpreted in respect of the company's claim against the insurer for such indemnification. Therefore, where a DPA is agreed by the company and the company seeks reimbursement under Side B for indemnification made to a director, the Conduct exclusion clause (for example) would not apply so as to prevent the company from obtaining such coverage. Furthermore, a Related Claims clause would not apply so as to preclude such coverage where the company has claimed under its Side C coverage, nor where a director has claimed under their Side A coverage, unless the policy is not composite in nature or does not provide such suitable severability language.

Where a director wishes to seek relief under section 1157 of the CA 2006, a company is permitted to provide a loan to the director in order to meet the costs of (criminal or civil) defence.[64] The company will need to obtain the insurer's consent prior to doing so, but 'in the absence of an express policy declaration, insurers could not deny reimbursement if the company has provided the fund in good faith'.[65] In any event, this is unlikely to occur where the company has agreed or wishes to successfully negotiate a DPA, for the aforementioned reasons.

17.3 *Ex turpi causa non oritur actio*

It may be argued that the maxim *ex turpi causa non oritur actio*[66] should preclude a company from being reimbursed for defence costs paid to its director(s) where the director(s) carried out the conduct for which the company – by way of a DPA – accepts criminal responsibility. The extent to which this may be permitted to be argued may depend on whether the conduct of the director is attributed to the company, or whether the company is a primary or secondary victim of the criminality. If the company is a primary or secondary victim, then this will likely not apply;[67] although the company may have agreed a DPA on the basis of such underlying wrongdoing, it would not be the company's own authorised and executed criminality upon which the claim against the insurer for reimbursement

63 ibid.
64 Companies Act 2006, s 250(1)(a)(i).
65 Paolini and Nambisan (n 60) para 8.41.
66 "No action can arise from a wrongful cause"; a person cannot profit from their unlawful acts.
67 *Bilta (UK) Ltd (in liquidation) v Nazir* [2015] UKSC 23 [7] (Lord Neuberger).

is based.[68] Further, it would not uphold the 'integrity of the legal system'[69] to allow the company to incur further losses as a result of the director's wrongdoing in such circumstances: a prohibition on indemnification would not be in line with public policy, nor would it be proportionate considering the company's victim status and the exact purpose of Side B cover.[70] Thus, the maxim would not apply.[71]

However, where the company is considered the criminal wrongdoer by virtue of the principle of attribution and obtained a DPA on this basis, and the director is being pursued by a third party for the same offence (in all respects),[72] this maxim may apply to preclude coverage. This will be a particular consideration where the DPA documentation names the relevant individual as a perpetrator of the company's criminality.

68 Whilst the director may be prosecuted for the offence of bribery, the company may have accepted criminal responsibility for its failure to prevent bribery (which is a strict liability offence). *See also* Rob Merkin, 'Lehman Brothers: Insurance and Reinsurance Implications' (2011) 121(3) BILA J 17, 21–22.

69 *Patel v Mirza* [2016] UKSC 42 [120] (Lord Toulson); *Bilta (UK) Ltd (in liquidation) v Nazir* (n 67) [172], citing *Hall v Hebert* [1993] 2 SCR 159 (Lord Toulson and Lord Hodge).

70 *Patel v Mirza* (n 69) [120] (Lord Toulson).

71 *Bilta (UK) Ltd (in liquidation) v Nazir* (n 67) [89], [172].

72 Not only for the same offence, but based upon the same facts, and so forth.

CHAPTER 18

Coverage under Side C

Side C provides coverage to the entity and was introduced first in the US in response to allocation disputes arising in regard to settlements involving insured individuals (under Side A) and uninsured corporations (**Section 3.2.1**). The following analysis of the impact of DPAs on Side C focusses on three central concepts: firstly, small to medium enterprises ("SME(s)") and DPAs, and affected senior individuals; secondly, the inclusion of securities-related offences within Part 2 of Schedule 17 of the CACA 2013 and the ability of a company to access cover; and thirdly, the impact of Side C response to DPA-related claims on the co-insured individuals under an ABC D&O policy.

18.1 The role of Side C in DPA-related circumstances

Access to DPAs as an alternative sanction for criminal wrongdoing is arguably comparatively lower for SMEs than larger companies. Increasing requirements and burdens involved in engaging in successful DPA negotiations, and thus associated issues with lack of funding, contribute to this imbalance. Further, corporate criminal liability standards make it far easier to prosecute SMEs.[1] It has been accepted quite vocally by the SFO that the DPA two-stage test, which prosecutors must meet prior to the preferring of an indictment, facilitates the expedited dealing with corporate criminal cases, saving time and money.[2] The reduced burden on prosecutors, particularly in respect of the evidential stage of the test, enables the penalisation of larger companies which might otherwise have evaded liability as a result of the flawed corporate criminal liability standards (recently the subject of much attention).[3]

1 In order to obtain a DPA, a lower evidential test must be met than the Full Code Test in the Code for Crown Prosecutors. This is beneficial when prosecuting larger companies with complicated structures which present evidential difficulties in regard to the directing mind and will; it is notoriously easier to prosecute SMEs as a result of this lack of structural complexity. *See* Crown Prosecution Service and Serious Fraud Office, 'Deferred Prosecution Agreements Code of Practice' (*Crown Prosecution Service*, 11 February 2014) <https://www.cps.gov.uk/sites/default/files/documents/publications/dpa_cop.pdf> accessed 9 June 2020, para 1.2 (regarding the evidential test); Law Commission, *Corporate Criminal Liability* (Law Com 2021) para 1.8 (regarding the comparison between larger companies and SMEs in prosecution).

2 This was reemphasised in a Cambridge Symposium event (hosted online due to COVID-19 restrictions) by SFO Principal Investigative Lawyer Anna MacIntyre and SFO Lawyer Irene Cummins. *See* Anna MacIntyre and Irene Cummins, 'The Effectiveness of DPAs as a Prosecutorial Tool to Date and for the Future' (online, Cambridge Symposium 9 September 2021).

3 The Economic Crime and Corporate Transparency Act 2023 extends the identification doctrine to include "senior managers" within the scope of the "directing mind and will" of the company (**Section 1.1.1**). *See* Economic Crime and Corporate Transparency Act 2023, s 196(1).

DOI: 10.4324/9781003456964-22

To reach the stage where the test can be met, however, companies will be required to engage in extensive cooperative efforts and to bear the exorbitant costs of investigation. Smaller companies may not have the access to resources which would facilitate this process (such as the use of artificial intelligence) and would be unlikely to be able to bear the burden of the typically multi-year investigative process before agreeing to further punitive sanctions. Thus, where SMEs self-report or, following the initiation of a criminal investigation, cooperate to the fullest extent with prosecutors, senior individuals – present and former – are considerably exposed: to criminal liability which may arise as a result of corporate cooperation, as the ability to identify the individual wrongdoers is typically far less complicated than in a larger company; to facing more civil claims as a result of the smaller nature of the business and connectedness with everyday functions; and to the collateral consequences that can arise following a failed DPA, such as loss of employment.

Side C coverage typically covers "Securities Claims", and it is unlikely that a larger company would (be able to) purchase Side C with greater breadth. However, Side C can be written on broader terms and provide corporate legal liability coverage for a greater range of wrongdoing. This is more prevalent in SMEs and is arguably all the more pertinent when contemplating access to funds and access to DPAs. In line with directors' general duties,[4] a director will be required to consider actions which are in the best interests of the company when corporate crime is revealed, and in the continuous endeavour to ensure that the company is adequately protected and prosperous. An SME director, if within the scope of their role, will likely consider purchasing broader Side C coverage, in order to keep pace with the increased prosecutorial focus on pursuance of corporate criminality and to be well-prepared should an investigation arise. Directors of larger companies will engage in similar evaluations and, though it may not be necessary in order to fund DPA negotiations, Side C might be a preference in order to avoid significant impact on liquidity.

Despite this rationale for broader entity coverage, its value in this context is entirely dependent on the policy's response to DPA-related claims and particularly the access to defence costs cover. To the extent that access to broader Side C coverage in obtaining defence costs and thus a reasonable chance at DPA negotiations may decrease the exposure of senior individuals within SMEs, where Side C is not drafted in such a way that it impinges on the individuals' cover, Side C coverage is discussed hereon.

18.1.1 Securities-related Claims

Article 2 of The Crime and Courts Act 2013 (Deferred Prosecution Agreements) (Amendment of Specified Offences) Order 2018 ("the 2018 Order") effected an amendment to Part 2 of Schedule 17 of the CACA 2013, which sets out the list of offences for which a DPA can be agreed. The 2018 Order interposed the inclusion of three offences from the Financial Services Act 2012:[5] section 89 regarding misleading statements; section 90 regarding misleading impressions; and section 91 regarding misleading statements in relation to benchmarks.[6] There had previously been provision for the agreement of

4 Companies Act 2006, ss 171–177.

5 As amended by The Financial Services and Markets Act 2000 (Market Abuse) Regulations 2016, SI 2016/680.

6 The Crime and Courts Act 2013 (Deferred Prosecution Agreements) (Amendment of Specified Offences) Order 2018, art 2(3); Crime and Courts Act 2013, sch 17 pt 2 para 26ZA.

DPAs for misconduct relating to financial transactions; however it was the outdated section 397 of the Financial Services and Markets Act 2000 which was outlined as opposed to its successor. The 2018 Order was thus introduced to '[effect] a technical correction of an anomaly' and allow the SFO and CPS to negotiate DPAs for the relevant misconduct as originally intended.[7] Despite the correction, which came into force on 8 October 2018, no DPAs have yet arisen on the basis of these offences.

The extent to which the amendment to the CACA 2013 impacts Side C depends on the policy's definition of "Securities Claims". If "Securities Claims" includes not only shareholder derivative actions (as is common) but also criminal proceedings instituted against a company for securities-related offences, then Side C may be triggered (subject to the scope of cover within the policy). It is quite typical that a Securities Claim definition under a Side C policy will take the following form:

> a Claim made against an Insured that is brought:
> (a) by any person or entity arising out of, based upon or attributable to the purchase or sale or offer or solicitation of an offer to purchase or sell any Securities of the Company; or
> (b) by a holder of Securities of the Company with respect to such holder's interest in Securities of the Company; or
> (c) derivatively on behalf of the Company by a holder of Securities of the Company.[8]

As is evident from the sample clause, coverage is largely focussed on shareholder-related claims. The definition may explicitly include 'criminal proceedings',[9] or those 'brought by any governmental or regulatory agency'.[10]

Securities Claims is often a standalone definition, but it will typically be referred to within the Claim definition, and the Side C Insuring Agreement will tend to follow the same style as Sides A and B.[11] Thus, Side C is subject to the same policy definition in respect of Loss and often subject to the same (and perhaps additional) exclusions. "Criminal proceedings" will include (part of) the DPA process and, thus, where included within the (Securities) Claims definition, Side C may respond upon notification by the

7 HL Deb 9 May 2018, vol 791, col 2GC (Baroness Vere of Norbiton).

8 WR Berkley UK Limited, 'Directors and Officers Liability and Company Reimbursement Insurance Policy' (*WR Berkley*, May 2018) <https://www.brokerdirect.co.uk/wp-content/uploads/2018/08/Directors-Officers-WRB_PolicyWording_V06_MAY18.pdf> accessed 23 November 2020, 9; GB Underwriting, 'Management Liability (D&O) and Company Reimbursement Policy Wording' (*GB Underwriting Ltd*, July 2014) <https://web.archive.org/web/20160413182237/http://www.gbunderwriting.co.uk/downloads/> accessed 17 December 2020, 6. In the Australian case of *Murray Goulburn Co-operative Co Ltd v AIG Australia Ltd* [2021] FCA 288, the underlying D&O policy defined "Security" as 'any security representing a debt of or equity interest in any Insured Entity', and the "Insured Entity" definition encompassed a trust, thus giving rise to a "Securities Claim" under the policy.

9 Ironshore, 'Directors and Officers Liability Insurance Policy With Public Company Securities Claims Coverage' (*Ironshore Insurance Services LLC*) <http://www.ironshore.com/pdfs/general/Public-D-OPolicyForm.pdf> accessed 17 September 2021, 3.

10 Zurich, 'D&O Corporate Directors' and Officers' Liability: Policy Document' (*Zurich Insurance plc*, April 2020) <https://www.zurich.co.uk/business/-/media/Business/Documents/Specialty-lines/710008.pdf> accessed 22 January 2021, 13.

11 For example: "*The Insurer shall pay on behalf of the Company all Loss which the Company shall be legally obligated to pay as a result of a (Securities) Claim first made against the Company during the Policy Period or the Discovery Period for a Wrongful Act.*"

insured company. The following analysis will also apply to broader Side C policies which provide coverage to a broader range of offences.

18.2 Policy application considerations

DPAs are quite often based on historic conduct which may require disclosure to the insurer, as a material circumstance,[12] during the application process. One of the DPA Code factors for prosecutorial consideration in offering a DPA is whether 'the offending is not recent and [the company] in its current form is effectively a different entity from that which committed the offences'.[13] This could mean that where fair presentation is made by new management during the D&O application process, the insurer is exposed to indemnification in a subsequent DPA-related claim where the new entity insured did not have knowledge of the extent of the underlying circumstances, or could not have been said to ought to have such knowledge.[14] Even if a disclosure is made 'which gives the insurer sufficient information to put … [it] on notice that it needs to make further enquiries for the purpose of revealing those material circumstances',[15] it may be unlikely that the insurer will be able to uncover historic misconduct if the prospective insured itself is unaware.

Though the knowledge of the company will be that of one or more of the individuals part of its senior management or responsible for the insurance,[16] even a company-wide questionnaire may not reveal the relevant wrongdoing. In order to mitigate this risk to the insurer, particulars to the policy will be negotiated and agreed upon before a company takes out cover, and part of that process may include agreeing upon a date for the Retroactive clause.[17] Such an exclusion minimises the risk to the insurer and may reflect a date of substantial change to the company insured. This is crucial to receiving indemnification for DPA-related claims, particularly where the underlying Wrongful Act is historic (as was the case for *Rolls-Royce*, for example). For insureds, a recent Retroactive clause date will present greater risk of non-covered liability. In the case of *Rolls-Royce*, the 12 offences subject to the DPA were committed over 24 years,[18] which demonstrates the potential impact of the exclusion. This is particularly so when combined with the Interrelated Wrongful Acts exclusion,[19] which would allow an insurer to group together the 12 offences

12 Insurance Act 2015, s 3(4)(a).

13 Crown Prosecution Service and Serious Fraud Office, 'Deferred Prosecution Agreements Code of Practice' (n 1) para 2.8.2(v).

14 Insurance Act 2015, s 3(4)(a).

15 ibid s 3(4)(b).

16 ibid s 4(3). If the offending director(s) were to remain within the company and in the directorship position, this would create issues as regards knowledge of the company if undisclosed at the application stage.

17 This operates to exclude Claims related to Wrongful Acts committed prior to the agreed date. *See* Larry Goanos, *D&O 101: Understanding Directors and Officers Liability Insurance* (Wells Media Group Inc 2014) 61–62.

18 *Serious Fraud Office v Rolls-Royce Plc* [2017] Lloyd's Rep FC 249 (Crown) [30].

19 In *Cove Partners LLC v XL Specialty Ins Co* No CV 15-07635 SJO (GJSx) (CD Cal Feb 2 2016), 'the interrelated claims provision, which provided that claims arising from the "same Interrelated Wrongful Acts shall be deemed to constitute a single Claim and shall be deemed to have been made at the earliest of the time at which the earliest such claim is made," read in conjunction with a prior litigation exclusion, operated to broadly exempt coverage'. *See* Troutman Sanders, 'D&O and Professional Liability: 2016: A Year in Review' (*Troutman Sanders*, 2016) <https://www.troutman.com/images/content/2/0/v2/200793/D%26O-ProfessionalLiability2016Review.pdf> accessed 1 December 2020, 5.

as "Interrelated" for the purpose of denying coverage (where the Retroactive clause date falls after the date on which the first offence was committed).[20]

18.3 Judgment stage

The prosecutor and the company are both free to withdraw from negotiations at any time. This means that there will be a mutual understanding that, where successful, the negotiations will proceed to the judgment stage. For the company defendant in the ensuing proceedings, consent (from the insurer) to settle would likely be needed prior to the judgment stage where a (Securities) Claim is deemed to have been made. Consent to settle would not be needed beforehand, at the point when the letter of formal invitation is received by the company, because at this point a final settlement is not in sight and both the prosecutor and the company can withdraw from negotiations at any time (unless "Claim" includes investigations). At this stage, the investigation by the prosecutor is still ongoing.

If investigations are not included within the (Securities) Claim definition, the judgment stage is the first point at which a Claim may be deemed to have been made, if inclusive of "criminal proceedings". Once the DPA is negotiated and agreed upon 'in principle'[21] by the prosecutor and company, the DPA proposal will face the court in a preliminary hearing for judicial approval, which is declared publicly in a subsequent open hearing (and the final judgment). The preliminary hearing is an opportunity for the prosecutor to seek a declaration of the Crown Court that a DPA can be obtained prior to the final approval and takes place 'after the commencement of negotiations ... but before the terms of the DPA are agreed'.[22] Although the preliminary hearing takes place before the terms are agreed, or 'settled',[23] the defendant company must consent to the proposal within the application documentation.[24] Despite the fact that the defendant company must provide consent to the proposal agreement, the company can withdraw from this late stage of negotiation at any time up until the final hearing/approval.[25]

The final hearing is referred to as the "open hearing" and is the point at which the final declaration is made. Court proceedings are instituted in the final hearing and automatically suspended[26] (proceedings are 'reinstituted'[27] if a DPA is breached). On the basis of a strict interpretation of "criminal proceedings" in policy wording, in line with the official terms used within the DPA process, a Claim would only be made against the company sufficient to trigger coverage within the final hearing. As criminal proceedings

---

20 Goanos, *D&O 101: Understanding Directors and Officers Liability Insurance* (n 17) 62.

21 Serious Fraud Office, 'Deferred Prosecution Agreements' (*Serious Fraud Office*, 23 October 2020) <https://www.sfo.gov.uk/publications/guidance-policy-and-protocols/sfo-operational-handbook/deferred-prosecution-agreements/> accessed 23 October 2020.

22 Crime and Courts Act 2013, sch 17 para 7(1).

23 Serious Fraud Office, 'Deferred Prosecution Agreements' (n 21).

24 Thus, also the application. *See* CrimPR 11.3(3)(h).

25 Serious Fraud Office, 'Deferred Prosecution Agreements' (n 21). Sir Brian Leveson told the House of Lords that in one of the first four UK DPA cases, he had not approved the proposed DPA in its first preliminary hearing and instead made points to the SFO for consideration in the continued negotiations, which were reflected in the second preliminary application. *See* Select Committee on the Bribery Act 2010, *The Bribery Act 2010: Post-Legislative Scrutiny* (HL 2017–19, 303) para 290.

26 Crime and Courts Act 2013, sch 17 paras 2(1)–(2).

27 Crown Prosecution Service and Serious Fraud Office, 'Deferred Prosecution Agreements Code of Practice' (n 1) para 12.8.

are not technically instituted within the preliminary hearing, an insurer may argue that a Claim has not been made at this point in the process. However, in an interpretation in line with typical D&O custom, criminal proceedings tend to comprise 'judgments'.[28] Though the judgments from preliminary hearings are not always published, those published are referred to as 'Approved Judgments'[29] between the prosecutor (applicant) and offending company (respondent). This therefore suggests that a Claim may be made at the point of the preliminary hearing. Despite this, if coverage is precluded at any earlier point throughout the process then it will continue to be precluded; if the investigation and judgment stages are considered to be two separate Claims, a Related Claims clause would exclude any following the first where the first was excluded based on the Conduct exclusion clause (due to their treatment as a single Claim).

Even if it is considered that a DPA is not a "settlement" (though often referred to as such),[30] a Consent to settle clause tends to be broad in requiring consent be sought before incurring liability in respect of a Claim.[31] As the company is still able to withdraw, it may be argued that consent would not need to be obtained in order to proceed with the preliminary hearing (if coverage has not already been precluded) unless policy wording requires: for example, where an insurer is looking to minimise any potential loss. If a Claim is deemed to have been made at the point of the preliminary hearing, it will remain the case that the insured will be required to obtain consent prior to incurring liability (including defence costs), and therefore some form of insurer consent would be required in any event.[32] Consent to settle would certainly be required prior to the final judgment/approval stage, following the completion of negotiations and the decision of the prosecutor that the approval stage should immediately follow.

As the company signs a confidentiality undertaking, consent from the insurer sought in advance of the public final approval stage may not *prima facie* be possible, as the preliminary hearing is held in private.[33] Despite this, a disclosure of the fact of DPA negotiations at such a late stage is likely to be considered to be required as part of the completion of DPA negotiations. With permission of the prosecutor,[34] the company could depart from

28 Kari McCormick and others, 'Insurance' (*Burges Salmon*, June 2014) <https://www.burges-salmon.com/-/media/files/publications/open-access/insuring_the_cost_of_prosecutions_and_regulatory_investigations.pdf> accessed 22 January 2021.

29 *Serious Fraud Office v Standard Bank Plc (now ICBC Standard Bank Plc) (Preliminary)* [2016] Lloyd's Rep FC 91 (Crown).

30 DPAs have frequently been referred to in the UK as "settlements". *See Director of the Serious Fraud Office v Airbus SE* [2021] Lloyd's Rep FC 159 (Crown) [4] (Dame Victoria Sharp); Select Committee on the Bribery Act 2010, *The Bribery Act 2010: Post-Legislative Scrutiny* (n 25) para 303; Lisa Osofsky, 'We're Defending the UK as a Safe Place for Business' (*The Times*, 30 June 2021) <https://www.thetimes.co.uk/article/were-defending-the-uk-as-a-safe-place-for-business-617f500fw> accessed 30 June 2021 (by the then-Director of the SFO); Colin King and Nicholas Lord, 'Deferred Prosecution Agreements in England and Wales: Castles Made of Sand?' (2020) (Apr) PL 307, 326 (by academics).

31 *See Vigilant Ins Co v Bear Stearns Cos Inc* 2008 NY Slip Op 02080, 10 NY 3d 170 (2008). *See also* Thomas H Bentz, 'A Buyer's Guide to Obtaining Comprehensive D&O Insurance Coverage' (*Holland & Knight*, 2014) <https://issuu.com/hollandknight/docs/holland-knight-d_o-insurance-covera> accessed 3 November 2020, 65.

32 This consent cannot be unreasonably withheld, and a decision to withhold consent at such a late stage following the insured's incurring of substantial costs throughout the investigative/negotiation process would likely be deemed to be unreasonable when considering the likely alternative of prosecution.

33 Crime and Courts Act 2013, sch 17 para 7(4). There have been only a few instances whereby news of preliminary approval has been announced prior to the final hearing, and this has not occurred in recent DPA cases.

34 Also the court to which the undertaking is made, if made in this way.

the undertaking only in order to inform the insurer. If this is when the insurer becomes aware of the extent of liability behind an earlier blanket notification (**Section 18.4.1.3**), this may be the point at which coverage is excluded under the policy in regard to the Conduct exclusion clause.[35] If this is the case, any earlier sums paid – for example in Mitigation Costs cover – would need to be repaid to the insurer.

The nature of the DPA is that a bill of indictment with one or numerous charges is preferred, but proceedings are suspended on the basis that a number of terms are met. The final judgment sets out the draft indictment of the alleged offences, and the fact that the statement of facts provided by the company would be treated as an admission to such offences should criminal proceedings resume.[36] Due to the maxim *ex turpi causa non oritur actio*, which prevents a legal person who commits an unlawful act from seeking indemnity against the liability which resulted from that act, indemnification of the company for costs incurred within the DPA will not occur (**Section 18.5.3**). Nonetheless, the Conduct exclusion clause under a policy would operate to exclude this possibility – invoked at this preliminary/final stage as a result of an admission by the company to the wrongdoing, contained within the statement of facts.[37]

A Conduct exclusion clause requiring only a "final adjudication or judgment" may see a different outcome. When a prosecution is deferred, the criminal proceedings are not "final" until the expiration of the DPA; the proceedings can be reinstituted at any point and are effectively paused pending the fulfilment of the DPA obligations.[38] Once the DPA has expired and is complete, under paragraph 11 of Schedule 17 to the CACA 2013, the prosecutor gives notice to the court that it does not want proceedings to continue.[39] Upon this expiry and discontinuation, the insurer would be able to argue that a final judgment has been made for the purposes of refusing coverage, or seeking reimbursement for any indemnification already advanced. However, a clause requiring only a "final adjudication" may leave an insurer exposed, as DPAs are commonly regarded as settlements, which do not constitute adjudications for this purpose.[40]

35 Where coverage is excluded at the point at which the insured seeks consent to settle, the "seeking" of such consent will be on the basis of adherence to the contractual obligation and honouring good faith, and may take the form of a notification of Circumstances.

36 The statement of facts would be treated as an admission under section 10 of the Criminal Justice Act 1967.

37 If the company is not able to disclose the fact of the DPA negotiations to its insurer, and thus the statement of facts, then the company will likely find that coverage is precluded at the final approval/judgment stage – where the insurer becomes aware of an admission to criminal conduct having been made by its insured to a prosecutor. Any defence costs advanced up to this point would therefore need to be repaid by the insured.

38 *Unencumbered Assets v Great Am Ins Co* 817 F Supp 2d 1014 (SD Ohio 2011), citing *Chubb Custom Ins Co v Triumph Capital Group Inc* No 04–1893–BLS2, at 3 (MassSuperCt Feb 9 2007). *See also* Kevin LaCroix, 'D&O Insurance: A "Final" Analysis' (*The D&O Diary*, 28 June 2015) <https://www.dandodiary.com/2015/06/articles/d-o-insurance/do-insurance-a-final-analysis/> accessed 23 October 2020.

39 However, no notice of discontinuance is needed where the court terminates the DPA (in respect of DPA breach). *See* Crime and Courts Act 2013, sch 17 para 11(5)(b). *See also* Crown Prosecution Service and Serious Fraud Office, 'Deferred Prosecution Agreements Code of Practice' (n 1) para 14.6.

40 *US Bank National Association v Indian Harbor Insurance Co* 2014 WL 3012969 (D Minn 2014); *JP Morgan Sec Inc v Vigilant Ins Co* 126 AD 3d 76 (NY App Div 2015). *See also Rochester Drug Co-Operative Inc v Hiscox Ins Co* 466 F Supp 3d 337, 354 (WDNY 2020).

18.3.1 Breach of DPA

Actions contrary to the DPA terms may constitute a breach: for example, a company has limited ability to contest third-party claims, as statements contradicting the DPA must not be made.[41] In order for a DPA to be obtained, a two-part test must be satisfied, including the evidential and public interest stages.[42] To resume criminal proceedings upon breach, the prosecutor must be satisfied that the Full Code Test under the Code for Crown Prosecutors is met for each charge[43] – a more rigorous standard – and the public interest consideration will be reassessed.[44]

Consequences following breach of a DPA are ultimately decided by the court, and thus the ensuing court proceedings would likely fall within the (Securities) Claims definition, if the definition includes "criminal proceedings". The company might be invited to agree proposals with the prosecutor to remedy the breach, which would require representation in court. The breach proceedings may be considered to be a Claim in their own right, or part of the original proceedings within the judgment stage (a single Claim) due to the way that proceedings in the final hearing are suspended[45] and then 'reinstituted'[46] upon breach. If not, under a Related Claims clause, any previous Claims made relating to the DPA may exclude coverage for related Claims regarding its breach.[47]

Without a Related Claims clause, the question of whether or not the breach proceedings would attract coverage is an interesting consideration. A breach of a DPA is not in itself a criminal act, but the nature of the breach means that a conviction – following reinstitution of proceedings – is likely[48] to result, and such conviction would preclude any coverage from being extended by virtue of the Conduct exclusion clause. If alternative measures are agreed by the company and prosecutor during the proceedings, indemnification should

---

41 *See for example* Serious Fraud Office, 'Amec Foster Wheeler Energy Limited – Deferred Prosecution Agreement' (*Serious Fraud Office*, 2 July 2021) <https://www.sfo.gov.uk/download/amec-foster-wheeler-energy-limited-deferred-prosecution-agreement/> accessed 2 July 2021, para 48. This may include insurance coverage disputes.

42 Crown Prosecution Service and Serious Fraud Office, 'Deferred Prosecution Agreements Code of Practice' (n 1) paras 1.2, 2.1–2.10.

43 This is not an absolute requirement in order to enter into the DPA negotiation process. Instead, it will be sufficient (for the purpose of meeting the evidential stage of the two-part test) for there to be at least a reasonable suspicion based on admissible evidence that the company committed the offence, with reasonable grounds to believe that a continued investigation within a reasonable time would provide further evidence which altogether would be capable of establishing a realistic prospect of conviction in accordance with the Full Code Test. *See* ibid para 1.2(i).

44 ibid para 12.9.

45 Crime and Courts Act 2013, sch 17 paras 2(1)–(2).

46 Crown Prosecution Service and Serious Fraud Office, 'Deferred Prosecution Agreements Code of Practice' (n 1) para 12.8.

47 Where the breach Claim is determined to have a sufficient causal link to the original DPA Claim (or underlying wrongdoing). In *Connect America Holdings LLC v Arch Insurance* 174 F Supp 3d 894 (ED Pa 2016), an Interrelated Wrongful Act clause could not be invoked as 'the acts alleged in the 2013 lawsuit did not share a sufficient causal link with acts alleged in the 2004 letter or 2009 lawsuit to preclude coverage under the corporate canopy policy'. *See* Troutman Sanders, 'D&O and Professional Liability: 2016: A Year in Review' (*Troutman Sanders*, 2016) <https://www.troutman.com/images/content/2/0/v2/200793/D%26O-ProfessionalLiability2016Review.pdf> accessed 1 December 2020, 6.

48 A conviction is arguably "likely" to follow a breach of a DPA, once proceedings are reinstituted and a trial is held, as the statement of facts would be admissible against them. *See* Crown Prosecution Service and Serious Fraud Office, 'Deferred Prosecution Agreements Code of Practice' (n 1) paras 6.4, 12.8. It is not necessarily guaranteed, however, particularly in respect of identification principle offences where the individuals from whom the *mens rea* is extracted have been acquitted in the interim.

not be precluded on the basis of a "final adjudication or judgment" – as the underlying proceedings (albeit deferred and essentially paused) have not been finalised.[49] If the breach leads to the reinstatement of criminal proceedings, the same application of the Conduct exclusion clause would apply, with a subsequent conviction constituting a final adjudication. Furthermore, the maxim *ex turpi causa non oritur actio* will likely continue to prevent the company from seeking indemnity against any liability resulting from their original criminal act, and therefore indemnification of the company for costs incurred in relation to the breach will not occur.

18.4 Claim definition including "Investigations"

Much of the prospective extension of coverage under Side C relating to the pre-approval DPA process will be dependent on the inclusion of investigations within the (Securities) Claim definition. This requires express provision, as even in cases of corporate indemnification of directors the question as to inclusion of investigations within the "Claim" definition arises.[50] A Claim definition including investigations will typically require that the investigation be a formal or official investigation against the insured, and that the insured is identified in writing as being a subject of that investigation. The clause may go further to state that there must be an understanding that 'a criminal, administrative or regulatory proceeding may be commenced'.[51] Typically, such definitions will specify that the investigation must be against an Insured Person (individual, not entity), and any reimbursement to the entity for investigation costs incurred will only be provided for under Side B (where the entity has incurred such costs on behalf of the individual insured). Where this is the case, the company would not be able to argue that costs incurred by it during an investigation into its own affairs would be covered under Side C,[52] unless contractually provided; this is unlikely, particularly in respect of Side C policies which offer coverage for securities-related Claims only (but may be included within policies providing broader coverage to SMEs).

The following analysis (under **Section 18.4**) will consider the pre-judgment stages of the DPA process and application of coverage where the (Securities) Claim definition includes "investigations". If policies do not bear such broad wording, a Claim will be deemed to be made during the judgment stage (if including "criminal proceedings"). Whether a Claim has been made will be relevant in respect of the type of notification made: where investigations are included within the definition, this will take the form of a Claim notification, and further policy requirements may be triggered (for example, to seek prior consent of the insurer whilst cooperating with prosecutors).[53] Where not so included, the company

49 Though it may be precluded on the basis of the admission within the statement of facts/DPA itself. *See also RSUI Indemnity Company v David H Murdock and Dole Food Company Inc* 2021 WL 803867, 36 (Del Mar 3 2021).

50 Guy Wilkes and Francis Kean, 'The Position of Individuals in Regulatory Investigations: A Changing Landscape' (2017) 1(2) Journal of Financial Compliance 172, 172–179.

51 Zurich, 'D&O Corporate Directors' and Officers' Liability: Policy Document' (n 10) 9. In any event, a Claim is not made against the insured until it is communicated to the insured. *See J Rothschild Assurance Plc v Collyear* [1998] All ER (D) 431 (QB) (Rix J).

52 An allocation clause would likely allow the entity to seek reimbursement for covered costs incurred, such as the costs incurred on behalf of individual insureds.

53 In a particularly broad policy, the simple notification of an investigation (even where "investigations" are not expressly provided for within the policy) may trigger a Claim, where Claim is defined as a written notice

will be required to make a notification of Circumstances. Notification of Circumstances will be required at each progressive stage in the process, as each stage may (or is reasonably likely to) give rise to liability,[54] though doing so may present difficulties. A Claim is required for the Advancement of Defence Costs extension to be triggered.

18.4.1 Notification

18.4.1.1 Pre-DPA criminal investigation and the self-report

The prosecutor's investigation into the criminal wrongdoing of the offending company will far precede the offer of a DPA. For a DPA to be offered, it is a precondition for the prosecutor to have established 'identification of the full extent of the alleged offending before negotiations can begin'.[55] A company notified that it is being investigated by prosecutors for suspected criminal wrongdoing will be obliged to report such information to its insurer by notification (of a Claim or Circumstance). For a company to be invited to enter into DPA negotiations, it must have displayed high levels of cooperation throughout the investigative process.[56] The increasingly crucial self-report not only weighs in favour of obtaining a DPA, but also of obtaining more lenient terms (such as a reduced fine). A self-report, however, does not guarantee a DPA;[57] there is a risk that the prosecutor elects to pursue a criminal conviction. Unless a Claim is made, consent to make a self-report will not be necessary unless specifically provided for within the policy. However, notification of Circumstances is particularly crucial as a self-report can be used in criminal proceedings against the company.[58]

"Self-Report Investigations"[59] may attract coverage, though this is likely to apply only to individuals.[60] D&O specialists Mark Sutton and Karen Boto have stated that insurers wishing to provide indemnification for internal investigations should consider sub-limiting and/or capping cover, 'perhaps at the point when wrongdoing is uncovered and a self-report is made, in order to manage their exposure'.[61] This suggests that an insurer may

that a third party intends to hold the insured responsible for a wrongful act. *See* Adolfo Paolini and Deepak Nambisan, *Directors' and Officers' Liability Insurance* (Informa Law 2008) paras 2.44–2.45.

54 *HLB Kidsons (a firm) v Lloyd's Underwriters subscribing to Lloyd's policy No 621/PK1D00101* [2008] EWCA Civ 1206 [72] (Rix LJ).

55 Serious Fraud Office, 'Deferred Prosecution Agreements' (n 21); Crown Prosecution Service and Serious Fraud Office, 'Deferred Prosecution Agreements Code of Practice' (n 1) para 2.2(ii).

56 Crown Prosecution Service and Serious Fraud Office, 'Deferred Prosecution Agreements Code of Practice' (n 1) para 2.8.2(i); *Standard Bank Plc (now ICBC Standard Bank Plc) (Preliminary)* (n 29) [30], [38], [52], [57]; *Airbus SE* (n 30) [68]–[69].

57 Skansen Interiors Ltd's parent company Skansen Group provided a self-report and made an extensive cooperative effort, but ultimately the subsidiary was denied a DPA on the basis that it would not have the resources to pay a fine forming part of the agreement. The company subsequently received an absolute discharge for the same reason that the DPA was refused. *See* Prina Patel, 'Blog: Skansen Interiors Limited: The UK's First Contested Prosecution Under S7 of the Bribery Act' (*JDSUPRA*, 26 April 2018) <https://www.jdsupra.com/legalnews/blog-skansen-interiors-limited-the-uk-s-66280/> accessed 30 April 2018.

58 For example, if DPA negotiations are unsuccessful. *See* Crown Prosecution Service and Serious Fraud Office, 'Deferred Prosecution Agreements Code of Practice' (n 1) para 4.6(ii).

59 Investigations following self-reports which are conducted by the entity itself.

60 Entities would most likely only be covered in this respect for losses incurred in meeting indemnification requirements (Side B). Internal investigation costs may fall within the definition of Loss, depending on policy wording, but as coverage does not begin until a Claim is made, any costs incurred in forming a self-report would likely need to be included by contractual provision.

61 Mark Sutton and Karen Boto, 'Guest Post: D&O Insurance Implications as Deferred Prosecution Agreements Take Off in the U.K.' (*The D&O Diary*, 30 January 2021) <https://www.dandodiary.com/2017/01/

look to preclude coverage from the point at which a self-report is made, which may just relate to investigation costs, but likely also to any future costs incurred in Claims related to the underlying wrongdoing within the report where the policy bears a Related Claims clause. A company could self-report to minimise liability, in the hope of obtaining a DPA, but incur more "personal" liability where the insurer refuses coverage.[62]

18.4.1.2 Invitation to enter DPA negotiations

The DPA Code sets out the requirements for the pre-negotiation period, whereby the prosecutor offers to enter DPA negotiations, the company accepts, and then undertakings regarding the terms of negotiations are made. Though the letter of invitation signals the start of the pre-negotiation period,[63] the actual negotiation period cannot begin until the company provides its acceptance of the invitation. Following acceptance, a second letter will be sent by the prosecutor to the company in respect of undertakings as to the terms of the negotiations. An indication of the potential terms is likely to have been given in the first letter, which outlines 'the basis on which any negotiations will proceed'.[64] The undertakings will predominantly concern the confidentiality of the process (**Section 18.4.1.3**).

For a DPA to be obtained, a two-part test must be satisfied.[65] The prosecutor must consider the test prior to offering a DPA, which demonstrates the extent to which an investigation will already have taken place, potentially triggering notification requirements.[66] Notification of an intention to enter into DPA negotiations may invoke the Conduct exclusion clause (on the basis of an admission of excluded misconduct), whilst an inability to notify could render the company unable to obtain an advancement of defence costs during a costly period of the DPA process. It is likely that the company will be considered to be bound by a duty of confidence prior to the signing of the undertakings,[67] as the first letter

articles/international-d-o/guest-post-insurance-implications-deferred-prosecution-agreements-take-off-u-k/> accessed 8 October 2021.

62 This highlights the importance of policy wording and the crucial role of the claims handler in advising and protecting the company's best interests.

63 The official starting point of the DPA negotiation process is somewhat confused. The DPA Code sets out that the prosecutor will first send the company a 'formal letter of invitation outlining the basis on which any negotiations will proceed', which constitutes the 'beginning of the DPA negotiation period'. However, the DPA Code then sets out that the letter must include a 'request for confirmation of whether [the company] wishes to enter into negotiations' and a timeframe in which the company must notify the prosecutor of whether or not it accepts the invitation 'to enter into negotiations'. *See* Crown Prosecution Service and Serious Fraud Office, 'Deferred Prosecution Agreements Code of Practice' (n 1) paras 3.1–3.2, 3.5.

64 ibid para 3.1.

65 The evidential stage of the test (the first part) requires either the evidential stage of the Full Code Test in the Code for Crown Prosecutors to be satisfied; or that there be at least a reasonable suspicion based on admissible evidence that the company committed the offence, with reasonable grounds to believe that a continued investigation within a reasonable time would provide further evidence which would altogether be capable of establishing a realistic prospect of conviction in accordance with the Full Code Test. The public interest stage of the test (the second part) requires the public interest to be properly served by a DPA, as opposed to the prosecutor not prosecuting the company, in accordance with the criteria set out in the DPA Code. The criteria include factors such as negotiations, cooperation, historical conduct, compliance programmes, actions of individuals, time of offending, disproportionate consequences of conviction, and public impact. *See* ibid paras 1.2(i)–1.2(ii), 2.1–2.10.

66 For example, where the Claim definition includes investigations. Notification of an investigation may constitute a Claim where "Claim" is defined as a "written notice" that a third party intends to hold the insured responsible for a Wrongful Act. *See* Paolini and Nambisan (n 53) paras 2.44–2.45.

67 A duty of confidence is imposed 'whenever a person receives information he knows or ought to know is fairly and reasonably to be regarded as confidential'. *See Campbell v Mirror Group Newspapers Ltd* [2004] UKHL 22 [14] (Lord Nicholls).

requires the company to give its 'confirmation of whether [it] wishes to enter into negotiations in accordance with the [CACA 2013] and [the] DPA Code',[68] with paragraph 3.6 of the latter setting out confidentiality requirements.[69] Thus, although the confidentiality obligations will not yet exist by way of signed undertakings, an implied acceptance to adhere will have been given upon confirmation. If it is the case that the first offer letter sent by the prosecutor has the requisite confidentiality attached – which is perhaps what was meant by paragraph 3.2 (setting out that the first letter signalled the start of negotiations prior to acceptance) – then the company will be bound by such confidentiality even before it accepts.[70] The impact of the obligation of confidence at such an early stage will predominantly affect notification requirements.

18.4.1.3 Disclosure of the fact of DPA negotiations

The SFO Operational Handbook outlines that the confidentiality of 'the fact of the negotiations taking place'[71] is central to the negotiation process and lists some of the risks of disclosure. Though it is outlined that the terms of the negotiations will be set out in undertakings signed by the company and the SFO, including terms in respect of confidentiality, it is not entirely clear (as not expressly set out) that for the company this will extend to confidentiality restrictions on the disclosure of the fact of the negotiations taking place.[72] However, a duty of confidence may nevertheless apply – so as to similarly restrict notification – as a result of the contents of the letter of invitation. If the undertaking does not extend to the fact of the negotiations and the letter of invitation does not impose an early duty of confidence, then the insured company will be able to disclose the negotiations to its insurer. For example, where the company is listed, and the fact of DPA negotiations is considered to be sufficient to trigger the requirement to make a disclosure of "insider information" to the public (**Section 1.1.3.1**). It may be the case that the insurer elects to refuse coverage at the point at which the company takes part in DPA negotiations, if the Conduct exclusion clause is deemed to be invoked.[73]

The following analysis will consider the various situations which may emerge if the fact of the DPA negotiations was to form part of the confidentiality undertaking, which is likely, considering the SFO's statement that this is 'central to the process'.[74] Companies are permitted[75] to depart from the confidentiality requirements in two circumstances.

68 Crown Prosecution Service and Serious Fraud Office, 'Deferred Prosecution Agreements Code of Practice' (n 1) para 3.5(ii).

69 ibid para 3.6.

70 It may just be the case that enforcement of the obligation differs.

71 Serious Fraud Office, 'Deferred Prosecution Agreements' (n 21).

72 The DPA Code outlines that the prosecutor will make an undertaking to the company that the fact of the negotiations will be confidential, but it is not expressly outlined (within the DPA Code or the SFO Operational Handbook) that the company must make an undertaking with the same term. *See* Crown Prosecution Service and Serious Fraud Office, 'Deferred Prosecution Agreements Code of Practice' (n 1) para 3.6(i).

73 If the taking part in negotiations is deemed to constitute an acknowledgement (or admission, where admission is more broadly defined) of wrongdoing and thus forms a basis for invoking the Conduct exclusion clause; or on the basis that this will only constitute a potentially covered Claim. Alternatively, the insurer may wait until an admission is more clearly/sufficiently made or for a "final adjudication or judgment". The approach taken will depend on policy wording.

74 Serious Fraud Office, 'Deferred Prosecution Agreements' (n 21).

75 That is, will not incur liability. *See* Crown Prosecution Service and Serious Fraud Office, 'Deferred Prosecution Agreements Code of Practice' (n 1) para 3.9.

Firstly, where 'required by law'.[76] This may see the company exercise its right to access a full defence, as provided for under Article 6(3)(b) of the ECHR.[77] Under this provision, a person[78] charged with a criminal offence has the right 'to have adequate time and facilities for the preparation of his defence'.[79] One could interpret 'facilities for the preparation of his defence' as including an advancement of defence costs, where the company would otherwise be unable to meet the costs of the defence.[80] Criminal proceedings are instituted at the point at which a bill of indictment is preferred by the prosecutor, charging the offender, with the consent of the Crown Court judge following DPA approval.[81] Though the charges succeed the investigation and DPA negotiation stages,[82] Article 6 has been interpreted by the ECtHR as including the investigative stage.[83] Despite the undertaking, the company would, by law, be *entitled* to share the fact of the DPA negotiations with its counsel if the policy is duty to indemnify, or with its insurer if the policy is duty to defend.[84] Though the insured may be entitled, the obligation to notify is not a *legal* requirement,[85] and therefore it may be argued that this provision could not be invoked on this basis.[86]

The other (and more likely) way in which a company can depart from the confidentiality undertaking is where 'required for the purposes of the DPA negotiations'.[87] The company will need to be represented by its legal representation throughout the negotiation

76 ibid.

77 Convention for the Protection of Human Rights and Fundamental Freedoms (European Convention on Human Rights, as amended) (ECHR) art 6(3)(b).

78 Including a company.

79 Convention for the Protection of Human Rights and Fundamental Freedoms (European Convention on Human Rights, as amended) (ECHR) art 6(3)(b).

80 '"Facilities" provided to an accused include consultation with his lawyer (*Campbell and Fell v. the United Kingdom*, § 99; *Goddi v. Italy*, § 31).' *See* European Court of Human Rights, 'Guide on Article 6 of the European Convention on Human Rights – Right to a Fair Trial (Criminal Limb)' (*Council of Europe*, 31 August 2020) <https://www.echr.coe.int/documents/guide_art_6_criminal_eng.pdf> accessed 25 November 2020, para 411; *Campbell and Fell v the United Kingdom* App no 7819/77 (ECtHR, 28 June 1984), para 99; *Goddi v Italy* App no 8966/80 (ECtHR, 9 April 1974), para 31.

81 Crime and Courts Act 2013, sch 17 para 2(1).

82 Which include the drafting of the statement of facts.

83 European Court of Human Rights, 'Guide on Article 6 of the European Convention on Human Rights – Right to a Fair Trial (Criminal Limb)' (n 80) para 43; *Dvorski v Croatia* App no 25703/11 (ECtHR, 20 October 2015), para 76.

84 'While duty to defend policies are somewhat common among private companies, public companies typically have a non-duty to defend policies.' *See* Lawrence Trautman and Kara Altenbaumer-Price, 'D&O Insurance: A Primer' (2012) 1(2) AUBLR 337, 351.

85 It is a contractual requirement to trigger coverage under the policy.

86 Where the company is seeking a new policy, there would be a legal requirement upon the insured to make such a disclosure – under the duty of fair presentation – though disclosure to the prospective new insurer would not impact the insured's coverage for this existing matter, which would be drawn from the earlier policy under which the notification of Circumstances was made (either at the point of self-report, invitation to enter into DPA negotiations, or entering into DPA negotiations; regardless of whether that notification was made in blanket form). The Prior Claims/Circumstances and Related Claims provisions of the new policy would operate to tie all new Claims made under the new policy period back to the previous policy for the purpose of excluding coverage under the new policy. *See* Insurance Act 2015, s 3 (regarding duty of fair presentation of risk); *Kajima UK Engineering Ltd v Underwriter Insurance Company Ltd* [2008] EWHC 83 (TCC) [99]; *Euro Pools plc (in administration) v Royal & Sun Alliance Insurance plc* [2019] EWCA Civ 808 [32], [43] (regarding Claims arising from an earlier notification of Circumstances being considered to have been made within the requisite period of insurance); *Cove Partners LLC v XL Specialty Ins Co* (n 19) (regarding the Related Claims and Prior Claims/Circumstances clauses).

87 Serious Fraud Office, 'Deferred Prosecution Agreements' (n 21); Crown Prosecution Service and Serious Fraud Office, 'Deferred Prosecution Agreements Code of Practice' (n 1) para 3.9.

process,[88] and it is a requirement for both the prosecutor and the company to be involved in the negotiations. Thus, to take place, legal representation is required and disclosure could be made to the company's counsel or the insurer directly,[89] as the company may be reliant upon an advancement of defence costs to be able to participate in negotiations. Where the company is not financially reliant upon advancement to participate in negotiations, this argument for the disclosure of the fact of DPA negotiations to the insurer has less weight. The way in which an insured company under a duty to indemnify policy, with the financial means to cover its own defence costs,[90] could meet its notification obligations without breaching the undertaking and its duty to cooperate with its insurer, is by making a blanket notification of Circumstances.

A blanket notification of Circumstances,[91] where permitted, would allow an extension of coverage for all subsequent Claims – providing that there is a causal link between the notified Circumstances and the Claims arising, and that the Claims are not otherwise excluded – even where the insured does not know the exact scale, cause, and/or consequences of the issue.[92] Standard policy wording which requires notification of Circumstances which 'might'[93] give rise to a Claim requires only a possibility of Claims arising in future. Use of a blanket notification would allow the insured to alert the insurer to the underlying wrongdoing and the potential for ensuing Claims, and to honour its obligations within its confidentiality undertaking. Bound by the undertaking, the insured would make a fuller disclosure to the insurer upon the conclusion of this confidential stage. Though this would not fully assist the insurer in its own investigation, such actions would be in good faith and would minimise any potential liability which may have been incurred upon a breach of the undertaking.[94]

A Cooperation clause requiring the provision of information to the insurer within a reasonable time may cause some dispute where an insured is unable to provide information relating to DPA negotiations on account of a confidentiality undertaking. It is an implied term that information will be provided within a reasonable time,[95] and thus the company

88 Due to its corporate legal personality and the existing rules on corporate representation in criminal cases. *See* Sarah Worthington, *Sealy and Worthington's Texts, Cases and Materials in Company Law* (11th edn, Oxford University Press 2016) 184–185.

89 The insurer would be informed directly in a duty to defend policy, as the insurer takes on responsibility for the defence of the insured and would need to be appropriately informed. Disclosure would be made to the company's counsel where the policy is duty to indemnify, and further made to the insurer.

90 Without being "required" to obtain an advancement from the insurer in order to do so.

91 'A "blanket notification" is a notification of an extremely broad problem, potentially without identifying the necessary plaintiffs or the specific problems experienced.' *See* Patrick Perry, 'Notification – The Fundamental Issues Arising' (*Clyde & Co*, April 2015) <https://www.clydeco.com/uploads/Files/Updates/CC007097_Notification_-_Fundamental_issues_arising-09.04.15.pdf> accessed 24 November 2020.

92 According to Clyde & Co, a blanket notification can be made for potential Claims 'known or unknown'. *See* ibid. *See also J Rothschild Assurance Plc v Collyear* (n 51); *HLB Kidsons (a firm) v Lloyd's Underwriters subscribing to Lloyd's Policy No 621/PKID00101* [2007] EWHC 1951 (Comm); *HLB Kidsons (a firm) v Lloyd's Underwriters subscribing to Lloyd's policy No 621/PK1D00101* [2008] EWCA (n 54); *Kajima UK Engineering Ltd v Underwriter Insurance Company Ltd* (n 86); *McManus v European Risk Insurance Co* [2013] EWHC 18 (Ch); *Euro Pools plc (in administration) v Royal & Sun Alliance Insurance plc* (n 86).

93 *See J Rothschild Assurance Plc v Collyear* (n 51). For an example of such policy wording, *see* WR Berkley UK Limited, 'Directors and Officers Liability and Company Reimbursement Insurance Policy' (n 8).

94 A breach of the undertaking may lead to legal proceedings seeking damages. *See* Julie Bowring, 'Solicitors' Undertakings Back in the Spotlight' (*Clyde & Co*, 3 March 2015) <https://www.clydeco.com/en/insights/2015/03/solicitors-undertakings-back-in-the-spotlight> accessed 27 November 2020.

95 *See for example Shinedean Ltd v Alldown Demolition (London) Ltd (in liquidation*) [2006] EWCA Civ 939 [1] (May LJ).

must endeavour to provide as much information as possible, as soon as possible. However, in making such a blanket notification, it is unlikely that the Cooperation clause will be deemed to have been breached, particularly where the insured has made efforts to comply and cooperate in all other means.[96]

As the undertaking is legally enforceable by the prosecutor and potentially the court, the company cannot be prejudiced by its insurer in adhering to its terms. Where made as an undertaking to the court, the obligations are governed by the Civil Procedure Rules.[97] As compliance is effected in line with the statutory instrument,[98] insurers would not be able to ultimately refuse coverage (when the insurer becomes aware of the claim's extent) under section 13A(3)(c) of the IA 2015; doing so would be in breach of the implied term that insurers must make payments due for claims within a reasonable time, having regard to any statutory or regulatory compliance. If the insured makes a notification (or regularly discloses) to the fullest extent possible within the parameters of the undertaking, which ceases to have effect upon the final hearing[99] (and is not imposed at the point of a self-report, when an original notification may have been made), then the insurer will not be able to preclude coverage (on this particular basis), by virtue of section 13A(3)(c)[100] and the insured having acted in good faith. Such a notification of Circumstances may preserve coverage for future linked Claims but would not provide relief in the form of advancement of defence costs.[101]

To avoid any dispute arising as regards compliance with the confidentiality undertaking, the company should endeavour to negotiate its parameters to allow disclosure to their insurers,[102] as an express term. Should concerns arise, this provision could be qualified by outlining that information will not be shared with co-insured individuals under the ABC policy, and that notification of intended or effected disclosure will be made to prosecutors to ensure transparency. Doing so would be in the best interests of the company, the prosecutor (in effecting negotiations), and potentially – depending on the scope – the directors.

If a broader notification is possible (for example, where a contractual right upon the insurer to compel disclosure by virtue of a Cooperation clause arises), as the pre-negotiation confidentiality undertaking is contractual in nature,[103] any liability arising from

96 Kevin LaCroix, 'Thinking About the Duty to Cooperate' (*The D&O Diary*, 25 October 2016) <https://www.dandodiary.com/2016/10/articles/uncategorized/thinking-duty-cooperate/> accessed 27 November 2020.

97 CPR.

98 Failure to comply is penalised by committal order, committing the party to prison, which if that person is a body corporate, is enforced against any director or other officer of the body. *See* CCR Ord 29, r 1(1).

99 The undertaking regarding the term of negotiations spans the period of negotiations, formally ending upon approval/refusal at the final hearing, though the public nature of the final hearing means that the part providing for confidentiality of the fact of negotiations would cease to have practical effect then anyway. *See* Crown Prosecution Service and Serious Fraud Office, 'Deferred Prosecution Agreements Code of Practice' (n 1) para 3.2.

100 Insurance Act 2015, s 13A(3)(c).

101 If a Claim is not deemed to have been made. Where a Claim is already deemed to have been made at the initiation of the investigation, this blanket notification may aid a continued advancement/defence where policy wording allows.

102 This would appear to be possible: 'Until the issues of confidentiality, use of and retention of information have been *agreed to the satisfaction of both parties*, and the agreement reflected in signed undertakings, the prosecutor must not continue with the substantive DPA negotiations' (emphasis added). *See* Crown Prosecution Service and Serious Fraud Office, 'Deferred Prosecution Agreements Code of Practice' (n 1) para 3.11.

103 In *Omers*, it was outlined that the defendant company (in these civil proceedings: Tesco Plc, parent company of Tesco Stores Ltd) was 'caught between its [disclosure] obligations … and its obligations to keep the

it may be excluded by a Contract exclusion clause (**Section 18.5.2**). It may be argued that coverage in respect of the liability incurred within the DPA (for example, a fine) and defence costs incurred throughout the process would be precluded, as such liability can only arise following the signing of the pre-negotiation confidentiality undertaking.[104] However, this interpretation is likely too broad, and the liability incurred in the DPA process too remote. The Contract exclusion clause will likely not apply where liability would have attached in the absence of the contract/agreement.[105] Though it may be argued that the undertaking unlocks the ability to incur such (DPA-related) liability, liability in respect of the criminal investigative process and/or proceedings would likely have been incurred in any event (particularly following a damning self-report). However, liability arising as a result of acts committed in respect of the undertaking – for example, its breach – would likely be subject to such an exclusion.

18.4.1.3.1 Statement of facts

Part of the negotiation process will be the drafting of the statement of facts, an extensive document outlining details of the wrongdoing which forms part of the DPA. There is no adjudication or assessment of the facts during the DPA court proceedings, and therefore the prosecutor and company must agree on the content within the statement of facts.[106] An insurer is likely to want to know the content of the statement of facts for the purpose of its own investigation, and such disclosure will be expected on the basis of the Cooperation clause which forms part of most standard policies.[107] Such disclosure may be difficult if it forms part of the company's confidentiality undertaking.

SFO Documents confidential and private, unless otherwise directed by the Court'. *See Omers Administration Corp v Tesco Plc* [2019] EWHC 109 (Ch) [1]. The latter part of this statement suggests that the pre-negotiation confidentiality undertaking may have been made to the court. If these undertakings are made between the parties in letter format, and then subsequently to the court, it is likely that the undertakings would be enforceable by the court (as a promise to it) and by either party upon breach in the law of contract. *See Independiente Ltd v Music Trading On-Line (HK) Ltd* [2007] EWCA Civ 111 [21]. In respect of the undertaking to the court: the SFO could institute proceedings as a claimant, as the CPS did in proceedings before Judge Goymer referred to in *R v M* [2008] EWCA Crim 1901 [11]. Where the undertakings are made between the company and prosecutor but are not subsequently made to the court, it is likely that the exercise of outlining such commitments in signed documents is intended to be contractual. In *Omers*, it was also outlined that the undertaking was 'given by acceptance of the terms of the SFO's letters', which may suggest (not knowing the content of the acceptance) that no further step was taken to make the undertaking to the court. *See Omers Administration Corp v Tesco Plc* [2019] EWHC 109 (Ch) [11].

104 The undertaking must be given before negotiations can proceed. *See* Crown Prosecution Service and Serious Fraud Office, 'Deferred Prosecution Agreements Code of Practice' (n 1) para 3.11.

105 For example, in tort. *See Omega Proteins Ltd v Aspen Insurance UK Ltd* [2010] EWHC 2280 (Comm). *See also* AIG PrivateEdge, 'D&O Coverage Section' (*AIG*, 2016) <https://www.aig.co.uk/content/dam/aig/emea/united-kingdom/documents/Financial-lines/PrivateEdge/privateedge-do-2016.pdf> accessed 23 November 2020, para 5.11(i): 'The Insurer shall not be liable to make any payment for Loss … arising out of, based upon or attributable to any liability of any Company under any express oral or written contract or agreement. This Exclusion 5.11 (Contract) shall not apply to … any liability that would have attached in the absence of such a contract.'

106 'The parties should resolve any factual issues necessary to allow the court to agree terms of the DPA on a clear, fair and accurate basis. The court does not have the power to adjudicate upon factual differences in DPA proceedings.' *See* Crown Prosecution Service and Serious Fraud Office, 'Deferred Prosecution Agreements Code of Practice' (n 1) para 6.2. *See also Director of the Serious Fraud Office v Amec Foster Wheeler Limited* [2021] Lloyd's Rep FC 353 (Crown) [11]. 'My approval of the DPA is simply a confirmation of those facts, the facts being admitted by [the defendant]': *Serious Fraud Office v Serco Geografix Ltd* [2019] Lloyd's Rep FC 518 (Crown) [29].

107 Requiring the insured to cooperate with the insurer.

The SFO Operational Handbook outlines that the confidentiality of 'information and material *provided by both parties* during the negotiations'[108] (emphasis added) is central to the negotiation process and details various examples of the risk of disclosure. However, it only specifies that 'information and material *provided by the SFO* as part of the DPA negotiations'[109] (emphasis added) must form part of the written confidentiality/nondisclosure undertaking of the company.[110] It can therefore be reasonably presumed that such exclusive wording is deliberate.[111] As the statement of facts does not constitute material provided *by* the SFO,[112] and in most cases will be agreed upon following the surrendering of documentation and information by the company, it can therefore be determined that the company is not precluded by the undertaking from disclosing the content to its insurer. Provided that the company is permitted to disclose the fact of the DPA negotiations (as the undertaking only exists for that period), the company may be able to disclose the contents.[113] This may not be the case, however, where the statement of facts is deemed to contain material provided by the prosecutor (for example, witness statements gathered in its own investigation).

18.4.2 Advancement of defence costs

For defence costs to be advanced under an Advancement of Defence Costs extension, a Claim must have been made against the insured, and no exclusion clause(s) invoked to exclude coverage. The following analysis continues to consider the Claim definition inclusive of investigations. A mandatory requirement upon the insurer to advance will require an exclusion clause to be (actually) invoked in order to refuse advancement.[114] Conversely, where the requirement to advance is discretionary, the insurer may refuse advancement even where an exclusion is not triggered, if the insurer perceives that it has realistic grounds to do so.[115] Should a duty to indemnify policy provide an advancement to a potentially covered claim, advancement will cease when an exclusion clause is triggered,[116] and a subsequent determination that the defence costs are non-covered will engage the insurer's right to recoupment of sums paid.

108 Serious Fraud Office, 'Deferred Prosecution Agreements' (n 21).

109 ibid.

110 This is also the case within the DPA Code. *See* Crown Prosecution Service and Serious Fraud Office, 'Deferred Prosecution Agreements Code of Practice' (n 1) paras 3.6, 3.9.

111 Furthermore, although the material provided by both parties – which may reasonably be taken to include the agreed statement of facts – is to be treated as confidential during the negotiations, the company's undertaking is limited only to nondisclosure of material provided by the SFO.

112 Unless it contains evidence gathered by the prosecutor.

113 The company would not be permitted to share the statement of facts with its insurer if it is prohibited within an undertaking from sharing the fact of the negotiations. This is not because the statement of facts itself is protected, but because the fact of the negotiations (to which the statement of facts drafting is a part) is. In such circumstances, a blanket notification would remain preferable. This would similarly be the case should a duty of confidence arise on the basis of such terms, even if not set out within a company's undertaking.

114 *Wilkie v Gordian Runoff Ltd* [2005] HCA 17; Paolini and Nambisan (n 53) paras 8.28–8.30.

115 *Silbermann v CGU Insurance Ltd* [2003] NSWCA 203. *See also* Paolini and Nambisan (n 53) para 8.26.

116 A duty to defend policy – which is unlikely under Side C – would require the insurer to continue providing a defence to the insured even where the underlying claim is only potentially covered, and thus where the Conduct exclusion clause is not officially triggered, defence will remain in place.

18.4.2.1 Pre-DPA investigation and the self-report

An insurer may refuse to advance during the investigative stage where the Conduct exclusion clause is deemed to be invoked. During the investigation, the company wishing to obtain a DPA will be required to cooperate so as to ensure 'that the full extent of the alleged offending has been identified'.[117] Such a level of cooperation to the point of surrendering all self-incriminating information (including the self-report) would require prior consent of the insurer,[118] which cannot be unreasonably withheld or delayed.[119] Following receipt of a request to obtain consent to admit liability, the insurer may deem the insured's self-incrimination an admission to the excluded misconduct. In policies requiring only an acknowledgement to invoke the clause, coverage would be precluded.[120] If the underlying Claim remains potentially covered despite the self-report, the insurer will have a continued obligation to advance in duty to indemnify policies which expressly provide for such particularly broad coverage.[121] However, it is likely that an insurer with a discretionary obligation to advance would exercise its right to refuse to do so.

Nothing in the DPA Code or SFO's website guidance suggests that an initial self-report would be treated as a formal admission in criminal proceedings. However, an extensive self-report would render any future defence or denial of wrongdoing difficult. Regardless, it may be considered by insurers to be an admission of criminal wrongdoing. A Conduct exclusion triggered by admission may exclude cover when evidence ('for instance of a written nature')[122] supporting allegations of the excluded conduct arises. A self-report made to a prosecutor will generally be in writing and will support the notion that the excluded conduct either had, or may have, occurred.[123] It will be crucial for an insured to understand the insurer's position on self-reports and what constitutes an admission (and excluded conduct) under the Conduct exclusion clause at the inception of the policy, so as not to act to the detriment of their own interests.

---

117 Crown Prosecution Service and Serious Fraud Office, 'Deferred Prosecution Agreements Code of Practice' (n 1) para 2.2(ii).

118 If a Claim is deemed to have been made.

119 The giving of consent does not necessarily amount to the insurer's acceptance of coverage liability.

120 From this point forward, analysis of the potential invoking of the Conduct exclusion clause will predominantly consider the typical requirements of a "final adjudication or judgment" and/or "admission". It can be reasonably presumed that where an admission is determined for the purposes of invoking the clause, a clause requiring an acknowledgement instead would bear the same consequences. Nevertheless, at many stages in the DPA process, it could be said that the companies involved acknowledge their involvement in wrongdoing excluded by the clause, as a DPA is a negotiated criminal justice tool.

121 Without such expression, only covered claims require advancement. *See Hulton & Co v Mountain* (1929) 28 LILR 249 (CA). *See also Wilkie v Gordian Runoff Ltd* (n 114); Paolini and Nambisan (n 53) para 1.31. If potentially covered claims generate advancement, a later determination that the costs are non-covered will require their repayment to the insurer. *See US Telepacific Corp v US Specialty Insurance Company* No 19-55828, at 2 (9th Cir Jun 17 2020). *See also Oldham v QBE Insurance (Europe) Ltd* [2017] EWHC 3045 (Comm). The insurer will have a duty to act in the defence of the insured in duty to defend policies in such circumstances. *See Montrose Chemical Corp v Superior Court* 6 Cal 4th 287, 295 (Cal 1993); *Buss v Superior Court* 16 Cal 4th 35, 47–48 (Cal 1997); *S Cal Pizza Co v Certain Underwriters at Lloyd's* 40 Cal App 5th 140, 252 Cal Rptr 3d 639, 639–640 (Cal Ct App 2019).

122 AIC, 'Directors' and Officers' Insurance: AIC Guide' (*Thomson Reuters Practical Law*, 26 August 2010) <https://uk.practicallaw.thomsonreuters.com/0-503-1690?transitionType=Default&contextData=(sc.Default)&firstPage=true&OWSessionId=2adf19263cf448e4913ed9ed3525deff&skipAnonymous=true> accessed 10 October 2023.

123 A typical policy will not require that an admission is made in writing to the insurer specifically, but will just require that it is made in writing.

18.4.2.2 Negotiation process

Defence costs are not necessarily advanced on an understanding that the insured is innocent but are to be repaid upon determination of excluded misconduct. A policy definition of "Defence Costs" will tend to provide for coverage for "reasonable fees, costs and legal expenses" incurred in the "investigation, defence, settlement or appeal" of a Claim. The negotiation process of a DPA arises during a criminal investigation,[124] and quite often runs parallel to regulatory investigations (such as by the FCA). The negotiation stage is, according to the DPA Code, prior to the institution of proceedings,[125] and follows a lengthy period of cooperation with the offender. Thus, a (Securities) Claim definition including "criminal proceedings" would not respond unless also inclusive of investigations.

The ability to obtain an advancement, or to be defended, by the insurer during the negotiation period may be crucial; the value of a Claim definition inclusive of investigations may be the source of an SME's ability to engage in negotiations. An invitation to enter into DPA negotiations is not a guarantee that a DPA will result,[126] and the company will be aware of the alternative reality of a possible conviction should negotiations fail. Where an insurer is aware that defence costs advanced are pursuant to a DPA, it will be aware that the claim will likely be precluded under the policy should the negotiations be successful.[127] *Prima facie*, the claim is non-covered; however the company may withdraw from negotiations and any prosecution may be unsuccessful.[128] The insurer may see it to be in its interests to defend the Claim, as numerous further Claims may emanate. The insurer may continue to provide a defence (costs) up until the expiry of the DPA, whereupon it would seek recoupment for sums paid; upon DPA breach, the insurer would be keen to ensure that a variation (and not a conviction) results. Alternatively, the insurer may exculpate its liability where the insured accepts liability,[129] or consent to the insured's acceptance of liability but elect not to provide coverage on the basis of an admission; the insurer may reconcile with the fact that future Claims will likely fall within a well-worded Related Claims clause.

18.4.2.2.1 Statement of facts

The process of drafting the statement of facts and correspondence with the prosecutor will be done with the assistance or oversight of legal representation, and therefore it is likely that the company will seek an advancement of defence costs. The statement of facts does not require formal admission of wrongdoing, but the company 'must admit the contents and meaning of key documents referred to in the statement of facts'.[130] Further, the state-

---

124 With a view to prosecution. *See* Crown Prosecution Service and Serious Fraud Office, 'Deferred Prosecution Agreements Code of Practice' (n 1) para 2.2.

125 ibid para 5.1.

126 ibid para 2.1.

127 Most likely as a result of a Conduct exclusion clause triggered by "admission" or "final adjudication or judgment", where applicable to the defence costs provision. However, indemnification for defence costs is not absolutely precluded where the Conduct exclusion clause is not suitably worded to respond, in cases where public policy would not require such preclusion.

128 A duty to indemnify policy providing advancement to potentially covered claims (or a duty to defend policy) would be preferable to the insured in these circumstances, but advancement will be dependent on the ability to notify.

129 Where liability is admitted without the insurer's consent. *See* Paolini and Nambisan (n 53) para 1.31.

130 Serious Fraud Office, 'Deferred Prosecution Agreements' (n 21). No admission of liability is often a condition precedent to coverage. *See Baulderstone Hornibrook Engineering Pty Ltd v Gordian Runoff Ltd*

ment of facts is considered an admission by the company under section 10 of the CJA 1967 in criminal proceedings brought against it for the relevant offence (for example, should a DPA not be agreed).[131] Confidentiality undertaking requirements may not allow the company to share the contents of the statement of facts with the insurer, even where disclosure of the fact of negotiations is permitted, but on the basis that the statement of facts in its entirety is often deemed to be an "admission" and is likely to be so by the insurer, coverage may be precluded.[132] For the company, the operation of a blanket notification may be useful here where a Claim is not deemed to have been made. Notifying the insurer holistically without mentioning the fact of DPA negotiations may allow for the obtaining of Circumstances Investigation Costs cover (though this would only provide interim relief and likely require repayment). However, if the company is able (**Section 18.4.1**) to notify of the fact of DPA negotiations (and just not the information and material disclosed), it must do so.

Where the insured is permitted to share the contents of the statement of facts, this would be in thorough adherence to the Cooperation clause. However, this would likely also then provide the basis upon which the insurer precludes coverage – by virtue of a written admission by the insured (Conduct exclusion clause) – which would render the company liable for any further defence costs incurred during the negotiation and judgment stages (and for the repayment of any advancement received). Though it has been said that '[t]here is a world of difference between giving a factual account of what happened, without giving any expression of opinion as to blame, and an admission of liability',[133] and in DPAs '[t]here is no requirement for formal admissions of guilt in respect of the offences charged by the indictment',[134] the statement of facts would still likely be considered an admission of liability for the purpose of invoking the Conduct exclusion clause.[135] Within the Beazley Side A DIC policy, it is noted in respect of the Conduct exclusion clause that: 'Formal written admission by the company in a deferred prosecution agreement statement of fact does not constitute formal written admission by an insured person';[136] this suggests that there is at least some policy interpretation that would consider the statement of facts to trigger the exclusion.[137] Even if the company elects not to share the statement of facts with its insurer during the negotiation stage, it is likely that the insurer will preclude coverage on the basis that the negotiation stage is ongoing and thus constitutes an acknowledgement

---

[2008] NWSCA 243; Robert Merkin, *Colinvaux's Law of Insurance* (12th edn, Sweet & Maxwell 2019) para 21-080.

131 Crown Prosecution Service and Serious Fraud Office, 'Deferred Prosecution Agreements Code of Practice' (n 1) para 6.4.

132 An admission may be 'evidence (for instance of a written nature) being non-covered supporting the contention that the alleged acts took place'. *See* AIC (n 122).

133 *Terrys v Trafalgar Insurance Co Ltd* [1970] 1 Lloyd's Rep 524 (M&CL) 526 (Rogers J).

134 Crown Prosecution Service and Serious Fraud Office, 'Deferred Prosecution Agreements Code of Practice' (n 1) para 6.3.

135 A formal admission in the Conduct exclusion clause need not equate to a guilty plea. Furthermore, the fact that the statement of facts attaches to the DPA, and would be considered a formal admission under section 10 of the Criminal Justice Act 1967 upon DPA breach, would provide further support of its nature as a mode of accepting liability for the content therein.

136 Beazley, 'Side A DIC Policy' (*Beazley*) <https://web.archive.org/web/20220421213351/https://www.beazley.com/documents/Wordings/Side%20A%20DIC.pdf> accessed 7 September 2021, 3.

137 Against the company.

or admission of the insured to having participated in the criminal conduct forming the basis of the negotiations.[138]

18.4.3 Access to pre-Claim coverage where "Investigations" are not within "Claim"

As D&O operates upon "Claims made", a policy not including investigations within the definition of "Claim" may transpire to be somewhat redundant to an insured entity involved in DPA negotiations. At the point at which a Claim would then be made, the company may have incurred such monstrous liability that its ability to meet the conditions of the DPA or continue in business would be vastly limited.[139] The question has arisen, posed by industry specialist Neil McCarthy: 'Would you rather have a small limit on circumstance investigation costs, or a full limit pre-investigation costs and a significant chunk of mitigation costs instead?'[140] Pre-Investigation costs (also known as "Self-Report Investigation" costs) would typically provide coverage for internal investigations where a self-report has been made or is in consideration.[141] This may therefore prove useful in the pre-negotiation stage but would likely cease to provide coverage thereafter.

Circumstance Investigation Costs would provide cover where a notification of Circumstances is sufficiently made, though would likely be capped and exhaust the aggregate limit of indemnity.[142] This would be useful in the negotiation stage where the company is only able to make a blanket notification, although the DPA investigation/negotiation process is expensive and the capped limit may not be sufficient. A blanket notification would need to be sufficient to give rise to such an extension of coverage, and this would be dependent on policy wording. Furthermore, this is not a common feature amongst D&O policies.[143] Where it is, however, this may provide some relief to an insured, and the capped limit may (at the application stage) be somewhat negotiable. Such a provision would not be considered a Claim but may lead to the preclusion of future related Claims where the Related Claims clause denotes 'any and all Claims and/or Investigations'.[144] The payment of such investigation costs would likely be subject to the policy's exclusion clauses (unless provided as a separate undertaking), and therefore a later invoking of the Conduct exclusion clause would require any sums paid under this policy extension to be repaid.

---

138 The insurer would be aware that the statement of facts will form part of the DPA negotiation process, and the insured will have requested consent to accept liability within it.

139 This is evidence of the potential unfairness to smaller businesses in respect of access to true justice (when compared with larger companies) and negotiated settlements.

140 Neil McCarthy, 'Smoke, Mirrors and Management Liability: Is More, Less and Less, More?' (*LinkedIn*, 18 April 2018) <https://www.linkedin.com/pulse/smoke-mirrors-management-liability-more-less-neil-mccarthy> accessed 20 January 2021.

141 Chubb, 'Elite' (*Chubb*, 2020) <https://www.chubb.com/uk-en/business/elite.html> accessed 20 January 2021.

142 To minimise the insurer's exposure. *See* Allianz Broker, 'Directors & Officers Liability Section' (*Allianz*, 2020) <https://www.allianz.co.uk/content/dam/onemarketing/azuk/allianzcouk/broker/docs/policy-wording/LD0008-directors-and-officers-liability-section-policies-incepted-prior-to-310717.pdf> accessed 22 October 2020, 15.

143 It is unlikely that for larger companies this broader scope would be offered in a hard D&O market, but nonetheless may provide an avenue for SMEs to be able to engage in DPA negotiations.

144 Allianz Broker, 'Directors & Officers Liability Section' (n 142) 10.

As an alternative, Mitigation Costs cover exists to provide an extension of coverage to insureds in pre-Claim situations where the necessity for defence costs coverage may arise. Mitigation Costs cover will only respond where mitigation is sought to be made by the insured in anticipation of loss being incurred of a type that would be covered under the policy, and that may occur if prior action is not taken.[145] Though the intent of such cover is to respond to loss that would otherwise be covered within the main insuring conditions of the policy, poor drafting could leave an insurer exposed to providing cover it had not foreseen.[146] Therefore, it will likely be drafted that insurer consent is required prior to the incurring of costs, and coverage will likely be subject to a capped limit. The requirement to trigger Mitigation Costs cover is likely to be notification of Circumstances. As this extension of cover is typically intended to be a collaborative and cooperative measure between the insured and insurer,[147] and consent is required prior to the incurring of costs, policy wording would need to be particularly broad to permit and respond to a blanket notification pre-Claim.[148] This would likely only be available to SMEs.

18.5 Indemnification

In order to receive indemnification, actual legal liability must be established. Where the company agrees a DPA, this will be 'compelling evidence' of liability.[149] If it is deemed that this (particularly prior to expiration) constitutes a settlement, as opposed to a judgment ascertaining loss, the insurer will be open to challenging whether the insured was truly liable.[150] The insurer may refuse indemnification if it determines that the insured was not actually liable, unless the policy provides for indemnification 'wherever liability is "ascertained" by judgment or settlement, even if on an objective analysis there was no legal liability'.[151] However, as the penalty imposed by the DPA will not be indemnifiable, the value of Side C (particularly to SMEs) will be the provision of defence costs and response to third-party civil claims. Defence costs are not subject to this liability principle, unless contractually expressed, and will instead be interpreted via contractual

145 'The indemnity provided by the insuring clause includes the Assured's defence costs and expenses, claimant costs … [and] Mitigation Costs … "Mitigation Costs" is also a defined term. Mitigation costs are defined as: "Mitigation Costs shall mean any payment of loss, costs or expenses reasonably and necessarily incurred by the Assured in taking action to avoid a third party claim or to reduce a third party claim (or to avoid or reduce a third party claim which may arise from a fact, circumstance or event) of a type which would have been covered under this policy (notwithstanding any Deductible amount)."' *See Standard Life Assurance Ltd v Ace European Group* [2012] EWCA Civ 1713 [2].

146 Debra Burford and Laura Cooke, 'Mitigation Costs Cover' (*AIG*, September 2013) <https://web.archive.org/web/20140903220148/http://www.aig.co.uk/financial-institutions-insights_2538_362207.html> accessed 21 January 2021, 3.

147 ibid 7.

148 Furthermore, if blanket notification was permitted by the insurer, and the clause required that coverage only be extended for losses that would otherwise be covered under the main policy conditions, a later determination that the coverage is non-covered may be considered to be contrary to good faith in certain circumstances.

149 *AstraZeneca Insurance Co Ltd v XL Insurance (Bermuda) Ltd* [2013] EWHC 349 (Comm) [65] (Flaux J).

150 ibid [65], [89], [109]–[110] (Flaux J). *See also Post Office v Norwich Union Fire Insurance Society Ltd* [1967] 2 QB 363 (CA) 373–376.

151 *AstraZeneca Insurance Co Ltd v XL Insurance (Bermuda) Ltd* [2013] EWHC (n 149) [65] (Flaux J). It has been questioned whether some DPAs should have been agreed, in respect of whether liability would have arisen in the first place, and therefore this will be pertinent. *See for example* Ross Dixon, 'Great Expectations?' (2021) 171(7939) NLJ 15, 16.

principles. Questions may arise as to whether defence costs must be recouped where a DPA expires and no conviction arises; however, the right of recoupment will arise as a result of the Conduct exclusion clause, which is drafted in reflection of public policy.

18.5.1 Financial penalty

A fine imposed within a DPA would not be covered in a typical D&O insurance policy.[152] Though the term "Loss" to a layperson may suggest the inclusion of financial penalties levied against a party and the consequential burden to pay, a typical D&O "Loss" definition will exclude criminal fines or penalties for public policy reasons: it would be contrary to the principles of justice to allow indemnification for financial penalties amassed for wrongdoing.[153] Though some policies may provide indemnification for civil fines and/or penalties, the criminal nature of the DPA would exclude this possibility. Though many D&O policies provide coverage for settlements,[154] thus within some "Claim" definitions, the true nature of the claim will reveal that the DPA is an alternative prosecutorial tool for criminal (thus excluded) settlement.[155]

18.5.2 Contract exclusion clause

Within *AL* (**Section 7.1.1**), Mr Justice Green in the High Court outlined that a DPA is a contract, within which contractual powers and duties are conferred upon both the prosecutor and company.[156] This position, however, is contested. The powers conferred upon the prosecutor, albeit by virtue of a DPA having been agreed and approved, exist independently of the DPA within Schedule 17 of the CACA 2013 and the Criminal Procedure Rules. Some powers become live when the company consents/agrees to a DPA, such as the power to apply to the court for approval, but the powers cannot be said to exist as a result of contractual conferral within the DPA. The company simply agrees to consent to the prosecutor's exercising of the "powers" under Schedule 17 of the CACA 2013, and to submit to the jurisdiction of the court and prosecutor's powers within the relevant statutory instruments in order to have the DPA approved. The company has an obligation to adhere to the terms of the DPA, but those terms are not contractually enforceable by the prosecutor or any other party upon breach.

---

152 This would nonetheless be excluded within the narrow form of the *ex turpi causa non oritur actio* maxim. 'In its narrower form it is that a claimant cannot recover for damage which is the consequence of a sentence imposed upon him for a criminal act; in its wider version it is that a claimant may not recover for damage which is the consequence of his own criminal act.' *See Safeway Stores Limited v Twigger* [2010] EWCA Civ 1472 [16], citing *Gray v Thames Trains Ltd* [2009] UKHL 33, citing *Worrall v British Railways Board* (CA, 29 April 1999). *See also* John Birds and Katie Richards, *Birds' Modern Insurance Law* (12th edn, Sweet & Maxwell 2022) para 14-07, citing *Hardy v Motor Insurers' Bureau* [1964] 2 QB 745 (CA) 760.

153 Kevin LaCroix, 'Executive Protection: D&O Insurance – The Insuring Agreement' (*The D&O Diary*, 5 August 2010) <https://www.dandodiary.com/2010/08/articles/d-o-insurance/executive-protection-do-insurance-the-insuring-agreement/> accessed 22 May 2018.

154 Goanos, *D&O 101: Understanding Directors and Officers Liability Insurance* (n 17) 63. DPAs have frequently been referred to in the UK as "settlements". *See* n 30.

155 A non-prosecution agreement overseas might however attract indemnification, should policy wording be broad enough.

156 *R (on the application of AL) v Serious Fraud Office* [2018] EWHC 856 (Admin) [52], [62], [93], [105].

Instead, breach is governed by Schedule 17 of the CACA 2013 and the terms are either varied or terminated (whereby a prosecution will likely follow). Some obligations, such as those relating to disclosure, will exist independently of the DPA and will simply form part of the DPA in order to ensure that the company is fully cooperative in ongoing investigations and/or proceedings, with the threat of breach proceedings if not. However, disclosure obligations will be enforceable by the relevant parties regardless of the DPA's existence. Furthermore, though there are legally enforceable elements to a DPA and powers conferred by law within the CACA 2013, a DPA is not intended to be a contract but a criminal penalty. The only exception to criminal law governance is the possibility of judicial review of prosecutorial decisions (but not the decision of the court to approve, or otherwise, a DPA).[157]

Coverage may nonetheless be precluded on the basis of a Contract exclusion clause.[158] A typical Contract exclusion clause will provide that defence costs remain indemnifiable,[159] which would allow for access to an advancement of defence costs, though any advancement made for a later determined non-covered claim will need to be repaid to the insurer. Typically, a Contract exclusion will preclude coverage for Claims arising from a contract and/or agreement, depending on policy wording. On the basis that a DPA does not constitute a contract, a Contract exclusion clause with restrictive language precluding coverage for "contracts" alone could not be invoked. It may be the case that such clauses with broader wording, allowing preclusion also for 'agreement[s]',[160] would be invoked. If this is the case, coverage for Claims 'arising out of, based upon, or attributable to'[161] any liability under the agreement would typically be precluded. However, often Contract exclusion clauses will not apply where liability would have attached in the absence of the contract/agreement.[162] An insured could reasonably argue that liability would attach in the absence of the DPA.[163] However, this argument would be circular, as the imposition of the fact that criminal liability would otherwise arise would invoke the Conduct exclusion (by admission), which will likely remain the insurer's first choice of assertion in precluding coverage in any event.[164]

157 Ministry of Justice, *Deferred Prosecution Agreements: Government Response to the Consultation on a New Enforcement Tool to Deal With Economic Crime Committed by Commercial Organisations* (Cm 8463, 2012) para 183.

158 As seen in *Omega Proteins Ltd v Aspen Insurance UK Ltd* (n 105).

159 'The Insurer shall not be liable to make any payment for Loss … arising out of, based upon or attributable to any liability of any Company under any express oral or written contract or agreement. This Exclusion 5.11 (Contract) shall not apply to … any Defence costs in connection with Corporate Legal Liability Cover and Company Extension 3.3(iii) [Breach of Contract].' *See* AIG PrivateEdge, 'D&O Coverage Section' (n 105) para 5.11(ii). 'The Insurer shall not be liable for any Loss or any Investigation Costs … arising out of, based upon, or attributable to any actual or alleged contractual liability assumed by the Company under any contract or agreement; provided that this Exclusion shall not apply to Defence Costs for a Claim brought against the Company.' *See* Allianz Broker, 'Directors & Officers Liability Section' (n 142) 19.

160 ibid.

161 ibid.

162 'The Insurer shall not be liable to make any payment for Loss … arising out of, based upon or attributable to any liability of any Company under any express oral or written contract or agreement. This Exclusion 5.11 (Contract) shall not apply to … any liability that would have attached in the absence of such a contract.' *See* AIG PrivateEdge, 'D&O Coverage Section' (n 105) para 5.11(i).

163 It is not always clear whether "liability" refers to civil obligations.

164 On the basis that negotiated agreements with suspected offenders in criminal law will most likely require an admission or acknowledgement of liability, it may be perceived that qualifying "agreements" within

18.5.3 Ex turpi causa non oritur actio *and public policy*

An insurer may argue that the maxim *ex turpi causa non oritur actio* (no action can arise from a wrongful cause) precludes a company from obtaining any indemnification under Side C where the company agrees a DPA, which will arise on the basis of a criminal offence. The Latin maxim is said to be the root of another maxim, which states that a person cannot profit from their unlawful acts.[165] Also known as the "illegality doctrine", the Supreme Court in *Patel v Mirza* laid down a new test for application to establish whether a claim is precluded, whilst outlining that the rationale of the doctrine is that 'it would be contrary to the public interest to enforce a claim if to do so would be harmful to the integrity of the legal system'.[166] The "range of factors test" is applied to evaluate the harm to the public interest, with consideration in denying a claim on the basis of criminality as to whether the underlying purpose of the prohibition transgressed is upheld, public policy, and proportionality of response.[167]

In considering public policy, one cannot be indemnified as a result of their deliberate criminal act;[168] this may be despite the fact that the person was aware that they were committing the action, but unaware that it was criminal.[169] In the case of a company, its actions are carried out by its directors (the organ), but the wider board may be unaware of the extent (and/or nature) of the actions of some of its members. The more flexible approach adopted in *Patel* may allow for consideration of the nature of the corporate criminality in assessing public policy for the indemnification,[170] which would likely be predominantly for defence costs incurred in criminal proceedings, and Losses arising from civil/regulatory/administrative proceedings. Where a DPA is based upon a fraudulent scheme inherent within, known, and authorised by the company, and thus where attribution of the director's(') acts occurs, public policy would lead to an application of the illegality doctrine.

Where a DPA is based upon conduct of a select number of directors and the board was unaware of the conduct (and did not authorise it), there may be scope for consideration as to whether the company can be considered to have acted deliberately, or whether it was a primary or secondary victim of the criminality for which it accepted responsibility. This may occur, for example, where the company agrees a DPA on the basis of a

---

a Contract exclusion clause with a definition is unnecessary in respect of DPAs, where exclusion is likely to be found elsewhere within the policy anyway.

165 Birds and Richards (n 152) para 14-02.

166 [2016] UKSC 42 [120] (Lord Toulson).

167 'In assessing whether the public interest would be harmed in that way, it is necessary (a) to consider the underlying purpose of the prohibition which has been transgressed and whether that purpose will be enhanced by denial of the claim, (b) to consider any other relevant public policy on which the denial of the claim may have an impact and (c) to consider whether denial of the claim would be a proportionate response to the illegality, bearing in mind that punishment is a matter for the criminal courts.' *See* ibid.

168 'If an act is manifestly unlawful, or the doer of it knows it to be unlawful, as constituting either a civil wrong or a criminal offence, he cannot maintain an action for contribution or for indemnity against the liability which results to him therefrom.' *See* Paolini and Nambisan (n 53) para 4.04, citing *Burrows v Rhodes* [1899] 1 QB 816. *See also Beresford v Royal Insurance Co* [1938] AC 586 (HL).

169 'It is clearly contrary to public policy to insure against the commission of an act, knowing what act is being committed, which is a crime, although the person committing it may not at the time know it to be so.' *See Haseldine v Hosken* [1933] 1 KB 822 (CA) 833 (Scrutton LJ).

170 In Delaware in the US, public policy does not necessarily bar indemnification for claims which bear an undertone of fraud, where the Wrongful Act covered under the policy arises as a result of fraud (for example, breach of duty). *See RSUI Indemnity Company v David H Murdock and Dole Food Company Inc* (n 49) 31.

"failure to prevent" offence. In *Safeway Stores Limited v Twigger*,[171] which precedes *Patel*, it was considered that the maxim only applies where the wrongdoer was '"personally" at fault',[172] which raises as yet undetermined questions regarding the liability of companies which can be classed as primary or secondary victims of their director's(') wrongdoing, and/or by strict liability.[173] In *Bilta v Nazir*,[174] Lord Mance considered whether a principal would be precluded from taking advantage of an agent's illegal acts; however this point awaits clarification.[175] Considering the application of the public conscience test,[176] if a company is to be properly regarded as a separate legal person within the law, it may be considered to be contrary to the 'integrity of the legal system'[177] to refuse indemnification in the circumstances.

The question of the purpose of the prohibition on indemnification, if to uphold public policy,[178] must be considered in line with the discussion above. In considering the proportionality of denying the company indemnification, one must '[bear] in mind that punishment is a matter for the criminal courts';[179] the company will have endured the imposition of a criminal penalty under the DPA. Though it is accepted that a criminal fine and penalty cannot be indemnified due to public policy,[180] arguably the unique circumstances which arise (as regards a DPA based upon a strict liability offence) may permit the indemnification of defence costs, and would not lead to exclusion in collateral consequential claims.

---

171 *Safeway Stores Limited v Twigger* (n 152).

172 ibid [19], citing *Moore Stephens (a firm) v Stone Rolls Ltd (in liquidation)* [2009] UKHL 39 [27]–[28] (Rimer LJ).

173 Arguably, liability imposed as a result of a strict liability offence still outlines some element of fault/wrongdoing. However, companies are in a unique position whereby strict liability can be incurred in respect of rogue individuals abusing the passive nature of the corporate shell. In *Askey v Golden Wine Co Ltd* [1948] 2 All ER 35, the defendant was not indemnifiable in respect of a strict liability offence, but it was abundant that he had acted intentionally/criminally. *See Safeway Stores Limited v Twigger* (n 152) [18] (Longmore LJ).

174 [2015] UKSC 23.

175 ibid [49] (Lord Mance). Lord Mance at paragraph 49 referred to an article which outlined that the maxim 'preclude[s] a principal from taking advantage of an agent's illegal acts' (*Ashmore, Benson Pease & Co Ltd v AV Dawson Ltd* [1973] 1 WLR 828): *see* Peter Watts, 'Stone & Rolls Ltd (In Liquidation) v Moore Stephens (A Firm): Audit Contracts and Turpitude' (2010) 126(Jan) LQR 14–20. This point awaits clarification, though in the meantime D&O insurers should bear in mind the importance of a carefully worded Conduct exclusion clause.

176 *Euro-Diam Ltd v Bathurst* [1988] 2 All ER 23 (CA). The public conscience test as set out in *Euro-Diam Ltd v Bathurst* was 'rejected' in *Tinsley v Milligan* [1994] 1 AC 340 (HL). *See* Law Commission, *The Illegality Defence in Tort* (Law Com CP No 160, 2001) para 5.19. However, 'it is suggested that the public conscience test is still useful in insurance cases': Birds and Richards (n 152) para 14-03.

177 *Patel v Mirza* (n 166) [120] (Lord Toulson).

178 Lord Kerr's interpretation of 'the underlying purpose of the prohibition which has been transgressed and whether that purpose will be enhanced by denial of the claim' was: 'the reasons that a claimant's conduct should operate to bar him or her from a remedy which would otherwise be available.' *See* ibid [120], [124] (Lord Toulson and Lord Kerr).

179 ibid [120] (Lord Toulson).

180 Some arguments may arise as to the indemnification of the company for a fine incurred in a DPA where the company is a primary or secondary victim of the underlying wrongdoing. Given the punitive nature of the financial penalty, the fact that the public interest is a relevant factor in the prosecutor's consideration of offering a DPA and the financial penalty imposed, and that the DPA must be considered by the approving judge to be in the interests of justice, it is unlikely that the argument as regards not applying the illegality doctrine will go this far. *See Singularis Holdings Ltd (in liquidation) v Daiwa Capital Markets Europe Ltd* [2019] UKSC 50 (regarding consideration of the indemnification of fines where attribution does not occur); Crown Prosecution Service and Serious Fraud Office, 'Deferred Prosecution Agreements Code of Practice' (n 1) paras 1.2, 8 (regarding the prosecutor's consideration of the public interest); Crime and Courts Act 2013, sch 17 para 8(1)(a) (regarding the judicial declaration).

This will be based upon a flexible *Patel* interpretation and will likely have value only where the Conduct exclusion clause is ambiguously phrased: for example, a clause excluding "wilful and dishonest" conduct may raise questions as regards a corporate strict liability offence.

18.6 Impact on individuals insured under Side A

18.6.1 Recoupment and subrogation

Where an insurer indemnifies for losses which are later deemed to be non-covered, recoupment may be sought.[181] Notably, however, this will not be possible if the insurer has paid pursuant to a settlement contract which prevents revisiting of the payment. Were recoupment to remain a possibility, this may be contemplated where the insurer believes that there were insufficient grounds for agreeing a DPA. This has been considered following the *Tesco Stores Ltd* DPA, for example, whereby agreement was reached on the basis of the same conduct for which three former directors were ultimately acquitted. Therefore, it will be crucial to ascertain whether cover is precluded (most likely due to the imposition of an exclusion clause or nondisclosure). The ability to seek recoupment may turn on the basis upon which the DPA was agreed and whether the company can be considered the perpetrator of the criminal conduct, or a primary or secondary victim of it, and/or liable for a strict liability offence.[182]

The insurer may pursue the individuals considered to have conducted the corporate offending. In respect of composite insurance, an insurer cannot generally exercise subrogation rights in the position of one co-insured as against another (here, for example, in the position of a company insured under Side C as against a (former) director insured under Side A, under an ABC policy). However, as losses caused by excluded conduct (for example, fraud) of a co-insured are not covered (by virtue of public policy,[183] and also a Conduct exclusion clause), subrogation rights may arise in relation to losses arising out of that conduct.[184] If the individuals insured under Side A are deemed to have engaged in such excluded and thus uninsured conduct, the insurer may exercise its rights of subrogation irrespective of the composite structure.

The insured cannot act in a manner which may prejudice the rights of the insurer and cannot reach any agreement which may undermine their rights.[185] Where the company agrees a DPA, the term disallowing the company from making statements contrary to the statement of facts may prejudice the insurer's rights of subrogation, which must be exercised in the name of the insured (i.e., the company). Such an exercising of rights – for

181 Thus, to the extent that the losses are indemnifiable under the policy, reimbursement will not be sought. *See Simpson v Thomson, Birrell* (1887) 3 App Cas 279, 284 (Lord Cairns LC).

182 Where liable for a strict liability offence, the company may have had no knowledge of the underlying wrongdoing and would simply be liable for a failure to prevent it. Though the failure to prevent incurs liability in itself, the loss can arguably be said to have been caused by (and rooted in) the underlying perpetrator of the wrongdoing.

183 *Burrows v Rhodes* (n 168). *See also Beresford v Royal Insurance Co* (n 168); Paolini and Nambisan (n 53) para 4.04.

184 *National Oilwell (UK) v Davy Offshore Ltd* [1993] 2 Lloyd's Rep 582 (CA) 614–616 (Colman J); *Netherlands v Youell* [1997] 2 Lloyd's Rep 440 (QB) 450–451 (Rix J). *See also* Alison Padfield, *Insurance Claims* (5th edn, Bloomsbury Professional 2021) para 12.4.

185 *Commercial Union Assurance Co Ltd v Lister* (1873–74) LR 9 Ch App 483.

example, against a (former) director – must be with the company's consent,[186] which when given would constitute a breach of the DPA (by authorisation of a contradictory statement by the company, or at least a representative of it).[187] To the extent that the insurer does not contradict the statement of facts, the DPA will not be breached. However, the insurer would risk causing a breach of the DPA if it did make such contradictions (for example, in an action against an individual), and this would potentially cause greater loss to the insurer (albeit subject to the right of recoupment upon exclusion on DPA breach).

18.6.2 Civil claims and policy composition

As demonstrated in the sample Securities Claim definition (outlined in **Section 18.1.1**), the standard definition will include civil claims, such as shareholder derivative actions. Where the relevant Wrongful Act and Loss (for example, defence costs) arising fall within the policy's definitions, the company will be covered under Side C. In a US case, Cognizant Technology Solutions Corporation ("Cognizant") entered into a $95 million (US) settlement agreement (not a DPA) with the SEC to resolve a consolidated putative securities class action complaint against it and some of its former officers. The company reported the following:

> A substantial majority of the settlement payment will be covered by the Company's insurers under the applicable directors and officers insurance policies, after which there will be no amounts remaining available to the Company under the policies applicable to this matter and the Company's ongoing indemnification and advancement obligations with respect to certain former officers of the Company.[188]

This suggests that the policy is responding under Side A and Side C (as the "applicable … policies"), but that the limit of indemnity is exhausted such that Side B and Side C will no longer respond; it is not entirely clear as to whether Side A has been exhausted. However, this demonstrates the response of Side C to securities-related civil claims. In the US, it is possible to agree civil DPAs and, should such an extension of the offering of DPAs in the UK arise in future, it may be the case that Side C becomes of greater value than contemporaneous defence costs advancement (prior to repayment) in DPA-related claims. However, the above Cognizant statement outlines the impact that such large payments made by insurers in response to settlements might have across the policy. An exhaustion of the Side B limit of indemnity will adversely impact the company's directors to the extent that they will then be reliant upon having suitable and responsive Side A cover. This may present further issues where the aggregate limit of indemnity between Side A and Side B is shared, which is 'usually' the case.[189] Thus, an expansion of DPAs to permit agreement based on civil liability – which is unlikely in the near future due to the tool's

186 The complexities of this are briefly discussed by Lord Justice Kerr in *MH Smith (Plant Hire) Ltd v DL Mainwaring (t/a Inshore)* [1986] 2 Lloyd's Rep 244 (CA) 246.

187 *See for example* Serious Fraud Office, 'Amec Foster Wheeler Energy Limited – Deferred Prosecution Agreement' (n 41) para 48.

188 John Kim, 'Form 8-K Cognizant Technology Solutions Corp: Current Report, Item 7.01' (*US Securities and Exchange Commission*, 7 September 2021) <https://www.sec.gov/Archives/edgar/data/1058290/000105829021000241/ctsh-20210907.htm> accessed 18 September 2021. *See also* Mike Koehler, 'Cognizant's $95 Million Ripple' (*FCPA Professor*, 16 September 2021) <https://fcpaprofessor.com/cognizants-95-million-ripple/> accessed 18 September 2021.

189 Wilkes and Kean (n 50) 180–181.

relative novelty in the UK – will require contemplation of the appropriateness of the entire ABC policy.

It will be vital for Side B and Side C to be drafted in a composite form, particularly upon reflection of the Cognizant settlement above, so as not to expose individuals insured under Side A to exclusions in coverage.[190] Without sufficient policy wording designed to 'insulate' individual co-insureds under Side A of an ABC policy, an insurer may seek to refuse cover to the co-insured on the basis of facts disclosed to it during the company's Side C claim.[191] This highlights the importance of rigorous severability language – and the composite policy structure – as it may not just be corporate conduct that is used as a basis upon which to refuse coverage to an individual, but also the information obtained during the corporate's insurance claim. It is also vital that each Side of coverage has separate limits of indemnity, or at least that the cover provided under Side A is ringfenced whilst the limits of Side B and Side C are shared (which remains unideal). This can be expressly effected by policy wording, to recognise the primary purpose of D&O cover (the protection of individuals); other protective measures can be taken, such as the Order/Priority of Payments clause.

190 Additionally, to encourage corporate indemnification where possible.

191 Wilkes and Kean (n 50) 181.

PART V

RECOMMENDATIONS AND CONCLUSIONS

The final part draws the book to a close, offering conclusions and recommendations on each key aspect covered throughout. Though an underlying theme of the book is the consideration of directors' liability, the final part of the book sets out a landscape of understanding and good practice for several stakeholders in the deferred prosecution agreement ("DPA") process, including directors, companies, lawyers, prosecutors, the judiciary, and – of course – the insurance world. Part V opens with a look to the impact of the DPA process on directors, drawing some comparisons to different jurisdictions and identifying vulnerabilities and exposure to liability. Upon this foundation, Part V moves to consider the impact of DPAs on directors' and officers' ("D&O") liability insurance. The contemplation of the complex ABC D&O policy is a key theme in this respect, ensuring that all facets of the traditional D&O policy are considered in determining consequences to coverage. Side A is discussed first, in determining the impact of DPAs on directors' access to cover, before moving to analysis of Sides B and C in considering any further collateral impact.

DOI: 10.4324/9781003456964-23

CHAPTER 19

DPAs and directors

It is crucial, in order to identify the position of individuals, to understand the governing legal framework of DPAs. As the UK framework is heavily influenced by that in the US, the differences in scope must be determined. The US DPA framework provides a backdrop for the UK model and sits within the wider concept of pretrial diversion. Originally introduced in the US to offer alternative methods of dealing with individual wrongdoing, PDPs continue to exist within the law and allow the diversion of wrongdoers (usually for low-level offences) to rehabilitation and out of the court system. The 1974 Speedy Trial Act[1] embedded a distinction between PDPs and DPAs within the law, requiring court approval of a written agreement between the prosecutor and wrongdoer.

As the use of DPAs in the US has turned to corporations, their use in individual cases has declined and memoranda governing their use (since the turn of the century) focus on corporations and the cooperation of corporates in assisting the prosecutor in their pursuit of implicated individuals. The SEC adopts a more flexible approach to the use of individual DPAs than the DoJ, though this tends to occur in relation to lower-level offending and is in respect of civil liability. Nevertheless, this provides some form of accountability, which has been a matter criticised in respect of criminal liability of implicated directors in corporate crime. Individuals are not to be protected by corporate DPAs, unless "exceptional" circumstances – an undefined term – arise. In respect of the public attitude and political will in the US, the use of DPAs for directors implicated in corporate crime is increasingly unlikely, particularly in respect of criminal sanction. The PDP does not offer much of an alternative in such circumstances, due to the implicit nature of offending.

In the UK, individuals are not able to agree DPAs (individually or as a co-defendant) pursuant to the statutory framework under Schedule 17 of the CACA 2013, despite relative levels of support for such an extension of the provision within the House of Lords during the debating stage. Furthermore, DPAs were not introduced with the intention to offer individuals any protection from prosecution. Conversely, the importance of individual prosecution has been consistently highlighted, for example, in post-legislative scrutiny of the Bribery Act 2010.[2] This is despite the fact that successful prosecution of individuals

1 Speedy Trial Act 18 USC § 3161 (Supp IV 1974).

2 Select Committee on the Bribery Act 2010, *The Bribery Act 2010: Post-Legislative Scrutiny* (HL 2017–19, 303) para 315.

DOI: 10.4324/9781003456964-24

post-DPA has occurred only in one instance thus far (the conviction of a third party to, and not a (former) director of, the offending company).[3]

Though some domestic police forces in the UK (for example, Durham Constabulary) elect to offer a form of PDP to individuals, this tends to be in respect of lower-level and first-time offending, much like the approach taken in respect of PDPs in the US. In regard to these programmes, the phrase "deferred prosecution" is often deployed despite the fact that prosecution does not appear to arise, judicial approval is not required, nor does the CACA 2013 apply. In any event, the use of such initiatives would, as in the US, unlikely offer an alternative to the prosecution of directors involved in corporate crime: the level of offending and political will would suggest little support for such extension. Drafting anomalies in approving judgments have previously led to a reasonable interpretation that individuals are protected by the respective DPAs; however, this is ultimately not the case when read in line with the DPA terms. In more recent UK DPAs, care has been taken in drafting to ensure that such lack of clarity does not arise, and it is set out that individuals are not protected by the agreement.

The position of UK company directors becomes complex where the prospect of a DPA arises, with potential conflict arising between personal rights and professional duties. Though the guidance surrounding DPAs (for example, the DPA Code and the SFO Operational Handbook chapter) is more discretionary in its language, regarding the position of implicated individuals remaining within a company that is negotiating and potentially agreeing a DPA, the judicial approach appears to be stricter. A distinction can be drawn between individuals under investigation and those prosecuted, and between lower-level employees and senior management. Where disciplinary action is sufficient – as opposed to removal from the company – such action must be taken, and those under suspicion will not be able to take part in the negotiation process. Those prosecuted will need to have left the company, as focus increasingly turns to the idea of the company being a new and/or reformed entity. In this respect, focus particularly turns to senior management to ensure that those culpable are removed, and it is likely that those under suspicion will face even greater scrutiny and consequences than lower-level employees.

Self-reporting is a substantial factor in favour of entering DPA negotiations and ultimately the offer of a DPA, but is not crucial. Cooperation of the company is key and includes the proactivity of senior management and the disclosure of information not otherwise known to or accessible by prosecutors. The self-report, and corporate cooperation in the DPA process, is designed to inculpate and thus impact individuals; the company is weaponised against individuals in taking an activist approach to overseeing the disclosure of evidence and in polarising any existing relationship. A power imbalance arises as a result of this weaponisation, as the surrendering of individuals to prosecutors will not necessarily be founded upon a basis of criminal activity. This was the case in respect of the *Tesco Stores Ltd* directors and also led a former *Serco Geografix Ltd* director to accuse the SFO of trying to retrofit a case against him post-DPA.[4] Where a company wishes to nego-

3 Roger Dewhirst was a third-party recipient of the bribe payments underpinning the corporate criminal wrongdoing. *See* Ruby Hamid and others, 'The DPA Challenge – The SFO's First DPA-Related Conviction of an Individual Bucks the Trend' (*Ashurst*, 10 March 2023) <https://www.ashurst.com/en/news-and-insights/legal-updates/the-dpa-challenge---the-sfos-first-dpa-related-conviction/> accessed 28 March 2023.

4 Oliver Gill, 'Abolish Serious Fraud Office Says Acquitted Ex-Serco Boss' (*The Telegraph*, 8 May 2021) <https://www.telegraph.co.uk/business/2021/05/08/abolish-serious-fraud-office-says-acquitted-ex-serco-boss/> accessed 13 May 2021.

tiate a DPA but remains closely connected to its wrongdoing – thus, not simply inheriting the legacy of wrongdoing of its "former" self – it has been argued that the lack of leniency provisions for individuals disincentivises self-reporting.[5] Leniency measures may be counterintuitive to the judicial approach and the intention behind DPA introduction but, on balance, safeguarding the position of individuals may offer a valuable alternative.

Whilst a director will not be able to agree a DPA in the UK, they may be offered protection under the leniency provisions within the SOCPA 2005 (sections 71 and 72) and SA 2020 (sections 74 and 387–388), following their admission of all available information and involvement in criminal activity. However, it should be noted that such provisions are used sparingly. Whilst leniency may be unlikely where a company is fully cooperating, particularly where it is a new entity, such measures may remain useful. A restricted use undertaking[6] may provide a less hostile approach to information gathering than the use of the SFO's section 2 powers,[7] and extrinsic evidence found remains admissible. However, such use of corporate information may be in breach of the director's section 175 of the CA 2006 duty,[8] and for former directors this will (by virtue of section 170(2)) arise where a profit can be established. Immunity[9] is unlikely to be used in the circumstances due to statutory interpretation and political will, and the alternative of reduction in sentence[10] generates risk as it is subject to judicial approval. Furthermore, risks arise where such leniency is not recognised in overseas jurisdictions, and particularly where double jeopardy is unrecognised. Nevertheless, use in directors' cases is not excluded by section 232 of the CA 2006.

In considering whether to self-report wrongdoing, or to notify a prosecutor of an internal investigation, directors will need to balance the factors set out under section 172 of the CA 2006 in considering what best promotes the success of the company. Relevant considerations will include the completeness of any report made, the timing of the report, and whether notification is compulsorily made to regulators. It may be that a self-report is made soon after discovery of wrongdoing in order to allow for a later evaluation of the nature of such wrongdoing (for example, whether it is criminal) and thereafter the consequences, such as a DPA. Whilst a DPA is not guaranteed, if the director(s) acts in good faith, breach of the section 172 duty will not arise. Whilst such considerations will be vital in respect of availing the company the best opportunity of successfully negotiating a DPA, should it be in the company's best interests, the duty – and that under section 175 – involves a prioritisation of the corporate interests above personal interests and thus may require self-incrimination. Were a director to make an incomplete self-report in order to further their personal interests, this may constitute a breach of the section 175 duty. In such circumstances, breach of the duty under section 171, to exercise powers conferred for a proper purpose, may also arise. If a conflict arises, a director has the option to disclose or resign, but upon resignation the former director will remain subject to the non-profit duty; this will include the use of information. Although section 175 is not breached if other

5 Select Committee on the Bribery Act 2010, *The Bribery Act 2010: Post-Legislative Scrutiny* (n 2) para 314.

6 Serious Organised Crime and Police Act 2005, s 72.

7 Criminal Justice Act 1987, s 2.

8 The duty to avoid conflicts of interest.

9 Serious Organised Crime and Police Act 2005, s 71.

10 Sentencing Act 2020, s 74.

directors authorise the matter,[11] those directors will themselves remain subject to the duty to promote the success of the company.

The decision to self-report encompasses the duty to act as a member, and not independently, of the board,[12] and must be exercised with reasonable care, skill, and diligence.[13] Though claims brought against current directors are relatively rare, former directors may be subject to claims by the company. Such a risk increases in a DPA context, where the company is weaponised against individuals, though would not be permitted if made solely for a political point. Furthermore, a director remaining within the role when knowledge of wrongdoing arises will face a precarious balancing of their professional duties, and the personal risk will be exacerbated when there is suggestion of their own involvement. In any event, the director must in good faith act in the best interests of the company and must prioritise the company's interests above their own or resign their position. If a director is implicated in the wrongdoing, it may be that resignation is ultimately in the best interests of the company if a DPA is likely to be preferential and is negotiable. In any event, an implicated director will not be availed the opportunity to participate in DPA negotiations.

As a director implicated would likely (practically) need to leave the company, particularly if prosecuted, and leniency measures provide little scope for protection (particularly with their current use), safeguards to the individual's right to defence are paramount. In respect of LPP, a company will not be able to assert privilege over documentation created in reasonable contemplation of DPA negotiations (for example, a self-report or interview transcripts), or over information disclosed to prosecutors during negotiations, which would be disclosed by way of limited waiver with the prosecutor's own disclosure obligations to individuals squarely in contemplation. Such an assertion of privilege may amount to a breach of the contractual pre-negotiation undertaking or of the DPA (if the process has so advanced, albeit that such breach will be indirect). Thus, the prosecutor need not force waiver. Should it become necessary to do so, contractual enforcement via the pre-negotiation confidentiality undertaking may enable the prosecutor to bring an action against the company for specific performance, to ensure that disclosure obligations to the individual are met, within the parameters of the limited waiver. The prosecutor is also empowered to refuse a DPA in such circumstances, not for a corporate decision not to waive privilege, but instead on the basis of the adverse implications and consequences arising from that decision. There will be some reliance upon the prosecutor's enforcement of such obligations, which was criticised in *AL*,[14] though such actions would be subject to judicial review.

Where joint privilege arises between the company and (former) director, both parties must consent to waiver (alongside any others sharing the joint privilege). A director's assertion of privilege may, however, be overridden where the director instructs the lawyer in furtherance of or to conceal their own criminal wrongdoing, or in breaching their directors' duties. A claim of privilege made in order to obstruct the company's ability to make

11 Companies Act 2006, s 175(4)(b).

12 Companies Act 2006, s 173.

13 Companies Act 2006, s 174.

14 Mr Justice Green highlighted concerns at the SFO's decision not to pursue Sarclad Ltd for what appeared to be a breach of the terms of cooperation within its DPA, in failing to make such disclosures. These concerns were shared by HHJ Testar in the application to the Crown Court to require the SFO to seek disclosure. *See R (on the application of AL) v Serious Fraud Office* [2018] EWHC 856 (Admin) [38].

a waiver pursuant to DPA negotiations may be considered a breach of the duty provided for by section 172 of the CA 2006. Failure to make a waiver, though not itself a ground to refuse a DPA, may inhibit the prosecutor's ability to fully understand the wrongdoing, thus leading to failed DPA negotiations. Moreover, a former director would be in a less precarious situation in this respect. A company may similarly attempt to obstruct an individual's defence by asserting privilege, for example, in order to minimise follow-on litigation. Doing so may, however, be considered a breach of the terms of the contractual pre-negotiation undertaking, or of the DPA, on the basis of the latter's inclusion of a term requiring cooperation in the prosecution of individuals.

A director will have a personal privilege against self-incrimination, founded within their right to a fair trial.[15] Such privilege is impacted by the SFO's powers under section 2 of the CJA 1987, which allow for the demand of compulsory disclosure of information and material, with criminal consequences for non-compliance. On balance, the consequences are somewhat mitigated in admissibility provisions. As a section 2 notice in respect of company affairs is addressed to an individual, a director addressee may find that the interview allows the opportunity to fulfil their professional duties under the CA 2006, whilst preserving their personal interests. The director would need to give a full and frank account within their interview and then consider invoking their privilege against self-incrimination in their personal proceedings, to avoid the risk of making inconsistent statements and thus rendering the interview disclosures admissible. Taking a literal statutory interpretative approach, a director should be able to make inconsistent statements in proceedings based upon the same offence as the investigation, though a purposive approach would negate this opportunity.

A director should be careful to avoid raising – and not allow those instructed on their behalf to raise – disclosures made pursuant to section 2 powers (or asking questions relating to the interview) in proceedings for which the interview was conducted, in order to avoid admissibility. An inescapable by-product of the use of section 2 is the admissibility of extrinsic evidence found, though a director can be wary in ensuring that only the information requested is disclosed in order to minimise such a risk. Though mitigating steps can be taken during the investigative stage into the company, upon DPA approval the position of the director will become increasingly difficult. As a common DPA term requires cooperation in the pursuit of individuals, and disallows the making of contradictory statements to the statement of facts, a continuing director may cause a breach of the DPA (and thus be in breach of their own directors' duties) where they invoke the privilege against self-incrimination with such adverse effect. Furthermore, it can be observed that, post-DPA approval, the ability of an implicated individual to remain within the company is realistically significantly challenging.

A company involved in DPA negotiations is somewhat protected should those negotiations prove unsuccessful, as the use of draft statement of facts will be restricted in respect of admissibility. Conversely, when a DPA is approved but thereafter breached, the statement of facts will be admissible against the company. Individuals implicated are not so protected: although reporting restrictions may be imposed on the publication of the statement of facts post-DPA approval, in anticipation of individual criminal proceedings, those restrictions may allow for admissibility if achievable within the parameters of the

15 Human Rights Act 1998, sch 1 pt 1 art 6.

orders. A statement of facts, if not subject to reporting restrictions, will be admissible as hearsay evidence against individuals implicated within it, as will other evidence obtained during negotiations. This may include the evidential basis of the DPA, such as interview notes, which would also be subject to the prosecutor's disclosure obligations to individual defendants. As the company will be required to cooperate in the prosecution of individuals, as a term of its DPA, the message within the statement of facts may be conveyed in any event by the use of witnesses. Though draft DPA documentation and the fact of negotiations will not be admissible against an individual should such negotiations prove unsuccessful, other evidence gathered will be. However, the company will not be bound to cooperate in the prosecution, and privilege may be claimed over some documentation. In any event, the (draft) statement of facts will not be attributed back to the director in order to establish their own *mens rea* and thus liability.

In respect of civil proceedings, post-DPA approval, the corporate DPA and statement of facts may be admissible against an individual as hearsay evidence, but other evidence will be admissible in limited circumstances. This will depend on confidentiality (though this may be mitigated by use of a "confidentiality club")[16] and private or public interest and relevance. Nevertheless, when a DPA is not agreed, the confidential nature of negotiations will mean that admissibility disputes in respect of third-party claims will rarely arise; where negotiations are known, disclosure will be limited to circumstances whereby the prosecutor owes such an obligation. Furthermore, admissibility of the statement of facts as hearsay evidence will be assessed in respect of its negotiated nature and thus credibility, though may be persuasive.

Until 2020, there was no guidance on the naming of individuals within DPA documentation; the SFO has since outlined that the necessity of naming will be the key consideration, alongside the possibility of reporting restrictions.[17] In the US, naming unindicted co-conspirators in legal proceedings against others is disapproved on the basis of a lack of forum for vindication, and alternatives such as anonymisation or adoption of pseudonyms are advised by the DoJ.[18] However, the latter may become convoluted where the individual is greatly involved in the relevant wrongdoing. Prosecutors may name individuals so as to make use of hearsay evidence in future prosecutions of those named, though this is discouraged. The ECtHR has similarly refuted such naming and held that the practice may be in violation of the named individual's right to respect for private and family life (thus protection of reputation) under Article 8 of the ECHR.[19] In the UK, the Supreme Court in *Khuja* outlined in the context of reporting that matters discussed at a public trial are not those in which a person named could have had any reasonable expectation of privacy, in respect of giving rise to the tort of misuse of private information, and that any Article 8 impact would be indirect and incidental where the individual is not directly involved in the litigation.[20] In such circumstances, great weight is placed upon the freedom of the

16 *Omers Administration Corp v Tesco Plc* [2019] EWHC 109 (Ch) [85], [111].

17 Serious Fraud Office, 'Deferred Prosecution Agreements' (*Serious Fraud Office*, 23 October 2020) <https://www.sfo.gov.uk/publications/guidance-policy-and-protocols/sfo-operational-handbook/deferred-prosecution-agreements/> accessed 23 October 2020.

18 The United States Department of Justice, 'Justice Manual > 9-11.130 –

19 *Vicent del Campo v Spain* App no 25527/13 (ECtHR, 6 November 2018) para 56.

20 *Khuja v Times Newspapers Limited* [2017] UKSC 49 [34].

press to report court proceedings. Notably, this was a majority view, and dissenting judges adopted a view akin to that of the ECtHR.

The approach taken in *Khuja* can be contrasted with DPAs, whereby open justice is not absolute and is restricted, and the agreed statement of facts is not subject to public scrutiny in the same way as evidence at trial. Article 8 will not be treated as having presumptive priority over Article 10 in the circumstances, but realistically Article 10 need not be impacted significantly beyond the existing provisions within the CACA 2013, and anonymisation – for which there is precedent – would be entirely proportionate. Furthermore, an individual unaware of DPA negotiations would not foresee the consequences, nor have access to a forum for vindication unless invited. This is a crucial consideration at the DPA drafting stage, as reporting restrictions act only as an interim safeguard of the individual's Article 6 right to a fair trial and do not protect against long-term consequences of identification, unless the judge elects to anonymise documentation suitably (post-individual acquittal and pre-lifting of restrictions).

Obvious identifiers need not be incorporated into documentation and, where necessary in the DPA hearing, case management powers can be exercised to ensure that rights are protected and to ensure the administration of justice. In respect of other means of referencing individuals, care must be taken to avoid identification by use of initials. Further, a tentative approach should be taken to specific reference to job title, accompanied by detailed personal employment information, which would allow for jigsaw identification. Reporting restrictions may remain pertinent where excerpts of the statement of facts are transposed into the approving judgment(s), though this should nevertheless be avoided where it may unnecessarily lead to identification of individuals. Outlining of the agreed facts of the corporate wrongdoing remains achievable in a managed and transparent way.

Where outrightly named without conviction, an individual may have a claim in tort for misuse of private information, on the basis of a reasonable expectation of privacy and their Article 8 right. An alternative action in tort for defamation would be unlikely to succeed, due to privileges in respect of court proceedings and criminal investigations, and the public interest. Data protection provisions would be unlikely to provide a forum for the rectification of a statement of facts whereupon the content relating to a named individual is later deemed to be inaccurate. Though the individual's own proceedings may act as an opportunity to clear their name, ultimate vindication where named will arise in the amendment of the naming documentation. Although the CACA 2013 places a condition of (avoidance of) breach in order for an amendment of the DPA, and thus statement of facts, to be made, and it has been ruled that the statement of facts cannot be altered or modified post-approval,[21] subsequent amendment and addendum to the *Airbus SE* DPA proves otherwise and allows a transparent modification to the documentation which can be freely reported upon (where not subject to restrictions) by the press. In the period between approval and expiry of the *Bluu Solutions Limited* and *Tetris Project Limited* DPAs – when reporting restrictions remained in place – the move to anonymise documentation upon individual acquittals further demonstrated judicial powers beyond the statutory framework.

Comments made by Lord Justice Edis in the *AFWEL* DPA approved judgment suggest the possibility of a substitution of one statement of facts for another upon the prosecution

21 *Serious Fraud Office v Tesco Stores Ltd* [2019] EW Misc 1 (Crown) [4].

of individuals (the substitution not effecting change in a move *towards* anonymity).[22] This is troubling as prosecution precedes conviction, and it must proceed that only those convicted of the relevant offence are named. Any amendment or substitution should not significantly alter the factual account, which would otherwise require a variation of the DPA and agreement of the company, as it would upon the company's breach be deemed a formal admission under section 10 of the CJA 1967. However, the removal of names within the statement of facts would constitute a revisable change upon their acquittal, as seen in the cases of *Bluu Solutions Limited* and *Tetris Project Limited* (pre-DPA expiry).

Aside from the amendment of the DPA and the statement of facts, the matter of naming implicated individuals in approved judgments presents increasing concern. In *Bluu Solutions Limited* and *Tetris Project Limited*, prior to DPA expiry, the statement of facts was published following the anonymisation of individuals upon their acquittal. However, upon the expiry of the DPAs, a subsequent "de-anonymised" judgment was published alongside the notice of discontinuance.[23] Within the de-anonymised judgment, individuals already *acquitted* in their own proceedings are named, and Mrs Justice May covers aspects of the statement of facts (thus allegations against those named individuals) in some depth. There is no requirement to publish a subsequent de-anonymised judgment in order to identify individuals, where an anonymised judgment has already been published approving the DPA. When the *Sarclad Ltd* DPA was approved, a redacted judgment was first published.[24] When the full version of the judgment was later published, individuals were not named (though arguably reference made to them by their job position was not a necessary step and could contribute to jigsaw identification).

Mrs Justice May takes steps within both issued judgments (anonymised and de-anonymised) to set out that no findings of fact are made by the court, but nonetheless presents the references to individual alleged conduct as having derived from '*facts* ... agreed between the SFO and the corporate Respondents'[25] (emphasis added). Whilst it is acknowledged that the "facts" 'have not been agreed by any of the individuals to which I refer in this judgment, nor have they been asked for their comments',[26] the names of the acquitted individuals remain attached to "facts" presented as to their part in the corporate criminal conduct. Such practice must be actively avoided, particularly where no mention of individual acquittals (even in post-judgment note) is made. If the publication of a subsequent approving judgment is deemed to be necessary, perhaps in order to de-anonymise the company itself (which may have been anonymised pending the outcome of proceedings against individuals), it follows that individuals should only be de-anonymised where they have been convicted. Prior to the expiry of the *Bluu Solutions Limited* and *Tetris Project Limited* DPAs, it had appeared to be the case that anonymisation was becoming standard practice. Interestingly – and likely the consequence of challenge to the decision to de-anonymise – just over two months after the de-anonymised judgment was published, it was removed from the SFO website (as well as any other detail referring to the

22 *Director of the Serious Fraud Office v Amec Foster Wheeler Limited* [2021] Lloyd's Rep FC 353 (Crown) [5].

23 *Director of the Serious Fraud Office v Bluu Solutions Limited and Tetris-Projects Limited* [2023] EWHC 1976 (KB).

24 *Serious Fraud Office v XYZ Limited* [2016] Lloyd's Rep FC 509 (Crown).

25 *Bluu Solutions Limited and Tetris-Projects Limited* (n 23) [16] (Mrs Justice May).

26 ibid.

acquitted individuals by name).[27] Anonymisation ultimately remains within the discretion of the prosecutors and judges, and it is becoming all the more clear that both must exercise this discretion in ensuring the anonymity of individuals, except where those individuals are convicted. As the de-anonymised version of the *Bluu Solutions Limited* and *Tetris Project Limited* judgment is currently unavailable on the SFO website, this must remain the case, and similar decisions must be avoided in future cases.

As DPA documentation may be admissible against individuals, it is all the more important that individuals are not identified by name. The zero percent success rate of UK prosecutions of (former) directors of DPA-agreeing companies demonstrates the unjustifiable approach to naming, and has collateral impact in respect of exposure to follow-on proceedings and personal circumstances. The onus is on the company, prosecutor, and judiciary to uphold a high standard of justice in ensuring that individuals are not named within the DPA documentation unless such individuals are convicted. If naming occurs and individuals are acquitted, the opportunity to amend or substitute the statement of facts can and must be exercised. Despite conflicting opinion as to the role and involvement of the judiciary in US DPAs, the role of the judiciary in UK DPAs is clear, and such influence will be crucial in ensuring the abidance by the anonymous or pseudonymous approach.[28] The provisions within the CACA 2013 allow for the conducting of the DPA process in a manner proportionate to the objectives and use of the tool, and taking the step to ensure anonymity, or adequate pseudonymity, would not impact freedom of the press to report any further than those existing provisions.

27 Serious Fraud Office, 'R v Bluu Solutions Limited and Tetris Projects Limited' (*Serious Fraud Office*, 2 October 2023) <https://www.sfo.gov.uk/cases/r-v-bluu-solutions-limited-and-tetris-projects-limited/> accessed 2 October 2023.

28 Notably, even in the US, the inherent supervisory power to ensure the administration of justice may encompass such considerations.

CHAPTER 20

Directors' D&O coverage

Consideration of the impact of DPAs on directors' liabilities naturally carries with it the necessity to consider the impact on D&O insurance. An "ABC" D&O policy represents three "Sides" of coverage, which all have the capacity to adversely impact the others. D&O insurance, under Side A, provides a comfort blanket of protection to directors and senior officers where the company cannot or will not indemnify. However, the development of the product has also led to the standard provision of entity coverage, under Side C, and reimbursement cover for the entity where indemnification obligations are duly met, under Side B. D&O will be of particular pertinence to an individual when a corporate DPA arises: Side B may respond where the company indemnifies its (former) directors, but Side A will be crucial in responding where the company cannot (or possibly will not) do so as a result of the agreement. Further, Side C considerations, such as the vast depletion of the policy limit of indemnity, may adversely impact the directors' ability to obtain coverage under an ABC policy. For the director, access to coverage under Side A will be of the utmost importance in the circumstances.

In respect of the precontractual duty of fair presentation,[1] a failure to disclose or misrepresentation could be detrimental to coverage. A director will typically be insured under a separate contract of insurance in respect of D&O coverage, and thus exposure is somewhat minimised as the applicable knowledge provisions under the IA 2015[2] will be those relating to individual insureds. However, risks remain where the knowledge of an individual responsible for the director's insurance is deemed to be the knowledge of the director. This is particularly risky in SMEs, whereby the person responsible for the insurance may be a director or senior officer with greater knowledge than a lower-level employee appointed to conduct such a task. Further, the director will be required to conduct a reasonable search of information in discovering what they ought to know. As the typical D&O policy is composite in structure, attribution to the company of senior management knowledge for the purpose of entity coverage will not impact the director's own Side A cover; the composite structure will mean that a remedy against one insured for breach of the duty of fair presentation will not automatically arise against a co-insured, though this remains a substantial risk within rare joint policies. This is further supported by the common "Severability of Application" clause. The impact of nondisclosure and

1 Insurance Act 2015, s 3.
2 ibid s 4.

 DOI: 10.4324/9781003456964-25

misrepresentation may ultimately be expressly outlined within policy wording, particularly in respect of fraudulent or dishonest conduct.

Being a Claims made policy, the typical Prior Claims and Circumstances exclusion will, in any event, exclude coverage for Loss arising from a Claim or Circumstance notified under a previous policy, disclosed within the policy proposal, or which ought to have been known and thus disclosed. Policy wording will depend on whether that which ought to have been known relates to knowledge of the specific insured or any insured under the ABC policy, and thus may lead to exclusion in coverage irrespective of policy structure. In this respect, a director insured under a policy taken out by the company should be wary of the individual responsible for their insurance and their own knowledge. Further, the director should take care to understand the wording of a Prior Claims and Circumstances exclusion, in ensuring that consideration of Circumstances (in particular) which ought to be known by co-insureds cannot impact severability provisions and thus any subsequent Claims made against them.

As notification of Claims and Circumstances (the latter which subsequently, by causal link, give rise to a Claim) is a condition precedent to indemnity, it is crucial to ensure that a satisfactory notification is made. The policy to respond will be that under which the notification is made. Hence, it is vital for directors to notify of Circumstances when they arise, as otherwise the director would need to maintain their own Side A coverage upon resignation and would be covered only if a newly notifiable Claim/Circumstance arises. A Circumstance notified must have a sufficient factual basis beyond mere concerns,[3] and in a DPA context may include an internal investigation (where not within the definition of Claim). Directors must be conscious of the continuing need to notify throughout evolving investigations so as to ensure the maintenance of a causal link to any subsequent Claims arising. When the scale and consequence of a problem are unknown, but might reasonably be expected to produce a Claim, a blanket notification may be made.[4] This may be particularly pertinent in respect of the unveiling of historic corporate misconduct within which a director is implicated: the precise nature of the misconduct (for example, whether it is criminal, or just malpractice) may not be appreciated at the point the misconduct is identified as "wrong".

Whilst LPP is somewhat protected by the precontractual duty of fair presentation, confidentiality held in information is overridden. Post-contract, a Cooperation clause will have the effect of bestowing a contractual right upon the insurer to override an insured's claim to privilege and to compel the production of documentation or information. Furthermore, any disputes as to privilege should be resolved prior to court proceedings, whereby loss of privilege could have a wider consequential impact. Even where an insurer does not have such a contractual right, the underlying facts remain notifiable. Therefore, a director with knowledge of DPA negotiations must notify their insurer of a Circumstance which may give rise to future Claims against the director, though this will likely take a blanket form as a result of the company's pre-negotiation confidentiality undertaking. With increased focus on the accountability of senior management, this is crucial. If unaware of negotiations, which would most likely apply only in respect of former directors or those subject to disciplinary procedures, such a notification obligation would not arise; the individual

3 *Euro Pools plc (in administration) v Royal & Sun Alliance Insurance plc* [2019] EWCA Civ 808 [43].
4 *Kajima UK Engineering Ltd v Underwriter Insurance Company Ltd* [2008] EWHC 83 (TCC) [99].

responsible for the director's insurance will unlikely be deemed to know of the negotiations on a literal interpretation of the IA 2015. Where the insurer becomes aware of disclosures made within a section 2 interview with the SFO,[5] such information may be utilised by the insurer in determining coverage. Furthermore, a duty to indemnify policy and separate representation of the insurer and the insured company will be crucial, as a joint retainer will remove confidentiality.

A composite policy is crucial for insured directors, not only in respect of precontractual disclosure (for example, regarding historic wrongdoing), but also to avoid being caught by exclusions to coverage imposed against co-insureds. Typically, a Severability in exclusions clause will achieve this aim, nonetheless. It is vital that insured directors understand the wording and impact of Interrelated Wrongful Acts and Related Claims clauses in regard to DPA-related Claims. The latter will be of particular pertinence, as many types of Claims can arise against directors post-DPA. Though such clauses typically apply to the particular insured, it is crucial to determine that this is the case and that Claims against or Wrongful Acts of the entity do not impact the director's access to cover. The Related Claims clause presents dramatic exposure to directors in respect of DPAs, particularly where a director is joined as a co-defendant in an action against the company (for example, civil proceedings or overseas criminal proceedings). If the clause is not removable, policy wording should provide that Claims will only be deemed a single matter where made against the insured as a sole defendant. However, this is somewhat unlikely, as the clause is designed to limit the insurer's scope of liability. Directors should be mindful of the risk of joint proceedings and the impact on the Related Claims clause: where severance of proceedings is possible, it should be sought so as to avoid prejudice to the director's own proceedings by way of restricted access to defence.

Civil claims for breach of directors' duties may arise in various circumstances in relation to a DPA: for example, where the director was personally engaged in the underlying wrongdoing, or where the director negatively interfered with self-reporting or negotiations. Side A is crucial where such claims arise, as the company is not legally permitted to indemnify its directors in this respect; Side A will likely respond, except where an exclusion is deemed to apply. The company is not legally precluded from making such a claim, despite an agreed DPA, but an Insured vs Insured exclusion clause may preclude cover where clear exceptions regarding derivative claims (for example), or provision of defence costs cover, are not provided for within the policy.

Cover in respect of criminal proceedings foremost depends on the inclusion of criminal proceedings within the Claim definition. Where a director is convicted of a criminal offence, public policy and the legal maxim *ex turpi causa non oritur actio* will preclude coverage for defence costs and any related costs arising as a result of the criminal action (for example, a financial penalty). This is further upheld by the typical Conduct exclusion clause within D&O policies, which precludes coverage for dishonest, fraudulent, and/or criminal acts (depending on policy wording). The Conduct exclusion clause is typically invokable by final adjudication or judgment, and a conviction not subject to appeal would be sufficient for this purpose. The Conduct exclusion may also be invoked by admission

5 Criminal Justice Act 1987, s 2.

where a leniency agreement under section 74 of the SA 2020, or a guilty plea, is reached.[6] The insurer's consent would need to be sought prior to admitting liability, and, in respect of the leniency agreement, a Contract exclusion clause would also serve to preclude coverage where inclusive of agreements.

Coverage pursuant to an acquittal will require the Wrongful Acts definition to encompass alleged, and not just actual, Wrongful Acts (as is common). Where a director is acquitted of a criminal offence, the liability principle (requiring actual legal liability) will not be invoked so as to preclude coverage. In respect of defence costs cover provided for within the Loss definition, entitlement to coverage arises as per contractual provision; this is effected by the contractual inclusion of defence costs cover within a D&O policy, and is founded upon business efficacy. Defence costs cover cannot be subject to the liability principle, or the scope test (which considers whether a Claim would fall within the scope of the policy, with a broad interpretation encompassing the application of exclusion clauses), as such cover would be rendered illusory in respect of successfully defended criminal actions (**Section 14.3**). As such, the scope test can be reframed in determining whether defence costs cover is triggered simply as a result of a Claim made, and not liability incurred (or which would have occurred had the Claim against the insured succeeded). Defence costs cover provided within the Loss definition can *bona fide* remain so, as it is simply the interpretative principle which can be distinguished from the remainder of the clause. Furthermore, the cover will remain subject to the fate of the claim and thus bound by any exclusion clauses invoked. If provided for as a separate undertaking, defence costs cover exists as a wholly separate form of cover, and thus exclusion clauses will apply only insofar as policy wording provides. In any event, a director insured will be required to obtain the insurer's consent prior to incurring defence costs. Where a director is not technically acquitted but instead granted immunity pursuant to a section 71 of the SOCPA 2005 notice, it is likely that the Conduct exclusion clause will be invoked on the basis of an admission so as to preclude coverage (as well as a broadly constructed Contract exclusion).

An insurer's rights of subrogation may be impacted post-DPA where the director remains with the company (and the DPA remains active) and as a result of policy composition. In the former instance, an insurer challenging the company's DPA or statements made within it may be considered a breach of the DPA term prohibiting contradictory statements. This will arise where the company is deemed to authorise, or fails to publicly repudiate, such a contest. In this respect, the insurer's rights may be further restricted by its good faith obligations, in light of the potential collateral consequences (such as breach of directors' duties, as subrogation requires the consent of the individual insured). Composite policy composition will mean that an insurer cannot exercise subrogation rights if the parties are both insured under the same policy (under Side A and Side C) and covered against the same risk. However, rights may arise where the loss is deemed to be caused by the uninsurable conduct of the company (for example, fraud), provided that the individual would have a cause of action.

6 In some jurisdictions, a guilty plea pursuant to a criminal prosecution is not deemed to be an admission of liability (this will, in any event, be policy wording dependent). *See Harbourfield Engineering Co Ltd v Falcon Insurance Co (Hong Kong) Ltd* [2003] HKEC 959; *Grace Electrical Engineering Pte Ltd v EQ Insurance Co Ltd* [2016] SGHC 23. *See also* Robert Merkin, *Colinvaux's Law of Insurance* (12th edn, Sweet & Maxwell 2019) para 21-080.

A duty to defend form D&O policy is relatively rare, and would negate the need for advancement of defence costs: the insurer would be required to defend potentially covered (but not non-covered) claims. Conversely, an insurer is only required to advance defence costs for covered claims in a duty to indemnify policy, and any other costs advanced are repayable upon determination that they are non-covered. Mandatory advancement requires contemporaneous advancement unless an exclusion clause is actually invoked, whereas discretionary (and not necessarily contemporaneous) advancement permits insurer discretion and may be refused on the basis of realistic grounds to believe that an exclusion would apply.[7] A Claim must have been made against the insured in order for the opportunity to arise, and consent must be obtained from the insurer (and cannot be unreasonably withheld) prior to incurring such costs.

Where a DPA is approved and a statement of facts is publicised, a discretionary advancement obligation presents far greater exposure to an insured director. In this respect, a mandatory obligation is in the insured's best interests, though any exclusion invokable by admission continues to present a risk unless specifically required to be made by the insured person (unless it is explicitly outlined that a DPA statement of facts would not be considered an admission of an individual in any event). An advancement provision not bound by exclusions would be optimal, though unlikely as the provision is typically an extension to the main insuring clause. Though a duty to defend policy may be optimal in respect of providing coverage for potentially covered claims, this is unlikely in practice.

The insurer may seek to invoke the Conduct exclusion clause against an insured director on the basis of the DPA statement of facts. Directors must be mindful to ensure that an admission will only trigger the Conduct exclusion clause when made "by the Insured (Person)". If not so restrictively worded, the statement of facts as an admission by the insured company may be sufficient to trigger the exclusion (even if efforts have been made to anonymise the account). Even where admissions must be "by the Insured (Person)", the document may be relied upon where it is deemed to contain admissions by the director, and the director's continued position within the company will be relevant in determining whether the account goes beyond the incidental inclusion of third-party material (for example, internal interview transcripts). Similar considerations will apply in respect of a director's contribution to a corporate self-report to prosecutors, and the director may need to seek the consent of the insurer to do so if making admissions. In any event, attribution principles will not apply in reverse so as to attribute the statement of facts to the director. Where the statement of facts is subject to reporting restrictions and published upon a director's acquittal, insurers may seek to refuse cover and demand recoupment of costs paid on the basis of its contents, though will be bound by good faith and policy wording in doing so.

Though an insurer may seek to rely upon an adverse judgment within civil proceedings or declaratory judgment against the director, in invoking the Conduct exclusion clause based upon a final adjudication or judgment, doing so on the basis of the DPA will be more challenging. The DPA must have expired in order to be deemed final, and the clause must provide for "judgments" as well as "adjudications": a DPA is not strictly an adjudication, as it is a settlement, but is subject to an approved judgment. In such circumstances, it is

7 *Silbermann v CGU Insurance Ltd* [2003] NSWCA 203.

in the best interests of an insured director to ensure that a final adjudication or judgment[8] must be made against "an Insured (Person)" and is not broader in scope.

Whilst an insurer may seek to rely upon the DPA statement of facts to preclude coverage, in determining the true nature of the claim, an insured may rebut this by challenging the nature of their liability as a type insured under the policy; this has been observed as a possible outcome in the context of the *Tesco Stores Ltd* DPA and related individual prosecutions.[9] An insurer may further consider an implicating statement of facts to be demonstrative of a failure of an insured director to disclose during the precontractual stage and, if so argued, public policy may restrict advancement. It is in the best interests of the insured director that policies follow the approach taken by Beazley in its sample Side A DIC cover,[10] in clearly setting out that the statement of facts does not constitute an admission (or knowledge) of co-insured persons.

An insurer may wish to conduct an investigation into an insured director's claim following a corporate DPA, but will be bound by the duty of good faith and the implied term requiring payment within a reasonable time (under section 13A of the IA 2015) in doing so. Whilst the insurer may have reasonable grounds to dispute liability, its actions during the process must be reasonable, and this will embrace consideration of whether any exclusion clauses (or nondisclosure) are deemed to arise.

The insurer's right to recoupment of defence costs is problematic in respect of duty to defend policies, and it has been argued that the policy should expressly provide for the right.[11] The right to such recoupment may be reliant upon the claim never having a prospect of coverage. In a duty to indemnify policy, costs paid are generally subject to the right of recoupment. If no such provision is outlined, an advancement provision existing as an extension to the main insuring clause will operate in such a way nonetheless, as such cover will be bound by the policy's definitions and exclusions. Where defence costs are provided for by way of separate undertaking, the provision for recoupment may differ in scope and will be dependent on policy wording.

In respect of the allocation of defence costs, it will be crucial to ensure that Side C has clearly defined separate limits, as an application of the reasonably related test may otherwise rapidly exhaust the director's limit of indemnity when the DPA process arises (**Section 15.5**). Though this may benefit uninsured directors, a policy without such defined limits is not in the best interests of the insured director. The reasonably related test may be advantageous in ensuring that multiple Claims made against a director (where the test successfully applies, and one of the Claims is covered under the policy) attract advancement. If an allocation clause does not exist, reliance upon the perceived nature of the

8 Taking influence from the US case of *Rochester Drug Co-Operative Inc v Hiscox Ins Co* 466 F Supp 3d 337 (WDNY 2020).

9 This argument arises in particular where a DPA is agreed on the basis of an identification principle offence, and subsequently the respective "directing mind and will" is acquitted in individual proceedings based on the same conduct.

10 Beazley, 'Side A DIC Policy' (*Beazley*) <https://web.archive.org/web/20220421213351/https://www.beazley.com/documents/Wordings/Side%20A%20DIC.pdf> accessed 7 September 2021.

11 *American Western Home Ins Co v Gjonaj Realty & Management Co* 192 AD 3d 28 (2d Dept 2020); Michael Zigelman and others, 'Jurisdictions Continue to be Split Over Insurer's Right to Recoup Defense Costs' (*Reuters*, 29 June 2021) <https://www.reuters.com/legal/legalindustry/jurisdictions-continue-be-split-over-insurers-right-recoup-defense-costs-2021-06-29/> accessed 18 August 2021.

claim could prove disadvantageous in respect of advancement, should DPA-related claims increasingly be considered to be non-covered.

It is vital that measures are taken to preserve directors' protection under ABC policies where DPAs arise and as they proliferate. This can be achieved by ensuring that the Order of Payments clause sufficiently prioritises Side A claims, with sufficient allocation provision (should multiple Claims arise simultaneously), and by clearly defined separate limits of indemnity. The provision of a separate tower for Side A with a separate limit, whilst ensuring composite policy composition, and providing directors' defence costs as a separate undertaking not bound by the fortunes of the main insuring clause(s), would provide optimal cover to directors. Where Side A coverage is insufficient, Side A DIC may provide an additional comfort blanket of protection, though may (depending on policy wording) simply be founded upon the terms of the primary policy unless express additions to coverage are made. Furthermore, the inclusion of defence costs within either product will be vital in DPA-related individual claims. If adequate scope of coverage cannot be obtained under Side A (DIC), directors may seek cover under alternative products such as Willis Tower Watson's "Directors' All Risk Cover" to ensure their personal protection.[12] As D&O is Claims made in nature, former directors must be vigilant in ascertaining whether the company continues to purchase insurance covering former directors and – if not – should consider purchasing their own Side A cover.

12 Willis Towers Watson, 'Directors' & Officers' Insurance' (*Willis Towers Watson*, 1 September 2020) <https://www.willistowerswatson.com/-/media/WTW/Insights/2020/09/directors-and-officers-insurance.pdf?modified=20200901122754> accessed 17 December 2020, 9.

CHAPTER 21

Companies' D&O coverage

An ABC form D&O policy represents a package of protection for directors and senior officers and also the corporate body. The "ABC" acronym represents the three different Sides (or "Insuring Agreements") of cover: Side A provides protection to the director; Side B provides for reimbursement to the company upon its own indemnification of the director; and Side C provides entity coverage (in typically limited circumstances). Where the coverage provided to a director under Side A is found within an ABC D&O policy, consideration of the response of Side A alone is insufficient in determining the impact of DPAs on the director's insurance coverage. Though *prima facie* the provision of directors' cover appears separate, under Side A, characteristics of the ABC policy may serve to diminish or prevent the extension of coverage. A shared limit of indemnity across the ABC policy could be detrimental to directors' access to cover, particularly where larger actions indemnifiable under Side C arise. Even where the limit is not shared, lack of sufficient severability wording could mean that an exclusion applied in refusing coverage to the entity is consequently triggered against directors. The impact of DPAs on Side B and Side C must therefore be considered in order to ensure that directors remain sufficiently protected. Not least, directors implicitly benefit where the entity holds Side B cover and circumstances arise whereby coverage can be extended: coverage is not extended to the directors, but directors will have been indemnified by the company for Side B to be triggered.

Side B consideration is important, as corporate indemnification of directors may ultimately be based upon reliance on the transfer of liability to the insurer. Where Side B cover is not in place, the corporate approach to indemnification of its directors may not be as forthcoming. A company would not be precluded from making a Side B claim where it has agreed a DPA on the basis of the relevant director's wrongdoing if the company itself is a primary or secondary victim of the wrongdoing. However, where the company is deemed to be the criminal wrongdoer by virtue of the principle of attribution, the maxim *ex turpi causa non oritur actio* may apply to preclude coverage. Furthermore, it is in the company's best interests to avoid naming directors within DPA documentation if it is to later rely upon Side B coverage, particularly in respect of an identification principle offence. The impact of the DPA – in respect of refused related claims under Side C – upon preclusion of cover under Side B is reduced by a composite D&O structure, and the application of policy definitions and exclusions to the underlying Claim made against the director (as opposed to the claim made by the entity).

DOI: 10.4324/9781003456964-26

Beyond statutory restrictions set out within section 234 of the CA 2006,[1] the terms of an active DPA may preclude a company from indemnifying its directors, thus reducing the response of Side B cover. The principal DPA terms of concern will be those regarding cooperation in the prosecution of individuals, and prohibiting contradictory statements. Though the US case of *Stein I* may bear some influence in the extent to which prosecutors can interfere with an individual's defence and funding of it (**Section 17.1**), typical UK DPA phraseology regarding contradictory statements will continue to have a negative impact on the access to corporate indemnification of serving directors. Even where a DPA is not agreed, such indemnification may be considered (indirectly) a factor in favour of corporate prosecution (and thus against DPA), particularly where the directors retain their position. Conversely, indemnification of former directors (no longer part of the directing mind and will) may be permissible where executed in adherence to contractual obligations, whilst publicly repudiating statements made. Though there will be certain costs non-indemnifiable by the company (for example, defence costs incurred in criminal proceedings leading to conviction), corporate indemnification (and thus Side B) will remain useful where Side A does not respond (for example, due to an exhausted limit).

Directors' duties will need to be borne in mind to ensure that the company is adequately protected by insurance, particularly when a DPA may arise. The value of Side C will predominantly be in defence costs cover (particularly the Advancement extension) and may be obtainable by SMEs due to broader terms of coverage, or by larger companies where coverage for Securities Claims (only) is broad enough to include criminal proceedings. Part of ensuring adequate protection may entail negotiation of the Retroactive clause date in ensuring that coverage could respond to historic misconduct, which is relevant in respect of DPA-related wrongdoing and the increased focus on companies being "new" entities at the point of negotiation and agreement.

Ex turpi causa non oritur actio will not necessarily automatically preclude Side C coverage, and a broadly phrased Conduct exclusion clause (for example, triggered by "wilful or dishonest" conduct) may permit indemnification of defence costs in respect of a failure to prevent offence where the wrongdoing was committed in a manner such that the company itself was a victim of its directors' misconduct. In any event, indemnification of the financial penalty within a DPA will not be possible. Notification will depend on whether the policy includes investigations within the Claim definition, and the scope of the pre-negotiation confidentiality undertaking. An inherent aspect of the DPA process is its confidentiality, with parties involved subject to a pre-negotiation confidentiality undertaking before negotiations are initiated. As such, negotiation of the terms of the pre-negotiation confidentiality undertaking to allow notification will be crucial. If investigations are included within "Claim" and the undertaking can be agreed so as to permit the notification of the fact of DPA negotiations, the insurer will likely invoke the Conduct exclusion clause by virtue of an admission on the basis of the statement of facts, which will be disclosable to the insurer in line with the Cooperation clause, or on the basis of the insured seeking consent of the insurer to admit liability. Furthermore, whether the Conduct exclusion is invoked at an earlier stage may depend on the wording of any self-report.

1 A company cannot indemnify a director for liabilities owed to the company itself or to an associated company, nor defence costs incurred in civil proceedings brought successfully against the director by the (associated) company (but can indemnify in respect of civil proceedings brought by third parties). Indemnification is not permitted in respect of penalties imposed by regulatory authorities. *See* Companies Act 2006, s 234.

If the Claim definition does not include investigations, and the company is not permitted to share the fact of DPA negotiations, a blanket notification will be in the company's best interests (where a contractual right upon the insurer to compel disclosure by virtue of a Cooperation clause does not arise). Where cover such as Circumstances Investigation Costs is included, this may allow for some extension of cover in circumstances where a company is bound by confidentiality, though it may also impact a broadly phrased Related Claims clause.

Defence costs cover will be the inherent value of Side C cover in respect of DPAs, but ultimately a duty to indemnify policy will only advance defence costs if specifically provided for and if there is a mandatory obligation upon the insurer to do so. The insurer may elect to defend the Claim in order to minimise liability, but any costs paid will be subject to the right of recoupment. If a DPA is agreed, a broadly phrased Contract exclusion clause (including agreements) may also be invoked to refuse coverage. The extent to which cover is refused is particularly relevant where an ABC policy's Related Claims clause is broadly drafted without sufficient severability.

An insurer may exercise subrogation rights in the position of the insured company against a co-insured individual where the individual is deemed to have caused the loss by wilful misconduct, fraud, or another type of uninsurable conduct. Where a Side A claim is refused (or where the director is convicted), this may provide a basis upon which to exercise such rights and will provide further exposure of the individual to liability. This right is somewhat restricted by DPAs, to the extent that the company (and therefore the insurer in the company's name) cannot make statements contradicting the content of the DPA whilst the DPA remains active. To do so would give rise to potential breach proceedings in respect of the DPA.

It is vital that the aggregate limit of indemnity within an ABC policy is split per Side of coverage, or that the limit of indemnity preserved for Side A is ringfenced. This will particularly be the case if UK DPAs are extended to civil violations, as Side C response will likely proliferate; this may be presently touted as unlikely, given the novelty of the provision, but could occur in the future. Further insulation of Side A cover by ensuring a composite policy structure and sufficient severability language throughout the policy, including in respect of the Related Claims clause and exclusions, will be critical in respect of the impact of DPAs and entity coverage on directors' access to Side A cover.

Since their introduction, the extent of the potential impact of DPAs on company directors has been the subject of real oversight. Such lack of clarity has adversely impacted numerous individuals in respect of criminal and civil proceedings, and has had reported collateral consequences on health and wellbeing. Areas of law posing unknown and unquantifiable liability not only undermine the legal system, and the pursuit of justice, but also pose stark consequences in respect of insurance cover. With inadequate, or unobtainable, cover in respect of increasing risks, the subsequent impact on industry discourages directorship and/or good corporate governance. When considering the impact of corporate DPAs on related individuals, the weaponisation of companies against directors and subsequent heightened exposure to liability is evident. Thus, in considering the position of company directors and the juxtaposing professional duties and personal interests, such clarity is all the more important. Lessons must be learnt by engaged stakeholders not only to protect individuals and insurers, but in order to safeguard the integrity of the DPA tool in its pursuit of equitable justice.

INDEX

Note: Page numbers in **bold** indicate tables

For Product Safety Concerns and Information please contact our EU
representative GPSR@taylorandfrancis.com
Taylor & Francis Verlag GmbH, Kaufingerstraße 24, 80331 München, Germany

www.ingramcontent.com/pod-product-compliance
Lightning Source LLC
LaVergne TN
LVHW080806011026
849160LV00015B/1544

* 9 7 8 1 0 3 2 5 9 9 5 4 0 *